Handbook of Psychobiography

HANDBOOK OF PSYCHOBIOGRAPHY

Edited by

William Todd Schultz

OXFORD
UNIVERSITY PRESS

2005

OXFORD

UNIVERSITY PRESS

Oxford University Press, Inc., publishes works that further
Oxford University's objective of excellence
in research, scholarship, and education.

Oxford   New York
Auckland   Cape Town   Dar es Salaam   Hong Kong   Karachi
Kuala Lumpur   Madrid   Melbourne   Mexico City   Nairobi
New Delhi   Shanghai   Taipei   Toronto

With offices in
Argentina   Austria   Brazil   Chile   Czech Republic   France   Greece
Guatemala   Hungary   Italy   Japan   Poland   Portugal   Singapore
South Korea   Switzerland   Thailand   Turkey   Ukraine   Vietnam

Copyright © 2005 by Oxford University Press, Inc.

Published by Oxford University Press, Inc.
198 Madison Avenue, New York, New York 10016

www.oup.com

Oxford is a registered trademark of Oxford University Press

Library of Congress Cataloging-in-Publication Data
Handbook of psychobiography / edited by William Todd Schultz.
p. cm.
Includes bibliographical references and index.
ISBN-13 978-0-19-516827-3

1. Psychology—Biographical methods.   2. Artists—Psychology—Case studies.
3. Politicians—Psychology—Case studies.   4. Psychologists—Psychology—Case studies.
I. Schultz, William Todd.
BF39.4.H36 2005
150'.72'2—dc22   2004012961

Printed in the United States of America
on acid-free paper

For the late Rae Carlson,
who long ago asked the question
"Where's the person in personality research?"
This book provides one answer.

Preface

It's been a long road to this book, full of potholes, hitchhikers, and map confusion, plus occasional stops for gas. Still, if you put your pedal to the metal, and keep it there, you tend to get where you want to be.

Alan Elms said it first: psychobiography is a way of doing psychology. It's an unusual way, an artful way, a more difficult than easy path, but it is a *way*. This book constitutes a show and tell (or rather, a tell and show). Part I, How to Write a Psychobiography, starts readers at the very beginning of the process. How to find psychological meaning in biographical data (Schultz), how to make use of current research in personality psychology when doing psychobiography (McAdams), how to choose theory wisely (Elms), how to judge the relative value of psychobiographical explanations (Runyan), how to conduct N > 1 psychobiographical analyses (Isaacson)—all these questions get answered. In the introduction (Schultz), psychobiography's usefulness for the field of psychology is explored, as well as definitions of good psychobiography, bad psychobiography, and optimal structure for the psychobiographical essay. After choosing a subject to focus on (Saddam Hussein, e.g.), my students typically ask: OK, now what? Where to go from here? Part I provides a roadmap. It's a blueprint for success.

The remaining parts of the book are divided up in ways matching the field's historical tendencies. In Part II, Psychobiographies of Artists, I introduce the terrain most explored by psychobiographers over the last 100 years. This précis is followed by chapters on artists that show, or exemplify, high-quality psychobiography in action: Alan Elms and Bruce Heller on Elvis Presley, myself on Sylvia Plath, Dan Ogilvie on J.M. Barrie (the author of *Peter Pan*), and James Anderson on Edith Wharton.

Part III, Psychobiographies of Psychologists, is introduced by James Anderson. Figures explored include Freud (by Alan C. Elms), Gordon Allport (by Nicole Barenbaum), Nietzsche (by Kyle Arnold and George Atwood), Erik Erikson (by Irving Alexander), and the operationist S.S. Stevens (by Ian Nicholson).

Part IV, Psychobiographies of Political Figures, is introduced by Alan Elms and Anna Song. Stanley Renshon explores the life of George W. Bush, Anthony Dennis tackles the "sum of all fears," Osama Bin Laden, Anna Song weighs in on Kim Jong-Il, and Betty Glad surveys a range of political "tyrants."

Those the least bit acquainted with the field of psychobiography will recognize in the above lineup all its leading voices, its most talented practitioners. As I say again in chapter 1, this book is the best the field has to offer. There has never been anything quite like it. It is the most sumptuous feast for anyone with even the slightest interest in psychobiography. So please dig in and get what sustenance you will from its pages.

I feel as if I could thank the whole planet. Let me start by expressing my appreciation and admiration to all chapter writers, who performed with the utmost grace and aplomb. Alan Elms, in particular, has been for me *sui generis*. His wisdom never ceases to "shock and awe" me. Simply, if not for him, these words would be buried somewhere unexhumable. Mac Runyan has also been a constant source of inspiration, as have Irving Alexander, Dan McAdams, Rae Carlson, Jim Anderson, Dan Ogilvie, and Nicole Barenbaum. The Society for Personology, to which most chapter writers belong, helped me solidify the courage of my convictions, and in a field such as this one, that's worth a lot. When I first started doing psychobiography I was surrounded by a worthy group of peers at UC Davis, including David Philhour, Phil Crabtree, and especially Eva Schepeler. I thank them, too. My students I can't possibly praise enough. Some—Miki Souza and Kate Hutslar—served as research assistants. Some read drafts of my work-in-progress; for that I thank Athena Phillips, James Martinsen, Jen Prag, the incomparable Sarah Sameh, and most of all, for roughly ten years of stellar conversation, the "moon-goddess" Selene Crompton-Rogers. One class at Lewis and Clark College was a special delight. Marina, Dana, Patience, Heather, and others really helped shore me up merely by virtue of their kind enthusiasm for what the field had to offer (as did the outstanding Christine Hooker, another Lewis and Clark student, now studying schizophrenia). At Pacific University Cathy Suroviak has been a constant ally, as have innumerable others, including Alyson Burns-Glover, Marc Marenco, and Tim Thompson. I learned much about people and what makes them do what they do from time spent as a mental health therapist at an inpatient psychiatric unit at Providence Hospital in Portland, Oregon. For all their support, good wishes, and insight I thank Orawan, Bill Blaylock, Connie Ross, Mary Lowes, Mary Gordon, Casey Weber, Jim Kuhn, Peter Meiers, Scott Stapely, Gladys Hawthorne, Cheryl Corwin, Gail Hughson, Scot Cook, Mary Murphy, and Glen Robichaud.

Catharine Carlin, my editor on this project, has been an absolute joy in all respects. I thank my lucky stars daily for having had her on my side. She is a true wonder, one of the liveliest minds I know.

I owe this book to Dan Ogilvie, and for that I bow respectfully.

Dr. John Deeney changed my life, and more than anyone else got me thinking about a career in psychology. Friends at Lewis and Clark College set the ball rolling. These include Thomas Schoeneman, Glenn Meyer, Clayton Morgareidge, Bill Rottschaefer, Sevin Hirschbein, and my eternal "best man," Carol Capelli. (Carol in particular was always good at keeping me sane.)

I thank my wife, Theresa M. Love, the genuine article, the artist who taught me the most about artists, and my two shining diamonds, Adrienne Emerald Bradstreet and Henry William Wilder.

And finally, I thank my parents, who surrounded me with books, and showed me how to love reading.

Contents

Contributors

Irving E. Alexander, Duke University
James W. Anderson, Northwestern University
Kyle Arnold, Long Island University
George Atwood, Rutgers University
Nicole Barenbaum, University of the South
Anthony Dennis, http://www.acpr.org.il/people/adennis.html
Alan C. Elms, University of California, Davis
Betty Glad, University of South Carolina
Bruce Heller, http://www. corporatecoachingintl.com/team.php3
Kate Isaacson, University of California, Davis
Dan P. McAdams, Northwestern University
Ian Nicholson, St. Thomas University
Daniel Ogilvie, Rutgers University
Stanley Renshon, City University of New York
William McKinley Runyan, University of California, Berkeley
William Todd Schultz, Pacific University
Anna V. Song, University of California, Berkeley

PART I

HOW TO WRITE A PSYCHOBIOGRAPHY

Introducing Psychobiography

The aim of psychobiography is simply stated, though immensely difficult to achieve: the understanding of persons. This is what psychobiographers spend their hours thinking and writing about: complex, creative, inevitably contradictory individual lives, many of them also at their end. If, to most research psychologists—those valuing above all else the examination of single variables and part processes in contexts of careful experimental control—psychobiographers are felt to be chasing the wrong rainbows, that says more about psychology than it does psychobiography. After all, if psychology ought to strive for anything, if it hoped one sunny day to step away from its labs, one-way mirrors, instruments, and apparatuses into the uncontrolled world of life, then saying something vital about people—not single-file nameless mobs, but actual individuals with a history—should be job one.

When I first started doing psychobiography under the guidance of Alan Elms at the University of California at Davis—indeed when I first heard the term even used—I quickly grasped its antidotal nature (it was a partial "cure" for psychology's "sicknesses" of reductionism, scientism, trivialness, and irrelevance), and also its radicalism. It was not quite permissible. Its subjects weren't anonymous. It had nothing to do with groups. It did not require statistics. It made little effort to discover general principles applicable either to everyone or to subsets of subjects. Rather, it was all about taking up one lonely life at a time and trying to make whatever sense one could of that life. One seeking mind, armed with theory and research, directed at the details of another—that is psychobiography. When one stops to consider, this is exactly where psychology proper came from. All the great names—Freud to Skinner—made zero apologies for adopting the individual as a primary unit of analysis. Psychobiography, then, is psychology's "return of the repressed." It puts the person back where she should be in personality: front and center, the most moving target imaginable.

The fact that you are holding this book in front of you says much about how far the field has come over the last twenty years. One wonders, tremulously: Is psychobiography entering the mainstream? Not quite yet, but this text constitutes a step in that direction. My hope in editing this volume, and the hope of its chapter writers, too, is that it will serve as the definitive introduction to the field and that it will guide those so inclined in the writing of psychobiographies of their own. What follows really is the best that psychobiography has to offer, in the words of its most talented practitioners, its "music-makers" and "dreamers of dreams" (as Arthur O'Shaughnessy put it). Those with ears will hear the song and find the import in its lyrics.

The immediate question I want to try answering in this introduction—at the risk of leapfrogging more elementary matters—was first asked by Alan Elms in his own pathbreaking book, *Uncovering Lives: The Uneasy Alliance of Biography and Psychology* (1994): Why would a psychologist want to do psychobiography at all? What is psychobiography uniquely suited to provide psychology with?[1]

First of all, if Murray and Kluckhohn (1953) are correct in asserting that we are all in some respects like all other people, like some other people, and like no other people, then psychobiography and related case-study approaches work to fill in that last cell of information, namely, how people are unique, or how they function and come to be irrespective of any reference group. Psychobiographers frankly, and I think perfectly reasonably, assume such knowledge can be valuable, that individuals are worth knowing in a deep way. Its subjects, moreover, are often exactly those people whom knowing more about, and as intimately as possible, may be seen as most profitable: the world's Gandhis and Hitlers, Picassos and van Goghs. These are the figures who define the limits and the architecture of the human mind, in all its horror or magnificence. We must know them, because to know them is to know ourselves. Apologies to Burt Bacharach, but what the world needs now, more than anything else, is a science (or art) of persons, a way to get out of our own heads into the mind of another, and then, when finished with that Herculean task, to return to ourselves, armed with what we now know. I am speaking, then, of two reasons for doing psychobiography, each arguing on behalf of the other: *to cogently know another person, and to know ourselves.* What could be more basic?

Theories, or at least hypotheses, also emerge out of psychobiography. The doing of science begins with what Karl Popper (1959) called a context of discovery, followed by a context of falsification. Psychobiographies produce inspirations, strong hunches, or insights, leading in time to formal propositions that can be tested against larger groups of people (if such an end is desired). Psychoanalysis emerged out of Freud's self-analysis combined with analyses of hysterical patients—as did Jung's analytical psychology. Maslow, Piaget, Erikson, Laing, Murray, Allport, Tomkins, and others made their way into theory in similar fashion. They started with a person, or a handful or persons, took the task of speculation seriously, then branched out from there, in the end articulating models of mind applicable—theoretically at least—to all of us.

Psychobiography is psychology's stiffest challenge. *It brings various findings to bear on single lives, discovering what works and what doesn't.* The latter outcome is maybe the most desirable. When something does not work—does not illumine a life's more shadowy corners—the concept in question can be tinkered with, moved however slightly in increasingly useful directions. Freud tried this with *Leonardo*. He used the artist as a testing ground for ideas on sublimation and homosexuality. Erikson (1969) did something similar with Gandhi. And Maslow (1972), extending his research on dominance behavior in primates to the lives of a select group of optimally functioning humans, resurfaced in his problem-centered program with the notion of self-actualization. Elms (see 1994, pp. 14, 221) invented the "superego trip" after assaying the life of John Foster Dulles. Murray (1981) dissected the Harvard mind, then came away with the Icarus complex. My own Orpheus complex derived from detailed analyses of the life and writing of James Agee and Jack Kerouac, respectively (Schultz, 1996). Theories drive research. Theory is what experiments aim to refute or provisionally confirm. Though it may sometimes seem otherwise, theories do not fall from the sky tightly bundled, wonderfully intact and complete. Works of art in the widest sense, they are, when it comes to it, made up. They are created. They may even spring from abject irrationality or madness (one thinks here of Jung, who flirted with psychosis to communicate more fluidly with archetypal motifs). Single lives work as powerful stimuli. They elicit thrillingly impudent speculations. Speculation is where the action is. We need to remind ourselves of that fact from time to time.

Here it helps to bring in another branch of research seemingly (but only seemingly) so dissimilar from the psychobiographical. I'm talking about neuroscience. There the single case is indispensable (Ogilvie, 2003, makes the same point). It yields speculations leading almost daily to novel notions of brain function. Split brain work by Gazzaniga and Sperry transformed how we think about the cerebral hemispheres. Its subjects were assembled from a small number of scattered callosum-severed epileptics. Ramachandran (1998)—no enemy of speculation—proposed the existence of a right-hemisphere-generated "anomaly detector" after investigating anosognosia (denial of paralysis) in a tiny set of right-parietal-damaged stroke victims. Going back even further, lesion work is what provided initial answers to questions of brain morphology or structure.

One can't deny the existence of some debate on this subject, but in neuroscience generally, the single case propels inquiry. It is the starting point for later extrapolations—and unapologetically so. Psychobiography will occasionally produce bad ideas (as has brain science). So what? No falsehood damages the waiting truth. Besides, bad ideas are plentiful; they come from everywhere, even scientific research on large numbers of anonymous undergraduates. To put it a little differently: The existence of bad psychobiography—or bad car repair, for that matter—says nothing about psychobiography *in principle*. As with any field of endeavor, one comes across both talented and untalented practitioners. Poor internists don't call the field of medicine to the carpet.

What else does psychobiography offer? *Relevance*. In Elms's (1994) nifty phrase, it "tests the statistically significant against the personally significant" (p. 12). Let's face it, all the research in the world—however shiningly scientific, however robust and rigorous and carefully controlled—only sits there on a library shelf, shiningly inert, unless it makes sense in this life here, or that one over there. Lives aren't lived in the laboratory, Elms also tells us, and moreover, "[e]xperiments and correlational studies, and statistical analyses of the data they generate, may identify significant variables in the lives of people-in-general. But I haven't encountered a psychologist yet who could put together a live person from those statistical body parts and honestly cry out, 'IT'S ALIVE!'" (p. 13). Rae Carlson (1971) goes further. One can study persons in experimental situations, she writes, but one can't study personality experimentally. Carlson's comment is more than a Mobius strip of language. She offers it in service of a larger point: To know a person requires interpretation, not variable manipulation. One needs to enter the life, its dead ends and detours, its accreting mound of biographical fact, with subjectivity and presuppositions (world-knowledge) intact. If we wish to discover why someone did what she did, or how she became what she became, or what drives her, then what we need to do is step out

of the lab and into an existential context. Gathering a life history, reading written products, analyzing dreams, journals, and letters, talking to intimates, inspecting creative work—these and others are requisite tasks.[2] Psychobiography is one way to complete them.

Assembling even a simulacrum of a person from the hiccups of mind that experimenters typically set their sights on delineating requires someone—a new-age William James—who can do the arithmetic, the adding up of findings. But psychology is full of Wundts and absent Jameses. We are less a discipline than a farrago of sub-disciplines, each dragging along behind it a set of specialized sub-subdisciplines and a lexicon sure to discourage intrepid party crashers. Psychology's disorder is multiple personality (or, as it's now called, dissociative identity). We speak in a cacophony of voices. It is a din never quite achieving melodiousness. But if Jameses do exist, if generalists are to be found anywhere, they often gather in the arena of psychobiography. Why? Because psychobiographers draw from disparate bodies of knowledge. They take what is useful and make use of it. In my chapter on the photographer Diane Arbus (see chap. 8 this vol.), it became necessary to look over research concerning the effects of depressed mothers on their daughters, the concept of sensation seeking, symbiosis and splitting as described by object-relations theorists, ontological insecurity à la R.D. Laing, and the development of an "as-if personality" in response to narcissistic parenting. Psychobiography is unique in the sense that it makes of the psychobiographer, whether he likes it or not, a generalist, a James. It is for this reason, one guesses, that Howard Gardner (1992) singles out what he calls the field's "person-centered quartet" (students of consciousness, the will, personality, and self) and charges it with the task of unification. *In taking one life at a time, psychobiography achieves assimilation; it integrates the discipline's split selves.* This integration is temporary, true, but temporary, piecemeal integration is better than none at all.

I don't think psychobiography needs to go on defending itself *ad nauseum*. Coarse, sustained defensiveness is never appealing. Plus, it just distracts from the work to be done. But every once in a while—and particularly in this context, the publication of a comprehensive collection of essays—it's helpful to remind critics (or tell them for the first time) what the field offers. Trumpeting the value of single lives, generating novel theories or just tweaking those already established, encouraging subdisciplinary assimilation through acts of application, psychobiography promises a return to relevance. As Elms (1994) reveals in his book's final paragraph, the doing of psychobiography led him not astray, but "home." "I think," he writes,

> I've found a route to [psychology's] very center, to the understanding of human beings in their full complexity. I know there are many routes to that center, including the various paths I abandoned as unsuited to my own skills and my own personality. But I look for increasing numbers of psychologists to join me along the path of psychobiography, until it becomes a well-traveled avenue. (p. 256)

This present volume, too, is all about trail building. Recommending trails for their scenicness, comparing one vista to another—such strategies can't hurt, though here, in particular, they read like choir preaching. In the end, as Buddhists say, paths are made by walking.

Truth in Psychobiography

A question my students ask, especially after immersing themselves in the vexing ambiguites of a life and finding "answers" different from those they've been primed to expect, concerns the subject of truth, or what form of it psychobiographers seek. They want to know what makes a psychobiography good. They want to know what psychobiographers regard as successful understanding.

I always applaud this question. It has a bracing effect. It requires that we examine assumptions about people and their interpretation. My belief is that the extreme deconstructionist line is dead. Psychobiography is a structuralist endeavor. Those practicing it assume that motives, scripts, unconscious ideas, personality conflicts, and so on are real things—actual, knowable

mental structures (not "author functions" or "tropes"). And some efforts at knowing generate better answers than do others. To say, as the archest deconstructionists do, that all reading is a misreading and all interpretations are equally flawed by virtue of what they leave out, is to celebrate (and encourage) pointlessness. It is smirky, winking surrender, an abdication of the responsibility to find something to believe in. I prefer belief to clever, arid disbelief. In the day-to-day world of relationships, of constant soft collisions with others, we live and make meaning through interpretation, tacit or explicit. What did mysterious person X really mean when she said that? This simple question encapsulates psychobiography's chronic posture. People are poems, I tell my students (a few eyes roll). And like poems, people may be interpreted in different ways, some even contradictory. Poems and people are not so much explained as understood. We make sense of them. We bring them to coherence. What is at first un-understandable becomes, in a flash, clear. We "get" what is being said. This meaning is often subtextual, too. It must be deciphered. And—here is the core assertion—some meanings are clearly better than others. But which? What constitutes successful meaning making? Runyan ventures one reply in chapter 6, as he examines competing opinions as to why van Gogh cut off his ear (a classic essay in the history of psychobiography). But we can anticipate a little.

To start with, everything we do is overdetermined. Every act, even the most quotidian, emerges out of a conspiracy of reasons. No single reason suffices, or it does so only very rarely. To make matters worse (or better yet, more interesting), different sets of reasons may motivate different facets of the same gestalt of action. So, van Gogh cuts off his ear because he hears voices, and because he wishes to mimic the scene on Calvary, say, but he gives his ear to a prostitute with an altogether different intent. We oversimplify when we seek single aims. Reasons are better described as concerted, as pluralities. Psychobiographers look for clusters of motives, not "the" motive. Even so, certain members of any motive cluster still are better than others—more explanatory, more incisive. What makes them so? First and foremost, they possess *co-*

gency (which I'll define momentarily; see Table 1.1). They persuade. In reading about them we find ourselves won over—just like jurists are won over by evidence for the prosecution, which also rises or falls on the establishment of motive (in general, jury persuasion is a fair analogy for the persuasion occurring in psychobiography).

Rhetorical strategies, or the structure of the psychobiographical narrative, play an important role. How one tells the story of the life directly affects the story's persuasiveness. For example, conclusions stated prior to supporting evidence always make me suspicious. Saying Saddam Hussein is a sociopath, and then listing facts in support of such a claim, tends to raise questions about how the facts have been assembled and which facts have been left out. It's always better to let conclusions follow naturally from an array of data: Give the reader the evidence, then suggest its meanings, and let the chips fall where they may. (A related point: Beware psychobiography by diagnosis. Diagnoses are always oversimplifications, ways of not understanding. And giving a name to a set of "symptoms" is both pathographic, excessively focused on the negative alone, and merely descriptive, never explanatory.)

More cogent psychobiographical essays are also relatively *comprehensive*. They illumine more features of the act in question. In chapter 15, on Freud's *Leonardo*, Elms shows why, for personal reasons, Freud was consumed (consciously and unconsciously) with thoughts of both sublimation and homosexuality, revealing how these two ideas—and the urgency with which Freud felt the need to explore them—had their roots in personal conflicts Freud worked through in the act of writing. Elms's interpretation accounts simultaneously for several aspects of Freud's behavior, not just one. The great success of the chapter derives, in part, from its comprehensiveness.

Psychobiographies persuade in another sense when their conclusions rest on a *convergence of evidence*. The more data supporting an interpretation, and the more various its sources, the better. The very best interpretations are those that seem almost inevitable, and what makes them seem inevitable is the way assorted lines of thought and opinion lead inexorably back to them. If my aim is to suggest that Sylvia Plath wrote her famous poem "Daddy" so that she may once and for all escape the hold that her dead father's image had on her, then I want to find support for this idea in what she says about the poem (in journals and letters), in what others said about the poem (say, her husband, Ted Hughes), in related poems about her father (there are many), in details drawn from her life at the time she wrote the poem, and in patterns of conflict from the biographical record. One line of evidence alone may tantalize, but to persuade it is necessary to cast one's net widely (for more on Sylvia Plath, see Schultz, chap. 11 this vol.).

What other qualities characterize good psychobiography? Cogent interpretations *make the initially incoherent cohere*. Puzzling details get accounted for, often strikingly. In her latest book

Table 1.1 Good Psychobiography Markers

Cogency	Basic intepretive persuasiveness, on the model of jury persuasion, for instance. The best psychobiographies leave the reader feeling ineffably "won over."
Narrative structure	Letting conclusions follow naturally from an array of data, for example.
Comprehensiveness	Interpretations illuminating more aspects of an act in question are more cogent than those failing to account for central details. The more reasons clarified, the better, especially in light of the fact that behavior of whatever kind is always "overdetermined."
Data convergence	The more data supporting a fact or an interpretation, and the more various its sources, the better.
Sudden coherence	The best interpretations make the initially incoherent cohere. Mystery's elucidation is psychobiography's most salutary aim.
Logical soundness	Freedom from logical inconsistency or self-contradiction.
Consistency	Jibes with the full range of available evidence and with general knowledge about human functioning.
Viability	Capacity to withstand attempts at falsification.

(*The Seal Wife*, 2003), Kathryn Harrison devotes a page or two to, of all things, an eerily ambulatory tongue—sneaking up on the book's main character, twisting and turning wetly. Lacking context, the image jars. It seems, at first, inexplicable, incongruous. Then one recalls Harrison's affair with her father (which she describes in her memoir, *The Kiss* 1997), and how that affair commenced with a "French kiss." At once the tongue makes sense. Its return in fiction coheres with the life. Superimposing one on the other—the life on the art—resolves perplexity. Mystery's elucidation is psychobiography's most salutary aim. The odder the detail one sheds light on, the more convincing the interpretation.

Other more obvious characteristics of the cogent interpretation include *logical soundness, consistency with the full range of available evidence and with general knowledge about human functioning*, and *survival of attempts at falsification* (the idea's ability, in other words, to withstand scrutiny). These and other criteria are taken up later by Runyan (see chap. 6 this vol.), so I don't elaborate on them here. The larger point is this: Criteria for judging an interpretation's effectiveness do exist. We need not throw up our hands in a posture of surrender, proclaiming—exhaustedly—that all interpretations are equal, their relative merits indistinguishable. To assume the latter is to assure psychobiography's demise—and to fly in the face of common sense. Life is about understanding other people. Psychobiography is no different. If anything, its sense-making efforts are more liable to succeed, since they derive from larger and public data sets. Psychobiography always has plenty of evidence at its disposal; its subjects are written about, talked about, pursued with assiduity. They are, in short, famous, surrounded by a "climate of opinion."

The Structure of the Psychobiographical Essay

By this point in the conversation my students start to feel a little more reassured, a little less lost and off-kilter. They accept psychobiography's value (they probably always did, actually). The wisdom of focusing on one life at a time makes intuitive sense to them. After all, what drew them to psychology was an interest in people. People are what they want to study (not variables or part processes). They also begin to see that interpretations can be judged in light of clear and reasonable criteria. A winnowing can occur, the bad differentiated from the good (with this task of winnowing students, in my experience, always excel). But when it comes to the possibility of writing their own psychobiographical essay, they freeze. How to begin? Where to start? These are the questions most often met with. The following chapters of this book provide both explicit and implicit answers. They exemplify how to proceed. Still, I'll venture a few ideas of my own.

I said already, mystery's elucidation is psychobiography's most salutary aim. Compelling psychobiographies begin with a *koan* (i.e., in the Zen tradition, a paradoxical, elusive phrase or episode requiring for its solution a leap to another level of understanding). Complicit fascination is what we hope to engender with that koan. Questions with fascinating effects do not always arrive on schedule, however. They tend to come unbidden; they surprise us. It's mutual: We find them, and they find us. I'll use one of my students, James Martinsen, as an example. James decided to write his thesis on Maurice Sendak. He began exactly as he should—by reading Sendak, by reading secondary literature on Sendak, by looking over interviews with Sendak, and by getting up to speed on Sendak's life. He became acquainted with his subject, in other words. Still, for all that, no koan presented itself. The life was spread out before him; lots of avenues seemed vaguely promising, but nothing riddling stepped into the breach. James lacked a core enchantment, something he could reveal in surprising ways. Then, as always seems to happen, in his reading James collided with a quote, a sentence or two in an interview. Sendak mentions how all his books, all his art, can be traced to a single infantile experience, some psychic territory "below the head" that, however hard he tries, he can't articulate, can't pin down. *Shazam*. James located his mystery. He decided then and there to try articulating what Sendak himself could not. He returned to the data with this goal—effing the ineffable—and let his ingenuity take it from there.

I don't know what's more difficult, locating the mystery or interpreting it. Each makes its own demands. Whatever the case, mystery coaxing is a key part of most every psychobiography. If we want to persuade by making the incoherent cohere, then let's be sure to conjure the most tantalizing incoherences we can find. Why did Freud go so uncharacteristically astray in writing on Leonardo? What is the origin of Nabokov's immensely entertaining but no less virulent hatred of psychoanalysis and of Freud, that so-called figure of fun? Who is the "shrouded stranger" menacing Kerouac in so many of his books, the cackling "Dr. Sax" of his childhood reveries? How to make sense of Emily Dickinson's dressing exclusively in white? Why, indeed, did van Gogh cut off his ear? Such questions—all of them koans—fascinate (or if they don't, you have the wrong book in your hands). They also illustrate an important difference between psychobiography and biography. The former most often targets one facet of a life at a time, a more or less discrete episode or event or action, not "the" life in all its yawning immensity (unless, as in rare cases, such as Erikson's books on Luther and Gandhi, one attempts a full-scale assessment of a life). Psychobiography's goals tend to be more modest than biography's—to illumine this one episode or event or action, to bring this one happening into clarity. The clarity sought is psychological in nature. It has chiefly to do with the subject's interior world, the effects of his life history on his mind and actions. The perspective is person centered, but not fatuously so. Historical, sociological, cultural, political, even economic factors all play some role in determining who we are and why we do what we do. There can be no denying that simple fact. But there can be no denying the fact of the psychological, either. That is where the psychobiographer sets up camp. That is his contribution to the whole.

Where to go after squeezing out the sparks of mystery? To the data again (in fact, it's a constant back and forth). As Alexander (1990) says, ask the data a question and let the data reveal themselves. Everything in the mystery's nimbus demands particularly close attention. The life itself suggests lines of theory or research to inspect—follow those leads. They are the tools for

going beyond the data toward its interpretation. Different ideas will emerge—insights, hunches, speculations—but patience, as they say, is a cardinal virtue. Don't foreclose on any one idea too soon. Psychobiography is an iterative process. Data lead to interpretations; more data lead to different and better interpretations; different and better interpretations lead to new ways of configuring the data—the process unfolds according to its own timetable, until one achieves what feels like the best fit, the most elegant coherence between the life, the work, and the link between the two.

Then it's a matter of structuring the story in its most arresting format. Decisions as to structure should be made consciously. How we present our case will either enhance or interfere with its capacity to persuade. There really is no *a priori* ideal framework with categories or components that simply get filled in (as one meets with in the experimental paradigm). In fact, the experimental paradigm—introduction, hypothesis, subjects, procedures, results, discussion—is ill-suited to the psychobiographical enterprise. We aren't doing an experiment. There are no procedures or statistical results. We are interpreting the poem of a person. I can speak only for myself, and others will speak for themselves in chapters to follow. I first show the mystery, seeking the reader's complicit fascination. I tell the reader what she needs to know about the mystery, explain why the mystery is so mysterious, and why it ought to be interesting or worth uncovering. Then I spread out all evidence germane to the mystery, careful at this point not to tip my hand (sometimes I'm still waiting for the dealer of the hand to finish!). The reader needs a chance to see what is there, to make her own sense of things, develop her own hunches. Once that occurs, interpretation directed by theory and research crafts out of incoherence a pleasing, often surprising, always artful whole—an elegant totality that simply feels like an answer. The parts must be seen to come together, the evidence to converge on a conclusion that, in concert with the evidence, appears almost impossible not to reach.

Two examples come right to mind. Ogilvie (2003), in his book *Fantasies of Flight*, looks at a number of persons attached to the idea of

getting off the ground and into air (myself, I prefer terra firma, and when I'm into air, all I can
think of is getting on the ground again). Ogilvie's
primary subject is J.M. Barrie, the author of *Peter
Pan*. He begins with Barrie's fictional fantasies,
in the process introducing flight desires as a
mystery worth unpacking (i.e., why do people
entertain such a weird wish anyway?). He reviews theory touching on the subject—Freud,
Murray, neuroscience. Then he unveils his own
perspective, his own model of flying fantasies,
returning once more to the data in order to make
a case for why his position produces the most
clarifying coherence. Ogilvie's is a nice example
of how theory can "arise," so to speak, from an
analysis of a handful of biographical subjects (he
adds to Barrie other flight afficionados).

Elms's (1994) essay on Allport employs a
similar framework. He tells how Allport first met
Freud, of the "pungent significance" of their
encounter, and how Allport tended to repeat the
story whenever he had the chance to (for much
more on Allport's meeting with Freud, as well
as how it both recapitulated and predicted similar sorts of meetings with other individuals
Allport admired, see Barenbaum, chap. 16 this
vol.). The meeting, combined with Allport's need
to talk or write about it, becomes the mystery.
What made this meeting so pivotal? What might
it tell us about Allport's personality and his
theory of personality? Elms interviews those who
knew Allport (including, as it happens, Dan
Ogilvie) and explores aspects of Allport's life and
theory building residing in the mystery's nimbus.

Then he superimposes his own viewpoint, a set
of insights that, again, make of scattered puzzle
pieces a clearly recognizable picture. The parts,
in other words, form a whole.

Ogilvie and Elms provide two examples of
psychobiography at its finest. Mystery is artfully
elucidated, theory and research reviewed, and a
novel synthesis introduced. The reader is won
over. Cogency is achieved.

Bad Psychobiography

Good psychobiographies really are plentiful. But
what makes a psychobiography bad? Which
practices should we avoid?

I'll start with one of my favorite poor strategies: psychobiography by diagnosis (or "pathography," touched on above; see Table 1.2). Let's
say a psychobiographer wants to make a case for
Marilyn Monroe having borderline personality
disorder. Symptoms form an orderly single-file
line, and each gets checked off predictably.
Marilyn suffers from chronic feelings of emptiness; her personal relationships are unstable; she
fears abandonment; her moods are volatile, labile; she entertains suicidal ideas. Voila! Aspects
of Monroe's behavior accord with a set of diagnostic criteria. Her life is given a new imprima-
tur: borderline. What does that reveal? Nothing
we don't already know. What is a diagnosis anyway but a shorthand description for pigeon-
holed behaviors? It doesn't succeed in
interpreting those behaviors; it merely names

Table 1.2 Bad Psychobiography Markers

Pathography	Psychobiography by diagnosis, or reducing the complex whole of personality to static psychopathological categories and/or symptoms.
Single cues	Excessive reliance on one piece of data in offering interpretations. The best insights are tied instead to sets of evidence, a nexus of supporting facts drawn from the biographical record.
Reconstruction	Inventing psychological facts inferentially for which no direct evidence exists. Often resorted to in the absence of verifiable data about childhood history.
Reductionism	Explaining adult character and behavior exclusively in terms of early childhood experience while neglecting later formative processes and influences. Childhood is doubtless often key, but it isn't ever the *only* key to personality.
Poor theory choice	Making use of theories utterly lacking experimental support or credibility within the field.
Poor narrative structure	Analyses artlessly presented with, say, conclusions stated prior to careful introduction of evidence.

them. It adds to the mystery, uncovering, really, nothing. So, *beware psychobiography by diagnosis*. In oversimplifying a life—something all labels do—psychiatric diagnosis succeeds by subtraction, by leaving things out. Good psychobiography leaves *in* as much as possible.

Interpretations relying on one piece of data also fail to persuade. To be sure, the vivid instance can sometimes captivate. It stands out. It draws attention to itself. Avoiding analyses of vivid instances altogether won't do. They make for a starting point—but that is all. Additional details need to be adduced. One dream, one memory, one action can't sustain an entire interpretation—or does so only perilously. Surrounding life events warrant consideration, as do comments made by friends and intimates about the dream, memory, or action in question. Similar dreams, memories, or actions that seem in whatever way related to the primary one likewise provide important contextualizing information. We want to know: Is this vivid instance a prototype for other instances met with in our subject's life? Does the vivid instance symbolize a pattern of sorts? The most famous example of bad psychobiography in the "vivid instance" vein is provided, funnily enough, by Freud. Enthralled, for personal reasons, by one of Leonardo's fantasies—of a bird visiting the artist in his cradle and thrusting its tail into his mouth—Freud rushes headlong into a proliferating farrago of speculations about, among other things, Leonardo's early life (about which almost nothing is known), his sexuality, even the Mona Lisa's enigmatic smile (see Elms, 1994). This bird Freud took to be a vulture. Later translations correct that error, revealing the bird to be a kite. Since many of Freud's interpretations derive exclusively from the presumed vulture visit, they fly merrily out the window once that vulture becomes a bird of an altogether different feather. The moral of the story is clear: Tie your interpretations to sets of evidence, to a web of supporting facts taken from the life. That way, if one piece of evidence fails—or is exposed as incomplete or excessively partial—other pieces remain, securing the interpretation's effectiveness.

Freud's error was actually compounded in this case. He relied too much on one fantasy (in fact, no one knows if it was a fantasy, a dream, a memory, or what). He also used that fantasy to reconstruct an entire infantile history. Such reconstruction signals bad psychobiography. It never succeeds.[3] Runyan (1982) suggests banning it altogether (I agree), or at least "keeping it distinct from events for which there is clear documentary evidence" (p. 208). Because Leonardo fantasized an infant in its cradle—presumably Leonardo himself—sucking a bird's tail feathers, Freud says, he must have spent his early years in the company of his real mother, the model for his later paintings that, through the act of painting, he hoped to elicit. This is reconstruction, and it is make-believe. We know nothing of Leonardo's first few years, and no amount of fantasy makes up for that fact. Runyan (1982) cites a similar make-believe in the case of Emily Dickinson. On the basis of comments made in letters, recurring metaphors, family correspondence, and Dickinson's tendency for seclusiveness—among other clues—Cody (1971) argues that Dickinson likely "experienced what she interpreted as a cruel rejection by her mother" (quoted in Runyan, 1982, p. 198). Trouble is, as Runyan notes, "there exists no record of any concrete instance in which Mrs. Dickinson took such an attitude toward her daughter" (p. 198). No educated guesswork prompted by analyses of patients with "scars similar to Dickinson's" compensates for this paucity of evidence. Psychobiography is all about interpretation. But what gets interpreted are facts—not inferred facts (which aren't really facts at all). So, *avoid psychobiography by reconstruction*. If the data aren't there, and if the only way to "find" them is to make them up, then do not write the psychobiography. Choose another subject.

Reductionism is yet another marker of a bad psychobiography, though here let's be very clear about what "reductionism" means. In this context, reductionism is at work in efforts "to explain adult character and behavior exclusively in terms of early childhood experience while neglecting later formative processes and influences" (Runyan, 1982, p. 209). Childhood can be key. We should never neglect it entirely. It may be trauma filled for some and doubtless influential for the development of personality. It might even be the most formative time period in any one subject's life as far as who that person becomes and why she does what she does. Childhood is almost always a factor; it isn't ever the only factor, however. At least not in good psychobiography it isn't.

Wilhelm Reich began as a Freudian but in time came to believe—and here he must have found himself in a distinct minority, perhaps of one—that Freud failed to place enough importance on sex. Or on orgasm, to be specific. For good health, Reich believed, and to shed the shackles of characterological armor, human orgasmic potency must increase. He postulated what he called "orgone energy," a cosmological vigor field capable of being harvested and concentrated for salutary gain (free atmospheric Viagra). To achieve this concentration he patented an Orgone Box, which he sold over the mail (I sat in one of these boxes a few times during days of graduate-school-inspired openness to experience, to nothing but soporific effect). He was arrested for fraud and died in prison, refusing to mount any defense. An event at age fourteen may account for some of the above. It was then that Reich learned of his mother's affair with one of his tutors (see Stolorow & Atwood, 1979). He confessed this discovery to his notoriously violent father, an action his mother responded to with suicide. In other words, "by acting on the basis of a narrow code of sexual morality Reich was responsible for the death of the one person he loved above all others" (quoted in Runyan, 1982, pp. 199–200). As an adult, he compensated—one might posit—by championing free sex and by opposing all antisexual, totalitarian "death forces" at work in the world. His theory was a repudiation of a childhood error of judgment. At least, *in part* it may have been, and this proviso is critical. Explaining Reich's theory and assorted other intellectual beliefs *exclusively* in terms of his mother's suicide when he was fourteen is reductionism. Surely what Reich stood for had numberless other roots as well. One event does not a life make—though, as I said, single events can be incredibly potent on occasion, as this one obviously was. But to argue that Reich's theory and assorted other intellectual beliefs stemmed *in part* from his mother's suicide when he was fourteen is not reductionism. In the latter way of looking at things, the suicide is accorded its due impor-

tance—only not exclusively, not in a way superseding all other contributing factors. It is one factor—likely the most important factor—but not the only factor. Reductionism reduces to explaining a lot by way of a very little (a single reason); in fact, psychobiography works best when it does exactly the opposite, namely, tracing mysterious gestalts of thought and action back to a variety of biographical vectors (remember, everything we do is overdetermined, or caused by a concert of reasons). So, beware the inverted pyramid: Do not rest a great parcel of attitudes on one tiny point. When you do, more often than not the parcel collapses of its own weight.

Theory can pose problems in psychobiography, too. *Choices of which theory or theories to use must be made judiciously, with attention paid (when possible) to the question of experimental support.* An analysis based on, say, penis envy would seem, *prima facie*, unconvincing. It assumes an unreasonable degree of credulousness in the reader and also, if dogmatically applied, flirts with both reductionism and reconstruction (evidence for penis wishes being indirect and inferential). Psychology is presently preparadigmatic and noncumulative. No agreed-upon theory unifies the field. And in fact, much theory is either unfalsifiable or lacking the kind of experimental support arising from attempted falsifications. Such facts make decisions on theory difficult. The best tack is to let the evidence point the way and then to apply theory nimbly, intelligently, and with every necessary qualification. Don't pretend the theory works perfectly if it does not. Use those aspects that seem valuable, and bracket everything else. A "hermeneutics of suspicion" is a healthy posture for sifting through evidence, and it works for applications of theory, as well. Don't let self-doubt cripple you, but do subject even your fondest interpretations (those especially, in fact!) to ongoing self-scrutiny. It's worth remembering that psychobiography is only as good as the theory on which it rests. If the theory isn't "true," or if it's applied luridly or tactlessly or, worse yet, gracelessly (which is to say, artlessly), or if its application lacks the requisite self-consciousness, then even when it seems to work, it doesn't: It won't inspire the reader's confidence, and though it suffices minimally, it will not persuade. One last point: Too much theory also dismays the reader. Jargon and heavy-handedness are a turnoff. They crowd the narrative and test the reader's patience unduly. This is a subtle point, but still worth putting across: *In many cases theory works best when it remains off-stage.* Though applying it every step of the way, let it stay in the background, the orchestra's invisible conductor. To hear the music we need not focus on the baton (although it still guides every note). For more advice on the difficult task of theory choice in psychobiography, see Elms (chap. 5 this vol.).

One last red flag is extrascientific but unignorable. Style matters in psychobiography. *The blend of plodding, generic, spuriously precise, clunkily objective and almost pusillanimous prose one comes to expect (with dread) of standard research-journal-style writing only undermines the effectiveness of the psychobiographical essay.* In psychobiography one tells a story about a life. Chances are, the life itself already entices, but the story adds to or subtracts from any initial intensity of interest. The most arresting, alluring subject (Elvis, let's say) arrives lumpily on the page if the prose dulls him up. To write psychobiography one acts not like a scientist but an artist (same goes, really, for *doing* it). Narration is required. One seeks the best form, not always beginning at the beginning. Details are dwelt on, caressed, finessed. One wallows in nuance, never rushing ahead to oversimplification or generalization. The reader must feel rising dramatic tension resolved by interpretation—the sudden opening of a door revealing the mystery's true source. What has been tremulously implicit all along at last finds words. If understanding people really is analogous to the interpretation of a poem, then we can't deny the essential artfulness of the psychobiographical enterprise. Like any artisan, we do best when we hone this artfulness, not ignore or avoid it.

The State of the Field

We've discussed the usefulness of psychobiography, the critical part played by mystery, the structure of the psychobiographical narrative, and features of good and of bad research.

Now, in this last section, I want to try synopsizing where the field currently stands. How healthy is it? Has it leveled out, or is it on the rise? And where is it headed? What other avenues of research has it tended to merge with or parallel?

A little personal history seems in order, only because it illustrates a more general past. I mentioned that I first discovered psychobiography in 1986 when, by some magic act of fate, I wandered into Alan Elms's seminar on the topic at UC Davis. I had little idea what to expect. The very word "psychobiography" was new to me, as it was, I assume, to others in the class. We were all of us doubtless quite curious. As most schools do, my undergraduate college more or less ruled out research not deemed "empirical"—a term my teachers took to mean (naively) experimental and statistical. Qualitative theses were implicitly disallowed—and, if brashly proposed, were just as brashly dismissed. If I wanted to read Freud, or to take up "big picture" questions of theory, the only department open to me was philosophy, a subject in which I wound up majoring (along with psychology). As an undergrad I was sometimes asked by psychology faculty to lecture on Freud. I did so happily. To be honest, I knew more about Freud than my psychology professors did (a discrepancy they worried little about). But they always regarded me as this funnily misguided zealot whose callowness eventually would wear off as I learned the amusing wrongness of my ways, and more or less got the joke. But I never did learn this. I never got the joke. And I started wondering who, in fact, was wrong and who right. I guess I became, there and then, a critic of my own field.

And finding out about psychobiography only solidified that stance. Here was another wonderfully taboo art (in 1986). I don't suppose a course like Elms's was offered anywhere else in the entire nation (except maybe Berkeley, where William Runyan taught). Why was that, exactly? What did psychology have against psychobiography? Those things already listed: It was hopelessly subjective, too enamored of the single case, interpretive, excessively reliant on psychoanalysis, and so forth. It was not experimental. It did not make use of statistics. It wasn't, in other words, psychology. Fortunately for me, at Davis in the mid-1980s lots of things that weren't psychology were nonetheless finding their way into the psychology curriculum. Charles Tart was lecturing on altered states, Thomas Natsoulas was teaching classes on consciousness and perception from Jamesian and Gibsonian perspectives, and yes, Alan Elms offered seminars on psychobiography. Into these orbits I gratefully drifted. Two years later, I felt just impudent enough to propose a psychobiographical dissertation—a path cleared by one of my stellar peers, Eva Schepeler. Unchecked fantasy fast became fettered reality, and the whip I reserved for self-flagellation was now in the department's meaty hands.

After much insider debate within my department and concerned lip biting over matters of precedent—none of which I was privy to, being only a grad student—Alan Elms managed to convince the faculty (my professors) that psychobiography was in fact a legitimate dissertation subject. I was allowed—as was Eva Schepeler before me—to form a thesis committee (replete with nonpsychologists even). The question apparently hinged once more on the definition of the word "empirical." This time Elms traced the term to its proper root—the British empiricists. To be empirical means simply to observe directly, and that is what I would be doing. What I observed was, in a word, text, or biographical data. And I interpreted these data through the lens of theory. Psychobiography, it was decided, was by this definition just as "empirical" as any other form of psychological research. The road thus opened up, I went on to write a thesis on the life and creative work of the American writer James Agee. I managed, that is, to do something quite unusual for a graduate student in a psychology department committed to the highest standards of experimental rigor: finish a dissertation focused on just one person, with no effort made to generalize my findings, and no statistical results section. (Eva Schepeler accomplished the same feat, finishing a groundbreaking psychobiographical dissertation on Jean Piaget.)

I look back on all this with a surfeit of mostly misplaced pride. My work changed nothing. It did not elicit an avalanche of psychobiographical thesis proposals. But it did force the department to take a hard, long look at what psychology really was, and in admitting psychobiography to the club, however provisionally and resentfully, department members allowed for the prospect of future qualitative proposals. Because mine went through, others might too. Psychobiography wasn't *really* psychology, but it was close enough not to get rejected out of hand.

When planning my thesis there wasn't much to draw on. Only one example of a clearly thoughtful and scholarly text on the subject existed, this being William Runyan's (1982) *Life Histories and Psychobiography: Explorations in Theory and Method.* In short order that book became my bible. If I didn't sleep with it at my side, I should have. Just being able to look at it on my shelf provided comfort. It said to me: Yes, one can actually do psychobiography responsibly, judiciously, intelligently, and convincingly. Runyan's book led me to Henry Murray's (1981) *Endeavors in Psychology*, a dense, sententious tour de force full of brash antipsychology criticism and prose that refused to sit still. I recognized Murray's art, thrilled to his championing of what he called personology, the inspection of one life at a time, over time. Then there was the late Rae Carlson, most famous for her polemical 1971 essay "Where Is the Person in Personality Research?" She seemed to be calling for exactly what I wanted to spend my time doing: analyzing not anonymous undergraduates in experimental settings, but fully lived lives, whole minds rather than part processes extracted from biographical context.

But these were voices in the margins. They were tolerated, looked at sideways, discovered and taken deeply seriously by the few. What they said seemed difficult to deny, but as anyone knows, awkward truths have a way of getting brushed aside by those too little enamored of ambiguity and contradiction. Today, as I compare past and present, the story is rather different. Intrepid graduate students dreaming of psychobiographical dissertations will find much more to go on. If I was slicing my canoe into a spoon-fed creek, they will meet a swelling river. The times, they are a changin', not necessarily radically, but still, as Nasby and Read (1997) observed a few years back, "Strange doings are afoot in personality psychology . . . The long silenced call has sounded again for the study of individual lives" (p. 788).

First, in 1988, the *Journal of Personality* devoted a special issue to psychobiography and life narratives, with chapters by Elms, Runyan, Carlson, Alexander, Anderson, David Winter, and McAdams—many of those included in this volume, in fact (see McAdams & Ochberg, 1988). This was one of those occasions when excitement proved perhaps a little short-lived. The decision by a mainstream personality journal to devote an entire number to the subject of psychobiography was a stunner (to me at the time); the effects this decision had on the field, however, are hard to adduce. We do know, based on a review of research, that between 1993–1995 a lonely two case-study-type articles appeared in any of five major personality journals (those assayed were *Journal of Personality*, *Journal of Research in Personality*, *Journal of Personality and Social Psychology*, *European Journal of Personality*, and *Personality and Individual Differences*). The venue in which they landed? *Journal of Personality*, in both cases. Predictably, the overwhelming majority of articles were questionnaire based, utilizing large samples (see Endler & Speer, 1998).

Still, in 1994 another signal event occurred. Alan Elms's *Uncovering Lives: The Uneasy Alliance of Biography and Psychology* appeared in print. Set alongside Runyan's, this book with chapters on Freud, Jung, Skinner, Nabokov, L. Frank Baum, Carter, Hussein, and George Bush Sr., among others—instantly became must reading for any psychobiographer. It was a second stellar example of psychobiography set forth with tact, cogency, and intelligence.

Then Demorest (1995) resurrected Henry Murray's concepts of the thema and unity-thema—pushed aside more or less by the competing trait variable—linking these with Tomkins's notion of "scripts." In the second half of the same essay Demorest pursued an idiographic method of personal script assessment informed by Alexander's notions of abstraction and sequencing (pp. 584–588). Relying on the saliency identifier of "primacy" (see Alexander, 1990) and on script theory yet again, Demorest and Siegel in 1996 published in the *Journal of Personality* an empirical case study of B.F. Skinner.

The same year saw a piece by David Winter (1996) on Allport, followed by a special section

in the *Journal of Personality* commemorating the centennial of Allport's birth, with several personological chapters (Winter, 1997; Barenbaum, 1997). Schaller (1997) looked at the relationship between fame and self-consciousness via the lives of Kurt Cobain, Cole Porter, and John Cheever. Barresi and Juckes (1997) recommended personology and narrative analysis as the "most promising methodology" for a science of persons.

In 1997 there came another special issue I recall being shocked by. The *Journal of Personality* devoted an entire volume to a case analysis of Dodge Morgan, who in 1986 at the age of 54 completed a solo circumnavigation of the world. Then in 1998 a forum consisting of four essays on mad King George appeared (Simonton, 1998).

It isn't hard to see that the above represents the commitment of one mainstream journal—*Journal of Personality*—to personology. In fact, to be more precise, what it represents is the commitment of one *editor* at that journal, Stephen G. West, to the field of personology, which he has over the years shepherded into the mainstream of personality research. Still, I'm encouraged (one's better than none), especially after adding to the mix activity outside psychology proper. From 1999 through 2003, I've contributed an annotated bibliography of psychobiography research to the fall issue of the journal *Biography: An Interdisciplinary Quarterly* (for a complete listing of these entries, see http://www.psychobiography.com/biblio.html). In 1999, 26 articles were indexed, along with 23 books on subjects from Who drummer Keith Moon to Mary Baker Eddy (the first year I did not search out dissertations with psychobiographical foci). In 2000 there were 46 articles in the bibliography, 15 dissertations, and 4 books. The 2001 index included the most entries by far (a partial artifact of the excellence of my research assistant at the time, Stefanie Page): 67 articles and 15 dissertations. I stopped this year looking for books and focused instead on relevant book chapters, of which I found 20 with a clear psychobiographical emphasis. In 2002 my database search was severely truncated due to various constraints on time. Still I met up with 24 articles, 20 books and book chapters, and 4 dissertations.

In 2003, 35 articles were tracked down, along with 3 books and 5 dissertations.

What journals do these articles come from? Mainly psychoanalytic, for the obvious reasons that applied psychoanalysis has always been valued in Freudian circles, and modern psychobiography began with Freud—his book on Leonardo and his case studies. *American Imago*, *Psychoanalytic Review*, and the *International Journal of Psycho-Analysis* are heavily represented in the index. But so are *Journal of Personality*, *Creativity Research Journal*, *Political Psychology*, *Clio's Psyche*, and *Biography: An Interdisciplinary Quarterly* (of course). The *Annual of Psychoanalysis* also recently devoted an entire volume to the subject of psychoanalytic psychohistory, with chapters from many of the field's leading practitioners (see Winer & Anderson, 2003)

Who are the subjects? They cluster into categories we find also in this volume: artists, politicians, and psychologists/thinkers, with few exceptions. Artists include Plath (more than any other), Dickinson, Tennessee Williams, George Eliot, Joyce, Rothko, Cezanne, van Gogh, Mahler, Mishima, Kahlo, Mondrian, Nabokov; politicians Adlai Stevenson, Clinton, Stalin, Gorbachev; psychologist/thinkers Freud (more than any other person over the four years canvassed), Jung (a close second), Harry Stack Sullivan, Wittgenstein, Bettelheim, R.D. Laing, mathematician Paul Erdos, and Gordon Allport.

Theoretical approaches? Chiefly psychoanalytic or object-relations based, but in recent years many researchers seem to be adopting what I would call a diagnostic bent, reducing the art of Plath, van Gogh, Dickinson, Hemingway, and others to assorted, usually mood-based mental illnesses. I find this a dangerous turn (for reasons discussed above). We don't get a good sense of the fluid dynamics of a life, its strengths and weaknesses, its infinite subtlety and grace, from one-sided pathographic "disease" sniffing. Even so, the return to pathography is real. One hopes the stay is a short one, only a detour on a far more scenic journey, the most insipid vista of the entire trip.

What all this suggests is that since 1995 especially, and energized by books such as Runyan's (1982), Alexander's (1990), and Elms's (1994), psychobiography in its various guises has flourished—both in the mainstream of psychology (thanks to Stephen G. West and the editorial openness of the *Journal of Personality*) and outside it, in scholarly arenas at large.

Another stimulus impossible to overlook is the success of Dan McAdams's life story model of identity and of narrative psychology generally, each hardly inhospitable either to qualitative-type research or to psychobiography. Sarbin's (1986) prediction is in the process of becoming at least partially true: narrative as root metaphor for the mind has taken hold. Scripts, means-end sequences, redemption/contamination sequences, forms of master narrative, scenes, imagoes—all such constructs are now commonplace (and appear with marked frequency in this volume). And more broadly, the idea that personality is a story we tell ourselves, and others, about ourselves is likewise difficult to miss in the literature. Those at the leading edge of this movement, if it can be called that, come out of a personological tradition (e.g., McAdams, Ruthellen Josselson, Irving Alexander, Gary Gregg, Jefferson Singer, and others). Consequently, as narrative research picks up converts, so too will psychobiography (and to some degree, vice versa). Also, as narrative research permeates the mainstream, psychobiography should do the same, as the guest of a guest invited to a party. An illustration of just this sort of courtesy privilege is the recent commitment by the American Psychological Association Press to the publication of the *Narrative Study of Lives* series (McAdams et al., 2001; Josselson et al., 2003). In these first two volumes—the only to appear thus far—psychobiography is strongly represented, with chapters on Oscar Wilde, Henry and William James, and Katherine Power, plus an entire book (Josselson et al., 2003) devoted to personological research methods.

The success of the narrative metaphor rubs off on psychobiography; at the same time, basic differences between the two approaches do exist. First, psychobiography is multimethodological and essentially theoretically anarchistic. One can do psychobiography historiometrically, reducing text to numbers. One can, as is most frequently the case, adopt a Freudian stance, or one derived from ideas in object-relations schools. Whatever the case, psychobiographers don't always or even usually employ a narrative based theory for making sense of lives. Also, most psychobiographers are structuralists (as explained above). When they talk about the biographies and minds of their subjects, they propose to discuss something *real*. In the most extreme narrative-based models, mind is text, and text is endlessly mutable. Self is story, and story is fiction. What's behind the story? Nothing, really. Story is all there is. A few psychobiographers may follow that line, but in my estimation, most do not. They approach the person as tangibly knowable, not as a text function.

So what's the verdict? And what might the future hold? As a discipline psychology remains means centered, and the method most centered on is experimental. That much is undeniable (though regrettable). As a subdiscipline, personality psychology, of which psychobiography forms a small part, is struggling. Still, if we look back 15 years and compare then to now, there can be no question: One finds far more activity in the psychobiography vein and more mainstream acceptance. Especially auspicious are the 39 psychobiography-inspired dissertations finished between 2000 and 2003, along with the 188 articles in scholarly journals (26 in 1999, 46 in 2000, 67 in 2001, 24 in 2002, and 35 in 2003. Also auspicious is the rise of narrative models, which in many cases ply their trade in psychobiographical domains.

And, lastly, the appearance of this book you now hold. For the first time a source exists combining clear methodological guidelines with exemplars of how to do the job right, a book that both "shows" and "tells." This can't help but encourage more work in the field. And it can't help but increase the odds that such work will be successful, leading to even more acceptance, more work, and more success. We shall see.

Notes

1. One could ask the opposite, too: What is psychology uniquely suited to provide psychobiography with? The answer is theories and research with which to undertake a psychobiographical analysis. Since the effectiveness of psychobiographies—analyses of persons—pivots around findings emerging out of psychological research (these are the findings that get applied to individual lives), it succeeds as far as psychology succeeds in providing tools of understanding. In one sense psychobiographies are only as sound as the theory and research on which they are based.

2. Allport reaches a similar conclusion: "If we want to know how people feel; what they experience and what they remember, what their emotions and motives are like, and the reasons for acting as they do—why not ask them?" (Barenbaum, 1994). Asking is a start. But answers to questions also typically require interpretation. One must go beyond text to subtext (on this Allport might disagree, given his objections to probing the unconscious. See Barenbaum, chap. 16 this vol.).

3. We still call it reconstruction even when what gets reconstructed is a more recent past. Lester (1998) applies several models of suicide to the life of Sylvia Plath, finding Aaron Beck's to fit her case best. Beck predicts, among other things, that the suicidal person's thoughts are arbitrary, and that, even so, she considers them valid and sees no alternatives. On this point Lester says, "We have to speculate on what Plath might have been thinking in the hours and days prior to her death, but it seems likely that a cognitive therapist would have judged her thoughts to be irrational" (p. 661). When the evidence isn't there, it isn't there. Manufacturing missing evidence is reconstruction, whether of infantile or adult history.

References

Alexander, I.E. (1990). Personology: Method and content in personality assessment and psychobiography. Durham, N.C.: Duke University Press.

Barenbaum, N.B. (1994, April 30). Personality theory and autobiography as narrative: The cases of Murray and Allport. Paper presented at the International Conference on Narrative Literature, Vancouver, B.C., Canada.

Barenbaum, N.B. (1997). The case(s) of Gordon Allport. Journal of Personality, 65(3), 743–755.

Barresi, J., & Juckes, T.J. (1997). Personology and the narrative interpretation of lives. Journal of Personality, 65(3), 693–710.

Carlson, R. (1971). Where is the person in personality research? Psychological Bulletin, 75, 203–219.

Cody, J. (1971). After great pain: The inner life of Emily Dickinson. Cambridge, Mass.: Harvard University Press.

Demorest, A.P. (1995). The personal script as a unit of analysis for the study of personality. Journal of Personality, 63(3), 569–591.

Demorest, A.P., & Siegel, P.F. (1996). Personal influences on professional work: An empirical case study of B.F. Skinner. Journal of Personality, 64(1), 243–261.

Elms, A.C. (1994). Uncovering lives: The uneasy alliance of biography and psychology. New York: Oxford University Press.

Endler, N., & Speer, R. (1998). Personality psychology: Research trends for 1993–1995. Journal of Personality, 66(5), 621–669.

Erikson, E.H. (1969). Gandhi's truth. New York: Norton.

Gardner, H. (1992). Scientific Psychology: Should we bury it or praise it? New Ideas in Psychology, 10(2), 179–190.

Harrison, K. (2003). The seal wife. New York: Random House.

Josselson, R., Lieblich, A., & McAdams, D.P. (Eds.). (2003). Up close and personal: The teaching and learning of narrative research. Washington, D.C.: APA Books.

Lester, D. (1998). Theories of suicidal behavior applied to Sylvia Ploth. Death Studies, 22(7), 655–666.

Maslow, A.H. (1972). The farther reaches of human nature. New York: Viking.

McAdams, D.P., Josselson, R., & Lieblich, A. (2001). Turns in the road: Narrative studies of lives in transition. Washington, D.C.: APA Books.

McAdams, D.P., & Ochberg, R.L. (1988). Psychobiography and life narratives [Special issue]. Journal of Personality, 56(1).

Murray, H.A. (1981). Endeavors in psychology (ed. E.S. Shneidman). New York: Harper & Row.

Murray, H.A., & Kluckhohn, C. (1953). Personality in nature, society, and culture. New York: Knopf.

Nasby, W., & Read, N.W. (1997). The life voyage of a solo circumnavigator: Integrating theoretical and methodological perspectives. Journal of Personality [Special issue], 65(4).

Ogilvie, D.M. (2003). Fantasies of flight. New York: Oxford University Press.

Popper, K. (1959). The Logic of Scientific Discovery. New York: Basic Books.

Ramachandran, V.S. (1998). Phantoms in the brain: Probing the mysteries of the human mind. New York: Quill.

Runyan, W.M. (1982). Life histories and psychobiography: Explorations in theory and method. New York: Oxford University Press.

Sarbin, T. R. (Ed.) (1986). Narrative Psychology: The storied nature of human conduct. New York: Praeger.

Schaller, M. (1997). The psychological consequences of fame: Three tests of the self-consciousness hypothesis. Journal of Personality, 65(2), 291–309.

Schultz, W.T. (1996). An "Orpheus complex" in two writers-of-loss. Biography: An Interdisciplinary Quarterly, 19, 371–393.

Simonton, D.K. (1998). Mad King George: The impact of personal and political stress on mental and physical health. Journal of Personality, 66(3), 443–493.

Stolorow, R.D. & Atwood, G.E. (1979). Faces in a cloud: Subjectivity in Personality Theory. Northvale: Aronson.

Winer, J.A., & Anderson, J. (2003). The annual of psychoanalysis, Vol. 31: Psychoanalysis and history. Hillsdale, N.J.: Analytic Press.

Winter, D.G. (1996). Gordon Allport and the legend of "Rinehart." Journal of Personality, 64(1), 263–273.

Winter, D.G. (1997). Allport's life and Allport's psychology. Journal of Personality, 65(3), 723–731.

Chapter 2

William McKinley Runyan

Evolving Conceptions of Psychobiography and the Study of Lives

Encounters With Psychoanalysis, Personality Psychology, and Historical Science

How are we to conceptualize the evolving relations between the study of individual lives and the discipline of psychology?

This question is more complex than it first appears. How to conceptualize the study of lives? How do we conceptualize the discipline of psychology? And how are we to conceptualize their evolving relationships? Much is at stake in the answer, with implications for what psychology might become. People bet their careers and their working lives on different answers to such questions.

This chapter attempts to tell a different story about psychobiography and the study of lives in relation to the discipline of psychology. It is not a traditional "rise of natural science" story, in which case studies are seen as being replaced by more rigorous quantitative and experimental methods. It is, instead, a story which respects the virtues of historical, interpretive, and narrative methods, as well as of quantitative and experimental methods.

Personal life histories are, I believe, involved in the creation and development of every tradition in psychology, including psychoanalysis, learning theory, behaviorism, humanist psychology, cognitive psychology, neuroscience, and the study of lives. The development of the study of lives is examined in this chapter in relation to the lives and careers of a number of people active in the tradition, including Henry Murray, Robert White, Gordon Allport, Alan Elms, and Jerry Wiggins. I also include elements of my personal experience interacting with supporters and opponents of the study of lives. These examples may resonate (or not) with readers reflecting on their own experiences encountering different "hard" or "soft" traditions in psychology over the years.

We are all faced with competing conceptions of psychology, back through the history of the discipline. Is psychology about the study of sensation and perception? Reaction times? Memory? The structural elements of consciousness? The unconscious? Learning? Behavior? Social psychological processes? Personality? Developmental processes and change? Cognition? Psychopathology? Therapy and change? Neuroscience? And/or is psychology about the study of persons and lives?

Each of these conceptions has been proposed (and more). Consensus has been difficult to achieve (Sternberg, 2005). There were early conceptions of psychology, such as Wundt's physiological and experimental psychology (Wundt, 1873–1874), that focus on the experimental study of sensation and perception and reaction times, with little or no attention given to persons or lives. The history of experimental psychology (Boring, 1929/1950; Hearst, 1979) follows the application of experimental methods from sensation and perception, to memory, to animal learning, to motivation, to cognitive science, to social psychology, to experimental psychopathology, and so on (Hearst, 1979).

One view is that experimental methods would spread and eventually be able to more rigorously cover the whole array of topics in psychology (Hilgard, 1987). However, over the last century there have also been a variety of countermovements, arguing that psychology needs a variety of alternative methods, from Dilthey's *Introduction to the Human Sciences* (1883/1988), to Freud's psychoanalytic case studies, to phenomenology, to the study of lives, to the dissident array of theorists concerned with the "whole person" (Hall & Lindzey, 1957). Cahan and White (1992) offer a brief survey of this set of "second psychology" or human science approaches and some of the tensions between natural science and human science visions of psychology.

The study of individual lives has not necessarily triumphed within psychology, but neither has it disappeared. It has evolved and reappeared in many different forms, and the study of lives has been actively growing in recent decades. At its best, this *Handbook of Psychobiography* could help organize and advance the psychological study of lives, as the *Handbook of Experimental Psychology* (Stevens, 1951) and the *Handbook of Social Psychology* (Lindzey, 1954) did for their areas.

This chapter is not an exhaustive history of relations between psychology and the study of lives. Rather, it discusses encounters that the study of lives has had with psychoanalysis, personality psychology, and historical science.

It seems to many that psychology ought to have something to do with the study of individuals, but this goal sometimes clashes with evolving conceptions of what counts as scientific. As Wundt said about William James's *Principles of Psychology* (1890), "It is literature, it is beautiful, but it is not psychology" (Fancher, 1979, p. 128). For more than a century, there have been worries about how the study of lives relates to science. Freud remarked that, even though trained as a neuropathologist, it still struck him "as strange that the case histories I write should read like short stories and that, as one might say, they lack the serious stamp of science" (Breuer & Freud, 1895/1955, p. 160). He consoled himself, however, with the thought that this came not from any preferences of his own, but was required by the subject matter (p. 160).

There is a long history of putting down or critiquing the study of individual cases. Lundberg (1926), for example, said that "(1) The case method is not in itself a scientific method at all, but merely the first step in the scientific method;

(2) individual cases become of scientific significance only when classified and summarized in such form as to reveal uniformities, types and patterns of behavior; (3) the statistical method is the best, if not the only method of classifying and summarizing large numbers of cases" (p. 61).

One of the most widely used methodology texts is Campbell and Stanley's *Experimental and Quasi-Experimental Designs for Research* (1963), which asserts that "one-shot" case studies

> have such a total absence of control as to be of almost no scientific value. . . . Such studies often involve tedious collection of specific detail, careful observation, testing and the like, and in such instances involve the error of *misplaced precision*. . . . It seems well-nigh unethical at the present time to allow, as a thesis or dissertation in education, case studies of this nature i.e. involving a single group observed at one time only. (pp. 6–7)

This book has had tremendous influence (Shadish et al., 2003), and been drawn on in many later textbooks. What is less known, however, is that Campbell (1975) later retracted this "earlier dogmatic disparagement of case studies" (p. 191).

It seems we need better ways of thinking about the role of case studies throughout the scientific enterprise, from initial impressions and interpretations of cases, through theory building interacting with quantitative and experimental research, and back to reinterpreting and intervening with individual cases in their social, cultural, and historical contexts. Do narrative accounts of lives "lack the serious stamp of science"? They may lack quantification and experimental control, but are these the only forms that scientific rigor can take?

My argument in this chapter, in a nutshell, is as follows. Lee Cronbach (1957) argued that there are two disciplines of scientific psychology, correlational and experimental, with the possibility of integrating them through studying person—situation interactions (Cronbach, 1975). In this chapter I argue that there is also at least a third discipline of scientific psychology, namely, historical-interpretive psychology. Historical-interpretive psychology employing narrative methods is used in clinical case studies, in psychobiography, and in the study of lives in particular social, cultural, and historical contexts. "Historical science," or the study of particular contingent sequences of events and processes, as developed by Stephen Jay Gould (1986), can help clarify the objectives and methods of the study of lives and their place in scientific psychology.

It is a mistake, even a "misinterpretation," to dismiss the case study as nothing more than "observing a single unit at a single point in time" (Campbell & Stanley, 1963). Ideally, there can be a whole history of accounts and interpretations of individual lives, with the collection of additional evidence, employment of new theory and research, critical evaluation of earlier accounts, and progress toward more adequate accounts, explanations, and interpretations (Runyan, 1988b). Studying and interpreting individual lives is not just a "one-shot" affair but can involve "quasi-judicial" procedures, analogous to procedures in courts of law, where people with different interests and different evidence argue for different conclusions. One example is the history of Freud biographies, from a classic early sympathetic biography by Ernest Jones (1953–57), to a more critical comparative historical analysis (Ellenberger, 1970), to more detailed biographical information about Freud and his followers (Roazen, 1975), to an enormous number of intellectually and politically charged alternative accounts of Freud and his work. Consider also the history of Darwin biographies, or the history of biographies of William James. The study of lives has intellectual challenges to deal with, but being limited to "one-shot" case studies is not high on the list. The history of reconceptualizing, recontextualizing, and reinterpreting is central in the psychological study of lives. As a method, it can be seen more clearly as scientific when compared with other "historical sciences" (Gould, 2002) such as evolutionary biology, archaeology, or historical geology.

When Henry A. Murray (1893–1988) came up for tenure at Harvard in 1936, with the manuscript for *Explorations in Personality* partially available, although not yet finished, one of Murray's supporters, Gordon Allport, argued

that Murray was the intellectual heir of William James and important to the development of a humanistically oriented psychology at Harvard (Triplet, 1983, p. 252). Another committee member, neuropsychologist Karl Lashley (1890–1958), strongly opposed the appointment, arguing that William James had done "more harm to psychology than any man that ever lived" and threatened to resign if Murray was given tenure (Robinson, 1992, p. 225). He saw Murray's as a case in which "the conflict between the older humanistic and philosophical psychology" (Murray) was in tension with "the attempt to evolve a more exact science through an objective and biological approach" (Lashley) (Robinson, 1992, p. 226). The tenure vote was split three votes to three, and to resolve the impasse Boring proposed that Murray be given two five-year nontenured appointments, which was done. By 1946, though, the department had split into two different groups, psychology (experimental) and social relations (social and clinical psychology with sociology and social anthropology).

Murray's two five-year appointments would have ended in 1947. In June 1945, Murray resigned from Harvard University. Behind the scenes, he was involved in formation of the new Social Relations department which began in 1946. In 1948, Murray published *Assessment of Men* (1948) on the Office of Strategic Services assessment program he had headed, and co-edited *Personality in Nature, Society and Culture* (Kluckhohn and Murray, 1948). He returned to his earlier biographical work on Melville, and published a 90-page Introduction (plus 75 pages of explanatory notes) to Melville's *Pierre* (Murray, 1949). In 1948, Murray returned to Harvard as a lecturer in Social Relations, with an appointment as full professor in 1950, until his retirement in 1962.

The tension between natural science and human science conceptions of psychology has not gone away. When I was in graduate school in clinical psychology and public practice at Harvard from 1969 through 1975, I was told by many that my interest in individual life histories was clearly *not* scientific. One professor said in response to my dissertation proposal on the study of life histories, "You may think you're flying to the moon, but instead, you're flying to the garbage dump." David McClelland, another professor, objected to my interests in conceptual and methodological issues in the study of individual lives and wrote me a letter on May 25, 1971, the end of my second year in graduate school, saying that these philosophical interests were not suited to the program. "So, I would urge you strongly to leave Harvard before you waste more time here, your time and our time." I declined the offer (Runyan, 2003). I assembled a more sympathetic dissertation committee, received some moral and intellectual support from Henry A. Murray and Robert W. White, both retired, and did a dissertation on "Life Histories: A Field of Inquiry and a Framework for Intervention" (Runyan, 1975). This was followed by work on methodological and conceptual issues in the study of lives (Runyan, 1978, 1981, 1982, 1983, 1984, 1988a, 1988b, 1994, 1997, 2002, 2003).

Conflicting views about the study of individual lives have not disappeared. In chapter 1 of this volume, the editor, William Todd Schultz, describes his experience as an undergraduate at Lewis and Clark College, where he received his bachelor of arts degree in 1985. His professors there ruled out research not deemed "empirical," interpreted to mean quantitative or experimental, with qualitative theses not allowed.

As a graduate student at the University of California at Davis, he was able to get a psychobiographical dissertation approved, but it was a struggle. He was supported by Alan C. Elms, a major contributor to psychobiography (Elms, 1976, 1981, 1994). As reported by Elms, the psychology department at Davis required that dissertations be based on empirical research, interpreted as quantitative or nomothetic research. Elms argued that, according to standard dictionary definitions, "empirical" meant "related to facts or experiences . . . based on factual investigation" (Elms, 1994, p. 242) and that psychobiography involved painstaking factual research. "There is no inherent difference between the many items of biographical fact collected about one individual in a life-historical study and the few facts collected about each of many individuals in the standard sort of 'empirical' psychological research" (p. 243). The department approved two dissertation committees

for psychobiographical dissertations, for Eva Schepeler in 1990 and William Schultz in 1992. Part of Schepeler's dissertation was published in 1993 as "Jean Piaget's Experiences on the Couch: Some Clues to a Mystery" in the *International Journal of Psychoanalysis*, and William Todd Schultz's 1992 dissertation was titled "A Psychobiographical Inquiry into the Life, Mind, and Creative Work of James Agee." Portions of Schultz's dissertation were published in *American Imago* (1999) and *Biography: An Interdisciplinary Quarterly* (1996), and he went on to edit this volume. Other psychobiographical dissertations have subsequently been approved at UC Davis for Kate Isaacson and Anna Song, two contributors to this volume. (I am serving as an outside member for Kate Isaacson's psychobiographical dissertation on John Bowlby and Mary Ainsworth.) With changing patterns of support and opposition, work in the study of individual lives has continued throughout the history of psychology. William James wrote *Principles of Psychology* (1890), reviewing and critically evaluating work in experimental and general psychology, but he also wrote *Varieties of Religious Experience: A Study in Human Nature* (1902), which relied largely on autobiographical accounts of religious experience. G. Stanley Hall (1844–1924) in his two-volume work on *Adolescence* (1904) made extensive use of adolescent autobiographies. Edwin G. Boring in *A History of Experimental Psychology* (1929/1950) provided numerous biographical portraits, and Boring was the force behind the throne in starting the series *A History of Psychology in Autobiography*, beginning with the first volume in 1930 edited by Carl Murchison, with volume 8 appearing in 1989 (vols. 6–8 ed. by Gardner Lindzey). In *The Use of Personal Documents in Psychological Science* (1942), Allport reviews a number of these early studies, dividing them into uncritical and critical uses of personal documents.

In this chapter, I do not attempt an exhaustive history of the evolving relationships between the study of lives and the discipline of psychology, but try instead to conceptualize the interaction in a way that may be useful for future work in the field. The following section briefly discusses relationships between psychoanalysis and psychobiography, while the third section examines the complex and changing relationships between personality psychology and the study of lives. The fourth section discusses potential contributions of "historical science" to the study of lives, while in the Conclusion, I review several main ideas about relations of the study of lives to the goals and methods of psychology.

This chapter is not a comprehensive review of the field, but rather, a review by one person, in one location, at one point in time. It is both informed by and limited by my own particular encounters with the study of lives and is thus only one view of psychology and the study of lives. Useful chapters could also be written about relations of the study of lives with history, sociology, anthropology, political science, or literature. This chapter needs to be complemented by the views of many others.

Several stages in my thinking which have shaped the particularities of this chapter include a doctoral dissertation seeking to conceptualize the study of life histories as a field of inquiry (1975), an article on the life course as a theoretical orientation (1978), and then a book on methodological and conceptual issues in psychobiography and the study of lives (1982). A next step was analyzing what constitutes "progress" in psychobiography, and the processes through which it can occur (1988b). This was accompanied by a book on the relations of psychology and historical interpretation, with a chapter on alternatives to psychoanalytic psychobiography, and a chapter on reconceptualizing relationships between history and psychology, with substantive examples from psychohistorical research on Nazi Germany (1988a). Another line of work attempted to clarify the place of the study of lives in relation to personality psychology (Runyan, 1997).

After the publication of Robinson's *Love's Story Told: A Life of Henry A. Murray* (1992), I was forced to come to terms intellectually and emotionally with a different interpretation of Murray (Runyan, 1994). Lawrence Friedman's biography of Erikson (1999), along with Sue Erikson Bloland's article on her father (1999), led me to re-interpret Erik Erikson, and I helped organize a symposium on Erikson with Freidman, Paul Roazen, and Sue Bloland at the Harvard Graduate School of Education on February 10, 2000. A complementary line of work was on personal and intellectual autobiography (2002, 2003). Since 1995, I have been doing archival research on relations between the life and work of several natural science and human science psychologists at Harvard, while learning much about the history of psychology from Sheldon H. White (Runyan, 2005). While not yet published, parts of this archival research will be drawn on in this chapter. The general point here is that there are evolving conceptions of psychobiography and the study of lives not only by decades in the field as a whole, but in smaller ways, within each person engaged in making their path through the field. Readers may, I hope, find this chapter useful in their own evolving understandings of psychobiography and the study of lives.

Psychoanalysis and Psychobiography

Psychobiography is often dated as beginning with Freud's *Leonardo da Vinci and a Memory of His Childhood* (1910/1957). This was preceded by Freud's work on *Delusions and Dreams in Jensen's "Gradiva"* (Freud, 1907/1959) and followed by shorter pieces on Goethe and Dostoevsky as well as Freud's book *Moses and Monotheism* (1939/1964). There were a number of other early psychoanalytic psychobiographies, such as several by Isidor Sadger (1908, 1909), and analyses of Shakespeare as revealed through Hamlet (Jones, 1910), Richard Wagner (Graf, 1911), the artist Giovanni Segantini (Abraham, 1912/1935), Amenhotep IV (Abraham, 1912/1935), Martin Luther (Smith, 1913), and Socrates (Karpas, 1915). Reviews of early psychoanalytic psychobiography are provided by Dooley (1916) in "Psychoanalytic Studies of Genius," Barnes (1919), Fearing (1927) and Barnes's *Psychology and History* (1925). However, Freud's study of Leonardo had more influence and received substantially more attention than any of these other efforts (Elms, 1994; Collins, 1997), while his work on *Moses and Monotheism* has received many reinterpretations in recent years (Bernstein, 1998; Yerushalmi, 1991). More details on the history of psychoanalytic psychobiography and psychohistory are provided in Elms (2003), Mack (1971), and Runyan (1982, 1988a).

Within psychoanalysis, many turned away from Freud's early drive theories, focusing instead on the role of the ego, object relations, and countertransference (Loewenberg, 1988). A recent special issue of the *Annual of Psychoanalysis* centers on psychoanalysis and history (Winer & Anderson, 2003). Co-editor James Anderson notes that psychoanalysts best known as psychobiographers remain Freud and Erik Erikson but that current psychoanalysts tend to rely more on other theorists in their clinical work (p. 79). Anderson (2003) reviews the relevance for psychobiography of such recent psychoanalytic theorists as Donald Winnicott (1896–1971), Otto Kernberg (1928–), and Heinz Kohut (1913–1981). The volume also includes autobiographical chapters by several writers in the field of psychoanalysis and biography, including Moraitis (2003), Runyan (2003), and Strozier (2003).

Personality Psychology and the Study of Lives

There is a "puzzling history" of relationships between personality psychology and the study of individual lives:

> Most simply, the study of individual persons and lives was one of the central concerns and motivating agendas for founders of the field such as Gordon Allport (1937) and Henry Murray (1938), but was then lost sight of in the 1950s and 1960s . . . as far greater attention was given to psychometric concerns and the experimental study of particular processes. (Runyan, 1997, p. 41)

There were exceptions, such as the work of Robert White (1952) or Erik Erikson (1958) on the study of individual lives, but the emphasis seemed more on aggregate psychometric or experimental work.

Major texts of the period gave relatively little attention to the study of individual lives. Hall and Lindzey's *Theories of Personality* (1957),

which eventually sold more than 700,000 copies, argues that the fruitfulness of personality theories "is to be judged primarily by how effectively they serve as a spur to research" (p. 27). A model for this book was Hilgard's *Theories of Learning* (1948), which outlines major theories of learning and the empirical research related to each of them. Mischel's *Personality and Assessment* (1968) argues for the superiority of experimentally based social learning theories over trait and psychodynamic approaches for the prediction and modification of behavior. It is noteworthy that an improved understanding of individual persons or lives was not emphasized in either of these influential books, or in a number of other personality texts of the time.

I speculated that the move away from the study of lives might be due to

> changing intellectual fashions about what it means to "be scientific," personal and temperamental preferences for particular kinds of research, the kinds of graduate students attracted to the field in the growing competition with clinical psychology after World War II, patterns of funding and grant support, and institutional processes determining who was or was not hired and promoted at Harvard, Stanford, Yale, Berkeley, and other major universities around the country. (Runyan, 1997, p. 42)

Since then, Barenbaum and Winter have conducted two useful reviews of the history of personality psychology, one a general history of personality psychology (Winter & Barenbaum, 1999), and the other, particularly relevant for present purposes, on the history of ambivalence toward case studies in psychology (Barenbaum & Winter, 2003). Their second review opens with a quote from R.S. Woodworth, long-term professor of psychology at Columbia University and author of the best-selling psychology textbook for 25 years, first published in 1921. In the revised edition of *Psychology* (1929), Woodworth begins with a life history of a woman novelist, Gene Stratton-Porter. He says he gave attention to the case history method in this introduction "not because it is the preferred method in psychology, for it is the least rather than the most preferred, but because it can give us what we want at the outset, a bird's-eye view of the field, with some indications of the topics that are deserving of closer examination" (p. 19).

It may not be a surprise that, as the author of a widely selling text on *Experimental Psychology* (1938), Woodworth thinks of the case history as the "least preferred" method. What was a surprise, though, when I went back to look at the book, is that the text defines psychology as the study of individuals; as the "scientific study of the activities of the individual . . . psychology takes the individual as a whole, and describes his activities" (p. 3). Who would have guessed? Such a definition is most congenial to personologists, but not one I would have associated with Woodworth. (The history of psychology can be full of surprises.) In my own view, as discussed below, the study of individuals is one of the four objectives of personality psychology, but many conceptions of psychology do not have the study of individuals as even one of the stated objectives of the field.

Personality as an area of psychology was formulated at least in part by Gordon Allport (1937) and Henry A. Murray (1938), both professors at Harvard. How did Allport initially conceive the field? As an undergraduate at Oberlin College, I took a summer course at Western Reserve University in 1967, in which the official text was Allport's *Pattern and Growth in Personality* (1961), a revision of his groundbreaking *Personality: A Psychological Interpretation* (1937). I found the book a mix of interesting topics, with impressive scholarship, but frustratingly elusive or noncommittal in some ways about Allport's particular beliefs or experiences. That summer, after my sophomore year, I was more drawn to Hall and Lindzey's *Theories of Personality* (1957), with its contending theoretical orientations and clearer links to empirical research.

I did not purchase my own copy of Allport (1937) until December 11, 1980 (the sales slip is still taped inside, in an effort to document historical particularities). Now, I find much of it of interest, particularly in relation to the current topic of relations between personality psychology and the study of individual lives. One passage caught my eye, providing a clearer sense

than I'd had before of Allport's view of relations between psychoanalysis and personality psychology. Allport seems to be arguing that his approach to personality psychology is a broader and more eclectic approach to personality than is psychoanalysis. In a footnote Allport says, "Devotees of psychoanalysis will no doubt be distressed to find here so tardy and so incomplete a review of the contributions of Freud and his many disciples, both orthodox and dissident" (p. 181). Allport then gives three reasons why his account of psychoanalysis is "so critical and so brief": that psychoanalytic concepts are drawn from neurotic and pathological material, that the parts valid for normal personality are incorporated elsewhere in the book, and that the story of psychoanalysis is too well known to need another exposition. Allport says that Franz Alexander's *The Psychoanalysis of the Total Personality* (1930)

> wrongly implies that psychoanalysis is equipped to deal with the *whole* of personality. The truth is that it deals only with a fraction of the phenomena encountered in a comprehensive study of the subject. But in spite of its narrowness the bulk of all literature on the psychology of personality is written from this one point of view. It is time the story be told in more eclectic terms! (p. 181)

In short, Allport is objecting to psychoanalysis because it is too exclusively based on psychopathology, because the bulk of all literature on personality is written from this psychodynamic perspective, and because a more eclectic view is needed. In addition to the intellectual side of this, there may be personal reasons for Allport's demurrals, such as his "traumatic" encounter with Freud in 1920 (see Elms, 1994, chap. 5 this vol.; Barenbaum, chap. 16 this vol.).

What was the place of the study of individual lives in Allports's view of personality psychology? And how did it relate to his interests in individuality? Allport starts his book with the sentence, "The outstanding characteristic of man is his individuality" (1937, p. 3). What did Allport mean by individuality? Individuality in temperament? In cultural interests? In biological constitution? In personal experiences? In values and strivings? He is concerned with how scientists can study this individuality with a combination of nomothetic and idiographic methods.

Allport outlines in a chart fifty-two different methods for studying personality (p. 370). In this chart, the methods of psychoanalysis or of "depth analysis," including psychiatric interview, free associations, dream analysis, and analysis of fantasies, are only six of the fifty-two different methods. Methods are divided into fourteen groups, with "depth analysis" as only one of the fourteen groups, the others including studies of cultural setting, physical records, social records, personal records, expressive movement, rating, standardized tests, statistical analysis, miniature life situations, laboratory experiments, prediction, ideal types, and synthetic methods.

One of these synthetic methods was the "case study," which Allport described as the "most revealing method of all" (Barenbaum, 1997). For a variety of reasons, however, Allport only published one long case study, *Letters From Jenny* (1965), and an autobiographical chapter (1967). After his autobiographical chapter was published, Allport wrote to Boring that "I think Carl Rogers comes through most clearly—no doubt because of his long practice in disclosing himself to his clients. By comparison, I find myself rigid and prosaic" (Nicholson, 2003, p. 181). I think Rogers' emphasis on individual subjective experience was meaningful to Allport, and at least one of the important meanings of individuality. In Allport's teaching file, I remember a quote along these lines: "Rogers practices what Allport preaches." It is not clear to me yet whether this is a statement Allport had heard or had composed himself.

Although drawn to the study of individuality, Allport had reservations about publishing case studies himself, or about encouraging doctoral students to do them as dissertations. Bertram Cohler, who received his Ph.D. from Harvard in 1967, reported that Allport cautioned him that "idiography was no country for young men," which Cohler interpreted as a statement about political realities, expressing some of Allport's ambivalence about case studies (Cohler, 1993, p. 134). However, from looking at Allport's papers in the Harvard Archives, I see that he frequently had students in his personality class do psychobiographical papers or final projects. In his notes, he says he could ask them to apply any of the theories in Hall and Lindzey's *Theories of Personality* (1957). Before the book was published, when he referred to it as Lindzey and Hall, he was distributing draft chapters to students and eliciting their critical feedback.

While Allport, with his chart of fifty-two methods, was aiming for a more eclectic approach than psychoanalysis, Murray was after something different. His project for *Explorations in Personality* (1938) was primarily about applying the more rigorous methods of academic psychology to some of the ideas of dynamic psychology, as well as developing his own conceptions of personality.

Robert White's conception of the study of lives was influenced strongly by Henry Murray, but also by Gordon Allport. Even though he received his Ph.D. in 1937, while lecturing at Harvard in 1940 White attended Allport's seminar titled "How Shall a Life History Be Written?" When White was appointed director of Harvard's new clinical psychology program in 1946, arrangements were made by Allport, as Murray was not then at Harvard.

As I came to understand it more over the years, the study of lives had somewhat different meanings for Henry A. Murray and for Robert W. White. For Murray, "the life history of a single man" is a unit the discipline of psychology needs to deal with, and the study of lives overlapped more with a romantic project of including the deepest human experiences within psychology, such as those of Jung, Melville, himself, and others. As opposed to "peripheralists" concerned with an objective approach to sensation and perception and overt behavior, Murray finds himself more sympathetic to "centralists" who are "especially attracted to subjective facts of emotional or purposive significance; feelings, desires, intentions" with a "craving to know the inner nature of other persons as they know their own" (Murray, 1938, p. 8). In Murray's view, academic psychologists were too concerned with the periphery of sensation and perception and not sufficiently attuned to the "driving forces which are basic to human nature" (1938, p. 341). As Murray charged in 1935 to the experimental psychologists of his time,

The truth which the informed are hesitant to reveal and the uninformed are amazed to discover is that academic psychology has contributed practically nothing to the knowledge of human nature. It has not only failed to bring to light the great, hauntingly recurrent problems, but it has no intention, one is shocked to realize, of attempting to investigate them. Indeed—and this is the cream of a wry jest—an unconcerned detachment from the natural history of ordinary mortals has become a source of pride to many psychologists. (Murray, 1935/1981, p. 339)

For Robert White, who found his home within Murray's vision of psychology yet had a different temperament and different priorities, the study of lives was something else. It overlapped more with the study of normal growth and development (White, 1952, 1972), the understanding of competencies and effective adaptation, the value of lives for teaching abnormal psychology and personality psychology (White, 1948/1964, 1974)), and the use of life history interviewing as a way of relating personally with students and others. For White, "[t]he study of personality includes the time dimension and is most perfectly represented in the study of whole lives in all their individuality" (White, 1972, p. 2).

White is known for early contributions to the study of lives as in his case of "Earnst" in *Explorations in Personality* (Murray, 1938), with papers titled "The Personality of Joseph Kidd" (1943), and for five memorable case histories in chapter 2 of *The Abnormal Personality* (1948/1964). This was followed by books on *Lives in Progress* (1952), *Opinions and Personality* (1956), *The Study of Lives* (1963) and *The Enterprise of Living* (1972), all of which contain conceptions and examples of the study of lives. White's (1987) memoir allows a glimpse of an earlier, more personal engagement with the study of lives.

White (1904–2001) was originally trained with a B.A. degree (1925) and an M.A. in history (1926) from Harvard. He planned to become a teacher of cultural and intellectual history. In a first teaching job as an instructor in history at the University of Maine (1926–

1928), he found himself not living up to his ideal of having a "helpful and understanding relation with students. Experience began to show that I did not know how to bring about such relations" (White, 1987, p. 1). With a shy and silent student from a poor family, with a homesick freshman who failed to return to school, and with a disruptive student he put down in class, White felt that his relations were ineffective or superficial. "Comfortably at home as I was with books, ideas, and music, I was not in good touch with the people around me. Suddenly I experienced a powerful need to understand better my students and my fellow teachers, not to mention myself" (1987, p. 2).

A catalyst for these desires to understand people better psychologically was the arrival in Maine of Donald MacKinnon (1903–1987), instructor in psychology who had begun graduate school at Harvard with Henry A. Murray. White admired MacKinnon's "clear mind, appropriate confidence, and willingness to set forth his convictions" as well as "the ease with which he seemed to size other people up" (1987, p. 2). White wondered "whether these qualities were the product of scientific training and graduate study in psychology. In retrospect I offer this idea as the surest proof that my thinking was fuzzy, but I more than half believed it" (1987, p. 2). As White later said, Donald MacKinnon converted him "from the history of nations to the history of individual lives" (White, 1972, p. v).

In a chapter titled "A Humanist Strays into Psychology," White (1987) speaks of the barrenness of mainstream experimental psychology for someone with his interests. The experimental tradition of Wundt and Ebbinghaus, as taught by Edwin G. Boring, chairman of the Harvard Psychology department, left him cold. Two promising professors were Henry A. Murray at the Harvard Psychological Clinic and Gordon Allport, who returned to Harvard from Dartmouth in 1930. "The straying humanist luckily found oases at the edges of the desert," White wrote (1987, p. 4).

After three years as an instructor in psychology at Rutgers (1930–1933), White returned to graduate school at Harvard in 1933. He had to choose between working with Allport or Murray, ultimately selecting the latter's research program, which he long felt was the right one. White received his Ph.D. in 1937 with a dissertation titled "Experimental Evidence for a Dynamic Theory of Hypnosis" and published six journal articles on hypnosis from 1937 through 1942. (Murray had also investigated the subject of hypnosis.) In the end, however, White did not find hypnosis a congenial topic and stopped working with it in 1938.

While doing his dissertation on hypnosis, White was also working with the group at the Harvard Psychological Clinic on what became *Explorations in Personality* (Murray, 1938), a task that he found far more engaging. White contributed the section on the "Hypnotic Test" (pp. 453–461), and he was the biographer of the one complete life history in the book in chapter 7, "Case History: Case of Earnst" (pp. 604–702).

How was this early project in the study of lives tradition conceptualized? The introduction to the chapter was written by Murray (pp. 604–615), while White was the "biographer" charged with the task of collecting the observations and test results of the subject and then fitting "them together as best he could into an interesting and understandable portrait." Murray goes on to say, "A 'portrait' meant a 'biography', since the notion was accepted generally that the history of the personality *is* the personality" (p. 604).

Like hundreds of thousands of other students across the United States, I was introduced to abnormal psychology and to the broader field of clinical psychology through Robert White's *The Abnormal Personality* (1948/1964). White had drawn on his interests in history and in the study of lives by providing two introductory chapters, first a historical introduction and then a "clinical introduction," consisting of five case histories in "realistic vividness." He raised the questions: "What does it mean to be psychologically disordered? How does it feel and how does it express itself in behavior? What are the symptoms? What sense can be made out of a disorder, and how can its causes be untangled?" (1964, p. 50).

In the second chapter, White provides five examples of "disordered personalities": Joseph Kidd, "a case of adolescent maladjustment with spontaneous recovery" (p. 52); Pearson Brack,

a bombardier in World War II suffering neurosis from combat stress; Bert Whipley, a career criminal who seemed to want to get arrested; L. Percy King, a psychotic with long-standing paranoid delusions who had been a state hospital patient for 28 years; and Martha Ottenby, a 56-year-old woman struck two years before with Pick's disease, a rare degenerative brain disorder. White writes that when psychological disorders occur in people, "we shall get a fairer impression of the problems if we start with case histories rather than with lists of symptoms or theoretical formulations" (p. 50). He asks that readers keep these cases in mind, as they read the later chapters of the book about particular disorders.

After the great popularity of White (1948/1964), which eventually sold more than 350,000 copies through its fifth edition (White & Watt, 1981), White considered a book on normal personality development, which became *Lives in Progress: A Study of the Natural Growth of Personality* (1952). The three lives discussed were those of Hartly Hale, physician and scientist; Joseph Kidd, businessman; and Joyce Kingsley, housewife and social worker. All had been students at Harvard or Radcliffe. In subsequent editions, White followed up their later development. The book was intended as a brief introduction to the whole field of personality, and these three case histories were used to "introduce and illustrate the general ideas" that make up a scientific account of personality.

The study of personality and the understanding of lives were conceived broadly, so *Lives in Progress* White (1952) includes discussions of "The Shaping of Lives by Social Forces" (chap. 4), "The Biological Roots of Personality" (chap. 6), and "The Psychodynamics of Development (chap. 8; White, 1966). White's professional affiliations at Harvard had included the Department of Psychology, the Psychological Clinic, and the Department of Social Relations. These three social structures may have helped him to attend to biological, psychodynamic, and social and cultural perspectives on the study of lives (White, 1966, p. iv).

I share White's view that personality can be influenced by biological, psychological, and social and cultural factors. However, what are the relations between "personality" and "the study of lives"? White, and Murray before him, often spoke as if they were the same thing. In my view, personalities are a part of, though not all of, life histories. I used to have debates about this with Murray, with me thinking that I'd won, and him probably thinking that he'd won, although sometimes it seemed to me he agreed with this distinction between personalities and life histories.

Murray and White sometimes say that "the history of the personality is the personality." One can agree with that. However, the history of the personality is not the same as the life history. The life history is a larger unit of analysis. It includes the history of the person interacting with contingent social, cultural, and historical contexts. This can be a valuable complement, even a humanizing component, to the hard science side of personality which emphasizes biological factors in evolutionary psychology, neuroscience, and genetic sources of personality.

Since the 1930s in the United States, the study of lives has been allied with personality psychology, as in the "personology" of Henry Murray, the study of lives of Robert White, Erik Erikson's work in psychobiography, or Gordon Allport's interest in how the psychological life history should be written. Personality psychology includes at least three different methodological traditions, the psychometric study of traits and individual differences, the experimental study of particular processes or classes of behavior, and the interpretive study of individual lives.

Mischel (1968) argued that experimental social learning approaches were superior to trait measurements or to psychoanalytic interpretation. This was followed by many psychologists stressing the virtues of person-situation interactionism. In recent years, there has been renewed emphasis in personality psychology on the measurement of personality, as with the five-factor theory (McCrae & Costa, 2003), while social psychologists often stress the value of experimental methods. The interpretive study of individual lives, however, too often falls by the wayside. Throughout the history of personality psychology, the study of individual lives has been regarded ambivalently and sometimes undervalued (Barenbaum & Winter, 2003). In this chapter, I focus on changing conceptions of psychobiography and the study of lives, while

arguing for the enduring value of historical-interpretive and historical science methods.

The personal and interpersonal story of the study of lives tradition is more complex than one might at first imagine. White's memoir, *Seeking the Shape of Personality* (1987), gives a largely positive account of his relations with Murray and the clinic. However, as White said in interviews and correspondence with Jim Anderson (2000), his relations with Murray were different than and more complicated than most people imagined. After World War II, when Murray returned to Harvard, he asked White to resign his new position as director of Harvard's clinical psychology program (Anderson, 2000) so that the position could be given to Don MacKinnon, one of Murray's first doctoral students, who had also been head of the O.S.S. Assessment Center near Washington, D.C. during World War II. White refused, and this event affected the later course of their relationship. It did not, however, prevent White from editing the volume on *The Study of Lives* (1963) in honor of Murray's seventieth birthday and writing an informative and sympathetic account of work at the Harvard Psychological Clinic (White, 1981). MacKinnon went on to found the Institute of Personality Assessment and Research at the University of California at Berkeley in 1949, where I showed up in 1975, finding the institute sympathetic to my interests in the study of lives, though I was then largely unaware of this complex web of associations.

While doing the research and theorizing, writing the papers, and relating to colleagues, participants may have only a partial knowledge of what is going on, and some of this may be inaccurate. When Henry Murray read Rodney Triplet's 1983 dissertation, "Henry A. Murray and the Harvard Psychological Clinic, 1926–1938: A Struggle to Expand the Disciplinary Boundaries of Academic Psychology," Triplet provided more details on Murray's tenure meeting than had previously been known. I heard Murray say about Boring, who Triplet reported voted against him, "That son of a bitch. He told me he'd done as much as he could for me." I found Murray the most charismatic and interesting psychologist I had ever met since encountering him early in graduate school in 1970. Forrest Robinson's (1992) biography of Murray, though, also revealed much about Murray's intellectual and personal life that I had not known and led me to understand more about his relations with Herman Melville, with Christiana Morgan, and with psychology. In reviewing the book, I had to rethink my relations to him and his work, parts of which are reflected in "Coming to Terms with the Life, Loves and Work of Henry A. Murray" (Runyan, 1994).

Even though I had talked with Robert White since 1969, read his publications and his memoir (1987), I did not understand the complexity of his relations to Murray until reading Jim Anderson's paper about White (1991/2000), as well as having a number of chances to talk with White during the last year of his life (2000–2001), conversations I hope to write about in a volume in honor of Robert White. This invitation to contribute a chapter on the history of psychobiography and the study of lives for this volume has also provided a welcome although demanding opportunity to reinterpret relations of the study of lives to the discipline of psychology. Every tradition in psychology can be understood in relation to its triple personal, social, and cultural contexts. In the following discussion, I'll say a little about the study of lives in relation to its personal contexts, with the somewhat different meanings that the study of lives had among founders of the tradition such as Murray, White, and Allport, down to a recent contributor to personology, Jerry S. Wiggins, with a little on myself and on William Todd Schultz in relation to Alan Elms along the way.

I'll try to provide glimpses of each of these individuals encountering the study of lives in relation to psychoanalysis, personality psychology, and historical science.

A Historical Sketch of Personology

A useful sketch of the history of personology is provided in Wiggins (2003). He identified major contributions by decade, from the field's origins with Freud (1910) on up through the present. In Table 2.1, I have slightly modified Wiggins's chart, by adding White's *The Abnormal Personality* (1948/1964), which was more

widely read than Murray's *Assessment of Men* (1948), and by subtracting one of my own books, *Psychology and Historical Interpretation* (Runyan, 1988a), which excellent though it may be, has not (at least not yet) had significant impact, though I do include a later chapter (Runyan, 1997). I added a number of other works that I see as significant contributions to the study of lives, such as those of Boring and Lindzey (1967), Meehl (1973), and several contributions since 2000, including this Handbook.

Jerry Wiggins is best known through his landmark volume *Personality and Prediction: Principles of Personality Assessment* (1973). He also co-authored a scholarly personality textbook (Wiggins et al., 1971) and edited *The Five-Factor Model of Personality* (1996).

How, one may ask, did Wiggins manage to move from a major psychometric text, a general personality text (with little attention to the study of lives), and a book on the five factor model, to doing a history of "personology" as one of five major *Paradigms of Personality Assessment* (Wiggins, 2003)? Is Wiggins's path of including the study of individual lives one that could be followed by others? In this book, Wiggins has experts apply five different approaches to personality assessment to the same subject, a flamboyant Native-American woman lawyer who grew up in an abusive family and spent time in prison yet managed to get through an Ivy League college, obtain a law degree, and become a successful defense lawyer in Arizona. How did Wiggins come to outline the history of personology and to apply five major approaches to the same person, things rarely done by personologists themselves? I don't know the whole story, but a few fragments are provided below. Wiggins was born in 1931, attended college at American University in Washington, D.C., and received a Ph.D. in clinical psychology from Indiana University in 1956. He taught at Stanford from 1957 through 1962, at the University of Illinois from 1962 through 1973, and from 1973 to retirement taught at the University of British Columbia.

Wiggins (2003) includes in his book a short section about his personal experiences with each of the five paradigms (pp. 16–22). His best-known ties are with the multivariate paradigm

Table 2.1 Historical Development Of The Personological Tradition
(*adapted from Wiggins, 2003*)

ORIGINS	Freud (1910) *Leonardo da Vinci and a Memory of His Childhood*
1930s	Dollard (1935) *Criteria for the Life History*
	Allport (1937) *Personality: A Psychological Interpretation*
	Murray (1938) *Explorations in Personality*
1940s	Allport (1942) *The Use of Personal Documents in Psychological Science*
	White (1948) *The Abnormal Personality*; Murray (1948) *Assessment of Men*
1950s	Erikson (1958) *Young Man Luther*
	White (1952) *Lives in Progress*
1960s	Boring, Edwin G. & Lindzey, G. (eds.) (1967) *A History of Psychology in Autobiography*, Vol. 5 (Allport, Murphy, Murray, Rogers, Skinner)
	Erikson(1969) *Gandhi's Truth*
1970s	Block (1971) *Lives Through Time*
	Meehl (1973) "Why I Do Not Attend Case Conferences"
	Levinson (1978) *The Seasons of a Man's Life*
1980s	Runyan (1982) *Life Histories and Psychobiography*
	McAdams & Ochberg (Eds) (1988) *Psychobiography & Life Narratives*
1990s	Alexander (1990) *Personology: Method and Content in Personality Assessment and Psychobiography*
	Elms (1994) *Uncovering Lives: The Uneasy Alliance of Biography and Psychology*
	Runyan (1997) "Studying Lives: Psychobiography and the Conceptual Structure of Personality Psychology"
2000–	McAdams, *The Person*, 3rd ed, (2001)
	Barenbaum & Winter (2003) "Personality" (ambivalence toward case studies)
	Wiggins (2003) *Paradigms of Personality Assessment* (5 paradigms applied to a single life)
	Schultz, W.T. (2005) this *Handbook of Psychobiography*

(Wiggins, 1973). When he moved from Stanford to the University of Illinois in 1962, he says he was on his way "to become a full-fledged member of the multivariate paradigm" (p. 20). This was to be "baptism by fire," though, as one of his first graduate teaching assignments was a lecture to the measurement section of the department. His fellow contributors to this section "included such superstars" as Raymond Cattell, Lee Cronbach, and Lloyd Humphreys. In a chapter on personality structure for the *Annual Review of Psychology* (Wiggins, 1968), he attempted to summarize Raymond Cattell's work, with substantial help from Cattell. Another influence was Donald Fiske, visiting at the University of British Columbia and co-teaching a graduate course on personality assessment, using Wiggins (1973) and Fiske's *Measuring The Concepts of Personality* (1971). Wiggins also has a 45-year association with Lewis R. Goldberg, and the Oregon Research Institute with Goldberg was a "home away from home." He also became friends with Paul Costa, who was the best man at his wedding to Krista Trobst.

Wiggins read first Freud in high school, "probably because of his emphasis on sex" (2003, p. 17). In his first year in college at American University, Wiggins wrote a term paper on "Hamlet and Oedipus," which he now sees as part of the personological paradigm. Over the Christmas break, he was made to feel welcome at the Library of Congress while researching this topic. When Lawrence Olivier's film on Hamlet appeared, he was able to impress a young lady by talking about its "Oedipal implications." By then, Wiggins said he often referred to James Agee's articles on film in *Partisan Review* and generally behaved "as an obnoxious teenage 'intellectual'" (p. 17). He maintained an interest in psychoanalysis while in a behaviorist graduate program at Indiana University, and when he became a faculty member at Stanford, he found senior figures such as Robert Sears and Ernest Hilgard had respect for it, and he was able to get funds for a brief psychoanalysis with a talented ego psychologist.

In encounters with the personological paradigm, Wiggins says he used Dan McAdams's

1990 personality text, *The Person*, to reorganize his undergraduate course along a personological orientation, and that students loved the book. McAdams also invited Wiggins to contribute an interpersonal perspective to a psychobiographical case in the *Journal of Personality* (Wiggins, 1997). Wiggins also says that I helped him to learn about life histories and psychobiographies and encouraged him to include his personal experiences with the different paradigms in this book.

I am flattered that Wiggins mentioned me as an influence, because his 1973 book *Personality and Prediction: Principles of Personality Assessment* (1973) was such a formative influence on my understanding of personality assessment. I remember finding the book in 1973, with its unusual red fish scale cover with gold lettering, in a bookstore in Amherst. With its rigorous analysis of the uses of personality assessment for predicting socially relevant behavior, including a historical overview of five American "milestone" studies in assessment, it introduced a new field to me. We first met when Wiggins was a visiting scholar at the Institute for Personality Assessment and Research at UC Berkeley in the late 1970s. We often ran into each other at later conventions of the American Psychological Association, and I'd hear about his book in progress as well as about his personal encounters with each of the different traditions. He was reluctant to include them in the book—"Who would be interested?"—but I encouraged him to include the stories as they were both humanly interesting and they illustrate the personal processes through which we are each exposed to different traditions. I wasn't sure what he'd decided but was delighted to see in the published book that he included a number of these encounters. If I had an influence on getting such an accomplished personality psychologist interested in the study of lives, and to integrate it into his understanding of the field, that's a worthy contribution.

The Study of Lives in Relation to Other Approaches in Personality Psychology

Once "personology" or the study of lives is again included as a topic within personality psychol-

ogy, how to understand its relationships with quantitative and experimental research in the field? Personality texts can be organized around general theories of personality (Hall & Lindzey, 1957), around general conceptual issues (Allport, 1937, 1961), around empirical research on substantive topics, around applications, or around various combinations of these approaches (e.g., Mischel, et al., 2004).

I'd like to suggest an alternative way of conceptualizing the structure of personality psychology, one that highlights the ways that theory and research relate to the study of individual lives. The central idea is that personality psychology is concerned with four major tasks or objectives: (1) developing general theories of personality, (2) studying individual and group differences, (3) analyzing specific processes and classes of behavior or experience, and (4) understanding individual persons or lives.

The top level of Table 2.2 outlines major theoretical orientations in personality psychology, including psychoanalysis starting around 1900, behaviorism beginning around 1913, culture and personality in the 1930s, psychometric approaches to personality in the 1950s, humanistic psychology in the 1960s, and cognitive in the 1970s.

The second level on individual and group differences has subheadings referring to major individual differences such as intelligence, types of psychopathology, personality traits, dimensions, and types, with a number of significant persons associated with each of these traditions. The bottom category in the second level is that of group differences, as by gender, age, race, class, culture, or historical periods. As I see it now, the study of individual differences may rely significantly on psychometric methods, while the study of group differences may rely not just on testing but more heavily on social, cultural, and historical analysis.

The third level includes specific processes and classes of behavior, with examples such as "dreams, slips, jokes, anxiety," all topics investigated by Freud; phobias, as investigated by behaviorists; honesty, researched by Hartshorne and May (1928); frustration and aggression, as studied at Yale in the 1930s; achievement motivation, as studied by David McClelland and col-

Table 2.2 The Study of Lives in Relation to Four Levels of Analysis in Psychology
(*items placed approximately by their historical time*)

	1900	1940	1980
Level 1 GENERAL THEORY	Psychoanalysis Behaviorism Culture & Personality	Psychometric Humanistic	Cognitive Behavior Genetics
Level 2 INDIVIDUAL & GROUP DIFFERENCES			
Intelligence:	Binet Terman	Wechsler	H. Gardner
Psychopathology:	Kraepelin	DSM I	DSM III
Traits/Types Dimensions:	Introversion/Extraversion Murray MMPI Meehl Cattell Eysenck Big Five		
Group Differences: (gender, age, race, class, sexuality, culture, historical period, etc.)			
Level 3 SPECIFIC PROCESSES & CLASSES OF BEHAVIOR	dreams slips jokes anxiety honesty phobias	achievement motivation frustration & aggression sex creativity anti-semitism emotions	social cognition stress & coping delay of gratification goal seeking suicide
Level 4 PERSONS AND LIVES			
Autobiographical Understanding:	Psychological theorists, researchers, therapists, clients (Freud, Jung, Horney, Skinner, Rogers et al.)		
Clinical Patients:	Freud's case studies Dora, Little Hans, Rat Man	Case Studies in Behavior Mod	DSM Casebook
Research Subjects:		Earnst	Lives in Progress Letters from Jenny
Biographical Figures:	Leonardo da Vinci Moses & Monotheism	The Early Mental Traits of 300 geniuses Melville Woodrow Wilson	Hitler Young Man Luther Van Gogh Stalin Gandhi's Truth Emily Dickinson Henry James Dostoevsky

leagues; delay of gratification, as studied by Mischel; and so on.

The bottom level of persons and lives has the four subcategories of autobiographical understanding, clinical patients, research subjects, and biographical figures, with selected examples of each of these four kinds of work in the study of lives.

The top row of level 4, autobiographical understanding, has been pursued by psychological theorists, researchers, therapists, clients, and developing persons. For example, there is substantial research on the self-understandings of theorists such as Freud, Jung, Helene Deutsch, Karen Horney, Carl Rogers, B.F. Skinner, and others and how this may be related to their theories of personality (Stolorow & Atwood, 1979; Demorest, 2005).

To provide an illustration of the self-understanding of therapists, consider *How Therapists Change: Personal and Professional Reflections* (Goldfried, 2001). This volume contains chapters by a number of therapists associated with the Society for the Exploration of Psychotherapy Integration on their changing theoretical orientations and clinical approaches, sometimes related to personal experiences. There are autobiographical chapters by Paul Wachtel,

Marvin Goldfried, Morris Eagle, Lorna Benjamin, George Stricker, Arnold Lazarus, Leslie Greenberg, Michael Mahoney, and others.

Self-interpretations of the work and life of psychological researchers, as well as theorists and clinicians, are contained in the series *A History of Psychology in Autobiography* (Vols. 1–8, 1930–1989). The series began in 1930 with a focus on experimental psychology, but by 1967, the fifth volume, edited by E.G. Boring and Gardner Lindzey, included contributors from a wider array of areas of psychology. The 1967 volume contained chapters by Gordon Allport, Gardner Murphy, Henry A. Murray, Carl Rogers, B.F. Skinner, and others. Volumes 6–8, edited by Lindzey, contained chapters from an array of psychological researchers and theorists, including Ernest Hilgard, David Krech, Margaret Mead, S.S. Stevens, Anne Anastasi, Jerome Bruner, Hans Eysenck, Donald Hebb, Herbert Simon, Roger Brown, Lee Cronbach, Barbel Inhelder, Eleanor Maccoby, Stanley Schacter, and Paul Meehl.

The second row is clinical patients, with examples of Freud's case studies of Dora, Little Hans, and the Rat Man, or the influential collection *Case Studies in Behavior Modification* (Ullmann & Krasner 1965), or the case books prepared to accompany recent editions of the *Diagnostic and Statistical Manual of Mental Disorders*. Accounts of mental illness from a first-person perspective include *The Inner World of Mental Illness* (ed. by Kaplan, 1964) or, in novelistic form, *I Never Promised You a Rose Garden* (Green, 1964). The third row is research subjects, illustrated with the case of "Earnst," written by Robert White in Murray (1938), White (1952), or Allport (1965). These are obviously not exhaustive lists, but a few illustrations of each of the four kinds of studies of individual persons and lives.

The bottom row is biographical figures, with examples of Freud's studies of Leonardo da Vinci (1910/1957) and *Moses and Monotheism* (1939/1964), to Catherine Cox's study, under Lewis Terman, to estimate *The Early Mental Traits of 300 Geniuses* (1926), to studies of Hitler starting with the O.S.S. in World War II with hundreds of later studies, to studies of Herman Melville by Henry Murray and others, to Erikson's influential *Young Man Luther* (1958) and *Gandhi's Truth* (1969), to the multivolume psychobiography of Stalin by Robert Tucker, to psychological interpretations of Vincent Van Gogh, Emily Dickinson, Henry James, and Dostoevsky.

Each level in the chart is associated with different methods. The second level, particularly the study of individual differences, is often pursued with psychometric and correlational methods. The third level, the study of particular processes and classes of behavior, is often studied with experimental methods, while the bottom level of individual lives is often associated with historical-interpretive methods. These, though, are rough associations, as topics in each row can be investigated with an array of methods.

To analyze relationships between these four enterprises in personality psychology, consider the task of trying to understand Adolf Hitler (a subject in the bottom row). In a valuable psychobiographical study, *The Psychopathic God: Adolf Hitler* (1977), Robert Waite draws on contributions from each of the top three levels. At the level of general theory, Waite draws most heavily on psychoanalytic theory, in discussing psychosexual stages in Hitler's development, Hitler's Oedipus complex, and the operation of defense mechanisms such as displacement and projection in Hitler's anti-Semitism. Waite also makes use of Erikson's psychosocial theory in discussions of trust and mistrust in Hitler's childhood, and discussions of identity crises and identity development in his adolescence and young adulthood.

At the second level of the chart, on individual and group differences, Hitler has been diagnosed medically and psychologically in a great number of ways. Diagnoses offered include Parkinson's disease, syphilis, and borderline personality. At the third level of particular classes of behavior and experience, Waite cites studies of anti-Semitism, survivor guilt, sexual perversion, masochistic behavior, and suicide to understand aspects of Hitler's behavior. (Additional details about interpretation of the Hitler case are in Runyan [1997].)

An alternative way of thinking about the relations of personality psychology to life stories, which has already had considerable influence, is provided by Dan McAdams in the third edition of *The Person* (2001). He uses a tripartite conception of personality around traits, characteristic adaptations (motivational, social-cognitive, and developmental), and their relations to integrative life stories or narrative identities (McAdams, 2001; see also McAdams, Chap. 4 this vol.)

Historical Science and the Study of Lives

While on sabbatical at Harvard in the spring of 1986, and again in the spring of 1990, I was much influenced by Stephen Jay Gould's arguments for the importance of "historical science" in both evolutionary biology and historical geology. In auditing lectures for his course titled "History of the Earth and of Life," I continually felt excited by the sense of these ideas having enormous implications for the social sciences and for our conception of psychology. I was affected particularly by Gould's *Time's Arrow, Time's Cycle* (1987), by *Wonderful Life: The Burgess Shale and the Nature of History* (1989), and an article on "Why History Matters" (1986). Most recently, Gould elaborated these themes in *The Structure of Evolutionary Theory* (2002), completed shortly before his death in May 2002.

What is Gould's conception of historical science? He argues that we often hold an oversimplified conception of "the scientific method," with images of a scientist in a "white lab coat twirling dials in a laboratory—experiment, quantification, repetition, prediction, and restriction of complexity to a few variables that can be controlled and manipulated" (Gould, 1989, p. 277). These are powerful procedures, but they are not adequate for explaining all of nature, particularly not for explaining complex sequences of historical events. Gould argues that "many large domains of nature—cosmology, geology, and evolution among them—must be studied with the tools of history" (p. 277).

Historical science is concerned with explaining complex sequences of historically contingent events and processes, which often can not be predicted, can not be exactly replicated, and can not be subsumed under general laws. If, for example, we want to understand why dinosaurs became extinct about 65 million years ago, one interpretive hypothesis depends on the discovery in the late 1970s that one or more asteroids hit the earth, changed its climate, and may have led to the extinction of dinosaurs, with evidence embedded in geological strata of the time.

Consider the evolution of humans. Gould argues that the whole history of life depends upon historically contingent sequences of events. If those comets that hit the earth had gone into different harmless orbits, then "dinosaurs still rule the earth, precluding the rise of large mammals, including humans" (p. 280). Given the multiple contingencies of evolution, capable of cascading down many different paths, "[w]e came *this close* (put your thumb about a millimeter away from your index finger), thousands and thousands of times, to erasure by the veering of history down another sensible channel" (p. 289).

Gould argues that Darwin was "the greatest of all historical scientists" (p. 282). He contrasts Darwin's methods with the "hypothetico-deductive" conception of science, central to experimental inquiry, given classic formulation in Carl Hempel's *Aspects of Scientific Explanation* (1965). In the history of psychology, the experimental psychology championed by Titchener and Boring won out over the human science psychology of Dilthey and the cultural-historical side of Wundt. The logical empiricism of Hempel, Nagel, and others was sometimes used as an ally of behavioral psychology (Smith, 1986). Gould's argument for historical science can be seen as an ally of "soft" or "human science" traditions such as psychoanalysis, phenomenological psychology, and the study of lives, making clearer appropriate standards of scientific rigor.

The relations between "natural science" and "historical science" are formulated in a useful way in Harvard's "core curriculum," with undergraduates required to take electives in both "science A" and "science B" (Keller, 1982). Science A courses (as described in the 1981–1982 Harvard catalogue) "are intended to introduce students to areas of science dealing primarily with deductive and quantitative aspects and to increase the student's understanding of the physical world." For example, Science A-16 is "Modern Physics: Concepts and Development" and Science A-25 is "Chemistry of the 20th Century."

Science B courses "are intended to provide a general understanding of science as a way of looking at man and the world by introducing students to complex natural systems with a substantial historical or evolutionary component." For example, Science B-15 is "Evolutionary Biology," taught by E.O. Wilson, and Science B-16 is "History of the Earth and of Life," taught by Stephen Jay Gould. Historical science appears in biological, physical, and social sciences. The goals of historical science—studying particular sequences of events and processes—and the methods of historical science for forming, critically evaluating, and constructing more adequate accounts and interpretations—have many analogies to, and implications for, the processes involved in advancing knowledge and understanding of individual lives.

After World War II, with the importance of technology in winning the war for the Allies, there was talk of "Science: The Endless Frontier," (Zachary, 1997). Just as there are unending possibilities for natural science inquiry, there may also be an "endless frontier" for human science inquiry, with the possibilities for historical science interpretations of individual lives interacting with their social, cultural, and historical contexts.

Conclusion: The Study of Individual Lives in Relation to the Goals and Methods of Scientific Psychology

The opening question of this chapter was: How are we to conceptualize the evolving relations between the study of individual lives and the discipline of psychology? I expressed a hope in 1982 that,

[i]n a view to the future, progress in the social and human sciences should be measured not solely by the development of more elaborate experimental and statistical procedures and the creation of increasingly comprehensive theories, but also by the development of more rigorous and insightful case studies and psychobiographies, and by advances in our understanding of individual lives. (Runyan, 1982, p. 246)

We are, it seems to me, considerably further along in that quest, with contributions by McAdams and Ochberg (1988), Alexander (1990), Jamison (1993), Elms (1994), Franz and Stewart (1994), McAdams et al. (2001), Josselson et al. (2003), Winer and Anderson (2003), Wiggins (2003), and now this first *Handbook of Psychobiography*. There are now also websites on psychobiography maintained by William Todd Schultz and on narrative psychology maintained by Vincent Hevern.

To summarize, in this chapter I have argued that the study of individual lives can move from being seen as a predecessor or an adjunct to scientific psychology, to being seen as one of the ultimate objectives of an appropriately scientific and humanistic psychology.

Scientific psychology can be conceived of as including not only the two disciplines of correlational psychology, and of experimental psychology, but also a third discipline of historical-interpretive psychology. Work in "historical science" can help to clarify the goals and methods of the study of lives, and perhaps in the human sciences more generally.

A brief review of relations between psychoanalysis and psychobiography was followed by a look at the complex and changing relations of personality psychology to the study of lives. The study of individual persons and lives was one of the central concerns and motivating agendas for founders of personality psychology such as Gordon Allport and Henry Murray, but in the 1950s and 1960s, the field turned more toward psychometric-correlational research and experimental studies. There was a surge of interest in the psychological study of individual lives by the 1980s, and this chapter argues that "historical science" can help bring the goals and methods of the study of individual lives into clearer focus. Recent personality textbooks, however, too often still neglect or marginalize the study of individual lives. Along with the accomplishments of correlational, experimental, and biological psychology, it is hoped that an increasing number of texts and overviews will include the "personological tradition" (as did McAdams, 2001, and Wiggins, 2003), review historical-interpretive and narrative methods, and include stories about individual lives as one of the starting points and end points of scientific psychology.

Acknowledgments

I thank Nicole Barenbaum, Mary Coombs, Alan Elms, William Todd Schultz, and members of the San Francisco Bay Area Psychobiography Working Group for their comments on an earlier draft of this chapter.

References

Abraham, K. (1935). Amenhotep IV (Ikhnaton): A psychoanalytic contribution to the understanding of his personality and the monotheistic cult of Aton. Psychoanalytic Quarterly 4, 537–549. (Original work published 1912)

Alexander, F. (1930). The psychoanalysis of the total personality. New York: Nervous and Mental Diseases Pub. Co.

Alexander, I. (1990). Personology: Method and content in personality assessment and psychobiography. Durham, N.C.: Duke University Press.

Allport, G.W. (1937). Personality: A psychological interpretation. New York: Holt.

Allport, G.W. (1942). The use of personal documents in psychological science. New York: Social Science Research Council.

Allport, G.W. (1961). Pattern and growth in personality. New York: Holt, Rinehart & Winston.

Allport, G.W. (1965). Letters from Jenny. New York: Harcourt, Brace, & World.

Allport, G.W. (1967). Gordon W. Allport. In E. Boring & G. Lindzey (Eds.), A history of psychology in autobiography (Vol. 5, pp. 3–25). New York: Appleton-Century-Crofts.

Anderson, J.W. (2000). The life of Robert W. White: A psychobiographical exploration (2nd draft). Unpublished manuscript. (Original manuscript dated 1991)

Anderson, J.W. (2003). Recent psychoanalytic theorists and their relevance to psychobiography: Winnicott, Kernberg and Kohut. In

J. Winer & J. Anderson (Eds.), The annual of psychoanalysis, Vol. 31: Psychoanalysis and history (pp. 79–94). Hillsdale, N.J.: Analytic Press.

Barenbaum, N. (1997). "The most revealing method of all": Gordon Allport and case studies. Paper presented at Cheiron, Richmond, VA.

Barenbaum, N., & Winter, D. (2003). Personality. In D. Freedheim (Ed.), History of psychology (Vol. 1, pp. 177–201). New York: Wiley.

Barnes, H.E. (1919). Psychology and history: Some reasons for predicting their more active cooperation in the future. American Journal of Psychology, 30, 337–376.

Barnes, H.E. (1925). Psychology and history. New York: Century.

Bernstein, R.J. (1998). Freud and the legacy of Moses. Cambridge: Cambridge University Press.

Bloland, S.E. (1999). Fame: The power and cost of a fantasy. Atlantic Monthly, November.

Boring, E.G. (1950). A history of experimental psychology (2nd ed.). New York: Appleton-Century-Crofts. (originally published 1929)

Boring, E.G., & Lindzey, G. (Eds.) (1967). A history of psychology in autobiography (Vol. 5). New York: Appleton-Century-Crofts.

Breuer, J., & Freud, S. (1955). Studies on hysteria. In J. Strachey (Ed. & Trans.), The standard edition of the complete psychological works of Sigmund Freud (Vol. 2, pp. 1–305). London: Hogarth Press. (Original work published 1893–1895)

Cahan, E.D., & White, S.H. (1992). Proposals for a second psychology. American Psychologist, 47, 224–235.

Campbell, D.T. (1975). "Degrees of freedom" and the case study. Comparative Political Studies, 8, 178–193.

Campbell, D.T., & Stanley, J.C. (1963). Experimental and quasi-experimental designs for research. Chicago: Rand-McNally.

Cohler, B.J. (1993). Describing lives: Gordon Allport and the "Science" of personality. In K. Craik et al. (Eds.). Fifty years of personality psychology (pp. 131–146). New York: Plenum.

Collins, B. (1997). Leonardo, psychoanalysis and art history. Evanston, IL: Northwestern University Press.

Cox, C. (1926). The early mental traits of three hundred geniuses. Stanford, CA: Stanford University Press.

Cronbach, L.J. (1957). The two disciplines of scientific psychology. American Psychologist, 12, 671–684.

Cronbach, L.J. (1975). Beyond the two disciplines of scientific psychology. American Psychologist, 30, 116–127.

Demorest, A. (2005). Psychology's grand theorists: How personal experiences shaped professional ideas. Mahway, N.J.: Erlbaum.

Dilthey, W. (1988). Introduction to the human sciences. Detroit: Wayne State University Press. (Original work published 1883).

Dooley, L. (1916). Psychoanalytic studies of genius. American Journal of Psychology, 27, 363–416.

Ellenberger, H.R. (1970). The discovery of the unconscious. New York: Basic.

Elms, A.C. (1976). Personality in politics. New York: Harcourt Brace Jovanovich.

Elms, A.C. (1981). Skinner's dark year and Walden Two. American Psychologist, 36, 470–479.

Elms, A.C. (1994). Uncovering lives: The uneasy alliance of biography and psychology. New York: Oxford University Press.

Elms, A.C. (2003). Sigmund Freud, psycho-historian. In J. Winer & J. Anderson (Eds.), The annual of psychoanalysis, special issue on psychoanalysis and history (pp. 65–78). Hillsdale, N.J.: Analytic Press.

Erikson, E.H. (1958). Young man Luther: A study in psychoanalysis and history. New York: Norton.

Erikson, E.H. (1969). Gandhi's truth. New York: Norton.

Fancher, R.E. (1979). Pioneers of psychology. New York: Norton.

Fearing, F. (1927). Psychological studies of historical personalities. Psychological Bulletin, 24, 521–539.

Franz, C. & Stewart, A. (Eds.), (1994). Women creating lives: Identities, resilience, and resistance. New York: Perseus.

Freud, S. (1955). Analysis of a phobia in a five-year-old boy. In J. Strachey (Ed. & Trans.), The standard edition of the complete psychological works of Sigmund Freud (Vol. 10, pp. 5–149). London: Hogarth Press. (Original work published 1909)

Freud, S. (1959). Delusions and dreams in Jensen's Gradiva. In J. Strachey (Ed. and Trans), The standard edition of the complete psychological works of Sigmund Freud (Vol. IX, pp. 7–95). London: Hogarth Press. (Original work published 1907)

Freud, S. (1957). Leonardo da Vinci and a memory of his childhood. In J. Strachey (Ed. and Trans), The standard edition of the complete psychological works of Sigmund Freud (Vol. Xl, pp. 63–137). London: Hogarth Press. (Original work published 1910)

Freud, S. (1964). Moses and monotheism: Three essays. In J. Strachey (Ed. and Trans), The standard edition of the complete psychological works of Sigmund Freud (Vol. XXIII, pp. 7–137). London: Hogarth Press. (Original work published 1939)

Friedman, L. (1999). Identity's architect: A biography of Erik H. Erikson. New York: Scribner.

Goldfried, M.R. (Ed.) (2001). How therapists change: Personal and professional reflections. Washington, D.C.: American Psychological Association.

Gould, S.J. (1986, January-February). Evolution and the triumph of homology, or why history matters. American Scientist, pp. 60–69.

Gould, S.J. (1987). Time's arrow, time's cycle. Cambridge, Mass.: Harvard University Press.

Gould, S.J. (1989). Wonderful life: The Burgess shale and the nature of history. New York: Norton.

Gould, S.J. (2002). The structure of evolutionary theory. Cambridge, Mass.: Harvard University Press.

Graf, M. (1911). Richard Wagner in the "Flying Dutchman." A contribution to the psychology of artistic creation. Schriften zur angewandten Seelunkunde, 9.

Green, H. (1964). I never promosed you a rose garden. New York: Signet.

Hall, C., & Lindzey, G. (1957). Theories of personality. New York: Wiley.

Hall, G.S. (1904). Adolescence (2 vols.). New York: Appleton.

Hartshorne, H. & May, M.A. (1928). Studies in deceit. New York: Macmillan.

Hearst, E. (Ed.). (1979). The first century of experimental psychology. Hillsdale, N.J.: Erlbaum.

Hempel, C.G. (1965). Aspects of scientific explanation. New York: Free Press.

Hilgard, E. (1948). Theories of learning. New York: Appleton-Century-Crofts.

Hilgard, E. (1987). Psychology in America: A historical survey. San Diego: Harcourt Brace Jovanovich.

James, W. (1890). Principles of psychology. New York: Holt.

James, W. (1902). The varieties of religious experience: A study in human nature. Cambridge, Mass.: Harvard University Press.

Jamison, K.R. (1993). Touched with fire. Manic-depressive illness and the artistic temperament. New York: Free Press.

Jones, E. (1910). The Oedipus complex as an explanation of Hamlet's mystery: A study in motive. American Journal of Psychology, 21, 72–113.

Jones, E. (1953–1957). Sigmund Freud. (3 volumes). New York: Basic.

Josselson, R., Lieblich, A., & McAdams, D. (Eds.) (2003). Up close and personal: The teaching and learning of narrative research. Washington, D.C.: American Psychological Association.

Kaplan, B. (Ed.) (1964). The inner world of mental illness. New York: Harper & Row.

Karpas, M.J. (1915). Socrates in the light of modern psychopathology. Journal of Abnormal Psychology, 10, 185–200.

Keller, P. (1982). Getting at the core: Curricular reform at Harvard. Cambridge, Mass.: Harvard University Press.

Kluckhohn, C. & Murray, H.A. (Eds). (1948). Personality in nature society and culture. New York: Knopf.

Levinson, D. et al. (1978). The seasons of a man's life. New York: Knopf.

Lindzey, G. (Ed.) (1954). The handbook of social psychology (2 volumes). Reading, Mass.: Addison-Wesley.

Loewenberg, P. (1988). Psychoanalytic models of history: Freud and after. In W. Runyan (Ed.), Psychology and historical interpretation (pp. 126–156). New York: Oxford University Press.

Lundberg, G.A. (1926). Case work and the statistical method. Social Forces, 5, 61–65.

Mack, J.E. (1971). Psychoanalysis and historical biography. Journal of the American Psychoanalytic Association, 19, 143–179.

McAdams, D. (1990, 2001, 3rd ed.). The person: An introduction to personality psychology. San Diego. Harcourt Brace Jovanovich.

McAdams, D., Lieblich, A., & Josselson, R. (Eds.). (2001). Turns in the road: Narrative studies of lives in transition. Washington, D.C.: American Psychological Association.

McAdams, D. & Ochberg, R. (Eds.) (1988). Psychobiography and life narratives. Durham, NC: Duke University Press.

McCrae, R. & Costa, P. (2003). Personality in adulthood: A five-factor theory perspective, 2nd edition. New York: Guilford.

Meehl, P.E. (1973). Why I do not attend case conferences. In P.E. Meehl, Psychodiagnosis: Selected papers (pp. 225–302). Minneapolis: University of Minnesota Press.

Mischel, W. (1968). Personality and assessment. New York: Wiley.

Mischel, W., Shoda, Y., & Smith, R.E. (2004). Introduction to personality: Toward an integration (7th ed.). New York: Wiley.

Moraitis, G. (2003). The ghost in the biographer's machine. In J. Winer & J. Anderson (Eds.). The annual of psychoanalysis (Vol. 31, pp. 97–106). Hillsdale, N.J.: Analytic Press.

Murchison, C. (Ed.). (1930). A history of psychology in autobiography (Vol. 1). Worcester, Mass.: Clark University Press.

Murray, H.A. (1938). Explorations in personality. New York: Oxford University Press.

Murray, H.A., with Staff (1948). Assessment of men. New York: Rinehart.

Murray, H.A. (Ed. with Introduction) (1949). Melville, H. Pierre, or the ambiguities. New York: Hendricks House.

Murray, H.A. (1981). Psychology and the university. In E.S. Shneidman (Ed.), Endeavors in psychology: Selections from the personology of Henry A. Murray (pp. 337–351). New York: Harper & Row. [Original published 1935]

Nicholson, I.A.M. (2003). Inventing personality: Gordon Allport and the science of selfhood. Washington, D.C.: American Psychological Association.

Roazen, P. (1975). Freud and his followers. New York: Knopf.

Robinson, F.G. (1992). Love's story told: A life of Henry A. Murray. Cambridge, Mass.: Harvard University Press.

Runyan, W.M. (1975). Life histories: A field of inquiry and a framework for intervention. Unpublished doctoral dissertation, Harvard University, Cambridge, Mass.

Runyan, W.M. (1978). The life course as a theoretical orientation: Sequences of person-situation interaction. Journal of Personality, 46, 569–593.

Runyan, W.M. (1981). Why did Van Gogh cut off his ear? The problem of alternative explanations in psychobiography. Journal of Personality and Social Psychology, 40, 1070–1077.

Runyan, W.M. (1982). Life histories and psychobiography: Explorations in theory and method. New York: Oxford University Press.

Runyan, W.M. (1983). Idiographic goals and methods in the study of lives. Journal of Personality, 51, 413–437.

Runyan, W.M. (1984). Diverging life paths: Their probabilistic and causal structure. In K. Gergen & M. Gergen (Eds.), Historical social psychology. Hillsdale, N.J.: Erlbaum.

Runyan, W.M. (Ed.). (1988a). Psychology and historical interpretation. New York: Oxford University Press.

Runyan, W.M. (1988b). Progress in psychobiography. Journal of personality, 56(1), 295–326. Also in Psychobiography and life narratives, McAdams, D. & Ochberg, R. (Eds). Durham, N.C.: Duke University Press.

Runyan, W.M. (1994). Coming to terms with the life, loves, and work of Henry A. Murray (review of F. Robinson, Love's story told: A life of Henry A. Murray). Contemporary Psychology, 39, 701–704.

Runyan, W.M. (1997). Studying lives: Psycho-biography and the conceptual structure of personality psychology. In R. Hogan et al. (Eds.), Handbook of personality (pp. 41–69). New York: Academic.

Runyan, W.M. (2002). On coming to understand my father: A personal and professional journey. In R. Pellegrini & T. Sarbin (Eds.), Between fathers and sons (pp. 77–89). Haworth.

Runyan, W.M. (2003). From the study of lives and psychohistory to historicizing psychology: A conceptual journey. In J. Winer & J. Anderson (Eds.), The annual of psychoanalysis, special issue on psychoanalysis and history (pp. 119–132). Hillsdale, N.J: Analytic Press.

Runyan, W.M. (2005). Toward a better story of psychology: Sheldon White's contributions to the history of psychology, a personal perspective. In D. Pillemer & S. White (Eds.) Developmental psychology and social change (pp. 59–82). New York: Cambridge University Press.

Sadger, I. (1908). Konrad Ferdinand Meyer. Wiesbaden.

Sadger, I. (1909). Aus dem Liebeleben Nicolaus Lenaus. Leipzig.

Schepeler, E. (1993). Jean Piaget's experiences on the couch: Some clues to a mystery. International Journal of Psychoanalysis, 74.

Schultz, W.T. (1992) A psychobiographical inquiry into the life, mind and creative work of James Agee. Unpublished doctoral dissertation, University of California at Davis, Davis, CA.

Schultz, W.T. (1996). An 'Orpheus complex' in two writers-of-loss. Biography: An Interdisciplinary Quarterly 19 (4), 371–393

Schultz, W.T. (1999). Off-stage voices in James Agee's Let Us Now Praise Famous Men—Reportage as covert autobiography." American Imago, 56 (1), 75–104.

Schultz, W.T. (Ed.) (2005). Handbook of psychobiography. New York: Oxford University Press.

Shadish, W., Phillips, G., & Clark, M. (2003). Content and context: The impact of Campbell and Stanley. In R.J. Sternberg (Ed.), The anatomy of impact: What makes the great works of psychology great (pp. 161–176). Washington, D.C.: American Psychological Association.

Smith, L.D. (1986). Behaviorism and logical positivism: A revised account of the alliance. Stanford, Calif.: Stanford University Press.

Smith, P. (1913). Luther's early development in the light of psycho-analysis. American Journal of Psychology, 24, 360–377.

Smith, M.B., Bruner, J.S., & White, R.W. (1956). Opinions and personality. New York: Wiley.

Sternberg, R. (Ed.) (2005). Unity in psychology: Possibility or pipedream? Washington, D.C.: American Psychological Association.

Stevens, S.S. (Ed.) (1951). Handbook of experimental psychology. New York: Wiley.

Stolorow, R.D. & Atwood, G.E. (1979). Faces in a cloud: Subjectivity in personality theory. Northvale, N.J.: Aronson.

Strozier, C.B. (2003). Autobiographical reflections on writing the biography of Heinz Kohut. In J. Winer & J. Anderson (Eds.), The annual of psychoanalysis, special issue on psychoanalysis and history (pp. 107–118). Hillsdale, N.J.: Analytic Press.

Triplet, R.G. (1983). Henry A. Murray and the Harvard Psychological Clinic, 1926–1938: A struggle to expand the disciplinary boundaries of academic psychology. Unpublished doctoral dissertation, Durham, N.H.: University of New Hampshire,   .

Ullmann, L.P. & Krasner, L. (Eds.) (1965). Case studies in behavior modification. New York: Holt, Rinehart & Winston.

Waite, R.G.L. (1977). The psychopathic god: Adolf Hitler. New York: Basic Books.

White. R.W. (1943). The personality of Joseph Kidd. Character and Personality, XI, 183–208, 318–360.

White, R.W. (1964). The abnormal personality, 3rd ed. New York: Ronald. (Originally published 1948).

White, R.W. (1952, 1966, 1975). Lives in progress: A study of the natural growth of personality. New York: Holt, Rinehart & Winston.

White. R.W. (Ed.) (1963). The study of lives. New York: Atherton.

White, R.W. (1972, 1976). The enterprise of living: A view of personality. New York: Holt, Rinehart & Winston.

White, R.W. (1974). Teaching personality through life histories. Teaching of Psychology, 1, 69–71.

White, R.W. (1981). Exploring personality the long way: The study of lives. In A. Rabin et al. (Eds), Further explorations in personality (pp. 3–19). New York: Wiley.

White, R.W. (1987). A memoir: Seeking the shape of personality. Marlborough, N.H.: The Homestead Press.

White, S.H. (2001). Developmental psychology as a human enterprise. 2001 Heinz Werner Lecture Series. Worcester, Mass.: Clark University Press.

Wiggins, J.S. (1973). Personality and prediction: Principles of personality assessment. Reading, Mass.: Addison-Wesley.

Wiggins, J.S., Renner, K.E., Clore, G.L., & Rose, R.J. (1971). The psychology of personality. Reading, Mass.: Addison-Wesley.

Wiggins, J.S. (Ed.) (1996). The five-factor model of personality: Theoretical perspectives. New York: Guilford.

Wiggins, J.S. (1997). Circumnavigating Dodge Morgan's interpersonal style. Journal of personality, 65, 1069–1086.

Wiggins, J.S. (2003). Paradigms of personality assessment. New York: Guilford.

Winer J. & Anderson J. (Eds.), (2003). The annual of Psychoanalysis, Vol. 31, special issue on psychoanalysis and history. Hillsdale, N.J.: Analytic Press.

Winter, D., & Barenbaum, N. (1999). History of modern personality theory and research. In L.A. Pervin & O. John (Eds.), Handbook of personality: theory and research (2nd ed.). New York: Guilford

Woodworth, R.S. (1929). Psychology (rev. ed.). New York: Holt.

Woodworth, R.S. (1938). Experimental psychology. New York: Holt.

Wundt, W. (1873–1874). Grundzuge der Physiologische Psychologie [Principles of physiological psychology]. Leipzig: Englemann.

www.narrativepsych.com. Last accessed September 16, 2004.

www.psychobiography.com. Last accessed September 16, 2004.

Yerushalmi, Y.H. (1991). Freud's Moses: Judaism terminable and interminable. New Haven, Conn.: Yale University Press.

Zachary, P. (1997). Endless frontier: Vannevar Bush, engineer of the American century. New York: Free Press.

Chapter 3

William Todd Schultz

How to Strike Psychological Pay Dirt in Biographical Data

Choosing a subject to think and write about is the first step in any psychobiography. At some point a person, for an untold surplus of reasons partly conscious yet usually mostly unconscious, starts waving at you, calling out from a distance. Come see about me! Sometimes you stop to wonder, Why this individual particularly? Or you wonder why later, after finishing your work, especially in cases when this individual seems to have a lot in common with other individuals who have waved and called in similar fashion before. Perhaps a certain type of person fascinates you uniquely, pulls on you in ways difficult to resist. Maybe the people you write about resemble you. Maybe you write about those you detest, with the aim (unconscious) of justifying your enmity. Maybe you write about people you admire, in possession of talents you wish you possessed. Whatever the case, this "why" question is worth mulling over. It may even constitute a place to start, or at least somewhere to sojourn as the process of research unfolds. As I discuss in my chapter on Diane Arbus (see Schultz, chap. 8 this vol.), it sometimes happens that the "why" factor interferes with "whats" and other "whys." Our own needs can get in the way, that is, leaving us dangerously cock-eyed. So be watchful. The doing of psychobiography occasionally careens into autobiography. And when that happens, as it did to Freud in his work on Leonardo, even the most elegantly assembled edifice goes up in smoke. Elms's (1994) advice works well as a general principle: best to select a subject for whom your feelings are neither strongly negative nor strongly positive. It's not possible to feel nothing. You won't sustain any interest at all lacking some in-

tensity of affect. The proscription is against letting that affect run away with you. Use it but don't abuse it, or better yet, don't let it abuse you.

Once you put your motives in order to the extent possible short of psychoanalysis, then the process of working with sources rises front and center. Sources must be various enough and sufficiently psychologically oriented to proceed. There will be times when you choose a subject about whom very little has been written or about whom what has been written relates not at all to his or her mental life or life history. You search long and hard but come up empty-handed. Then what? Sad to say, you simply start over with someone new. No amount of interest—your own or the world's—compensates for lack of evidence. At the very least, a detailed biography is a must. Lacking that, there just isn't enough to go on. You need data to interpret.

But let's say you are lucky, and having chosen as your subject Kingsley Amis, for instance, you discover a biography, a book of letters, a memoir, a memoir by Amis's son Martin, and a long list of fiction titles, poems, literary criticism, and accounts of Amis's life. You are now on solid ground. In fact, what you face is truly quite daunting, but in a different sense. In front of you there lies not a paucity but a superabundance of relevant material. You find yourself at a critical juncture. Now the question is how to identify within this mound of biographical, psychological, and literary data those that deserve special emphasis—episodes or events of unique saliency. Which interpretable moments—and these are numberless—ought to be singled out for closest scrutiny? On one hand, you might simply go

42

forward intuitively, focusing on factors catching your interest for whatever reason. That strategy may well suffice in certain cases, when intuitions are especially finely tuned and guesses educated. On the other hand, one may do better yet to rely on some sort of system for sifting through and winnowing out facts of a life, letting the system guide you, in effect making your choices for you. That is this chapter's burden. Its aim is to provide the psychobiographer with two slightly overlapping strategies for working with biographical data and highlighting those of unusual prominence and psychological importance. Irving Alexander's (1990) indicators of saliency are introduced first, followed by my own concept of the prototypical scene. Both methodologies serve as guides for the delineation of life events most mysterious, most revealing, and therefore most in need of elucidation.

Selecting Saliencies

All lives are momentous, packed with events. The overwhelming majority of these events we dismiss as irrelevant or else unimportant as far as who the person is or how she became what she became. They don't really matter, in other words. They make no difference in the life, or at least seem not to make a difference (rarely some may turn out to; we don't know for sure). Other events we judge to be central, constellating, defining, nuclear. Our sense is that they shape the person and, in combination, form a major component of personality. What's inessential from the standpoint of knowing someone and what is, on the other hand, core to the person are judgments we make moment by moment in life, and almost always unconsciously. We can't say for sure why we zeroed in on one event as opposed to any other, but zero in we do. This data selection process can be done more deliberately, however, or, as I put it above, less intuitively (not that intuition always leads one astray).

As soon as one enters the orbit of a life and begins to acquaint oneself with that life's details, a realization slowly dawns: There are too many damn details! Alexander's (1988; 1990) "textual indicators of psychological saliency" were invented to reduce this embarrassment of riches.

Based for the most part on strategies used in psychoanalysis, and in some cases on Freudian concepts directly, these cues or pointers for homing in on uniquely meaningful utterances can be relied on while wending one's way through any set of biographical data—diaries, letters, autobiography, even biography, and fiction. They serve as markers. They point to events we may want to reexamine, or take up later in more detail. They reduce the signal-to-noise ratio and thus help us "hear" our subjects a little more clearly. Using these pointers we less often go astray, and increase our chances of striking psychological pay dirt.

The pointer of primary usefulness is, in my experience, frequency or repetition (see Table 3.1). For Freud, repetition denotes neurosis. Doing the same thing over and over again, or dreaming the same dream recurrently, or writing books always containing the same egoist female character—such actions signal the presence of a core conflict demanding disguised expression. Freud named this tendency the "compulsion to repeat" or the "repetition compulsion." In his system repetition emphatically did not lead to mastery or overcoming of the conflict. It was purely defensive, one of the surest indications of the reality of the death instinct. Whatever one thinks about repetition's potential for growth, when we detect it in a life, we should pay special attention. Patterns or scripts that occur with frequency comprise nuclear constituents of personality.

An example of frequency provided by Elms (1994) and explored in detail by Barenbaum (chap. 16 this vol.) is trait theorist Gordon Allport's repetitive retelling of a story about his meeting Freud. Elms makes the case that this meeting, "pungent" in its "significance" (according to Allport), not only reveals much about Allport's personality but also led him to invent a personality theory with assumptions directly challenging those made by Freud. The theory, then, was (at least partly) what Freud would have called a "reaction formation"—a "psychological attitude diametrically opposed to a repressed wish" (Laplanche & Pontalis, 1973, p. 376).

Elms (1994) includes another nice example of frequency in his chapter on Nabokov, who made the most of every opportunity to proffer "extreme and insistent denunciations of Freud," many of these included in forewords to his novels. As Elms

Table 3.1 Irving Alexander's (1990) "primary indicators of psychological saliency"

1. *Frequency*	Any repeated communications, themes, scenes or events or happenings, means-end sequences, relationship patterns, conflicts, obsessions, and so on (see, e.g., Barenbaum, chap. 16 this vol., on Allport's repeated references to his meeting with Freud).
2. *Primacy*	What comes first in a text occasionally tells us more than anything else, or tells us something uniquely significant (see, e.g., Anderson on Wharton's earliest memory, chap. 13 this vol.).
3. *Emphasis*	The effort by a subject to, in effect, italicize a happening in some way. This can assume the form of over-, under-, or misplaced emphasis (e.g., Bill Clinton taking great pains to emphasize how he "did not have sex with that woman").
4. *Isolation*	The so-called "come again?" criterion, at issue when material jarringly stands out from surrounding text, and thus seems not to fit at all, as in the example of Kathryn Harrison's "ambulatory tongue" (this chap.)
5. *Uniqueness*	Material that is marked by the subject as unprecedented or somehow especially singular (e.g., "I have retained just one memory from my childhood," or "One incident always comes to mind from the period of my adolescence").
6. *Incompletion*	When a subject begins a story but neglects to finish it, in effect trailing off without adding necessary details, a kind of avoidance to reach conclusion.
7. *Error, distortion, omission*	The act of getting, say, a memory wrong, or distorting what really happened, or else omitting certain relevant facts altogether (see, e.g., for error in particular, Elms & Heller on Elvis, chap. 10 this vol., and Schultz on Plath, chap. 11 this vol.).
8. *Negation*	Strenuous disavowal especially in the absence of any positive assertion to the contrary, a kind of "Gertrude Rule," in the sense of "protesting too much" any given psychological or biographical fact—for instance, George W. Bush's assertions that he is not his father (see Renshon on Bush, chap. 22 this vol.).

declares, "For a man who rejected Freud so vehemently, Nabokov was astonishingly preoccupied with him" (p. 164). And of course, the question is why?

One of Nabokov's critics called his Freud bashing "obsessive." This brings to mind another point worth making regarding the frequency cue. Sometimes key repetitions come across as obsessions, particularly, I think, when the subject is an artist. I say something similar in a later chapter on Diane Arbus (see Schultz, chap. 8 this vol.), but it bears mentioning here as well: It is always useful to ask of an artist (or a politician, or a theorist) what is her obsession? What subject does she return to over and over again? For photographer Diane Arbus, the answer is eccentrics; for poet Sylvia Plath, the answer is her father. For Freud, the answer is sex; for Erikson, the answer is identity. Obsessions tell fundamentally revealing stories. Stay on the alert for them, maybe above all else. And when you find them, ask yourself what they mean for your subject, whoever he or she might be.

One final observation about the frequency pointer: Repetitions need not be literal or exclu-sively textual in nature. The children's author and illustrator Maurice Sendak habitually drew engorged moons (which he himself identified as breasts) in the corners of many of his frames—hence, a pictorial repetition of psychological import (see Martinsen, 2003). Kerouac included in several of his books—*Dr. Sax, On the Road*—a shrouded, black-caped shadow figure, a dark traveler who "ghosted" Jack's fictional alter-ego (see Schultz, 2003). This seems best described as a symbolic repetition. One can even focus on repetitions of musical form. Along such lines, a student of mine once wrote an essay on Kurt Cobain's tendency to compose rock songs with suddenly shifting dynamics—a smoothly melodic, pianissimo section followed by crashing, bar-chord atonality ("Smells Like Teen Spirit," e.g.).

Anyway, the point is that repetitions assume many forms. Don't look only for the textual.

Primacy is another of Alexander's indicators of psychological saliency. What comes first in a text occasionally tells us more than anything else, or tells us something uniquely significant. Psychoanalysis attaches importance to earliest memories, and more recently McAdams (1993) does the same in his life story model and interview protocol. Not all "first things" of any kind are revelatory, but some are, or may be, so paying attention to them can't hurt. I find this pointer applying most usefully to autobiographical writing, especially when an autobiography begins with an event or happening, and not chronologically (e.g., "I was born in," etc.). A few days ago I bought at an estate sale two autobiographies by men I know very little about: Robert Evans, erstwhile production chief of Paramount Pictures, and Frank Lloyd Wright. The books are *The Kid Stays in the Picture* (1994) and *Frank Lloyd Wright: An Autobiography* (1977). Out of curiosity I checked this morning how each began, and in both cases the answer was telling, revealing, in a way illustrating the value of primacy as a cue to meaning. Evans recounts how he managed to full-Nelson Henry Kissinger into attending the premiere of *The Godfather*—which Evans had produced—despite the fact that the North Vietnamese offensive had just begun. Evans's wife at the time, Ali McGraw, had the same day returned from shooting *The Getaway* with Steve McQueen. The premiere goes splendidly; Ali, though exhausted, looks radiant; Kissinger is drolly charismatic; and the film, as we know, in time is regarded as a masterpiece of cinema. "Holding Ali tightly in my arms, I felt," Evans recalls, "I was the luckiest man in the world. It was the highest moment of my life. Was I dreaming? I was. It was all a facade. The beginning of the end" (p. 11). We learn in Peter Bart's foreword to the book how, after *Godfather*, Evans became increasingly obsessed with his work, developed a reliance on painkillers and so-called "vitamin shots," and found that his wife Ali was having an affair with McQueen. "The Gatsby-like image began to fade," we are told. And this fade-out followed directly on the heels of the highest moment of Evans's life. Evans begins with a peak experience, only to contrast it with the nadir to come. He is a winner about to lose big. Disaster hangs in the air like one of Sendak's full moons.

Wright starts his autobiography with a memory of a moment shared with his uncle. The two make their way across a snow-covered field, his uncle assuring him, "Come, my boy, and I will show you how to go" (Wright, 1977,

p. 23). The destination is a "point upon which he [Wright's uncle] had fixed his keen blue eyes." Uncle walks straight, neither to right nor left—"possessed." But the boy, Wright, breaks free from the man's grasp, running willy-nilly to collect bunches of weeds, their "delicate clusters of dark bronze heads" having caught his eye. The two reunite at the top of a hill. The uncle shoots Wright a "stern look." He points to the straight path he had taken, then contrasts it with the boy's "wavering, searching, heedful line embroidering the straight one like some free, engaging vine as it ran back and forth across it" (p. 24). Wright says Uncle John's meaning was clear: neither to right nor to left, but straight, is the way. Yet Wright, the boy, is troubled. "Uncle John had left out something—something that made all the difference to the boy." What? What had Uncle John left out? And why did it make all the difference? Is Wright telling us that the searching, more adventurous and risky line is in fact preferable to heading directly toward one's goal? Does the anecdote symbolize Wright's feeling about his art? Does his Uncle's reaction (reproof) to the weed bunches Wright offered anticipate the world's initial reaction to his architecture? I don't know the answers to such questions, and I don't know if Wright returns to this reminiscence later in his book in order to draw out its meaning (as I said, I bought the book only a few days ago!). But by looking closely at how the autobiography begins, we do get a sense of the sorts of themes that may emerge as the greater story takes shape.

In both cases—Evans's and Wright's—the decision of where to begin was doubtless made with a great deal of thought. The intent is to start in such a way as to foreshadow, and also to compress in one anecdote major features of the entire life story, or at least its central themes. Indeed, whenever autobiographies commence with a specific episode, I suggest (following Alexander) looking at the episode extra-carefully, and asking, simply, Why? Why did he or she start here? The answer can lead to promising hypotheses and jump-start inquiry.

Alexander also recommends the pointer of emphasis. This fact seems obvious enough: When our subjects italicize some happening, we ought to mark it as salient. The matter gets a little more complex. Alexander subdivides the cue into the components over-, under-, and misplaced emphasis. We should stay alert for occasions when something apparently mundane is given fierce attention (overemphasis), when something that seems like a major life experience is passed over with little comment (underemphasis), or when an irrelevancy is stressed with undue force (misplaced emphasis). Over three pages devoted to her descent into depression and bulimia, Kathryn Harrison in *The Kiss* (1997) repeatedly mentions the "green vinyl chair" she likes to sit on in her college room. Why keep referring to the chair and its greenness? Why such over- and misplaced emphasis? Later in this chapter I answer these questions in the process of examining Harrison's "prototypical scene."

When, in poring over the details of a life, we suddenly meet with puzzling content, something that seems not at all to fit, we've probably, knowingly or not, noticed an instance of isolation. Elms (1994) jokingly suggests renaming this the "come again?" criterion. We could also call it the "sore thumb" cue—isolated material simply, and jarringly, sticks out. Maybe the best example is a Freudian slip. Such speech errors are at odds with their surrounding content, and they call attention to themselves as a direct result. Again, they don't fit, so we need to ask, What is their motive or purpose? What are they "doing there?"

For Freud isolation is a mode of defense that "consists in isolating thoughts or behavior such that their links with other thoughts or with the remainder of the subject's life are broken" (Laplanche & Pontalis, 1973, p. 232). The goal is to deprive an idea of its associative connections to repressed material; isolating it, or splitting it off, makes it less likely to remind us of something we'd rather forget. Indeed, the subject rarely notices consciously the thought's relation to earlier trauma—and that is the whole point. If he did notice, the defense would be ineffective.

An excellent illustration of isolation comes from the writer Kathryn Harrison. Harrison's novel *The Seal Wife* (2003) concerns a weather-mapper named Bigelow who in the icy anonymity of Alaska falls in love with a native, and mute, Aleut. The book has its surreal moments, and we aren't ever certain whether the Aleut is real or a

sort of "silky," but no passage compares with the ambulatory tongue as far as bizarreness goes. Bigelow imagines it giving chase. The tongue, belonging to a repulsive store owner named Getz, sneaks up on him, follows him around corners, pokes at him, and flashes him the universal sign for cunnilingus. In this instance, "come again?" seems like a clearly justifiable response. What is this tongue doing in the book? What accounts for its mobile malevolence? Readers of Harrison's notorious *The Kiss* (1997) may be in position to hazard a guess. That book, a memoir, describes her consensual affair with her own father, commencing in an airport when Harrison was nineteen. Seeing her visiting father to his gate, she offers a chaste kiss. Her father has different ideas. He sticks his tongue in her mouth. Harrison has told me that she identifies with Bigelow (K. Harrison, personal communication, March 16, 2003). That being so, when the tongue chases him sinisterly, the scene recapitulates Harrison's anguished subjection at the hands of her father.

Harrison's example raises an important point. Isolation can serve as a useful marker. But as in psychoanalysis, the task for the psychobiographer is to restore the link between the isolated fragment and the web of unconscious ideas for which it stands. If we don't ever associate what is initially dissociated, the cue can't serve its optimal purpose, which is revelation, the uncovering of deep meaning.

Still another pointer is uniqueness. As Elms puts it, "if you have many biographical data that say one thing and you suddenly come across something that says another, it's worth a closer look" (1994, p. 246). Something unique may also be isolated, but not necessarily. Uniquenesses need not jar, and they don't always seem like slips. They don't, in other words, precipitate "come again?" reactions, though one does notice their singularity. As an example Elms (1994) points to Leonardo's one childhood memory, or fantasy, of a bird visiting him in his cradle and thrusting its tail into his mouth.

Incompletion is in evidence when a subject, say, starts a story and then stops in the middle, or changes the subject, or in whatever way fails to see a thought through to its conclusion. And like the other pointers, incompletion may apply outside merely textual domains. When an artist has difficulty completing works—as did Leonardo, to take just one example—that may be telling. Even writer's block can, depending on the context, represent a form of incompletion. (And if so, we might ask, Why is she blocked? Does it relate to the content of the work? Does it relate to the motive her work subserves?) Mozart was reluctant to complete *Requiem*, some say because he felt he'd die if he did. Gary Snyder took decades to finish his "Mountains and Rivers" poem—why such dilation? I suppose incompletion is easiest to grasp when regarded as a form of avoidance. We don't finish things we'd prefer not to think about or have to do, or whose content leads to thoughts that provoke guilt or anxiety.

Error, distortion, omission, and negation might also signify the presence of psychologically salient material. Nothing happens by accident, according to Freud (or does so exceedingly rarely). So when we make a mistake—fail to mail a letter, dial one friend's number when we meant to dial another's, call our spouse "mom" or "dad"—it is never "innocent" in nature. "Mischievements," as Freud called these missteps, are motivated. We commit them for a reason or usually for several reasons combined, and the reasons, or motives, are generally unconsciously driven. In her journals Sylvia Plath (1993) muses, when pursuing types of suffering and psychological pain, "no one I ever loved has died"—but that isn't so. Her father died a week after she turned eight. An odd error, to say the least, and maybe revealing. (For other examples of Plath errors, see Schultz, chap. 11 in this vol.) Also in her journals, she mentions reading Freud's essay "Mourning and Melancholia," which has to do with the relationship between loss, depression, and suicide. The one childhood loss Plath experienced was her father's death. But for reasons I believe particularly potent, she misunderstands the essay, applying it not to her dead dad but to her still living (at the time) mother. A motivated misreading? I think so.

Errors and/or distortions can assume infinite forms. Subjects might misdate an event. They might contradict themselves. They might exaggerate tendentiously. They might even lie, I suppose, an act of certain importance psychologically.

Freud may go too far. Some mistakes do seem pretty insignificant. After all, we can't analyze every stubbed toe. Still, it will not hurt to treat errors as provisionally meaningful until we convince ourselves otherwise. Plath's, for instance, one would err in overlooking.

Omission means just what it sounds like it would. Elms (1994) refers to it (cleverly) as the "Sherlock Holmes Rule": "Sometimes we should ask more questions when a dog doesn't bark than when it does" (p. 246). Leaving things out can be accomplished by way of incompletion (defined above). But omissions can also function as total (or partial) lacunae: an absence of expectable content. Apparently the photographer Diane Arbus avoided ever talking about her poet brother, Howard Nemerov, and vice versa. Why? Sisters are supposed to mention their brothers from time to time, aren't they? When they assiduously do not, we ought to take note.

Negation refers to the suspiciously emphatic, sometimes also incongruous "NO!"—especially when "no" is said in the absence of any question. When Allport told Freud of the "dirty boy" on the train, Freud asked ultra-Freudianly, "Was that little boy you?" And in reply Allport spent his life saying no, no, a thousand times no! Again and again he felt the need to make it clear: "I am not that little boy." Think of negation as the "Gertrude rule" (as in Hamlet). Sometimes people simply "protest too much."

Oscar Wilde was imprisoned for homosexuality. He had an affair with Lord Alfred Douglas, Douglas's father pressed charges, Douglas urged Wilde to countersue, and Wilde did—and famously lost (Schultz, 2001). In his letter from prison—subsequently titled *De Profundis* (1996) —Wilde repeatedly tells Douglas, "I do not blame you; I blame myself." After a while, the protests start to seem excessive; Wilde's magnanimity the reader begins to doubt.

As I said above, after we select a psychobiographical subject, thoughts turn to the data and how to winnow out the trivial from the telling. Usually we are dealing with an excess, of fact and of opinion. What content can we set aside and safely ignore, and what privilege? There is no failsafe answer. And it's difficult even to consider the question in a theoretically neutral fashion (some regard dreams as the royal road to the unconscious, others as epiphenomenal brain burps that the cortex dutifully, but meaninglessly, shapes). Alexander's cues are not atheoretical; they draw, as advertised, on Freud. But they also derive from common sense. We emphasize what's important, for instance, and when we leave things out, we often do so tendentiously. So as common-sensical, Freud-inspired guides to identifying psychological saliencies, they come in handy. I use them in all my psychobiography courses and with uniformly positive results. Students always have questions when it comes to qualitative data; Alexander's is one model for organizing and prioritizing it. Use of saliency cues may lead to misses (how could it not?). But it also leads to lots of hits. In a field where hits can be hard to come by, that's saying something.

Now I'd like to shift focus slightly. The use of pointers for homing in on especially interpretable moments or events leads to the identification of potentially numberless saliencies. We might discover ten, we might discover hundreds. But is it possible to prioritize still more finely? Are some saliencies more striking than others? And could there even exist, possibly in every life, one and only one "supersaliency," a single scene encapsulating all the core parameters of a life story? I believe so. Or at least I'm willing to hypothesize as much. I call these constellating memories prototypical scenes, because in them one finds revealed the outline for, and model of, a life. They are a blueprint, a kind of personality X-ray allowing us to peek transdermally. In a moment I want to talk about how one locates prototypical scenes in lives, and then provide a number of examples. But before doing so, a reference case for what I'm trying to get at may be useful.

Diane Arbus is best known for her photographs of subjects she referred to, without malice, as freaks (see Schultz, chap. 8 this vol.). Her earliest memory, and the only memory from before age ten she discusses in any detail, predicts this later artistic preoccupation. It also qualifies as a prototypical scene. Arbus tells interviewer Studs Terkel,

I always had governesses. I had one I really loved until I was seven and then I had a succession of ones I really loathed. I remember

going with this governess that I loved—liked—to the park [Central Park in NYC], to the site of the reservoir which had been drained; it was just a cavity and there was this shanty town there. For years I couldn't get anyone to remember this, but finally someone at the Museum of the City of New York said yes, there was this shanty town. This image wasn't concrete, but for me it was a potent memory. Seeing the other side of the tracks holding the hand of one's governess. For years I felt exempt. I grew up exempt and immune from circumstance. The idea that I couldn't wander down . . . and that there is such a gulf. I keep learning this over and over again. . . . My brother and I never went far afield . . . the outside world was so far. Not evil, but the doors were simply shut. You never expected to encounter it. For so long I lived as if there was contagion. I guess you would call it innocence, but I wouldn't call it pretty at all. (quoted in Bosworth, 1995, pp. 278–279)

Though not concrete, the memory is "potent." There is, moreover, the insinuation, or at least the possibility, that no shanty town ever existed in that reservoir cavity, that Arbus's recollection is more fantasy than reality, a construction. The scene symbolizes family tensions—Arbus's parents were unavailable. Her father owned Russek's department store, and had little time for his kids, and her mother was prone to occasional crippling depressions. When she could take notice of Diane and Howard, she found them both strange and hard to understand, likely because of their giftedness. Governesses, then, became for Diane and Howard parent surrogates. Arbus is clear that she loathed most of hers, and though she wants initially to say she loved Mamselle (the governess referred to above), she retracts that effusion, replacing it with the word "liked"—to use the term "love" would put Mamselle in direct competition with Diane's mother, thus engendering anxiety and guilt, I would guess. The taboo shadow-world represented by the shanty town reminds Arbus of her alienation as a rich girl. She wants to explore it, to "wander down" into what seems a disguised image of the unconscious itself, only Mamselle says no. Certain doors have been sealed against

Diane. Her family has conveyed to her a fear of contagion. The resulting sense of exemption and immunity she finds unpretty. So as an adult, and an artist, she devotes herself to reversing the equation. Her pictures of transvestites, albino sword swallowers, Jewish giants, Russian midgets, twins, triplets, strippers, and masked retardates on Halloween emerge from immersion in contagion, identification with what as a child she felt exempt from. At seven she could not wander down, French nanny by her side; as an artist she finally makes the descent, lives inside the cavity for hours and days at a time, her camera a talisman and a license. She made certain she was no longer innocent or immune.

I regard this scene as prototypical because of the way in which it succeeds as an encapsulation of so many conflicts and motives met with in Arbus's life and art. It comprises a summary. Her absent (or present by way of conspicuous absence) parents, her sense of exemption and its implied alienation from the world, her wealth, her loneliness and sadness, her art's dedication to finding beauty in ugliness, to the documentation of a Dante-esque underworld most would never see if not for Arbus herself—all these facts the prototypical scene compresses into one supersalient happening. It isn't entirely quixotic to say that to know this one scene is to know Diane Arbus. As a configuration, its sweep really is enormously inclusive.

By Alexander's standards, Arbus's scene is salient, marked by qualities of uniqueness and primacy, for starters, but it's also prototypical—supersalient—because of the richness and range of information it condenses. This brings up an important point: All prototypical scenes are salient, but not all salient scenes rise to prototypical status. And this proposition, in turn, brings up a question: Which saliencies are prototypical, and why?

Some prototypical scenes can be identified through the use of pointers similar to those outlined by Alexander. After all, prototypical scenes may be unique, emphasized by their subjects, marked by isolation or incompleteness, and so on. Some, however, may not possess any of these characteristics, though by relying on other telltale cues, one still can know them when one sees them.

(1) Prototypical scenes generally are recalled vividly, with specificity and emotional intensity (see Table 3.2). As additional examples will show, colors usually are emphasized, characters are carefully positioned, dialogue with transcript-type detail occurs. Focus, in other words, is intense, surrounding scenes retreating into comparative deconcentration or dispersion (as in a photograph). Regarding emotional intensity, such scenes are never lukewarm. Though not necessarily dramatically conveyed, affective tone lends clear atmosphere to the proceeding. Arbus's scene, for example, is recalled ruefully, her deprivation (the outside world being sealed) and loneliness (no one present but paid governess) emphasized. It isn't, as she says, a "pretty" picture. Innocence bequeaths unreality.

(2) Prototypical scenes also interpenetrate. By this I mean something a little more precise than just repetition. Interpenetration implies permeation; the prototypical scene permeates. One finds it leaking into a number of different contexts or activities or personal products. Plath's scene (described shortly) appears in a poem, a novel, a journal entry, and a letter; Kathryn Harrison's prototypically prototypical scene (also described shortly) occurs in a book of fiction and in a memoir. So it isn't only that the subject tells others about the scene repetitively; more definingly, the scene works its way into a range of psychological or artistic settings, either overtly or allusively. This isn't the most felicitous of analogies, but in the sense of transmission from one location to another, one could say that prototypical scenes metastasize. They travel. It's as if, because of their importance and the attention they command, they remain chronically on the ready for retrieval, like a Broadway stand-in who might get called to duty any moment, with or without warning.

(3) Prototypical scenes also ordinarily issue from developmental crises in the nonpathological sense of "crisis" meant by Erikson (i.e., each psychosocial stage entails a "decisive encounter" between a person and a particular sort of conflict, e.g., the one between identity and role confusion). Arbus's scene may illustrate, for instance, the conflict between initiative and guilt —she wants to explore, to inspect the darkness,

Table 3.2 W.T. Schultz's keys to identifying "prototypical scenes"

1. *Vividness, specificity, emotional intensity*	Such scenes are never "lukewarm" emotionally. Focus is intense, color emphasized, dialogue recounted with precision, characters carefully positioned.
2. *Interpenetration*	Such scenes permeate or leak into a number of different contexts or activities or creative products (stories, poems, novels, memoir).
3. *Developmental crisis*	Such scenes entail a "decisive encounter" between a person and a particular sort of conflict, for instance identity vs. role confusion or initiative vs. guilt.
4. *Family conflict*	Such scenes more specifically focus in on conflict within the family, between, say, a daughter and father or two brothers or a son and mother.
5. *Thrownness*	Such scenes place the subject in a situation that violates the status-quo. Something anomalous or surprising transpires, producing a feeling of disequilibrium. The normally taken-for-granted suddenly can't be; old ways of making sense do not suffice. Repetitive story-telling thus allows one to extract meaning from the event, to decrease its unfamiliarity, the anxiety it provokes.

to see a world that has been concealed from her, but to do so would risk contagion and the contempt of her parents, who forbid her such contact, and of her surrogate parent, Mamselle. Her instincts and native curiosity Arbus is asked to override. The implicit moral is that the two worlds—rich and poor, light and dark, above and below ground—must never merge. Initiative Erikson equates with a posture of being "on the make"; this perfectly captures Arbus's later attitude as she sought out photos that, in order to get them, required the utmost tolerance for risk and capacity for daring.

(4) Prototypical scenes most often depict family conflict, directly or indirectly. Arbus's isn't the best example in this case, though I do think conflict lingers slightly off-stage in the scene she recollects. Arbus's parents delegated her care to paid others, many of whom Arbus detested. She was raised by women she did not like because her mother (and father) hadn't the time or the desire to do the job themselves. Arbus doubtless recognized this as a form of abandonment, and I'm sure there were occasions when that recognition angered or depressed her, or both. So the conflict the scene expresses, allusively, is between a child who wants to be loved and encouraged, her intuitions and desires taken seriously if not indulged, and a pair of parents who either, in the father's case, have little time for their kids or, like the mother, find them perplexing and faintly embarrassing on account of their originality. Another conflict regards wealth. Money made Arbus guilty. "I've always been ashamed of making money," she tells Terkel, "and when I do make money from a pho-

tograph, I immediately assume it's not as good a photograph" (quoted in Bosworth, 1995, p. 279). The shanty town was a reminder of her privilege, her family's wealth and its associated costs, most of which she resented. "You see, I never suffered from adversity. . . . I was confirmed in a sense of unreality" (p. 279). Arbus's desire was to break free. She sought what might be thought of as the reality of adversity. It became, for her, an antidote to the unreality of walled wealth.

There is a photo by Arbus I find strangely haunting, and in certain respects it evokes her prototypical scene. It's called "a flower girl at a wedding, Conn. 1964" (Arbus, 1972). The girl appears to be around seven or so—roughly Arbus's age when she visited the Central Park reservoir cavity. She wears a flower tiara and what looks like a white fur jacket. She holds a wicker basket. Her eyes are dazed; she stares absently, abstractly beyond the photographer, not so much at her. We wonder, what is she thinking? Thin arms of nearby bushes reach out at her from the left and from below. And the background, her mind's metaphorical content, is fog shrouded, crepuscular, dotted with indistinct pines or cedars. The girl's glowing getup contrasts with the world outside. She is white, bright, carefully assembled; it (the world) is growing darker and more menacing by the second, the fog seemingly advancing toward her feet, intent on enveloping her. This, I think, is Arbus. To all appearances she looks to be the perfect picture of a lucky girl, pretty and rich, but in her eyes we see the darkness. It's touched her, and she will disappear into it.

(5) Finally, in all the examples provided below, prototypical scenes creatively rehearse varying degrees of thrownness. What I mean is, the subject recalling the scene finds him- or herself in a situation that violates the status quo, in which something anomalous or surprising transpires. The feeling is of disequilibrium; the normally taken-for-granted suddenly can't be; old ways of making sense of things do not suffice. Just like in Thomas Kuhn's theory of scientific revolution, where anomalies provide the stimulus for developments of theory, in the individual, too, events that are initially un-understandable call for more conscious efforts at narration. Repetitive storytelling is one way to extract meaning from the event and to decrease its unfamiliarity, the anxiety it provokes. Kerouac gets slapped by his beloved and otherwise saintly brother Gerard (see below). How could Gerard have done such a thing? What does the slap say about him? About little Jack? How to assimilate the slap into previously existing mental frames for who Gerard is and what he stands for?

The model prototypical scene will possess these five features: (1) specificity and emotional intensity, (2) interpenetration, (3) developmental gravity, (4) family conflict, and (5) thrownness, or violation of the normally taken for granted. Not every such scene contains every single element. Judgment calls sometimes need to be made. Psychobiography, after all, is more art than science. But if these scenes can be tracked down and worked with, mined for meaning, they stand a good chance of either generating psychobiographical hypotheses (they may reveal what we don't yet know) or confirming pre-existing interpretations (they may underscore what we already felt to be true). At this chapter's conclusion I discuss similar concepts contained in the literature and why and how the prototypical scene is unique among them and also explore a number of theoretical/methodological questions the idea may raise. But first, more examples are in order, as a way of fleshing the concept out more fully. I begin with the Southern writer Truman Capote, most famous for his nonfiction novel *In Cold Blood* (and also for being famous), then turn to Kathryn Harrison, Jack Kerouac, and Sylvia Plath. Other examples of the use of prototypical scenes can be found in this volume (see, e.g., Ogilvie, chap. 12, and Barenbaum, chap. 16).

Truman Capote

The writer John Knowles, Capote's neighbor and famous in his own right for the classic novel *A Separate Peace* (2003) says,

> Truman often talked about himself. Oh, my God, yes. . . . Just after I first met him, Truman began telling me his life story. This terrible, tragic story. The central tragedy (as he saw it) in his life is a scene: Truman is two years old. He wakes up in an utterly strange room, empty. He yells, but he's locked in there. He's petrified, doesn't know where he is—which is in some dumpy hotel in the Deep South—and his parents have gone out to get drunk and dance; they have locked this tiny little boy in this room. That was his image of terror, and I think it was his way of symbolizing the insecurity of his youth—this image of that kind of abandonment. (quoted in Plimpton, 1997, p. 26)

Then here is Capote himself, from a conversation with Lawrence Grobel:

> It was a certain period in my life. I was only about two years old, but I was very aware of being locked in this hotel room. My mother was a very young girl. We were living in this hotel room in New Orleans. She had no one to leave me with. She had no money and she had nothing to do with my father. She would leave me locked in this hotel room when she went out in the evening with her beaus and I would become hysterical because I couldn't get out of this room. (quoted in Grobel, 1985, p. 48)

Knowles is right on: The hotel room scene symbolizes the insecurity of Capote's youth—and his adulthood. It was, indeed, his image of terror and abandonment. It also, like all prototypical scenes, compresses the core parameters of Capote's life story into one determining constellation. It's a chorus of voices converging on a single note.

Figure 3.1. A fresh-faced Truman Capote in Venice, circa 1950. (Getty Images)

Capote has always been clear on the fact that "there was a great absence of love" in his childhood (see Schultz, 2001). His mother was pregnant at seventeen and later became alcoholic and committed suicide; his father he seldom saw at all. He was raised by his mother's family, a not utterly unhappy circumstance inspiring much of his early, more "fantastic" writing, like his first novel "Other Voices, Other Rooms" (1948). "I always thought of myself as a kind of two-headed calf. . . . I was an only child, very sensitive and intelligent, with no sense of being particularly wanted by anybody. . . . My mother wasn't unkind to me; she simply had other interests. . . . I wasn't neglected financially. . . . It was just a total emotional neglect. I never felt I belonged anywhere" (Inge, 1987, p. 117). In interview after interview—and Capote sat for hundreds—he never wavers when asked, as he often was, about his greatest fear or most frightening experience: "betrayals, abandonments" (p. 354).

The only way people can ever hurt me is if I let them get too close to me. . . . I do think rejection is the unkindest thing people do, and maybe it stems from my childhood when I was shoo'ed from one family to another for different reasons. . . . It's a very powerful trauma, rejection, or to be the recipient of any kind of deliberate cruelty. . . . [Reading some] bad review of something, that doesn't bother me at all. But if I feel somebody has betrayed me in some way or been disloyal about something, I get terribly upset about it. (pp. 316, 306, 178)

Then in remarks bearing directly on the point: "Because of my childhood, because I always had the sense of being abandoned, certain things have fantastic effects on me, beyond what someone else might feel. . . . Every morning I wake up and in about two minutes I'm weeping. . . . I'm so unhappy. I just have to come to terms with something. There is something wrong. I don't know what it is" (quoted in Clarke, 1988, p. 498).

There isn't time to explore this vein as deeply as it warrants, but themes of abandonment showed up in Capote's fiction too. There was, in other words, clear interpenetration of content and symbolism. One of his first stories, and still his most famous, was called "Miriam." It's an eerie tale of a mysteriously motherless little white-haired girl resembling, in numerous incidentals, a female version of Truman (who was often mistaken for a girl anyway, or dressed up as a girl by his aunts). Miriam manages to insinuate herself into, then promptly destroy, the life of a widow, Mrs. H.T. Miller. At the story's enigmatic finish, Mrs. Miller appears on the brink of madness, the girl's Myrmidon, pathetically powerless to say "no." What does it all mean? That Capote's used his gift to turn the tables. Instead of the forgotten and forgettable two-year-old at the mercy of his mother's narcissistic needs, he is the utterly indomitable Miriam, reducing the widow to a jabbering parody of the victimized "senior." The story is an act of revenge. No one's going to lock Miriam in a room.

Capote's last book, the one he famously failed to finish and that many felt never even existed, was *Answered Prayers*, published in 1988 in the form of fragments assembled from magazine excerpts. The book's narrator is P.B. Jones. Jones is a genius, about as tall as a shotgun—just like

Capote—and is, funnily enough, shopping a book called *Answered Prayers*. He also, like Capote did, comes to know many of society's elite, and over time they tell him their secrets—stories that with Jones's finessing make up the bulk of the book. It is episodic and anecdotal in the extreme (but nearly always wickedly amusing).

Capote bequeaths to Jones his childhood: "I was a baby abandoned in the balcony of a St. Louis vaudeville theater" (1988, p. 4). Raised by nuns—nonsecular versions of Capote's aunts—Jones grew to be a "favorite," though "they never realized how conniving I was." For example, Jones says "when I left the orphanage, ran away, I didn't leave a note or ever communicate . . . again; a typical example of my numbed, opportunistic nature" (p. 5). He ventures a similar self-analysis later:

I didn't say good-bye to anybody, just left; I'm the type, and a type by no means rare, who might be your closest friend, a buddy you talked to every day, yet if one day you neglected to make contact, if you failed to telephone me, then that would be it, we'd never speak again, for I would never telephone you. I've known lizard bloods like that and never understood them, even though I was one myself. (p. 30)

In both these pre-emptive abandonments, Jones leaves an older woman whom he actually likes: in the first instance Sister Martha, who taught English and was convinced of Jones's gift, in the second Alice Lee Langman, a writer who befriends Jones, even allowing him to live with her. Jones's creed in fact duplicates Capote's in life: preclude potential betrayals and abandonments by betraying and abandoning prophylactically. That's what the real *Answered Prayers* was for Capote. By tattling on all the trillionaires who considered him their pocket Merlin, and the "swans," as he called them, who cherished their witty gay confidante, Capote chose self-destruction over destruction. When book excerpts appeared, Capote got dropped like a hot potato. He claimed he didn't care, but his drinking and drug use increased, as did his level of depression. In short order he was a mess. He fried the fancier fish, but he got swallowed by a whale.

Capote made use of a single scene to suggest the isolation of his childhood. In his life he feared more than anything else betrayal and abandonment—a repeat, in other words, of the hotel lockup. His fiction, especially early on, was written "to escape from the realities of my own troubled life, which wasn't easy. My underlying motivation was a quest for some sense of serenity, some particular kind of affection that I needed and wanted. . . . I never felt I belonged anywhere" (quoted in Grobel, 1985, p. 46). The prototypical scene runs through the work in the form of call and response; the work was a reply to anticipatory panic. Capote was in a position to use his writing defensively, to "escape," to allay his greatest fear, as in "Miriam" and *Answered Prayers*.

All the indicators are present in this scene: specificity and emotional intensity, interpenetration, developmental gravity, family conflict, and thrownness, or violation of the normally taken for granted (in the sense that a child typically may take for granted that he will not be locked in a room by himself for long periods of time, and by his own mother, no less!). Something else to notice, and it's a feature of prototypical scenes generally: As memory is a construction and in some cases a fabrication, remembered prototypical scenes are part fact, part fantasy. Most often they likely contain whispers of truth, or even howls, but they are also, to varying degrees, imaginative products. We embellish as necessary. We add or subtract, focus or blur, amplify or mute. At the same time, it's important to realize that some such scenes will be utterly veridical, scarcely imagined at all; others will be utterly fanciful, scarcely valid at all. It makes no difference, though, as far as the scene's importance and/or function, which is to summarize, constellate, and express (parsimoniously) life themes. In conveying this concept, I sometimes hear from students, "But who knows if it really happened at all? Capote was two, for heaven's sake! How could he possibly remember an event like that one? In fact, isn't it the case that narrative memory doesn't really kick in till around three or four???!!!" Good points, every one. But reality or dream, to Capote the hotel scene said it all. It was his magnum opus. If it never even happened, he still made use of it whenever he needed a quick reminder of who he was. And thus, it also tells us who he was.

Kathryn Harrison

Harrison's prototypical scene was the first I ever came across. In other words, it was the inspiration for the idea, along with a few other scenes that followed in quick succession. I think its centrality in the story of her life is indisputable. It condenses so much, and therefore says so much—an entire life writ small. On the other hand, it also raises questions, the most interesting of which Harrison herself asked me after reading a draft of an earlier chapter. I'll get to her demurral shortly. First, the scene itself. Harrison includes it in her autobiographical novel *Thicker Than Water* (1991; her first book) and in her memoir about her affair with her father, *The Kiss* (1997). In *Thicker Than Water* the incident seems deliberately bookmarked by memories of sex. Harrison speaks of "being fucked" for the first time, and thinking of her mother, of the "whole brilliant unknown territory of sex traversed in somnambulence." She says she "drove men to violence so that perhaps they could awaken me" (p. 178). Then the scene appears.

[My mother] drove us to the gynecologist's gray-walled office on the fifteenth floor of a skyscraper in West Los Angeles. Through the tinted windows and the summer smog, the city below looked cool and elusive, half-hidden under a blue shroud. Toward the ocean, where the pall lifted, I could see traffic crawling on the tiny distant freeway. My mother was in the examining room when the doctor broke my hymen so he could fit me properly for the device. He used a series of graduated green plastic phalli. First a tiny, little boy-sized one, then larger and larger ones, until he withdrew one whose shaft had been discolored by a smear of blood. My mother leaned against the wall, watching. She stood just to the left of a poster that revealed the most intimate, cellular level of human communion, one triumphant sperm breaking through the egg's thin, eager wall. I writhed on the table as the doctor swabbed my genitals with disinfectant.

Then, after producing the correct size of diaphragm and instructing me on its insertion, the doctor left the room, taking my mother with him, so that I might climb painfully down from the table and try to put it in correctly by myself. . . . It sprang out of my grasp, skidding along the floor, twice before I got it in. . . . But I didn't use it. I thought of it as hers. She was the one who had wanted it. (pp. 179–180)

Harrison follows this with more about her (or, to be more precise, her character's) sexual history, recalling "all the boys who fucked me, some reaching for me with love on their faces, some with anger, one disgustedly." She says she continued to think of her mother every time and of "the constant message of my childhood. Do not make the mistakes your mother did. Do not get involved with the Wrong Boy" (p. 180).

As noted, the scene also finds its way into *The Kiss* (1998), which appeared roughly six years later. There Harrison repeats, in exactly the same words, her childhood's "constant message": "Don't make the mistakes your mother did" (p. 41). *The Kiss*'s gynecologist seems reluctant to use the green plastic penises, of a color that "exists nowhere in nature." He asks Harrison's mother if she's sure. Is this what she (mother) really wants done? Yes, mother replies. Harrison reaches the foregone conclusion, "This doctor deflowers me in front of my mother" (p. 43). The very next scene finds Harrison talking to her father on the phone, preparatory to his visit—a visit culminating in a highly sexual kiss at the airport that commences the affair.

A few other details drawn from the memoir refer back to the gynecologist scene. First, Harrison expresses shock at discovering her father's uncircumcised penis, which she "can't help but find alien, unclean"—just like the alien-appearing green phalli. Second, she connects a later suicide attempt to the gynecologist visit, saying "I think I took [the pills] so that my body would die along with what else was murdered that day—girlhood, hope, any notion of being safe anywhere, with anyone" (p. 186). Third, in the kiss's wake Harrison tries registering for college, her roommates fluttering excitedly around her, but finds she can "do none of what I, as a student, am supposed to do" (p. 72). She spends the better part of two weeks, days and nights as well, sleeping upright, her arms encircling her knees—all the while in a "green vinyl-upholstered chair," its back to the wall (p. 72). The green here may sound incidental. On the other hand, judging by the way Harrison emphasizes the detail of the chair and its greenness—describing it five times over a short four pages—and because of what the chair is intended to symbolize—passivity, alienation, shock—my guess is that it's anything but.

In the gynecologist visit we meet with all the earmarks of prototypicality. The scene's recalled with harrowing specificity—the gray-walled office on the fifteenth floor, the blue shroud of the hidden city below, the green phalli, the poster on the wall, the realization in the deflowering's wake, "Do not make the mistakes your mother did, do not get involved with the Wrong Boy." It interpenetrates, appearing in two books six years apart, and spreading associatively over similarly stigmatized happenings (like the suicide attempt). Family conflict is at the scene's core—the diaphragm is not something Harrison wanted—and the scene's also developmentally decisive, occurring when Harrison was fifteen and just becoming sexually active. Her mother drove her to the doctor's office, her mother said "yes" when the doctor wavered, her mother stood by as the procedure unfolded—so the scene also conveys a strong attitude of thrownness. The deflowering is something that was done to Harrison. She didn't even use the diaphragm. She thought of it as her mother's. Against her will and her own wishes she was violated.

This one scene really says it all, or if it doesn't quite say it all, it sure says a lot. We get the culpable mother. Though Harrison's passivity and desire (as a fifteen-year-old) to please surely abetted things, the diaphragm was her mother's doing. She made it happen, not Harrison. And several years later, she also made the incest happen. By virtue of inaction, she provides the context for the "kiss." Mother can't take father to the airport because she has a headache (the single most stereotypical reason, one might add, for declining sex). "You drive him," she tells Harrison. "He seems more interested in your company than in mine" (p. 66). "Oh good,"

Harrison's father says when he learns of the change of plans. Then at the gate he sticks his tongue in his daughter's mouth.

We get symbolic descent into utterly unnatural "sex," with her father's uncircumsized, "alien" and "unclean" penis later recalling the green phalli. We get the violating doctor who asks the mother's permission. Harrison's father was also a doctor—a Ph.D.—and he was also given tacit permission. We get the "Wrong Boy." Harrison does in fact commit her mother's mistake. She has sex with the supremely "Wrong Boy"—her own father. We get the somnambulance of sex itself and also its wrongness, its violence, its secretiveness. We get the murder of hope, the danger of being anywhere, with anyone—even one's mother, father.

Prototypical scenes summarize lives and life conflicts; they are shorthand for a much longer "text," the life story. Harrison's truly is a stellar example.

But it's also interestingly problematical. Thinking I was really on to something, and thrilled by the chance for once to share my work with its subject (all my prior subjects were dead!), I sent Harrison an earlier chapter on the prototypical scene that appeared in 2002 (see Schultz, 2003). She was amazingly gracious. "I'm never opposed to opportunities for self-awareness," she said. We struck up a correspondence. What she said about the gynecologist visit, and my assertion regarding its centrality, was characteristically incisive: "In some essential way I'm living a second life, and you're responding to the first one. . . . Intentionally I destroyed the unhappy young woman I was, used my father as he used me, accomplices in the psychic murder of that unfortunate girl in the gynecologist's office" (K. Harrison, personal communication, December 13, 2001). What Harrison's asking, and it's a question one can't possibly avoid, is whether one scene is enough for every life. Can we outgrow a prototypical scene? Does each life transition require its own prototype event? And more peripherally, can one really, whether intentionally or not, destroy prior versions of oneself, rendering the prototypical scenes encapsulating those prior versions more or less insignificant? I have to say, I don't know the answers to these questions. I'm inclined to believe that for most lives, one scene is enough, for the reason that most lives seem to lack the sort of radical disjuncture or discontinuity referred to by Harrison. Most of us do not live second, third, fourth lives. Most of us, moreover, do not murder prior versions of who we were, either. We bring them along with us, like by-products or impurities. And I'm not so sure Harrison's psychic murder succeeded. After all, as I discussed above, the "tongue" still trails her.

One final observation before moving on to the next scene: My conversations with Kathryn Harrison have never been anything but rewarding. But in general, living psychobiographical subjects are not always preferable to dead ones. Their willingness to answer questions or respond to ideas pro or con does not lead ineluctably to enhanced validity, as many seem to believe. Most people do not know themselves very well. Their motives may be as obscure to them as they are to us—even obscurer. They may be defensive. They may want to be thought of in ways that conflict with who they really are. They may even lie. Dead or alive, people are complicated. Dead or alive, we still read them the same way. We still work with text—what people say and write.

Jack Kerouac

The name Kerouac calls to mind the image of a carefree hipster romantic wandering the highways of the East and West, stopping now and then to guzzle Tokay and scribble pithy haiku, thumb pointing permanently north, lips curved into a permanently beatific grin. Nothing could be further from the truth. Loss was Kerouac's stimulus; the atmosphere he breathed was gloom, a word appearing in his work maybe more than any other. Mnemosyne was his muse, and what he strove always to remember, to conjure, and when unsuccessful in those two tasks, to replace, was the vision of his dead brother Gerard, who passed away when Kerouac was four (Gerard was nine). By all accounts Gerard was a saint. Nuns tended his bedside in order that they might hear from him Christlike parabolic sighs of wisdom. Birds flew to his hand fearlessly. He nursed trapped mice. He saw visions of angels. To Kerouac he was Buddha, Christ, and brother—

ideal self, too—rolled up into one utterly unearthly introject.

Not surprisingly, Kerouac's prototypical scene centers on Gerard. But it isn't a paean to Gerard's saintliness. It's more a dirge, a song of lament. And it's definitely a violation, maybe even wished for, of the hallowed family script. It appears in the book devoted to Gerard, *Visions of Gerard* (1991): Gerard instructs Jack,

> Always be careful not to hurt anyone—never get mad if you can help it—I gave you a slap in the face the other day but I didn't know it when I did it"—
>
> (That'd been one of the last days when he felt good enough to get up and play with his erector set, a gray exciting morning for all-day work, gladly he'd at the breakfast crumb-swept newspapers of the table begun to raise his first important girder when I importunately rushed up tho gleefully to join in the watching but knocked the whole thing over scattering screws and bolts all over and upsetting the delicate traps, inadvertently and with that eternal perdurable mistakenness we all know, he slapped my face yelling "Decolle donc!" (Get away!) and must have instantly regretted it, no doubt that in a few minutes his remorse was greater than my disappointed regret—). (p. 104)

They make up "at the sad and final mortal window," Jack and "holy Gerard." Do you forgive me for hitting you? Gerard asks. Yes, says Jack, "tho I was too littly naive to know what it meant forgive, and hadn't really forgiven him, holding back that reserve of selfly splendor for future pomp" (p. 105).

Even before *Visions of Gerard*, in a letter to Neal Cassady that Kerouac calls a "full confession of my life," the scene surfaces. Gerard is the letter's primary focus. Kerouac refers to his death as, oddly, "the agonized cock of the matter." He then says, "Neal, the death of this child was a loss that must be impossible for you and I to calculate in the souls of my mother and father" (Kerouac, 1995, p. 253). Here is the scene:

> Just before he died he slapped me in the face. It was the last thing I remember before he

died. It was a gray morning, my sister was going to school, breakfast was being removed from the table. Gerard sat at his erector set before the most magnificent structure of his brief career: it was huge, towering, a crane of some sort, arranged and hung in strange new ways and calculated to do a thousand strange feats. . . . But I had to come along and grab at his little arrangements: knock a subsidiary structure down, push the little wrench on the floor, whatever it was, disturbing him so suddenly that with understandable rage he impulsively tightened inside and his hand shot out and slapped me in the face. "Get away from here!" he cried. I mooned over that in the parlor. . . . I don't know what happened from there. Bill Burroughs claims according to his amateur psychoanalysis of me in 1945 that I resented the slap in the face and wished Gerard would die, and he died a few days later. (p. 259)

I couldn't agree with Burroughs more.

It's interesting to compare the two versions. The color gray recurs, as does Gerard's "get away [from here]." The erector set structure differs slightly: in the scene as recalled in 1950 (in the Cassady letter) it is huge, towering, with a phallic crane, whereas in *Visions of Gerard* we hear only about the raising of the first important girder (girders are horizontal support beams, so in fact they would not get raised at all). In 1950 Kerouac grabs at Gerard's arrangements—destroys them deliberately, in other words. In *Visions of Gerard* Kerouac rushes up to watch, and accidentally knocks the contraption over. The later version thus increases Gerard's guilt: what Jack did was inadvertent, the slap more unjustified than if Jack had knocked the structure over on purpose (as he does in the initial iteration of the scene).

But back to Burroughs's amateur psychoanalysis: The slap is the last thing Jack recalls about his brother (uniqueness). In the letter and in *Visions of Gerard* it is followed directly by Gerard's death, which four-year-old Jack eagerly and excitedly announces to his father and the entire neighborhood, "Gerard is dead! Gerard is dead!," as though spreading gospel. Proximity suggests causality. Gerard slaps Jack, Jack wishes

silently, unconsciously, that Gerard would die, and Gerard does precisely that. Gerard's lasting gift is guilt. Jack's anger killed him. Also, Jack betrayed him by living. It was he who should have died, not Gerard. Anyone but Gerard! Since the slap precedes by a day or two Gerard's death, its effects are irreversible. No wonder, then, that Gerard becomes a haunter: "Why did I secretly believe he hated me after all?" Kerouac asks. "He who had been my kind brother had also been my hater in the night; . . . failing to destroy me, . . . he had no other recourse but to haunt me in the night. I feel that to him, I was the knower of his death" (1995, p. 272). Then later,

Judas is me, Jesus is Gerard. What have I gone and done; and what hath God wrought? I never asked to be Judas and I'm sure that Judas never did. . . . But if I hadn't been born then how could I have betrayed Gerard; for I betrayed him merely by living when he died. He was an angel, I was a mortal; what he could have brought to the world, I destroyed by my mere presence; because if I had not lived, Gerard would have lived. (p. 282)

The only way for Jack to atone was by writing; the only reason he ever wrote at all, he tells

Figure 3.2. Jack Kerouac listening to himself on the radio, 1959. (Copyright John Cohen/ courtesy Deborah Bell Photographs, New York City)

us in *Visions of Gerard*, was for Gerard—"write in honor of his death." And Gerard appears constantly. In Kerouac's first book, *The Town and the City* (1983), he is Julian; he is also Dr. Sax, the shadow-haunter standing wild-haired over Kerouac's crib, as well as the "Shrouded Traveler" of *On the Road* (1991), pursuing Kerouac across the desert; he is Neal Cassady too, for as Kerouac repeats at least six times in two or three pages of *Visions of Cody* (about Cassady), "Cody is the brother I lost" (see Kerouac, 1972, pp. 318–321). In fact, Cassady, Gary Snyder (Japhy Ryder in *The Dharma Bums*, 1991), and countless other heroes Kerouac lists in his oeuvre with religious devotion—all can be seen as Gerard substitutes. Jack is even Gerard. The two look very much alike, as Jack explains at one point; and as Jack relates when preparing to start *Visions of Gerard*, "my brother is my true self as Bodhisattva Hero— the mournful idealistic little boy in the gloomy rain" (Kerouac, 1999, p. 367).

Like Zen masters will do, Gerard slapped Jack awake. From that moment Jack's noble suffering began. And he's "going to be made to appreciate it, like a Fallen Angel"—Samsara's "sorrow parade."

Sylvia Plath

Plath's father, Otto, the expert on bees and the inspiration for a series of poems known by critics as the "bee sequence," died roughly one week after Sylvia turned eight. On that day Plath "went into the dirt," she tells us, "into the lightless hibernaculum" where she wintered for twenty years (see the poem "Electra on Azalea Path"). She spent her artistic life knocking "for pardon" at her dead father's "gate." Like Kerouac did vis-à-vis Gerard, she felt her love killed her father. "It was my love did us both to death," she wrote (Plath, 1981). In dreams of deformity and death she records in her journal, she is (she conjectures) punished for this "murder," an act she repeats symbolically in what some consider the *Guernica* of modern poetry, "Daddy."

All this being so, it makes fine sense that Plath's prototypical scene centers on her dad— on, specifically, a visit to his grave. The event is recorded in her journal, is included in her novel

The Bell Jar (1981a), and provides the stimulus for the poem "Electra on Azalea Path." There is interpenetration, in other words. The visit occurs on March 9, 1959, in the wake of what Plath describes as a "lugubrious" session with her therapist that left her "much freed":

> A clear blue day in Winthrop. Went to my father's grave—a very depressing sight. Three graveyards separated by streets, all made within the last fifty years or so, ugly crude block stones, headstones together, as if the dead were sleeping head to head in a poorhouse. In the third yard, on a flat grassy area looking across a sallow barren stretch to rows of wooden tenements, I found the flat stone, "Otto E. Plath: 1885–1940," right beside the path, where it would be walked over. Felt cheated. My temptation to dig him up. To prove he existed and really was dead. How far gone would he be? . . . Left shortly. It is good to have the place in mind. (Plath, 1993, p. 298)

Roughly ten days later she refers to facing "dark and terrible things" in therapy. She mentions fantasies of "killing and castrating" her father. "How to lay them?" she asks, "to stop them operating through the rest of my life? I have a vision of the poems I would write, but do not. When will they come?" (p. 299).

In "Electra on Azalea Path" she refers to the graveyard visit as the day she "woke" from her wintering. Before then, before she proved to herself that Otto really was dead, she had lain "small as a doll in my dress of innocence/ . . . dreaming your epic, image by image/ Nobody died or withered on that stage" (1981, p. 116).

The Bell Jar's trip to find her father's grave is prefaced by the interestingly ambiguous declaration, "I had a great yearning, lately, to pay my father back for all the years of neglect, and start tending his grave" (Plath, 1981a, p. 135). When she locates the stone she remembers she "had never cried for [my] father's death." She lays her face to the marble, howls her loss "into the cold salt rain." The next sentence is this: "I knew just how to go about it"—"it" meaning suicide.

The visit Plath finds depressing; she feels cheated. The flat stone is located in such a way as to encourage "walking over." In the numerous poems about her father Plath describes him as "hieratical," "maestro"-like, as a "fixed vortex" on the air, straddling oceans, "riveting stones, air, all of it, together." He is, in "Daddy," marble-heavy, a "bag full of God." The list of father metaphors goes on and on. The point is, Plath's fearsome daddy introject had little in common with the flat marker looking across to rows of wooden tenements. If it was good to have that realization in mind—the fact that, as her mom averred, her father had died "like any man"—this may have had mostly to do with bringing the myth down to earth, taming the "man in black" imago. Indeed, Plath does speak of "paying her father back for the years of neglect"—for, in other words, dying on her and not playing any role in her life, in effect abandoning her (and the death was unnecessary, to make matters worse; for more on that, see Schultz, chap. 11 this vol.). She imagines killing her father and does just that in the poems, especially "Daddy."

I address this possibility more fully in chapter 11 on Plath, but one way to stop these fantasies from "operating through the rest of [her] life" was by allowing them entry into consciousness through the medium of the art. When Plath

writes "Daddy, I have had to kill you," she refers primarily to the introject she tries hating into valuelessness. The other option might be to die to get back to her father—a tack she tried, and also wrote about ("at twenty I tried to die, and get back, back, back to you"). In *The Bell Jar* the visit leads directly to a suicide attempt. Again, proximity suggests causality. She finds her father, and then she resolves to die. She needs to know he's really dead. She can't live without this knowledge. But she has to die to get it.

Plath's mourning at her dead father's grave is her prototypical scene. It's also a fair description of the chief motive for her poetry.

Conceptual Questions: Brief Replies

The prototypical scenes described and analyzed above do a decent job of illustrating the concept's value for psychobiography. They also nominate a number of questions, particularly as regards the idea's generalizability.

First, can we really propose that each life has one and only one prototypical scene? I raised this question before in the case of Kathryn Harrison. My provisional answer? Yes. The idea is that these scenes serve as quick and effective summaries of self. They pack a wonder of information into one small identity suitcase. And with each creative rehearsal, each retelling, they become even more privileged, more representative, more easily accessed. Springing so readily to mind, and doing their job so well, these scenes—partly because they constitute a violation that must be made sense of—never stop asserting themselves. If we find their pull difficult to resist, we do so nostalgically, with gratitude. They remind us, and others, who we are and where we came from. In rare cases of sudden identity explosion and rebirth via, for instance, conversion, epiphany, trauma, or even psychotherapy, one might choose to pack the scene away like an old family album. It doesn't do the trick anymore, one figures. It's the old "me," the "me" I left behind. (This was more or less Harrison's position.) But the question is, Has the scene truly become less prototypical? How replaceable is it? Embedded in this is a larger question: Can the new self

Figure 3.3. Sylvia Plath (Corbis).

destructively update the old? Are some discontinuities more apparent than real? I worried this thorny question in an earlier chapter on Oscar Wilde, who made out of his prison experience an opportunity for self-revelation (Schultz, 2001). A new Wilde was heralded. Yet how new was he? And where did the old Wilde go? I'm not sure. It may be that stories change, but prototypical scenes remain the same. (Harrison committed psychic murder, but the tongue slavered on.)

Another question: What motivates the cultivation of prototypical scenes? Whence the drive to construct just one? It is in the nature of self to proliferate. Personality is a sort of oil spill. Like Jung said, the energy finds its gradients. Helpless theorists of who we are, we tend toward eclecticism. But eclecticism always breaks down in the face of its own illogic. Dissonance is its inevitable end result. And dissonance's remedy is consonance (it's hard to live cacophonously). The best theories are parsimonious. They possess the elegance of simplicity. The same goes for the best theories of self. After all, one can suffer from too much narration. More story is not always beneficial. It leads to confusion, dislocation, alienation, even delusion (i.e., imposing meaning on meaninglessness). The prototypical scene is the principle of parsimony in action. It is grounding. It unifies themes, like a collage. It brings pieces together. From time to time we need simple reminders, more signal and less static. That's precisely what the prototypical scene provides. It's a dissonance-decreasing distillation. It fashions a unity out of diversity. At times in the life cycle, especially early on, the ideal personal myth benefits from qualities of openness and differentiation. Premature foreclosure, the cutting off of identity options, will not do, particularly for adolescents. But as McAdams (1993) explains, early adulthood demands refinement, integration, reconciliation, coherence (pp. 271–273). One refashions the life story "in a way that brings the different characters together in some manner, or in a way that makes their oppositions even starker, so as to find unity and purpose" (p. 272). Excessive openness of story equals incoherence.

A final question centers on trauma: Is there such a thing as a happy prototypical scene? I want to say yes. But the proviso is "thrownness."

No thrownness, no prototypical scene. Because these scenes depict a violation of the status quo—a contrast, an affront, a confrontation with a recalcitrant reality—they perplex, focus, and captivate attention. They become, in a word that works very nicely, riveting. And as such, they nominate themselves for prototypicality. We habituate to and overlook the familiar. It's just more of the same. Novelty transfixes, and it also tends to raise anxiety levels by virtue of its unexampledness. Turbulence is at the heart of prototypical scenes. But turbulence need not always be unhappy (unless one happens to be sitting on a plane). What it can't be, in this case, is bland. The affect is what the scene amplifies (as script theorist Silvan Tomkins might say). So again, affective intensity and thrownness are key. From these one might derive happiness or sadness; one might rise above or sink down; one might grow or get stuck. Arbus's life, for instance, was a sort of triumph over the privation of privilege that her scene underlines. She reversed the formula. Unfortunately, after going down, she couldn't get back up (see chap. 8, this volume).

Other Cues That Point to Pay Dirt

Saliency pointers and prototypical scenes provide a roadmap. So do a handful of other indicators worth keeping an eye out for.

But first a few more words about saliencies. To locate the most psychologically salient material is not to understand it. It's a start, but only that (the same goes for prototypical scenes). Alexander (1990) also examines ways of transforming salient extractions into units—a number of consecutive sentences that form an entity through shared content, microscopic stories with an introduction, an action, and an outcome—or fragments, whose story line is somehow disturbed (p. 24). Units can be mined for means–end sequences; fragments can not, since they tell no meaningful story (e.g., "My brother has to be, without doubt, the dumbest guy in the world but beside that he's okay"). Alexander provides the following example of a unit taken from an interviewee:

You know, something happened to me today that really upset me and brought to mind the memory of a time when as a child I didn't speak to my father for close to two weeks. My boss called me in to discuss a report which I had just finished after a week of productive and satisfying effort. He chose to dwell on a minor point which he thought might contain an error. This made me very angry and I sat there dumbfounded. (p. 24)

If one were to rewrite this sequence in its most general or abstract form, the pattern might go something like this: independent effort leads to satisfaction (positive affect), which is interrupted by criticism from an authority, leading to anger and perplexity (negative affect). Then, in cases where transformed bits selected by salience criteria reveal sequences with repetitive properties, one gets a good sense of the fixity and generality of what seemed at first like disparate units. We want always to ask ourselves: How powerful are the subject's sequences, and how pervasive? The prototypical scene might be used in similar fashion; its embedded sequence would be expected to summarize others contained in a subject's less core scenes. In either case, the scene—salient or prototypical—is a primary unit of analysis. As with dreams, its latent content can be inferred as one goes beyond surface features. Or, one can stick with the surface, extrapolating means–end movements and the role played by affect, how positive turns negative or vice versa.

McAdams (1993) also outlines a number of strategies for examining stories, those narratives we offer when asked to explain who we are. His life story interview protocol asks subjects to detail eight key events—what he calls, collectively, "nuclear episodes"—any of which the psychobiographer might focus in on. These include peak experiences, a term borrowed from Maslow— high points or wonderful moments (as in the Robert Evans example at the "Godfather" premiere). Low points or worst moments, so-called nadir experiences, also naturally warrant attention (Capote in the hotel room seems like a definite nadir). What makes the highs so high for any subject, the lows so low? And how do subjects respond to the highs and lows? Such questions move inquiry along. Turning points, because of

their tendency to "symbolize a significant change" of self-understanding, likewise can't help but prove edifying. What turned, and why? "Who" survived the turn, and "who" got left behind? Did the turn affect the art a person made, the ideas he championed, the political positions he espoused? All these things we want to know. McAdams recommends the highlighting of earliest memories, important childhood memories, important adolescent memories, and important adult memories. Imagine your subject sitting across from you. Then, relying on your knowledge of the life, imagine her responses. What early memory has she singled out? (In Arbus's case it was the reservoir visit). What childhood memory, adolescent memory, and so on? McAdams's protocol provides a set of questions one may want to "ask" and divine answers to.

One might also, following McAdams's recommendations, search out themes of agency or of communion in key events. Some subjects seem to be exceptionally strongly disposed toward power, autonomy, mastery, and achievement. They cultivate a dominant, forceful style. They command attention in social settings. They cherish courage and valor. These people are agentic. Communion is the path of love and intimacy. Those scoring high on this trait exhibit warmth and friendliness. They listen carefully. They cherish compassion. They espouse beliefs in world peace, human interdependence, and equality. When it comes to the recollection of key events, people with strong power motives favor themes of strength and impact, status, autonomy, and accomplishment. Those with a need for intimacy gravitate toward scenes of love/friendship, dialogue/sharing, care, and unity/togetherness.

Nuclear episodes may also "signal the emergence or development of a particular life-story character" (McAdams, 1993, p. 298). A man high in power motivation might highlight the "warrior" imago. He sees himself (figuratively) as going to war. He's in constant battle. Communal imagoes include the lover, the caregiver, and the "chum."

Recently McAdams, like Alexander, has turned his attention to story sequences (see McAdams & Bowman, 2001). These, McAdams says, are likely to be "both the causes and the consequences of different levels of psychosocial adaptation"

(p. 29). Depressed and nongenerative people may incline toward what McAdams calls "contamination" sequences: a good experience is "spoiled, ruined, sullied" by an emotionally negative outcome. Those who feel relatively satisfied with their lives (who are, in other words, well adapted psychosocially) might sequence stories more "redemptively": the bad is made good. Pain leads to pleasure, growth, learning, self-improvement.

Nuclear episodes, themes of agency or communion, and story sequences of, for instance, redemption or contamination all illumine "authorial" choices made in the writing of a novel that is a life. For McAdams identity is story. We are the myth we create and continually revise. I don't agree. I can't help but see the story as a portal into something deeper, story being what Freud called "manifest" or surface content. The story's a start, not an ending. But that's what this chapter is about: how to start the psychobiographical process. We first uncover the myth; then we make sense of it.

Tomkins's (1987) script theory also provides a framework especially useful for psychobiographers. Scripts, like McAdams's stories and story sequences, are sets of rules for organizing and magnifying affect-laden families of scenes. Limitless in number, more self-validating than self-fulfilling, they are selective in the number and types of scenes they order, incomplete even within the scenes they magnify, both inaccurate and accurate in terms of their interpretation of events, and continuously reordered depending on their type. Tomkins foregrounds several common possibilities. Affect scripts concern the control, management, and salience of affect. Affluence scripts govern positive affect scenes, contamination scripts ambivalent scenes that resist decontamination, and antitoxic scripts purely negative affect scenes (with limited success). Ideological scripts "attempt an account for how life should be lived and the place of human beings in the cosmos" (p. 160). They represent faith, whether religious or secular. Commitment scripts "involve the courage and endurance to invest and bind the person to long-term activity and to magnify positive affect in such activity" (p. 167). Toxicity scripts address scenes of sufficient negative affect density and threat that they must be opposed, excluded, avoided, or defeated. Nuclear scripts—with commitment and ideological scripts the type most explored by Tomkins—"utilize a self-defeating double-strategy of both minimizing negative affect and of maximizing positive affect, and so do neither" (p. 168). They arise from "the unwillingness to renounce or mourn what has become irresistibly seductive and the inability to recover what has been lost" (p. 197). As such, they are involved in "idealized defenses against idealized threats to idealized paradises" (p. 197).

If we want to stay alert to the appearance of trademark story sequences or key events, we would also do well to remain watchful for types of scripts. A difference between McAdams and Tomkins—however slight—is the centrality of affect. To Tomkins affect is positively key. We script either to amplify (in the case of single scenes, like the prototypical scene) or magnify (in the case of families of scenes that are co-assembled) feelings. Homing in on types of scripts therefore requires that we do the same with respect to affect. And that is tremendously valuable. We don't want only to know which stories get told most; we also want to explore how subjects react to particular qualities of feeling, and how feelings reliably produce sets of responses (i.e., scripts). Scripts are patterns of reaction, preferred modes of self understanding. They validate personality. Knowing some of the forms they take and what these forms may mean in the context of a life allows us to know the life itself—in uniquely dynamic fashion.

Last Words

So there you have it. I promised "strategies for working with biographical data and highlighting those of unusual prominence and psychological importance." Now these very same have been arrayed before you. Of course, locating what to interpret, number one, and advancing cogent interpretations, number two, are very different tasks. The former, while scarcely easy, is still quite a bit easier than the latter. But in what follows advice as to the latter, as well as numerous distinguished examples of how to achieve it, both are in generous supply.

My feeling has always been that we learn most about effective interpretation by reading what strike us—usually purely intuitively—as effective interpretations. Some psychobiographical essays just seem right; they uncannily persuade. We find ourselves seduced by the happy gestalt they produce. When this happens, when we feel won over, it is always—without fail—uniquely instructive to ask why. What about the chapter made it so appealing? The structure of the narrative? The organization and presentation of the evidence? The employment of theory and the artful way it got applied? The biographical sources? The way what had seemed to be so chaotic ineffably assumed coherence? Take as your model the chapters that convince you. Ask how they did it, then aim for the same with your own work. The quality of cogency is hard to put into words. But as they say, we know it when we see it. And when we see it, we need to take notice, to learn as much as we can from those rare exemplary instances of unusual illumination.

References

Alexander, I. (1988). Personality, psychological assessment, and psychobiography. Journal of Personality, 56(1), 265–294.

Alexander, I. (1990). Personology: Method and content in personality assessment and psychobiography. Durham, N.C.: Duke University Press.

Arbus, D. (1972). Diane Arbus: An aperture monograph. New York: Aperture.

Bosworth (1995). Diane Arbus: A biography. New York: Norton.

Capote, T. (1966). In cold blood. New York: Random House.

Capote, T. (1988). Answered prayers. New York: Plume.

Clarke, G. (1988). Truman Capote: A biography. New York: Simon & Schuster.

Elms, A. (1994). Uncovering lives: The uneasy alliance of biography and psychology. New York: Oxford University Press.

Evans, R. (1994). The kid stays in the picture. New York: Hyperion.

Grobel, L. (1985). Conversations with Capote. New York: NAL Books.

Harrison, K. (1991). Thicker than water. New York: Avon.

Harrison, K. (1997). The kiss. New York: Avon.

Harrison, K. (2003). The seal wife. New York: Random House.

Inge, T. (1987). Truman Capote conversations. Jackson: University Press of Mississippi.

Kerouac, J. (1972). Visions of Coy. New York: McGraw-Hill.

Kerouac, J. (1991). On the road. New York: Penguin.

Kerouac, J. (1991). Visions of Gerard. New York: Viking.

Kerouac, J. (1991). The Dharma Bums. New York: Penguin.

Kerouac, J. (1995). Selected letters: 1940–1956. New York: Viking.

Kerouac, J. (1999). Some of the Dharma. New York: Penguin.

Laplanche, J., & Pontalis, J.B. (1973). The language of psychoanalysis. New York: Norton.

Martinsen, J. (2003). Where the wild things are: A psychobiography of Maurice Sendak. Unpublished manuscript.

McAdams, D.P. (1993). The stories we live by. New York: Morrow.

McAdams, D.P., & Bowman, P.J. (2001). Narrating life's turning points: Redemption and contamination. In D.P. McAdams, R. Josselson, & A. Lieblich (Eds.), Turns in the road: Narrative studies of lives in transition (3–34). Washington, D.C.: APA Books.

Plath, S. (1981a). The bell jar. New York: Bantam Books.

Plath, S. (1981b). The collected poems. New York: Harper & Row.

Plath, S. (1993). The journals of Sylvia Plath. New York: Avon.

Plimpton, G. (1997). Truman Capote: In which various friends, enemies, acquaintances, and detractors recall his turbulent career. New York: Talese-Doubleday.

Schultz, W.T. (2001). Why Truman Capote fried the fancier fish in Answered Prayers. Unpublished manuscript.

Schultz, W.T. (2001). De Profundis: Prison as a turning point in Oscar Wilde's life story. In D.P McAdams, R. Josselson, & A. Lieblich (Eds.), Turns in the road: Narrative studies of lives in transition (pp. 67–89). Washington, D.C.: APA Books.

Schultz, W.T. (2003). The prototypical scene: A method for generating psychobiographical hypotheses. In R. Josselson, A. Lieblich, & D.P. McAdams (Eds.), Up close and personal: The teaching and learning of narrative research (pp. 151–176). Washington, D.C.: APA Books.

Tomkins, S. (1987). Script theory. In J. Aronoff, A.I. Rabin, & R.A. Zucker (Eds.), The emergence of personality (pp. 147–216). New York: Springer.

Wilde, O. (1996). De profundis. London: Dover Editions.

Wright, F.L. (1977). Frank Lloyd Wright: An autobiography. New York: Horizon Press.

Chapter 4

Dan P. McAdams

What Psychobiographers Might Learn From Personality Psychology

Personality psychology is *the scientific study of the whole person*. The ultimate goal of personality psychology is to provide a valid account of an individual person's life (Allport, 1937; McAdams, 2001a). In a similar vein, psychobiographers aim to provide psychological accounts of individual human lives, especially the lives of famous or controversial persons. In applying psychological concepts to the particular life, psychobiographers often put into practice ideas that are of central concern to personality psychology (Runyan, 1990). You might think, therefore, that psychobiography and personality psychology would have much in common. You might expect that personality psychologists would find many illuminating case examples in the literature of psychobiography and that psychobiographers might draw upon contemporary personality theory and research to inform their explorations of the individual human life. You might even envision a lively and critical dialogue between the "fields" of personality psychology and psychobiography. But if you thought, expected, or imagined any of this, you would be wrong.

With a few notable exceptions (e.g., Ogilvie, 2003; Schultz, 1996), personality psychology and psychobiography today have little to do with each other. To the extent that there is a relationship between the two, it might best be described with such words as "contempt" or "avoidance." Hard-nosed (and perhaps hard-headed) personality researchers may contemptuously dismiss psychobiographical efforts, claiming they are fanciful, unsubstantiated, and nonscientific. Psychobiographers may avoid the entire field of personality psychology, save psychoanalytic theory and its offshoots, because they assume it traffics mainly in trivial generalities and methodological technicalities. Both viewpoints are not without merit. Critics of psychobiography (e.g., Stannard, 1980) have little difficulty finding egregious examples of wild speculation and baseless claims. And critics of personality psychology have taken the field to task for its tendency toward reductionism and its preference for simplistic (though objective) methods and measures (e.g., Block, 1995). Even the most empirically minded personality psychologist often finds it difficult to stay awake as he or she reads through an issue or two of any scientific personality journal. It is also true that while personality psychologists typically identify themselves as "scientists," many psychobiographers see what they do as, partly, an "art." Personality psychologists aim to develop theories and test hypotheses that may be applied to many different people, while psychobiographers focus on one particular person at a time. To borrow Allport's (1937) old distinction, personality psychologists are oriented more toward the *nomothetic*, whereas what psychobiographers do is, by necessity, *idiographic*.

Nonetheless, it seems odd that even the best psychobiographies and the brightest examples of important personality research rarely seem to take each other into consideration. For all their differences in emphasis, after all, both endeavors aim to comprehend the whole person. In an effort to build a relationship between psychobiography and related efforts, on the one hand, and contemporary personality psychology, on the other, a number of scholars have strongly urged personality psychologists to open their minds and their research programs to the possibilities of case-based research, narrative methodologies, and the use of biography in the study of lives (Carlson, 1988; McAdams & West, 1997; Nasby & Read, 1997; Wiggins, 2003). There is some evidence to suggest that personality psychologists have begun to listen and learn, for recent years have witnessed an opening up of the field and a flourishing of conceptual and methodological diversity (McAdams, 2001a). Perhaps it is time, then, for psychobiographers to listen, as well, and to learn what lessons they might glean from a careful reading of contemporary research and theorizing in personality psychology. If a constructive (and constructively critical) dialogue between personality psychology and psychobiography is ever to emerge, both sides will need first to learn what the other has to offer.

The explicit and immediate goal of this chapter is to suggest a few lessons that psychobiographers might draw from contemporary personality psychology. The implicit and long-term goal is to urge biographers, life writers, and all those individuals who find human individuality so fascinating to consider much more carefully and critically what the scientific study of human individuality—that is, personality psychology—has to offer. It is still true that people who look to psychology for guidance and insight regarding the mysteries of individual lives typically look no further than Freud and the psychoanalytic tradition. Most psychobiographers still draw mainly on Freud, or what they think Freud said (Elms, 1994). While the psychoanalytic tradition has generated many stimulating ideas for psychology as a whole, Freudian theory and its derivatives (e.g., Jung, ego psychology, object-relations theory) are no longer dominant forces in personality psychology. This is not to suggest that psychobiographers (or anybody else, for that matter) should abandon psychoanalytic concepts. But in limiting themselves to one particular theoretical tradition, psychobiographers may miss opportunities to enrich their interpretations with a wide range of well-researched concepts about human personality that offer important new insights and ask new and important questions.

Historical Context

Personality psychology emerged as a distinctive field in the behavioral and social sciences in the 1930s with the publication of canonical texts by Allport (1937) and Murray (1938), the establishment of the journal *Character and Personality* (now the *Journal of Personality*), and the coming together of such disparate lines of inquiry as German character studies, British and American surveys of individual differences, psychoanalytic essays and case studies, and anthropological explorations of culture and personality (McAdams, 1997; Winter & Barenbaum, 1999). The putative founders of the field—Gordon Allport and Henry Murray—envisioned a discipline that was hospitable to psychological biography. Although Allport was suspicious of all things Freudian, he championed the use of personal documents in psychology (Allport, 1942) and the study of the single case (Allport, 1965). Favorably disposed to both Freud and Jung, Murray employed biographical methods and case studies, and he devoted many years of his life to a psychobiographical exploration of Herman Melville (Murray, 1949, 1951). Among Murray's many collaborators in developing the influential methods and concepts that came out of *Explorations in Personality* (Murray, 1938) was Erik Erikson, who went on to write two of the most highly regarded psychobiographies: *Young Man Luther* (Erikson, 1958) and *Gandhi's Truth* (Erikson, 1969).

Allport and Murray believed that personality psychologists might undertake intensive biographical studies of the single case to illustrate personality concepts and to refine or reformulate theory. Exemplified in Freud's many clinical case studies and Robert White's (1938) case of "Earnst," the psychologist might illustrate the power of a particular idea—be it the Oedipus complex or a particular constellation of psychogenic needs—through an in-depth case study. In these kinds of analyses, the key theory or concept would be worked out ahead of time; the analysis would involve the application of the extant theory or concept to the life; the interpretive move would be from the general theory to the more particular life. But in-depth biographical studies of the single case might also be used to discover or develop theory, a point that Allport strongly urged. Through induction, a psychologist might formulate more general propositions from the concrete data of the case. According to Allport, personality psychologists should approach the individual case with an open mind, ready to learn new things and develop new theories from the particulars of a person's life.

The particulars of a person's life have always been the grist for the psychobiographer's mill, going all the way back to Freud's (1910/1957) psychobiography of Leonardo. Psychobiographers since Freud have usually tried to arrange and interpret these particulars according to such concepts as the Oedipus complex, psychosexual stages and early family dynamics, the conflict between instinctual expression and societal oppression, internalized objects and unconscious mental representations, the developmental process of separation/individuation, and other ideas that have enjoyed strong currency in psychoanalytic circles. Indeed, many early psychobiographers saw their work as an exercise in *applied psychoanalysis* (Runyan, 1988). Although the earliest practitioners of psychobiography were psychiatrists and practicing analysts, scholars from many other disciplines—history, political science, literary studies, anthropology, sociology—quickly took up the challenge of interpreting the lives of the famous and the notorious through a psychoanalytic frame.

Interest in psychobiography grew slowly in the first half of the twentieth century but increased substantially after about 1950 (Runyan, 1988). As psychobiographies became more and more popular, critics began to highlight important problems and shortcomings. Psychobiographers were too quick to pathologize their subjects, many critics claimed, often reducing genius or leadership or other admirable qualities of human life to diagnostic categories, personality disorders, or dysfunctional family relations. Some psychobiographers overemphasized the influence of early stages of development or singular incidents in the biography, rather than examining the entire pattern of a life set in time and social context. Still others based their conclusions on inadequate evidence or the imaginative reconstruction of unknown events, especially events from childhood. Standards for good psychobiography eventually

emerged (Alexander, 1990; Anderson, 1981, 2003; Elms, 1988; Runyan, 1982; see also Schultz, chap. 1 this vol.), even as many psychobiographers continued to violate them. While the practice of psychobiography remained highly controversial, some scholars observed that meaningful progress in psychobiographical inquiry could nonetheless be discerned. For example, Runyan (1988) documented advances in the understanding of particular lives as psychobiographers brought forth new evidence and used new data collection procedures, published critical examinations of the evidence in particular cases, tested competing interpretations, revised life history accounts in light of new developments, and incorporated a greater array of social, political, and historical factors in their interpretations.

In the meantime, the field of personality psychology developed along a very different trajectory. Although the pioneers of the 1930s and 1940s showed interest in biographical methods and the application of broad theories to the individual life, personality psychologists moved in the direction of laboratory methods and psychometrics after World War II, as they eschewed the study of lives and focused their attention on a handful of key personality constructs (e.g., achievement motivation, anxiety, field-independence, response bias; but for exceptions, see White, 1963). Despite important advances in measurement and method in personality psychology in the 1950s and 1960s, critics of the field began to doubt the efficacy of personality constructs, essentially arguing that situational factors (but not personality variables) determine what people do (Mischel, 1968). Many questioned the need for personality constructs (and personality theory), and by the 1970s the field of personality faced an intellectual crisis. Defenders of the field, however, launched strong counterattacks in the 1980s, and new evidence was adduced to suggest that well-defined and operationalized measures of personality constructs were reliable and valid predictors of behavior, especially when behavior was aggregated across different situations (Epstein, 1986). Developments in many different areas led to a resurgence of important research and creative theorizing in personality psychology in the 1980s. Since that time, the field has witnessed the revival of interest in personality traits, advances in the conceptualization of so-cial-cognitive variables in personality, and the emergence of narrative-based theories and methods in the study of lives. All three of these developments suggest important implications for the practice of psychobiography.

A Contemporary Framework for Personality

Research and theory in personality psychology today may be organized into three areas or levels (Hooker, 2002; McAdams, 1995, 2001a). The three levels specify three kinds of descriptions and explanations that psychologists (and other persons) might offer in answering the question, "What do I know when I know a person?" In their scientific efforts to know persons, person-ality psychologists may know, or learn about, dispositional traits, characteristic adaptations, and integrative life stories, respectively. Traits provide a dispositional sketch of human individ-uality, adaptations fill in many of the details, and integrative stories tell what a person's life may mean in the overall. As displayed in Table 4.1, personality itself may be construed as a unique and evolving arrangement of traits, adaptations, and stories situated in a particular social and historical context (McAdams, 2001a).

At Level 1, *dispositional traits* are broad, in-ternal, and comparative features of human indi-viduality that account for consistencies perceived or expected in behavior and experience from one situation to the next and over time. Typically assessed via self-report questionnaires or ob-server ratings, dispositional traits position an individual on a series of bipolar, linear continua that describe the most basic and general dimen-sions upon which persons are typically perceived to differ. A large and diffuse corpus of research suggests that individual differences in basic traits consistently predict behavioral trends (Matthews & Deary, 1998) and important life outcomes (e.g., Barrick & Mount, 1991). Trait scores show substantial heritability (Loehlin et al., 1998) and considerable stability over time, especially across the adult life course (Costa & McCrae, 1994; Roberts & Friend-Delvecchio, 2000). In recent

years, a consensus has emerged to suggest that most personality traits can be grouped into five large clusters, often called the Big Five: extraver-sion/introversion, neuroticism, conscientious-ness, agreeableness, and openness to experience.

At Level 2, *characteristic adaptations* are mo-tivational, social-cognitive, and developmental facets of human individuality that are contextual-ized in time, place, or social role. They include current goals and motives, values and beliefs, coping strategies and mechanisms of defense, in-ternalized representations of relationships, inter-ests and domain-specific skills, developmental tasks, and other particularized features of person-ality that spell out the specific ways in which in-dividuals adapt to the contingencies of daily life. Characteristic adaptations typically speak to what people want (or wish to avoid) in daily life and how they go about trying to get what they want (or avoid what they do not want) in particular situations and with respect to particular people, groups, organizations, and social roles (Cantor & Zirkel, 1990; Little, 1999; Mischel & Shoda, 1995). Less stable and more contingent than dis-positional traits, characteristic adaptations fill in many of the details of human individuality and typically express much more directly than do traits the important ways in which people *change* over time.

If dispositional traits sketch the outline and characteristic adaptations fill in many of the details of human individuality, what is left to know in knowing persons? One thing that is left is *meaning*. What does a life mean? More spe-cifically, what does a person's life mean *to the person*? A growing number of social scientists have recently argued that individuals living in modern societies typically provide their lives with some sense of meaning and purpose by construct-ing internalized narratives of the self, or life sto-ries (Cohler, 1982; Giddens, 1991; McAdams, 1985, 2001b; Polkinghorne, 1988). At Level 3 of personality, *integrative life stories* tell how a person reconstructs the past and anticipates the future as a *narrative identity* complete with self-defining scenes, characters, plots, and themes. Like traits and adaptations, the inter-nalized and evolving stories that modern people work on are integral aspects of their personal-ity. To know a person well is to know his or

Table 4.1 Three Levels of Personality (from McAdams, 2001a, p. 10)

Level	Definition	Examples
Dispositional traits	Broad dimensions of personality that describe assumedly internal, global, and stable individual differences in behavior, thought, and feeling. Traits account for consistency in individual functioning across different situations and over time.	Friendliness Dominance Tendency toward depression Punctuality
Characteristic adaptations	More particular facets of personality that describe personal adaptations to motivational, cognitive, and developmental challenges and tasks. Characteristic adaptations are usually contextualized in time, place, situation, or social role.	Goals, motives, and life plans Religious values and beliefs Cognitive schemas Psychosocial stages Developmental tasks
Life stories	Internalized and evolving narratives of the self that people construct to integrate the past, present, and future and provide life with some sense of unity, purpose, and meaning. Life stories address the problems of identity and integration in personality—problems especially characteristic of modern adulthood.	Earliest memory Reconstruction of childhood Anticipations of future self "Rags to riches" stories

her traits, adaptations, and stories, all set in a particular social, cultural, and historical context.

Level 1: Dispositional Traits

The establishment of the dispositional trait as an indispensable construct for describing and explaining human individuality is arguably the most important advance in personality psychology in the past 20 years. Although Allport (1937) viewed the concept of the trait as a cornerstone idea for personality psychology, traits fell on hard times in the 1960s and 1970s, as critics came to view trait labels as little more than linguistic artifacts and attribution errors. A substantial body of research conducted in the past two decades, however, shows that these critiques were rather more clever than true. It is increasingly clear that dispositional traits organized under the Big Five umbrella represent relatively stable and broad dimensions of personality that predict general trends in what people do, feel, and think. The dispositional traits subsumed within the Big Five framework capture basic individual differences in behavior and experience that have been documented in many different cultures (Church, 2000). Furthermore, neuroscientists have begun to link certain trait dimensions—especially those related to extraversion (dominance, sociability, and positive affectivity) and neuroticism (anxiety, depressive-

ness, and negative affectivity)—to brain processes and mechanisms such as dopaminergic pathways and the functions of the amygdala.

What might psychobiographers learn from recent research and theorizing on dispositional traits? Let me suggest a simple first lesson: *A full psychobiographical account of an individual's life should begin with a dispositional profile.* A step in this direction was recently taken by Ogilvie (2003), who provided a rudimentary Big Five profile for J.M. Barrie, the author of *Peter Pan*. Biographers have also occasionally used single trait concepts to contrast different individuals with each other. For example, Freud is generally seen as more extraverted than Jung (Steele, 1982), and Henry James more introverted than his older brother William (Edel, 1985). But these comparisons rarely attempt to be comprehensive or systematic, and they virtually never draw in any kind of sophisticated way from the empirical research literature regarding traits.

Whereas shorter psychobiographical essays and chapters may seek to solve a single mystery in a person's life (Elms, 1994), more extended (e.g., book-length) efforts typically try to provide a more comprehensive account. A dispositional profile is especially important, I believe, for the kind of full-bodied and ambitious psychobiographies that are usually published as books or monographs. Authors of full psychobiographies bring psychological concepts and theories to bear in painting a broad portrait of a person's life. Whatever other ideas they wish to explore, these authors would do well to delineate general cognitive, emotional, and behavioral trends in their subjects' lives in terms of the kinds of dispositional traits set forth in the Big Five scheme.

Psychobiographers might begin by identifying those few traits within the Big Five framework upon which their subjects appear to exhibit a very high or very low position. (Table 4.2 presents one version of the Big Five framework.) The trait definitions provided in the Big Five are more precise and concrete than the casual and inconsistent attributions that are often made by biographers. By locating their subjects at precise points in a Big Five conceptual space, psychobiographers can offer their readers an easy-to-assimilate sketch of basic personality trends, a sketch that might be profitably compared to dispositional sketches offered by other biographers for the same and different subjects. (Such interbiography comparison might promote the kind of progress and interchange in the field of psychobiography envisioned by Runyan [1988], and it might also open up exchanges between psychobiographers and personality psychologists who study traits.) Psychobiographers can organize different incidents and tendencies in their subjects' lives within particular trait categories. More important, they can show the conditions under which a given subject *may act in opposition to his or her dispositional profile*. Traits are not absolutes; the highly extraverted person does not act in an outgoing and sociable manner in every situation in life. Gross or unexpected departures from a dispositional pattern are likely to be especially interesting in a psychobiography. Such departures may provide the biographer with a wonderful opportunity to explain something that on first blush may seem inexplicable.

While dispositional profiles are indispensable for a full *description* of human individuality, they can also be useful as *explanations*. This is why it is important for psychobiographers to obtain some working knowledge of research on personality traits. Empirical studies document expected and sometimes surprising relationships between different traits, between traits and behavior, and between traits and important life outcomes. As

Table 4.2 The Big Five Trait Categories (after Costa & McCrae, 1994)

E: Extraversion (vs. introversion)
Warmth
Gregariousness
Assertiveness
Activity
Excitement seeking
Positive emotions
N: Neuroticism (vs. emotional stability)
Anxiety
Angry hostility
Depression
Self-consciousness
Impulsiveness
Vulnerability
O: Openness to experience (vs. conventionality)
Fantasy
Aesthetics
Feelings
Actions
Ideas
Values
A: Agreeableness (vs. antagonism)
Trust
Straightforwardness
Altruism
Compliance
Modesty
Tender-mindedness
C: Conscientiousness (vs. unconscientiousness)
Competence
Order
Dutifulness
Achievement striving
Self-discipline
Deliberation

just one example, research on extraversion consistently shows a positive link between this trait and experiences of positive affect. Not only are extraverts consistently more outgoing than introverts, but they also report more experiences in life (both social and nonsocial) that bring pleasure and joy (e.g., Lucas & Diener, 2001). At the same time, extraverts do *not* report fewer experiences of *negative* affect than do introverts. (Negative emotional experiences seem more closely linked to the trait of neuroticism, which itself is independent of extraversion.) Some trait theorists group extraversion and the tendency toward positive affectivity within a single *behavioral approach system* whose brain correlates may include relatively higher cortical activity in the left frontal regions and reward sensitivity mediated by the neurotransmitter dopamine (Revelle, 1995). Psychobiographers, therefore, might expect that their most extraverted subjects should have little trouble finding pleasure and joy in life. Again, deviations from this expected pattern would provide an interesting opportunity to explain why.

How do traits come to be? This question leads to a second, albeit negative, lesson that psychobiographers might draw from personality psychology: *Shared family influences are* not *good explanations for the development of traits*. Research on twins (identical and fraternal, raised together and apart) shows that at least half of the reliably measured variance in most personality trait distributions can be accounted for by genetic differences between people. In looking to explain the remaining portion of the variance, researchers have examined many different kinds of environmental influences. The search for simple environmental explanations for the development of traits has, so far, been a failure. While it is not clear how environments do influence traits, it is becoming increasingly clear that the kinds of simple family influences that common belief suggests are important for shaping personality traits—variables such as maternal or paternal warmth or discipline and other general characteristics of families that siblings in the family share—play almost no role!

Most students and many clinical psychologists simply do not believe the data here—data showing that shared environmental influences typically account for no more than 5% of the variability in trait scores (Dunn & Plomin, 1990). Let me translate this to psychobiography: Erikson (1958) was probably wrong when he suggested that Martin Luther's tendency toward compulsivity (a subtrait of conscientiousness in the Big Five, perhaps with some neuroticism thrown in) was partly determined by the strictness Hans Luther showed as Martin's father. Hans may have been especially strict and authoritarian, and Martin may have developed similar traits, as well as compulsivity, as he grew older. But Luther's development with respect to these traits likely had little to do with the way Hans acted as a father. Indeed, the development of the traits probably had much more to do with the fact that Hans gave Luther something much more powerful for the shaping of traits—his genes.

Research on the determinants of traits does not suggest that environments have no influence. Rather, it suggests that the influence is complex, and that the aspects of the environment that may have the greatest influence may *not*, Freud to the contrary, reside in the family (Harris, 1995). To be fair, most research on the development of personality traits does not examine environments of extreme deprivation or horrific abuse. It is certainly possible that, under extraordinary family conditions, shared environment influences may come to rival genetic effects and factors outside the family. Occasionally a psychobiographer may find that a subject's family environment is so incredibly bizarre or deprived that one can not escape an explanation for traits that emphasizes shared family environment. But my sense is that this kind of family environment is rarer than psychobiographers think and, to be more contrarian, that some psychobiographers endeavor to pathologize family environments in order to give them ready explanations for the origins of basic traits.

Contemporary research suggests that psychobiographers would develop more valid explanations by looking outside the family, or to contingent patterns within the family, for environmental influences on traits. Many researchers today believe that *nonshared* environments play an underappreciated role in the development of traits. Nonshared environments include external factors that siblings in the same family do not share—such as peer groups, teachers, lucky breaks and fateful accidents, and the many environmental effects that seem to push children in the same family into different directions when it comes to personality traits. Indeed, some nonshared environmental factors do play themselves out within the family, as well—such as birth order and differential treatment of children in the same family. In this regard, Freud's claim that he was "the indisputable favorite of his mother" (in Jones, 1961, p. 6) suggests, as Freud seemed to know, a defensible candidate for a nonshared environmental influence in Freud's own life.

From childhood dimensions of temperament to stable individual differences in the adult years, traits may evolve according to a process that

Caspi (1998) calls "developmental elaboration." The process is complex and many-faceted, but stripped to its essentials it may go like this: Genotypes give rise to inborn differences in temperament; the social environment "responds" to those temperaments in ways that often (though not always) reinforce and articulate the dimensions that already exist; temperament dimensions are further articulated and elaborated into full-fledged personality traits as the maturing person comes to select and construct his or her own environments in ways that are often (though not always) consistent with those trait dimensions, further reinforcing and articulating those same dimensions. To take a simple example, the baby owning a genotype that provides for a relatively cheerful and outgoing temperament elicits from the environment more smiles and social interaction than a more inhibited baby (blessed with a different kind of genotype) elicits from the environment, perhaps reinforcing and accentuating differences between the two babies. As the cheerful child sets out along a particular developmental pathway, he or she encounters many environments that are sympathetic with the tendency toward cheerfulness and outgoingness (in part because the child shares genes with the parents, who structure an environment that is consistent with their own—and ipso facto the child's—genotypes). As the little-extravert-to-be grows older, he or she chooses to spend more time with people and pursue more joy-inducing experiences than a little-introvert-to-be is likely to choose, by virtue now of the fact that the extravert- and introvert-to-be are different both genetically and in terms of the environments that their genotypes have, as it were, engendered. And on it goes.

My example is oversimplified and suggests, unintentionally, that the inborn differences in temperament drive development the entire way. In reality, many different environmental factors may compete with each other in the elaboration of inborn differences, leading to unexpected and interesting developmental pathways. After all, not all cheerful one-year-olds grow up to be extraverts. Nonetheless, psychobiographers need to trace the many different environmental influences that may shape traits over the long haul. In tracing the development of dispositional traits,

psychobiographers would do well, therefore, to look beyond singular events and downplay shared family environments in favor of explanations that show how early temperament differences are elaborated and articulated into full-fledged dispositional traits over time.

An example from the life of Mary McCarthy illustrates an approach that is compatible with this point of view (Gelderman, 1988). Born in 1912, McCarthy lived her first six years with two parents who cherished her and valued her assertive temperament style. In 1918, within 24 hours, both her parents died during the great influenza epidemic. For the next five years, Mary and her three younger brothers stayed with her paternal grandmother's sister and that woman's husband. Living with this couple, the Shrivers, was a nightmare for Mary. They showed no affection for her, and they strongly discouraged her outgoing and domineering ways. The Shrivers beat the children regularly and forbid Mary from playing with the neighborhood kids. It is likely that Mary's strong-minded and unyielding tendencies antagonized the Shrivers further, motivating them to be especially harsh and controlling with her. After five years, Mary's maternal grandparents learned what was going on, and they arranged for Mary to come live with them. Again, the environment changed dramatically. The grandparents were kind and indulgent, but they were unable to give Mary the undivided attention she craved. With her grandparents, Mary seemed to become less assertive overall in that she no longer faced an authority at home against whom to rebel. But she also became more rebellious at school. In sum, Mary's temperamental style evolved over a decade or so as it shaped and was shaped by the different kinds of environments she encountered and engendered. Her sunny assertiveness grew darker over time. It also grew more selective as it morphed into a tendency toward defiance in the face of oppressive authority.

Level 2: Characteristic Adaptations

The two greatest strengths of the trait concept—breadth and stability—double as its two biggest weaknesses. As broad dispositions that account for general consistencies in behavior across many different situations, traits are not well equipped to describe or explain inconsistencies, contingencies, and particularities (Thorne, 1989). Traits help in accounting for what a person will do, think, or feel in general, but they do not and cannot provide the kind of detail, context, and dynamics that may be required to describe precisely what a person does, thinks, or feels in a particular situation, and *why*. As relatively stable individual differences that demonstrate substantial longitudinal continuity over the adult life course, traits do not go very far in accounting for personality change and development. It is true that mean levels of conscientiousness and agreeableness appear to increase slightly while neuroticism may decrease slightly from early to middle adulthood (Helson & Klohnen, 1998). But these normative developmental patterns in broad traits do not capture the many other nuanced ways in which persons change and grow over time. A full accounting of human individuality should *begin* with traits. But it can not *end* there.

Over the past 20 years, personality psychologists have made impressive strides in measuring and understanding motives, goals, strategies, beliefs, values, interests, schemas, and a range of other characteristic adaptations in an effort to account for what traits cannot account for. The various approaches they have developed travel under many different names—for example, *social-cognitive* theory (Cantor & Zirkel, 1990), *cognitive-affective systems* theory (Mischel & Shoda, 1995), *self-determination* theory (Deci & Ryan, 1991), *life span motivational* approaches (Freund & Baltes, 2000), *personal action* psychology (Little, 1999), conceptualizations of *possible selves* (Markus & Nurius, 1986) and *self-with-other* (Ogilvie & Ashmore, 1991), and various developmental approaches that emphasize stages, seasons, or trajectories in the life course. The different research programs these approaches have generated emphasize many different concerns, but they almost all share an interest in the contextualized particularities of human lives and how those particularities can change, in both predictable and unpredictable ways, over time.

What might psychobiographers take away from the sprawling literature on characteristic adaptations in personality? A first lesson is

readily derived from the distinction between adaptations (Level 2) and traits (Level 1): *Meaningful personality change in the adult years is more likely to occur in people's goals, motives, beliefs, and strategies rather than in the broad outlines of their behavioral, cognitive, and affective styles.* Compared to dispositional traits, characteristic adaptations are more strongly and directly shaped by environmental contingencies, developmental demands, and social roles, especially in the adult years. As a person's social world changes over time, it should not be surprising to find that his or her motives, goals, beliefs, and strategies may also change. For example, Oscar Wilde's overall style of interacting with others seemed to change little over his life (dispositional traits); yet he came, over time and chiefly because of his experiences in prison, to despise the same shallowness and artificiality that he once had made the basis of his philosophy of the artistic life (Schultz, 2001).

A more recent example is Ronald Reagan. Under the influence of his new wife Nancy, Reagan transformed himself from a moderate liberal to a champion of political conservatism (Morris, 1999). The content of his beliefs, as well as his life goals, changed markedly in Reagan's 30s and 40s. Interestingly, what may not have changed at all was the overall *style* of his thought—a tendency to make sense of the world with a few strong principles while overlooking complexity and contradictions. At Level 1 of personality, Ronald Reagan remained relatively low on the dispositional trait of openness to experience. At Level 2, however, he transformed himself from a pro-union liberal searching for Hollywood stardom to a staunch conservative who sought and achieved high public office—a personality change that was of no small import for the history of the United States in the second half of the twentieth century.

The case of Ronald Reagan raises the question of what indeed constitutes change in personality. Some psychologists might argue that a shift in political values and life goals is too superficial or limited to constitute a "real" personality change. Indeed, some trait psychologists have suggested the same (e.g., Costa & McCrae, 1994). They see broad dispositional variables as *the* fundamental dimensions of personality.

From this point of view, characteristic adaptations are nothing more than situationally informed derivatives of basic traits. I believe, however, that this view is unrealistic and wrongheaded. It is unrealistic because in decreeing that dispositional traits are the only "real" dimensions of personality and showing that these dimensions are increasingly stable as people age, the trait-is-everything viewpoint sets the bar too high for personality change. Changes in characteristic adaptations may often represent important personal transformations that have a huge impact on people's self-conceptions and on the social ecologies within which their lives are situated. Indeed, a great deal of what constitutes change in psychotherapy is change in goals, strategies, and beliefs. The prioritization of traits is wrongheaded, furthermore, because research shows conclusively that motives, goals, beliefs, and other characteristic adaptations do not map neatly onto personality traits (Winter et al., 1998). Level 2 in personality is not just more specific than Level 1. It is also different in kind. It deals with the kind of motivational, cognitive-social, developmental, and strategic aspects of human individuality that do not find a clear expression in the language of dispositional traits.

The language of Level 2 is a language of contingency, context, change, conflict, and complexity. It is a language that speaks to the intrapsychic and interpersonal dynamics of daily action. It is a language that accommodates psychoanalytic conceptualizations, but only to a point. Contemporary research on strivings and goals, for example, explores the kinds of motivational dynamics and conflicts that have always been at the heart of the psychoanalytic tradition (Emmons & King, 1988; Little, 1999). Attachment research explores internalized object representations of the sort described by Fairbairn and Kohut (Main et al., 1985). Personality and cognition researchers have recast the distinction between conscious and unconscious functioning into one between explicit (on-line, cold, slow but precise) and implicit (off-line, hot, fast but impressionistic) functioning, supporting a crucial Freudian insight (Epstein, 1994). At the same time, however, contemporary research on characteristic adaptations departs from most psychoanalytic approaches—and indeed most of the grand theories of personality proposed in the first half of the twentieth century—in at least one very important aspect: *domain specificity*.

The trend in findings from studies of characteristic adaptations is away from the universal processes and integrative mechanisms featured so prominently in Freud, Jung, Adler, Horney, Sullivan, Kohut, Rogers, Maslow, and Allport and toward specific manifestations in particular domains (Cantor & Zirkel, 1990; Little, 1999). Many social-cognitive approaches to personality, for example, view persons as complex, multitasking organisms who solve many different problems and work on many different life projects at the same time and over time. These approaches look skeptically upon broad assertions regarding basic needs, fundamental complexes, or universal patterns of human individuality. Instead, human beings have evolved to meet many different and competing demands and agendas (Tooby & Cosmides, 1992). No single goal, schema, defense mechanism, motivational pattern, or value cluster provides the key, integrative construct for understanding the person. Furthermore, the multiple and conflicting demands of modern life ask people to play many different and conflicting roles (Gergen, 1992). Characteristic adaptations are defined and lived out in particular contexts—a coping strategy that is used in one kind of situation (when interacting with strangers) but not others; a goal that drives behavior during one period of life (adolescence) but not another (midlife); a set of beliefs that proves serviceable when assuming social role A (leadership positions) but not social roles B, C, and D.

Biographers often describe multiple roles and orientations in their subjects' lives. For example, biographers of Abraham Lincoln have marveled at the many different and seemingly contradictory personae he adopted over time—from the rail splitter of his youth, to itinerant lawyer, to local politico, to presidential candidate, to commander-in-chief of the Union forces in the Civil War (e.g., Donald, 1995). A common interpretive strategy for dealing with this kind of multiplicity is to search for some form of hidden unity that lies beneath the diversity. The different roles and orientations may be seen as surface or manifest characteristics that can be explained away by invoking deeper, latent forces. Research on characteristic adaptations, however, suggests the possibility that some lives defy explanations invoking deep unity, that some individuals really are contradictory, that some self-constructions really are multiple and contingent.

Research on characteristic adaptations provides a wealth of constructs and insights that might be creatively employed in making psychological sense of multiplicity and contingency. As one example, de St. Aubin (1998) drew from research and theory on the Level 2 concept of *generativity*—the midlife concern for and commitment to promoting future generations—to explore Frank Lloyd Wright's development as an architect and as a father. De St. Aubin showed how Wright expressed generativity in multiple and confusing ways in different life domains and how both his greatest successes and his greatest failures in life reflected contradictions in his characteristic approach to generativity.

The lesson here for psychobiographers is clear: *Motivational, social-cognitive, and developmental interpretations of the single life must allow for multiplicity, contradiction, and domain specificity.* The psychobiographer who looks for a common or core set of motives, goals, strategies, or beliefs—especially a "fundamental" psychodynamic pattern derived from childhood—runs the risk of oversimplifying the subject and ignoring contingency, context, change, and the local specificities of the particularized life. Research on characteristic adaptations cautions against grand efforts to find the one "key" idea to explain the single life. Yet the drive to provide this kind of reductionistic explanation for a full life is powerful. Readers expect biographers to develop a psychological thesis for the case; they expect a clear, take-home message. Psychological theory is supposed to make a confusing life understandable. But the most skilled psychobiographers formulate interpretations that show multiple variations on a set of well-defined themes. The variations are just as important as the themes, for it is typically the variations that reveal the intricately contextualized and contingent nature of a life.

Level 3: Integrative Life Stories

As research on dispositional traits and characteristic adaptations has proceeded apace over the past 20 years, a growing number of personality psychologists have turned their attention to a third way of thinking about human individuality. Beginning with Tomkins's (1979) script theory, personality psychologists started to appreciate and consider the role of *narrative* in human lives. Tomkins conceived of the person as a playwright who, from birth onward, constructs *scenes* and *scripts* in life in order to magnify emotion and make meaning over time. From Tomkins's perspective, life is organized and narrated as if it were an ongoing story, complete with settings, scenes, characters, plots, and themes. Emphasizing similar ideas, McAdams (1985) formulated a *life-story model of identity*, contending that individuals living in modern societies begin to construct and internalize integrative life narratives in late adolescence and young adulthood and continue to work on these identity stories into the later years of the life course. Singer and Salovey (1993) identified *self-defining memories* as key autobiographical scenes in the life story—episodes that capture vivid emotional experiences and express unresolved identity issues. Hermans (1996) formulated an influential *dialogical* theory that construes personality as a *polyphonic novel* giving voice to multiple facets of the self. An upsurge of interest in narrative theories (e.g., Barresi & Juckes, 1997) and narrative-based methodologies (Craik, 1997) in personality psychology today dovetails with an interdisciplinary movement in the social sciences called the *narrative study of lives* (Josselson & Lieblich, 1993; Josselson et al., 2003; Rosenwald & Ochberg, 1992). The narrative study of lives seeks to write, interpret, and disseminate people's life stories with an eye toward understanding what those stories say about the people themselves and about culture.

At Level 3 in personality, a life story is the developing person's own internalized and evolving narrative of the self. From the standpoint of the subject, it is the story of *my* life *as I see it*. The life story is subjective in two senses. First, it is the subject's own narrative construction of self—and not the construction or interpretation offered by an observer, be that observer the subject's mother or biographer. Second, the life story departs markedly from any kind of objective chronicle of a person's past in that it selects and constructs only those events from the past that the subject deems worthy of selection and construction, and links those events to an imagined future. The life story, therefore, is more like a personal myth than an objective biography (McAdams, 1993), even though the subject believes the story to be true. Indeed, the story is true, in a psychological sense. It aims to give a coherent sense of who (and why) a person is, was, and will be. Among other functions, life stories reconstruct the past and anticipate the future in ways that provide an individual with some semblance of meaning and direction in life. Life stories provide much of what Erikson defined as ego identity. They tell a person who he or she is, was, and may be; they spell out how a person is similar to and different from others; they integrate a life in time; they help to specify a psychosocial niche in the world; they consolidate choices and commitments; they make a particular life sensible and tellable in a world—the modern world—wherein many different lives might be lived and many different stories told. Beginning in late adolescence and young adulthood, then, life stories provide modern men and women with *narrative identities*.

What might psychobiographers draw from narrative theory and research in personality psychology and the narrative study of lives? The fact is, most psychobiographers already keenly appreciate narrative. Indeed, they are storytellers themselves. Psychobiography may even be defined as "the systematic use of psychological (especially personality) theory to transform a life into a coherent and illuminating story" (McAdams, 1988, p. 2). Referring to his monumental biography of Henry James, Edel (1978) wrote that when "the biographer can discover a myth, he has found his story. He knows the meaning of his material and can choose, select, sift, without deceiving himself about the subject of his work" (p. 2). But the interpretive story the psychobiographer tells about his or her subject is not necessarily the same as the story the subject might tell—that is, the third-person narrative that becomes a psychobiography itself is not synonymous with the subject's (first-person) narrative identity. Indeed, the two may conflict dramatically, as when the biographer maintains that the subject was deceiving him- or herself,

and perhaps others, in maintaining a "false" sense of self. Relatedly, individuals may sometimes invent characters and make up false stories about their own lives, as in the case of Lillian Hellman (1973), who seems to have created events for her memoir, *Pentimento* (1973), that simply never happened. It is, of course, the biographer's literary right to prioritize his or her own narrative interpretation over and against what the biographer imagines the subject's own story might have been. But Lillian Hellman notwithstanding, the biographer should not be too quick to ignore or dismiss a subject's narrative identity. I would argue that good psychobiography needs to incorporate what the psychobiographer imagines to be the subject's own narrative identity, along with what the psychobiographer imagines to be the subject's traits and characteristic adaptations.

An important lesson regarding Level 3 in personality, therefore, is this: *Psychobiographers' third-person accounts of their subjects' lives should aim to uncover, interpret, incorporate, and critique subjects' first-person narrative identities; the story the psychobiographer tells should creatively engage the story the psychobiographer thinks the subject told.* For some psychobiographies, the aim may be to make explicit a story that the subject tells or told implicitly. In looking for the subject's narrative identity, psychobiographers should pay closer attention to late adolescence and adulthood, and perhaps less than they commonly pay to the earliest years. McAdams's (1985, 1993) life-story model of identity suggests that experiences in infancy and childhood provide material for the life story, but the life story itself does not begin to take shape until society demands that a person begin to formulate a meaningful and coherent life—in modern societies, late adolescence and young adulthood (Arnett, 2000). Furthermore, cognitive developmental research shows that the skills necessary for creating a narrative identity are not consolidated until the late-adolescent years (Habermas & Bluck, 2000). In late adolescence and young adulthood, people living in modern societies put together aspects of their lived and imagined experience with those cultural narratives that they find most compelling or imposing to create unique life stories. The stories are influenced by early experience to be sure, but they are just as much products of personal agency and culture (Franz & Stewart, 1994; Gregg, 1991). Psychosocially constructed, edited, updated, and reformulated over time, narrative identities are personal and cultural *texts* —written, read, and lived in an evolving cultural context characterized by its own favored, and suppressed, modes of discourse about what it means to live a life worth living.

Life-narrative research suggests a number of different interpretive frames for analyzing, classifying, and critiquing life stories. For example, McAdams (1985, 1993) identifies the dimensions of narrative *tone*, *theme*, and *complexity*. Tone refers to the overall emotional quality of a story, ranging from the optimism and joy found in comedy and romance to the darker affective expressions of tragedy and satire. Stories with a generally positive affective tone suggest that characters are born into a world that is fundamentally secure and that, despite obstacles along the way, the plots of their lives will result in happy endings. Stories with a more negative tone signal danger and distrust, especially in the early chapters, and they lead the reader to expect that even the noblest strivings or yearnings in life will be frustrated in the end.

Spelling out what characters strive to accomplish in stories, narrative themes (or *thematic lines*; McAdams, 1985) may be classified according to Bakan's (1966) distinction between *agency* and *communion*. Agentic themes are about self-expansion, achievement, power, and the like; communion is about the strivings for love, friendship, and community. Personality researchers have developed ways to measure agentic and communal themes in life-narrative accounts, and they have conducted studies linking these themes to other characteristics of personality and life outcomes (e.g., McAdams et al., 1996; Woike, 1995). For example, research suggests that individuals with strong power motives (Level 2 in personality) tend to create life stories prioritizing the agentic themes of self-mastery, impact, and personal accomplishment, whereas individuals high in intimacy motivation tend to create more communal life stories emphasizing romantic love, friendship, interpersonal dialogue, and caring for others.

Tone and theme go to the *content* of life stories; complexity refers to life-story *structure*. Complex life stories incorporate a larger number of plots and characters and articulate a greater number of distinctions than do simpler life stories. Research suggests that individuals who show higher levels of ego development (Loevinger, 1983) and score higher on measures of openness to experience tend to craft more complex autobiographical accounts, compared to those lower in ego development and openness to experience (McAdams, 1985; McAdams et al., 2004).

Another interpretive construct for making sense of life stories is the personal "imago" (McAdams, 1985). An imago is an idealized personification of the self that functions as a main character in the life story. (This usage of the term may be contrasted to Jung's, who viewed the imago as akin to a universal archetype of the collective unconscious; in McAdams's theory, imagoes are highly personalized and culturally shaped personifications of selfhood.) In modern society, people's life stories often contain more than one imago, as if the self were partitioned into multiple protagonists (McAdams, 1985) or voices (Hermans, 1996). Each imago expresses its own values, beliefs, goals, roles, and preferred modes of interaction. While one imago may take center stage during, say, an early chapter in the life story (e.g., "the lover," "the warrior"), another may assume prominence later in the story ("the sage," "the peacemaker"). The interaction and conflict between and among different imagoes helps to structure a story's plot and define the key contrasts, obstacles, and challenges in a life story (see also Gregg, 1991). Furthermore, by implicitly constructing a narrative identity with multiple imagoes, the individual expresses what postmodern theorists such as Gergen (1992) call the multiplicity of contemporary selfhood within a single story of the self. In this way, especially integrative life stories solve the perennial identity problem, identified by William James, of the self's need to be many things and one thing at the same time (Knowles & Sibicky, 1990).

In his biography of Alfred Hitchcock, Spoto (1983) identifies two main characters, or imagoes, that define a central conflict in the famous director's life story. One protagonist is the consummate perfectionist, bold and meticulous, who mastered and revolutionized the craft of film making. The other is the 300-pound glutton, cruel and alienated, who was a physical slob and an emotional cripple. Spoto argues that these two personifications are revealed in the many instances in his films in which Hitchcock sets up antagonistic doubles. The duality also played itself out in Hitchcock's ambivalent treatment of women. Leading ladies such as Grace Kelly and Kim Novak played roles as flawless paragons of feminine elegance, but women were also savagely raped, mutilated, and debased, as in the famous shower scene in *Psycho* and the last attack on Tippi Hedren in *The Birds*. Hitchcock also projected the two self-personifications onto his two favorite leading men—Cary Grant and Jimmy Stewart. Grant represented the suave and sophisticated man of the world who always got the girl. By contrast, Stewart was the theorist of murder in *Rope*, the chair-bound voyeur in *Rear Window*, and the obsessed and guilt-ridden pursuer of romance in *Vertigo*. While Grant personified the fastidious perfectionist who made his way in the world with style and grace, Stewart hinted at the darker imago of the brooding, inept fat boy, a character who, Spoto maintains, dominated the life story in Hitchcock's childhood chapters and then made its way back to center stage in the director's final years.

Going back to Tomkins (1979), life-narrative researchers have paid close attention to those particular scenes or episodes that stand out within the story in bold print (Singer & Salovey, 1993; Thorne & McLean, 2003). Tomkins was especially intrigued by what he called *nuclear scenes*. Typically appearing in childhood chapters of the life story, nuclear scenes begin with positive emotion, often as the child interacts with trusted others in a way that initially provides "stimulation, guidance, mutuality, support, comfort, and/or reassurance." But things turn suddenly bad with the appearance of "an intimidation, or a contamination, or a confusion, or any combination of these which jeopardize the good scene" (Tomkins, 1987, p. 199). What begins, therefore, as joyful or exciting turns frightening, disgusting, contemptuous, shameful, or sad. Tomkins suggested that

nuclear scenes can lead to larger nuclear scripts, which are broader life-story patterns formed in an effort to reverse the nuclear scene, to turn the bad scene into a good scene again. In some life stories, however, the attempt to undo the contamination is, at best, only partially successful, and the protagonist ultimately appears fated to repeat the pattern of the nuclear scene again and again. Not surprisingly, life-narrative research suggests that contaminated nuclear scenes of the sort described by Tomkins are associated with depression and lower levels of self-reported mental health (McAdams et al., 2001).

If some life scenes narrate the move from good to bad, others tell how bad events eventually turn good. In a *redemption sequence*, a character in the life story is delivered from suffering to an enhanced, emotionally positive state (McAdams et al., 2001). Redemption sequences are positively associated with self-reported mental health, and among midlife American adults they are positively linked to generativity, or a strong concern for and commitment to promoting the well-being of future generations (McAdams et al., 1997). In the same way that contaminated childhood scenes may suggest broader nuclear scripts (Tomkins, 1987), strong redemptive sequences may signify broader life-narrative patterns or story types. Research on the life stories of highly generative—that is, especially productive and caring—midlife American adults shows that the redemptive sequences readily found in these narrative identities are often accompanied by the following: (1) a childhood sense of feeling special or advantaged; (2) an early sensitivity to the suffering or oppression of others; (3) the consolidation of a simple but compelling personal ideology in adolescence and the commitment to that ideology through the adult years; (4) tension between agentic and communal strivings in adulthood; and (5) anticipating growth and fruition for the future.

Described in Table 4.3, McAdams (in press) labels this life-narrative pattern *the redemptive self*. The redemptive self may represent a characteristically *American* way of narrating a caring and productive life at midlife. As highly generative American adults shape their lives into redemptive narratives, they implicitly draw upon

Table 4.3 The Redemptive Self: Six Themes Characterizing Life Stories Constructed by Highly Generative American Adults (McAdams, in press; McAdams et al., 1997)

1. Early advantage	As a young child, the story's protagonist enjoys a special advantage or blessing that singles him or her out in the family or vis-à-vis peers. From an early age onward, the protagonist feels that he or she is special in a positive way.
2. Suffering of others	Early in the story, the protagonist witnesses the suffering or misfortune of other people and feels sympathy or empathy for them. Objects of the protagonist's concern might include the sick, dying, disabled, mentally ill, economically disadvantaged, or any of a number of other groups or individuals that might require special care or help.
3. Ideological steadfastness	By adolescence, the protagonist has established a clear and coherent belief system that governs his or her life. The belief system, often rooted in religion, remains relatively stable and steadfast over time. Once the belief system is established, the protagonist does *not* experience profound ideological doubt, uncertainty, or crisis.
4. Redemption sequences	Bad or affectively negative life events are immediately followed by good or affectively positive outcomes. The bad scene is redeemed, salvaged, made better by what follows.
5. Power versus Love	As an adult, the protagonist repeatedly finds that strong agentic desires to distinguish the self by having a positive impact on the world repeatedly conflict with equally strong communal desires to form loving relationships and be accepted by others as an equal.
6. Prosocial future	In looking to the future chapters of the life story, the protagonist sets goals that aim to benefit society in general or its institutions.

an optimistic and highly individualistic understanding of the life course that celebrates personal redemption through the discourses of atonement (religion), emancipation (politics), recovery (medicine), self-actualization (psychology), and upward social mobility (economics). These discourses have their origins in such canonical American texts as the spiritual autobiographies of the New England Puritans, Benjamin Franklin's autobiography, Emerson's nineteenth-century lectures and essays on "self-reliance," Horatio Alger stories, the Gettysburg Address, and the powerful narratives written by escaped slaves before the American Civil War. Variations on the same themes run through twentieth-century American autobiography and fiction, American television and movies, and the burgeoning literature of American self-help. Translated into myths of national identity, these themes are reflected in such quintessentially American notions as "the chosen people," "manifest destiny," and "the American dream." The life stories constructed by highly generative American adults today employ rich metaphors and ways of thinking about identity that Americans have both cherished and contested, found both inspiring and problematic, for more than 300 years—from the Pilgrims to Oprah.

Certain kinds of life scenes (e.g., contamination, redemption) may signify broader life narrative patterns (e.g., nuclear scripts, redemptive narratives), and these narrative patterns may illuminate psychological and social themes that speak to the meanings of individual lives and culture. Bringing these ideas to the practice of psychobiography, Schultz (2003) entertains the possibility that some life stories contain single scenes capturing *the* essential themes and dynamics of a life. Schultz provides guidelines psychobiographers can use to identify what he calls the *prototypical scene* in a life, and he illustrates his approach by examining autobiographical accounts from Kathryn Harrison, Jack Kerouac, Truman Capote, and Sylvia Plath (see also Schultz, chap. 3, this vol.). For Schultz, the search for prototypical scenes can yield at least two dividends. First, an especially representative, encapsulating scene reveals in a nutshell some of the most salient aspects of tone, imagery, theme, and plot in a person's narrative identity. From the standpoint of the subject's first-person account of his or her own life (the narrative identity that he or she may have worked on over the life course), the prototypical scene may reveal the essential parameters of the self-defining myth.

Second, the prototypical scene may help the psychobiographer generate new hypotheses and insights for the psychobiography itself. Schultz is aware that the story the psychobiographer ultimately tells is not synonymous with the story the subject of the psychobiography may have told about his or her own life over time. But exploring what that latter story might have been can greatly enhance the former, providing the psychobiographer with conceptual tools to enrich and deepen the interpretation of the single life.

Conclusion

Once upon a time, personality psychology had little more to offer the world beyond the grand personality theories proposed in the first half of the twentieth century. Grouped under broad paradigmatic rubrics such as "psychoanalysis" (Freud, Jung, Adler, Horney, Sullivan, Erikson), "humanism" (Allport, Rogers, May, Maslow), factor theories (Cattell, Guilford, Eysenck), and "behaviorism" (Miller & Dollard, Skinner, Bandura), these all-purpose theories provided authoritative statements about human nature, individual differences, and personality development (see Hall & Lindzey, 1957). That these frameworks enjoyed very little scientific support did not temper their adherents. Each theory offered a comprehensive viewpoint that might be pitted against its rivals; to choose one (e.g., existentialism) was often to reject another (e.g., social learning theory). Psychobiographers and others aiming to use a psychological lens to apprehend the individual life looked to these broad theories for guidance and insight. In that the psychoanalytic tradition offered the richest theories and the most innovative concepts for understanding the individual life, it should come as no surprise that psychobiographers drew most heavily on the writings of Freud and those depth psychologists who followed him. That they continue to do so speaks both to the continued viability of the psychoanalytic tradition and to the intellectual disconnect between psychobiography and personality psychology today. This chapter takes aim at that disconnect.

It no longer makes any sense, if indeed it ever did, to think of personality psychology as being neatly divided into alternative theoretical schools or camps, each with its own view of human nature, individual differences, and personality change. Although some undergraduate textbooks in personality still dutifully trot out each grand theorist one chapter at a time, scientific research and theorizing in the field of personality psychology looks nothing like these books. Instead, research and theorizing center on a wide range of dispositional traits, characteristic adaptations, and life-story issues that together present an impressive and exciting array of concepts heretofore untapped by psychobiographers.

The constructs I have featured in this chapter—dispositional traits, characteristic adaptations, and life stories—hold one huge advantage over yesterday's grand theories, including the psychoanalytic frameworks most favored by psychobiographers. In a word, the advantage is *science*. I have focused on personality concepts that are embedded in a rich and evolving scientific discourse, wherein constructs are operationalized, hypotheses tested, and theories are continually reformed and refined as a result of consensually validated rules of discovery, inference, and justification. I do not ask that psychobiographers draw *all* their insights from the scientific study of human individuality. Psychobiographers should feel free to tap many different intellectual sources—from feminism and critical theory to psychoanalysis to evolutionary psychology. My more modest aim is merely to suggest that psychobiographers begin to look in the direction of a scientific field with which they should have some affinity, that they begin to take seriously the proposition that contemporary research and theorizing in personality psychology might help to inform their best efforts to make sense of the individual life. The field of personality psychology itself has recently begun to consider biographical assessments, case-based methods, and other approaches to inquiry that would seem near and dear to the psychobiographer's craft. Psychobiographers might wish to return the favor.

Acknowledgments

Many thanks to Jim Anderson and Todd Schultz for comments on an earlier draft of this chapter.

Preparation of the chapter was aided by a grant to the author from the Foley Family Foundation.

References

Alexander, I.E. (1990). Personology: Method and content in personality assessment and psychobiography. Durham, N.C.: Duke University Press.

Allport, G.W. (1937). Personality: A psychological interpretation. New York: Holt, Rinehart, & Winston.

Allport, G.W. (1942). The use of personal documents in psychological science. New York: Social Science Research Foundation.

Allport, G.W. (1965). Letters from Jenny. New York: Harcourt, Brace, & World.

Anderson, J.W. (1981). Psychobiographical methodology: The case of William James. In L. Wheeler (Ed.), Review of personality and social psychology (Vol. 2, pp. 245–272). Beverly Hills, Calif.: Sage.

Anderson, J.W. (2003). A psychological perspective on the relationship between William and Henry James. In R. Josselson, A. Lieblich, & D.P. McAdams (Eds.), Up close and personal: The teaching and learning of narrative research (pp. 177–197). Washington, D.C.: APA Books.

Arnett, J.J. (2000). Emerging adulthood: A theory of development from the late teens through the twenties. American Psychologist, 55, 469–480.

Bakan, D. (1966). The duality of human existence. Boston: Beacon Press.

Barresi, J., & Juckes, T.J. (1997). Personology and the narrative interpretation of lives. Journal of Personality, 65, 693–719.

Barrick, M.R., & Mount, M.K. (1991). The Big Five personality dimensions and job performance: A meta analysis. Personnel Psychology, 44, 1–26.

Block, J. (1995). A contrarian view of the five-factor approach to personality description. Psychological Bulletin, 117, 187–215.

Cantor, N., & Zirkel, S. (1990). Personality, cognition, and purposive behavior. In L. Pervin (Ed.), Handbook of personality: Theory and research (pp. 135–164). New York: Guilford.

Carlson, R. (1988). Exemplary lives: The use of psychobiography for theory development. Journal of Personality, 56, 105–138.

Caspi, A. (1998). Personality development across the life course. In W. Damon (Ed.), Handbook of child psychology (5th ed.), Vol. 3: Social, emotional, and personality development (pp. 311–388). New York: Wiley.

Church, A.T. (2000). Culture and personality: Toward an integrated cultural trait psychology. Journal of Personality, 68, 651–703.

Cohler, B.J. (1982). Personal narrative and the life course. In P. Baltes & O.G. Brim, Jr. (Eds.), Lifespan development and behavior (Vol. 4, pp. 205–241). New York: Academic Press.

Costa, P.T., Jr., & McCrae, R.R. (1994). Set like plaster? Evidence for the stability of adult personality. In T.F. Heatherton & J. Weinberger (Eds.), Can personality change? (pp. 21–40). Washington, D.C.: APA Books.

Craik, K.H. (1997). Circumnavigating the personality as a whole: The challenges of integrative methodological pluralism. Journal of Personality, 65, 1087–1111.

De St. Aubin, E. (1998). Truth against the world: A psychobiographical exploration of generativity in the life of Frank Lloyd Wright. In D.P. McAdams & E. de St. Aubin (Eds.), Generativity and adult development (pp. 391–428). Washington, D.C.: APA Books.

Deci, E., & Ryan, R.M. (1991). A motivational approach to self: Integration in personality. In R. Dienstbier & R.M. Ryan (Eds.), Nebraska symposium on motivation: 1990 (pp. 237–288). Lincoln, Nebr.: University of Nebraska Press.

Donald, D.H. (1995). Lincoln. New York: Simon & Schuster.

Dunn, J., & Plomin, R. (1990). Separate lives: Why siblings are so different. New York: Basic Books.

Edel, L. (1978). Biography: A manifesto. Biography, 1, 1–3.

Edel, L. (1985). Henry James: A life. New York: Harper & Row.

Elms, A.C. (1988). Freud as Leonardo: Why the first psychobiography went wrong. Journal of Personality, 56, 19–40.

Elms, A.C. (1994). Uncovering lives: The uneasy alliance of biography and psychology. New York: Oxford University Press.

Emmons, R.A., & King, L.A. (1988). Conflict among personal strivings: Immediate and long-term implications for psychological and physical well-being. Journal of Personality and Social Psychology, 54, 1040–1048.

Epstein, S. (1986). Does aggregation produce spuriously high estimates of behavior stability? Journal of Personality and Social Psychology, 50, 1199–1210.

Epstein, S. (1994). Integration of the cognitive and psychodynamic unconscious. American Psychologist, 49, 707–724.

Erikson, E.H. (1958). Young man Luther. New York: Norton.

Erikson, E.H. (1969). Gandhi's truth. New York: Norton.

Franz, C., & Stewart, A.J. (Eds.). (1994). Women creating lives: Identities, resilience, resistance. Boulder, Colo.: Westview Press.

Freud, S. (1957). Leonardo da Vinci and a memory of his childhood. In J. Strachey (Ed.), The standard edition of the complete psychological works of Sigmund Freud (Vol. 11, pp. 59–137). London: Hogarth Press. (Original work published 1910)

Freund, A.M., & Baltes, P.B. (2000). The orchestration of selection, optimization, and compensation: An action-theoretical conceptualization of a theory of developmental regulation. In W.J. Perrig & A. Grob (Eds.), Control of human behavior, mental processes, and consciousness (pp. 35–58). Mahwah, N.J.: Erlbaum.

Gelderman, C. (1988). Mary McCarthy: A life. New York: St. Martin's Press.

Gergen, K.J. (1992). The saturated self. New York: Basic Books.

Giddens, A. (1991). Modernity and self-identity. Stanford, Calif.: Stanford University Press.

Gregg, G. (1991). Self-representation: Life-narrative studies in identity and ideology. New York: Greenwood Press.

Habermas, T., & Bluck, S. (2000). Getting a life: The emergence of the life story in adolescence. Psychological Bulletin, 126, 748–769.

Hall, C., & Lindzey, G. (1957). Theories of personality. New York: Wiley.

Harris, J.R. (1995). Where is the child's environment? A group socialization theory of development. Psychological Bulletin, 102, 458–489.

Hellman, L. (1973). Pentimento. New York: New American Library, Inc.

Helson, R., & Klohnen, E. (1998). Affective coloring of personality from young adulthood to midlife. Personality and Social Psychology Bulletin, 24, 241–252.

Hermans, H.J.M. (1996). Voicing the self: From information processing to dialogical interchange. Psychological Bulletin, 119, 31–50.

Hooker, K. (2002). New directions for research in personality and aging: A comprehensive model for linking levels, structures, and processes. Journal of Research in Personality, 36, 318–334.

Jones, E. (1961). The life and work of Sigmund Freud. New York: Basic Books.

Josselson, R., & Lieblich, A. (Eds.). (1993). The narrative study of lives. Thousand Oaks, Calif.: Sage.

Josselson, R., Lieblich, A., & McAdams, D.P. (Eds.). (2003). Up close and personal: The teaching and learning of narrative research. Washington, D.C.: APA Books.

Knowles, E., & Sibicky, M.E. (1990). Continuity and diversity in the stream of selves: Meta-phorical resolutions of William James's one-in-many-selves paradox. Personality and Social Psychology Bulletin, 16, 676–687.

Little, B.R. (1999). Personality and motivation: Personal action and the conative evolution. In L.A. Pervin & O. John (Eds.), Handbook of personality: Theory and research (2nd ed., pp. 501–524). New York: Guilford.

Loehlin, J.C., McCrae, R.R., & Costa, P.T., Jr. (1998). Heritabilities of common and measure-specific components of the Big Five personality factors. Journal of Research in Personality, 32, 431–453.

Loevinger, J. (1983). On ego development and the structure of personality. Developmental Review, 3, 339–350.

Lucas, R.E., & Diener, E. (2001). Understanding extraverts' enjoyment of social situations: The importance of pleasantness. Journal of Personality and Social Psychology, 81, 343–356.

Main, M., Kaplan, N., & Cassidy, J. (1985). Security in infancy, childhood, and adulthood: A move to the level of representation. Monographs of the Society for Research in Child Development, 50(1 & 2), 66–104.

Markus, H., & Nurius, P. (1986). Possible selves. American Psychologist, 41, 954–969.

Matthews, G., & Deary, I. (1998). Personality traits. Cambridge: Cambridge University Press.

McAdams, D.P. (1985). Power, intimacy, and the life story. New York: Guilford.

McAdams, D.P. (1988). Biography, narrative, and lives: An introduction. Journal of Personality, 56, 1–18.

McAdams, D.P. (1993). The stories we live by. New York: Morrow.

McAdams, D.P. (1995). What do we know when we know a person? Journal of Personality, 63, 365–396.

McAdams, D.P. (1997). A conceptual history of personality psychology. In R. Hogan, J. Johnson, & S. Briggs (Eds.), Handbook of personality psychology (pp. 3–39). San Diego, Calif.: Academic Press.

McAdams, D.P. (2001a). The person: An integrated introduction to personality psychology (3rd ed.). New York: Wiley.

McAdams, D.P. (2001b). The psychology of life stories. Review of General Psychology, 5, 100–122.

McAdams, D.P. (in press). The redemptive self. New York: Oxford University Press.

McAdams, D.P., Anydioho, N.A., Brown, C., Huang, Y.T., Kaplan, B., & Machado, M.A. (2004). Traits and stories: Links between dispositional and narrative features of personality. Journal of Personality, 72, 761–784.

McAdams, D.P., Diamond, A., de St. Aubin, E., & Mansfield, E. (1997). Stories of commitment: The psychosocial construction of generative lives. Journal of Personality and Social Psychology, 72, 678–694.

McAdams, D.P., Hoffman, B.J., Mansfield, E., & Day, R. (1996). Themes of agency and communion in significant autobiographical scenes. Journal of Personality, 64, 339–377.

McAdams, D.P., Reynolds, J., Lewis, M., Patten, A., & Bowman, P.J. (2001). When bad things turn good and good things turn bad: Sequences of redemption and contamination in life narrative, and their relation to psychosocial adaptation in midlife adults and in students. Personality and Social Psychology Bulletin, 27, 472–483.

McAdams, D.P., & West, S. (1997). Introduction: Personality and the case study. Journal of Personality, 65, 757–783.

Mischel, W. (1968). Personality and assessment. New York: Wiley.

Mischel, W., & Shoda, Y. (1995). A cognitive-affective system theory of personality: Reconceptualizing situations, dispositions, dynamics, and invariance in personality structure. Psychological Review, 102, 246–268.

Morris, E. (1999). Dutch: A memoir of Ronald Reagan. New York: Random House.

Murray, H.A. (1938). Explorations in personality. New York: Oxford University Press.

Murray, H.A. (1949). Introduction. In H. Melville, Pierre, or the ambiguities (pp. xiii–ciii). New York: Farar Straus.

Murray, H.A. (1951). In nomine diaboli. New England Quarterly, 24, 435–452.

Nasby, W., & Read, N. (1997). The inner and outer voyages of a solo circumnavigator: An integrative case study [Special issue]. Journal of Personality, 65 (4).

Ogilvie, D.M. (2003). Fantasies of flight. New York: Oxford University Press.

Ogilvie, D.M., & Ashmore, R.D. (1991). Self-with-other representation as a unit of analysis in self-concept research. In R.A. Curtis (Ed.), The relational self (pp. 282–314). New York: Guilford.

Polkinghorne, D. (1988). Narrative knowing and the human sciences. Albany, N.Y.: SUNY Press.

Revelle, W. (1995). Personality processes. Annual Review of Psychology, 46, 295–328.

Roberts, B.W., & Friend-DelVecchio, W. (2000). The rank-order consistency of personality from childhood to old age: A quantitative review of longitudinal studies. Psychological Bulletin, 126, 3–25.

Rosenwald, G., & Ochberg, R. (Eds.). (1992). Storied lives: The cultural politics of self-understanding. New Haven, Conn.: Yale University Press.

Runyan, W.M. (1982). Life histories and psychobiography: Explorations in theory and method. New York: Oxford University Press.

Runyan, W.M. (1988). Progress in psychobiography. Journal of Personality, 56, 295–326.

Runyan, W.M. (1990). Individual lives and the structure of personality psychology. In A.I. Rabin, R.A. Zucker, R.A. Emmons, & S. Frank (Eds.), Studying persons and lives (pp. 10–40). New York: Springer.

Schultz, W.T. (1996). An "Orpheus complex" in two writers of loss. Biography: An Interdisciplinary Quarterly, 19, 371–393.

Schultz, W.T. (2001). De Profundis: Prison as a turning point in Oscar Wilde's life story. In D.P. McAdams, R. Josselson, & A. Lieblich (Eds.), Turns in the road: Narrative studies of lives in transition (pp. 67–89). Washington, D.C.: APA Books.

Schultz, W.T. (2003). The prototypical scene: A method for generating psychobiographical hypotheses. In R. Josselson, A. Lieblich, & D.P. McAdams (Eds.), Up close and personal: The teaching and learning of narrative research (pp. 151–176). Washington, D.C.: APA Books.

Singer, J.A., & Salovey, P. (1993). The remembered self. New York: Free Press.

Spoto, D. (1983). The darker side of genius: The life of Alfred Hitchcock. New York: Ballatine.

Stannard, D. (1980). Shrinking history: On Freud and the failure of psychohistory. New York: Oxford University Press.

Steele, R. (1982). Freud and Jung: Conflicts of interpretation. London: Routledge & Kegan Paul.

Thorne, A. (1989). Conditional patterns, transference, and the coherence of personality across time. In D.M. Buss & N. Cantor (Eds.), Personality psychology: Recent trends and emerging directions (pp. 149–159). New York: Springer-Verlag.

Thorne, A., & McLean, K.C. (2003). Telling traumatic events in adolescence: A study of master narrative positioning. In R. Fivush & C. Haden (Eds.), Autobiographical memory and the construction of a narrative self (pp. 169–185). Mahwah, N.J.: Lawrence Erlbaum.

Tomkins, S.S. (1979). Script theory. In H.E. Howe, Jr., & R.A. Dienstbier (Eds.), Nebraska symposium on motivation (Vol. 26, pp. 201–236). Lincoln, Nebr.: University of Nebraska Press.

Tomkins, S.S. (1987). Script theory. In J. Aronoff, A.I. Rabin, & R.A. Zucker (Eds.),

The emergence of personality (pp. 147–216). New York: Springer.

Tooby, J., & Cosmides, L. (1992). The psychological foundations of culture. In J.H. Barkow, L. Cosmides, & J. Tooby (Eds.), The adapted mind (pp. 19–136). New York: Oxford University Press.

White, R.W. (Ed.). (1963). The study of lives. New York: Prentice-Hall.

Wiggins, J.S. (2003). Paradigms of personality assessment. New York: Guilford.

Winter, D.G., & Barenbaum, N.B. (1999). History of modern personality theory and research. In L.A. Pervin & O. John (Eds.), Handbook of personality: Theory and research (2nd ed., pp. 3–27). New York: Guilford.

Winter, D.G., John, O., Stewart, A.J., Klohnen, E.C., & Duncan, L.E. (1998). Traits and motives: Toward an integration of two traditions in personality research. Psychological Review, 105, 230–250.

Woike, B.A. (1995). Most-memorable experiences: Evidence for a link between implicit and explicit motives and social cognitive processes in everyday life. Journal of Personality and Social Psychology, 68, 1081–1091.

Chapter 5

Alan C. Elms

If the Glove Fits
The Art of Theoretical Choice in Psychobiography

For the past twenty years, I've regularly taught an undergraduate course on psychobiography. Students in this course must write a brief but original psychobiographical term paper on a subject of their choice. Most students quickly choose a subject who meets the assignment's basic requirements: he or she must be publicly known for some kind of achievement (political, scientific, artistic, criminal, or whatever), and the student must be able to obtain a substantial amount of biographical information. But then, because this is to be a *psycho*biographical paper and not merely a biographical sketch, each student faces the problem of which psychological concepts, or what psychological theory, to apply.

By the time they get around to writing a rough draft, my students have already been exposed, in class and in assigned reading, to a variety of short and long examples of psychobiography, and to several different theories of personality. But the relationships between these examples or theories and a student's chosen subject may not be at all obvious. Indeed there may be little apparent connection between, let's say, Erik Erikson's analysis of Gandhi and the student's typical term-paper choice of Madonna or Charles Manson. So students often come up after class to ask, "How do I choose a theory?"

I've already told them that psychobiography is a scientific enterprise, based on empirical data and involving the iterative testing of hypotheses. So they seem to assume, or at least to hope, that choosing a theoretical approach is a straightforward procedure, neatly diagrammed in some text or handbook, or available as a software pro-

gram. I do often refer them to Hall and Lindzey's classic personality theory text (Hall et al., 1998), which summarizes a variety of theories not covered in class. But I also tell the students that what they're looking for may not be easy to find. I don't usually tell them—and maybe I should—that theoretical choice in psychobiography is more art than science.

That goes for my own theoretical choices, and for those of most other professional psychobiographers. I say "most others," because some psychobiographers start out being committed to a particular theory, then stay with it regardless. Either they force the theory onto a chosen biographical subject, no matter how the biographical data may resist, or they keep looking around until they find a subject who fits their theory. I don't see anything inherently wrong with the latter approach. I think we benefited, for instance, from Erik Erikson's recognition that Martin Luther would be a good illustration of Erikson's already developed concepts of identity crises (1958), and that Mohandas Gandhi was more concerned with generativity issues, appropriately handled by another part of Erikson's theoretical system (1969). But I generally operate on the assumption that no single theoretical approach can capture the entirety of human personality, and that the concepts of many theorists are needed to deal with the full range of psychological diversity. So in doing psychobiography, my preference is to start with the *subject*—to study a subject who has made important contributions to a field of endeavor, but about whom certain psychological mysteries remain concerning the connections between his or her private developmental history and those public achievements. Having located such a subject, the next question I need to address is the same one my students keep asking: How do you choose an appropriate theory?

I still don't have a table or checklist or statistical procedure to show me and others how to do that. Maybe my office neighbor, the distinguished historiometrician Dean Simonton, will eventually come up with a neat statistical approach to the problem. But until that far-off date, the choice of theory is going to be an artful choice, a blend of knowledge, skill, and creative intuition. To illustrate how such artful choices come about, this chapter briefly reviews a number of examples from my own psychobiographical research, and occasionally from the research of others. My emphasis on my own work may appear unduly narcissistic, and perhaps it is. But it also strikes me as the most efficient way to proceed, because I already have some understanding of why I made a particular choice of theory in various specific cases. Published psychobiographical studies, my own and others, seldom explain how that happened. Because of space limits in journals or for other reasons, they may simply present a biographical case history and then apply a single theoretical approach that appears to fit, with no discussion of alternatives or of the earlier pursuit of false leads.

The examples I've chosen illustrate several possible strategies for finding a psychological theory that may apply to a given case. More than one theory may work well with different kinds of data or different aspects of the subject's life. So these strategies should be regarded as potential leads or "jump-start" suggestions, not as firm rules or guidelines to achieve the absolute best choice.

Let Your Subject Be Your Guide

In choosing a theory, you may not have to start from scratch. Your subject will have lived with himself or herself for a lifetime, and may already have developed or discovered a congenial theory that explains key aspects of that life. Psychobiographers of psychological theorists are most likely to benefit from such a theoretical head start, but literary figures and even the occasional politician may also provide a certain amount of insightful self-reflection.

My initial example here was my own first psychobiographical study. During my first year of graduate school, my major professor, Irving Janis, started a seminar week by having us read a large part of Freud's *Interpretation of Dreams* (1900/1958). Then we got a homework assignment: to diagram Freud's interpretation of his own "specimen dream" (the first dream he interpreted in detail), which has come to be known as the Dream of Irma's Injection. Professor Janis also suggested that we add to our diagrams any further interpretations of the Irma dream that might occur to us. He didn't tell us that he had planned this assignment as a particular kind of didactic device, to show us how hard it would be to improve upon Freud's complex interpretation. Nor did we know that during the following week, he'd have us read Erik Erikson's paper on the same specimen dream (1954), to show us how much more Erikson could get out of Freud's dream by examining the identity issues buried deep within it.

At that point I had never even heard of Erik Erikson. But in my spare time I had been reading the recently published volume of Freud's letters, edited by his son Ernst (E.L. Freud, 1960). I knew from those letters that Freud's wife Martha was pregnant with their sixth child when Freud dreamed the Irma dream. Freud himself interpreted the dream as mainly involving issues of professional conscientiousness. In his published free associations he made only vague allusions to his unsuccessful attempts to avoid impregnating Martha. As I later heard from Henry Murray, Erikson deliberately avoided the pregnancy issue in his published reinterpretation of the dream, because Erikson's analyst Anna Freud forbade him to discuss it—she had been the fetus in question. But while I was completing my homework assignment, it occurred to me that I could use Freud's ideas about dream symbolism to interpret several puzzling elements in the dream: symbolic acts and objects that referred to the pregnancy, to Freud's concerns about his wife's health, and especially to his sexual frustrations prior to and during this difficult time in his marital relationship. So I put all that in my big poster-board diagram of the dream.

Professor Janis was impressed by my response to the homework assignment, though not impressed enough to encourage me to run out and write a psychobiographical journal article. I came away from the experience feeling that if there was anyone to whom Freud's theories about sexual dream symbolism, sexual sublimation, and related matters could be usefully applied, Freud was the subject on whom they were most likely to work. These ideas percolated down through accumulations of additional biographical data over the next decade or so, until they finally resulted in my first substantial psychobiographical paper (Elms, 1980).

Sometimes a psychological theorist goes so far as to write his own autopsychobiography, using his own personality theory, and does it better than anyone else could have. I think the best example here is Erik Erikson's autobiographical account of his youthful identity crises (1970). He was a child whose stepfather pretended to be his real father, until Erik discovered the truth by accident (and never learned his biological father's identity). Then as a young man he went through several sharp changes of direction in career and cultural environment, finally involving his forced emigration from his native Germany to Denmark and then to America. At first Erikson may not have consciously recognized these personal foundations for his emerging theoretical perspectives. But when the concept of identity crisis became central to his thinking, with lots of support from his clinical and psychobiographical cases, it didn't take him long to apply it back to himself.

Don't Let Your Subject
Guide You Astray

While psychological theorists may be astute observers of certain phenomena in themselves and others, they are only human and therefore may have minor or major blind spots, especially about themselves. I first became aware of such blind spots in studying two very different theorists: C.G. Jung and B.-F. Skinner. (They resembled each other only in signing their names with their first two initials.)

Few psychobiographies employ Jungian theory, and on the whole I've found them uninteresting. They usually emphasize widely shared archetypes at the expense of any subtle analysis of the individual biographical subject's life. (Jung did likewise in his clinical practice.) But I have been impressed by Ravenna Helson's two short papers (1979, 1984) about women writers of classic children's fantasy stories. Helson emphasized concepts of midlife development of self, a process Jung called individuation, rather than standard symbolic archetypal analysis. For both Mrs. Molesworth and Edith Nesbit, the writers Helson studied, literary creativity flowered at midlife as the women's lives were transformed. A midlife developmental emphasis seems quite appropriate for such subjects, and Jungian theory provides more useful constructs along those lines than, for instance, Freudian theory.

Some fifteen years ago, I began to look at Jung's 1925–1926 journey through East Africa and down the Nile. He made this trip at age fifty, so I thought it might be productive to apply those same Jungian midlife developmental concepts to an analysis of his psychological responses to the journey. Jung himself, in his autobiography (1963), described his eventual realization that he had embarked upon this six-month journey to avoid dealing with certain elements of personal crisis back home. But instead of holding those crises at bay, the journey raised questions about himself that touched upon "every possible sore spot in my psychology" (p. 273). That certainly sounded like a midlife crisis to me, and I suspected that Jung had responded to it with further self-individuation as well as with various expansions of his theories.

But as I gradually reconstructed the trip in some detail, drawing upon Jung's unpublished writings and other sources, I found that Jungian theory didn't help me much in understanding his reactions to the trip. Mostly, he sought out confirmations of previous insights, rather than opening himself to new ones. He came back from the journey with his personal problems still unresolved, his theoretical perspectives hardly enlarged. I'm continuing to work on his journey and have published little of my detailed analysis so far. At this point I'd have to say that a recurrence of early narcissistic personality issues, of the sort that George Atwood and Robert Stolorow (1993) have attributed to Jung, provides a better explanation of his reactions to the African trip than his own theory of midlife individuation.

Then there's the case of B.-F. Skinner, the most famous psychologist of his generation. As an undergraduate psychology major, I was educated in a mainly Skinnerian psychology department, and I continued to read his work closely even when I entered a graduate program with a rather different orientation. When Skinner's autobiography began to appear in multiple volumes, I was intrigued by his efforts to avoid "mentalistic" accounts of his inner life and to emphasize instead the external events and circumstances that shaped his behavior. Yet one of the most striking chapters in the autobiography's first volume involved a time in his life that he described, with genuine emotion and with obvious reference to inner depression, as the "Dark Year" (Skinner, 1976).

The Dark Year was a period in which, most importantly, the young Skinner's efforts to become a fiction writer failed miserably. In the autobiography's second volume (Skinner, 1979), the chapter that first caught my eye concerned his next serious attempt at fiction, the writing of the novel *Walden Two* two decades later (Skinner, 1948). That writing project went unusually quickly and smoothly. Skinner's expressions of strong emotion (this time enthusiasm and intense satisfaction) again seemed a far cry from a strictly behaviorist, nonmentalistic account of his life. Reading the two chapters together, I was struck by how much the Dark Year bore all the earmarks of an adolescent identity crisis, while *Walden Two* came at a time when he seemed to be experiencing another identity crisis, at midlife.

The Dark Year had happened at just the right time for a classic Eriksonian identity crisis. It centrally involved occupational choice, as well as Skinner's strong feelings of being out of place in his family and in the community to which they had recently moved. When I carefully reviewed Erikson's criteria for such crises, I was surprised to find that Skinner's account of the Dark Year fit in all significant particulars Erikson's description not just of an ordinary identity crisis, but of a *severe* identity crisis, close to pathology. Further, Skinner's eventual resolution of the crisis fit Erikson's description of how such severe crises are often resolved: by an enthusiastic commitment to a strong ideology—in Skinner's case, to radical behaviorism.

When I discussed the Dark Year with Skinner, he reluctantly conceded that he and Erikson did seem to be describing the same kind of phenomenon, though in rather different language. But Skinner was not at all willing to concede what I went on to suggest with regard to *Walden Two*: that he had written the novel in response to a renewal of those adolescent identity issues as he entered midlife. I still think I was right on both counts. Erik Erikson thought so too, I will immodestly add. He had known Skinner ever since their early days at Harvard, and he was delighted with my Eriksonian analysis of Skinner's psychological development. Indeed, he sounded as though he felt an old score had thereby been settled in this battle of dueling theories.

To be fair to Skinner, I should note that he continued to insist, with some eloquence, that his Dark Year and his responses to it could be accounted for in strictly behaviorist terms—no identity theory need apply. He told me that the third and final volume of his autobiography would present a detailed behavioristic analysis of his entire life history, identifying more clearly than before the reinforcement patterns and environmental cues that had led him to behave as he did. But he eventually concluded the autobiography (in four volumes, not three) without ever providing that sort of organized and detailed behavioristic account. No one else has offered such a behavioristic psychobiography either, of Skinner or of anyone else. I think that has failed to happen because it's simply impossible to do. I do believe in the power of partial reinforcement, and I can sometimes identify at least loosely the "reinforcement schedules" that have shaped or sustained a particular behavior pattern in a given individual's life. Skinner intermittently did so for aspects of his own behavior. But trying to explain an entire life course in behavioristic terms would involve at least as much retrospective speculation (about patterns of positive and negative reinforcement, partial reinforcement schedules, extinction of learned responses, and so on) as the wildest psychoanalytic interpretation.

Follow the Bliss, Follow the Anger

Joseph Campbell, the Jungian cultural scholar, used to encourage his readers and viewers, "Follow your bliss": pursue the enthusiasms that bring you the deepest satisfaction. In deciding which motivational theories to apply to a psychobiographical subject, one good approach is to look for a theory that highlights the activities or goals the subject desired most. If your male subject's relationships with women centered on control rather than sex, look at Adler's (1930) theories or David Winter's (1973) empirical research on power motives. If your female subject loved to fly and was fascinated by fire from early childhood, take a close look at Henry Murray's (1981) concept of the Icarus complex or Dan Ogilvie's (2003) work on fantasies of flight.

But in my experience as a psychobiographer, an approach at least as productive as "follow the bliss" is "follow the anger." What makes your subject offended, angry, outraged—and repeatedly so, over long periods or most of a lifetime, under circumstances where most people would soon simmer down?

One of my favorite subjects in this regard has been Gordon W. Allport. Allport was one of psychology's most influential advocates of studying the individual personality in all its idiosyncratic glory. In important ways he was one of my role models, a champion of the kind of psychology I continue to practice. He was a kindly and a Christian man, in the best sense of that term. But one little characterological hang-up wouldn't let go of him: He despised Sigmund Freud and all of Freud's concepts about unconscious motivation. Allport expressed his strong rejection of Freud by telling the story, over and over and over, of how as a young man he had dropped by to see Freud as one of Vienna's tourist highlights. To make conversation at an awkward moment, Allport told Freud about encountering a little boy on the tram a few minutes earlier, a little boy who had a well-developed dirt phobia. Freud promptly asked, "And was that little boy you?" Hundreds of times over the next forty years, Allport told this anecdote and then insisted that Freud had made an unwarranted, outrageous interpretation of Allport's innocuous remarks.

Meanwhile, Allport's audiences, at least those who knew him well or could watch this neat and prissy professor tell the story, realized that Freud's quick interpretation was dead on (Elms, 1994, pp. 72–84).

I've explored the several foundations of Allport's sustained outrage (which he also expressed at length in several anti-Freudian books and papers): his strong cleanliness concerns in childhood and adulthood, his distress at being thought of as a "little boy" in other contexts, his vigorous rejection of any characterization of himself that might deny his unique individuality. In other words, I found plenty of evidence that he had personal and in some ways Freudian reasons for denying that he or any other "normal adult" was significantly ruled by unconscious motives. Allport also had his enthusiasms, his genuinely positive contributions to psychology and to society, and I respect those. But he could have developed a good deal more self-insight, and perhaps greater freedom from those unconscious motives, by paying more attention to the deeper sources of his anger toward Freud.

Wondering why some people spend so much psychological energy hating Freud carried me on to a very different psychobiographical subject: Vladimir Nabokov, the great Russian-American novelist, best known as the author of *Lolita*. Nabokov has been one of my favorite writers ever since I first read *Lolita* as a college sophomore. Early in my psychobiographical career, I thought of doing *something* on Nabokov, but the breadth and the brilliance of his published work were daunting. Where to start? As I thought about the possibilities, I realized I had long been bothered by Nabokov's insistence on making mean fun of psychotherapists in his fiction and nonfiction, and especially by his vicious verbal attacks on Freud. So I decided to puzzle out where that personalized hostility to Freud came from. In reading or rereading most of Nabokov's fiction and autobiographical works, I found his hostility toward Freud so pervasive that the project began to grow into a full-sized book, well beyond my available time and limited literary expertise. So I focused my attention much more narrowly, at least for the time being: on a single story by Nabokov, titled in the standard English translation "Cloud, Castle, Lake" (Nabokov, 1995).

At first I had a Freudian interpretation of the story vaguely in mind, because it contains several obvious sexual symbols—sausages as penises, and so on. But as I read the story repeatedly, I noted a more sustained pattern of symbolism. Its several scenes may be taken as vividly describing the unhappy protagonist's discovery of a symbolic womb in the form of a beautiful little house in the forest, his growing desire to stay there forever, and his forced rebirth into the real world in a painful passage through a twisting birth canal. Once that story's symbolism became evident, I had no difficulty spotting a variety of return-to-womb and painful-birth images in Nabokov's autobiographical accounts of his childhood, his traumatic ejection from Russia during the Revolution, and his escape from Nazi Germany with his Jewish wife and small son shortly before he wrote "Cloud, Castle, Lake." Such birth-related imagery led me in two theoretical directions, both useful in analyzing Nabokov's fiction and his anger toward Freud: Henry Murray's (1938) concept of a "claustral complex" and Freud's (1918/1955) concept of "the narcissism of minor differences." I won't go further into these explanatory constructs here (see Elms, 1994, pp. 167–182). But I think they explain a lot about Nabokov, and I would not have explored them if I hadn't been pursuing his obsessive anger toward Freud. (Of course, Nabokov's response to such applications of psychological theory would have been sheer outrage—more fuel for my analytic fire.)

Stay Ready to Change Theories in Midstream

If you start your psychobiographical project by looking for a subject who exemplifies your chosen theory, you may have to change horses—that is, subjects—in midstream. Not every subject will prove to be a good example of any given theory, and you may find that you've wasted a lot of research time on a subject who falls outside your framework. But if your research is initially subject-centered—if your intent is to understand a given individual by the best means available—your initial choice of theory need not turn out to be a disaster. Indeed, if you remain open to

theoretical shifts when the biographical facts refuse to fit your initial theory, you may well end up with a stronger psychobiographical case than in the theory-centered approach.

One of my first attempts to do political psychobiography was a study of Henry Kissinger (Elms, 1976, pp. 136–148). A term often used to describe Kissinger by political commentators, close colleagues, and long-time enemies is "Machiavellian." So I began my research with the idea of seeing how well his public behavior and personal history matched the defining criteria of the "Machiavellian personality," emerging from the empirical studies of Richard Christie and Florence Geis (1970). In Kissinger's case, I didn't have to change my theoretical approach in midstream; he fit the Machiavellian personality template in all particulars. In doing further research on him a decade and nearly two decades later (Elms, 1986; Elms, 1994, pp. 229–231), I saw no need to abandon my initial choice of Machiavellianism in pulling together a great variety of data, including Kissinger's own voluminous writings about himself and his manipulation of others.

During the later research, I had a happy inspiration: why not compare Kissinger with Alexander Haig, his chief lieutenant in the White House, who later became Secretary of State himself? I initially assumed, mostly on the basis of journalists' characterizations, that Haig was another Machiavellian, though not as smooth an operator as Kissinger. But the more I learned about Haig, the more evident it became that another personality type fit him much better: the authoritarian personality (Adorno et al., 1950). The most persuasive evidence for that conclusion, forcing me to abandon my initial assumptions about Haig's Machiavellianism, was his own memoir of his time in the Reagan White House, a book rather oddly titled *Caveat* (1984). ("Caveat," of course, is Latin for "Let him beware"—a warning seldom voiced by Machiavellians as they practice their deceits on others.) The book was suffused with Haig's anxieties about where he stood in the White House hierarchy, his struggle to establish a rigid hierarchical structure that he could then control, and his anger when such efforts failed because others wouldn't play by the rules. Kissinger loved to play games of power in the White House and abroad, and delighted in outfoxing his opponents with devious moves. Haig demanded that his opponents accept his rules, assuming he could then force them to acknowledge that according to the rules he was King of the Hill. When President Reagan was shot and Secretary of State Haig proclaimed, "As of now, I am in control here, in the White House," he was not being a smoothly manipulative Machiavellian but a crudely assertive authoritarian. When the rest of the White House hierarchy and the national press laughed at that attempt to change the game's rules, Haig was on his way down and out.

A more recent instance of starting with one theoretical model and shifting to another in midstream (or at least two or three steps into the current) comes from my research on two science fiction writers, Cordwainer Smith and James Tiptree, Jr. Neither writer ever became well known to the general public during their lifetimes, whether by those pseudonyms or by their real names. But within the science fiction world their work remains highly valued, often anthologized, and strongly influential on other writers.

In several ways Smith and Tiptree had remarkably similar personal histories. Both were born to world-traveling parents who put them on display as children. Both had little peer contact in childhood, as they traveled from country to country in the company of adults, and felt painfully isolated as a result. Both repeatedly contemplated and sometimes attempted suicide. Both served as military intelligence operatives and later worked for the CIA. Both developed an intense interest in psychology and then became successful science fiction writers under carefully guarded pseudonyms. Cordwainer Smith was in real life a China expert named Paul Linebarger. James Tiptree, Jr., was in real life a professional artist and Ph.D. experimental psychologist named Alice Sheldon.

When I began to compare these two writers, in terms both of their personal histories and of their science fiction stories, I thought perhaps attachment theory would help. There was that big issue of psychological isolation, in their early histories and in certain key stories. Furthermore, I had the distinguished attachment theorist Phil Shaver in my department, to give me a hand when I needed help in applying the theory.

But I never got far enough into the attachment mainstream to struggle with the undertow. It may yet happen that attachment theory will tell me something insightful about either Smith or Tiptree, or perhaps both. But it didn't say much to me in the first few weeks I tried it on them.

Then I had another of those happy inspirations (maybe I should call them epiphanies). Why not look at how Smith and Tiptree differed as well as how they resembled each other, and find a theory that made sense of those differences? Most of Smith's stories, as I thought more about them, conveyed quite a different tone from Tiptree's stories. At the simplest level, Smith's stories generally ended happily for his protagonists, while Tiptree's didn't. But more subtle distinctions could be teased out. In Smith's "happy endings," the protagonist was often forced to accept a prosaic reality, or at least what passes for prosaic reality in the science fiction world. At the same time, his protagonists typically had struggled against great odds, lived up to their commitments, and went beyond them, doing much good for people or creatures ignored or rejected by the powers-that-be. Tiptree's stories offered empathy to such downtrodden creatures and sometimes concluded with a facetiously happy ending. But the Tiptree stories were by and large depictions of defeat, failure, tragedy on a massive scale—stories of optimism crushed by catastrophe.

In addressing these contrasts between Smith's and Tiptree's fictional worlds, I thought to look again at a favorite paper by Rae Carlson (1988). Her paper contrasted two basic psychological scripts that her mentor Silvan Tomkins had identified in his version of script theory. Some people develop what Tomkins called a *nuclear* script that guides them in their life path: They learn early on that any really promising, truly gratifying situation in their lives will eventually lead to disaster—and sure enough, if they believe that, it usually does. Other people develop a *commitment* script: Even though things may look grim in the short run, these people feel they can probably get through the bad stuff and achieve their objectives if they just carry on—and sure enough, that often happens, too.

I'd had a hard time reading Silvan Tomkins in his original, high-density papers and books (e.g., Tomkins, 1987). But Rae Carlson spent much of her later career translating Tomkins into plain English. In the paper that came to mind, she contrasted Nathaniel Hawthorne and his consistent *nuclear* script with Karl Marx's social-worker daughter Eleanor Marx and her consistent *commitment* script. And there I had an answer to my theoretical hunt: Cordwainer Smith's prevailing psychological script was a commitment script, whereas James Tiptree, Jr.'s was a nuclear script. That was true of the bulk of their fiction, and it was true of much in their lives, early and late. Finding the right theory here, more by intuition than anything else, then enabled me to organize much of the knowledge I already had about both writers and to make sense of their differences despite their more obvious similarities (Elms, 2000). Those are the sorts of things a good theory ought to do.

I should note here that I don't depend only on my own intuitions of what is artful in theory selection. I do continue to think of myself as an empirical scientist, so I usually make reality checks by submitting my psychobiographical accounts to other knowledgeable people before I publish. That means checking my conclusions with living subjects when I can, as with B.-F. Skinner and Henry Murray (Elms, 1987)—though I don't necessarily accept their verdicts about themselves when I've got plenty of evidence to the contrary. It may also mean consulting with close friends and relatives of a subject who is already dead. In the case of Gordon Allport, for instance, I got plenty of confirmation from his former graduate students and colleagues that my picture of Allport as a dirtphobic, neatness-obsessed individual was reasonably accurate. (I also got a caution from his son that there was a good deal more to Allport than that.) And when I can, I personally cross-check with other biographers and psychobiographers, who often know much more about a subject than they've published so far.

As an example of the latter, I asked Julie Phillips, who is currently writing the first full-scale biography of James Tiptree, Jr., to look at my application of script theory to Tiptree. Phillips (personal communication, July 29, 1998) told me that although my characterization of Tiptree as operating from a nuclear script has some validity, I sometimes sounded as if I was forcing "square facts into round holes." I've kept

that cautionary comment in mind as I've written further about Tiptree (Elms, 2004). Sometimes, it seems to me, Tiptree was as round a peg as anyone could find to fit into the round hole of the nuclear script. At other times she was a sort of oval peg, and at yet other times a rectangular peg, but never a totally square one. I don't expect a broadly stated personality theory to fit anyone perfectly at all times. I'm happy if it fits pretty well at certain important times in the subject's life and work. I'm especially happy if it fits better than any other theory in sight.

Let Others' Errors Provoke and Inspire You

Psychobiography is, like other scientific and artistic endeavors, an iterative field, which builds upon the work of others and perhaps in the long run shows progress in understanding given subjects (Runyan, 1988, pp. 318–320). Sometimes that means adding to and expanding the research and interpretations of other scholars concerning a given subject's psychology. Sometimes it means deciding that a previous scholar has taken the wrong track in his or her choice of a theory or a personality diagnosis and bringing a new perspective to bear instead.

One example of the latter is my work on another science fiction writer, Jack Williamson (Elms, 1994, pp. 117–130). Williamson's active writing career has encompassed a longer time span than any other science fiction writer ever— longer, probably, than any other American writer in any field. His first story appeared in 1928. As of 2004, he is still publishing solid and sometimes prize-winning work at age 96. He is also remarkable among science fiction writers for having undergone a full-scale psychoanalysis nearly seventy years ago—partly to get past writer's block, if you can believe it. The analytic treatment significantly influenced the content of Williamson's subsequent writing, as well as helping him cope with (if not totally resolve) his psychological problems.

I began a psychobiographical study of Williamson because I had long enjoyed his fiction, because I came to know him personally, and because in his published autobiography

(Williamson, 1984), he suggested that his psychoanalytic treatment was represented symbolically in one of his classic novels. I didn't have any clear theoretical approach in mind when I began to put together a paper on him, but Williamson almost inadvertently provided me with a direction to pursue. He had mentioned in the autobiography that his psychoanalyst at the Menninger Clinic had published a paper on his case, of course disguising his identity. Apparently nobody in the science fiction world had ever read the published case—a good thing, since the disguise was rather thin. Williamson offered to tell me where the case had been published fifty years earlier and to show me an unpublished account he had written at that time of how the analysis went from his perspective.

I read the published case history with the idea that it would give me greater insight into Williamson's personality and psychological functioning. What it mainly gave me was insight into the therapist's personal biases—he was quite hostile toward the kind of literature Williamson was writing and publishing at the time—and into the therapist's narrow diagnostic perspective. Perhaps the therapist shouldn't be faulted for the latter. He was apparently a new psychiatric resident, with little experience treating patients on his own. He diagnosed this patient as having a "schizoid personality," dangerously close to slipping into full schizophrenic psychosis, especially if Williamson kept on writing those nasty "horror stories." Williamson had no intention of quitting his career as a science fiction writer, and he didn't really agree with the diagnosis. But he stayed with the therapy for several months, and even went back to the same therapist for further treatment a couple of years later.

I didn't agree with the diagnosis either. From my acquaintance with Williamson, but even more from his autobiography and his unpublished contemporary account of the therapy, he didn't strike me as likely ever to have been close to psychosis. Further, although he had been socially withdrawn in his youth and was still a quiet, introverted man when I came to know him, the diagnosis of "schizoid personality" didn't fit. Diagnostic categories had been elaborated and fine-tuned in the half-century since Williamson

had been treated, and though I don't ordinarily look at the *Diagnostic and Statistical Manual of Mental Disorders* (*DSM*, the American Psychiatric Association's diagnostic bible) for psychobiographical inspiration, I decided this was a good time to do so. When I did, I found that my—and Williamson's—uneasiness about the therapist's diagnosis was justified, and that a similar-sounding but distinctive diagnosis was more appropriate: not "schizoid personality" but "avoidant personality."

According to the *DSM* descriptions, people with schizoid personalities are emotionally cold, indifferent to others, withdrawn because they don't care. People with avoidant personalities are socially withdrawn too, but that's mainly because they fear rejection; they really do want contact with others (Millon, 1981, p. 304). It was clear both from Williamson's autobiography and from his social behavior—I knew him, after all, because he had actively participated in the Science Fiction Research Association's annual conferences for many years—that he was "avoidant" and not "schizoid." Williamson himself felt that was a fairer diagnosis when I explained it to him, and it also seemed a better fit with the many protagonists of his fiction. (It's also a pretty good description of many science fiction fans, who attend multiple conventions each year to socialize with other avoidant personalities, more comfortable in each other's presence than in the "mundane" social world.)

In a final example of choosing a theory as a response to another writer's erroneous conclusions, I'll turn from science fiction to fantasy—and back to Freudian symbolism, with which I began this chapter. I once had the opportunity to take an intensive two-week workshop on folklore research from the great folklorist Alan Dundes, who also happens to be the most Freudian folklorist in the field (see, e.g., Dundes, 1980). As part of the workshop, each participant had to come up with a folkloric research project and then present it to the group and to Professor Dundes. This time my recent reading had included Bruno Bettelheim's book about fairy tales, *The Uses of Enchantment* (1976).

I really liked most of Bettelheim's chapters suggesting how specific fairy tales can help children deal with stressful developmental issues. But his discussion of "Goldilocks and the Three Bears" bothered me. Bettelheim didn't like the story very much, though it's one of the most often-told fairy tales. Empathizing with the character he described as "poor, beautiful and charming Goldilocks" (p. 218), he discussed the story mainly in terms of Goldilocks struggling to move past Oedipal issues in order to cope with adolescent identity problems. That interpretation struck me as not at all convincing. When my daughters were little, they had strongly empathized with the bears, not with Goldilocks. So had I as a small child, and so had the friends I asked as adults to recall the story, and so did their children.

Then I asked myself, "At what age is this story especially appealing to children? What psychological issues are a special concern to them at that time, as well as to the bears in the story?" The age range, it seemed to me, was definitely preschool, and the issues included cleanliness training, maintaining environmental and behavioral order, and distress about disruptions of order—in short, *pre*-Oedipal issues, especially involving what Freud called anality. All sorts of things then clicked into place, and they made sense to Alan Dundes as well. Another homework triumph!—especially when my anal interpretation of "The Three Bears" was prominently featured in the *Journal of American Folklore*, my only publication to date in that journal (Elms, 1977).

I didn't discuss individual psychology in that published paper. But beyond the fairy tale lies a true psychobiographical story, still waiting to be written. Though "The Three Bears" has traditional folktale sources, the form in which we know the story was determined largely by the English poet Robert Southey, who first put it into print. At some point after I published my anal analysis of the story, I thought it might be interesting to check out Robert Southey himself. He was a famous poet and essayist in his time, but most of his work has been forgotten. His one lasting contribution to English literature is this remarkably anal version of "The Three Bears." Might that have something to do with his personality?

I soon found that as a child, Southey had been raised by an aunt who was dirt-obsessed—per-

haps I should say, cleanliness-obsessed. Further, the aunt appears to have succeeded in passing this obsession on to Southey himself, though perhaps in somewhat milder form. I haven't yet gotten around to putting together all the psychobiographical pieces of "Southey and the Three Bears." Southey is for the most part a pretty boring writer, and detailed information on his childhood is scarce. But I suspect that when I do complete that paper, my theoretical choice will still be not so much a matter of Bettelheimian post-Oedipal ego development as of Freudian pre-Oedipal anality, for Southey as well as for his very tidy bears.

Conclusion

Before I ever wrote a word of the first draft of this chapter, I titled it "If the Glove Fits"—another artful choice. The O.J. Simpson murder trial was much in the news at the time, and I thought perhaps I could begin and end the paper with a clever adaptation of Johnnie Cochran's doggerel summation of the case for the defense. Now that I've written and revised and sat on the chapter for a while, and then written it out again, I'd say the title fits even better than I had anticipated, with no reference necessary to a long-past trial.

Think about a person's life and work as two hands, controlled by the same individual consciousness and probably by the same individual *un*conscious. Think of a theory as a pair of gloves—or, better yet, let's think of a variety of theories as several pairs of gloves, differing in size and style and material. For a particular individual, no one pair of gloves will be a perfect fit in all regards. Finger lengths will vary; finger thickness will differ, from finger to finger and hand to hand; skin sensitivity will respond to different fabrics in various subtle ways. So you try this or that pair of gloves on your subject's hands—not through precise measurements, not by trying every possible pair, but by intuition and informed guess and iterative approximation and gradual elimination of possible fits in various directions. You won't find a perfect fit, in gloves or theories, ever. You may be tempted by the latest fashions, even if they're more pretty than practical. But some gloves will fit better than others, and certain theories will hardly need stretching to fit a given personality. You could keep trying on gloves forever, but sooner or later you should find a pair that stands up to heavy use. And then, if the gloves fit, you must commit!

References

Adler, A. (1930). Individual psychology. In C. Murchison (Ed.), Psychologists of 1930 (pp. 395–405). Worcester, Mass.: Clark University Press.

Adorno, T.W., Frenkel-Brunswik, E., Levinson, D.J., & Sanford, R.N. (1950). The authoritarian personality. New York: Harper & Row.

Atwood, G.E., & Stolorow, R.D. (1993). Faces in a cloud: Intersubjectivity in personality theory (Rev. ed.). Northvale, N.J.: Aronson.

Bettelheim, B. (1976). The uses of enchantment. New York: Knopf.

Carlson, R. (1988). Exemplary lives: The uses of psychobiography for theory development. Journal of Personality, 56, 105–138.

Christie, R., & Geis, F. (1970). Studies in Machiavellianism. New York: Academic Press.

Dundes, A. (1980). Interpreting folklore. Bloomington: Indiana University Press.

Elms, A.C. (1976). Personality in politics. Boston: Little, Brown.

Elms, A.C. (1977). "The three bears": Four interpretations. Journal of American Folklore, 90, 257–273.

Elms, A.C. (1980). Freud, Irma, Martha: Sex and marriage in the "dream of Irma's injection." Psychoanalytic Review, 67, 83–109.

Elms, A.C. (1986). From House to Haig: Private life and public style in American foreign policy advisers. Journal of Social Issues, 42 (2), 33–53.

Elms, A.C. (1987). The personalities of Henry A. Murray. Perspectives in Personality, 2, 1–14.

Elms, A.C. (1994). Uncovering lives: The uneasy alliance of biography and psychology. New York: Oxford University Press.

Elms, A.C. (2000). Painwise in space: The psychology of isolation in Cordwainer Smith and James Tiptree, Jr. In G. Westfahl (Ed.), Space and beyond: The frontier theme in science fiction (pp. 131–140). Westport, Conn.: Greenwood Press.

Elms, A.C. (2004). The psychologist who empathized with rats: James Tiptree, Jr. as Alice B. Sheldon, Ph.D. Science Fiction Studies, 31, 81–96.

Erikson, E.H. (1954). The dream specimen of psychoanalysis. Journal of the American Psychoanalytic Association, 2, 5–56.

Erikson, E.H. (1958). Young man Luther. New York: Norton.

Erikson, E.H. (1969). Gandhi's truth: On the origins of militant nonviolence. New York: Norton.

Erikson, E.H. (1970). Autobiographic notes on the identity crisis. Daedalus, 99(4), 730–759.

Freud, E.L. (Ed.) (1960). Letters of Sigmund Freud. New York: Basic Books.

Freud, S. (1900). The interpretation of dreams (ed. & trans. J. Strachey). New York: Basic Books, 1958.

Freud, S. (1918). The taboo of virginity. In J. Strachey (Ed. & Transl.), The standard edition of the complete psychological works of Sigmund Freud (Vol. 11, pp. 193–208). London: Hogarth Press, 1955.

Haig, A.M., Jr. (1984). Caveat. New York: Macmillan.

Hall, C.S., Lindzey, G., & Campbell, J.B. (1998). Theories of personality (4th ed.). New York: Wiley.

Helson, R. (1979, September 1). Mrs. Molesworth and the wingless bird of alchemy: A Victorian midlife crisis. In M.J. Meadow (Chair), Symbol and imagery in growth and healing. Symposium presented at the annual meeting of the American Psychological Association, New York City.

Helson, R. (1984). E. Nesbit's forty-first year: Her life, times, and personality growth. Imagination, Personality, and Cognition, 4, 53–68.

Jung, C.G. (1963). Memories, dreams, reflections (rec. & ed. A. Jaffé; trans. R. & C. Winston). New York: Pantheon.

Millon, T. (1981). Disorders of personality: DSM-III: Axis II. New York: Wiley.

Murray, H.A. (1938). Explorations in personality. New York: Oxford University Press.

Murray, H.A. (1981). American Icarus. In E.S. Shneidman (Ed.), Endeavors in psychology: Selections from the personology of Henry A. Murray (pp. 535–556). New York: Harper & Row.

Nabokov, V.N. (1995). Cloud, castle, lake. In The stories of Vladimir Nabokov (pp. 426–433). New York: Knopf.

Ogilvie, D. (2003). Fantasies of flight. New York: Oxford University Press.

Runyan, W.M. (1988). Progress in psychobiography. Journal of Personality, 56, 295–326.

Skinner, B.-F. (1948). Walden two. New York: Macmillan.

Skinner, B.-F. (1976). Particulars of my life. New York: Knopf.

Skinner, B.-F. (1979). The shaping of a behaviorist. New York: Knopf.

Tomkins, S.S. (1987). Script theory. In J. Aronoff, A.I. Rabin, & R.A. Zucker (Eds.), The emergence of personality (pp. 147–216). New York: Springer.

Williamson, J. (1984). Wonder's child: My life in science fiction. New York: Bluejay Books.

Winter, D.G. (1973). The power motive. New York: Free Press.

Chapter 6

How to Critically Evaluate Alternative Explanations of Life Events
The Case of Van Gogh's Ear

Late Sunday evening December 23, 1888, Vincent Van Gogh, then 35 years old, cut off the lower half of his left ear and took it to a brothel, where he asked for a prostitute named Rachel and handed the ear to her, asking her to "keep this object carefully."

How is this extraordinary event to be accounted for? Over the years, a variety of explanations have been proposed, and more than a dozen of them will be sketched below. What sense can be made of such a variety of interpretations? Is one of them uniquely true, are all of them true in some way, or, perhaps, are none of them true? And how can we know? This incident is examined in order to explore the problem of alternative explanations in the study of lives (Allport, 1961, 1965; Hogan, 1976; Murray et al., 1938; Runyan, 1978, 1980a, 1980b; White, 1963, 1975) and to contribute to a growing literature on the logic and methodology of psychobiographical studies (e.g., Anderson, 1981; Crosby, 1979; Elms, 1976; Gedo, 1972; George, 1971; Glad, 1973; Izenberg, 1975; Lifton & Olson, 1974; Mack, 1971; Mazlish, 1968; Meyer, 1972). The discussion is intended to raise basic issues encountered in applying personality theories to the life of a single individual, whether a historical figure, a research subject, or a clinical patient.

A Variety of Explanations

1. One explanation of Van Gogh's behavior is that he was frustrated by two recent events: the engagement of his brother Theo, to whom he was very attached, and the failure of an attempt to establish a working and living relationship with Paul Gauguin. The aggressive impulses aroused by these frustrations were first directed at Gauguin but then were turned against himself (Lubin, 1972).

2. A second interpretation is that the self-mutilation resulted from a conflict over homosexual impulses aroused by the presence of Gauguin. According to this account, the ear was a phallic symbol (the Dutch slang word for penis, *lul*, resembled the Dutch word for ear, *lel*), and the act was a symbolic self-castration (Lubin, 1972; Westerman Holstijn, 1951).

3. A third explanation is in terms of Oedipal themes. Van Gogh was sharing a house with Gauguin, and Gauguin reported that on the day before the ear mutilation Van Gogh had threatened him with a razor but, under Gauguin's powerful gaze, had then run away. According to this interpretation, Gauguin represented Van Gogh's hated father and that, failing in his initial threat, Van Gogh "finally gratified his extraordinary resentment and hate for his father by deflecting the hatred on to his own person. In so doing Van Gogh committed, in phantasy, an act of violence on his father with whom he identified himself and at the same time he punished himself for committing the act" (Schnier, 1950, p. 153). Then "in depositing his symbolic organ at the brothel he also fulfilled his wish to have his mother" (pp. 153–154).

4. Another interpretation is that Van Gogh was influenced by bullfights he had seen in Arles. In such events the matador is given the ear of the bull as an award, displays his prize to the crowd,

and then gives it to the lady of his choice. The proponent of this interpretation, J. Olivier (in Lubin, 1972), says: "I am absolutely convinced that Van Gogh was deeply impressed by this practice. . . . Van Gogh cut off the ear, his own ear, as if he were at the same time the vanquished bull and the victorious matador. A confusion in the mind of one person between the vanquished and the vanquisher" (p. 158). Then, like the matador, Van Gogh presented the ear to a lady of his choice. (The following explanations, unless otherwise noted, are also from Lubin's [1972] comprehensive analysis.)

5. In the months preceding Van Gogh's self-mutilation, there were 15 articles in the local paper about Jack the Ripper, who mutilated the bodies of prostitutes, sometimes cutting off their ears. "These crimes gave rise to emulators, and Vincent may have been one of them. As a masochist instead of a sadist, however, it is conceivable that he would reverse Jack's act by mutilating himself and bringing the ear to a prostitute" (Lubin, 1972, p. 159).

6. Van Gogh was emotionally and financially dependent on his brother Theo, and usually spent the Christmas holidays with him. This year, however, Vincent learned that Theo would spend the holiday with his new fiancée and her family. One interpretation suggests that Van Gogh's self-mutilation was an unconscious strategy for holding on to his brother's attention, and a way of getting Theo to come and care for him rather than spending the holidays with his fiancée.

7. Van Gogh had recently been painting a picture of a woman rocking a cradle, using Madame Roulins as his model. He felt great affection for the Roulins family and may have envied the love and attention their children received. In mutilating himself, Van Gogh may have been attempting to obtain care and love from these substitute parents. The immediate response of Madame Roulins is not known, but Monsieur Roulins came to Van Gogh's aid on the night of the injury and helped to care for him afterward.

8. Van Gogh had a great sympathy for prostitutes and identified with their status as social outcasts. One suggestion is that his self-mutilation was a reflection of this identification. "In June, just a few months before butchering his ear, he had written that 'the whore is like meat in a butcher shop': when he treated his own body as 'meat in a butcher's shop,' he reversed their roles, identified himself with the whore, and showed his sympathy for her" (Lubin, 1972, p. 169).

9. Vincent felt that his mother saw him as too rough and as a bad boy. During the psychotic state surrounding this incident, primitive symbolic thought processes may have led Van Gogh to cut off his ear from a desire to be perceived more positively by his mother. "Because the unconscious mind tends to regard protuberances as masculine and aggressive, removing the protuberant part of the ear may have been to inform the prostitute, a substitute for his mother, that he was not an aggressive, hurtful male—the 'rough' boy whom his mother disliked—but helpless, penetrable, the victim of a hurt" (Lubin, 1972, p. 173).

10. It is likely that Van Gogh experienced frightening auditory hallucinations during his psychotic attack similar to those he experienced in other attacks. Afterward, while in the sanatorium, he wrote that other patients heard strange sounds and voices as he had and speculated in one case that this was probably due to a disease of nerves in the ear. Thus, in a psychotic state, Van Gogh could have felt that his own ear was diseased and cut it off to silence the disturbing sounds.

11. In the Garden of Gethsemane scene in the Bible, Simon Peter cut off the ear of Malchus, a servant of the high priest, who had come to seize Christ. This scene had been on Van Gogh's mind. He attempted to paint it in the summer of 1888 and also mentioned it in a letter to his sister in October. In his delirium, Van Gogh may have acted out the scene at Gethsemane, carrying out the roles of both victim and aggressor.

12. Another explanation is that Vincent identified with the crucified Jesus and that the Virgin Mary lamenting over the dead body of Christ represented Vincent's mother. "In giving the mother surrogate, Rachel, a dead segment of his body, Vincent symbolically repeated the scene on Calvary" (Lubin, 1972, p. 179).

13. Vincent Van Gogh lived in the shadow of a dead brother, also named Vincent, who died at birth exactly one year before Vincent the painter was born. It is suggested that Vincent had the feeling he was unloved by a mother who continued

to grieve over an idealized lost son. Killing part of himself may have been an attempt to win his mother's love. Vincent's self-mutilation "represented a symbolic death, exhibiting Vincent in the image of his dead brother, the first Vincent—someone mother adored. As a gift, the severed ear was specifically the gift of a baby, a dead baby. Thus it was both a reliving of wishes to unite him with mother and a bitter mockery of his mother's attachment to her dead son" (Lubin, 1972, pp. 182–183).

What to Make of These Alternative Explanations?

Here are thirteen different psychodynamic explanations for why Van Gogh cut off his ear and gave it to a prostitute, and additional interpretations have been proposed (Lubin, 1972; Nagera, 1967; Schneider, 1950; Schnier, 1950; Untermeyer, 1955; Westerman Holstijn, 1951). There is also a substantial list of biological explanations for Van Gogh's disturbances (Monroe, 1978; Tralbaut, 1969). How should we interpret these alternative explanations? Are all of them true, are some true and some false, or, perhaps, are none of them true? Do the various explanations conflict, so that if one is chosen then one or more of the others must be rejected, or do a number of them supplement each other? Is there, perhaps, some other explanation that would replace all of these possibilities? Do we end up with a feeling that we understand Van Gogh's behavior, that we know why he acted as he did?

Individuals may vary widely in their responses to this material. From one point of view, it is a richly woven tapestry connecting a single event to many themes, conflicts, symbols, and unconscious wishes and processes in Van Gogh's life. According to the principle of "overdetermination," which suggests that actions typically have multiple causes and meanings, this material can be seen as a rich set of complementary explanations for Van Gogh's behavior. Lubin (1972) for example, after discussing a number of possible explanations, suggests that

there may be truth in all of these suggestions. One's motivations include the superficial fac-

tors that are well known to oneself as well as deep, troubling factors that one would vehemently deny when confronted with them. Man carries his conflicts from one period of life to the next, and each stage of development puts its mark on the next. (p. 163)

From the standpoint of overdetermination, it would be surprising to find a single explanation for any human action, and events can be expected to have more than one cause, more than one meaning. At other points, Lubin states that "various aspects of Vincent's life converged in this single episode" (p. 155) and that what we have is a set of "interrelated" explanations (p. 182).

A second way of making sense of these multiple explanations is to note that several of the different explanations are concerned with different aspects or features of the larger episode. For example, the choice of an ear may have been related to Van Gogh's observation of bullfights, the fact that it happened at Christmastime may have been associated with the presentation of the ear as a gift, and his choice of a prostitute as the recipient may have been related to recent publicized accounts of Jack the Ripper. A substantial number of interpretations, however, are concerned with similar aspects of the event. His choice of the ear has been related to his observation of bullfights, the newspaper accounts of Jack the Ripper, the ear as a phallic symbol, a belief that auditory hallucinations may have come from diseased nerves in the ear, and his concern with the Gethsemane scene.

A third approach is to work from the assumption that several of these explanations may be valid while the others are not, and that procedures for critically evaluating alternative explanations are needed in order to assess their relative credibility. The doctrine of overdetermination may be correct in that psychological events often have multiple causes and meanings, but to assume that all possible interpretations "are ultimately members of one happy family is to abandon critical thinking altogether" (Hirsch, 1967, p. 164). For therapeutic purposes, it may be useful to explore as many meanings as possible for a single event, but for scientific or explanatory purposes, it is necessary both to critically assess the plausibility of alternative explanations and then to examine the extent to which the remaining explanations supplement or conflict with one another.

A fourth possible response is to think that all of this symbolic interpretation is somewhat arbitrary, perhaps even hopelessly arbitrary. If interpretations can be generated merely by noting similarities between the event in question and earlier events and experiences, then connections "are embarrassingly easy to find" and "the number of possible (and plausible) explanations is infinite" (Spence, 1976, pp. 377, 379). It can be argued that the process of interpretation is so loose and flexible that it can be used to explain anything, and its opposite, not only once but in many different ways. A milder version of this criticism is that the process of psychodynamic interpretation is perfectly legitimate but that it has been used with insufficient constraint in this particular example.

The Critical Evaluation of Explanatory Conjectures

This incident forcefully raises several basic questions about the logic of explanation in psychobiography. What procedures exist, or can be developed, for critically evaluating alternative explanations of life events? How can we know whether we do or do not have a "good" explanation of a particular event or set of events in a life history? The Van Gogh example is useful in that it pushes the explanatory endeavor further than usual by suggesting a wide range of possible interpretations, with supporting evidence for each. In doing so, it raises with unusual clarity questions about the generation of explanatory hypotheses, about the critical evaluation of such hypotheses, and about the choice among, or integration of, a variety of explanatory possibilities.

It seems helpful, following Popper (1962), to distinguish between the processes of conjecture and refutation and to make a distinction between the processes of generating and critically evaluating explanatory conjectures. The literature on Van Gogh provides an excellent example of the processes of explanatory conjecture and can also be used to illustrate the process of critically evaluating such conjectures. Consider, for example, the hypothesis that Van Gogh may have been influenced by contemporary newspaper accounts of Jack the Ripper. This particular explanation depends on the assumption that Van Gogh read these stories in the local paper, that he noticed the ear-cutting detail mentioned in two of the fifteen stories, that it made a lasting impression on him, and that it influenced him the night he mutilated his own ear. This explanation depends on a chain of assumptions, none of which has direct empirical support, which leaves this particular conjecture relatively unsubstantiated.

In comparison, the probability that he was influenced in his actions by visions of a matador and bull may be somewhat higher (although still perhaps low on an absolute basis) in that his letters indicate that he had attended bullfights in Arles. There is evidence that he had at least witnessed this scene, and that it had made an impression on him, whereas we can only presume that he may have read about Jack the Ripper and his cutting of ears.

Consider also the theory that he identified with a prostitute by treating his own body like meat in a butcher shop. The phrase "the whore is like meat in a butcher's shop" occurred in a letter in June 1888, 6 months before the ear-cutting incident. Without further supporting evidence that this image occurred to Van Gogh nearer in time to the ear-cutting incident, there is little reason to believe that it played a significant part in his self-mutilation.

Part of the evidence supporting an Oedipal interpretation of the incident also seems open to question. Gauguin did not report that Van Gogh threatened him with a razor until 15 years after the incident; indeed, in Gauguin's account to a friend four days after the event, this was not mentioned. Gauguin left Arles for Paris immediately after Van Gogh's self-mutilation. It has been suggested by Rewald (1956) that Gauguin was concerned about the propriety of his conduct and may have invented the threat story later as a justification for having abandoned Van Gogh in a moment of crisis.

In yet another explanation, Untermeyer (1955) suggested that Van Gogh "had cut off an ear and sent it to one of the prostitutes he and Gauguin had visited. It was a Christmas present, a return for being teased about his over-sized ears" (p. 235). There are several reasons for being suspicious of this particular explanation. As far as I have been able to determine, there is no evidence that Van Gogh was teased by the prostitute about the size of his ears. This highly relevant circumstance is not mentioned in such primary sources as Van Gogh's letters or Gauguin's memoirs or in far more extensive biographies of Van Gogh, such as Tralbaut's (1969) or Lubin's (1972), which contain detailed analyses of the ear-cutting episode. Furthermore, the same paragraph containing this assertion has at least two other factual errors in its description of the incident. Instead of supposing that Untermeyer's book of ninety-two biographical sketches has access to information unavailable to scholars such as Tralbaut, who has spent more than fifty years studying and writing about Van Gogh, it seems more reasonable to conclude that there is no reliable evidence supporting this explanatory conjecture and that the evidence was fabricated in order to produce a plausible account. Similar criticisms may be made of Meier-Graeffe's (1933) story that the prostitute had earlier asked Van Gogh for a five-franc piece, he had refused, and that she then said that "if he could not give her a five franc piece he might at least honour her with one of his large lop-ears for a Christmas present" (p. 163).

An explanation not based on such unreliable evidence rests on Van Gogh's report several months later in the sanatorium that other patients heard words and voices, just as he had, probably because of diseased nerves of the ear. Such beliefs may have played a part in the ear-mutilation episode.

Perhaps the single most strongly supported explanatory factor in Vincent's breakdown was the perceived loss of his brother's care. Specifically, the ear-cutting incident and two later mental breakdowns coincided with learning of Theo's engagement, his marriage, and the birth of his first child. In each case, Vincent was threatened by the prospect of losing his main source of emotional and financial support, as it seemed that Theo might redirect his love and money toward his new family (Tralbaut, 1969).

A masochistic response under situations of rejection or loss of love was not alien to Van Gogh. In 1881, he had visited the parents of Kee

Voss, a woman he loved but who was avoiding him. When he heard that Kee had left the house in order to avoid seeing him, Van Gogh "put his hand in the flame of the lamp and said, 'Let me see her for as long as I can keep my hand in the flame'" (Tralbaut, 1969, p. 79). They blew out the lamp and said that he could not see her. These other incidents make it seem more likely that Van Gogh's self-mutilation was influenced by a perceived loss of love from his brother.

It is no easy task to winnow through a range of explanatory hypotheses, and given limitations in the accessible evidence about historical events, it is sometimes impossible to directly test every explanatory conjecture. However, substantial progress can still be made in identifying faulty explanations and in gathering corroborative evidence in support of others. Explanations and interpretations can be evaluated in light of criteria such as (a) their logical soundness; (b) their comprehensiveness in accounting for a number of puzzling aspects of the events in question; (c) their survival of tests of attempted falsification, such as tests of derived predictions or retrodictions; (d) their consistency with the full range of available relevant evidence; (e) their support from above, or their consistency with more general knowledge about human functioning or about the person in question; and (f) their credibility relative to other explanatory hypotheses (Bromley, 1977, chap. 8; Cheshire, 1975; Crosby, 1979; Hempel, 1965, 1966; Sherwood, 1969).

For each explanatory problem we can imagine a tree of explanatory inquiries, with the trunk representing the initial question or puzzle, each limb representing an explanatory conjecture, and smaller branches off the limb representing tests of that particular hypothesis or conjecture. Any single explanatory hypothesis can be submitted to a variety of tests, with each test providing partial, although not definitive, corroboration or disconfirmation of the hypothesis.

The least developed inquiries would consist of a trunk with a single limb, representing a single explanatory conjecture that has received little or no critical examination. A comprehensive explanatory inquiry would resemble a well-developed tree, containing a great variety of explanatory conjectures, with extensive testing of each explanatory hypothesis. This picture of an ideal tree, or of a fully rational explanatory inquiry, provides a framework for assessing the progress of particular explanatory inquiries and for visualizing what has been done in relation to what could be done.

The Search for Single Explanations

Psychobiographical studies of individual lives are often criticized for being open to a variety of explanations. For instance, it is claimed that Freud's case studies "suffer from the critical flaw of being open to many interpretations" (Liebert & Spiegler, 1978, p. 50). Popper (1962) states:

> Every conceivable case could be interpreted in the light of Adler's theory, or equally of Freud's. . . . I could not think of any human behavior which could not be interpreted in terms of either theory. It was precisely this fact—that they always fitted, that they were always confirmed—which in the eyes of their admirers constituted the strongest argument in favour of these theories. It began to dawn on me that this apparent strength was in fact their weakness. (p. 35)

Similarly, Gergen (1977) says: "The events of most people's lives are sufficiently variegated and multifarious that virtually any theoretical template can be validated. The case study simply allows the investigator freedom to locate the facts lending support to his or her preformulated convictions" (p. 142).

These criticisms are, I believe, overstated and apply most readily to poorly developed explanatory inquiries. It may be possible to interpret any life with any theory, but often only at the cost of distortion or selective presentation of the evidence. Any explanatory conjecture can be made, but not all of them stand up under critical examination. In legal proceedings, self-serving explanations of the course of events by a guilty defendant often crumble under rigorous cross-examination. Similarly, explanations of a life history using a particular theory sometimes fail to stand up under critical examination. For example, the disorders of George III had widely been seen as manic-depressive psychosis until Macalpine and Hunter

(1969) persuasively reinterpreted them as symptoms of porphyria, a hereditary metabolic disturbance. Even if some evidence can be found in a life history that is consistent with a wide variety of theories, this does not mean that all of these theories provide an adequate interpretation of the events in question.

Critical testing of the claims and implications of various explanations can lead to the elimination of many of them as implausible or highly unlikely. Ideally, this process will lead to a single well-supported explanation. In some cases, though, even after a great number of unsatisfactory conjectures are eliminated, more than one explanation that is consistent with the available evidence may remain. We are sometimes faced with "many possible explanations, all of which may be equally valid theoretically and which the facts equally fit, and when this happens there is no way we can say which explanation is the most correct" (Pye, 1979, p. 53).

This problem may not be frequently encountered in everyday practice, where minimal resources are available for inquiry, where investigation ceases once a single plausible explanation is reached, or where inquiry stops once an interpretation consistent with a prevailing theoretical orthodoxy is produced. However, if an explanatory problem is extensively investigated, if it is approached from a variety of theoretical perspectives, or if it touches on conflicting social and political interests, it becomes more likely that a variety of alternative explanations will be generated.

Conclusion

It is sometimes suggested that interpretation of single cases is little more than an arbitrary application of one's theoretical preferences. No doubt this happens at times, but *any* method can be poorly used. Effective use of the case study method requires not only the formulation of explanations consistent with some of the evidence but also that preferred explanations be critically examined in light of all available evidence, and that they be compared in plausibility with alternative explanations. After the implausible alternatives have been eliminated, more than one explanation consistent with the available evidence may remain, but this is far different from saying that the facts can be adequately explained in terms of any theoretical conjecture.

When faced with a puzzling historical or clinical phenomenon, investigators are sometimes too ready to accept the first psychodynamic interpretation that makes previously mysterious events appear comprehensible. The case of Van Gogh's ear illustrates the dangers of this approach, as further inquiry often yields a variety of other apparently plausible explanations. When this happens, it is not sufficient to suggest that all of the explanations may be simultaneously true; this situation, rather, requires that the alternative explanatory conjectures be critically evaluated and compared in terms of their relative plausibility.

In some cases, critical analysis of the range of possible interpretations may enable us to reject all but one of the alternatives, but in other cases, we may end up with a "surplus" of explanatory possibilities, each of which is consistent with the available evidence, and with no apparent means for deciding among them. The psychobiographical enterprise must, it seems, steer between the Scylla of inexplicable events and the Charybdis of phenomena open to a troubling variety of alternative explanations.

Despite these difficulties, the problem of developing explanations of events in individual lives deserves our critical attention as it is inevitably encountered in everyday life and is a crucial task within personology, psychobiography, and the clinical professions. Further work is needed both on the intriguing epistemological question of what degrees of certainty can and cannot be attained in the explanation of events in individual lives and on the methodological problem of how best to develop such explanations.

References

Allport, G.W. (1961). Pattern and growth in personality. New York: Holt, Rinehart, & Winston.

Allport, G.W. (1965). Letters from Jenny. New York: Harcourt, Brace, & World.

Anderson, J.W. (1981). The methodology of psychological biography. Journal of Interdisciplinary History, 11(3), 455–475.

Bromley, D.B. (1977). Personality description in ordinary language. New York: Wiley.

Cheshire, N.M. (1975). The nature of psychodynamic interpretation. London: Wiley.

Crosby, F. (1979). Evaluating psychohistorical explanations. Psychohistory Review, 7(4), 6–16.

Elms, A. (1976). Personality in politics. New York: Harcourt Brace Jovanovich.

Gedo, J.E. (1972). The methodology of psychoanalytic biography. Journal of the American Psychoanalytic Association, 21, 638–649.

George, A.L. (1971). Some uses of dynamic psychology in political biography. In F.J. Greenstein & M.L. Lerner (Eds.), A source book for the study of personality and politics. Chicago: Markham.

Gergen, K.J. (1977). Stability, change, and chance in understanding human development. In N. Datan & H. Reese (Eds.), Life-span developmental psychology: Dialectical perspectives on experimental research. New York: Academic Press.

Glad, B. (1973). Contributions of psychobiography. In J. Knutson (Ed.), Handbook of political psychology. San Francisco: Jossey-Bass.

Hempel, C.G. (1965). Aspects of scientific explanation. New York: Free Press.

Hempel, C.G. (1966). Philosophy of natural science. Englewood Cliffs, N.J.: Prentice-Hall.

Hirsch, E.D., Jr. (1967). Validity in interpretation. New Haven, Conn.: Yale University Press.

Hogan, R. (1976). Personality theory: The personological tradition. Englewood Cliffs, N.J.: Prentice-Hall.

Izenberg, G. (1975). Psychohistory and intellectual history. History and Theory, 14, 139–155.

Liebert, R.M., & Spiegler, M.D. (1978). Personality: Strategies and issues. Homewood, Ill.: Dorsey Press.

Lifton, R.J., & Olson, E. (Eds.). (1974). Explorations in psychohistory. New York: Simon & Schuster.

Lubin, A.J. (1972). Stranger on the earth: A psychological biography of Vincent Van Gogh. New York: Holt, Rinehart, & Winston.

Macalpine, I., & Hunter, R. (1969). George III and the mad business. New York: Pantheon Books.

Mack, J.E. (1971). Psychoanalysis and historical biography. Journal of the American Psychoanalytic Association, 19, 143–179.

Mazlish, B. (1968). Clio on the couch: Prolegomena to psychohistory. Encounter, 31, 46–64.

Meier-Graeffe, J. (1933). Vincent Van Gogh: A biographical study (trans. J. Holroyd-Reece). New York: Blue Ribbon Books.

Meyer, B.C. (1972). Some reflections on the contribution of psychoanalysis to biography. In R. Holt & E. Peterfreund (Eds.), Psychoanalysis and contemporary science (Vol. 1). New York: International Universities Press.

Monroe, R.R. (1978). The episodic psychoses of Vincent Van Gogh. Journal of Nervous and Mental Disease, 166, 480–488.

Murray, H.A., et al. (1938). Explorations in personality. New York: Oxford University Press.

Nagera, H. (1967). Vincent Van Gogh: A psychological study. London: Allen & Unwin.

Popper, K.R. (1962). Conjectures and refutations: The growth of scientific knowledge. New York: Basic Books.

Pye, L. (1979). Letter to the editor. Psychohistory Review, 8(3), 50–53.

Rewald, J. (1956). Post-impressionism from Van Gogh to Gauguin. New York: Museum of Modern Art.

Runyan, W.M. (1978). The life course as a theoretical orientation: Sequences of person-situation interaction. Journal of Personality, 46, 569–593.

Runyan, W.M. (1980a). Alternative accounts of lives: An argument for epistemological relativism. Biography, 3, 209–224.

Runyan, W.M. (1980b). A stage-state analysis of the life course. Journal of Personality and Social Psychology, 38, 951–962.

Schneider, D.E. (1950). The psychoanalyst and the artist. New York: International Universities Press.

Schnier, J. (1950). The blazing sun: A psychoanalytic approach to Van Gogh. American Imago, 7, 143–162.

Sherwood, M. (1969). The logic of explanation in psychoanalysis. New York: Academic Press.

Spence, D.P. (1976). Clinical interpretation: Some comments on the nature of evidence. In T. Shapiro (Ed.), Psychoanalysis and contemporary science (Vol. 5). New York: International Universities Press.

Tralbaut, M.E. (1969). Vincent Van Gogh. New York: Macmillan.

Untermeyer, L. (1955). Makers of the modern world. New York: Simon & Schuster.

Westerman Holstijn, A.J. (1951). The psychological development of Vincent Van Gogh. American Imago, 8, 239–273.

White, R.W. (Ed.). (1963). The study of lives. New York Atherton Press.

White, R.W. (1975). Lives in progress (3rd ed.). New York: Holt, Rinehart, & Winston.

Chapter 7

Kate Isaacson

Divide and Multiply: Comparative Theory and Methodology in Multiple Case Psychobiography

Since the inception of psychobiography as a method for studying lives (Freud, 1910/1957), the field has primarily focused on in-depth empirical analyses of the single case. Over the course of the last century, analytical approaches and methods have grown more complex, taking into account an ever-increasing set of variables, including context, the environment, and close relationships. The field has begun to move away from exclusive analysis of the single case and is now, with more frequency than ever before, focusing on both interactions between people and comparisons among small groups of people.

Several psychobiographers have already adopted the analysis of multiple subjects as an appropriate tack for their studies (e.g., Schultz, chap. 3 this vol.). As the field of psychology in general focuses more on close relationships (e.g., at-tachment theory) and interaction schemas (e.g., Baldwin, 1995), psychobiographers will likely be rewarded with even more sophisticated theoretical tools with which to undertake multiple case comparative psychobiographical research.

Though, as noted, such studies do seem to be increasingly common, so far the psychobiographical literature has been silent regarding precise methods for multiple subject analysis. The comparative approach has yet to be articulated systematically. In this chapter I accordingly offer a model for the psychobiographical study of two or more lives, specifically addressing the ways they are distinct entities and, importantly, how they converge. I also provide guidelines for comparative psychobiographical studies, including a discussion of types of multiple case studies, advantages offered by this approach, theoretical models one might draw upon to enhance such a study, and a discussion of classic examples of the multiple subject approach.

Why Study More Than One Life?

Psychobiographical inquiries concern themselves with a common goal, understanding the individual life by identifying the specific psychological patterns within individuals and the dynamics between individuals and their environments. At this level of analysis, one might understand an individual better by examining the role of significant others in his or her life story in a single case psychobiography, or by actually seeing him or her through the eyes of a significant other in a multiple subject psychobiography. The role of subject and object is the main criterion establishing the need for a multiple case psychobiography. If each person in your study is taken as *both subject and object*, then it would seem you have good grounds for the endeavor. Or, alternatively, if you place each figure in the role of "subject," then analyze each in his or her own right, once again you have the makings of a multiple psychobiography. For example, Doris K. Goodwin's treatment of the Roosevelts in her psychobiography *No Ordinary Time* (1994) takes a comparative approach to each figure, analyzing each separately and then conducting post hoc analyses. If, on the other hand, you are attempting to understand your subject by elucidating the role played in his or her life by significant others, you may not need to conduct a full-blown multiple-case psychobiography because it isn't necessary to complete separate analyses of each subject. The simple act of taking the perspective of other characters in the life of your main character does not establish your study as a multiple subject psychobiography.

Perhaps the most common type of multiple case psychobiographical study (addressed in more detail below) is one relying on comparison. Political psychobiographers sometimes compare two leaders to provide more richly contextual profiles of each. Jerrold Post recently edited a compendium of psychobiographical studies, by different researchers, of both Saddam Hussein and Bill Clinton (*The Psychological Assessment of Political Leaders* 2003). Betty Glad (chap. 24 this vol.) compares and contrasts a number of historical and modern day tyrants. Howard Gardner, over the years, has conducted a number of side-by-side studies of "creatives" and geniuses. And Alan Elms includes a handful of useful comparative-type chapters in *Uncovering Lives* (1994).

How do dual subject psychobiographies differ from psychobiographies of single subjects? A multiple case psychobiography is more than a discrete collection of single subject psychobiographical studies. The defining feature is that multiple subject studies provide not only complete psychobiograpical analyses of the individual lives, that is, n = 1 within-subject assessments, but also move beyond each life to draw comparisons *between* subjects. In statistical analyses, we ordinarily call this distinction one of design, as studies are often either within-subjects or between-subjects enterprises—but by using this model in a different context multiple case studies offer both perspectives. Each inquiry looks at more than one subject either to compare/contrast them, or because they significantly interact. So though they vary widely in form from study to study, multiple case psychobiographies have two necessary components: individual psychobiographical analyses and comparative analyses across subjects. This latter component may also include analyses of the interaction between the subjects.

How does a multiple subject psychobiography differ from a small statistical study with an ample amount of data on each subject? Is it nomothetic? Is it idiographic? It actually enters a new category. Allport referred to this methodology as "morphogenic," a dimensional commitment to study common elements between all subjects and to examine the development of patterned structures out of common elements (for an example and discussion see *Letters from Jenny*, 1965). The multiple subject study similarly benefits from some of the strengths of the nomothetic approach by creating a comparison group, for which general laws and principles can be discovered; but because each subject is approached with idiographic means, no meaningful data on, or understanding of, the whole life is lost.

As is well known, psychobiographical studies typically use an iterative method. Through this approach theories are developed and further refined *throughout* the process of data collection and theory testing in order to find the best "marriage" of data and theory (for more on the iterative nature of psychobiography, see Schultz, chap. 1 this vol.). There are two main ways to proceed iteratively in a multiple case study:

1. *Serial iteration*: This involves separate data sets for each subject, and discrete idiographic hypotheses for each, as well. The side-by-side creation of comparison on each subject (separate idiographic theory formation) is then followed by cross-comparison of hypotheses across subjects.
2. *Parallel iteration*: In this method, all of the data for the subjects are pooled and are treated as a single set. The researcher then generates a single narrative through the iterative method, about all subjects.

To summarize, the central benefit of multiple subject psychobiography is that it affords analysis of the interaction between two or more people, comparision of two or more significant lives, and assessment of validity, or at least an enhanced perspective on a single historical outcome (e.g., the creation of a scientific theory or a collaborative writing venture). In any event, $N > 1$ offers the prospect of a deeper understanding of each life under analysis.

Choosing to Conduct a Multiple Subject Psychobiography

So, let's say you've decided to conduct a multiple subject psychobiography. In order to be truly effective, you need to figure out exactly *why you are looking at more than one subject*, and *what relationship your subjects have to one another*. This will help you guide your data collection, select your theory (or theories), and construct your analyses. Some common subject pairings are these:

1. Looking at an outcome or work that is the product of two individuals
2. Looking at both parties of a relationship
3. Comparing two people who have something significant in common (e.g., politicians, writers)
4. Looking at an historical, political, social, or cultural movement
5. Using comparative psychobiography for theory building, testing, and development

In addition to these five most common *pairings* of subjects, there are also two main *types* of multiple subject psychobiographies: (1) direct/indirect contact among the subjects under analysis and (2) categorical or single-dimension pairing. The means of distinction revolves around the relationship between the subjects. To place your study you need ask yourself, why have I grouped these individuals together? Also, you must clarify why one life might shed light on, or enhance the understanding of, the other. Let's look a little more closely now at these two categories.

1. Direct/Indirect Contact

The first type of pairing involves subjects whose lives have some sort of dynamic effect on one another—for instance, Sylvia Plath and Ted Hughes, or Diego Rivera and Frida Kahlo. These subjects may come into direct contact with one another, as in the case of a marriage or a family study (e.g., Mazlish's [1975] study of James and John Stuart Mill), or they may interact from a distance, as in the case of G.H.W. Bush and Saddam Hussein (Elms, 1994), or G.H.W. Bush and Mikhail Gorbachev (Winter & Herman et al., 1991).

When lives directly or indirectly overlap a range of comparisons are possible. One can explore any one of the five common vicissitudes described above, but other equally promising avenues open up as well. First, *reactions to and renditions of a single event can be compared.* This might tell us about each subject's means of processing information, and his/her tendencies regarding cognitive interpretation. If external sources of data are available, issues of validity might be broached with respect to the integrity of the information provided by the subject. Second, *the comparison can shed light on the relational style and interpersonal proclivities of each subject.* Data about, and interpretations of, the "other" can be directly assessed vis-à-vis the eyes of each subject; analyses of transactions can be contextually analyzed and reinforced by the psychological patterns and life theories already developed on each subject. Further, the interaction data can assist the iterative enterprise *by providing a continued basis for theory testing and development.* Third, a *theoretical model might be used to specifically explore the interpersonal relationship between the two subjects.* For example, narrative analysis, psychosocial theory, or attachment theory (interpersonal scripts or working models) might clarify issues regarding the place and function each subject has in the life story of the other. The comparative analyses may reveal similar or different roles and functions for each subject in the perspective of the other. Fourth, in some cases *the subjects may either be co-players or counterplayers in the life of the other.* I discuss many of these broader possibilities in more detail below.

2. Categorical Pairing or Single Dimension Comparison

If the lives of one's subjects do not come into direct or indirect contact, then pairing has most likely occurred because each person has something significant in common with the other. This similarity of whatever kind makes comparison of the lives useful. The basis for such a study might relate to commonalities, or dialectical differences, in the areas of: career (e.g., politicians, musicians, writers, artists, or scientists); sociohistorical context (e.g., American expatriates in

Paris in the 1920s or contemporary Scientologists); race (e.g., eminent African Americans); gender roles (e.g., stay-at-home fathers); economic class (e.g., the urban poor); and so on. A primary advantage of the comparative approach in these cases is that it provides the researcher with the ability to assess the similarity of the subjects on one variable, and to comparatively explore similarities and individual differences on a variety of other variables. For instance, one might choose to conduct psychobiographical studies of two politicians, Abraham Lincoln and Bill Clinton, and through comparison, explore themes of family background, early educational experiences, motives, political styles, interpersonal styles, personal writings, romantic relationships, reactions to political adversaries, and post-presidency pursuits. The basis for comparison is the subjects' common role as U.S. President. The results of the comparison will ideally be integrated into, or inform, the evolving research on each subject, and provide the groundwork for comparison in the final psychobiographical accounts.

What can the comparison of two ostensibly unrelated lives add to the understanding of each life? For example, how might studying the lives of 2 philosophers, even from different eras (e.g., Sartre and Socrates or Confucius and Camus), lend insight into both? First, articulating the similarities and differences in lives richly satisfies at least one, and in some ways two, of the main aims of the study of personality: we learn how a person is in some ways like some other people, and in some ways like no other people (see Kluckhohn & Murray, 1953). Evolving accounts of each life offer a detailed and contextually vivid basis for the tandem comparison of motives and values, development and changes, antecedents and outcomes, and basic personality and behavioral patterns. In some cases this will provide for a richer understanding of the person than that achieved by other methods, including psychobiographical studies of single subjects and mid-level nomothetic studies of individual differences, which often focus on delineating a reduced number of decontextualized life variables for comparison. Either of the above types—direct/indirect contact or categorical/single dimension pairing—might fortuitously use a comparative

approach to enhance iterative psychobiographical research on each subject. For example, if one happens to be studying two researchers who co-developed a theory (i.e., Watson & Crick), the multiple case method provides a basis for idiographic comparison relating to how each subject came to the research area, and how each developed subsequent to the articulation of the theory. The comparative framework also might include an account of how each subject interacted with the other throughout their period of joint research and theory development. The final narrative account of each individual life may even clarify questions relating to authorship and specific contributions to the theory.

The practice of multiple case psychobiography of whatever sort is also particularly useful if one wishes to clarify a theory or test its utility by applying it to notably different subjects. Using subjects who are similar can help establish reliability, while utilizing subjects different from one another creates a perspective on the broadness of the range of a theory's applicability. For instance Schultz developed his notion of the prototypical scene (see Schultz, chap. 3 this vol.) after encountering identical types of invasive memories in the lives of a subset of writers and artists, including Kathryn Harrison, Truman Capote, Jack Kerouac, Sylvia Plath, and Diane Arbus. Theory testing and development is an extraordinarily important and necessary function in personality psychology, one that is often—and sadly—overlooked. Psychological research most often focuses on broad, decontextualized part-processes; keeping theory in mind is critical, however, if researchers hope ever to produce cohesive (rather than idiosyncratic) interpretations of their results and establish relevance related to overall directional developments in the field. Ultimately, there comes a time when all research findings need to be integrated and assessed in the context of the "whole," especially when this "whole" is a human life. If one proposes to explain a system as complex as individual personality, integrated theory is essential. Case studies and multiple case psychobiographies provide the ideal format to put theories to the test by applying them to real lives, to ensure they actually enhance our evolving understanding of human experience.

Issues of Theory: One or Many?

Psychobiographical approaches include a range of subjects, theoretical approaches, and research questions. In essence, the best way to describe the enterprise is to say that psychobiography is a diverse and evolving methodology of *ways of looking* at individual, or sets of individual, lives. One strength of the psychobiographical model is its inherent flexibility in accommodating a variety of theoretical and analytical approaches from personality-social psychology. Because of this, the toolbox of theories from which psychobiographers draw is always up to date and on the cutting edge of research. The unique patterns presented by the individual life or lives under analysis can be powerfully explored and idiographically represented. Multiple theories may be used to explain different aspects of any individual life. Although multiple subject psychobiographies are in no way limited in the potential theoretical models according to which the data can be analyzed, the key questions for the studies may guide the selection and use of theory toward those focusing on relationships or interactions. In the case of psychobiographical studies used for theory exploration and development, the theory of interest will serve as the de facto model for approaching the lives under study. These objectives allow for the identification of a rather abridged list of theories that may prove useful for multiple case analysis.

Object Relations Theories.   Attachment theory, an object relations theory, is one of the most significant approaches to personality theory in the early 21st century, and a principal framework for the study of close relationships. This may provide the most useful framework for assessing interpersonal schemas and working models and the events that lead to their development and change. It also seems reasonable to take the basic themes of attachment theory and look at how each played out in the lives of subjects. For example, attachment theory addresses issues of maternal separation, anxiety-avoidance, secure base, coherence, and explorative behavior, as well as interpersonal relationships with parents, friends, and romantic others. As Bowlby (1979) envi-sioned it, the theory is relevant "from the cradle to the grave."

Other Relationship Theories.   Relationship theories are enjoying a renaissance in psychology. Previous studies of relationships have included a variety of models and variables that may prove useful to a multiple subject study. Kelley (1983) describes a relationship as "a pair's degree of interdependence" (frequency, diversity, and strength of meshed interconnections). This definition allows for a broad application of theory to many types of subject pairings, from intimate to more formal involvement. Comparative studies can be executed as a means of relationship analysis, in which case the relationship itself would rightly be the variable of interest. There are three levels of a relationship analysis. The *macrocontext*, which is the overall context in which the subjects exist; the *mesocontext*, the relationship settings; and the *microcontext*, the pair's own intimate environment, constructed over time by the partners's unique interaction (Levinger & Levinger, 2003). The analysis of dyadic interaction at each level, from the environment to the specific rules and norms created by the relationship, can lead to important revelations about each subject. Aron's (1992) relationship identity theory regarding inclusion of self in the other might be an especially valuable guide for deciphering relationship dynamics.

Psychobiographers often neglect systematically dealing with the complex dynamics presented by environmental variables in the lives of their subjects (relationships, context, time, norms). Given the narrative goal of psychobiography, this last frontier must not, however, be excluded. It is important to piece together environmental context and the conditions in which subjects thrive or struggle. The many interactive systems in the life of the individual can be accounted for within the psychological ecosystem of the subject.

One way to conceptualize influential relationships is via a systems theoretical approach. A truly systematic mindset can describe a coherent version of these principles, and demonstrate how they increase the effectiveness of their service. In this way, the psychobiographer would use systems theory to assess relationships between two people, and their complex sequences and patterns of interactions, or communications. The goal is to understand environmental effects and what they mean, and to fully explore dyadic interpersonal interactions in cardinal relationships.

Interaction Theories.   Interaction theories offer a relatively comprehensive analysis of exceptionally complex phenomena: interactions and relationships. They are ideally suited to two interacting subjects. For example, long term partners develop relationship-specific norms to solve interdependence problems. Tomkins' Script Theory (1987) focuses on the development, maintenance, and evolution of schemas and scripts regarding the relationships between personal experiences and affect. Most couples develop their own relationship norms that govern both the relationship and extra-relationship involvement (Buunk, 1987), therefore such norms should be a useful guide to the study of relationship interactions. Similarly, partners adopt rules concerning the distribution of resources—equity, equality, or need—and experience discomfort when these standards are violated (Walster et. al., 1978). Because many allocation rules are relationship specific, and as such idiosyncratic, an ideal way to investigate these rules is through a multiple case study. For example, in a communal relationship the norms guiding behavior are need based rather than contribution based (Fiske, 1992). These are normal adaptations that regulate interaction by promoting specific expectations about partners' motives and by prompting specific motives and behavior in response to specific interdependence patterns.

Players and Counterplayers.   As Elms has explained, "At times, the psychobiographer can understand crucial events in a subject's life only by looking at a counterplayer's activities as well" (1994, p. 207). The concept of a "counterplayer" was first introduced by Erik Erikson (1969) in his psychobiography of Mahatma Gandhi. Counterplayers are people who work in some way to oppose the life goals of an individual, and do so to such a degree that they assume a symbolic place in his or her life. They become, in effect, a kind of "nemesis." (Gandhi's counter-

player was a one-time friend who joined the opposing side of a labor dispute). Counterplayers "become occupied for a time with what they see as our role in *their* game, and they play to beat us" (Elms, 1994, p. 206). The feeling is often mutual, as in the case of Saddam Hussein and George H.W. Bush (Elms, 1994), though malice or even reciprocity of the role is not necessarily implied (i.e., my counterplayer may not regard me in the same way). The history of psychology, and of eminent individuals for that matter, is often marked by the presence of counterplayers. They on occasion facilitate an important shift in identity or orientation (e.g., Jung and Freud), or lead to a self-conscious blaze down a specific career or research path, as in the cases of Allport and Freud (see Barenbaum, chap. 16 this vol.), or James and Wundt (Anderson, 1981). Freud alone served as counterplayer to some of the greatest psychologists of the twentieth century.

If counterplayers impede our progress toward life goals, coplayers facilitate it. Psychobiographical studies have often focused on coplayers without labeling them as such, for example, the study of the friendship of Vita Sackville-West and Vera Brittain (Paul, 1991). Representing the flipside of the adversarial counterplayer, the coplayer is a person who consistently smooths our way. For example, a coplayer might be a valuable mentor who helps clarify and create opportunities for career development (e.g., the early relationship between Freud and Jung). In contrast, the presence of a counterplayer can be even more striking psychologically, given that people in opposition tend to display a good deal about their own self concept, identity, and motives in the act of positioning themselves against the other.

Conclusion

Psychobiography provides various *ways of looking* at lives. Multiple-case psychobiography, then, represents an evolving perspective in the study of lives—an alternative to the single case ($N = 1$) design most commonly used in the field. Psychological theorists and researchers have increasingly emphasized the role that relationships and dyadic interactions play as essential components in the context of human lives. Psychobiographical studies can explore and reflect these questions by considering interactions through multiple case studies.

In this chapter I describe a method of *parallel iteration* for conducting psychobiographies of interacting subjects. Paired with the recent advances in theories of close relationships, such an endeavor should be even more liable to reap benefits of enhanced insight and understanding of the individual life. Likewise, comparative case studies conducted in tandem, or via *serial iteration*, offer a method for investigating the commonalities of significant lives from a single discipline or field—e.g., the arts or psychology.

This nexus of theoretical trends and psychobiographical trends is no accident. The strength of psychobiographical study is that it is uniquely poised to take advantage of theoretical developments in a diversity of fields, not only from psychology but also in related areas such as history, political science, and critical theory. Psychobiography is intrinsically interdisciplinary in allowing the canvas of the human life to be explored and interpreted from the broadest possible perspective. Moving away from exclusive reliance on the single case, and allowing for the incorporation of more relational models of self, has the effect of broadening the range of possible analyses. This sort of broadening can only have a salutary impact on the field.

Although formal guidelines for comparative psychobiographical studies have, until now, not been articulated explicitly, Erikson's introduction of the concept of the "counterplayer" was a positive first step. It provided at least a preliminary roadmap for the treatment of the "other" in the study of the individual, at the same time outlining two typical roles and functions important "others" can play in individual lives. This chapter goes beyond Erikson to explore other avenues for comparative life studies research. As work in the comparative vein increases, additional models and prescriptive/proscriptive guidelines should slowly emerge, each making its own contribution to what is an evolving approach to the study of lives. This continual striving for authentic understanding reinforces the tradition of the psychobiographical enterprise in that the goal is ultimately to understand each life course in all its uniqueness, turns, and nuances.

I regard the multiple-case approach as progressive in the sense that the analysis of two (or more) lives in tandem can, in many ways, substantially increase our understanding of any single life in isolation. (See Runyan, 1991, for the presentation and explanation of a sequential procedure for generating and critically evaluating alternative explanatory conjectures and progress in psychobiographical accounts of lives.) In this chapter, I discussed five *main reasons* one might conduct a multiple subject psychobiography—for instance, because the subjects were co-creators of a significant scientific theory. Next I described the two *types* of relationships between multiple case subjects—that is, they either interact with each other in a way that is deemed significant or they are paired according to some common dimension, like field of achievement or notoriety. The goal of delineating the types of multiple case studies is to provide guidelines for a more focused and rigorous study of multiple subjects, as well as to put up some road signs for *possible types* of studies for future psychobiographers.

Finally, I referenced studies from the annals of psychobiography in which a multiple-case approach provided an advanced perspective, without which the studies would have been greatly diminished. These studies provide the historical precedent for this chapter and for the evolution of the field. There are so many novel questions we can ask in multiple subject studies, and such studies also give rise to a number of exciting new ways we can seek to understand human lives. George & George (1964), for instance, discovered a great deal about the personality of Woodrow Wilson by examining his connection with Colonel House. Similar gains have been made by looking closely at a number of complex and mutually self-defining relationships (e.g., Murray and Allport). It is not the striving for a multiple subject psychobiography that is new —only a detailed consideration of how it differs from the single case approach, and an articulation of the method. I hope this chapter has offered some inroads for charting this new direction.

References

Allport, G.W. (1965). Letters from Jenny. New York: Harcourt, Brace, Jovanovich.

Anderson, J.W. (1981). Psychobiographical Methodology: The Case of William James. Review of Personality and Social Psychology, 2.

Aron, A., Aron, E.N., & Smollan, D. (1992). Inclusion of other in the Self Scale and the structure of interpersonal closeness. Journal of Personality and Social Psychology, 63, 596–612.

Baldwin, M. (1995). Relational schemas and cognition in close relationships. Journal of Social & Personal Relationships, 12(4), 547–552.

Bowlby, J. (1979). The making and breaking of affectional bonds. London: Tavistock.

Buunk, B. (1987). Conditions that promote breakups as a consequence of extradyadic involvements. Journal of Social and Clinical Psychology, 5(3), 271–284.

Carlson, R. (1988). Exemplary lives: The use of psychobiography for theory development. Journal of Personality, 56, 105–138.

Elms, A.C. (1994). Uncovering lives: The uneasy alliance of biography and psychology. New York: Oxford University Press.

Erikson, E.H. (1969). Gandhi's truth. New York: Norton.

Fiske, S.T. (1992). Thinking is for doing: Portraits of social cognition from Daguerreotype to laserphoto. Journal of Personality and Social Psychology, 63(6), 877–889,

Freud, S. (1957). Leonardo da Vinci and a Memory of his Childhood. In J. Strachey (Ed. & Trans.), The standard edition of the complete psychological works of Sigmund Freud (Vol. 2). London: Hogarth Press (Original work published 1910)

George, A.L., & George, J.L. (1964). Woodrow Wilson and Colonel House. New York: Dover.

Goodheart, W.B. (1994). C.G. Jung's First Patient: On the seminal emergence of Jung's thought. Journal of Analytical Psychology, 29.

Karen, R. (1994). Becoming attached: First relationships and how they shape our capacity to love. New York: Warner Books.

Karpas, M.J. (1915). Socrates in the light of modern psychopathology. Journal of Abnormal Psychology, 10, 185–200.

Kelley, H.H. (1983). The situational origins of human tendencies: A further reason for the formal analysis of structures. Personality and Social Psychology Bulletin, 9, 830.

Kluckhohn, C., & Murray, H.A. (1953). Personality Formation: The Determinants. In C. Kluckhohn & H. Murray (Eds.), Personality in nature, society, and culture (2nd ed., pp. 53–67). New York: Alfred A. Knopf.

Levinger, G., & Levinger, A.C. (2003). Winds of time and place: How context has affected a 50-year marriage. Personal Relationships, 10(3), 285–306.

Mazlish, B. (1975). James and John Stuart Mill: Father and son in the 19th century. New York: Basic Books.

McAdams, D.P. (1988). Biography, narrative, and lives: An introduction. In D. McAdams & R. Ochberg (Eds.), Psychobiography and life narrative. Durham, N.C.: Duke University Press.

McAdams, D., Josselson, R., & Leiblich, A. (2001). Turns in the road: Narrative studies of lives in transition. Washington D.C.: American Psychological Association.

Mendelsohn, G.A. (1985). La Dame aux Camelias and La Traviata: A study of dramatic transformations in the light of biography. In R. Hogan & W. Jones (Eds.), Perspectives in personality (Vol. 1). Greenwich, Conn.: JAI Press.

Murray, H.A. (1938). Explorations in personality. New York: Oxford University Press.

Paul, E. (1991). Women's psychosocial development: The role of marriage and friendship in two lives. In Perspectives in Personality: Approaches to understanding lives (Vol. 3, Pt. B). London: Jessica Kingsley Publishers.

Post, J. (2003). The psychological assessment of political leaders. University of Michigan Press.

Runyan, W.M. (1982). Life histories and psychobiography. New York: Oxford University Press.

Runyan, W.M. (1991). "Progress" as an approach to epistemological problems in the study of lives. In Perspectives in Personality: Approaches to understanding lives (Vol. 3, Pt. B). London: Jessica Kingsley Publishers.

Tomkins, S.S. (1987). Script Theory. In J. Aronoff, A.I. Rabin, & R. Zucker (Eds.), The emergence of personality. New York: Springer, pp. 147–216.

Walster, E., Walster, G.W., & Berscheid, E., in collaboration with William Austin, Jane Traupmann, Mary K. Utne. (1978). Equity: theory and research. Boston: Allyn and Bacon.

Winter, D.G., Herman, M.G., Weintraub, W., & Walker, S.G. (1991). The personalities of Bush & Gorbachev measured at a distance. Political Psychology, 12, 215–245.

Chapter 8

William Todd Schultz

Diane Arbus's Photographic Autobiography
Theory and Method Revisited

It is not my childhood that I seek, but the childhood of my art. As much as to say, Mommy, where do images come from?

> Howard Nemerov, Journal of the Fictive Life

All this making of the eye which will see in the light is carried out in the dark. It is a preparing in darkness for use in light.

> Howard Nemerov, quoting Charles Sherrington, in Journal of the Fictive Life

This chapter is an ambitious one for the reason that I want to try doing two things simultaneously—without, I hope, short-changing either aim. My focus is the life and art of photographer Diane Arbus, best known for her pictures of subjects she often referred to, without malice, as "freaks," and for her suicide in 1971, in the wake of a series of decidedly eerie photographs taken at homes for the mentally retarded, many of these on Halloween. I want to use her case as a way of illustrating the doing of psychobiography from the ground up, from inception to conception to completion (not that any psychobiography ever reaches closure). What is typically subtextual will be made explicit here, the intention being to share process-related, tactical decisions regarding, among other things, where to begin in the study of a life, how to prioritize biographical data, and choice of theory. At the same time I present interpretations of Arbus's life and work that came to light in the course of a psychobiography seminar I taught in spring of 2002. What emerges is a hybrid enterprise: part method primer, largely generalizable to other analyses of artists (though photography is in many respects unique as an art form), and part speculative interpretation geared at unearthing the subjective origins of a deeply mysterious and maybe even unusually personal body of artistic work.

Arbus makes for a daunting study. The very nature of her art presents complications. When Pollock paints—or Plath writes poems, or Mozart composes music—there is just one person in the room. This one person does something to an object; he/she conjures, visualizes, fantasizes, makes things up. Pollock's canvas has no eyes, however much its emptiness leers. Arbus's "canvas" looks back. She is *not* alone.[1] Her art is mostly collaboration—conscious and unconscious intersubjective arrangement, mutual posturings—and her subjects sometimes did resist, occasionally even actively. They did not like what she was "doing" to them. Some felt less photographed than "Arbused." So in looking at, say, a picture of a face, the subject up for analysis is a relationship, the picture a subtle negotiation. At least in part, this relationship *is* the subject. Arbus's daughter, Doon, recalled, "Even if she was only with [her subjects] for a few hours or knew them for years, she exchanged secrets with them. Often what they told each other, neither had shared with intimate friends. . . . It was as much what people drew from her that excited her as what she could draw out of them" (Arbus, 1972, p. 44). That fact and its assorted emergent properties both need to be kept in mind. It nicely complicates our job.

Photography is also a strangely adventitious art form. In looking at photographs, often what one seems to be asking about them, even without knowing it, is "how and why a man or a woman aiming a camera in a certain way at a

112

certain segment of visual reality will occasionally, mysteriously, produce a work of art" (Malcolm, 1997, preface). Elements of risk and chance abound; photographers find pictures as much as they make them. As Arbus realized so clearly, they see things other people do not.[2] Cartier-Bresson speaks of the "decisive moment," that split, eroding second when a gesture or expression is at its highest peak of intensity, and the picture's composition achieves the appearance of good form (Malcolm, 1997, p. 37). Photographer Gary Winogrand, an opponent of posed and stylized photography, points to the photographer's understanding of *possibilities*. He can't know, when he takes a picture, that it will work, that it will be a *photograph*. All that is clear is that he has a chance. "I photograph," Winogrand explained, "to find out what something will look like photographed" (Malcolm, 1997, p. 33). The psychobiographical question is this: Why does a particular photographer find pictures where and when she finds them? Why some decisive moments and not others?

Regarding the biographical record, we have at our disposal just one full-length biography of Arbus. That biography was written without the cooperation of Arbus's daughter, Doon, or that of her husband, Allan Arbus, both extremely important witnesses (Arbus's brother, the poet Howard Nemerov, did consent to interviews, as did her mother, Gertrude, and her sister, Renee). Arbus remains, therefore, in crucial respects mysterious. Even her suicide, judging by the biography, is incompletely understood. As an artist Arbus thrilled to secrets, especially the prospect of their unmasking. That was her work's aim. As biographical subject, Arbus's secrets have been left tantalizingly intact. She lacks transparency. Even her writing retains an elliptical quality (e.g., "Nothing is ever the same as they said it was. It's what I've never seen before that I recognize," or "Nothing is ever alike. The best thing is the difference. I get to keep what nobody needs"; see Arbus, 2003). As Arbus's friend and lover Marvin Israel once put it, "She was many things to many people" (quoted in Bosworth, 1995).

Our task as psychobiographers has much in common with Arbus's task as an artist: Which mask is most real? Who, exactly, is she? Can she

even be known, and how might the inspection of her photographs help this knowing along?

Let's begin at the beginning.

First Steps

In all psychobiography, the first question has to be this: What is the first question? Where to begin? Once the decision gets made to study a figure such as Arbus—so unsettling in many respects, both because of her subject matter (eccentrics) and because of the way she died (suicide)—how best to initiate the process of knowing her better? This can be generalized: What do we know when we know a person (as McAdams once asked), and how do we get there, anyway?

The prospect of starting out can be unnerving. One worries over possible missteps, particularly the kind with the potential to doom the total endeavor. After all, how we start often predicts where we wind up. And in psychobiography, we want to be sure to take the most scenic route. Here my students' response provides immediately helpful guidance. Their preliminary query—one that caught me a little off guard, though it shouldn't have—concerned, not Arbus, but me (of all people). They wanted to know what drew me to my subject, why I found her so mysterious and inspiring. In short, what were my personal feelings about Arbus? I don't relish talking about myself in front of large groups of people. My plan was to start the class elsewhere, and far more impersonally. On the other hand, I'm glad the question got asked. It served as a nice reminder of something that usually—and potentially disastrously—falls to the wayside as psychobiographers lose themselves in the life of another. For the fact is, before beginning an analysis of any psychobiographical subject, one really must explore as deeply as possible any *personal motives* for undertaking the task. These motives, often marginalized or even ignored, doubtless steer inquiry. We may secretly wish to vindicate our subjects, attack them, love them, or participate vicariously in their fame. Our pursuit of their secrets may be a way of pursuing our own, a working through of conflicts and anxieties. All such matters warrant careful unpacking. The more we know about what we want, the more we control its subterranean framing of the questions we ask and answer. The best, and in some ways most surprising, example of a person who did not do this unpacking as much as he should have is Freud, in his famous book on Leonardo (Freud, 1964). Elms (see chap. 15 this vol.) has shown how Freud saw himself in Leonardo more than he saw Leonardo and therefore reached a number of conclusions about the artist that seem more autobiographical than psychobiographical.

I'm not sure when I first saw Diane Arbus's photos. I've always been drawn to eccentricity, to the extremes—the limit cases of human experience—so somewhere along the way I must have come across her twins and triplets, her masked retarded subjects shuffling crepuscularly, her cross-dressers and monkey lovers, her soothsayers and albino sword swallowers. Maybe they claimed their own special spot in my unconscious, along with its other "freaks." I do remember, in college, hatching a plan with my photographer friend Tina Rahr to travel around downtown Portland in search of images of "weirdos." Two privileged college kids ferreting out authenticity. She would take the photos, and I would write the accompanying text—just like Arbus did for several of her magazine spreads, most notably "The Full Circle" (see Arbus, 1984). And like Arbus, I too imagined eccentrics belonging to some secret confederacy, a family with a steep price of admission. They knew something I did not—they were both me and not me—and like Arbus, I felt that by some convoluted magic they succeeded in being more real, more committed to their own intensification of personality, absorbed in their fakery, whereas I, and my friends, simply felt fake.

Then I learned that one of my favorite writers kept a copy of Arbus's book *Untitled* (1995) next to her writing desk. (This is the series of photos taken at homes for the mentally retarded between the years 1969–1971.) I always felt these pictures represented a spooky departure for Arbus, a shift in style and subject matter that even, conceivably, held the key to much of her earlier work. The writer agreed, and this agreement instantly set my mind in motion; I felt I had identified a mystery, and mystery—enigmatic riddles of self—lies at the very heart of psychobiography.

Mystery's elucidation is psychobiography's most salutary aim.

Our next step in the class was to ask how we ought to engage the data, and how, more specifically, to sequence it. Which murky river—the biography or the art—should we first dip our toes in? If we start with the life, we bias our perception of the photography. We won't see the work naively. But if we start with the art, we lack context, and in the end our aim is to contextualize. Sometimes knowing a thing or two about the artist helps one to see her art more clearly.

Then we noticed that the only reason we were planning to spend so much time with Arbus was not because of her life so much, but because of the work she did. Arbus is *Arbus* for the reason that she took photographs people found arresting (or even disturbing). A similar point applies to Picasso, Plath, Mozart, and so on. The art is what peaks our interest in the personality. It is what leads us to seek correlations with the life, to ask about the person behind the public performance. That realization provided our orienting posture. We began the way most people begin to know Diane Arbus: by looking at her work and asking what were its most salient features.

Can one recommend the above as a general methodological principle of psychobiographical research vis-à-vis art and artists? I don't see why not. *Start with the work.* Get to know it well by spending time with it. Stare at, for example, the photographs. Look like an artist would (this form of looking requires all the creativity one can muster). Try to see what Arbus saw, why she chose one print over dozens of others. Learn all you can. Notice themes and patterns—also incongruities, marginalities. As James Agee once said: "Perceive simply the cruel radiance of what is" (Agee, 1941). Or Susan Sontag: practice an erotics of perception (i.e., use your senses fully, intellect aside). Then go to the life and do the same, returning once more—repeatedly, iteratively—to the work, allowing each to quicken the other in a delicate back and forth process of superimposition, of interpenetration. Watch the whole materialize. Let the data reveal themselves.

Another "first step" question concerns theory, namely, which to make use of (this subject is explored in detail in Elms, chap. 5 this vol.). My feeling is that this is better understood as a "last step" concern. Such isn't always the case, but the life more often than not dictates theoretical choices. Besides, interpretation follows immersion in the facts; it won't do to rush things. We come to a life with implicit models of self intact—that can't be helped. But before making explicit theoretical commitments, we first spend as much time as necessary with the raw materials, simply letting them lie there, unassembled. Then, when ready, we let the life point the way.

An example might be Maurice Sendak. This writer/illustrator seemed to very deliberately make use of insights gained during psychoanalysis as a way of developing his subject matter; he explored in his work what he was realizing in his therapy, and what he was realizing in his therapy had a lot to do with deeply infantile desires, many centered around the breast, eating, oral sadism/incorporation, and symbiosis. That being the case—and Sendak himself said it *was* the case—an obvious theory candidate would seem to be psychoanalysis, or some variant of what is called object-relations theory. Now, I don't feel one should always respect the wishes of the subject when it comes to theory. Skinner, for example, seems open to psychoanalytic considerations, a prospect he would abjure. But in most cases the subject's preferences make for a decent starting point. So, don't rush theory, and when it seems most sensible, *let the biography be your guide.*

The Work

Next we turned our attention to the work. Over two class sessions we viewed seventy of Arbus's photographs presented in rough chronological order. The class's task was to pick out themes—formal or content based. We noticed these things, some obvious, some not so obvious: The pictures were almost exclusively of people. The photos were in black and white. There were many shots of couples, even of twins and triplets, and of faces. A lot of the people in the photos were wearing masks or exploring identity. The expressions on the faces were intense, insolent, vaguely sad, confrontational, as if daring us to look back at them. In many of the pictures bodies appeared seamlesssly to blend together, to fuse, achieving physical symbiosis. It was difficult to tell where

one body ended and another began. And, of course, we all noticed Arbus's obsession with eccentrics.

Obsession is key.[3] We always want to know: *What is an artist obsessed with?* What does she seem to be working on most urgently, most repetitively? Since we return to subjects for a reason, repetition denotes lack of resolution, an unfinishedness. Such questions aren't always easy to answer. The best art captivates because of its ambiguity, its impenetrability. It grips us most when it flaunts its mystery. In fact, the luckiest thing for an artist, as Wilde once observed, is to be misunderstood. At the same time, it won't ever do to underestimate the obvious, and Arbus seems most obviously obsessed with human oddities, as she called them; with the "anomalies, the quixotic, the dedicated, who believe in the impossible, who make their mark on themselves, who-if-you-were-going-to-meet-them-for-the-first-time-would-have-no-need-of-a-carnation-in-their-buttonhole" (quoted in Southall, 1984).

At any rate, as it usually does, the art provided us with a set of orienting mysteries concerning Arbus. What drew her to these human addities? Why did she focus on couples, many symbiotically entwined? What made the mask such a compelling subject? Finally, how to make sense of the photos of the mentally retarded? Where they really a departure? How did Arbus feel about them, what did she say about them? Could they have had something to do with her suicide? Armed with questions such as these, we took up the biographical record. What would be the effect of superimposing the art on the life, and vice versa?

The Life

At this point the class read Patricia Bosworth's (1995) biography of Arbus, coming to the life with absolutely no pre-existing knowledge (to my anguished surprise, not a single student had ever heard of Diane Arbus). As for this task, it should be noted: Biographical molehills have a way of becoming mountainous; the data based on interviews, memoirs, secondary literature, gossip, autobiography, ex-therapist's confidences, and so on, tend to proliferate and accrete semi-spookily. Not to mention the arduous task of winnowing out these data sets, deciding which fact to privilege over another. The enterprise, in other words, has the capacity to overwhelm. So the place to begin is with some kind of system for dealing with the manifest superabundance of biographical material. For this Irving Alexander's (1990) "textual indicators of psychological saliency" and my own concept of the "prototypical scene" best fit the bill (each of these is described more fully in Schultz, chap. 3 this vol.).

Alexander suggests relying on a set of pointers or cues, many derived from psychoanalysis, that indicate the relative saliency of life events. These include primacy (what comes first in a text), emphasis (what is either over- or under-emphasized), uniqueness (events that are anomalous and/or unrepeated or deliberately singled out), frequency (episodes that either literally or metaphorically recur), omission (relationships or facts that go suspiciously unremarked on), incompletion (a failure to finish a line of thought), negation (the particularly urgent denial of an event's importance), and error or distortion (getting facts of one's own life wrong). The use of such cues when working one's way through life history information has the effect of increasing the signal-to-noise ratio; they help to home in on what is most important. From there, interpretations begin to develop. But the point is this: Before we hazard any interpretation, we first need to identify what's worth interpreting. We want, in other words, to linger over the right stuff.

One can also stay on the lookout for what I call "prototypical scenes" in a life. Each life has one, *and only one*. In this single scene (an episode or event) the core parameters of an entire life story are embedded and encapsulated. The prototypical scene is the blueprint of a life; it summarizes nuclear conflicts and personality patterns (see Schultz, chap. 3 this vol.). How do we know prototypical scenes when we "see" them? They possess the following characteristics: (a) their "telling" is vivid, imbued with detail, even verbatim dialogue; (b) they are affectively intense; (c) they interpenetrate, are repeated in various forms and various contexts; (d) they possess developmental gravity, issuing from trademark developmental crises or encounters; (e) they depict conflict, usually of a familial sort;

and (f) they allow their authors a chance to creatively rehearse "thrownness"—something done to the subject that he or she finds surprising or confusing or unmerited, thus requiring repeated narration as a way of making the experience understandable and assimilable. Prototypical scenes are not necessarily straightforwardly factual. They may be partly invented or tendentiously elaborated. Still, whatever their relative mixture of fact and fiction, they nicely and effectively constellate a life. We return to them, to the act of their narration, whenever we feel the need to tell ourselves or others who we are. In fact, that is their chief function: self-definition. They are accurate even if totally imagined.

Armed with these systems—and, as I said, it is important to have some system ready to hand before immersing oneself in the potential black hole of a life—one may begin to inspect the biography gingerly. In the case of Arbus, what the class found was the following.

(a) She repeatedly sought out the strange or anomalous, fringe people and fringe experiences. "My favorite thing is to go where I've never been," she once wrote, where there is "absolutely no method for control" (Arbus, 2003). She told Lisette Model, her teacher/mentor, "I want to photograph what is evil"—which her daughter, Doon, interprets as "forbidden . . . too dangerous, too frightening, or too ugly for anyone else to look at" (Arbus, 1972, p. 52).

(b) She consistently expressed feelings of isolation, both in her family and among her peers and schoolmates. Bosworth notes how Arbus's parents regarded her sister, Renee, as the "normal one" and Howard (her brother) and Diane as "different" (Bosworth, 1995, p. 185). Arbus herself said, "[As a kid] I was confirmed in a sense of unreality which I could only feel as unreality. . . . The world seemed to me to belong to the world. I could learn things but they never seemed to be my own experience" (p. 5). Her alienation, then, was both from the world and from her own mind.

(c) Terror aroused her uniquely. She sought it as a way of facing her fears and overcoming her shyness. Her daughter, Doon, writes: "Her finest moments were adventures attended by traces of fear. So, in a sense, she liked being afraid because there was in it the possibility of something terrific" (Arbus, 1972, p. 53). Her aim in her work to scrutinize the perverse, alienated, and extreme forced her to confront frightening people and situations. Her brother, Howard, noted, "She was terrified most of the time" (quoted in Bosworth, 1995, p. 131). Likewise, Gay Talese: "She was obviously courting danger" (p. 234).

(d) She was obsessed with the question of what was real, what was most authentic. "Even at the age of eleven," Bosworth (1995) observes, "she was aware of the duplicity in herself and her classmates, and she would write about it angrily in her autobiography" (p. 24). More than anything else, she strove to penetrate people's masks, to capture with her photographs slipping moments of unprotected, uncanny authenticity— contradictory, ambiguous, but also real. She spent hour upon hour photographing a blind, bearded giant named "Moondog," son of an Episcopal minister. The blind, she felt admirably, "can't fake their expressions. They don't know what their expressions are, so there is no mask" (p. 164). On another occasion a friend once asked Arbus to snap his picture. She refused, saying, "It would take five hundred exposures before I'd get you without your mask" (p. 178).

(e) Early relationships with parents and siblings can, of course, be especially formative, and the class zeroed in on these, as well. Arbus's mother, Gertrude Nemerov, was felt to be unreachable, perhaps partly due to depression. Bosworth (1995) depicts her lying in bed most mornings, drinking coffee and smoking (p. 10). The mother herself explained, "I simply could not communicate with my family. I felt my husband and children didn't love me and I couldn't love them. I stopped functioning. I was like a zombie" (Bosworth, 1995, p. 36). As with her sister and brother, Arbus's care was delegated to a series of governesses, some she liked, others she disliked.

(f) And her father, David Nemerov, Arbus saw as constantly putting on a "front," acting, for example, richer than he really was (he was merchandizing director and part owner of Russek's Fifth Avenue). But there was more here, too: Friends remarked on the "flirty" nature of Arbus's relationship with David, on the fact that

they seemed silently attracted to one another. Arbus herself discloses a fantasy of incest, according to Bosworth (1995, p. 27). So if the dad was a "phony," he was also, for Arbus, an oddly attracting one.

(g) All students expressed a sense of Arbus's duality. She was sometimes dirty and disheveled, sometimes extremely nicely dressed; she was intensely shy, yet strikingly bold and adventurous, an "explorer"; she was weak and needy, especially regarding her most important love relationships, but fiercely independent in her work. She seemed, in essence, to lead two lives: the single mother of two girls, and the nocturnal adventurer/seductress, prowling the darkest dungeons of New York City for pictures of oddballs, taking bus rides to circuses to shoot midgets and albino sword swallowers, visiting nudist camps where, to make photographs, she stripped too. This was an observation we mulled over for some time. Since all of us "contain multitudes," since we all are, at times, different people, depending on the circumstance, and since self is, maybe at root, a divided thing even in the "normal" mind, it may be wisest not to seek in our subjects anything resembling coherence. Truman Capote once claimed to be consistently inconsistent. The same goes for Arbus (and for psychobiographers, as well).

(h) Last, the class commented on Arbus's tendency to seek out experiences of symbiosis (also met with in her work). Her most important relationships were flagrantly intense, characterized by blending and fusion. She lost—or found— herself in others, most likely through a heated process of projective identification combined with idealization (i.e., she saw herself in others, identified with this mirror image, and then idealized it). She needed more than anything else a "secure base" to which she could reliably return as necessary for emotional refueling.

Reading backward (one feels) from the pictures to the life, Bosworth (1995) sees Diane and brother Howard as "twins," sealed in fate by their quirky intellects. She says the siblings were "inseparable," coveting some unspoken "secret experience" that "bound them close together" (p. 12). They "created rich fantasies which they shared with each other and no one else"—as twins often do (p. 12). And oddly enough, in adulthood "each rarely told anyone of the other's existence" (p. 13). So, whatever "primitive, non-verbal" connection the siblings cultivated contained, beyond that, qualities of the taboo. The relationship was intensely private, Nemerov explains (p. 13). In thinking back to a portrait he and Diane sat for when Howard was seven and Diane four, Howard associated "a little, a very little, sexual experimentation with my sister" dating to about that time, adding "it is possible, however, that this memory merely covers something of the sort that happened much earlier, at the time of the portrait" (Nemerov, 1965, p. 80). Bosworth (1995) goes on to record how, in late 1968, Arbus longed to photograph a couple afflicted with *folie a deux*: "She looked for this phenomenon in twins, husbands and wives, brothers and sisters, and a couple in a mental institution" (p. 277). This pursuit mirrors the "madness" she and her brother secretly shared by virtue of their giftedness. In aiming to explore this madness-of-two, Arbus seems to be asking, Can one love intensely without courting delusion?

At the age of 14 Diane met Allan Arbus, a 19-year-old working by day as a copy boy in the Russek's art department and attending City College at night. Almost instantly, "Allan became the most important person in Diane's life, the crucial relationship," her sister, Renee, confided. "Allan brought beauty and passion into her life. He became her guide, her mentor, her reason for being" (quoted in Bosworth, 1995, p. 34). She called him "swami." His word was gospel. Alex Eliot recalled, "[H]e'd keep telling her, 'Finish your sentence, girl, don't let your thoughts hang'" (p. 44). After their marriage, and while working together as fashion photographers—Diane did the conceptualizing and posed the models, and Allan took the pictures—"they were considered by everyone who knew them a shy young couple who seemed almost symbiotically close" (p. 71). A rumor even persisted that they were blood relations, first cousins who had fallen deeply in love (p. 71). As with Howard, Diane and Allan were "like twins," Bosworth (1995) writes, "sharing secrets, forbidden pleasures, little indulgences" (p. 73). When the marriage broke apart, Diane did too. "I am going to be numbed," a friend recalls her utter-

ing with intense foreboding (p. 153). The loss of the relationship presaged a loss of feeling.

Arbus's relationships with her daughter, Doon, and her subsequent mentor and lover, Marvin Israel, also are characterized by Bosworth (1995) as symbiotically intense. Tina Fredericks recalled, "[S]he could never see Marvin [who was married] as much as she wanted to. . . . [S]he wished he could be available for comfort and advice twenty-four hours a day" (pp. 202–203). Her friend "Cheech" (a pseudonym) said, "Diane changed when she met Marvin. . . . She absolutely worshipped him. . . . Diane was always saying 'Marvin this' and 'Marvin that.' . . . Marvin Israel began obsessing her" (p. 170). As for Doon, photographer Bruce Davidson remarked, "I've never seen such a symbiotic mother/daughter relationship. They were intensely close—fascinated by each other and bugged by each other" (p. 216). If Arbus sought mollifying merger, she elicited the same need in others so inclined. Israel recalled, "Everyone who ever cared about Diane became very possessive of her" (p. 205). Friends allude to the sexual atmosphere circling around her and her insinuating way with those she found desirable. A woman she met on the street exclaimed, "We became friends instantly. It was as if we had always known one another. . . . Our friendship was metaphysical, rapturous. We were all things to each other. . . . We exchanged secrets, ideas, memories" (p. 77). Looking for any and all kinds of connection, Arbus sought sex with as many people as possible, "because she was searching for an authenticity of experience, and [for her] the quickest, purest way to break through a person's facade was through fucking," John Putnam explained (p. 206).

All such psychological saliencies seem, in their own way, deserving of careful scrutiny. They tell us much about the person and the art. They suggest strategies for beginning the process of superimposition, of folding the life over the photography and vice versa. But first, before we move ahead to the task of interpretation (the real crux of the matter), we might pause for a moment to mull over the question of how theory and research—carefully applied—deepen our understanding of the biographical record. We have the life spread out before us, its most striking elements illumined. The job, at this point, is to make sense of it. What do the facts mean? How can theory get us from the facts to the art? The next section builds that bridge.

Theory

Most superficially—and this is not a place to end inquiry, or even, for that matter, a very good place to begin—we can start diagnostically. What *type* of person was Arbus? One asks this with the proviso firmly in mind: Diagnoses are never explanations, never interpretations, but merely shorthand ways of checking off sets of characteristics. In fact, when it comes right down to it, diagnoses encourage *mis*understandings. By their very nature they leave things out, they oversimplify, they turn a complex life into a name, a static clinical entity. This is at once their lure and their danger. Was John F. Kennedy a narcissist? Was Marilyn Monroe a borderline personality? Is Saddam Hussein a sociopath? These questions put personality in a stranglehold when, in fact, what we aim for as psychobiographers, what we hope our writing achieves, is the feeling that a subject has come alive. Diagnoses are deadening. Only in bad psychobiographies are they given any sort of prominence. Thus, *beware psychobiography by diagnosis*! (See also Schultz, chap. 1 this vol., for more on this particular proscription, along with other examples of bad psychobiography.)

Obviously Arbus was at times depressed—in her early years, in the "fashion years" while doing work she found dispiriting (she was, in effect, constructing then the fronts and poses she found so disturbing), and toward the end of her life, when in desperation she took to phoning her mother for advice on how she might get over her black moods. When she began her own work on eccentrics there commenced a "hypomanic" phase—increased activity, excitement, energy. She was at last doing the kind of work that later became her signature; she felt "like an explorer"; Bosworth (1995) describes her "living in an almost constant state of euphoria" (p. 175). At most, this observation invites us to regard her work as an antidote. It was a rejection of the stylized fashion world, of a photography de-

voted to "masks" and professional models. That human oddities thrilled her and made her feel uniquely alive comes as little surprise in context.

We also know, because she said so, that Gertrude Nemerov (Arbus's mother) suffered incapacitating bouts of depression. As noted above, she felt on these occasions unlovable and unloving, like a zombie. Research on depressed adolescents of depressed mothers reveals, first of all, that "one of the best empirically supported predictors of depression in youth is having a depressed mother" and that "half or more of the child and adolescent offspring of depressed women experience depressive disorders" (Hammon and Brennan, 2001, p. 1). More specifically, depressed children of depressed mothers encounter more difficulty in social domains, particularly relationships with family members. These children also show elevated rates of conflictive interpersonal and life events and more evidence of dysfunctional cognitions. They have fewer friends and participate in fewer social activities. They report—as Arbus did—less secure and more dismissing and fearful thoughts about relationships in general. Interestingly, depressed children of depressed mothers are more, not less, positive about their romantic appeal, indicating (one guesses) an especially urgent hope for just those kinds of relationships (for review, see Hammon and Brennan, 2001).

Outside the clinical realm, we could also think of Arbus as sensation seeking. This is a concept invented by Marvin Zuckerman (1971). Sensation seeking subsumes the factors "thrill and adventure seeking, experience seeking, disinhibition, and boredom susceptibility." Those scoring high on thrill and adventure seeking endorse statements such as "I sometimes like to do things that are a little frightening." With this Arbus would no doubt agree (she liked, as we saw, to go places she had never been, dangerous places). Experience seekers "prefer friends who are excitingly unpredictable" or people who are "homosexual," or "artists" and "hippies." Again, this seems to describe Arbus and the sorts of friends and subjects she courted. Disinhibition items include these: "I enjoy the company of real swingers" and "I like wild uninhibited parties" in which "keeping the drinks full" is key. Here

Arbus departs from the concept, or at least from some of its constituents. She did not drink or do drugs—rare for an artist. And although she sought out a relatively high number of sexual partners—another item included in the description of disinhibition—she did so less out of sensation-seeking than from a desire for authenticity of self-expression. At best, then, Arbus is a modest match for this dimension. Last, those susceptible to boredom prefer paintings that "shock or jolt the senses" and "dislike routine kinds of work"; they wish they "didn't have to waste so much of a day sleeping." Another decent match with Arbus.

So, if Arbus is in fact a sensation seeker, the question is: What does that tell us about her personality? Not a lot. Construct validity research done on the concept reveals that sensation seeking correlates with hypomania and impulsivity; that psychiatric patient groups tend on the whole not to be sensation seeking; that sensation seekers are not typically anxious or neurotic; and that, among numerous other correlations, sensation-seeking individuals are more "field independent," with heightened spatial abilities and capacities for form perception (Zuckerman, 1971). Once we learn that Arbus is a sensation seeker, that fact helps us predict a few other things about her, things related in certain ways to sensation seeking itself.

The idea behind the concept concerns optimal levels of stimulation, or individual differences in need for arousal. Arbus's sensory thermostat, in other words, was set too low; her baseline state was one of relative sensory deprivation. To reach adequate levels of arousal, she needed to seek out especially arousing experiences—thrills, adventures, and so on. Why did Arbus take pictures of people she called "freaks"? What made the eccentric so captivating? Why such a determined search for sex? In order to *feel*, one might say. Again, these drives would function antidotally. They counteract an emptiness, the numbness Arbus dreaded. This possibility introduces the question of functionality—always helpful to pursue. That is, we often move understanding forward by asking what our subjects get out of the things they do psychologically. What positive effects derive from their behavior? Arbus probably had some insight into this particular

dynamic. She had read and admired poet Edith Sitwell's book on "eccentrics" (defined rather photographically as "the Ordinary carried to a high degree of pictorial perfection"). There Sitwell recommends the study of human oddities as a cure for melancholy. She writes:

We may seek in our dust heap for some rigid, and even splendid, attitude of Death, some exaggeration of the attitudes common to Life. This attitude, rigidity, protest, or explanation, has been called eccentricity by those whose bones are too pliant. But these mummies cast shadows that do not lie in their proper geometrical proportions, and from these distortions dusty laughter may arise. (Sitwell, 1964, p. 20)

Arbus must have paid special attention to that passage. It confirmed her wish that her work be restorative. She reacted negatively to antidepressants; alternatively, photographing eccentrics might have seemed, to her, a more natural remedy for darkness. Notice, however, that while sensation seeking accounts for a portion of what drove Arbus motivationally, as a way of illuminating the content of her art it holds little appeal. It fails to answer the question, Why photograph anomalousness in people, rather than take up, say, hang gliding or do drugs? To get at these questions, we need to look elsewhere, to move beyond the purely diagnostic. In terms of theory proper, then, what model (or models) seems most applicable to the particulars of Arbus's life? Which theory should we interpret her with?

Here symbiosis points the way (in theory choice, as I said, *let the life guide you*). As we saw, Arbus sought out and in some ways got ensnared in symbiotic relationships with significant others—her brother, perhaps; her daughter, Doon; her husband, Allan Arbus; her mentor Marvin Israel; and even those known more at acquaintance level. She pursued merger. That fact tells us something about her sense of self or, more to the point, her comfort with her essential integrity. Erich Fromm (1941) was one of the first psychoanalytic theorists to discuss symbiosis in detail. He saw it as one particular mode of "escape from freedom." In fact, for Fromm symbiosis is "at the basis of both sadism and masochism" (p. 180). Being the union of one individual self with another self, it results, first of all, in the loss of the self's integrity. The sadist seeks security by "swallowing" another; the masochist, by being swallowed. In one case (masochism) the self is dissolved; in the other (sadism), the self is enlarged by making another self parasitical. "It is always the inability to stand the aloneness of one's individual self," Fromm explains, "that leads to the drive to enter into a symbiotic relationship with someone else" (p. 180). Such is not positive freedom, according to Fromm. Quite the contrary, since by seeking symbiosis, freedom is relinquished; the person tries to "overcome his aloneness by eliminating the gap that has arisen between his individual self and the world" (p. 161). Also, this particular mode of escape is characterized by its compulsivity; individuality is surrendered again and again as a means of escaping "threatening panic" (p. 162). Applying this line of thought to Arbus requires that we find, in her, evidence of an incapacity to tolerate aloneness. This evidence does exist. The prospect of what personologist Henry Murray called "insupport" panicked her. She needed her symbiotic attachments in order to weather tough times. Her search for sex can be interpreted similarly, and, as I explore later, so can her art, to the degree that she merged with her subjects or took pictures that served as projections of her fears and desires.

Symbiosis is a form of "object relationship"— that is, a way of interacting with the "objects" of one's drives, those significant others one identifies with, idealizes, or loves, and whose qualities one introjects (or makes part of oneself). In object-relations theory the basic motivational thrust generating mind or personality is object seeking, the need to establish and maintain connections with others.

Another way of relating to objects—one stressed most by the Kleinian school of thought—is called "splitting." To protect the good parts of people from the bad, and to keep the fantasized "bad" from destroying the "good," one splits objects into parts, in effect halving or compartmentalizing them. These parts are introjected—taken back into the self—producing, in turn, a split sense of self: The bad self is kept separate from the good self. Personality becomes a thing

divided. This is just what the class perceived most strikingly in Arbus: her dividedness. She was fearful and fearless or, as Israel put it, many things to many people—a shape shifter. Arbus's art also confirms splitting. On her photos of twins and triplets she commented: "Triplets remind me of myself when I was an adolescent. Lined up in three images: daughter, sister, bad girl, with secret lusting fantasies, each with a tiny difference" (quoted in Bosworth, 1995, p. 217). And after reading and admiring R.D. Laing's *The Divided Self* (1962), a phenomenologically informed rendering of schizophrenic experience, Arbus had the idea of doing "monologues by mad people under his guidance with his translations of the sense of what they were saying or doing and my photographs of how they looked or behaved" (quoted in Southall, 1984).

If Arbus cycled back and forth in her object relations between symbiosis and splitting, if she was exquisitely attuned to masks, personal "fronts," and phoniness in herself and others, and if what she valued more than anything else was masklessness, then these facts combined speak to a core inflammation of self. Self was for her both problematical and intoxicating to behold.

For Winnicott, another object-relations theorist, a robust sense of self develops through the provision by caretakers of a safe and responsive human environment in which the child experiences himself as authentic and alive. False selves represent compliant adaptations to the standards and expectations of others. Arbus, of course, felt all this acutely. She was, as she said, confirmed as a child "in a sense of unreality which I could only feel as unreality. . . . The world seemed to me to belong to the world. I could learn things but they never seemed to be my own experience" (Arbus, 1972, p. 5). Her problem was to define what was hers, to embody her own knowing, to discover what belonged to her. Photography seems curative in that she speaks of seeing things nobody else can or would, things that wouldn't exist but for her photographing them. The pictures were her "slight corner" on the "quality of things" (p. 15). They were her experience, what she alone could possess. She said, "I've come to believe you can only really learn by being touched by something" (quoted in Bosworth, 1995, p. 280).

When Arbus speaks directly of self, when she writes of her own experience, always her thoughts drift toward a Zen-like selflessness, a deeply private, unknowable, incognito self. She said, for example,

> Very often knowing yourself isn't really going to lead you anywhere. Sometimes it's going to leave you kind of blank. Like, here I am, there is a me, I've got a history, I've got things that are mysterious to me in the world, I've got things that bug me in the world. But there are moments when all that doesn't seem to avail. (Arbus, 1972, pp. 7–8)

She refers, also, to this ineluctable lacuna between the intended self and the self-as-seen-by-others:

> Everybody has that thing where they need to look one way but they come out looking another way and that's what people observe. You see someone on the street and what you notice about them is the flaw. . . . Our whole guise is like giving a sign to the world to think of us in a certain way but there's a point between what you want people to know about you and what you can't help people knowing about you. And that has to do with what I've always called the gap between intention and effect. I mean if you scrutinize reality closely enough, if in some way you really, really get to it, it becomes fantastic. . . . Something is ironic in the world and it has to do with the fact that what you intend never comes out like you intend it. . . . What I'm trying to describe is that it's impossible to get out of your skin into somebody else's. And that's what all this [the photography] is a little bit about. (pp. 1–2)

There is the guise, and there is the identity left after everything else gets stripped away, and it was between the two that Arbus sought to insert her camera. She was all about capturing an emptiness that, Zen-like, achieved magical pregnancy. The pictures were "a little bit about" the fact that you can't ever really become someone else—though in her life, her relationships, that form of becoming was something she sought.

Her family Arbus always portrays as lacking, even discouraging, anything resembling truth.

Her mother was baffled by her children's strangeness, their noses pressed in books; she "had a hard time figuring out what they were talking about," and her depressions kept her painfully vacant (Bosworth, 1995, p. 10). Her father "was something of a phony" committed to keeping up appearances. "My father was a frontal person," Arbus said, "a front had to be maintained. . . . I remember vaguely family conferences which took place behind closed doors. Like loans negotiated and things like that. . . . For years I felt exempt. I grew up feeling immune. . . . I never saw a real bread line. I saw it in the movies." Also: "The outside world was so far from us, one didn't expect to encounter it. The doors were shut. I guess it was innocence, but I don't think of it as anything pretty at all: the less you experience, the better. . . . That sense of being immune was painful." Then finally: "You grow up split between these two things—thinking that you're utterly average and inclusive or that every human emotion has its echo in you" (these quotes are an amalgam drawn from Terkel, p. 88, and Bosworth, 1995, pp. 277–280).

Now we get a better sense of the challenge Arbus faced: how to mend a rent experience, how to craft coherence out of splitness, how to inhabit her reality by capturing someone else's without losing herself in the process. She aims for a lucidity she naturally possessed before unreality arrived on the scene. As she explained, "I grew up thinking all my minimal conjecture was true. I thought I'd been born knowledgeable; that what I knew came from beyond the grave. I mean before birth. I didn't want to give up that wisdom for the ordinary knowledge of experience, which is the way I confirmed the way my parents brought me up" (quoted in Bosworth, 1995, p. 279). This was a challenge she faced in life and in her art. About the latter she noted: "There are always two things that happen. One is recognition and the other is that it's totally peculiar. But there's some sense in which I always identify with [my subjects]" (Arbus, 1972, p. 1). This last sentence moves us into the final phase of the chapter. The question becomes: How do we read Arbus in the viewfinder? How is what she saw in others a projected version of her own self, a secretly complicit, covert autobiography?

Provisional Interpretations

"Freaks"

Best to begin where Arbus herself began, with those she called "freaks." The fashion collaboration with her husband, Allan Arbus, had grown for Diane emotionally intolerable. It left her depressed, frustrated, and artistically ungratified. She had begun to take her own pictures and pursued a relationship with *Esquire*, which at the time was itching to get more edgy and risky in terms of content. In a long letter to the magazine, Arbus (quoting Edith Sitwell) proposes a series of photos of "eccentrics." This was November 1960. What do these eccentrics have in common? They comment pregnantly on life, criticize the world's arrangement with their contorted expressions or gestures. They contest or even refute the normally taken for granted. They revolt, like the

> irate lady who appears at night pulling a red kiddies express wagon trimmed with bells . . . , the Mystic Barber who teleports to Mars and says he is dead and wears a copper band around his forehead with antennae on it to receive his instructions from the Martians . . . , [or] a very cheerful man with only half a beard and someone who collects woodpecker holes as well as a lady in the Bronx who has trained herself to eat and sleep under water. (quoted in Southall, 1984, pp. 156–157)

These are "Characters in a Fairy Tale for Grown Ups" (as Arbus described them in Southall, 1984, p. 157). *Esquire* chose not to use the spread, though a version of it did appear in 1961 in *Harper's Bazaar* under the title "The Full Circle," along with an accompanying text—wonderfully detailed and beautifully written—by Arbus herself (Arbus, 1961).

If we ask, Why eccentrics? we need to acknowledge right off the bat that *no single answer will do*. As Freud explains, all actions, however large or small, are "overdetermined." Analyzing, say, a single dream image, one prepares to find at its source several condensed motives, never just one. This axiom also applies to the interpretation of art: Artists make the choices they do for a variety of reasons. Several reasons may be si-

multaneously apposite either because of the fact of overdetermination, or because each reason addresses a slightly different facet of the act in question.

In seeking out this concert of reasons, *proximity* can sometimes be revealing. What was happening in Arbus's life when she formed the idea of photographing eccentrics? She had ended her professional relationship with her husband. Human oddities, signifying revolt, in some ways seem like the perfect antifashion. If the fashion industry was all about constructing facades, making things look pretty, selling a dream—in short, about "fronts," precisely what Arbus deplored when she saw it in her father—then eccentrics made for a shot of reality in all its contorted "ugliness." Freaks were the latent content beneath the dream world of the happy family. They were the unarticulated underside and, as such, the antidote. They were the reality with which to contest the unreality Arbus felt confirmed in. It is telling, in this context, to note Arbus's mother's response to the *Harper's Bazaar* spread. She could not see why Diane took photographs of "such people" (Bosworth, 1995, p. 184). Eccentrics even bring to mind Arbus's earliest memory, one she recalled vividly and told on numerous occasions. Her governess had taken her to the dried up cavity of a reservoir in Central Park where a tin-shack Shanty Town lay revealed. This was truly "the other side of the tracks." Diane apparently wanted to investigate, though her nanny would not let her (Bosworth, 1995, p. 10). The "investigation" was only postponed; Arbus made the descent as an adult with her camera (for more on Arbus's prototypical scene, see Schultz, chap. 3 this vol.).

At the same time, eccentrics from another angle simply recapitulate the same quality of grotesqueness met with in fashion. As Arbus wrote in yet another proposal, "Beauty is itself an aberration, a burden, a mystery, even to itself" (quoted in Southall, 1984, p. 168). Both in beauty and in its antithesis Arbus was drawn to the same basic anomaly. As one reviewer noted, "She seems to respond to the grotesque in life. Even her glamour shots . . . look bizarre"; another reviewer finds an "emphasis on the hidden" (quoted in Southall, 1984, p. 165). These thoughts return us to the idea of the "front." Fronts Arbus reacted to with singular distaste. Her father was the front's epitome. Eccentrics and even sinisterly glowing model types therefore signify at some elemental level repudiation of the father and of the family facade of complicit silence and respectability Arbus felt as stultifying. Freaks as an initial artistic expression were Arbus's prison break.

Another stimulus worth exploring is the film *Freaks* by Todd Browning, released initially in 1932. MGM pulled the movie from distribution a few weeks after it appeared, but when it resurfaced several decades later, Arbus naturally discovered it and watched it repeatedly. The plot and the central characters reveal why. We meet, for instance, with several of Arbus's later subject types: a sword swallower, Siamese twins, a bearded lady, the "Living Torso," and a person who is half man, half woman. And we learn how freaks are a family, and a tenaciously loyal one at that. These misshapen misfits obey a very strict code of ethics: offend one freak, offend them all. When the film's villain, a "big" trapeze lady called Cleopatra, toys with the affections of a midget in order to get at his inheritance (she and her behemoth boyfriend plot to murder the dwarf), the freaks sit in grim judgment, united in their betrayal. They rise as one and, through some sort of contrived magic, succeed in turning Cleopatra into a chicken. This reversal is presaged by the dwarf's scathing accusation: "Dirty slimy freak." Who are we asked to side with? Freaks, of course, the truly moral family unit. Who is fraudulent? The big lady and her "normal" conspirators. Browning's attitude is mirrored in Arbus's work. In her most cited comment on the subject, Arbus explained (1972, p. 3),

Freaks was a thing I photographed a lot. . . . I just used to adore them. I still do adore some of them. . . . They made me feel a mixture of shame and awe. There's a quality of legend about freaks. . . . Most people go through life dreading they'll have a traumatic experience. Freaks were born with their trauma. They've already passed their test in life. They're aristocrats.

The family universe—a source of conflict for Arbus personally and something she must have responded to strongly in the film—is doubt-

less central. In her own home Arbus (and her brother) were regarded as freakish. They were too smart, too gifted. Somehow their brilliance was an affront, an awkward secret fact. One of Arbus's most famous photos—of the Jewish giant in his home—conveys arrestingly Arbus's own alienation. She took pictures of this man for almost a decade. That fact alone attests to her subject's intense importance. She felt she never could get him "just right," until at last she captured the tableau she'd been wishing for, a perfect encapsulation of her own childhood: the giant in his living room, head bent at ceiling level, his two contrastingly "midget" parents looking up at him in alarmed consternation. She says about the picture: "You know how every mother has nightmares when she's pregnant that her baby will be born a monster? I think I got that in the mother's face as she glares up at Eddie, thinking, 'Oh my God, no!'" (Bosworth, 1995, p. 194). This glaring mother is Gertrude Nemerov, and Eddie, the elephant in the living room, is Diane.

Other pictures make the same critical comment. In the photograph titled "A family on their lawn one Sunday in Westchester, N.Y. 1968," the father hides his eyes—another "frontal" husband—the mother obliviously sun worships, while their child, bored and forgotten, flashes them both his striped ass. And in "A young Brooklyn family going for a Sunday outing, N.Y.C. 1966," mother, father, and bonneted baby (fingers forming an accidental peace sign) have their normalcy betrayed by a waist-high, wall-eyed son clutching his penis. In this photo the mother in particular appears utterly waxen—vacant, pompadoured, with two perfectly drawn eyebrows floating like black quotation marks. Even Arbus's most famous picture—of a boy with a toy hand grenade in Central Park—seems autobiographical in the sense that behind him, as if exploding Athena-like out of his head, stands a blurry, menacing mother—his unconscious, in a sense. Meanwhile, off to the side can be glimpsed another blurry family, out for a stroll. (Not without insight, Norman Mailer once said of Arbus, "Giving her a camera is like putting a live grenade in the hands of a child.") All these families seem to be hiding a similarly combustible secret. There is, on the one hand, what they want us to believe about them, how they superficially appear, their "front," but then, on the other, the freaky detail that explodes the conceit. Recall how Arbus said: "There are always two things that happen. One is recognition and the other is that it's totally peculiar. But there's some sense in which I always identify with them" (Arbus, 1972, p. 1). What she identifies with in these photos is the peculiarity, the need we recognize in her subjects to express honestly the flaw they have been denied for so long (the trauma they were born with). Arbus is the "baby monkey" in the picture, the monster her mother gave birth to and dressed in pretty clothes.

Eccentrics as antifashion and protofashion, as emblems of the grotesque that goes unexpressed, as mirroring projections of family secrets—all these elements form a portion of Arbus's intent. But these human oddities also represent self-realization at its purest, a florid intensification of personality against all odds. It wasn't "just any old freak" that caught Arbus's attention. After all, freaks can be as boring and ordinary as so-called normal people; in their society the same class distinctions apply. There are real eccentrics, real aristocrats, and fake eccentrics—eccentrics playing a trick on us unbelievingly. Arbus discussed these matters with the writer Joseph Mitchell, whom she never actually met but took to phoning with regularity. They talked about the subject for hours. Diane said she imagined freaks were "a link to a strange, dark world—to an underworld." In shooting them she hoped to get at "what couldn't be defined" and "what was missing in an image" (Bosworth, 1995, p. 177). What especially drew her to a subject, according to the escape artist "Amazing Randi," was not weirdness per se but a "commitment to weirdness" (quoted in Bosworth, 1995, p. 165). She sought out eccentrics who believed in their fakery; more than anything, the freak needed to be sincere. So, in addition to everything else, in this work Arbus was all about zeroing in on personalities that had somehow managed to escape the strangleholds of culture and family. They were existentially embodied. They believed in who they were, something Arbus could not quite do. They answered a question at her core: how to possess a role unflinchingly, how to rise above impersonation. And unlike Arbus herself,

they were fearless. In their uncanniness—and the uncanny is always a powerful tonic—they laid down a mesmerizing prescription for the empty, melancholic self. Self in extremis against self as buried implosion.

Splits and Fusions

Arbus was taken with the work of the renegade psychiatrist/phenomenologist R.D. Laing, as noted already.[4] It is easy to guess why. In writing that "our normal adjusted state is too often the abdication of ecstasy, the betrayal of our true potentialities," and that "many of us are only too successful in acquiring a false self to adapt to false realities," he must have spoken to her in uniquely potent fashion (Laing, 1962, p. 12). He diagnosed her alienation. Much of Laing's work is devoted to the family, more specifically, to the assorted ways in which parents put their children in a checkmate position in response to which the only viable option is madness as a form of revolt, a way of saying "I refuse to participate." Psychosis is for Laing a strategy one adopts in order to live in an unlivable situation.

In *The Divided Self* (1962), which Arbus read and admired, Laing is concerned primarily with the "false-self system," with how we come to be unembodied and ontologically insecure, and in the book's grueling final chapter, with the "schizophrenogenic mother" and "family" who bequeath to the patient Julie a "death-in-life existence in a state approaching chaotic nonentity" (p. 195; also see below). As Laing asks in a passage that could have been written expressly for Arbus: "What can happen if the mother's or the family's scheme of things does not match what the child can live and breathe in? The child then has to develop its own piercing vision and to be able to live by that . . . or else become mad" (pp. 189–190).

The ontologically insecure person adopts a falseness bordering on parody. His every mechanized move symbolizes exactly what he rejects—deadness. Clinging to the most tenuous of identities, he fears absorption (what Laing calls "engulfment") and loss of being should he risk relating with another person openly. Reality in its impingement is felt as "implosive"; it looms menacingly as in fever. And though dreading being turned into a thing by the reifying gaze of another, he fashions a pre-emptive "petrification" of personality as a means of self-protection. His aim is not gratification of self but self's preservation. This becomes, ironically, a matter of life and death. If, like Julie, he chooses a "death-in-life" existence, then at least he chooses it, the deadness is his, not a sentence imposed from without.

The book is filled with richly detailed case studies in the existential/phenomenological tradition, with careful attention paid to the structure of the patient's lived experience. Laing's aim, he says, is to show that the schizoid person can be understood, to find interpretable psychological meaning in what others regard, and dismiss, as mere "symptoms." Arbus doubtless saw herself in these people—she refers to Laing's "extraordinary knowledge," his "empathy"—even though it would be wrong to regard her as schizoid or, least of all, "mad." Identification explains her desire in 1969 to photograph Laing's patients, to capture how they "looked or behaved" (Southall, 1984). There is James: "Other people were necessary for his [literal] existence." Like Arbus, he lived a polarity between "complete isolation or complete merging of identity" (Laing, 1962, p. 53). There is Mrs. D: "She was very afraid that she was like her mother, whom she hated." Baffled and bewildered, nothing she did "had ever seemed to please her parents." She was "unable to discover, as she put it, 'what they wanted me to be'" (p. 59). Her parents were "completely unpredictable and unreliable in their expression of love or hatred, approval or disapproval" (p. 59). About his own and Diane's parents, Howard Nemerov notes, "Everything in our house was based on approval, not love. This made us feel rather helpless because we never knew whether Daddy would approve or disapprove of something we did" (Bosworth, 1995, p. 12). Howard said his motto was, "Do what you're told and they'll leave you alone" (p. 13). Become, in other words, compliantly unreal. Next is Peter, who made no difference in his parents' lives. They "simply treated him as though he wasn't there"; his mother "hardly noticed him at all" (Laing, 1962, pp. 120–121). The central issue for him had crystallized "in terms of being sincere or being a hypocrite; being genuine or playing a part" (p. 124). As we've seen, Diane's

parents were likewise essentially self-obsessed. Her father "showed little warmth or interest in his children" (Bosworth, 1995, p. 11); her mother "wanted her only to do the right thing, the correct thing" (p. 25).

Then there is Mrs. R. Her parents, too, "were always too engrossed in each other for either of them to take notice of her" (Laing, 1962, p. 54). She grew up wanting to fill this hole in her life, "to be important and significant to someone else," in contrast to her abiding memory of herself "as a child that did not really matter to her parents, that they neither loved nor hated, admired nor were ashamed of" (p. 54). Eerily like Arbus, she was married at seventeen to the first man who really noticed this, feeling finally triumphant and self-confident under the warmth of her husband's affections. But then he left, and her panic returned. Laing concludes:

The pivotal point around which all her life is centred is her lack of ontological autonomy. If she is not in the actual presence of another person who knows her, or if she cannot succeed in evoking this person's presence in his absence, her sense of her own identity drains away from her. Her panic is at the fading away of her being. (p. 56)

Laing concludes with Julie, who felt "unreal," whose father had withdrawn himself emotionally, who was accepted only when she behaved falsely or "good" (i.e., as though existentially dead) and whose choice lay between merger/symbiosis and an alienating, parabolical madness. In the end Julie "splits" into what Laing calls "molar" units—partial assemblies or partial systems, each with its own stereotyped personality. Terrified of the intense anxiety occasioned by integration—the prospect of internal *folie a deux*—she sought refuge, instead, in "unrealness" (p. 197).

All these cases mirror what we have already discovered in Arbus: self-engrossed parents, a sense of unrealness, a distaste for masks, falseness, and fronts, fears of being alone and related needs for merger with others, a split self-image— indeed, a "divided self." These were the pivotal points around which her life centered, to use Laing's terminology. And these central issues naturally found their way into her art; she sought her own "piercing vision," a picture of the world she could live with, a more valid interpretation of reality.

We can start with the "Identical twins, Roselle, N.J. 1967," one of her most famous images (it was selected for the cover of her self-titled book, *Arbus*, 1972). The first thing most people notice about this photo, my students included, is that the twin girls, though "identical," express even more starkly what Laing referred to as partial assemblies—two antithetical personalities. There is the cheerful, optimistic, self-confident and self-possessed togetherness—integration—of the girl on the right, her white stockings pulled up tight, her haloed hair, the endless openness of her carefree gaze. Then there is the "left" self: lips pressed into a near grimace, eyelids lowered ever so slightly, her hair comparatively disarranged, her stockings drooping. These girls merge physically—they share a middle arm—but they diverge psychologically, expressing the right-sided "front"—the good girl—and the left-sided bad girl shadow.

"Triplets in their bedroom, N.J. 1963" creates the same impression. Again, the torsos blend. Arms are "shared," legs almost invisible beneath enveloping skirts. The three girls fuse Cerberus-like; they are one populous unit on guard in Hell. While the girl on the left looks almost puzzled, inquisitive, wondering—though infinitely civilized—the girl on the right sits defiant, cold, taunting. The middle child—a compromise self—projects self-satisfied pliability, her lips curling into a smile. We meet here with Freud's tripartite structure: id, ego, superego. We wonder, too, for how long this middle girl can mediate the conflicting demands of the sisters who sandwich her. These two photos, obviously similar in terms of subject matter, share additional incidental features: all five girls seem to be wearing what look like identical white hair bands. Thus, in even minor respects, the two pictures invite us to see them as one, expressing perhaps the same fundamental psychological reality. "Triplets remind me of myself," Arbus said; no doubt the twins did too. As all artists do, in these pictures Arbus expelled, then manipulated, her own internal drama, allowing it to look back at her. Yet one surmises it was

rather taunting too—this projected congress of characters—in that integration seems, at best, a fraught, unlikely outcome.

Arbus worked this theme tenaciously—identical opposites, binaries, disintegrated fusion. It was her Zen koan, the puzzle she collided with to the very end, until the photos of the retarded—discussed below—supplied a solution she could understand yet not abide. The "young man and his girlfriend" balance their identical hot dogs. Lunch conjoins them, though she has already hazarded a hungry bite. "Two girls in matching bathing suits" flaunt their angry sameness. Are they one, or two? Couples appear with regularity—nude, dancing, sitting on park benches—in every case tangled, either holding hands or crossing legs or with arms encircling shoulders. And masks, too, underscore Arbus's core intention—she wanted to "get" people at their most unconcealed, but intuited, as did Wilde before her, that the mask sometimes tells us more than any face. "Nudist lady with swan sunglasses" presents the same disjunction. Here is a woman denuded who nonetheless manages to conceal. She is natural and fake simultaneously. About nudists in general Arbus wrote interestingly: "After a while you begin to wonder. . . . They seem to wear more clothes than other people" (Arbus, 1972, p. 5). The purity of their self-expression is belied by their outhouses, their "mangy woods," the lake bottom that oozes mud "in a particularly nasty way" (p. 5). Even nudists, that is, have a lot to hide. Wilde comes in handy again: "Being natural is a pose."

If we go back to Arbus's "The Full Circle" (1961), self-proliferation once more rises to the fore. The five singular people she chronicles both in pictures and in her own text ask "what it is to become whoever we may be." "Privileged exiles" all (like Arbus herself), these living metaphors are more than what they seem—enormous, possessed, fearless, strong. With their tattoos, Uncle Sam outfits, and so on, they clone themselves, become twins, triplets, quadruplets; they multiply their personalities. Arbus quoted one: "The facets of a man's life so vary . . . that he appears to live his life as a succession of characters—in different dramas . . . and his innermost secrets are hidden in Time. . . . The personal history of anyone is merely a legend, imperfectly understood" (see Southall, 1984, p. 20) Uncle Sam declares: "Last year this time I was Nobody, now I'm Somebody. . . . I am what I call a Personality, . . . I have a suggestion for you: I could be other people." (see Southall, 1984, p. 20) Miss Cora Pratt, the Counterfeit Lady, seems like the article's centerpiece. As with Arbus, her mother cannot bear her, and her brother thinks she's divine. Cora's "real self" is Polly Bushong, but Polly, daughter of a socially prominent New England gentleman, can't fight off the urge to "occasionally [become] someone else." Thus toothy, wigged, loudmouthed Cora surfaces, typically by prearrangement with her hosts, to "commit the most unerring blunders" and tread where angels fear to. Cora/Polly seemed to unnerve Diane. Bushong recalled, oxymoronically:

> Diane Arbus was awful nice to me. Sweet. She spent all day photographing me in the garden. . . . But before she left she asked me a couple of times was I really sincere about having those two people inside myself? I kept telling her I was sincere, but I guess she didn't believe me. . . . Actually, I didn't mind, because I don't see how you could label me a freak. (quoted in Bosworth, 1995, p. 180)

Dividedness—the self as split entity—and fusion, dividedness' beckoning antidote, this was Arbus's albatross. Masks, fronts, nudity, symbiosis, "unreality," personality's proliferation —so many lines of evidence, indicators met with both in the life and in the work, converge unmistakably upon the same central theme: how to possess, or as Laing would say, embody and/ or integrate one's lived experience, how to be everything, or everyone, at once. Though he didn't follow his own dictum in this case, Freud (1964) in his book on Leonardo warns the potential psychobiographer against crafting conclusions out of isolated facts. (see Elms, chap. 15, this vol.) That is sound advice. With Arbus, the data fortunately come from all directions. Let us note explicitly: When searching out our subject's core concerns, we need to *focus on what the totality of facts tells us*, or how assorted lines of inquiry—never only one—can be seen to form a compelling gestalt. When it comes to evidence in psychobiography, the more, the merrier.

Untitled

We now approach what is perhaps the most revealing work of all, Arbus's photos of the mentally retarded taken between the years 1969 and 1971. There seems to be little doubt that this series of work was indeed a departure for Arbus. As Janet Malcolm (1997) has observed in her wonderful book *Diana & Nikon*, these pictures, when first included (though not in their entirety) in "Diane Arbus," (1972) "gave off a special aura: one sensed that Arbus was doing something new and had somehow raised the stakes" (p. 183). Doon Arbus, in *Untitled*'s afterword, reaches the same conclusion: "Almost from the beginning, [Arbus] recognized in these pictures something new. . . . The discovery set her free." Moreover, "none of her other photographs . . . looks quite like these do." Arbus herself wouldn't have disagreed. As she wrote in an undated letter to her then ex-husband Allan: "I took the most terrific pictures. The ones at Halloween . . . of the retarded women. . . . FINALLY what I've been searching for. . . . I think about doing a book on the retarded. . . . It's the first time I've encountered a subject where multiplicity is the thing" (quoted in Southall, 1984).

These are enormously interesting comments. First, they underscore the work's incongruity; it seems to stand in isolation from what had gone before. That fact connotes saliency in Alexander's terms (see chap. 3 this vol.). It tells us we need to pay special attention. Second, what Arbus says about the work raises intriguing questions. What, exactly, made these photos so unusual? What did she find in them, what is it she was "searching for?"

Malcolm feels that, with *Untitled*, the burden of "journalistic betrayal" had been lifted from Arbus. She could not help but get these subjects "right." The "simple-minded," Malcolm writes, "are also the pure-hearted; they will not betray themselves, because they have nothing to betray." They are who they are, purely and simply. They "don't worry about not knowing enough." This revelation, as Malcolm imagines, must have brought Arbus great "relief" (1997, p. 187). But did it really? Malcolm goes on to note how Arbus had always worked as a participant observer. It was very important for her to get to know her subjects, to form relationships with them, to hear their "life story." If she took photos of nudists, she got nude too (camera dangling from her neck). This leads Malcolm to pose what I regard as the central question concerning the *Untitled* series: "How do you become a participant observer at an institution for the retarded? How do you pare yourself down?" (pp. 187–188). Artistically, one might take the pictures as if knowing nothing about photography—"as a child holding a camera in unsteady hands" (p. 188). Or, the "purposeful frontality" of the photos might "enact the quality of straightforwardness by which [Arbus's] encounters with the retarded were evidently marked" (p. 188). Still, artistic strategies aside, how did Arbus react *psychologically* to this subject matter shift? In identifying with these people, in seeing herself reflected back in the pictures, what did she find, and how did she adjust? Eccentrics, an alternative aristocratic family, recapitulated her own childhood freakishness; twins, triplets, and the like portrayed her dividedness. What about the mentally retarded? What message did *they* convey?

One fact that helps to move this inquiry forward concerns Arbus's ambivalence. Initially, it is true, Arbus found her subjects' "extreme innocence," their total lack of self-consciousness, intoxicating. Bosworth (1995) says, "Their complete absorption in what they were doing . . . delighted and moved her. She went back to photograph them again and again" (p. 299). A friend, T. Hartwell said, "Diane was obviously very moved by these pictures. 'These people are so angelic,' she kept telling me'" (quoted in Bosworth, 1995, p. 306). Yet in June 1971, a month or so before her suicide, Arbus had reversed her position. As she told her mentor Lisette Model, she now hated the pictures. Unlike her previous subjects, the mentally retarded did not collaborate with her in the making of the photographs—"they didn't look her in the eye, they didn't acknowledge her presence, nor were they charmed or seduced by her" (Bosworth, 1995, p. 312). On July 10, Diane visited Nancy Grossman and Anita Siegel's loft. She was apparently "extremely distraught." She said her work was giving her nothing back: "My work doesn't do it for me anymore." Grossman relates:

She had spent months photographing these mental retardates and she was exhausted, drained from the experience, and the pictures were no good—out of control. She could not confront these subjects as she had in the past—it was a new thing for her. She didn't know what it meant. (Bosworth, 1995, pp. 318–319)

One solution to the problem of self is to invent a new one, to construct your own "legend." You can take off your clothes, the trappings of normalcy, as Arbus's nudists did; you can invent an alter-ego, as did Polly Bushong; you can dress up like a woman, as did Arbus's transvestites. You could even wear a mask and hide, as did many of her other subjects. Splitting is another option—the trumpeting of one's dividedness, as with the twins and triplets. Or symbiosis, a possibility Arbus explored in her life and work. All such strategies in the end restore personality's primacy, even in fragmentation. They represent a search for authenticity, the effort to make oneself more real, more genuine. What the mentally retarded showed Arbus—what she thrilled to initially as a true revelation but finally could not quite abide—was complete unself-consciousness. They were uninvented. In their absorption they became no-self. As Zen Buddhists say, "Form is emptiness; emptiness is form." Self is an illusion. The mirror, in this case, was clear; or better yet, there was no mirror at all—nothing to wipe dry, no place for dust to cling. If Arbus's art was a search for self, as I believe it was, and if her subjects filled her up by seeing her into being, by clarifying her own predicaments, then what her last work summoned was oblivion. When she told friends her work was not "doing it" for her anymore, what she meant was exactly this: It was not completing her. She stopped being a collaborator and became, invisibly, a witness. I suppose one could say, if her subjects paid her no attention, she ceased to exist.

This all seems strangely fated. Every road to self winds up at the same location: illusion, myth, story. The mentally retarded took it one step further. They had nothing to betray, as Malcolm explained. There was no story, no legend. They were pure. For whatever reason, no-self as a solution to the problem of self was not something Arbus could embrace. The gap between intention and effect always had fascinated her. With the

Figure 8.1. Diane Arbus in November, 1970. Behind her can be seen several shots from the Untitled series taken at homes for the mentally retarded. (Copyright © Saul Leiter, courtesy Howard Greenberg Gallery, New York City)

mentally retarded there was no gap, because there was no intention.

These last pictures recall Arbus's first, and thus complete the circle, suggesting, in some respects, a continuity within the discontinuity. One of the first pictures Arbus took was of a dog. This dog came at twilight every day in the summer at Martha's Vineyard; the photos of the retarded likewise shimmer and float crepuscularly. She said of the dog, "I just remember it was very haunting. He would come and just stare at me in what seemed a very mythic way . . . just looking right through you. I don't think he liked me. I did take a picture but it wasn't very good" (Arbus, 1972, p. 8). This haunted "looking right through you"—this describes the mentally retarded, as well. They looked, but they did not look back.

New Developments

Shortly after finishing this chapter, I got word of a new Arbus exhibition opening at the San Francisco Museum of Modern Art (October 25, 2003, through February 8, 2004). It was to be a mixture of mostly old photographs combined with a number of never-before-released pictures. It would also, as is the custom nowadays, be accompanied by publication of a new book,

titled, somewhat ominously for me, "Revelations" (Arbus, 2003). Why ominous? Because I figured my "revelations" might require serious revision in light of "Revelations." There would be much to add, reconsider, rewrite. A massive overhaul of all my thoughts seemed in the offing.

On the other hand, in some ways this new development was a good thing, and at the very least it illustrates an interesting methodological point: The emergence of new material allows for a kind of hypothesis testing. New facts can be seen as either supportive or falsifying. Ideas can be compared against material unavailable for review as the ideas were being formulated.

So, naturally, I bought the book immediately and went through it with tremulous anticipation. Was I wrong or right?

The Arbus estate's disdain for the unauthorized 1995 Bosworth biography is no secret. In fact, as Malcolm (2004) explains in her recent review of *Revelations*, Bosworth's book was "almost universally disliked." It offered—many felt—a portrait of Arbus as "brooding and morbid and sexually perverse, slightly absurd as she runs about asking her friends if they know of any 'battered people' or 'freaks' she can photograph." As if to make up for this mischievement, *Revelations* includes letters, diary entries, and compositions by Arbus herself—some of which Bosworth had access to, and some she did not. Malcolm's take on this new "solid gold" cache of primary material is exactly the same as mine. "Guess what?" she asks. "Arbus comes out looking just as brooding and morbid and sexually perverse and absurd" (Malcolm, 2004). Funnily enough, though the new book was obviously intended as a corrective to Bosworth's melancholic unsubtleties, it actually essentially confirms her vision. No new Arbus emerges; rather, we meet with more of the same.

Still, a few details warrant consideration for what they add to the picture of Arbus offered in this chapter. Among the most interesting are these:

(a) In 1950 Arbus made a double-exposure of her daughter, Doon (Arbus, 2003, p. 130), that eerily presages her later photograph of the New Jersey twins. The right-side Doon is joyful, amused, relaxed, content; the left-side version is, in contrast, unsmiling, faintly perturbed, internally preoccupied, troubled by something. Twins as a psychological theme began early on, it would appear. And the fact that Arbus manufactured an image of her daughter's dividedness seems, in light of their apparent symbiosis, to confirm Arbus's own sense of the same, discussed at length in this chapter. Also underscoring Arbus's fascination with twins is a comment about photographing a "twins convention" (p. 159) as epitomizing an "eccentric event."

(b) The intensity of the "freaks" motif is likewise underscored. Arbus wrote that she was "obsessed" with it (p. 154). She is said to have filled three notebooks with thoughts about the idea (thirty-nine notebooks in total exist, composed of quotes from her readings, plans for work, appointments, and so on). Regarding the project, (which became "The Full Circle, 1961") she notes feeling "alternately haunted and blessed" (p. 157), in a "queer empty excited state" (p. 156).

(c) In this chapter I make a case for eccentrics symbolizing Arbus's sense of herself within her family as freakish in various respects, suggesting, for instance, that the "Jewish giant" in the room with his two oggling parents is in some ways Arbus herself. A quote from Arbus directly confirms this idea. She wrote of how she wanted to shoot "overprivileged children of tycoons [i.e., children just like Arbus] who are almost as too-muchblessed [sic] as freaks" (p. 160). That remark forms an equation that was only implicit until now.

(d) More emerges on the subject of Arbus's fascination with falseness, too. She wanted to take pictures of "pseudo-places"—"false deserts" and "real mirages."

(e) The symbiosis theme is touched on, as well. She refers, for instance, to a "silent dialogue all our lives" between herself and her brother, Howard Nemerov.

(f) Finally, there is even more on the nature of her relationship with her subjects. I am "a magic mirror," she revealed, "who reflects what anyone wants to believe because I can't believe they believe it" (p. 169).

There is much more, of course, including revealing contact sheets for some of her most famous photos (of the twins, of the boy with the hand grenade), insights about her relationships (especially the one with Marvin Israel), and even

a morbidly clinical reprinting of her autopsy report. Cause of death is listed as "incised wounds of wrists with external hemorrhage. Acute barbiturate poisoning" (p. 225). An editorial note typical of the attitude of her estate avers how her suicide seems "neither inevitable nor spontaneous, neither perplexing nor intelligible" (p. 225). The message seems to be, per usual, that both in life and in death she was and will always be ununderstandable. This is Doon's position, to be sure. As she explains in the book's afterword, "The photographs needed me . . . to keep track of them, to safeguard them . . . from an onslaught of theory and interpretation, as if translating images into words were the only way to make them visible" (p. 299). Moreover,

> the photographs were eloquent enough to require no explanation, no sets of instructions on how to read them, no bits of biography to prop them up. The relevant things about her were in them anyway. . . . The person she was seemed best left to the vagaries of our private mis-recollections, and of little use to anyone in encountering the pictures. (p. 299)

Malcolm in her 2004 review of the book calls such ideas "breathtakingly silly." "Theory and interpretation, far from threatening works of art, keeps them alive," she wrote. Being in the business of interpretation and theory, I of course agree with Malcolm. Arbus is no more unintelligible than anyone else. In fact, she may be *more* intelligible than most other people by virtue of the fact that she spread her mind out so vividly in the pictures she made, in her art, something most people, not being artists, simply do not do. And for an artist who speaks of identifying so intensely with all her subjects, who tells us she is their magic mirror, the contention that her life is somehow out of bounds or "of little use" in understanding her work seems almost preposterously obstreperous.

Doon Arbus seems intent on discouraging understanding except of the sort leaving her mother entirely "out of the picture." She seems to regard any such attempt as dismissive, reductive, vulgar, cruel, or otherwise impolite. But there's another way of seeing understanding, the drive to explore mysterious aspects of another person's life. It may be less an act of violence than an act of love. At least it is for me. The psycho-biographer's job, after all, is to *sympathize*.

Author note: The Estate of Diane Arbus did not respond to several requests to reprint photographs in this chapter. Most of the pictures I refer to in the foregoing can be found in Arbus (1972).

Notes

1. Even portraiture differs in basic ways from photography. The latter confronts an "object" that is far more recalcitrant. When Arbus photographs a face, say, there is only so much she can do if she wants to make this face look unlike itself (unless she were to intentionally distort the image in some way). Picasso, on the other hand, in painting Gertrude Stein can make her look any way he wishes; she is infinitely plastic; she is a more passive object of per-ception than is the photographic subject, who in Arbus's case especially is a subject-participant.
2. "I do feel I have some slight corner on some-thing about the quality of things. I mean it's very subtle and a little embarrassing to me, but I really believe there are things which nobody would see unless I photographed them" (Arbus, 1972, pp. 15).
3. And to be clear, I am not using this term in its pathological sense.
4. This fact calls to mind another methodologi-cal tip: *Read what your subjects read* and especially respond to, then explore the question of why. Sometimes this leads to insights not achieved other-wise. Elsewhere (chap. 11 this vol.), I look closely at Sylvia Plath's reaction to an essay by Freud.

References

Agee, J. (1941). Let us now praise famous men. Boston: Houghton-Mifflin.

Alexander, I. (1990). Personology: Method and content in personality assessment and psychobiography. Durham, NC: Duke University Press.
Arbus, D. (1972, October). Diane Arbus, photographer. *Ms Magazine*, 44, 52–53.
Arbus, D. (1961). "The full circle." Harper's Bazaar, November. Pp. 133–137, 169–173, 179.
Arbus, D. (1995). Untitled. New York: Aperture.
Arbus, D. (1972). Diane Arbus: An Aperture Monograph. Millerton, NJ: Aperture.
Arbus, D. (1984). Magazine work (ed. Doon Arbus & Marvin Israel). New York: Aperture.
Arbus, D. (2003). Revelations. New York: Random House.
Bosworth, P. (1995). Diane Arbus: A Biography. New York: Knopf.
Fromm, E. (1941). Escape from freedom. New York: Holt, Rinehart, & Winston.
Hammon, C. & Brennan, P.A. (2001). Depressed adolescents of depressed and non-depressed mothers. Journal of Consulting and Clinical Psychology, 69(2), 284–294.
Laing, R.D. (1962). The divided self. New York: Penguin.
Malcolm, J. (1997). Diane & Nikon: Essays on photography. New York: Aperture.
Malcolm, J. (2004, January 15). Good pictures. New York Review of Books, 51(1) 4–7.
Nemerov, H. (1965). Journal of the fictive life. New York: Rutgers University Press.
Sitwell, E. (1964). Taken care of. New York: Atheneum.
Southall, T.W. (1984). The magazine years, 1960–1971 (152–175). In D. *Arbus, Magazine work* (ed. Doon Arbus & Marvin Israel). New York: Aperture.
Terkel, S. (1970). Hard times: An oral history of the great depression. New York: Pantheon.
Zuckerman, N. (1971). Dimensions of sensation seeking. Journal of Consulting and Clinical Psychology, 36(1), 45–52.

PART II

PSYCHOBIOGRAPHIES OF ARTISTS

Chapter 9

Nothing Alive Can Be Calculated
The Psychobiographical Study of Artists

Attitudes toward psychobiographies of artists tend to fall into two general camps: Some see nothing wrong with such a practice; others see everything wrong with such a practice. My sentiments lie with the former position, but I've thought a lot about the reasoning behind the latter, having been faced with it a few times in the course of my researches. Those who reject psychobiographies of artists by definition seem concerned, first and foremost, with issues of framing. That is, they feel too much information about the deeper motives of the artist, or even the artist's biography, interferes with perception of the art. Not only is such information unnecessary, they say, it also sullies the art itself, detracting from intrinsic qualities felt to be of higher purity. In short, art must stand on its own. All one needs to do is look at it. Everything about the artist is there to begin with, in the photograph or painting or poem. To add is to subtract.

Such arguments have mainly to do with which "frames" to privilege, I always feel. To appreciate a photograph, it does help to know about composition, about the placement of figure, about qualities of light and darkness or of color, about manipulations possible through the use of particular lenses, about the kinds of experiments that go on in the darkroom, as well as the history of photography. These frames even the most hardcore champion of purity rarely denounces. The psychological/biographical frame, however, is a totally different story. But why? Why single that frame out for special abuse? Maybe because it appears to suggest that the artist is not in complete control of her art, that she is at the mercy of forces outside awareness. Or because psychobiog-

raphy occasionally, when done poorly, reduces art to disease, treating the work as a symptom, a form of psychological defense against insight. Or even, quite simply, because it is impolite—some may argue—to rummage about in a stranger's psychology, insensitive and tactless, a form of dressed-up gossip.

These thoughts have some merit. Psychobiographers sometimes look a little too avidly for signs of disturbance in their subjects. And no small amount of presumption is required of those whose career demands that they spend most of their time imagining and making sense of a person who never asked to be understood or made sense of, and may even resent the very idea of such a thing. But speaking for myself, it has never been my experience that knowing about the life and psychology of an artist ever diminished my appreciation or respect for the art. Quite the contrary, in fact. These almost seem, at least phenomenally, like two very different types of knowing: One can practice what the writer Susan Sontag called an "erotics of perception" without taking the extra step of thinking about what one sees. I see the work first; then if, and when, I want to, I think about the person who made it, going back and forth in the process according to my moods. When I look at art I'm not the least bit distracted by a need to explain it or interpret it. I'm more involved in trying to figure out if I like it or not. And, speaking for myself again, liking the artist has absolutely nothing to do with liking the art he produced, though others admittedly may feel more dissonance about such a prospect than I.

What benefits come from psychobiographies of artists? We thereby better understand the elusive psychology of art, for starters. Artistic states are psychological states, after all, and no psychologist would be interested in pronouncing them out of bounds, any more than she might pronounce, say, near-death experiences out of bounds. Plus, psychobiographies of artists do advance understanding of a particular type of person, one who is most creative, most able to give form to what is initially formless. According to some psychologists (Maslow, for example) creativity is one sign of the optimally functioning individual. Thus, to examine the life of the artist is to discover more about what makes a person ideally psychologically healthy, in some cases. I tend to approach art as similar to dreaming or daydreaming in various respects (not identical with, but similar to). Analyzing how it happens, its characteristics and mechanisms, can lead to a more complete picture of the nature and function of fantasy—how contents get combined and condensed or displaced, how symbols acquire meaning, how personal experience achieves universality. Finally, theories of personality are most successful when most inclusive. They need to aim for scope and range. The artist is in some ways the prototypical outlier. As a fringe personality, his life reveals otherwise inaccessible truths about *personalities*, their forms and dynamics.

One could go on. But when it comes right down to it, the debate seems academic in the worst sense of the term. The purists' defense of purity, of the need for psychologists to restrain themselves, to stop trespassing over the artist's life, meets with a public hungry to know more. For when people thrill to art, especially when enigmatic or somehow paradigmatic, one of the very first things they want to hear about is the life of the person behind it. Who could have taken such a photo, painted such a painting, written such a poem? Where did she get her ideas? What was his life like? What was she intending to say? And, in what ways is he the same as, or different from, me? Psychobiography provides answers to these questions. And the questions show no sign of stopping. The way psychobiographers can be most useful is by continuing to perfect their own art, to venture answers more and more judicious, thoughtful, and incisive. Maybe what the purists decry most is bad psychobiography. This is in fact what psychobiographers decry most, as well. So as the field develops, resistance should weaken. The answer to critics of psychobiography is always, as Alan Elms (1994) once said, better psychobiography. Not less, but more, and better.

It's customary to begin dating modern psychobiography with Freud's book on Leonardo (1964). That relatively short examination of what was then known—not a lot—about the artist's life and work set a standard for what to do right and what to do wrong (see, for details, Elms, chap. 15 this vol.). The Freudian approach to the lives of artists is by now well known. Art, like dreams, expresses latent content. It can be read or seen as a secret history. It makes use of condensation, displacement, thematic affinity, symbolism, and other dream-derived mechanisms. It is dreaming while awake—a lucid dream. It must, therefore, be interpreted. The code of the art reveals, when properly cracked, unconscious ideas and energies, many dating back to childhood. Just as we don't immediately know the true meaning of our dreams, artists do not typically know the true sources of their art. Some may be more tuned in than others, but obscurity is the rule. A percentage of artists even avoid such knowledge, figuring that to know too much about what drives them would only interfere with process.

To take a Freudian approach to art is to assume that the work says more than it seems to on the surface. One needs to go beyond what is simply there, to make the implicit explicit. The search is for hidden coherences, the motives that the art simultaneously conceals and reveals. As Freud explained, despite all apparent randomness, surface contents always allude to the depths that produce them. The trick is to penetrate veiled references. In the land of Freudian theory, every day is Halloween; we find the real person when we strip off the disguise.

My chapter on Sylvia Plath (chap. 11 this vol.) exemplifies this method. Plath's father Otto died when Sylvia was a child. The "id" is loathe to relinquish its love objects, Freud maintained, so when one dies, it takes the object inside, makes the object part of itself as a way of maintaining the relationship in fantasy. Plath loved this father-imago, but she also hated it—Otto—for leaving her. Plath's efforts to kill herself are seen as acts of murder; she wanted not so much to die but to kill the image tormenting her. The poetry, then—or at least those poems on the subject of the father, and there are many—is homicidal. By killing her father artfully, in effigy, Plath hoped to live. But the shot backfired. Killing the part, the Otto introject, was self-murder. The part, after all, was *in* Plath; *it was she*, not a separate entity.

The poetry, then, codifies an interior struggle to take the measure of an inner object. Its imagery is treated as personal mythology that transposes latent conflict. The aim is to discover the symbolism's hidden meaning, or the "why" lying behind the symbolism.

Object-relations theory, developing in Freud's wake, also zeros in on the artist's early life— "relations" with inner "objects" representing key figures from childhood, most notably the mother and the father. These so-called introjects form and shape the self; self, then, is a relational entity, a fantasy-invested congress of characters interacting mainly unconsciously, sometimes splitting off from one another, sometimes merging into turbulent gestalts (see, for an example of this approach, chapter 8, this volume, on the subjective origins of Diane Arbus's photography). Art is a projection of this inner world. Winnicott, Kohut, and Kernberg are three such theorists from the object-relations camp who have proven especially influential. A nice review of how these theorists might be used to make sense of a life is provided in Winer & Anderson (2003).

Another way of doing psychobiography of artists begins with the assumption that lives are stories, that we narrate identity through the use of scene-enhancing scripts. The trick here is to discover how certain stories or story sequences (good scenes go bad, bad scenes go good) organize self-experience and become self-fulfilling or self-constellating. For Freud, manifest content was useful only as a portal to what was latent; narrative psychologists don't take this line. They stick with the surface, finding in it particular scripted patterns that reliably recur (without asking exactly *why* they reliably recur). One does not so much go beyond story but brings it out more clearly, discovering patterns, favored imagoes (interior characters), recurrent metaphors, and most of all, as mentioned above, story se-

quences. In short, what one tries to locate is a life script, the novel or play for which and in which one's subject functions as a major character. Those championing this approach include, most recently, Dan McAdams, Ruthellen Josselson, and Jefferson Singer, among many others, and more remotely, Silvan Tomkins, the inventor of what is called script theory.

Ogilvie (chap. 12 this vol.) typifies this method. He singles out one particular incident in J.M. Barrie's life—Barrie's "prototypical scene"—and then shows how that scene got recapitulated in Barrie's fiction, most notably the story of Peter Pan. The scene organizes major aspects of Barrie's life, in other words, and his writing. Tomkins might have called this episode "nuclear," in that something potentially good went very, very bad, so that Barrie spent much of his energy trying to make the bad good again. Was he successful? Probably not. In his desperation, he gradually became not so much himself but his dead brother, and also took on aspects of his mother's autobiography to boot. Interestingly, Ogilvie (2003) starts by applying Freud to Barrie's life, and then discards psychoanalysis in favor of a method more narrative in nature, because—and this is a decision all psychobiographers make from moment to moment—a script-based approach seemed like a better, more promising fit. We see theory emerge in real time.

Yet another way of organizing a psychobiography of an artist requires the combination of synchronic with diachronic analyses, or what personologist Henry Murray in a similar vein called "proceedings" and "serials." One begins with a single work, such as Elvis's original performance of the song "Are You Lonesome Tonight?" (see Elms & Heller, chap. 10 this vol.). Then one asks, in the instance of Elvis, what other songs he recorded around the same time, and how those songs may or may not share similar themes or express similar conflicts. The life also can be evaluated synchronically: What was Elvis experiencing psychologically when first recording "Lonesome?"

These aims accomplished, one turns next to diachronic-type questions: How does Elvis's initial recording of the tune compare to later recordings (here there were, overall, eleven). Do patterns emerge? Are similar errors made? And are the errors made consistently, in certain sections of the song as compared with others? Do the locations of the errors make sense psychologically? Do they seem, that is, to be psychologically motivated? As Elms and Heller (chap. 10 this vol.) point out, single events isolated from context and in time can doubtless be revealing, but "long enterprises" across an individual's life span, intermittent temporal sequences of psychologically related events, potentially tell us quite a bit more. A fuller understanding of a single event, Elms and Heller write, can be achieved "by seeing [that event] as the last installment in one of the many long-running serials that constituted [a person's] life, and by searching through the preceding installments in that serial to locate its common themes."

As in so much of psychobiography, then, we begin with a mystery, an enigmatic and in some way paradigmatic instance. Then we trace the spread of the mystery across the life, its residual interpenetrations, the way it uncannily depicts life themes and conflicts. Two challenges must be met: First, the mystery has to be identified, and that isn't always easy; second, its "arc" has to be carefully traced. Think of the single instance as a ricocheting bullet. One explores the circumstances surrounding its firing and then follows its careening path, leaving no vector unexamined.

Psychobiographies of artists may also take a functionalist tack. They can ask what an artist got out of her art, what role the art played in her psychological life, how it allowed her to deal with or to escape conflict. No doubt art is sometimes defensive. Like the unexamined dream, it lays conflict out metaphorically without necessarily allowing one to see that conflict correctly and objectively for what it is. Doing art can even cause problems for the artist; it sometimes has all the earmarks of wheel spinning, a grim repetition of themes and sequences that never come to any sort of resolution. Most people tend to regard art as somehow intrinsically therapeutic. It is not. It has that potential if used teleologically, but at the same time, most artists aren't particularly interested in seeing their work as an avenue for self-understanding. They simply want the art to be good. In rare cases, however, art seems to represent a "working through" in the psychoanalytic sense of the term. Deliberately the artist portrays her life in fiction, say, and then learns by writing how to overcome life challenges. Anderson (chap. 13 this vol.) is a study in just this sort of restitution. As a child Edith Wharton was isolated, lacking the sort of person in her life with whom she could share her talents and ideas. She later found herself in a marriage that only cemented these frustrations; her husband was unstable and seemed at a loss as far as appreciating her gifts was concerned. She felt, again, estranged and alone. The writing of *Ethan Frome* allowed her to express this frustration, and in the end it led to divorce; the book revealed something to her that she acted on in life. She moved forward positively. The art offered a solution.

So, keep an eye out for function. Ask yourself, What does this artist get out of his art? What does it "do" for her? And when it stops doing for him what it used to, why? Is the art a form of escape (defensive), or is it a way of working through (restitutive)? For more on this particular distinction, see Elms (1994).

I do want to mention a final approach to psychobiographies of artists, one I've discussed already in an earlier chapter (chap. 1 this vol.). More and more researchers seem content merely to diagnose their subjects with one or another mental "illness" (most often from the mood disorder category). So, for instance, van Gogh is called "bipolar," Sylvia Plath a "borderline personality," and the list goes on and on (sadly). This tack is useless for a number of reasons. First of all, it fails to make sense of the art itself. Calling van Gogh bipolar tells us nothing about why he painted what he did. Second, it is pathographic, ignoring by definition its subject's strengths. Third, such "disease" sniffing rarely achieves anything resembling an explanation. To give someone a name or label simply replaces sets of behaviors with "syndromes" that, themselves, only summarize the behaviors they pretend to replace.

I finish this chapter by examining two questions that come up repeatedly in psychobiographies of artists. First is the matter of medium. Each art form presents its own special complexities for the psychobiographer. Some media allow for more transparency than do others. Writers provide huge amounts of verbal material. Not only can we inspect their work—poetry, fiction, plays—but we also have access, if the writer happens to be famous enough, to journals, letters, autobiographies, reminiscences by friends and lovers, and so on. Writers leave behind a relatively thorough record of thought and communication, in other words. Sometimes it seems there's almost too much to go on. But this superabundance is good. As I've said already, the more data, the better. And so, not surprisingly, most psychobiography of art concerns itself with writers. Verbal material just seems pre-eminently interpretable. It's what we are used to dealing with. We live in a logocentric world.

But what if the artist is a musician or an abstract painter? Here the going gets tougher. Elms and Heller (chap. 10 this vol.) demonstrate one strategy for analysis of musical content in their chapter on Elvis. They home in on errors, but of a verbal sort. One might also inspect the emotional tone of a piece of music, or the context of its composition, or even its dynamics. John Lennon was into primal scream therapy when he recorded his first solo album in the early 1970s, *Plastic Ono Band*. As one might expect, on several numbers, especially the first, titled "Mother," one meets with a lot of angry-sounding howling. Lennon lost his mother as a child, so psychologically, his pain makes obvious sense. One has to be careful about reading backward from a suicide, but many of the lyrics of Nirvana's Kurt Cobain take on eerie importance in light of how his life ended. One wishes he were telling the truth, for instance, when he sang over and over (on the song "Come as You Are"), "I don't have a gun."

In one of my courses in psychobiography I focused for several weeks on Jackson Pollock. Most people aren't aware that when Pollock's career began, his work was mainly figural, although bizarre. Paintings like *Moon Woman Cuts the Circle*, *Guardians of the Secret*, and *Male and Female* seem relatively open to psychological interpretation based on themes in Pollock's life. In fact, Jungians found symbols galore, mostly numerical, in this work but they were effectively dismissed by art historians (Pollock had undergone Jungian analysis, though by all accounts he did not do much, if any, reading of Jung). That is not to say, of course, that other

approaches would not achieve more viable results. Later, during his "Jack the Dripper" phase, Pollock's painting drastically changed. Figures were missing, or at least hard to find (see figure 9.1). Form arrived randomly, a result purely of technique; drips splashed across a horizontal canvas lying flat on the ground, Pollock hunching over. The paintings lacked a "horizon," as Kurt Vonnegut once put it. What to do with this work? Can it be held to carry a psychological message? Frankly, I'm not sure. One can assess psychologically what led to this turn in Pollock's art, but in using the art as a way of reaching psychological conclusions about the man, it's hard to know how to proceed. Not impossible, but hard.

The ultimate question faced by psychobiographers of artists is this: Is psychology indispensable to an understanding of art work? Any answer depends of what one means by understanding. This same issue has surfaced with some urgency in the field of philosophy, stimulated, it seems, by Ray Monk's biographies of Wittgenstein and Russell. Conant (2001) puts the matter clearly:

> Some conclude that "everything that is relevant to an understanding of a philosopher's work is to be found in the pages he wrote. To look beyond the pages he wrote to anything of a more "personal" nature, whether said to a friend, or written in a diary or in private

Figure 9.1. Jackson Pollock, cigarette in mouth, poses for portrait in front of one of his paintings, January 3, 1949, in New York City. (Getty Images)

correspondence, is to look for something that is not part of the work, and thus without bearing on the task of seeking insight into what is happening on the pages of the philosopher's work. (p. 19)

We can be curious about the lives of great men and women, and we can seek to understand how these lives came to assume the shape they did, but we should not confuse the task of understanding these lives and what happens in them "with the utterly distinct task of learning to understand the philosophical works written by the individuals who happened to live those lives" (p. 19). These two activities—getting to know the life and getting to know the work—should be kept wholly apart, and never confused. They should be, that is, "compartmentalized" (Conant's term).

I disagree with this compartmentalist line, and so does Conant, for that matter. Good reasons for why are adduced by Anderson (chap. 13 this vol.). On the other hand, it does make decent sense to say that a theory or philosophy can be understood intellectually without resort to review of the theorist's or the philosopher's life. Ideas make sense, persuade, provide insight, and generally rise or fall regardless of the individual expressing them—just as the reader need not know my biography to find what I am saying here either valid or invalid. Of course, if one happens to be doing psychology, these same ideas can be dissected as a means of shedding light on the person propounding them. Art, however, is not primarily philosophical or intellectual theory. It is a whole-mind operation, like dreams. It is a personal interpretation of reality that, in the best cases, achieves universality. It is a way of seeing. While some artists work in a more transparently emotional fashion than others, to reject psychobiography in principle as a way of understanding art more thoroughly would be a rather obstreperous gambit.

Chapters that follow make this fact plain. Can one read Plath's "bee sequence" poems truly insightfully, making maximum meaning out of them, without the knowledge that Plath's father was a bee expert? Or what about Barrie? Does one get more out of *Peter Pan* after learning of Barrie's brother's death and his relationship with his mother in its wake?

Or take the case of the painter Max Ernst. At the age of fourteen, he was "strangely affected" by the death of a favorite cockatoo on the same day as the birth of a sister (Chilvers, 1998). Later, referring to himself in the third person, he wrote that "[i]n his imagination Max coupled these two events and charged the baby with the extinction of the bird's life" (p. 196). Chilvers notes, "A dangerous confusion between birds and humans became fixed in his mind and asserted itself in his drawings and paintings" (p. 196). He even came to identify himself with "Loplop," a bird-like creature that features in many of his works. Now, one can look at these works without any biographical context whatsoever, and one can find them arresting, beautiful, successful, or whatever. But the point is, we get something *more* out of our viewing, we understand what we see more thoroughly, with the fearsome Loplop's curious frame in place. Nothing is subtracted from the experience of beholding the art, but something is added. The "subtraction by addition" formula compartmentalists espouse simply does not hold up.

There are two different ways (at least) of knowing art. We have Sontag's "erotics of perception" and the relatively intellectual effort of interpretation. Psychobiographers certainly need practice at erotic perception; all work on art begins with experience, immersion in the medium. But interpretations arriving on the heels of this intense form of engagement are themselves just more immersion. To bracket them off, or to equate them with blindness, is to deny the fundamental fact that artists are driven to express. And they express what they care about deeply (in most instances). Arbus spoke of the gap between intention and effect. Her aim was to bridge it, not enlarge the chasm. And that is an excellent description of psychobiography's aims, as well.

References

Chilvers, I. (1998). Oxford dictionary of 20th century art. New York: Oxford University Press.

Conant, J. (2001). Philosophy and biography. In J.C. Klagge (Ed.), Wittgenstein: Biography and philosophy (pp. 10–39). Cambridge: Cambridge University Press.

Elms, A.C. (1994). Uncovering lives: The uneasy alliance of biography and psychology. New York: Oxford University Press.

Freud, S. (1964). Leonardo da Vinci and a memory of his childhood. New York: Norton.

Ogilvie, D.M. (2003). Fantasies of flight. New York: Oxford University Press.

Winer, J.A., & J. Anderson (2003). The annual of psychoanalysis, Vol. 31: Psychoanalysis and history. Hillsdale, N.J.: Analytic Press.

Chapter 10

Alan C. Elms & Bruce Heller

Twelve Ways to Say "Lonesome"

Assessing Error and Control in the Music of Elvis Presley

In the current edition of the *Oxford English Dictionary* (2002), twenty-two usage citations include the name of Elvis Presley. The two earliest citations, from 1956, show the terms "rock and roll" and "rockin'" in context. A more recent citation, from a 1981 issue of the British magazine *The Listener*, demonstrates the usage of the word "docudrama": "In the excellent docudrama film, *This Is Elvis*, there is a painful sequence . . . where Elvis . . . attempts to sing 'Are You Lonesome Tonight?'" (The ellipses are the OED's.)

This Is Elvis warrants the term "docudrama" because it uses professional actors to re-enact scenes from Elvis's childhood and prefame youth. But most of the film is straight documentary. The "painful sequence" cited by *The Listener* and the OED is an actual concert performance, occurring late in the film and in Elvis's life. It remains painful to watch: Elvis, his face puffy and wet with sweat or tears or both, his elaborate jumpsuit bulging at the seams, struggles with one of his most popular songs. He repeatedly forgets words and whole lines of the lyrics, replacing them with crudely self-abnegating jokes.

That particular performance occasioned widespread comment, not only during the film's theatrical release in 1981 but also in later biographical works on Elvis. As one example of film commentary, the noted critic Pauline Kael (1984) wrote (after expressing admiration for the young Elvis's performances):

By the end of the picture, in 1977, the heavyset, forty-two-year-old celebrity-god Elvis Presley is a gulping, slurring crooner, faltering on the lyrics of "Are You Lonesome Tonight?" . . . [H]e sweats so much that his face seems to be melting away. . . . [T]he dissolving face . . . recalls De Palma's pop-culture horror movie *Phantom of the Paradise*. (p. 201)

As an example of biography, Albert Goldman (1981) concluded his scurrilous best-seller *Elvis* with a description of the same scene:

He is smiling but sweating so profusely that his face appears to be bathed in tears. Going up on a line in one of those talking bridges he always had trouble negotiating, he comes down in a kooky, free-associative monologue that summons up the image of the dope-crazed Lenny Bruce. . . . For thirty or forty seconds of mental free-fall, you are up in that padded cell atop Graceland watching Elvis blither with tightly shut eyes as he voices all the crazy ideas that come thronging into his dope-sprung mind. (p. 591)

Other critics and biographers have similarly asserted or implied that Elvis's difficulties with the song during this performance came from his heavy drug use, and perhaps more generally from his deteriorating brain as he neared death, less than two months away.

Closer study of this performance, however, suggests that Elvis's forgetting and replacing of the song's lyrics were not merely a matter of random drug-induced memory loss, but were in large part psychologically motivated. Set within the context of his previous performances of the same song and related songs, his final recorded

142

performance of "Are You Lonesome Tonight?" provides evidence that issues central to his earlier psychological development remained significant until the end of his life.

Elvis's Early Songs: A Synchronic Approach

Psychobiographical studies of musicians present special problems. Psychobiography typically involves close study of words written or spoken by the subject. Musical lyricists provide plenty of well-chosen words for analysis, so studies of figures such as Bob Dylan or Stephen Sondheim may resemble studies of nonmusical literary creators. But without simultaneous consideration of the music that goes with Dylan's or Sondheim's lyrics, the psychobiographer omits aspects of their creativity that are central to their public success and perhaps to their private psychology. Composers of wordless or primarily wordless music present even greater problems. A few psychobiographers have written impressive studies of such composers: for example, Maynard Solomon (1995) on Mozart, Solomon (2001, 2003) on Beethoven, and Peter Ostwald (1985) on Schumann. But their analyses of the personal origins of nonverbal and nonprogrammatic music must remain largely speculative. Difficulties of a different sort face the psychobiographer of a subject who performs music mostly composed by others. In one of the few such studies, Ostwald (1997) developed an insightful analysis of Glenn Gould's piano artistry. But Ostwald necessarily relied on knowledge gained from a long and close personal friendship with Gould, as well as on Gould's own published writing and interviews, to interpret the psychological foundations of his idiosyncratic performances.

Elvis Presley falls into an intermediate category. He was principally a performer of others' musical compositions, though an unusually expressive and distinctive performer. He never wrote an entire song by himself, though he sometimes suggested song ideas to others, or encouraged them to write songs that expressed his current emotional concerns. He personally selected the songs he recorded and performed onstage (though not those he performed in films). His manager and his record producers tried when possible to limit his choices to songs for which they and he owned publishing rights. But Elvis often insisted on recording songs that he recalled from earlier listening, sometimes all the way back into childhood, and his choices were final.

Further, even though Elvis did not write the songs he recorded, he sometimes adapted existing songs to his own purposes. He deliberately changed words, phrases, and entire lines of some lyrics, as well as omitting lines or verses that didn't suit him. His choices of songs and his modifications of their lyrics can yield the sorts of personal data that make psychobiographies of creative artists possible. For instance, he spontaneously chose Arthur Crudup's jump blues "That's All Right, Mama" for an intense recorded performance at a time when his musical career was just getting started. The song's lyrics assert that the singer is willing and ready to evade his parents' (especially his mother's) attempts to control his sexuality, yet the lyrics also confuse mother and lover by calling both "Mama." This complex of Oedipal and personal control issues in one brief song, not widely popular before he recorded it but described by Elvis as one of his personal favorites, encapsulates a pattern of motives and conflicts that remained with him until his death.

Examination of other songs Elvis recorded during the same period in his life—in what might be called a *synchronic* approach to psychobiography (following Saussure, 1916)—can broaden and deepen our understanding of his principal concerns at that time. Over a two-year period, he recorded a total of ten songs that Memphis record producer Sam Phillips judged to be worthy of commercial release on his Sun Records label. Several unreleased recordings from the same period, when Elvis was nineteen years old to not quite twenty-one, went with him when Phillips sold his contract to RCA Victor. Most of those recordings were issued under the RCA label soon afterward. That entire set of early recordings made by Elvis in the small Sun Records studio (available as a CD collection titled *Sunrise*) is now regarded by music critics and knowledgeable fans as among Elvis's best: musically powerful, emotionally expressive, pioneering rock and roll.

Among the ten Sun Records releases, two are light-hearted but rather explicit assertions of sexual prowess—songs of the older male adolescent, as Elvis was at the time. Five are songs of abandonment, in three of which the singer triumphs, either by getting his woman back, by getting another woman, or by getting revenge. The remaining three songs, including "That's All Right, Mama," are love songs in which mother and sexual lover are symbolically or linguistically intermingled. In "Baby, Let's Play House," for instance, the singer repeatedly asks his "baby" to come on back and play house, that is, to play mama and papa with him—a remarkably Oedipal song for a singer whose favorite nickname for his mother was "Baby." It would have been easy for Elvis as a three-year-old to see himself as having won a sudden victory in the Oedipal conflict, when his father went off to prison for over a year and his mother thereafter directed her attention and affection mainly toward Elvis. Of course, the victory was not final: His father did return, though marked as an ex-con and as something of a failure ever after. Further, the role even of temporary victor must not have been a totally comfortable one for little Elvis. There was always the possibility that his mother would disappear as his father had, if Elvis wasn't a good boy.

Another Sun release, "Milkcow Blues Boogie," seems particularly expressive of the resulting confusion of Elvis's emotions. The song, an old blues number first recorded by Kokomo Arnold, begins with a metaphor directly combining maternal and sexual imagery: "Now if you see my milkcow, please drive her on home, / I ain't had no milk and butter since that cow been gone." The song then mixes lamentations of abandonment, such as "But don't that old moon look lonesome when your baby's not around," with verses of angry retribution for being abandoned, in which the singer again confounds sexual and parental roles:

Well, I tried to treat you right, day by
    day,
Get out your little prayer book, get
    down on your knees and pray,
'Cause you're gonna need me,
You're gonna need your lovin' *daddy*
    here some day,
Well, then you're gonna be sorry you
    treated me this way.

From one verse to the next, the singer sounds at times like an abandoned child, an adolescent resenting parental control, and a mistreated adult lover. It's a song that Elvis says "don't *move* me" when sung as a slow blues number. But when he transforms it into a fast "boogie," a song of happy revenge, it appears to tap into his deepest emotions.

Some critics have asserted that Elvis's music changed sharply, becoming commercial and emotionally vitiated, when he began to record for RCA Victor. In fact, he largely continued, over the next three years, to sing and to record with much the same intensity as at Sun Records, choosing songs that displayed similar emotional concerns. His first hit for RCA, "Heartbreak Hotel" (by Mae Axton and Tommy Durden), is a bitter dirge of rejection, depression, and loneliness unto death. In its first verse, the singer introduces a powerful metaphor that he elaborates through succeeding verses: his residential address, "Heartbreak Hotel" on "Lonely Street," which reflects an inner landscape, a state of mind, rather than a geographical locale. In the second verse, he describes other heartbroken lovers like himself, crying in the darkness and so lonely they could die. The third verse adds the bellhops and desk clerks to the roster of those abandoned by love and hope. (In his first televised rendition of the song on February 11, 1956, Elvis intensified the hotel staff's depression by substituting the words "they pray to die" for the recorded version's less vivid "they could die.") In the last verse, the singer directly addresses his audience, inviting them to "take a walk down Lonely Street" if their baby leaves them too.

Elvis preferred the flip side of "Heartbreak Hotel," a neatly structured song titled "I Was the One" (by Aaron Schroeder, Claude DeMetrius, Hal Blair, and Bill Pepper). That song is just as emotionally desolate, describing the arc of a romance in which the singer teaches his lover to kiss, to touch, to cry, until he has her "as perfect as could be. / She lived, she loved, she laughed, she cried, / And it was all for me." In the final verse, however, someone teaches her to lie, and she thereby breaks his heart. The song remarkably anticipates the course of Elvis's relationship with Priscilla Beaulieu beginning four years later, but as of 1956 Elvis had had little experience with having his heart broken. One might wonder why he inhabits this song so personally, even telling an interviewer it is his favorite of the songs he has recorded (Osborne, 1999, p. 10). But as with "That's All Right, Mama," the lyric's central focus is on control and evasion of control. Thus, for Elvis the song's "I" may well have been not the singer but his mother Gladys. She had indeed tried to shape his behavior as closely as she could to her specifications—so closely that she left him no options except "to lie" about his sexuality and his anger, feelings that he could release only in secret or onstage in front of millions.

Elvis's first record album for RCA was in large part leftovers from Sun and covers of current or recent hits by other singers. When he was given the opportunity to record a second album entirely from scratch, he made several idiosyncratically personal choices. In the sharpest deviation from his rock-and-roll rebel image, he insisted on including Red Foley's "Old Shep," a sad country ballad about a boy and his faithful dog. Elvis had first sung the song publicly at age ten, and he apparently continued to sing it on various occasions in junior high and high school. The song describes the intense attachment between boy and dog, and then the inevitable loss when Old Sheppy grows old and ill. The singer tries to put the dog out of his misery, but cannot pull the trigger and lays down his gun. Shep nonetheless goes "where the good doggies go," to a Dog Heaven fantasized by the singer as "a wonderful home."

In its original form (recorded by Foley in 1940), the song had an understandable appeal to the young Elvis. Not only did it give him a long-term devoted friend, Old Shep, as he never had in real life; it also described them as freely roaming the fields together, something Elvis's strict mother Gladys would never have allowed. (As a child, Elvis briefly had a dog named Tex; it was put to death when it developed mange [Osborne, 1999, p. 84].) But the original lyrics apparently did not fully meet Elvis's needs. When he recorded the song at age twenty-one, he made several significant changes in Foley's verses. Late in the song, at a point when the singer is about to lose control of the relationship, Elvis reasserts control: as the dog is dying, he has Old Shep come to him rather than vice versa. (In the original, "I went to his side and I sat on the ground"; in Elvis's version, "He came to my side and he looked up at me.") But curiously, Elvis then confesses guilt for an act that is not in the original song. As the dying Shep lays his head on the singer's knee, the original states, "I stroked the best friend that a man ever found." Elvis substitutes, "I had struck the best friend that a man ever had," that is, by the act of aiming his rifle at Shep's head, even though he failed to shoot. Finally, Elvis omits an entire verse that describes Shep's awareness of his own imminent death; instead, without transition, the dog is imagined as already in Heaven.

These changes and omissions reflect even more pointedly than the original some of the powerful complexities of Elvis and Gladys's relationship. From a psychodynamic perspective, we can see Old Shep not only as a man/boy's canine "best friend" but as a substitute for Elvis's mother (whom he often called "my best girlfriend"). The fantasy of freely roaming the "hills and meadows" may then be interpreted not only as escape from maternal control but also as an unresolved oedipal wish. As with his earlier Sun Records choices and consistent with Elvis's developmental history, the song symbolically confuses (or fuses) his mother with an alternative affectionate object, and struggles with the conflict between separation and attachment (*freely roaming the fields together*).

"Are You Lonesome Tonight?": The Beginning

We could easily continue this synchronic analysis of Elvis's song choices during his early career. But we want to demonstrate a *diachronic* approach as well (Saussure, 1916): looking at his performances of a single song across time, to see whether that approach tells us anything further about his personality. Perhaps the best example in this regard is his intermittent performances of the song with which we began this chapter: "Are You Lonesome Tonight?" Elvis sang the song often—not at every concert he performed, but at certain key moments throughout his professional career. His many recordings of "Are You Lonesome Tonight?" show how he *chose* a song to perform, *intentionally modified* portions of the original lyrics (starting with his first performance of the song), *unintentionally or impulsively* modified other parts of the lyrics (by forgetting or spontaneously substituting words), and *framed* the song with comments that displayed his feelings about its lyrics, the quality of his performance, or his internal state and broader life circumstances at the time.

"Are You Lonesome Tonight?" was written in 1926 by Lou Handman and Roy Turk. Lyricist Turk borrowed several lines from Shakespeare and some inspiration from Leoncavallo's *I Pagliacci*. The song took a somewhat unusual form for its day, with the first three verses sung, followed by a lengthy spoken bridge, after which the third verse was repeated in song. It quickly gained popularity, with at least three singers recording it in 1927. The Carter Family did a country version in 1936 (with the sung lyrics considerably rewritten and absent the spoken bridge). Gene Austin, best known for "My Blue Heaven," included it in his stage shows in the 1930s. Three recordings of the song appeared in 1950: by Don Cornell (again omitting the spoken bridge), by the Blue Barron Orchestra (with the band's regular vocalist Bobby Beers singing and Chicago disk jockey John McCormick reciting the spoken bridge), and by Al Jolson, in one of his final albums. (Though various sources list Jolson as first recording the song or performing it on film sometime in the 1920s, there is no actual evidence of it in his performance history before the April 28, 1950, recording [Kiner & Evans, 1992].)

This brief history of the song is significant for two reasons. First, the song was brought to Elvis's attention by his manager, Col. Tom Parker, who did not ordinarily intrude into Elvis's choice of material. Parker apparently suggested the song because it was a favorite of his wife, Marie (Jorgensen, 1998, p. 127). She knew it through Gene Austin's stage performances; Parker had been an advance man and quasi-manager for Austin in the late 1930s. (Elvis may have been more impressed by Marie's liking for the song than by the Colonel's recommendation. Elvis was reportedly fond of

Marie, and may have later named his daughter Lisa Marie partly in her honor.) Second, as Austin never recorded the song, Elvis likely based his own performance on one of the most readily available recordings: either Al Jolson's melodramatic presentation (Spedding, 1986; Leavey, 2000) or the Blue Barron Orchestra's very similar arrangement (Worth & Tamerius, 1990, p. 351; Escott, 2002). Elvis later joked in a stage comment (see version 7, below) that *he* had recorded the song in 1927, so he seems to have known something of the song's early history; but the original 1927 recordings had been long out of print by 1960. Whether he relied on Jolson's or Blue Barron's recording to learn the song, he made several deliberate modifications in the lyrics (as noted under version 1, below) when he began to perform it himself.

Elvis began singing the song informally during his U.S. Army service in Germany (Jorgensen, 1998, p. 117). According to Priscilla Presley, he sang it during her first evening with him, six months before he recorded it (Presley & Harmon, 1985, p. 29). His studio performance of the song took place during one of his first recording sessions after discharge from the Army, at around 4:30 a.m. on April 4, 1960, in RCA's Studio B in Nashville. Earlier that night, Elvis had recorded one of his biggest hits, "It's Now or Never," displaying a new command of his voice with English lyrics set to the music of the quasi-operatic standard "O Sole Mio." Over the course of the same night, efficiently and in a wide range of styles, he recorded most of the songs for one of his finest albums, *Elvis Is Back*.

Elvis insisted on special preparations for recording "Are You Lonesome Tonight?" The studio lights were turned off and he sat in the darkness, accompanied only by acoustic guitar and bass, with vocal backing from the Jordanaires. (Guralnick [1999, p. 65] says drums were also included, but no drums are audible on close listening.) He needed only five takes, using perhaps half an hour of studio time, to finish the recording that has since sold many millions of copies. Ever the perfectionist in his studio work, Elvis angrily rejected RCA's initial remix of the song for single-record release. He insisted that it be mixed again to his specifications, because "his voice had been brought up unnecessarily at the expense of the background vocals" (Guralnick & Jorgensen, 1999, p. 157).

Those special circumstances suggest that the song had even greater significance for Elvis than most of the carefully chosen selections of the *Elvis Is Back* sessions, his triumphal return to his recording career. The further history of his performances indicates that "Are You Lonesome Tonight?" was, or became, a song of intense personal meaning for him. Of his many "live" or public performances of the song, ten are available on officially released long-playing albums, CDs, and videotapes. (Though other performances may be available on bootleg albums or via illegal Internet transmission, no effort has been made to collect them for this chapter.) The following list includes descriptions of the two complete takes officially released from the original studio recording session, plus these ten live performances. The circumstances of each recording are noted, along with some indication of salient events in Elvis's life at the time the recording was made (see Table 10.1).

"Are You Lonesome Tonight?": Diachronic Data

Version 1.   RCA Studio B, Nashville, April 4, 1960, takes 1 and 2. In take 1, Elvis gets through the first line and a half of the lyrics before he is interrupted, apparently by a producer or technician. (This take is not counted in our tabulation of Elvis's errors.) In take 2, Elvis sings and speaks the song's lyrics with only one minor difficulty: In the spoken line "Honey, you lied when you said you loved me," he hesitates between "you" and "lied," and his voice breaks slightly on the word "lied." In this and subsequent performances of the song, he modifies the original spoken bridge in several ways. He omits two lines completely: "Then came the day you went away, / And left me all alone." He also changes two phrases: "Fate had me play a lover" becomes "Fate had me playing in love," and "In the part of a broken clown" becomes "With emptiness all around." These are evidently intentional changes and therefore will not be counted as errors, though they may suggest some of Elvis's personal sensitivities.

Version 2.   RCA Studio B, Nashville, April 4, 1960, take 5. According to Ernst Jorgensen (1998, p. 125), the final bar of an earlier take was spliced into this take to produce the official single release. This official release is the baseline for all subsequent citations of Elvis's "errors"—that is, his deviations from this master recording of the song.

The session that produced versions 1 and 2 took place a month after Elvis's return to America from his two-year tour of Army duty, most of it spent in Germany and all of it away from recording studios. A week prior to the session, he had appeared on nationwide television as the widely advertised guest on a Frank Sinatra musical special. Early in Elvis's Army hitch, his mother had died unexpectedly. Fairly late in the hitch, he met fourteen-year-old Priscilla Beaulieu and began the serious courtship that would eventually result in their marriage.

Version 3.   Bloch Arena, Honolulu, Hawaii, March 25, 1961. This concert was a fund-raiser for the *U.S.S. Arizona* Memorial in Pearl Harbor. It was also Elvis's first and last public performance between his Army induction in 1958 and his return to Las Vegas showrooms in 1969. Earlier in the same week, Elvis had recorded the soundtrack album for one of his most financially successful films, *Blue Hawaii*. The only available recording of the Pearl Harbor benefit concert is poorly done, with female fans' screams often drowning out Elvis's voice. Under the circumstances, it's not surprising that he begins to joke a little during the spoken bridge of "Are You Lonesome Tonight?" He says, "You seemed to change, you got fat" (instead of "you acted strange"), and "you've lost your hair" (rather than "I'm standing there"). He also drops two lines of the spoken bridge entirely.

Version 4.   NBC Studios, Burbank, California, 6 p.m. show, June 27, 1968. This performance before a small invited audience, with Elvis accompanied by two members of his original band and several friends, was taped for use in what became known as the "Comeback Special," a nationwide television broadcast. As the band begins to play the introduction to "Are You Lonesome Tonight?" Elvis says, "Dead serious, boy." He interrupts the song's third line to say jokingly, "Lip still does that, man, you know?" When he reaches the spoken bridge, he slurs its first line, "I wonder if—you're lonesome tonight?" After the band members laugh at this, Elvis simply returns to singing "Are you sorry we drifted apart?" the line he had interrupted with the joke about his crooked grin. He repeats the remainder of the sung verses without ever returning to the spoken bridge.

Version 5.   NBC Studios, Burbank, California, 8 p.m. show, June 27, 1968, also for use in the "Comeback Special." This time there are audible screams from the audience as he sings the first line, "Are you lonesome tonight?" He follows the screams by singing, "Does your hair look a fright?" and laughs. In the fourth line, he omits the word "stray" from "Does your memory stray," and instead says (apparently about a nearby audience member), "Man, she's pretty," followed by a whistle. When he gets to the point at which he would ordinarily recite the spoken bridge, he instead sings "Woh woh woh woh," then "La da da da da," with the band laughing; then he returns to "Does your memory stray" and the rest of the sung verses. He goes even beyond version 4 by eliminating the spoken bridge entirely.

Versions 4 and 5 were recorded under especially difficult circumstances for Elvis. He had not performed before a "live," non-movie-set audience since the single Pearl Harbor benefit concert seven years earlier. Though Col. Parker had recruited an especially supportive audience (mostly NBC employees and fan club presidents), they were disconcertingly close to Elvis in the small television studio. Further, the performances were being filmed for a major TV special, officially named "Singer Presents Elvis" after its major sponsor, the sewing machine company. But it was indeed, as it came to be called, a Comeback Special, demonstrating that Elvis still had what it took as a performer after years of musically inferior films and a decade without a concert tour. He was extremely nervous during filming of the concert special, especially in the small-audience setting. The show's producers encouraged him to joke with members of his old band as he performed, in order to reduce his anxiety.

Version 6.   Las Vegas International Hotel Showroom performance, supper show, August 24, 1969. Elvis introduced "Are You Lonesome Tonight?" by saying, "I'd like to do this song especially for Colonel Parker's wife. She's in the audience tonight and she's had an operation, and I'm glad she got a chance to come over and see the show. Miz Parker, I'm really glad you're here tonight. I'll do this song especially for you." He then performed the song without error, except for the omission of the line "I loved you at first glance."

Version 7.   Las Vegas International Hotel Showroom performance, midnight show, August 24, 1969. Elvis prefaced this performance of "Are You Lonesome Tonight?" by saying, "Good evening. [Screams from audience.] Hoo boy. [More screams; he laughs.] Good evening, ladies and gentlemen. This is my first live appearance in nine years. [Applause] Thank you. I appeared dead before, but this is my first live one—and one of the first records I ever recorded—way back in 19—27, I think it was." He chuckles, then begins to sing. As with version 6, the only error in his performance of the spoken bridge is his omission of the line, "I loved you at first glance."

Versions 6 and 7 were by no means Elvis's first "live appearances" in nine years; versions 4 and 5 were also "live" in the usual musical performance sense. But his four-week run at the Las Vegas International Hotel, starting with an invitation-only opening night gala on July 31 and continuing with two shows a night thereafter, marked his first public performances before large audiences since the Pearl Harbor benefit in 1961. Success with Las Vegas audiences was important to Elvis, since he (and others) regarded his previous appearances there in 1956 as a flop. As with the Comeback Special, he felt extremely nervous on the first nights of the 1969 Las Vegas engagement. But as he neared the end of the run, he was (according to Guralnick & Jorgensen, 1999) "almost wholly at ease onstage" (p. 262). He had begun to offer the audience an extra treat every evening, a jokey autobiographical commentary between songs. However, Col. Parker felt Elvis was getting too loose with this banter and wrote a note warning him to watch his language, especially at "the dinner show when there are a great many children" (quoted by Guralnick & Jorgensen, 1999, p. 262). Marie Parker was at the dinner show on July 24, and for all Elvis knew, she might show up at the midnight show as well. As we indicated earlier, Elvis originally recorded the song because it was her favorite. So whatever he felt about the Colonel's warning, he had good reason to be on his best behavior in performing the song.

Version 8. Las Vegas International Hotel Show-room performance, midnight show, August 26, 1969. Elvis hums several bars from the song "Surrender" ("La da da da da," etc.), and then says, "I ain't gonna do that song" and moves immediately into "Are You Lonesome Tonight?" In the sung verses, he first replaces "Do you gaze at your doorstep and picture me there?" with "Do you gaze at your bald head and wish you had hair?" He begins to laugh in the middle of the line, "Is your heart filled with pain?" and laughs again at the end of each of the next two lines, dropping the final word in each line, then says (laughing), "Oh Lord Lord." This unusual disruption of the sung verses does not carry promise for the spoken bridge—and indeed, as soon as he says the first words of the bridge, "I wonder," he starts laughing as he drops phrases and lines from his recitation. The phrase "if you're lonesome tonight" disappears in laugh-ter, then virtually all the rest of the spoken bridge. The only line he manages to speak in full is "And I had no cause to doubt you"; otherwise he is laughing heartily, with occasional side re-marks: "Oh God—Oh man I tell you—Oh Lord," and "Oh Lord—Oh sing it, baby." At what would ordinarily be the end of the spoken bridge, still laughing, he moves back into the sung verses: "Shall I come back [laughs] again? Tell me dear, are you lonesome [laughs]?" He repeats the final sung verse in full, laughing during the last line. Then he says, "Whew! That's it, man, fourteen years right down the drain, boy I tell you. Four-teen years just shot right there, man, I tell you."

This performance has come to be known among Elvis fans as "Are You Laughing To-night?" Played widely on British radio, it became a sort of novelty hit there. Several accounts of this almost total ruination of the song have sug-gested that Elvis felt moved to hilarity by the

wordless obbligato he had asked either Cissy Houston (Guralnick, 1999, p. 354) or Millie Kirkham (Jorgensen, 1998, p. 285) to sing as accompaniment to the song during the Las Vegas run. But she had been singing that accompani-ment for weeks without provoking a similar re-sponse from Elvis—as demonstrated by his near-perfect performance of the song two nights before in versions 6 and 7. A more likely provo-cation for his laughter was the Colonel's heavy-handed hint to Elvis to get his onstage comments under control. As with his mother's insistent attempts to make him behave like a good boy, Elvis responded to the Colonel passively offstage, but (after going out of his way to please Mrs. Parker) aggressively misbehaved onstage.

Version 9. Las Vegas International Hotel Show-room performance, midnight show, August 12, 1970. Elvis sings the first verse, then shouts, "Sing it, Armond!" (referring to Armond Mo-rales, the bass singer for the Imperials, a gospel quartet Elvis had hired to accompany him dur-ing this concert series). Elvis continues with the next line, then repeats the joke, "Do you gaze at your bald head and wish you had hair?" Band members laugh at the joke, and Elvis continues with the sung verses. He interrupts the "Tell me, dear" line with a sort of quick trill in the middle, "Woo woo woo woo," then adds a sung "Oo oo oo oo oo" to the line's end. He laughs, the audi-ence claps, and he says, "Thank you. Well, we got that out of the way, now we can go on with the show. [He laughs again.] What? [An audience member asks for a specific song.] Oh, yeah, yeah. There's about 26 others I forgot, let's see. Punt. We'll punt, is what we'll do." He entirely omits the spoken bridge, and does not return to the sung verses; instead he moves on to a serious and impassioned performance of the Simon and Garfunkel hit "Bridge Over Troubled Water."

Elvis's four-week August run, his second Las Vegas run in 1970, was arranged partly to give a large Hollywood production crew the oppor-tunity to film rehearsals and stage performances for a full-length Elvis concert movie, *That's the Way It Is*. For potential use in the film, Elvis ran through many songs, including some new to his repertoire and others dating back as far as his Sun Records days. He was, as the film shows, at the top of his nightclub-style form, lean and vigorous. "Are You Lonesome Tonight?" was clearly not intended to be one of the stage show's major production numbers; he tossed it off almost casually, and it did not appear in the film.

Version 10.   The Coliseum, Hampton Roads, Virginia, April 9, 1972. This performance is almost perfect. As Elvis begins the spoken bridge, he makes an unclear comment, apparently to his band: "Talk to me baby" or something of the sort. After the line "Act One was where we met," he sniffs audibly. In the line beginning "Honey, you lied," he hesitates between "you" and "lied," just as in version 1. At the end of the song, he simply tells the audience, "Thank you. Thank you for listening."

This concert was part of a two-week tour of venues ranging from Buffalo, New York, to Albuquerque, New Mexico. A major reason for the tour was the making of another concert film, titled *Elvis on Tour*. Elvis may have been unusually careful with the song's performance because of its potential use in the film, though that possibility had not led to a complete performance in version 9. Life events may also have had an impact: Three months earlier, Priscilla had initiated a separation; then six weeks before the Hampton Roads concert, she told Elvis she was involved with her karate instructor and wanted a divorce (Guralnick & Jorgensen, 1999, pp. 304–305; Nash, 2003, p. 270). Shortly before the concert, reflecting these concerns, Elvis recorded several separation-and-regret songs, including "Separate Ways" (written at his request by one of his oldest friends, Red West), "For the Good Times," and "Always on My Mind." Singing a carefully low-key version of "Are You Lonesome Tonight?" onstage, with a hesitation in the phrase "You lied," fit right into his general mood.

Version 11.   Civic Center Arena, Pittsburgh, Pennsylvania, December 31, 1976. This performance was taped by an audience member; a shrieking woman near the recorder often intrudes on Elvis's singing. But Elvis's performance overall was so good that the fan's recording (the only one available) has been given an official

release by an RCA subsidiary label aimed at Elvis collectors. On this recording, as soon as Elvis sings the song's first line, "Are you lonesome tonight?", the shrieking woman (who sounds more intoxicated than impassioned) shouts, "I *am* lonesome!" She screams similarly clever answers to the lyric's questions through the entire song, often followed by laughter from other audience members. Elvis maintains his singing and his spoken recitation until the line, "Act One was where we met"; he laughs after "Act" and repeats the word as he goes on. With an occasional laugh he continues the recitation until "Act Two": "You seemed to change, Charlie, you acted strange. Why—[dropping the phrase, "I've never known"]. Honey, you lied when you said you loved me, you dirty ss—[dropping "And I had no cause to doubt you."] But I'd rather go on hearing your lies [dropping "Than to go on living without you."] You gonna make a bad some man's [inaudible word]. Now the stage is bare, And I'm standing there, [drops "With emptiness all around"], Just me and Charlie—good luck." He completes the song without further alterations.

The "Charlie" of these joking remarks was Charlie Hodge, Elvis's onstage assistant and sometime harmony singer, who provided him with guitars, water, and scarves (the latter for wiping away sweat before Elvis tossed them into the audience). The jokes also appear in part to refer to the obnoxious female fan and her interference with the song. (Of course, Elvis was used to screaming female fans, but this one was so persistent and attracted so much attention from others in the audience that he sounded unusually close to overt anger. Later in the concert, as he began his introduction to another song, a different fan shouted, "Play it." Elvis responded with a mixture of humor and threat in his voice: "Don't tell me to play it. I will when I get ready, you understand me.") Beyond the screaming fan, Elvis's additions and omissions in this version of "Are You Lonesome Tonight?" can again be seen as responses to recent events in his life. Linda Thompson, his most serious love interest since his divorce, had recently terminated their relationship, and his rather difficult new girlfriend, Ginger Alden, was in the audience. Whereas version 10 took place during a period when Elvis seemed "chastened, brooding, almost perplexed" about the failure of his marriage (Guralnick, 1999, p. 459), his problems with women at the end of 1976 were immediate and on the boil.

Version 12.   Rushmore Civic Center, Rapid City, South Dakota, June 21, 1977. The film *This Is Elvis* shows him entering an auditorium in Lincoln, Nebraska, on the night of June 20, just before the scene shifts to his singing "Are You Lonesome Tonight?" However, though Elvis is wearing the same jumpsuit in both scenes, Ernst Jorgensen (1998, pp. 406–407), on the basis of documentary evidence, identifies the song's filmed performance as taking place in Rapid City the next night. Elvis sings the initial verses perfectly. But on the fourth line of the spoken bridge, he says, "Fate had me pay—playing in—pl-pl-pl—bl-bl-bl-bl—plus tax" (unintentional stutter, followed by intentional stutter, followed by joking substitution). He omits the next three lines, then says, "You read your lines so li—cleverly [laughs], And never missed a cue. Then came Act Two. You forgot the words, You seemed to change, you fool, you acted strange, And why I've never known. Or why I ever did it. Honey—who am I talking to? You lied when you said you loved me, you ss—And I had no cause to doubt you. But I'd l-wl-wl-wl-rrrr—Rather go on hearing your lies [laughs] Than to go on living without you. Now the stage is bare, And I'm standing there, without any hair. Ah, no. Ah—[laughs, omitting "With emptiness all around."] If you won't come back to me, hnh—Aw, the heck with it!" [omitting "Then they can bring the curtain down."] He then sings the final sung verse perfectly.

Interpreting Elvis's Errors

Version 12 is, of course, the performance with which we began this chapter, the performance often cited as the ultimate evidence of Elvis's decline and total collapse as a performer. Two of his final concerts were filmed for use in a CBS television special, arranged by Col. Parker. The directors of the film *This Is Elvis,* Andrew Solt

and Malcolm Leo, clearly chose this performance of "Are You Lonesome Tonight?" to demonstrate Elvis's decay. To intensify (if not exaggerate) the effect, they spliced into the filmed performance his introduction to the same song from his disastrous performance two nights earlier. Well after this spliced-together introduction and Rapid City performance of "Are You Lonesome Tonight?" became the standard instance of late Elvis, drugged and nearly dead, it was deleted from further releases of the *This Is Elvis* film, and RCA stopped marketing the soundtrack album. The soundtrack of the CBS television special is currently available on CD, but no video version has been officially released, for reasons explained to fans by the Presley estate:

> Because of the severity of Elvis's health problems at the time the special was shot, Elvis was far from his best in the way he looked and the way he performed. . . . The true fans look at this through the eyes of love, respect and understanding. . . . But this is not so with much of the general public and the media. . . . They already emphasize and exaggerate the tragedy and sadness of the last years of his life too much. Right now, the emphasis for us is to remind them of all that came before. (Elvis Presley Enterprises, 2004)

By the time of these last performances, the forty-two-year-old Elvis was an overweight, exhausted, depressed, definitely middle-aged man, whose hair had turned gray though he still dyed it black. He was a prescription drug addict, obviously in physical decline and near death. (Indeed, he had begun to resemble his mother in the last months before her death at age forty-six. She had also become obese, exhausted, and depressed, abused diet pills as well as alcohol [according to Dundy, 1985; Hopkins, 1980; Nash, 2003], and dyed her gray hair black.) But the concerns he expressed in his final filmed and recorded performances of "Are You Lonesome Tonight?" were not unique to his immediate circumstances; he had struggled with much the same concerns through most of his life. His labile affect (at times he appeared to laugh and cry simultaneously), the intentional spoiling of the song with jokes about aging, the unintentional slips, the lapses of memory, had all been present in previous performances of this particular song—though in less sharply etched detail than in this performance.

As shown in *This Is Elvis*'s version (of version 12), he denigrates his own guitar playing before he begins the song: "I'm going to actually play the guitar. I know three chords, believe it or not. But I faked 'em all for a long time." (He was actually not a bad guitar player, but he had expressed similar feelings before. In an interview at which his father was present, shortly before Elvis left the Army, he said, "I was never very good on the guitar, was I, Daddy?" His father responded, "Then you've fooled a lot of people" [Fort Worth *Star Telegram*, February 20, 1960]). Elvis then jokingly—or perhaps not so jokingly—expresses fear of being exposed as a fraud: "They may catch me tonight." Some members of the audience detect a double entendre here and squeal with delight. He follows with an open acknowledgment that "if you think I'm nervous, you're right." Having thus begun a string of emotional disclosures, he makes the most revealing one of all, by identifying his personal concerns with the concerns of the song: "And then we did a song called 'Are You Lonesome Tonight?' And I am, and I was." Then, apparently seeking distance from the feelings of loneliness he has just expressed, he focuses on a broken nail, picks at it, says, "Damn!", changes it to "Darn!" and finally, his mother's son to the end, apologizes for his lapse in good taste and begins to sing.

As the song was written, the concerns in the lyric and in the spoken bridge are the same: rejection, loss of control, and the pain of abandonment. But their locus is different. The introductory lyric expresses a fantasy that the singer's former lover is lonesome for him and, her heart filled with pain, sits at home yearning for reunion. The spoken bridge, however, presents at some length a grim reality: It is the singer who has foolishly fallen in love "at first glance," has been lied to and then abandoned. And yet he would rather continue the relationship, even if fraudulent, than live without his ex-lover. She is so important to him that in spite of his ambivalence he cannot let her memory go—just as

Elvis could never escape from his emotional enmeshment with his mother Gladys, even though she had abandoned him in death. The singer says he would rather die than live without his woman; this in fact was what ultimately happened to Elvis. The grim prospects described by the spoken bridge are then denied by a restatement of the sung lyric fantasy that the singer's lover yearns for him and awaits his return. Through this concluding fantasy, Elvis savors the image of his ex-lover experiencing the sense of abandonment that he had repeatedly experienced in reality. By projecting his feelings onto the woman (or women), he rids himself of these feelings at least in part. By reversing the role relationships, he maintains the illusion of control, avoiding the recognition of his vulnerability and the pain of abandonment that the spoken bridge insistently expresses.

When comparing omissions, alterations, and substitutions in the final performance with his original studio recording, we note that Elvis sings the lyric (where the singer is in control) perfectly, without error. But in the spoken bridge (where the singer is vulnerable, expressing his loss), Elvis makes many significant, largely unintentional, errors. He mangles the line "Fate had me playing in love." He omits the next three lines: "With you as my sweetheart. / Act one was where we met. / I loved you at first glance." Then he slightly but saliently garbles the next line, "You read your lines so cleverly." In this portion of the song as written, the singer moves from his initially stated hope that his departed lover still yearns for him, to describing his experience of her abandoning him. Elvis's loss of control in his recitation parallels the singer's loss of control as depicted in the song. In addition to omitting or garbling these lines, Elvis also unintentionally says "pay" for "play" and then, attempting to rescue the situation, jokingly substitutes the words "plus tax" for "in love." This attempt at regaining control further highlights his difficulty in managing feelings of rejection. It reflects Elvis's history of filling internal emptiness with possessions, satisfying his longing for love by buying emotional fealty through expensive gifts, and trying repeatedly to assure himself that at least a few people love him without regard to his wealth.

In the next segment of the bridge, unconscious contents appear to intrude, as Elvis jokingly/angrily blames his lover in the song for forgetting the words, when of course he is the one who has done so. He continues his angry tirade, inserting "You fool!" in the line "You seemed to change, you acted strange." As with the previous intrusion, "You fool!" may refer not only to his lover but to Elvis as well. His voice exaggerates these self-criticisms to make them funny, but again, tears appear to flow. Then after confessing ignorance about the reason for his lover's change, Elvis castigates himself directly, as he wonders "Or why I ever did it?"—why he ever fell in love with her in the first place, and perhaps why he ever chose his life path of performing onstage before an oblivious audience. Finally, realizing he has been verbally wandering, he attempts to regain control through reality testing; he asks, "Who am I talking to?" Unfortunately, nobody is there to respond, even though he is the center of supreme adulation by the thousands of fans who pack the arena. He is profoundly alone. Without Gladys, without Priscilla, without Linda Thompson, he has no one. He had told an early interviewer about such feelings when asked about marriage. He hoped to find the right girl soon, Elvis had said, because "I get lonesome, right in the middle of a crowd" (Farren & Marchbank, 1977, p. 65). (His current girlfriend, Ginger Alden, had proven by then to be an unreliable companion, more interested in getting special treatment for her family than in Elvis himself. He introduces her after the song, but when the audience applauds her, he says, "Sit down, Ginger—that's enough for her.")

Elvis then returns to the bridge, completing the line he had interrupted: "You lied when you said you loved me." He alters the first word of the next line, as if he were going to curse his fantasy lover: "You s . . ." Then he catches himself and says the line appropriately, only to garble the third word in the next line, "But I'd rather go on hearing your lies." He attempts to control the slip by intentionally rolling the garbled "r." But his unintentional loss of control again suggests a personal emotional reaction to the content of the song: He is angry at having been lied to, perhaps by every woman he has ever trusted.

In the next section, he avoids references to the loneliness he most fears by substituting a joking reference to aging, which he had often used in concert: "Without any hair," replacing "With emptiness all around." Given his psychological state, appearance, and physical condition, however, this "joke" is more pathetic than humorous. Finally, avoiding the ultimate loss of control—death—he omits the last line of the bridge, "Then they can bring the curtain down." Elvis ends by singing the remainder of the lyric beautifully, fervently. Though he has largely lost control of the spoken bridge, he is now able to regain control via the lyric fantasy that his ex-lover is indeed lonesome tonight—lonesome for him.

Why was this song so emotionally potent for Elvis? We suggest that its story line is the repetitive story line of Elvis's life. Recapitulating his early and subsequent emotional experience, it describes the singer's intense, ambivalent attachment to a woman who betrayed and abandoned him without his fully knowing why. Consumed with anger and yearning, unable to regain his lost love or to establish new attachments, he becomes lonely, depressed, deteriorates physically ("without any hair"), and approaches the final curtain of Act Two: death.

Our interpretation of Elvis's errors as psychologically meaningful may seem unnecessary or even far-fetched. But such an interpretation is strengthened by the diachronic evidence that, of his nine *other* recorded or filmed concert performances of "Are You Lonesome Tonight?" from 1961 to 1976, most involve similar memory "failures," substitutions, alterations, or joking with the words of the song, usually involving similar imagery of abandonment, loss, and deterioration. Table 10.1 illustrates this pattern of errors, as shown in the lines of the spoken bridge that he most often altered or omitted. (The count of total errors per line includes version 12, but the same pattern is present when only versions 3 through 11 are tabulated to compare with version 12.)

Again, Elvis made very few alterations or errors in the sung lyric (when he, as the singer, is in control). He made many more during the spoken bridge (when he, as the singer, is vulnerable). In addition, the line numbers in boldface

Table 10.1 Cumulative Errors in Ten Concert Performances of "Are You Lonesome Tonight?", Compared with Elvis Presley's Studio Recording (right column)

Version #										Total Errors per Line	Lyrics, Line Number	Elapsed Time on CD (minute:second)
3	4	5	6	7	8	9	10	11	12			
											[Sung:]	
										0	Line 1	0:13
		*								1	Line 2	0:18
	*									1	Line 3	0:22
		*								1	Line 4	0:31
										0	Line 5	0:36
										0	Line 6	0:41
										0	Line 7	0:50
					*	*				2	Line 8	1:00
					*					1	Line 9	1:09
					*					1	Line 10	1:14
					*	*				2	Line 10	1:19
											[Spoken:]	
		*			*	*				3	Line 12	1:31
*	*					*				3	Line 13	1:36
*	*				*	*				4	Line 14	1:39
*	*				*	*				4	Line 15	1:42
*	*				*	*			*	5	Line 16	1:44
*	*				*	*		*	*	6	*Line 17*	1:46
*	*	*	*		*	*		*	*	8	**Line 18**	1:50
*	*				*	*		*	*	6	*Line 19*	1:52
*	*				*	*				4	Line 20	1:55
*	*				*	*			*	5	Line 21	1:58
*	*	*			*	*		*	*	7	**Line 22**	2:00
*	*	*			*	*		*	*	7	**Line 23**	2:04
*	*				*	*		*	*	6	*Line 24*	2:09
*	*				*	*		*		5	Line 25	2:14
*	*				*	*		*	*	6	*Line 26*	2:18
*	*	*			*	*				5	Line 27	2:22
	*	*			*	*				4	Line 28	2:27
*	*	*			*	*				5	Line 29	2:30
*	*	*			*	*		*	*	7	**Line 30**	2:32
	*	*			*	*				4	Line 31	2:37
	*	*			*	*			*	5	Line 32	2:40
											[Sung:]	
						*				1	Line 33	2:46
					*	*				2	Line 34	2:49
					*	*				2	Line 35	2:54

in Table 10.1 (those lines altered or omitted in two thirds or more of the live performances) tell a poignant story, consistent with our interpretation:

I loved you at first glance (Line 18) states Elvis's initial, intense attachment;

You seemed to change, you acted strange (Line 22), his betrayal and rejection;

And why I've never known (Line 23), his feelings of victimization and implicit anger;

With emptiness all around (Line 30), his painful, depressive loneliness.

In addition, the remaining lines that were changed or omitted in more than half of the live performances (Lines 17, 19, 24, and 26, italicized in Table 10.1) touch upon a related and also sensitive issue for Elvis: lying to or being lied to by his lover. He had sung about the negative impact of such lies as early as "I Was the One" in 1956. He had felt the necessity to lie (or at least to omit potentially incriminating information) far back into his relationship with his mother, and even earlier he had seen the dangers of lying when his father was sent to prison for forgery. He had felt bitterly betrayed by Priscilla's lying about her extramarital relationship, even though he had been lying to her about his relationships all through their courtship and marriage. He had good reason to believe that Ginger was lying to him in similar ways.

We have suggested elsewhere (Heller & Elms, 1994) that the personality of Elvis's mother was shaped by such negative factors as her childhood experiences in a highly dysfunctional family, the unanticipated stillbirth of her first child (Elvis's twin brother), and the felony conviction of her husband. The fearfulness and sustained depression that Gladys developed as a result surely influenced the quality of her mothering toward Elvis. Research on attachment suggests that mothers with the sorts of ambivalent family relationships she had experienced often raise insecure or emotionally disorganized children (Ainsworth et al., 1978; George & Solomon, 1999), and that unresolved depression in a maternal caregiver may increase the child's insecurity, interfering with the normal process of separation-individuation (Main, 1988).

Elvis as a young child appears to have internalized Gladys's unfulfilled dreams and wishes as a sense of mission. As he reached adolescence, these internalizations began to affect his behavior more and more forcefully. He aspired to become *somebody*, to give Gladys the life his father Vernon was unable to provide. But as he did so, the conflict unresolved in the initial separation-individuation process reasserted itself with a vengeance. Becoming successful—individuating —at this level meant becoming a potent, adult male, with the potential for commitment to a mate of his own choosing. In order to do this, Elvis could not remain Gladys's "baby," dependent on and loving only her the way he had done as a child. This, then, was Elvis Presley's double bind: to become a successful adult, capable of autonomous functioning and mature attachments, and to remain Gladys's baby. If he was age-appropriately independent,

he feared wounding her and being abandoned; if he remained her baby and dependent, he feared being engulfed and developmentally stuck. In response to this irresolvable conflict, Elvis developed the feelings of emptiness, depressive longing, self-recrimination, and anger often expressed in his musical performances, most vividly in his final performance of "Are You Lonesome Tonight?"

Alternative Approaches

But need we resort to such psychologizing in order to explain why Elvis repeatedly and at times disastrously wrecked his delivery of that song? Perhaps there are simpler explanations. Three such possibilities immediately come to mind:

(a) *Maybe he had a poor memory in general, or a poor memory at least for spoken rather than sung material.* The first part of this supposition is manifestly untrue. People who worked with Elvis at various stages in his career have often remarked on his amazing memory for thousands of song lyrics and melodies. The second part of the supposition is untrue as well. The directors of his films were impressed with his memory for entire scripts, including not only his own but others' roles in his movies, as well as long sequences of dialogue from other films that he especially liked.

(b) *Perhaps he was encouraged (or reinforced) by audience laughter to repeat the same errors in the spoken bridge when he performed it again.* To some degree this may be true. But he appears not to have regularly repeated the occasional errors he made in delivering other songs, even though fans laughed and then applauded at his recovery on those occasions too. Further, his particular pattern of forgetting the spoken-bridge material (as illustrated in Table 10.1) is specific to certain issues in his personal life; it does not seem congruent with any identifiable pattern of "reinforcement" delivered by the fans' laughter and applause.

(c) *As the critics and biographers have said or implied, maybe he was so stoned and/or badly deteriorated, especially during that final filmed performance, that he couldn't remember much of anything, let alone all those words in the spo-*

ken bridge. Again, there is something to this explanation, but it doesn't take into account either the overall pattern of errors in the previous live performances of "Are You Lonesome Tonight?" or the rest of his final filmed concert. In that concert, as shown both in the *Elvis in Concert* TV special and in the *This Is Elvis* movie, Elvis was able to perform a variety of other songs with little or no error. An interesting example is his performance, several songs later, of "My Way," which has a long series of verses and little lyrical repetition. As in some earlier concerts where he performed that song (a fairly recent addition to his repertoire), Elvis begins to sing with a page of lyrics in hand. But after briefly glancing at the page a couple of times, he tosses it aside, performing the rest of the song without error and with evident confidence. Further, his remaining concerts on that tour—the truly final, though unfilmed, concerts of his life—were by various reports effectively done, especially the very last one (which apparently did not include "Are You Lonesome Tonight?"). His physical shape was still poor, and he no doubt continued on a heavy drug regimen. But as long as the songs he sang were not so directly concerned with issues of betrayal, loss, control and lack of control, he was able to deliver charismatic and, as most fans saw them, exciting performances.

We have cited as inspiration for our approach the ideas of the linguistic theorist Ferdinand de Saussure (1916), who proposed that related events be studied both synchronically (in the same time frame) and diachronically (across time). For those who prefer to take their inspiration for psychobiographical research from a psychological theorist, we recommend Henry A. Murray (1981, pp. 32–33). Murray proposed that personality psychologists study not only *proceedings* (single psychologically meaningful events) but also *serials*: "long enterprises" across an individual's life, seen as intermittent temporal sequences of psychologically related events. As Murray would have argued, observing a single proceeding such as Elvis's final performance of "Are You Lonesome Tonight?" can give us some insight into Elvis's psychological state—as, evidently, film critic Kael, biographer Goldman, and docudrama directors Leo and Solt all concluded. But as Murray would have gone on to argue, a much fuller understanding of what that single event meant to Elvis, and what it revealed about his personality, can be achieved by seeing it as the last installment in one of the many long-running serials that constituted his life, and by searching through the preceding installments in that serial to locate its common themes. The errors Elvis made, his hesitations, his confessions during the song's final performances were not so much a revelation of his conscious confusion and failing health at that moment, as they were a confirmation of the lifelong sources of his underlying emotional pain.

Discography

The twelve performances of "Are You Lonesome Tonight?" discussed here are all commercially available, mainly under the RCA/BMG corporate label. Version 1 is on the CD set *Elvis Today, Tomorrow & Forever*. Version 2 is available on many CD collections, including *Elvis 30 #1 Hits*. Version 3 is in the boxed set *Elvis Aron Presley*. Version 4 is on the CD set *Memories: The Comeback Special*. Version 5 is on the CD *Elvis: A Legendary Performer, Volume 1*. Version 6 is on the CD set *Elvis Live in Las Vegas*. Version 7 is on the *Elvis in Person at the International Hotel* disk of the two-disk set, *From Memphis to Vegas*. Version 8 is in the *Elvis Aron Presley* boxed set and in the *Collectors Gold* CD set. Version 9 is on the CD set *That's the Way It Is Special Edition*. Version 10 is available only on the videotape and DVD titled *Elvis: The Lost Performances*. Version 11 is available as part of the complete concert in a two-CD set on the Follow That Dream label, *Elvis: New Year's Eve*. Version 12 is available, with varying amounts of pre- and postsong remarks by Elvis, on the *Elvis in Concert* CD, some but not all videotapes of the *This Is Elvis* film, and the out-of-print *This Is Elvis* soundtrack album.

References

Ainsworth, M.D.S., Blehar, M.C., Waters, E., & Wall, S. (1978). Patterns of Attachment. Hillsdale, N.J.: Erlbaum.

Dundy, E. (1985). Elvis and Gladys. New York: Macmillan.

Elvis Presley Enterprises, Inc. (2004). Frequently Asked Questions: Status of the TV Special Elvis in Concert (1977). Retrieved September 7, 2004, from http://www.elvis.com/elvisology/ faq/faq.asp?qid=27.

Escott, C. (2002). Elvis today, tomorrow & forever [Liner notes for CD set]. New York: RCA BMG Heritage.

Farren, M., & Marchbank, E. (1977). Elvis in his own words. London: Omnibus Press.

George, C., & Solomon, J. (1999). Attachment and caregiving: The caregiving behavioral system. In J. Cassidy & P.R. Shaver (Eds.), Handbook of attachment, 649–670. New York: Guilford Press.

Goldman, A. (1981). Elvis. New York: McGraw-Hill.

Guralnick, P. (1999). Careless love: The unmaking of Elvis Presley. Boston: Little, Brown.

Guralnick, P., & Jorgensen, E. (1999). Elvis day by day. New York: Ballantine Books.

Heller, B., & Elms, A.C. (1994). Elvis Presley: Character and charisma. In G. DePaoli (Ed.), Elvis + Marilyn: 2 x Immortal, 73–97. New York: Rizzoli.

Hopkins, J. (1980). Elvis: The final years. New York: St. Martin's Press.

Jorgensen, E. (1998). Elvis Presley: A life in music. New York: St. Martin's Press.

Kael, P. (1984). Taking it all in. New York: Holt, Rinehart, & Winston. (Originally published [Review first published June 1, 1981.])

Kiner, L.F., & Evans, P.R. (1992). Al Jolson: A Bio-Discography. Metuchen, N.J.: Scarecrow Press.

Leavey, M.I. (2000). Al Jolson—the world's greatest entertainer. Retrieved September 10, 2003, from http://www.jolson.org/stage/voice/ep/ep.html.

Main, M. (1987, June). Lack of resolution of mourning as related to disorganization in infancy. Paper presented at conference on attachment, King's College, University of London.

Murray, H.A. (1981). Endeavors in psychology (ed. E.S. Shneidman). New York: Harper & Row.

Nash, A. (2003). The colonel. New York: Simon & Schuster.

Osborne, J. (1999). Elvis word for word. Port Townsend, Wash.: Osborne Enterprises.

Ostwald, P. (1985). Schumann: The inner voices of a musical genius. New York: Orion.

Ostwald, P. (1997). Glenn Gould: The ecstasy and tragedy of genius. New York: Norton.

Oxford English Dictionary [CD-ROM] (2nd ed.). (2002). Oxford: Oxford University Press.

Presley, P.B., & Harmon, P. (1985). Elvis and me. New York: Putnam.

Saussure, F., de. (1916). Course in general linguistics (trans. R. Harris). New York: Open Court Press.

Solomon, M. (1995). Mozart: A life. New York: HarperCollins.

Solomon, M. (2001). Beethoven (2nd rev. ed.). New York: Schirmer Books.

Solomon, M. (2003). Late Beethoven: Music, thought, imagination. Berkeley, Calif.: University of California Press.

Spedding, C. (1986). The Spedding tapes: Robert Gordon. *Details*, November.

Worth, F.L., & Tamerius, S.D. (1990). Elvis: His life from A to Z. Chicago: Contemporary Books.

Chapter 11

William Todd Schultz

Mourning, Melancholia, and Sylvia Plath

Writing an essay on Sylvia Plath is a lot like taking up the subject of Marilyn Monroe or Hitler. One has the feeling of arriving late or, worse, uninvited to a party packed with people, all nursing finely wrought opinions of one sort or another for which they might even be willing to die. There is, one quickly senses, an enormous amount of catching up to do. What's left to say that can be the least bit unexpected, the slightest bit revisive? And when one combs the margins, and as the margins grow ever more marginal, so too do most ideas residing there. In fact, the more limited the aim, the more precise the question asked, the more jejune it proportionally becomes. Slim chance for a large statement, in other words.

Plus, there is so much to canvas—multiplying mountains of opinion, some worth thinking about, some not at all. Even a partial list of required reading includes Plath's (1993) first journals with their elliptical taint (editorial excisions); the newly released (2000), unabridged journals (excisions restored); Plath's "letters home" to her mother (more ellipses); the poems, of course (Plath, 1999; 1981b); the stories; the one novel *The Bell Jar* (1981a); Ted Hughes's occasional reluctant weighings-in, along with his last book of poems, *The Birthday Letters* (1998); the blizzard of memoirs and reminiscences written by intimates and mere acquaintances alike, some who scarcely knew Plath; and the numberless biographies, each with its own barely concealed agenda. Maybe the best book of all is Janet Malcolm's masterful and delightfully debunking *The Silent Woman* (1995), a sort of un-biography on the perils of biography that somehow says more about Plath than the various prior versions of her life put together.

In classes I steer students away from essays on thoroughly ransacked lives: the James Deans, Charlie Mansons, Kafkas, and Poes of the psycho-biographical universe. Everything surprising about them has long passed into boredom. Try something more manageable, I always say. Or find someone who's so far evaded the peeping eyes of the body-snatchers. Well, in this instance I did not follow my own advice. And luckily enough, against the odds I came across a question about Plath that to my knowledge has not been sufficiently explored (or, if so, only glancingly). The question also seemed anything but marginal. In fact, it was central. It concerned not only Plath's art, but also her personality organization and her suicide.

In a 1998 special issue of the journal *Death Studies*, these subjects—the art, the personality, and the suicide—receive exhaustive treatment. Lester (1998), for one, applies fifteen theories of suicide to Plath, finding Shneidman's, Murray's, and Beck's each to fit her case especially well (Beck's was most successful, with a score of 8.5 out of a possible 10).[1] But strangely, given the facts of Plath's case, Lester sets aside Freud, with his central focus on loss—even though "the major traumatic event for Plath in her early years was the death of her father [Otto Plath]," and despite the fact that half of the suicides in Lester's sample had experienced "the loss of a parent or significant other before the age of 15" (p. 663). He goes on to note, while still avoiding the idea's obvious ramifications vis-à-vis Freud, that Plath seems to be conscious of psychodynamic processes that many people remain unaware of—for example, her resolution of the Oedipal conflict by marrying a father-substitute . . . . Plath's poems (and her novel and journals as well) provide a rich source of clues to her psychodynamic processes, such as her identification with her father. (p. 659)

An additional weakness of Lester's essay is its penchant for diagnosis. Because Plath in the last months of her life was writing "at a frantic pace," she was "probably in a manic state" and would "probably be diagnosed today as having a bipolar affective disorder" (p. 659). Later that "probability"—already easily contestable, since (a) frantic writing hardly equals mania and (b) in reality Plath showed almost none of the cardinal symptoms of a manic episode—transmogrifies into fact, as Lester informs us that "*as a manic depressive*, Plath may also have been anticipating a really severe depressive episode after the manic state she had been in recently" (p. 660; emphasis added). These are surmises—weak ones—masquerading as truth. We might also reflect on the fact that naming something does not of itself constitute an explanation for the thing named. Psychobiography by diagnosis almost always leads nowhere except directly back to the labeled "condition."[2] As a strategy, it must be identified and then rejected. (See, for more on the perils of psychobiography-by-diagnosis, Schultz, chap. 1 this volume.)

In the same special issue, Runco (1998) applies what he calls a "psychoeconomic" hypothesis to Plath's art and suicide, proposing the use of "temporal and psychic investments" of creators to predict behavior. Closer to the point, the more an individual has invested in something—say, poetry—the more she has to lose and the less likely she is to remain flexible and creative. Plath started to write at age nine, in the wake of her father's death, and worked single-mindedly and uncompromisingly at her art right up to the days immediately preceding her suicide, so clearly she had "invested a large amount of time and energy in her work" (p. 641). This investment was perhaps unusually personal, too, given the confessional nature of her poems and of the novel *The Bell Jar* (plus assorted stories). A little confus-

ingly, Runco also brings in his concept of "discount rates," or the "interest rate that a person uses to discount benefits received in the future [from creative works]" (p. 641). One who discounts the future heavily "would be unwilling to make costly investments today in exchange for benefits to be received only gradually in the future" (p. 641). There exists, in simpler words, an inability to delay gratification, or even to keep at one's work when not meeting with hoped-for approval because of it. But this does not jibe with what we know about Plath. If she was "discounting the future [so] heavily," why was she writing like a demon in the days before she killed herself? Runco asserts: "She clearly was unwilling to invest any more in her creative potential" (p. 641). Yet isn't this manifestly untrue? She was making precisely this investment every morning when she rose in the wee hours while her children still slept in order to scrawl out the blistering poems of *Ariel* that made her name. These grinding investments stopped only when she died, not before. Like Lester does, Runco notes the correlation between loss and creativity (the early loss of one parent is common among creative persons) but considers more important Plath's immersion in and devotion to her writing—that is, again, her degree of "investment" in her work and the sense in which she had quite a bit to lose because of this investment. The stakes were high, Runco reminds us.

Shulman (1998) follows a psychoanalytic line in his assessment of Plath's suicide. Yet while noting that "her life was greatly affected by her father's death when she was 8, such that it initiated a chain of events [including, most notably, a symbiotic attachment to her mother combined with a compulsive drive for achievement and praise] eventually resulting in her own death," and while duly recording the established link between early parental loss and later suicidal behavior, he stops just short of zeroing in on the precise meaning of these facts for Plath, though his essay contains plenty of hints as to what that meaning might be. Predisposing suicide factors he lists include a wish to join her father in death, alienation, perfectionism, self-hate, and the failure of her marriage to Ted Hughes.

In this necessarily truncated review I'll include one more effort to size up Plath's art and suicide, partly in order to give a sense of the range of opinion existing on the subject, and partly to show just how bad the occasional bad psychobiography can be. In what is doubtless one of the most reductionistic and irresponsibly inferential case studies I've ever had the misfortune to discover, Thompson (1990) finds that a close reading of Plath's poems, journals, and letters reveals that "she was almost certainly [sic] suffering from a severe form of the hormonal disorder now recognized as premenstrual syndrome, or PMS" (p. 221). This summary judgment arrives on the heels of an earlier assertion to the effect that "the 'Electra-complex' hypothesis offered Plath by traditional psychology was, and is, finally inadequate." In point of fact, this was Plath's own hypothesis (as we shall shortly see); it was not foisted on her by "traditional psychology," whatever that means. And if the "Electra-complex" hypothesis is "finally inadequate," Thompson's paper does little to show us why or how—she assumes instead that credulous readers will take her word for it.

In due course, we discover that PMS produces no less than 150 physical and psychological symptoms (p. 222).[3] Was Plath occasionally irritable, tense, anxious? Indeed. Therefore, she suffers from "all the major symptoms of PMS." What about her "sore throats"? PMS. Her "clumsiness"? PMS. Her "backaches"? PMS. Her "itchiness"? PMS. That irritating "ringing in her ears"? PMS. For as we know, a "lowered resistance to infections during the premenstruum [is a] hallmark of the condition" (p. 223). Thompson seems to possess a preposterously uncanny ability to know exactly when Plath is entering the late luteal phase of her menstrual cycle. When Plath writes her letters to her mother—missives marked by the disguised alacrity so typical of "letters home" to parents—she is in the "symptom-free phase of her cycles" (p. 226). When she toils as a guest editor for *Mademoiselle*—a stint famously described in *The Bell Jar*—"Plath's hormonal balance was in a state of serious disruption" (p. 226). As she comes upon Ted Hughes in suspiciously whispery conversation with a Smith coed about which she later vents her jealous rage—that, the journal entry on the incident, was "probably [written during] her premenstrual week" (p. 229).[4] As so often happens in bad psychobiography,

these assorted "probably's" gradually lose all qualification. Plath in her poems makes frequent use of the metaphor of the moon (hardly unique to her). Well, for Thompson, this is because "the power of the menstrual cycle to control Plath's psychic landscape was an absolute reality" (p. 232). In a similarly amusing aside, Thompson judges poet A. Alvarez's admittedly "correct assessment" of Plath (as someone crying out for help) to be fatally marred by the fact that "he could not have known that Plath's reality had a biochemical basis" (p. 231). In short, if Plath in her work speaks of rising with her "red hair," if she invokes the moon, if she notices the petals of poppies (labias all), if the dawn landscape finds itself perturbed by a "splash of red"—such imagery reveals these to be "menstrual poems" (p. 237).

Maybe the most disturbing aspect of this article occurs at its end. We learn there that Plath in her last letter to her mother mentions being referred to "a woman doctor" by her very good local doctor. Of course, nobody has any way of knowing who this woman doctor was. Thompson, however, presumes her to be a psychiatrist (some evidence for this does in fact exist), then even suggests a name, Katharina Dalton—a London physician, apparently, who at the time was "successfully treating severe cases of PMS with progesterone therapy" (p. 244). Plath, needless to say, never saw the doctor to whom she had been referred. On February 11 she committed suicide. Thompson's final sentence—so self-assured, so judgmental of Plath's previous treaters, so pompous in the context of an essay riddled with utterly unconvincing "probably's"—informs us, sanctimoniously, that Plath thus "died in the only city in the world where she could have received effective medical treatment" (p. 244). Thompson's special knowledge, it appears, would have saved Sylvia's life.

What I want to do here, in this chapter, is take Plath's word very seriously and see where it leads us. I agree with Lester—she was unusually insightful about her own moods and their source. Her doctor calls her a "model patient" with a rare ability to "understand her own struggle against suicidal depression" (Stevenson, 1989, p. 297). In her journal she works extremely hard and with characteristic diligence to apply insights emerging out of psychotherapy, in short, to make sense of herself, her life and mind, and her relationships with her mother and father especially. In late December 1958 she reveals a fact and an opinion that together provide this chapter's direction. She writes: "Read Freud's 'Mourning and Melancholia' this morning after Ted left for the library. An almost exact description of my feelings and reasons for suicide" (Plath, 1993, p. 279). Now, I agree with the always wise Janet Malcolm. Plath in her journals tends to portray herself as "the heroine of a great drama"—in this case of an Oedipal variety, one of the greatest dramas ever (Malcolm, 1995, p. 100). Regardless, the fact that Plath finds Freud's model of depression so uniquely serviceable—an "almost exact description"!—remains exceptionally striking (as does the fact that Plath in one respect misread the essay, for reasons I discuss later). And so, like I said, I suggest we listen to Plath herself and discover to what degree Freud's words in the essay cited work to illuminate not only Plath's depression and suicide but also her poetry. The best place to start is where Plath did. What exactly does Freud's "Mourning and Melancholia" (1915) propose?

The Shadow of the Object

To begin with, it is remarkable that Plath picked up this essay at all, unless it was recommended to her by her treating psychiatrist, Ruth Beuscher, who attended her at McLean, where she spent three months after her suicide attempt, and with whom she had gone back into psychotherapy (Malcolm, 1995, p. 151). Freud was a brilliant writer, but this short piece is Freud at his most densely metatheoretical, laboring to develop a connection between melancholia and the oral stage of libidinal development, the way in which the ego picks out an object and cannibalistically devours it. (The essay, then, is more accurately concerned with pre-Oedipal than with Oedipal conflicts. It has nothing at all to do with what Thompson disparagingly calls the Electra-complex hypothesis.)

Freud starts as he often does, by treating mourning as a prototype for melancholia (much as he took hysteria to be a prototype for dreams, and dreams to be a prototype for the whole of mental life). He also drops any claim for the essay's general validity; he speaks only of melancholias of an "indisputable psychogenic nature" (1915, p. 243). Why compare melancholia to mourning? Both frequently develop out of the same exciting cause: loss. For Freud, mourning is not pathological (but expectable) and is generally overcome after a lapse of time. Also, mourning lacks melancholia's aspect of self-reviling. In mourning, "it is the world that has become poor and empty," whereas in melancholia, this sorry fate falls to "the ego itself" (p. 246).

In what does the work performed by mourning consist? The loved person gone, the mind must now relinquish all attachments to him. Not an easy task, however. It is in the nature of the mind never to willingly abandon any "libidinal position" (or, emotional fixation), even when a substitute love object beckons. The "id" prefers to cling; libido is adhesive. Still, in the end reality "gains the day" (p. 244). It takes time, but bit by bit we detach from lost loved ones. Reality defeats romantic imagination.

"Dissatisfaction with the ego on moral grounds is the most outstanding feature" of melancholia, Freud observes (p. 248). One part of the mind sets itself over and against the other, judges it critically—takes it, in other words, as its object. Here Freud ventures a speculation on which the rest of the essay turns. His contention is this: The self-accusations met with so frequently in the melancholic do not apply to the patient himself, but to someone else, someone the patient has loved or should love. What looks to be self-reproach is in fact reproach against a loved object (i.e., person). The dynamics may be reconstructed as follows. Plath, for instance, loved her father Otto. This love was shattered when Otto died (under circumstances to be explored later). Plath, at age eight, responded by identifying with her father, devouring his image rather than fully displacing her love onto someone else, a substitute. As Freud explains, "[T]he shadow of the object falls upon the ego, and the latter can henceforth be judged by a special agency [that Freud later called the superego], as though it were an object, the forsaken object" (p. 249). Also, by taking flight into the ego, erecting an image of the person now gone, love—as it always aims in its pleasure-seeking to do—"escapes extinction" (p. 257). It persists, in a sense psychotically, in its loving of a thing dead.

An alteration such as this of the usual course of mourning requires, first, an especially strong fixation to the loved object and, second, a disposition to narcissistic object choice (i.e., a regressive substitution of identification for object love). The first condition is self-explanatory. What does Freud mean by the second? That some people never quite give up a very early form of ("oral") loving characterized by ingestion, as it were, of the person loved. They carry with them in a mental mausoleum the history of their loving, a psychical congress of romantic attachments. Death of love is the birth of the image. And these images (introjects, as they are called) are not simply left alone like buried mementos. Hate born of the ambivalence characteristic of all love relationships, and of mental life in general, now comes into the open; we set about abusing and debasing the substitute internal object. Via this circuitous path of self-punishment, the melancholic takes revenge on the person who, by dying, refused his love.

Sadism, for Freud, solves the riddle of suicide. (And it is a riddle for the reason that the immensity of the ego's self-love would appear to rule out self-destruction.) We can succeed in killing ourselves only when we take ourselves as an object. In other words, we don't so much kill ourselves as we kill the hated introject. All suicide, then, in this formulation, is really murder–suicide. Murder is the primary aim; suicide is achieved by indirection. The introject has become a part of us. When we kill it, we unintentionally kill ourselves. It really does seem to be true: In Freud, the suicide doesn't quite want to die. He wants, rather, to kill.

What brings this hatred to a close? Three eventual possibilities. The melancholic kills herself, for one. Second, the fury simply spends itself. Or, third, the fixation of the libido to the object loosens through the act of disparagement and denigration. The object, in this last scenario, is "abandoned as valueless" (p. 257). Freud's prescription for the melancholic would seem to be just this: go on raging. Free yourself from the object's hold by hating it into worthlessness. When Plath writes "Daddy, I have had to kill you," in a poem ("Daddy") called by one critic the *Guernica* of modern literature, she follows Freud's advice to the letter. This realization in fact suggests our next step. How closely does Freud's model fit Plath's case? To what degree is she correct in calling it an "almost exact description" of her feelings? A very high degree, in my opinion (with one important caveat).

The Girl Who Wanted to Be God

Asking what the reading of this essay meant to Plath requires, first, that we explore the nature of Plath's relationship with her father prior to his death. We need to revisit her first seven years, in other words—a difficult job. Data will be scarce and of uncertain accuracy, yet not, as it turns out, utterly nonexistent. In a long historical introduction to *Letters Home*, Plath's mother, Aurelia Plath, tells us Otto wanted his first child to be a daughter since "little girls are usually more affectionate" (1976, p. 11). When this girl obligingly arrived, Otto was hard at work on the expansion of his doctoral thesis into a book. It appeared in 1934 under the title *Bumblebees and Their Ways*. Next came an invited chapter called "Insect Societies" (Aurelia wrote the first draft). Her father thus preoccupied, Sylvia "attached herself to Grampy," becoming his "greatest delight" (p. 13). In Aurelia's eyes Sylvia was a healthy, merry child—"the center of attention most of her waking time" (p. 13).

The year after Sylvia's brother's birth, Otto fell ill. He was losing weight, had a chronic cough and sinusitis, and was "continuously weary" (p. 15). He refused steadfastly, however, to consult a physician, fearing a diagnosis of lung cancer. Moaning in pain from cramped leg muscles, he deteriorated both physically and emotionally. The children were mostly kept away out of concern Otto's condition might frighten them, but before bedtime Sylvia would occasionally play piano for her father, improvise dances, show him her drawings, or recite rhymes or poems for him. From early on, words were used by Plath as a poultice, rhymes and poems as medicine.

At last Otto's sickness was diagnosed: a "far-advanced state of diabetes mellitus" (p. 19). Sylvia helped with his care. A home health nurse altered an old uniform for her and called Sylvia her assistant. She would bring her father cool drinks now and then, and show him drawings she made for him, as before. In October, a few weeks before Sylvia's eighth birthday, Otto's gangrened leg was amputated. On November 5 he died from a pulmonary embolism.

Aurelia Plath waited a day to tell the children. On getting the news, Sylvia apparently looked at her mother sternly for a moment and then exclaimed, "I'll never speak to God again" (p. 22). (Considering how in her adult poetry Plath would stress Otto's godlikeness, this comment may apply as much to her father as to any diety.) Later she made her mother promise never to remarry. Viewing her husband at the funeral parlor and finding him unrecognizable, looking like a "fashionable store manikin," Aurelia chose not to take her children to the funeral (a decision Plath found fault with in her writings). By October 26, 1942 (a day before Sylvia's tenth birthday), Aurelia Plath had sold the family home in Winthrop and purchased a small, white frame house in Wellesley, Massachusetts. With this, Plath once wrote, her Edenic life by the sea came to an inglorious end. "This is how it [her vision of her seaside childhood] stiffens. My father died, we moved inland. Whereon those nine first years of my life sealed themselves off like a ship in a bottle—beautiful, inaccessible, obsolete, a fine, white flying myth" (p. 272). In the myth's place Plath inserted a substitute romantic world—poetry. "There is a voice within me," she wrote in 1948, "that will not be still" (1993, p. 31). A diary entry from 1948 records her wish to be omniscient. She muses, "I think I would like to call myself 'The girl who wanted to be God'"—more merciful, perhaps, than the one who took her godlike father from her (p. 37).

The above is Plath's mother's version of Sylvia's first years, brought out, along with *Letters Home*, to elide. The idea behind the book, Janet Malcolm (1995) explains, "was to show that Plath was not the hateful, hating ingrate, the changeling of *Ariel* and *The Bell Jar*, but a loving, obedient daughter" (p. 33). As such salvage efforts often will do, this one backfired. A fresh new harpy appeared on stage: that "barnacled umbilicus" and paralyzing placenta of the mother, as Plath later described her in the poem

"Medusa," grasping with "eely tentacles" across the Atlantic. Aurelia Plath says in the same introduction: "Between Sylvia and me there existed—as between my own mother and me—a sort of psychic osmosis which, at times, was very wonderful and comforting; at other times an unwelcome invasion of privacy" (p. 28). The generationally derived narcissistic symbiosis implied by this aside will come up again soon.

To return to the question of Plath's father, we can look past her mother's perceptions to Sylvia's as reported in her journal, many of these nurtured by several years of intense analysis. But even before her psychotherapy, Plath possesses clear insights. She ruminates on her "dead father who is somewhere in you [meaning Plath herself], interwoven in the cellular system of your long body which sprouted from one of his sperm cells uniting with an egg cell in your mother's uterus." She goes on: "You remember that you were his favorite when you were little, and you used to make up dances to do for him as he lay on the living room couch after supper" (pp. 25–26). She guesses that, had her father lived, she would have been made to know botany, zoology, and science. In the event, she leaned abnormally to the humanities personality of her mother instead, feeling the "echo of her voice, as if she had spoken in you [again, in Plath herself]" (p. 26).

Recall the two preconditions set by Freud for pathological mourning: an intense fixation to the love object, and a predilection for narcissistic object choice. Plath helped in her way to nurse her father; she thinks of herself as his favorite, her mother calling her the center of the family's attention; she associates Otto with an idyllic seaside childhood brought to abrupt terminus by his death. As Malcolm (1995) relates, the death of Plath's father is perceived by many as "the shadow-event of her life, the wound from which she never recovered" (p. 34). Plath's fixation to Otto's memory is lent further support by the intensity of her later need to see his headstone. This graveyard visit I've described as Plath's "prototypical scene," a blueprint constellating the core parameters of her life story (Schultz, 2003; see also Schultz, chapter 3, this volume). It is dutifully recorded in *The Bell Jar*, in her journal, and in the poem "Electra on Azalea Path." The poem is particularly declarative.

Among other things, in it Plath tells us, "the day you [Otto] died I went into the dirt"—along with the bees sleeping out a blizzard "like hieratic stones." Otto's death was also Plath's. Her fixation rises to identification. Small as a doll, she lay dreaming his epic, image by image and with grim fastidiousness. She concludes self-judgmentally: "I brought my love to bear, and then you died"—not like a god, but "like any man" will. "It was my love," she feels, "that did us both to death" (Plath, 1981b, pp. 116–117).

Under usual circumstances, a daughter's intense fixation on the object of her father would seem axiomatic; parents are our first love objects, and subsequent refindings of objects simply recapitulate dynamics active in the parent–child relationship. But what about Freud's second precondition, narcissistic object choice? Is there reason to believe self was problematical for Plath, that ordinary boundaries between her and significant others tended defensively to blur? The answer is yes on both counts. Shulman (1998) devotes a section of his essay on suicide to Plath's narcissism, noting that her diaries reveal a grandiosity protecting self-esteem; a tendency on the part of Aurelia Plath to treat her daughter more like an echo than an autonomous being (as Aurelia's mother had treated her, too); and felt needs for perfection along with a corresponding sense of shame for weakness (pp. 604–606). However exaggerated, mawkish, or histrionic Plath's journals may be, especially early on, and however much she used them as an vehicle for unchecked self-mythology (beliefs many critics endorse), the simple quantity of passages centered on identity and its various crises argues against hyperbole. Hughes is doubtless right when he describes his wife as a "person of many masks," some "camouflage cliche facades," some "involuntary defensive mechanisms," and understands the journal's story to be one of the "death of the old false self in the birth of the new real one" (see introduction to Plath, 1993, p. xiv). The sense of hollowness and/or artificiality so core in narcissism is everywhere. "And I sit here without identity: faceless," Plath wrote in 1950. "Now I know what loneliness is, I think. . . . It comes from a vague core of the self. . . . I am lost. . . . Life is loneliness, . . . despite the false grinning faces we all wear" (pp. 17–19). In

another, even more apposite section Plath tells herself,

> I do not love; I do not love anybody except myself. That is a rather shocking thing to admit. . . . I am, to be blunt, in love only with myself, my puny being with its small inadequate breasts and meager thin talents. I am capable of affection for those who reflect my own world. How much of my solicitude for other human being is real and honest, how much is a feigned lacquer painted on by society, I do not know. I am afraid to face myself. (Plath, 2000, p. 98)

She wants to know, and asks over and over, "Why is my flow of inner life so blocked? How can I free it? How can I find myself and be sure of my identity?. . . How can I know who I am?" (pp. 288–289).

This vexing emptiness Plath filled with prizes, awards, scholarships, grades—in short, with tangible achievements never quite silencing the abyss's howl (and Plath was keenly aware of the roots of her perfection seeking, as well as its dead-endedness). The psychic osmosis of Aurelia's own mother relationship was extended, as it usually will be, to her daughter. Francis McCullough, editor of the first journals (1993), sizes up Plath's struggle: "Sylvia often fused her life with her mother's," she wrote, a fact complicating her efforts to "feel a separate person, an individual self." (264–265) The lure of symbiosis was felt in her relationship with her husband, too: "It's rather as if neither of us, or especially myself, had any skin, or one skin between us." Reaching her own power required "breaking out of the symbiosis" (Plath, 2000, pp. 264–265).

These things, then, are clear: Plath's intense devotion to her father's image, along with a regressive ("oral") tendency toward the narcissistic object choice to which Freud in his essay refers. In loving, Plath sought and devoured reflections (in some ways like Diane Arbus; see Schultz, chap. 8 this vol.). She perceived this. Love objects—father, mother, husband—she introjected and also fused with. The question Plath obviously focused on in her therapy (implied by the portion of Freud's essay she pointed to as an exact description of her suicidal feelings) is this: what to do about these introjects and how to waylay them?

The final sections of her journal record that struggle—the effort to apply lessons learned in therapy to her life. Principally she devotes herself, starting around December 1958, to practicing hatred for her mother, letting the hatred out, a vocation she undertakes with terrible single-mindedness after getting her therapist's permission and, one guesses, encouragement. For the moment she feels "terrific." She takes the position that she can't love this "walking vampire," but only pity her. She—Aurelia—gave herself to her children; now she wants them to return the favor. Her mother killed her father, Plath reasons, "the only man who'd love me steady through life" (Plath, 2000, p. 431). She hates her for that, for sure. He was an ogre, he was old, but "it was her fault" he died. She is, for all that, an "enemy," a "murderer of maleness" (p. 433). Lying in her bed Plath thinks what a luxury it would be to "kill her, to strangle her skinny veined throat" (p. 433). But for murder she's too nice. "I tried to murder myself instead," she says, "to keep from being an embarrassment to the ones I loved and from living myself in a mindless hell" (p. 433). Of her mother's narcissism Plath retains zero doubt: "I want to grab my life from out under her hot itchy hands. My life, my writing, my husband, my unconceived baby. She's a killer. Watch out. . . . She wants to be me: she wants me to be her: she wants to crawl into my stomach and be my baby and ride along" (p. 433). In between the vitriol she keeps wondering "what to do with hate for mother. . . . how to express anger creatively?" (pp. 437–438).

Plath would sometimes write in response to a prompt provided by her husband or by herself. These journal sections have the same feel to them. They read like an essay assignment (situation: you hate your mother; now say why and how much and what you'd like to do to her in return). The mother hate crowds out all other loci of anguish, the analysis taking the form of an inverted pyramid, everything leading back ineluctably to the vampire node at bottom. This is why, when Plath later records her reading of the Freud essay, she seems in her interpretation of it to go surprisingly astray. As I said earlier, it's a difficult piece, dense and metatheoretical. But

stripped to its essence, it speaks of loss, followed by introjection of the lost love object, followed by self-hatred. However, Plath, so consumed with her mother hate, misses the essay's central point. Rather than relating it to the loss of her father—the most obvious line to take—she (mis)understands the essay as suggesting "a transferred murderous impulse from my mother onto myself" (p. 447). She cites a "vampire" metaphor Freud used when, in fact, nowhere in the essay does such a term even appear. What she has lost, she implies tortuously, is not a father but a mother's love. Her grief is over that, not over her father dying and "deserting me forever" (p. 447).

That Plath commits this error, twists the essay's meaning according to her own idiosyncratic demands of the moment, in effect reaching a recondite conclusion in place of a far more obvious one—these considerations raise the question of the error's motive.[5] The journal entry in which she discusses the Freud piece is filled with thoughts of the father—how she identifies Hughes with Otto, how Otto deserted her. Still, when it comes to the essay's value for her, Plath returns once more to the mother theme, leaving the father suspiciously out of the picture. This is psychological defense, its aim the substitution of one hate for another easier to avow. In one of the journal's earlier sections, Plath even asks, "What do I know of sorrow? No one I love has ever died" (p. 33)—a very odd remark that she fails to correct, its oddness revealing an obvious blind spot.

The shadow of the father in fact haunts many of the journal's therapy-related sections, despite the more explicit attention paid to vampire Aurelia. He appears many times in dreams. In the first—a dream of her mother's that Plath records in careful detail—Plath is dressed as a chorus-girl prostitute. Otto, brought alive "to relive the curse of his old angers," slams out of the house enraged, ostensibly to bring Plath home. But in his fury he drives off a bridge and is seen "floating dead, face down and bloated, in the slosh of ocean water by the pillars of the country club." Everybody was then "looking down from the pier at them. Everybody knew everything" (p. 432). What Plath means by the cryptic last line she reveals later, confessing that her dreams are "guilty visions of him or fears of punishment" for having "killed and castrated my father" (p. 476). Plath's recklessness, her sexuality—Aurelia's dream tells us—precipitated her father's drowning. Another dream—this one Plath's—has Plath dragging gravestones away with a rope, then finding herself in a corridor filled with corpses, half-decayed yet clothed in coats and hats. She wakes screaming at the "horror of the deformed and dead," standing among them "in the filth and swarming corruption of the flesh" (p. 459). She observes, "A cold corpse between me and any work at all," referring no doubt to the dead and deformed Otto.

Still more dreams follow. In one Otto makes an iron statue of a deer that comes alive, though with a broken neck. It must be shot. "Blamed father for killing it," she says, "through faulty art" (p. 510). Another depicts men in costume, one with his back turned and a great phallic sword in his hand, with which he hacks off legs at the knees, "men falling down like ninepins with their legstumps and lower legs scattered" (p. 470). The legless are meant to dig their own graves with the stumps. "This is too much," Plath tells herself. The assorted deformities implicate the father, who lost his gangrened leg before dying. In dreams he beats at the door of Plath's consciousness, and she resists by focusing instead on her vampire mother, repressing by means of distraction. As long as she pre-emptively keeps only her mother in her sights, training attention on this one source of anger to the exclusion of others, the lost father is spared and by implication redeemed. For the time being, the "father worship" Plath refers to in the journals is simply too valuable to explode.

If in dreams Otto returns as a reminder of a debt unsettled, he also appears in Plath's art. On New Year's Eve, 1958, Plath summarizes a story she's working on, later named "The Shadow," about a "complicated guilt system whereby Germans in a Jewish and Catholic community are made to feel, in a scapegoat fashion, the pain, psychically, the Jews are made to feel in Germany" (p. 453). She wonders, "How does her father come into this? How is she guilty for her father's deportation to a detention camp?" In the story itself a girl named Sadie—a name suggesting sadism, according to Plath—bites a boy's leg

in self-defense—a bout of rough-housing has gotten out of hand. Sadie and her family are scorned by their neighbors. All of a sudden no one talks to them anymore. The reason why is finally revealed to center on Sadie's atheist German father. "My mother says it's not your fault for biting Leroy," the boy's sister tells Sadie on their way to school. "My mother says it's because your father's German." Sadie confronts her mother with this news. Mother tells her that her father "may have to go away from us for a while" because, during wartime, people get frightened of enemies in their midst. "There are places out West for German citizens to live in during the war. . . . Your father has been asked to go to one of those" (Plath, 1980, 150). God won't let it happen, Sadie exclaims; her mother overrides her, "God will let it happen." Sadie answers dully: "I don't think there is any God, then. . . . Not if such things can happen" (p. 151).

The story thinly disguises Otto's death, here represented as deportation ("going away"), and Plath's having been the innocent cause of it, just as she was in the chorus-girl prostitute dream. The last few lines about God even mimic Plath's reaction on being told of her father's dying: "I'll never speak to God again." Plath knows her guilt is the story's true motor, but in the journal, at least, she never makes the connection between "The Shadow"'s surface and its depths. She sees it as political allegory instead.

The Bell Jar (1981a) was also written during this time period. There the father-shadow looms, as well. The book's centerpiece is a visit to Esther's father's grave, prefaced by this aside:

> I thought the most beautiful thing in the world must be shadow, the million moving shapes and cul-de-sacs of shadow. There was shadow in bureau drawers and closets and suitcases, and shadow under houses and trees and stones, and shadow at the back of people's eyes and smiles, and shadow, miles and miles and miles of it, on the night side of the earth. (p. 120)

At the graveyard she thinks of all the things her father would have taught her if he hadn't died (things she was actually studying on her own at the time—botany, German, and a little later, bees).

She says with interesting ambiguity, "I had a great yearning, lately, to pay my father back for all the years of neglect, and start tending his grave" (p. 135). It's Plath herself who is the victim of neglect, not the grave; her father does need paying back, but for dying and deserting her, not for having his stone ignored. She remembers she never cried for her father's death, nor did her mother, who just smiled and said "what a merciful thing it was" (p. 137). She laid her cheek "to the smooth face of the marble and howled my loss into the cold salt rain" (p. 137). The very next line lands sharply on the page: "I knew just how to go about it." "It" refers to suicide. Proximity of content implies psychological causality: Her father's death is what makes her suicide necessary. She visits his grave, and then she makes her attempt, in a way closely paralleling her real first suicide effort. As Plath wrote in the poem "Daddy," "At twenty I tried to die / And get back, back, back to you. / I thought even the bones would do" (Plath, 1981b, p. 224).

Something else, inessential out of context, seems noteworthy. A few paragraphs after the section on shadow, and when mulling over various means of suicide—one being cutting—Plath muses, "It was as if what I wanted to kill wasn't in that skin or the thin blue pulse that jumped under my thumb, but somewhere else, deeper, more secret, a whole lot harder to get at" (p. 121). Then later, imagining shooting herself, she realizes, "I wouldn't have a clue as to what part of me to shoot at" (p. 127). These two asides I find peculiarly significant. They have everything to do with the true target of Plath's self-hate. They refer to something inside her, a *part*, a deeper, secret shade she feels she must kill. Here we circle back to Freud's essay, which Plath partly misunderstood, but in other ways understood perfectly well. Suicide is murder. The self dies indirectly. What we really aim to kill is the introject, that lost object now inside us, that part we took in as an appeasement for loss. The bull's eye was not Plath's mother, but her dead father, the man crowding his way into her dreams, the man at the center of her art, the shadow under the stone, at the back of her smile.

The journal inches its way toward these insights, though without quite rising to explicit awareness about them. At one point Plath theo-

rizes, "If you are angry at someone else, and repress it, you get depressed. *Who am I angry at? Myself. No, not yourself. Who is it?*" (p. 437). (Her answer is her mother again, though father seems equally likely.) She thinks back to a run-in with her husband—a case of his being gone when she needed him—and the "furious access of rage" she knew in response. "Isn't this an image of what I feel my father did to me? . . . It was an incident only that drew forth echoes, not the complete withdrawal of my father who deserted me forever" (p. 447). (This entry occurs on the same morning Plath read Freud's essay.) She realizes that all her life she has been "stood up emotionally" by the people she loved most: "daddy dying and leaving me . . . . Why do I feel now I should be guilty, unhappy: and feel guilty if I am not?" (p. 455). Then again: "the guilt, need for punishment is absurd" (p. 468). Most tellingly, perhaps, she wonders, "What good does talking about my father do? It may be a minor catharsis that lasts a day or two but I don't get insight talking to myself. What insight am I trying to get to free what? . . . I may have all the answers to my questions in myself but I need some catalyst to get them into my consciousness" (p. 474). Finally, she records what I think is the central question, the one most vital regarding her art, which she feels intermittently to be blocked, unrealized: "What inner decision, what inner murder or prison-break must I commit if I want to speak from my true deep voice in writing?" (p. 469).

The question of "what inner murder" is where we turn our attention next. But before heading in that direction, let's review briefly. With the appearance of the unabridged journals in 2000, a more fully developed picture of Plath became possible. Many of the cuts previously made by Hughes served, one can now see clearly with the two versions side by side, to protect Aurelia Plath, Sylvia's mother. Excisions restored, it is she who emerges as Plath's cobra-headed "Lady Death," even, in Plath's fantasy world, a witch. But despite the fierce interest in accessing her mother rage, and though Plath goes so far as to partly misread an essay by Freud in order to hate her mother still more deeply, Otto has his way of worming into what Plath called her Greek drama. We have seen that she dreamt of him repeatedly through the year 1959 and regarded those dreams of deformity and death as punishment for her feeling of having loved her father to death, as she put it in the poem "Electra on Azalea Path." She wrote a story, "The Shadow," symbolizing father loss and her reaction to it. She visited her father's grave and then incorporated that experience into both a poem and her novel. Throughout it all she keeps wondering, Who am I angry at? Why do I keep punishing myself? What part do I seek to kill? What inner prison break must I commit? And indeed, "What insight am I trying to get [in order] to free what?"

This chapter has been a pursuit of the question of how reading Freud's essay helped Plath to understand her feelings of suicide and her art. There is very good evidence that Plath fixated on the image of her father, that she was prone to making narcissistic object choices, and that the father introject was an unusually active complex in Plath's mental life—the part, as I said, she was really trying to kill as she sought to "get rid of the accusing, never-satisfied gods" surrounding her "like a crown of thorns" (Plath, 2000, p. 502). All that established, we look now at how Plath with her poetry actually seemed to apply recommendations made in the last section of Freud's essay, the one concerning what to do with the introject and how to advance beyond melancholia. Or, to quote Plath: the need Freud saw in the melancholic for "inner murder."

Killing Daddy

One can read in sequence the poetry written between winter 1958 and winter 1959, the period during which Plath was back in psychotherapy (she read the Freud essay in December 1958). On February 19, 1959, she begins "Suicide Off Egg Rock," about a man who walks into the water to die, "his blood beating the old tattoo / I am, I am, I am . . ." (Plath, 1981b, p. 115). The sun striking the water like a damnation, everything shrinking in the sun's corrosive ray, he finds "No pit of shadow to crawl into."

One month later Plath finishes "Electra on Azalea Path," the poem she wrote to do "justice" to her father's grave (though in the end she rejected it as too forced and rhetorical). It is a story

of identification and of guilt. The day her father dies Plath does too—for twenty years, in fact, she went into the dirt, into the "lightless hibernaculum" with the bees, worming back toward her mother's heart. But in a durable whiteness she dreams Otto's epic, just as, at the time, she was dreaming of him in life. She even refers in the poem to one such dream (about the chorus-girl prostitute), writing "My mother dreamed you face down in the sea" (p. 117). (That dream is described in the journal entry dated December 12, 1958). As described above, the poem's final stanza has Plath asking for forgiveness from her dead father, a request made necessary by her realization that, when a child, she believed like children do that she had magically killed him: "O pardon the one who knocks for pardon at / Your gate, father—your hound-bitch, daughter, friend. / It was my love did us both to death" (p. 117). The final line is interesting in context. With it she ties her love for her father not only to his death but also to hers as well. Loving him is killing her or even has already done so. But she says the same thing later, too, in "Daddy" (i.e., I died to get back to you).

In early March she finishes "Man in Black," preceded by "The Beekeeper's Daughter," an Oedipal allegory in which Plath speaks of "My heart under your foot, sister of a stone" (p. 118). The former poem inaugurates a preference to surface later, also: Otto is always in black and, again, shadowy. Majestically and more godlike than ever, Plath's father strides out, straddling the ocean itself in his "black coat, black shoes" and "black hair." "Till there you stood," she wrote, "fixed vortex on the far / Tip, riveting stones, air, / All of it, together" (p. 120). In her journal Plath calls this a "love poem." She also speculates that the "dead black" in the poem "may be a transference from the visit to my father's grave" (p. 478).

"The Colossus" has Plath piecing her father together, "a blue sky out of the Oresteia" arching above them (p. 129). Maybe he is an oracle? A mouthpiece of the dead or of some god or other? Whatever the case, her labor has taken thirty years, and she is "none the wiser." She says with striking appositeness: "My hours are married to shadow" (a shadow that, as she writes in "Poem for a Birthday," has been shaped by ten fingers into a bowl).

The man in black lends all these poems his thundering pulse, and he returns expectantly in a series of efforts called by Plath critics "the bee sequence"—a set of five poems on the father, followed in short order by Plath's most famous poem of all, "Daddy." In "The Bee Meeting," the first of these poems written in October 1962, the month of Plath's birthday, she is taking part in a dark ritual, or being initiated, more specifically, by "villagers" who resurface with murderous intent at the end of the poem "Daddy"—the rector (spiritual head of a church), the midwife, the sexton (church maintenance man, alternate meaning, a "gravedigger"), the agent for bees. "That man in black" Plath takes to be the rector. All in fact nod their "square black" visored heads in fields of creamy bean flowers with "black eyes" (p. 211). Plath is given an Italian straw hat and a black veil: "they are making me one of them," she observes eerily. Though exhausted, a "pillar of white in a blackout of knives," she does not flinch.

"The Arrival of the Bee Box" puts Otto in a coffin too heavy to lift—just as, in "Daddy," he is "Marble-heavy," a "bag full of God" (p. 222). When seen into through a grid the box—locked, dangerous, "dark, dark" and exitless—conveys the "swarmy feeling" of African hands shrunk for export, "black on black." The noise is most appalling, like a Roman mob—in "The Colossus" Plath had compared her father to a "Roman Forum"—but Plath "can't keep away from it." She has, she concludes, ordered a "box of maniacs." Yet they can die; she need feed them nothing; she in her moon suit and funeral veil is the owner (an assertion she will complicate later).

In another of these poems, "The Swarm," the bees, now out of the box, which after all was "only temporary," swarm in a "black ball" with their "black intractable mind" near a "black pine tree" seventy feet high. They must be shot down; the "knives are out for" them. At last they fall dismembered to a tod of ivy, walking their plank into a "new mausoleum" (tod means death in German).

With the last poem in the sequence, "Wintering," Plath's six jars of honey winter in "a dark without window" next to rancid jam and bottles of empty glitter—a lightless hibernaculum recalling the one Plath "wintered" into when her father

died. The "black" is bunched into this room like a bat. If in "Daddy" she barely dares to breathe or "achoo," having lived in Otto's "black shoe" for thirty years, in this room too, the one with the honey, she "could never breathe in," so filled it is with appalling objects, "black asininity" and decay (p. 218). She says, very tellingly, "It is they [these black objects] that own me" (reversing her earlier judgment). The cold sets in. The bees, all women, one ball of "black mind," carry their dead. They have "got rid of the men." Still the question lingers: "Will the hive survive to enter another year?"

Plath is ordering a very dark world here. The man in black, the shadow daddy Plath married—I'm referring to Otto, not Hughes—has become a ball of bees, black-minded, black-eyed, swarming seventy feet up in a black pine. But Plath owns the blackness. It can die for lack of food. It can be shot or stabbed. Or maybe not. In the final poem the black owns her, and a matter of months before her suicide she wonders will she survive.

It's hard to think of a better metaphor for the father introject than a ball of black bees that Plath both owns and doesn't own. In "Daddy" he is a ghastly statue with a gray toe big as a Frisco seal. As before, she prays to recover him from the waters he straddled, and in which, in dream, he drowned. "I have always been scared of you," she says—his Aryan eye, "not God but a swastika / So black no sky could squeak through" (p. 223). She pictures him at the blackboard, the "black man" who bit her heart in two. She reminds us how, at twenty, she tried to die to get back to him: "I thought even the bones would do." But she survived: "They pulled me out of the sack, / And they stuck me together with glue."

Next comes a transition of great import. Plath says, "then I knew what to do. / I made a model of you, / A man in black with a Meinkampf look. / And a love of the rack and the screw. / And I said I do, I do" (p. 224). This model Plath made, most critics have taken to mean, without the least bit of complication, her husband Ted Hughes, to whom, of course, she had said I do. But there's another possibility, suggested by knowledge of Plath's having read Freud, and by the modeling of Plath's father in the bee sequence and before.

The "man in black" she made and married was not Hughes, or not only Hughes, but the menacing introjected father; it was the introject to whom she said I do. As she declares in "The Colossus," a poem in some ways "Daddy's" precursor, "my hours are married to shadow." Plus, when Plath very deliberately calls this model a "man in black," referring to an earlier image she considered a transference from her visit to her father's grave, here again Plath tips us off as to subtext.

She says, Daddy, I'm through. "If I've killed one man, I've killed two—/ The vampire who said he was you / And drank my blood for a year, / Seven years, if you want to know" (p. 224). As before, others have taken the two murders to refer to Otto and Hughes, respectively. But again, there's an alternative way to read the line. We already know about how Plath feels she killed her father—she loved him to death—and how her dreams of deformity and death constituted punishment for the act. That is, by way of the kind of irrationally egocentric omnipotence young children often assume in relation to death, Plath fantasized having murdered her father in life. He is the one who drank her blood, he is the "vampire" who died when Plath was seven. The other man Plath kills—the one who, when he was a ball of bees, she thought of starving, shooting, and stabbing—is once more not Hughes, or not only Hughes, but the father image, the introject inside her, born of loss. In fact, that message is clear. The villagers from the first bee sequence poem even return, this time to dance and stamp on daddy, who lies back with a stake in his heart.

"Daddy, daddy, you bastard, I'm through," Plath concludes. But with what? As Plath says in a reading of the poem prepared for the BBC, with "the awful little allegory" she "has to act out" before she "is free of it" (Plath, 1981b, p. 293). What Plath is doing with "Daddy," and also to some extent in the bee sequence as well, is just what Freud recommended to the melancholiac in the last pages of "Mourning and Melancholia." She is hating the introjected object into valuelessness and getting "through with it" (i.e., abandoning it) thereby. The image must be murdered for self-hate to come to an end.

Hardly coincidentally, four days after "Daddy" Plath tries working the same psychic magic with her mother. She writes "Medusa," another act of poetic murder. Steaming over the sea, squeezing the breath from the blood bells of the fuchsia, Plath's mom leaves her gasping for air, dead and moneyless, overexposed like an X-ray. "Green as eunuchs," her mother's wishes hiss at her sins. "Off, off, eely tentacle," she says. But this time the ending remains ambiguous (whereas in "Daddy," daddy is doubtless dead). When Plath writes in this case, "There is nothing between us," we don't know if she means the relationship is finally mercifully over, or if she's simply noting an ongoing symbiosis. Whatever the case, in "Medusa" as in "Daddy," Plath is after what she called "inner murder," a prison break from the stranglehold of the introjected object.

"The Jailer" came a day later, five days after "Daddy," in that white hot fever-filled several months of poetry writing the results of which led Plath to tell her mother she was a genius, not without good reason. She has been "drugged and raped," knocked out of her mind, she writes, "into a black sack where I relax, foetus or cat" (p. 226). She dies "with variety—/ Hung, starved, burned, hooked." The tables have turned. If before she shot, starved, and stabbed the "black ball" of bees, the maniac in a box connoting the daddy introject, now it is Plath in the black sack, being drugged, raped, hung, starved, burned, and hooked. She can kill the introject—that shadowy *part*—but it can kill her, too.

Two men people this poem. One, the jailer of the title, rattles his keys. The other is of more interest in light of the task of inner murder. This man she imagines "Impotent as distant thunder/ In whose shadow I have eaten my ghost ration" (p. 227). (In "Electra on Azalea Path" she calls herself the "ghost of an infamous suicide.") Then with two simple lines Plath suggests "daddy" may have survived the poetical stake in the heart, the villagers dancing and stamping on him, and that perhaps she isn't quite "through" with him after all: "I wish him dead or away / That, it seems, is the impossibility" (p. 227). On the other hand, she asks, "What would he do, do, do without me?", echoing "Daddy's" opening line, "You do not do, you do not do." Again, the message seems to be this: The inner object she sometimes owns, and sometimes she is its minion, like with the bees.

"Lady Lazarus," with its recitation of Plath's suicide history and its famous line "Dying / is an art, like everything else," was written during the week of Plath's birthday, late October 1962. It is directed to an unnamed antagonist, an "enemy" that at first seems like an anonymous, imagined audience of people, but who then becomes "Herr Doktor, Herr God, Herr Lucifer." Since the Germanic Otto Plath was a professor with a Ph.D., and since Plath in earlier poems had referred to him repeatedly as both a god and a devil, in this poem her invisible interlocutor is doubtless her father. It is he whom she tells, at the end, to "beware." It is to him she says, "I eat men like air," utilizing a metaphor suggestive of narcissistic devouring, the "swallowing" of the dead love object.

If Otto is the nuclear core of Plath's poetry, he is also the major figure in Ted Hughes' book of poems about his wife, titled *Birthday Letters* (1998), written over a period of twenty-five years and addressed, with two exceptions, to Sylvia. As the book jacket explains, Hughes is largely concerned with "the psychological drama that led both to the writing of [Plath's] greatest poems and to her death." And it's true: Hughes' book is his own psychobiography of his late wife, in poetic form. It makes available the beliefs he had guarded closely for so long, against all biographical body-snatchers (except, notably, Janet Malcolm (1995), the first to approach Hughes sympathetically, and the first to put his voice front and center).

"The Shot" provides an early indication of what's to come. Hughes tells his wife "Your worship needed a god. . . . Your Daddy had been aiming you at God / When his death touched the trigger" (Hughes, 1998, p. 16). In the resulting flash, Hughes says, Plath saw her whole life. She "ricocheted . . . with the fury of a high-velocity bullet." But Hughes knows, and I agree, that he—Hughes—was never the bull's eye the undeflected, "nickle-tipped" god-seeking missile sought. He was not who Plath wanted to kill. Her real target, says Hughes, "Hid behind me. Your Daddy, / The god with the smoking gun. For a long time / Vague as mist, I did not

even know / I had been hit. / Or that you had gone clean through me—/ To bury yourself at last in the heart of the god" (p. 17). Elsewhere, Hughes refers to the mystery of Plath's hatred, how she had danced for her father "to sweeten his slow death and mix yourself in it" (p. 26).

"Dream Life" registers Plath's nightly terrors, her dreams, many reviewed above, "of a sea clogged with corpses, / Death-camp atrocities, mass amputations" (p. 141). In each night's sleep Plath descended unafraid, Hughes writes, into her father's grave, harboring a truly Orphean heartache, and fighting the same urge to look back. "Your sleep was a bloody shrine, it seemed. / And the sacred relic of it / Your father's gangrenous, cut-off leg. / No wonder you feared sleep" (p. 141). Calling to mind "The Jailer," discussed above, Hughes says "You were the jailer of your murderer—/ Which imprisoned you" and "you wanted to be with your father in wherever he was," "you walked in the love of your father."

In one of the book's final poems, "A Picture of Otto," Hughes movingly confronts the shade who not only haunted his dead wife—his body "full of [her] arrows" though it was her blood "that dried on him"—but his own life, as well. They meet in a dark adit, an almost horizontal entrance to a mine that is Otto's family vault. "I never dreamed, however occult our guilt / Your ghost inseparable from my shadow / As long as your daughter's words can stir a candle" (p. 193). "I understand," Hughes says, "you never could have released her. / I was a whole myth too late to replace you" (p. 193).

The poems tell this story: Plath "mixed" herself in Otto's death, the imprisoned jailer of her own murderer, her life of father worship requiring the invention of substitute gods who, being too mortal to take the fury of her love, "more or less died on impact, . . . sound-barrier events along [her] flight path" (p. 16). But Daddy was her actual target, the man behind all the other men, with Plath's prison break possible only when the jailer killed her murderer. Hughes, when writing about the poem "Daddy," understands with terrible clarity that Plath's healing was also her demise: "Healed you vanished / From the monumental / Immortal form / Of your injury: your Daddy's / Body full of your arrows.

/ Though it was / Your blood that dried on him" (p. 180). When we kill the introjected object, when we murder the murderer, since he is really only us, and we his owner, then we die too—the murder becomes a suicide. Our blood dries on the object.

Summary and Conclusions

Plath's life and death struggle was with inner objects or introjects—of both her mother and her father—that, being a writer, and being prone to self-mythologizing and self-dramatizing as most writers by definition are, she invested with qualities serving to make these objects even more powerful and more destructive. Her mother, as we saw, was a witch, a vampire, an eel, a "barnacled umbilicus," her father a god and a demon, a black ball of bees, a "man in black," a "shadow." Hate got the best of Plath. She was a peculiarly angry writer. When she asked of herself in her journal what to do with her hate for her mother and how to use her anger creatively, these were questions of terrific import. Really, Plath's life depended on how she answered them. And in the end, whatever else may have been happening in her life, she seemed to have no answer.

Though she partly misapplied it, Plath lived Freud's essay to the letter. Early loss resulted in the introjection of the lost love object (Otto); introjection resulted in self-hate driven by ambivalence toward the object (more on this in a second); and the effort to murder the object—that *part* Plath despaired of naming—led to suicide. Plath also—I think consciously—tried taking up Freud's recommendations to the melacholiac. Perhaps to get his advice was her reason for reading the essay in the first place; at the very least, it must have derived from a wish to better understand her predicament. In several of her poems, but especially noticeably in "Daddy" and "Medusa," written days apart, Plath clearly aimed to hate her father and mother into valuelessness, at the same time to allow her fury to spend itself. At "Daddy's" finish she even exclaims, "Daddy, Daddy, you bastard, I'm through," as if death by effigy—creative murder—might once and for all declaw or even forever silence this introject (although a matter of days later, in "The Jailer,"

Plath finds this task impossible). There were rational reasons for Plath to hate her father, most centering on the manner of his death. Putting it simply, Otto Plath did not have to die. Had he acted more reasonably and less cravenly in response to emerging symptoms—if he had seen a doctor—chances are he would have lived, or at least stood better odds of doing so. His was a death by indirection, maybe even what suicidologist Shneidman calls a "sub-intentioned death" (death hastened by inaction or immoderation). For Plath this must have been hard to understand, and even harder to forgive. It must have seemed that Otto did not love her enough not to die, or that he died on purpose. In murdering him—"Daddy, I have had to kill you"—she's saying goodbye to a parent she tried at first to worship but decided was unworthy and deeply disappointing, not worth the effort.

When Plath turned on the gas taps and lay her head in the oven on February 11, 1963, as her two small children slept in a nearby room—which Plath had sealed against the fumes—she placed her head on a "little folded cloth" (Stevenson, 1989, p. 296). In "Stings," part of the bee sequence written in October 1962, Plath has assembled her honey machine. About halfway through the poem, she stops abruptly to note: "A third person is watching. / He has nothing to do with the bee-seller or with me. / Now he is gone / In eight great bounds, a great scapegoat" (p. 215). It seems the bees sting this scapegoat, finding him out, "molding onto his lips like lies, / Complicating his features." Plath says: "They [the bees] thought death was worth it, but I / Have a self to recover, a queen." At the time Plath judged suicide's payment for murder too high. But what strikes me about this third person, this scapegoat, especially in relation to the "little folded cloth" Plath set her head on while preparing to die, is that on his head, instead of a hat, he wore a "square of white linen." So did Plath, it seems, when she died.

Notes

1. The shallower the theory, the higher its score. Shneidman is without doubt the world's leading authority on suicide. Still, to falsify his primary motivational factor—escaping *psychache*, or unbearable psychological pain/anguish—requires no

less than the discovery of a set of improbably cheerful self-murderers. At times he seems to be positing little more than the fact that unhappy people kill themselves more than happy people (although I'm simplifying). And Beck's high score benefits from a good deal of murky decision making. For instance, the rationality of Plath's thinking in the days preceding her suicide is unguessable. Undeterred by lack of evidence, Lester opines: "It seems likely that a cognitive therapist would have judged her thoughts to be irrational and the conclusions drawn from them invalid" (p. 661). An overly generous determination, to say the least.

2. I once had the pleasure (or displeasure) of witnessing this exchange between a patient's attending psychiatrist and her family: "Doctor, can you tell us why X hears voices and why she does such strange stuff?" Doctor: "Well, it is because she has a disease called schizophrenia." Family: "Oh, I see. But, how do you know she has schizophrenia? For sure, I mean?" Doctor: "Because she hears voices and does strange stuff."

3. Naturally, Thompson is unaware of the fact that the more "symptoms" a disorder possesses, the less adequately understood it is, and the less likely it is to actually be a disorder at all. In fact, for a crushing debunking of the entire PMS syndrome, see Caplan (1995).

4. This dating of cycles is based on journal entries referring to things like cramps and faintness, and on Plath's periodic references to her period. We are meant to be reassured by tabulations such as these: "Taking April 21 as Day 1 of her cycle, May 22 would have been Day 32. She probably began menstruating shortly thereafter (the moods of her journal entries at this time indicate a cycle of thirty to forty days). The incident on June 11 probably occurred at, or shortly after, ovulation" (p. 247). Equally "probably," none of these assertions is correct.

5. There is another possibility, though it still points to a misreading, and an even more glaring one at that. The only time Freud in his complete psychological works uses the word "vampire" occurs in his book *Totem and Taboo*, in a section devoted to the "taboo upon the dead" and its virulence among most primitive peoples. There he discusses taboos against handling a corpse and uttering a dead person's name. He reviews prohibitions applying to mourners, whose "presence is unlucky. If their shadow were to fall on anyone, he would be taken ill at once" (Freud, 1950, p. 53). In some cultures, Freud says, whoever looks upon a widow dies a sudden death, so to prevent this fatal catastrophe "the widow knocks with a wooden peg on the trees as she goes along, thus warning people of her dangerous proximity" (p. 53).

The essence of taboo is a fear of demons, according to Freud, on the supposition that a dearly loved relative at the moment of his death "changes into a demon, from whom his survivors can expect nothing but hostility and against whose evil desires they must protect themselves by every possible means" (p. 58). (In a remark that seems suspiciously on point, Plath in May 1959 records a decision to change the title of her poetry collection to "The Devil on the Stairs," feeling that it better "encompasses my book and 'Explains' the poems of despair," Plath, 2000, pp. 482–483.) The dead, filled with a lust for murder, seek to drag the living into their train. All the dead are "vampires," in fact, with a grudge against the living, and a desire to injure them and "rob them of their lives" (Freud, 1950, p. 59). Why this transformation of the dead into demons? The "true determining factor," Freud says, "is unconscious hostility" (p. 63). The demons are projections of hostile feelings harbored by survivors against the dead; projection thus "turns a dead man into a malignant enemy" (p. 63).

Perhaps what Plath really read by Freud is the above work (clearly relevant), not "Mourning and Melancholia" which, like *Totem and Taboo*, makes use in its title of alliteration. If so, that would require the presumption of two errors: She mistakenly names the title of the work she was reading, and once again, she mistakenly applies Freud's ideas on projection, unconscious hostility, and mourning to her mother, not her dead father. Whatever the case, the point remains: Plath reaches a recondite conclusion in place of a far more obvious one, and the error made is defensively motivated.

References

Caplan, P. (1995). They say you're crazy. New York: Addison-Wesley.

Freud, S. (1915). Mourning and melancholia. In J. Strachey (Ed. & Trans.), The standard edition of the complete psychological works of Sigmund Freud, v. 14, 1914–1916. London: Hogarth Press. (Originally published 1915)

Freud, S. (1950). Totem and taboo. New York: Norton.

Hughes, T. (1998). Birthday letters. New York: Farrar Straus Giroux.

Lester, D. (1998). Theories of suicidal behavior applied to Sylvia Plath. Death Studies, 22(7), 655–666.

Malcolm, J. (1995). The silent woman: Sylvia Plath and Ted Hughes. New York: Vintage.

Plath, S. (1976). Letters home: A correspondence 1950–1963. New York: Harper/Row.

Plath, S. (1980). Johnny Paris and the Bible of dreams. New York: Harper Colophon.

Plath, S. (1981a). The bell jar. New York: Bantam Books.

Plath, S. (1981b). The collected poems. New York: Harper & Row.

Plath, S. (1993). The journals of Sylvia Plath. New York: Avon.

Plath, S. (1999). Ariel. New York: Harper-Perennial.

Plath, S. (2000). The unabridged journals of Sylvia Plath. New York: Anchor.

Runco, M. (1998). Suicide and creativity: The case of Sylvia Plath. Death Studies, 22(7), 637–654.

Schultz, W.T. (2003). The prototypical scene: A method for generating psychobiographical hypotheses. In R. Josselson, A. Lieblich, & D.P. McAdams (Eds.), Up close and personal: The teaching and learning of narrative research (pp. 151–176). Washington, D.C.: APA Books.

Shulman, E. (1998). Vulnerability factors in Sylvia Plath's suicide. Death Studies, 22(7), 597–614.

Stevenson, A. (1989). Bitter fame: A life of Sylvia Plath. Boston: Houghton-Mifflin.

Thompson, C. (1990). "Dawn poems in blood": Sylvia Plath and PMS. Triquarterly, 80, 221–249.

Chapter 12

Margaret's Smile

A few guidelines usually govern my activities when I conduct case study research: (a) permit the person who is the object of my investigation to take the lead as far as he or she is able to go, (b) suspend any notions regarding how the study will work out, (c) be open to surprises, (d) use the problems that arise as opportunities to learn about and welcome developments in surrounding disciplines, and (e) estimate how much time it will take to complete the project, triple it, and be prepared to triple it again.

I didn't think I would need to consult my guidelines when I embarked on a study of James M. Barrie. I intended it to be a simple investigation with a specific focus on the possible Oedipal origins of Barrie's famous story about Peter Pan. My original purpose went no further than to locate and organize some new material for a course in personality psychology that I have taught for many years. In the context of a field deeply rooted in the tradition of psychometric science wherein variables instead of people are the preferred units of analysis, I felt it would do no harm to expose my students to "old" ways of thinking about personality development, if only in the form of interludes or breaks between lectures on scale construction and research designs.

I was particularly interested in finding an example of Freud's idea that the unconscious knows no time, that childhood conflicts remain active in adulthood, and that the contents of dreams and fantasies are often shaped by their unrelenting search for expression. The more vivid and familiar the example, the better, and although time had eroded some of the details, I recalled that James Barrie's earliest construction of Peter Pan had some Oedipal components in it, so I set forth to refresh my memory.

Brushing Up on Peter Pan

Consulting some notes I had written years before led me to rediscover that the book titled *Peter Pan* (Barrie, 1911/1967) was published nine years after another book written by Barrie, *The Little White Bird* (1902). The latter contains a story within a story about Pan named Peter trapped on an island in London's Kensington Park. This was Peter Pan's first appearance in print. Bear with me as I summarize a portion of the story.

The opening chapters of *The Little White Bird* introduce readers to the mysterious Captain W., a retired military officer in his mid-forties, and his six-year-old playmate, David. During one of their outings, the Captain points out the island in the Kensington Garden on which all the birds that become boys and girls are born. He informs David that no one who is human can be on that island, except for Peter Pan, the forerunner of the more familiar Peter Pan. Peter can reside on the island because he is only part human. Peter is "ever so old" and "always the same age," and still possesses every one of his baby teeth. He was born long ago and is one week old, having never had a birthday, "nor is there the slightest chance he will ever have one." The reason for this, one presumes, was parental carelessness. Adequate precautions had not been taken to prevent Peter from escaping through a window in his nursery and flying back to Kensington Garden.

Peter was an enigma on the island. Fairies ran away from him when he approached them. Birds ignored him, thinking him to be quite odd. Every living thing shunned him. He did not consider himself to be a bird for he had no feathers, only itchy places on his shoulders where his wings had once been attached. And not for a moment did he think himself to be human.

One friendship, however, did develop. That was with an old codger of a bird, Solomon Caw, whose primary responsibility was to direct other birds to the mothers who would rear them as children. Solomon referred to Peter as "poor little half-and-half." When Peter spoke of his urge to return to his mother, wise Solomon simply said "good-bye," words bringing to Peter's attention the fact that he had no means of returning. "You will never be able to fly again, not even on windy days. You must live here on the island always," Solomon informed Peter. "You will always be Betwixt-and-Between," Solomon said, and the narrator observes, "that is exactly as it turns out to be" (Barrie, 1902, p. 166).

Solomon was wrong about one thing. In fact, for a time, Peter was able to fly again. The fairies warmed up to Peter in response to his providing them with some special service, and the Queen fairy granted him two wishes. His first wish was to go to his mother, but to return to the garden if he found her disappointing. The Queen said that she could give him the ability to fly home but she couldn't open the door. Peter assured her that his mother always kept the window open in the hope that he would someday return. Thereupon the fairies tickled him on his shoulder blades and rejuvenated his ability to fly. He intended to head directly to his mother's home, but as he flew over the housetops, Crystal Palace, Regent's Park, and other notable landmarks, it occurred to him that his second wish might be to remain a bird. Upon ending the detour and reaching his home, Barrie writes:

The window was wide open, just as he knew it would be, and in he fluttered, and there was his mother lying asleep. Peter alighted softly on the wooden rail at the foot of the bed and had a good look at her. She lay her head on her hand, and the hollow pillow was like a nest lined with her brown wavy hair. He re-

membered, though he had long forgotten, that she always gave her hair a holiday at night. How sweet the frills of her nightgown were. He was very glad she was such a pretty mother.

But she looked sad, and he knew why she looked sad. One of her arms moved as if it wanted to go round something, and he knew what it wanted to go round. (Barrie, 1902, p. 202)

As Peter fumbled through some of his old drawers, one of them creaked and his mother woke up and he thought she said his name. He decided that if she said "Peter" again he would cry "Mother," and run to her. But she spoke no more. She slept once again with tears on her face. Her sadness made Peter miserable. So, sitting on the rail at the foot of her bed, he played a lullaby on his pipe and he "never stopped playing until his mother looked happy" (p. 204).

Peter returned to his mother's bedside at night a few more times and played her a kiss on his pipe. In time, he decided against his second wish, to be forever a bird, and told the fairies "I wish now to go back to mother for ever and always." They tickled his shoulders and he flew directly to the window. But the window was closed. Bars had been placed on it. Peering in, he saw his mother sleeping peacefully with her arm round another little boy.

Peter called, "Mother! mother!" but she heard him not; in vain he beat his little limbs against the iron bars. He had to fly back, sobbing, to Kensington Garden, and he never saw his dear again. What a glorious boy he had meant to be with her. Ah, Peter, we who have made the great mistake, how differently we should all act at the second chance. But Solomon was right; there is no second chance, not for most of us. When we reach the window it is Lock-out Time. The iron bars are up for life. (p. 208)

Close Enough?

The story of Peter Pan's first appearance was a bit different than I had remembered. It would require some theoretical doctoring to make it into an Oedipal tragedy, though some of the critical elements were there.

The story was written when Barrie was in his early forties, and from a psychodynamic perspective, the theme of a child being locked out of his mother's bedroom could be discussed as a product of early-formed memories finding an avenue for expression in a fantasy written by a middle-aged adult. I speculated that it reflected Barrie's experience of having been replaced by the birth of another boy depicted in the story as being held in his mother's arms as she slept peacefully in her bed. Little Barrie, Jamie they called him, had been replaced by a sibling and his suffering had festered over many years. It appeared that Sir James Barrie had written a story that would serve my purpose.

Some detective work enabled me to confirm my prediction. Barrie's mother gave birth to another child when Jamie was three years old. It was a girl, not a boy, but let's give the author some liberty with the details.

Bolstered by my success, I could now argue that Jamie had been in the phallic stage of psychosexual development when his sister was born. We know that during this period boys experience a renewed interest in their mothers and that this interest is now sexualized. It can be presumed that Mr. Barrie had a competitive edge over Jamie regarding having access to his mother, and just when Jamie is in the throes of fantasies of how best to get rid of Daddy, another child is born. The competition had become overwhelming.

The only question that remained was how to interpret the flying part? Freud answered that question directly in his psychobiography of Leonardo da Vinci when he wrote, "The wish to be able to fly is to be understood as nothing else than a longing for sexual performance" (Freud, 1910/1964, p. 76). So the boy flapping his wings against the bedroom window represents a flying phallus attempting to snuggle up close to its mother.

Having suitably penetrated the latent content of Barrie's story, all that would be needed were a few items of embellishment. For sure, I would mention that several years after the publication of *The Little White Bird* Barrie added several new characters, notably Captain Hook. Peter Pan repeatedly outmaneuvers and humiliates Hook and takes over his ship. With the introduction

of the father clothed in a pirate's garb, the Oedipal triangle was complete.

A Psychobiographic Trap

Elsewhere I have written about the problem of being guided by theoretical inferences in case study research and then using these inferences as *data* to complete the analysis (Ogilvie, 2003, esp. chaps. 6, 8). Psychobiographers who set forth to analyze lives with the goal of providing support for their preferred theoretical positions are particularly vulnerable to this trap. That is what I had done. I sought evidence that the original version of Peter Pan expressed components of an Oedipal dilemma, found some of the elements I was looking for, inferred some others, and edited the story to suit my aims. Not bad for an afternoon's work. My lecture was set in my mind . . . and was never delivered.

Back to the Beginning

I was thrown off-purpose when I looked for evidence to confirm the prediction that Barrie's mother had given birth to another child when Jamie was a boy. The library shelf I consulted contained many other books by and about Barrie and I lingered too long. I knew that my ideas regarding a short-term project were over when I read a book Barrie had written in memory of his mother titled *Margaret Ogilvy by Her Son J.M. Barrie* (Barrie, 1901). It contained hints of an alternative interpretation of Peter Pan being barred from entering his mother's bedroom that, if pursued, could prove fatal to an Oedipal interpretation. Nearly two years of research resulted in a very different story.

Jamie Barrie was born in 1860 in a small cottage in Kirriemuir, Scotland. For his first three years, he was the youngest of seven living children. Two other children, both girls, had died early in their lives. His older brother, Alick, was attending Aberdeen University. Four sisters lived at home. Mary was fifteen, Jane Ann was thirteen, Sara was six, and Isabella was two. David, age seven, had been sandwiched between the four daughters. Margaret, the final child in the family, was born three years after Jamie.

Jamie's father, David Barrie, was a weaver who was successful enough in the trade to provide for his large family. David, Mr. Barrie, had married his wife Margaret when he was twenty-seven and she was twenty-one. Eighteen years later, Jamie was born.

These and many other facts are easy to obtain because J.M. Barrie has been written about so extensively. He was one of the most successful literary figures in Great Britain during the turn of the twentieth century. He began his career as a journalist who wrote daily columns for several newspapers. Gradually the writing of books and plays, many of which were staged in both London and New York, replaced that routine. *Peter Pan*, the book and the play, brought him fame, but during his lifetime he also was well known for his other works.

As mentioned above, one of his books was titled *Margaret Ogilvy*. Margaret Ogilvy was his mother's name, as it was customary in Scotland for wives to retain their maiden names. Ostensibly, the book is about Barrie's mother, who had died one year before it was written, but its primary focus is on Barrie's relationship with her. It is as much autobiographical as it is biographical.

Barrie begins by reporting that a set of six new chairs arrived at the same time he was born. The chairs were a big investment for his mother, and he imagines her whispering to him that they were just the beginning. She had great things in mind and "what ambitions burned behind that face." In turn, Barrie imagines himself declaring that he is there to help. She was a happy woman in those days, "placed on earth by God to open minds of all who looked to beautiful thoughts." What he recalled of his first several years was all hearsay. Full consciousness of his mother did not arrive until he was six years old. It was then, in 1866, that news arrived that her son David, seven years older than little Jamie and barely known to him, had been killed in a skating accident. Barrie wrote, "I knew my mother for ever now."

Margaret Ogilvy never recovered from the tragedy. Although she had several other children, David had been special. He was handsome and ruddy and possessed other qualities that brightened his mother's day, every day. Nobody could replace him. Margaret's grief became the focus of the family's attention, and Jamie's oldest sister, Mary, stepped forward to nurse her mother. One day, shortly after David's death, Mary, desperate for a solution, went to Jamie and told him to go to his mother's bedside and tell her she still had another boy. Jamie entered the dark room and stood there fearful as no sound came from the bed. Suddenly he heard a listless voice saying, "Is that you?" The tone hurt Jamie, so he gave no reply. Again, "Is that you?" Convinced that she was speaking to her dead son, Jamie replied, "No, it's not him. It's just me." He heard his mother turn over and cry.

Over the ensuing days, weeks, and months (lifetime, one could say), Jamie spent much of his time trying to make his mother forget David. A quotation cited earlier from *The Little White Bird*, "So, sitting on the rail at the foot of her bed, [Peter Pan] played a lullaby on his pipe and he never stopped playing until his mother looked happy" is transparently derived from this period in his life. He would do anything to lift his mother's spirits, then and much later. As he declares in the book, everything he ever wrote, all of it, was for his mother. He was always mindful of the prospects of gaining her approval, of bringing a smile to her lips, when she read his works.

But six-year-old Jamie was not yet writing. The way he tried to make her laugh was to go to her bedroom and reenact something that he had done elsewhere that had amused someone, hoping his antics would make her smile. Barrie wrote that she did laugh now and then. On such occasions he would rush to his sister and beg her to come and see the sight, but by the time she came "the soft face was wet again." He could remember only one time he made her chuckle in the presence of a witness. The project was so important to him that he kept a paper and a pencil handy so he could keep a running account of the number of times he was able to amuse his mother.

Mary encouraged Jamie to try to talk with Margaret about David as she lay in her bed thinking of him. Frequently Margaret was willing to do that, so much so that Jamie sometimes interrupted her stream of fond memories by crying out, "Do you know nothing about me?"

He then worked on a different strategy and attempted to bluff Margaret into thinking that he was David. The character he played was born from Margaret's nostalgic memories of her dead son. She spoke of David's cheery way of whistling and described to the child sitting at her bedside how David would stand with his legs apart and his hands in his pants pockets when he puckered up his lips. Thereupon, after Jamie perfected his own whistle, he disguised himself by slipping into David's ill-fitting clothes and entered his mother's room. "Listen!" he cried out triumphantly. He stretched out his legs, plunged his hands into the pocket of the trousers and began to whistle.

Jamie was so desperate to capture the attention of his mother that he pretended to be someone else, his dead brother. Despite his heroic efforts then and throughout his mother's lifetime, "I had not made her forget the bit of her that was dead; in those nine and twenty years he was not removed one day farther from her." Still struggling to remove the iron bars guarding the nursery, to obtain the unobtainable kiss that his mother hid from him, Jamie vowed to make his mother proud of him. "Wait till I'm a man," Jamie said to his mother, "and you'll never have reason to greet again." ("Greet" being the Scottish word for "grieve.")

The truth of the matter is that Barrie was terrified by the prospect of growing up. "The horror of my boyhood was that I knew a time would come when I would have to give up the games." Look at what happened to David when he grew up. He gave up more than games. But what Jamie feared most was how he would be able to survive if he failed to remove those dreadful tears from his mother's face. The tears and enduring sadness became objective evidence that his mother was unavailable to validate his existence, to confirm that he was a person of worth. The prospect of growing up under the shadow of being unworthy of his mother's love was unthinkable.

Margaret and Jamie created a temporary solution to their problem. Together, they discovered a way to periodically escape the emotional turmoil that had been triggered by the family tragedy. Throughout the many days that Jamie spent at his mother's bedside, an opening into a conversational safety zone emerged that involved Margaret reminiscing about her childhood. These conversations lightened Margaret's mood and offered Jamie an avenue for becoming engaged

Figure 12.1. Barrie with his mother.

with his mother . . . or at least engaged in the life of a little girl who later became his mother.

In addition to relishing and making elaborate mental records of his mother's accounts of her childhood, Jamie became an avid reader of books and poetry. He was so consumed by this hobby that he began to collect photographs of poets. One day he showed his collection of pictures to an old tailor friend of his. Upon viewing the photographs, the tailor quoted these lines from Cowley: "What can I do to be forever known, / And make the age to come my own?" Inspired by the passage, Jamie hurried home, rushed his mother from the company of some visitors who had dropped by, and repeated the lines. In jest, he asked her if that is the kind of person she would like to be. Margaret replied, "No, but I would be windy of being his mother." Hope at last. Knowing that he already could weave stories well enough to please her, the die was cast. Jamie was to be a writer. "I would be windy of being his mother," she declared. Jamie interpreted that statement to mean I would be "windy" of being *your* mother if you were to become famous.

A route to her heart had been discovered. Barrie's pen replaced the pipe that Peter Pan used for the purpose of removing sadness from his mother's face.

Prototypical Scenes

Barrie's recollections of the reaction of his mother to David's death makes the event a candidate for what Todd Schultz has labeled a prototypical scene (for much more on this particular concept, see Schultz, chap. 3 this vol.). Schultz views a prototypical scene as one that "anchors" a life (Schultz, 2003). It is a scene that achieves a kind of "supersaliency" by virtue of its oft-told status, embellishments, and interpenetrations with other memories and its packaging of core themes that both characterize and unify a person's life. A prototypical scene is a fundamental or primal scene that both sponsors and attracts other self-defining memories cohering to its basic form. It encapsulates personal concerns and provides a nest for other memories that seek meaningful places in the individual's master story. It centers most often on family conflict, and in some cases, according to Schultz, it may be as much fiction as fact.

As I let Barrie take the lead instead of allowing theory to shape my thinking—a commendable practice for any psychobiographer—he led me to consider the possibility that Margaret's reaction to David's death and the impact it had on Jamie's relationship with her may have provided the makings of a blueprint for his life. In this new context for constructing a psychological portrayal of Barrie, I also saw the prospects of altering the course of a tradition of reducing a life to a set of recycled themes by instead treating prototypical scenes as sources of innovative improvisations that carry traces of the past into the activities and passions of the "now," and vice versa.

It had been relatively easy to drop any further efforts to squeeze the episode of Peter Pan being barred from his mother's bedroom window into the Oedipal model. The dramatic shift in Margaret's relationship with Jamie and the degree to which she became the primary focus of his life had all the markings of a prototypical scene, and that became a far more attractive avenue to explore. But I was aware that one of the major problems in case study research involves a loosening of the boundaries between an investigator and the object of his or her investigation. It sometimes comes down to the question of who, in fact, is the subject of the investigation. Perhaps I selected Jamie's predicament because it reflected something about my own experiences that might open the door to studying Barrie, as pretense for declaring "truths" that could be more pertinent to my life than to his. This is not an easy dilemma to guard against, but some steps can be taken. In this instance, it was fortunate that three other people who had written about Barrie had identified Margaret's shift in her relationship to Jamie as a major turning point in his life.

The three people include Denis Mackail, Barrie's principal biographer; Robert Sapolski, a biologist and neuroscientist; and Jackie Wullschlager, a British literary scholar.

Denis Mackail

At the request of Barrie's two literary executors, Denis Mackail was provided access to all the information about Barrie retained after his death. These materials included large boxes containing Barrie's note pads, diaries, rough drafts of and revised copies of his novels and plays, letters to his mother, correspondence with other authors, and the results of interviews with many individuals who had been personal and/or theatrical acquaintances of Barrie. Mackail organized this mass of information into a long and sometimes tedious biography, *The Story of JMB* (Mackail, 1941) that, in addition to describing landmark events in Barrie's life, included such details as the scores of cricket games, opening and closing dates of plays, and who had been seen in Barrie's company at various social events.

In the mix of Mackail's extensive treatment of the events in Barrie's life, he created a profile of Barrie that includes the following personal characteristics. Barrie was a short and oftentimes desperately lonely man. Barely five feet tall, he was extremely sensitive about his size. He suffered prolonged bouts of depression throughout his life. Headaches were nearly daily occurrences, and he rarely missed a seasonal cold. Mackail consistently describes Barrie as moody and anxious. At the same time, he could also be quite humorous, both in person and in his writings. He was a crowd pleaser, but shortly after the crowd was pleased, he would retreat to his smoke-filled residence and pace the floors. Through it all, through the depression, the headaches, and fevers, particularly during his early to mid-adult years, Barrie applied himself to his trade.

Mackail attributes Barrie's devotion to his work to the aftermath of the shock of David's death. Mackail (1941) writes, "And Jamie would do anything—anything on Heaven and earth—to get that look off her [his mother's] face" (p. 51). Mackail frequently returns to Margaret's reaction to David's death and to the ghost that haunted Margaret Ogilvy. He emphasizes her living son's (Jamie's) vow that she must never again be disappointed. Jamie's early attempts to make Margaret happy marked the "beginning of 29 years of incessant and unalterable devotion" to her (p. 23). Mackail repeats what Barrie himself had observed. Everything he wrote was for his mother, and the primary purpose behind his writing was to make her proud of him.

Robert Sapolski

Sapolski is a Professor of Biological Sciences and Neuroscience at Stanford University. He is one of the world's leading figures in the area of stress-related illnesses. It is common knowledge that stress can take a toll on physical health, but Sapolski understands stress/health connections in the context of what happens beneath the skin, at the level of brain centers, hormones, neurotransmitters, and enzymes. In addition to being an excellent scientist, Sapolski is adept at conveying state-of-the-art developments in science for public consumption without sacrificing the integrity of his scientific discipline. One of the keys for doing that successfully is to provide common examples of topics under consideration. In the process of doing just that, Sapolski refers to J.M. Barrie in a chapter titled "Dwarfism and the Importance of Mothers" in *Why Zebras Don't Get Ulcers* (1998).

The chapter describes how growth can be inhibited during periods of stress. Examples are given of stunted growth of children who received adequate nutrition but inadequate handling in orphanages in Great Britain and elsewhere, particularly during major wars when there was an abundance of homeless children. In some institutions, the children were fed healthy diets, but they were rarely provided the kinds of creature comforts afforded by being picked up and caressed. Sapolski also writes about more severe conditions of child abuse and how in some cases it leads to a condition called "stress dwarfism." In the context of describing that condition at the organic level, Sapolski mentions having run across occasional references to Peter Pan and Tinker Bell in books on growth endocrinology. Mystified by these references, he found an explanation buried in a chapter of a textbook on the topic of how severe psychological stress can trigger psychogenetic dwarfism. Sapolski writes that the chapter

gave an example that occurred in a British Victorian family. A son, age thirteen, the beloved favorite of the mother is killed in a skating accident. The mother, despairing and bereaved, takes to her bed in grief for years afterward, utterly ignoring her other six-year-old son. Horrible scenes ensue. The boy, on one occasion, enters her darkened room; the mother, in her delusional state, briefly believes it is the dead son—"David, is that you? Could that be you?"—before realizing: "Oh, it is only you." On the rare instances when the mother interacts with the younger son, she repeatedly expressed the same obsessive thought: the only solace that she feels is that David died when he was still perfect, still a boy, never to be ruined by growing up and growing away from his mother. (p. 91)

Sapolski argues that Jamie Barrie seized upon the idea that by remaining a boy forever, "by not growing up, he will at least have some chance of pleasing his mother, winning her love. Although there is no evidence of disease or malnutrition in the well-to-do family, he ceases growing. As an adult, he is barely five feet in height, and his marriage is unconsummated" (Sapolski, 1998, p. 92). With this example in hand, Sapolski describes the growth-stopping physiological mechanisms triggered by stress that can result in the rare condition of stress dwarfism.

I am intrigued by Sapolski's hypothesis that Barrie was a victim of stress dwarfism as a result of having been shut out of his mother's life. Building on his knowledge of endocrinology, Sapolski describes Barrie as an exemplary case of persons who suffer from traumatic experiences severe enough to stunt their growth. However, I do not believe that there is sufficient information about the average heights of members of the Barrie and Ogilvy families to allow one to conclude that J.M.'s small stature was fully the result of stress. As shown in the photograph of Barrie and his mother, J.M. is taller than Margaret (see Figure 12.1). Thus, a genetic explanation for J.M.'s size is hardly out of the question.

Jackie Wullschlager

Wullschlager's book *Inventing Wonderland* (1995) deals with the lives and literary works of several authors, Barrie included, whose books for children reflected changes in British culture occurring as the Edwardian era gradually replaced the Victorian era in the late 1800s up to 1914, when World War I ushered in a new reality. Idealization of children marked both the Victorian and Edwardian eras, so Barrie's portrayal of a lad who would never grow up was a perfect match for the Zeitgeist. Barrie's observation that "nothing happens after we are twelve matters very much" was in harmony with the themes of childhood adventures contained in *Treasure Island*, *Kidnapped*, *Tom Sawyer*, and other novels of the late 1800s that featured boy heroes who easily outwitted adults. Barrie's personal obsession with childhood and its fortuitous convergence with Edwardian fascination with playful boys paid off handsomely for the son of Margaret Ogilvy.

At age sixty-two, in 1922, Barrie wrote, "It is as if long after writing Peter Pan its true meaning came to me—desperate to grow up but can't" (Wullschlager, 1995, p. 131). Wullschlager identifies the source of Barrie's ambivalence, the desire to grow up countered by a desire not to grow up, to be the same episode spotted by Mackail and Sapolski. Sobbing on the stoop one day, he is sent to his mother's room by his sister Mary to console Margaret by reminding her that she had another son. "Is that you?" Margaret asks

in a listless voice when Jamie entered her dark room. He gave no answer. "Then the voice said more anxiously, 'Is that you?' again. I thought it was the dead boy she was speaking to, and I said in a little lonely voice, 'No, it's no' him, it's just me.' Then I heard a cry, and my mother turned in bed, and though it was dark I know she was holding out her arms" (Wullschlager, 1995, p. 118).

In summary, all three scholars, each for their special aims, independently concur that events initiated by David's death had an enduring impact on Barrie. I consider myself to be in good company when I grant "prototypical" status to this episode in Barrie's life. However, it is not time to rest on one's laurels when one believes that a prototypical episode has been located. The next step is to root out the consequences of the event. Again, the best strategy is to let Barrie take the lead.

At His Mother's Bedside

Earlier, I referred to the hours upon hours, days upon days during his youth, when Jamie sat at the foot of his mother's bed as she regaled him with stories of her childhood. This had become her primary diversion from her dreadful sadness over David's death, a way to suspend the shock that the tragedy had delivered to her system. Margaret's stories offered an avenue of escape for Jamie, as well, because they took his mind far away from the time his mother had brought David back in his coffin. Her stories were of a time twenty to thirty years before Jamie had been born.

Biographer Mackail (1941) writes that Jamie "feels safer in the past, where nothing like that (the tragedy and Jamie's sense of maternal abandonment), he feels, can ever happen. He doesn't only listen to her stories but . . . he struggles to enter into them until he virtually succeeds" (p. 24). "Virtually succeeds" says it well, a phrase elaborated on in the following passage: "The reason why my books deal with the past instead of with the life I myself have known is simply this, that I soon grow tired of writing tales unless I can see a little girl, of whom my mother has told me, wandering confidently through the pages. Such a grip has her memory of her childhood had upon me since I was a boy of six" (Barrie, 1901, p. 25).

Prominent among the memories Margaret described to her son was the death of her mother when she was a mere child of eight, and how it fell upon her shoulders to cook, clean the house, mend the clothes, and manage the daily chores of a household that included herself and two Davids: her father and her younger brother. David, Sr. was a stonemason whose income relied on dawn to dusk devotion to his work. One of Margaret's favorite and often repeated memories involved carefully preparing and hand delivering her father's dinner to him at his work in her white pinafore and magenta frock.

Many of Margaret's stories were told to Jamie inside the walls of her darkened room. On her better days, days when she was strong enough to get out of bed and venture outside, she would take Jamie to the cottage of her youth and introduce him to the sights, sounds, buildings, sheds, streets, and paths that unleashed a host of seemingly endless memories. She spoke of her father's church, ministers and parishioners, ushers and elders, and social gatherings where legends of specters and spirits were passed along. Jamie learned a great deal from his mother about how his church was special, what distinguished it from at least three other splinter groups (all housed in different locations in the small town of Kirriemuir) that many years before had been united under the name of the Original Seceders. David Ogilvy's sect was known as the Auld Lichts (Old Lights), two words that would become well known in Great Britain near the turn of the twentieth century as they were contained in the title of Barrie's first triumphant book, *Auld Licht Idyls* (1888).

Jamie did not listen passively to Margaret's stories. He lived them. He imagined himself to be the little girl in a clean and neatly mended frock skipping down the path with her father's lunch container grasped firmly in her hand. In his mind, he was the girl who took loving care of her brother, who listened to legends and wondered about specters that wandered through the hills and secretly performed miraculous services for people in conditions of pain or impoverishment.

At the age of forty-one, Barrie wonders what memories may sustain him in his old age. He concludes that it will not be his life that comes sweeping back, but his mother's, "a little girl in a magenta frock and white pinafore . . . singing to herself, and carrying her father's dinner in a flagon" (Barrie, 1901, p. 207).

The stories Margaret Ogilvy related to her son over several years provided him with ideas that he would subsequently use in his quest to become "forever known." They escalated the career of a young, hard-working and oftentimes witty journalist to the level of book author whose works brought him early fame.

The first indication of what was to come was a failed initiative. A year before he went to college, Barrie wrote the better part of a three-volume novel and sent it to a publisher. The fee for publishing the manuscript was much more than Barrie could afford. He handled the disappointment, later expressing relief that the novel was never published, calling it exceedingly "dull" (Barrie, 1901, p. 51). More difficult to justify, although the comment should have come as no great surprise, was the publisher's statement of encouragement to the "clever lady" who had written it.

After obtaining a Masters in Arts at the University of Edinburgh, it was anticipated that Barrie would move into a career in teaching like his older brother Alick had done or become a minister, a role that the Barrie family believed that David had been destined to fill. But J.M. never wavered from his promise to himself that he would become an author whose mother would be "windy" of his achievements. His college years at Edinburgh had been lonely ones, and the most frequently appearing phrase in his daily journals was "grind, grind, grind." All the grinding and the enormous amount of energy that went into his writing provided him with the discipline needed to cope successfully with the pressure of producing a minimum of two articles a day in his first staff job with the *Nottingham Journal.*

Despite his shyness and the severity of his headaches, Barrie followed up on the recommendation of his sister, Jane Ann, by applying for the position of "leader writer" for the *Nottingham Journal.* Soon after his arrival in Nottingham, he began a routine of writing at least 1,200 words of prose a day, every day, without a break, for eighteen months. Keeping his pledge to his mother with a vengeance, the industrious journalist wrote fiction under the name of Hippomenes every Monday. A Modern Peripatetic authored Thursdays' columns.

During this period, acquaintances had to be careful about what they said in his presence lest their words and comments appear the next day in the *Journal*. Barrie needed material for his copy and could weave the most mundane happenings into a clever tale. Accuracy meant nothing to him. Nor was he the slightest bit concerned about the sensitivities of people who triggered a story. It was the story that mattered, and the boundaries between actual events and what might have happened were never fixed.

After a year and a half devoted to writing fiction, commentaries, and book and play reviews, the twenty-four-year-old Barrie was suddenly back in Kirriemuir. For cost-savings reasons, the *Nottingham Journal* had released its ambitious staff writer.

An accomplished author now with over a thousand articles in print but none credited to his name, J.M. Barrie remained unknown. He fought his loneliness, his headaches, his depression, and family suspicions that he would never become self-supporting in his chosen profession and continued to write, write, write. Most of his stories were composed as first-person accounts of events of some elderly character who was drawing upon and sometimes mocking his own memories. He sent these works to newspaper and magazine editors and became accustomed to not hearing back.

The drought was broken on November 17, 1884, when he received word that *St. James's Gazette*, a prominent newspaper in London, had published one of his submissions. Payment would be forthcoming. The article was titled "An Auld Licht Community," an alteration of the title he had given it, and, of course, the author was not named. With his foot now in the door, Barrie sent other articles and stories to Editor Greenwood at the *Gazette*. One of them that was rejected was returned with a note from Greenwood stating, "But I liked that Scottish thing. Any more of those?"

There were a lot more of those. With the assistance of his mother, he restored her (and his)

old memories, and his pen took charge of the rest. Soon thereafter "An Auld Licht Funeral" was published. "Auld Licht Courtship" followed that. Then came "An Auld Licht Scandal," "An Auld Licht Wedding," and more, with the author's name now attached to each.

Despite Editor Greenwood's preference for Barrie to mail the articles from Scotland, Barrie was convinced that residence in London was a prerequisite for fame. Margaret was worried about the move because of the discrepancy between her son's physical appearance (reed thin, short, and younger looking than his actual age) and whatever one might imagine his appearance to be, based on his writings. Nonetheless, Barrie arrived in London in spring 1885. Undaunted by the curious looks of publishers as they gazed in wonder at the anxious young man who tormented them to read his copy then refused to accept "no" as the final word, Barrie kept returning to the doorsteps where his works had been rejected until some, and eventually quite a few, editors took interest in the often humorous works of the boyish man.

As Barrie crowded articles into several newspapers, he began to merge some Auld Licht stories that had been published in *St. James's Gazette* into a book titled *Auld Licht Idyls*. That book, released in 1888, was an immediate success. J.M. had taken a giant step in the direction of answering his question about how to become known. Within a year, a second novel (in all there would be four based on his *Auld Licht* "memories") was published. Titled *A Window in Thrums* (1896), the book was hailed in a front-page review of the *National Observer* as a "book of genius."

You and I know that these works were co-authored. Barrie, of course, deserved and received credit for authorship, but a little girl whose life his mother had described during the years of his youth had guided his prose. In an effort to temporarily escape the trauma of David's death, Barrie had entered the Wonderland of his mother's childhood. Just as he had briefly endeavored to become David so that Margaret might love him, he entered into the mind and body of a girl whose life was fashioned and refashioned by the memories of his mother. He saw the scenes and dramas described to him. He "met" the characters that had shaped her life. He shared her experiences doing daily chores. He witnessed weddings and funerals, listened in on debates and feuds between different breakaway sects of the same church denomination. He imagined characters so vividly that he knew the lengths of their beards, their mannerisms, their quirks and foibles. He thought the thoughts of that little girl, traveled her paths, and shivered when she was cold. "I have seen many on-dings of snow" Barrie writes, "but the one I seem to recall best occurred nearly twenty years before I was born" (Barrie, 1901, p. 32).

Incorporating of the Object

I remember encountering the idea of "incorporating the object" in psychoanalytic literature in years gone by, and I also remember dismissing the concept as one of those convoluted terms psychoanalytic theorists use to mystify outsiders. It annoyed me that a secret language was being perpetuated. I wondered how long it would take for the speakers of the language to realize they were operating under a pretense of actually communicating with each other. I figured that most of them never would, and who was I to interfere with their game? Leave them be, I thought. They have their harmless circle of friends, and as long as they are nice to their children, take good care of their patients, and don't bother me with concepts like "incorporating the object," I'll just walk away.

Eating crow is one of my specialties. Barrie forced me to reconsider my bias.

But the question now is what "object" did Jamie incorporate? He did not attempt to "become" his mother. That is clear. Instead, he appears to have taken in or "swallowed" his mother's memories by way of a gradual, day-by-day process of imagining what it would be like to have been the child his mother described to him and then becoming that child. Margaret, or more accurately, a subjective Margaret whom Jamie had never known, was internally installed, piece by piece, story by story, as the next best option to failed attempts to get her to smile.

In the book *Fantasies of Flight* (2003) I speculate more fully than I am able to do here about how Jamie's sense of self had been brought to the

brink of destruction when Margaret turned away from him. He felt hollowed out by the disappearance of a vital player in his intersubjective world. Margaret's happy face and particularly her smile had been internalized as cues associated with his well-being, and he struggled to bring them back when she became overwhelmed with sadness. His partner in the life-giving process of co-regulating his feelings had vanished. It was then that he installed a new sense of self, a replacement part, if you will, and saw the world through the eyes of a little girl carrying a flagon with food for her father's lunch.

Although this "new" subjective self had little capacity to co-regulate his feelings, it did an excellent job of co-authoring his early books. But his borrowed self was a poor substitute for his sense of self that once flourished in the flow of its merger with Margaret. Here Heinz Kohut's theory of the importance of mirroring a child's sense of grandiosity is relevant (Kohut, 1977). Jamie lost his mirror when Margaret turned away from him. An important feature of that mirror had been Margaret's smile, and his only hope for restoring his previous sense of sense of self was to restore that smile.

Jamie the child and James the adult continued to return to Margaret's bedside for the purpose of checking to see if the smile had returned. Until the very end of Margaret's life, Barrie never ceased in his efforts to bring his core sense of self back to life and have it resume its proper position. The only way that could happen was to resurrect the facial cues that previously had evoked feelings of being united with an object that had been associated with his survival.

The Arrival of Peter Pan

Throughout his adult life, Barrie was never without a writing pad in his pocket for entering notes for plays and stories and for recording scraps of passing thoughts. Many of these notebooks were among the items made available to Mackail when he undertook the monumental task of writing *The Story of JMB*. One of the pads contained an entry where Barrie referred to "a little box inside me that nothing opened until later years it did of its own accord. Just trifles in it, but I made a game with them for many years" (Mackail, 1941, p. 77). That notation was entered in 1926, when Barrie was sixty-six years old. It was in reference to Peter Pan's debut in *The Little White Bird* twenty-five years earlier.

I doubt that the little box sprang open of its own accord. It had some assistance. The keys to the box can be found by knowing about some of the circumstances of Barrie's early adulthood life.

In his late twenties and early thirties, Barrie was well known in the London literary pool for having written several novels and some lightweight, funny plays. Since he was involved in auditions and the productions of his plays, he became acquainted with young, attractive actresses anxious for cast positions. Bowled over by their beauty, he charmed them with his wit, praised them for their good looks, and targeted some for sentimental letters. Recognizing the lovesick tone of these letters, only a few responded to his romantic overtures. Those who did, those who came back to laugh at his antics and be amused by his stories and his curious way of speaking, became puzzled by his sudden retreat into dark and distant thoughts. The discrepancy between the bold openness of his letters and shutting down in person was bewildering. In part, he retreated into concerns about his mother and the roller coaster quality of her health. Whenever one of the daily letters he received from his sister, Jane Ann, mentioned a worsening in Margaret's condition, Barrie would drop his work and travel from London to Kirriemuir to be at his mother's bedside.

At age thirty-four, Barrie became ill during one of these visits. A cold turned into pneumonia, and he fought for his life. For two years prior to his illness, Barrie had been seen in the company of Mary Ansell, an ambitious and strikingly attractive actress who had starred in a play that Barrie had written. Mary went to Barrie's home in Scotland and stayed with him during his lengthy convalescence. In midsummer, 1984, British newspapers reported that J.M. Barrie and Mary Ansell had been married in a private ceremony at the groom's home.

There is evidence from his private notes that Barrie was either not interested in or was incapable of making love. Sex is in the province of grownups and, as Barrie so frequently said, he didn't want to grow up. A contributing factor is the likelihood that he wanted Mary to serve as a replacement mirror for the one that had been shattered when his older brother had died. Whether or not those dynamics played a part in their troubled relationship, Mary terminated the marriage fifteen years later by having an affair with another man.

One might think that the marriage could have been salvaged after Barrie was released from his responsibility to visit Margaret's bedside. Margaret died in 1899, five years into Barrie's marriage, and within a little over a year he memorialized her in the book *Margaret Ogilvy*. The book gives every appearance of closing that long chapter of his life. He writes, for example, "Everything I could have done for her in this life I have done since I was a boy: I look back through the years and I cannot see the smallest thing undone" (Barrie, 1901, p. 203).

But the compulsion to check the expression on Margaret's face did not come to an end. The game was not over. Fortunately for the generations of children who have enjoyed Peter Pan, Margaret's death resulted in a fantasy enactment of the script that had taken Barrie to her bedside for 29 years. One year after Margaret was memorialized, Peter Pan, half human, half bird, arrived. Peter's first adventure was to fly to his mother's bedroom and attempt to make her look happy by playing her a lullaby. The "little box" inside a lonesome middle-aged man had opened, and it remained open for many years to come.

References

Barrie, J.M. (1888). Auld licht idyls. New York: International Book Co.

Barrie, J.M. (1896). A window in Thrums. New York: Dodd & Mead.

Barrie, J.M. (1901). Margaret Ogilvy by her son J.M. Barrie. New York: Charles Scribner's Sons.

Barrie, J.M. (1902). The little white bird. New York: Charles Scribner's Sons.

Barrie, J.M. (1967). Peter Pan. New York: Puffin Books.

Freud, S. (1964). Leonardo da Vinci and a memory from his childhood (Alan Tyson, trans.). New York: Norton. (Original work published 1910)

Kohut, H. (1977). *The restoration of the self.* New York: International Universities Press.

Mackail, D.G. (1941). *The story of JMB.* New York: Charles Scribner's Sons.

Ogilvie, D.M. (2003). *Fantasies of flight.* New York: Oxford University Press.

Sapolski, R. (1998). *Why zebras don't get ulcers: An updated guide to stress, stress-related diseases, and coping.* New York: Freeman.

Schultz, W.T. (2003). The prototypical scene: A method for generating psychobiographical hypotheses. In D. McAdams, R. Josselson, & A. Lieblich (Eds.), *Up close and personal: Teaching and learning narrative methods.* Washington D.C., APA Press.

Wullschlager, J. (1995). *Inventing wonderland: The lives of Lewis Carroll, Edward Lear, J.M. Barrie, Kenneth Graham, and A.A. Milne.* New York: Free Press.

Chapter 13

James William Anderson

Edith Wharton and *Ethan Frome*
A Psychobiographical Exploration

An Isolated Childhood

The novelist Edith Wharton published an autobiography that never gets beneath the surface. But she also left behind some unpublished pages that are far more revealing. These begin:

> My first conscious recollection is of being kissed in Fifth Avenue by my cousin Dan Fearing. It was a winter day, I was walking with my father, & I was a little less than four years old, when this momentous event took place. My cousin, a very round and rosy little boy, two or three years older, was also walking with his father; & I remember distinctly his running up to me, & kissing me, & the extremely pleasant sensation which his salute produced. With equal distinctness, I recall the satisfaction I felt in knowing that *I had on my best bonnet.* . . . Thus I may truly say that my first conscious sensations were produced by the two deepest-seated instincts of my nature—the desire to love & to look pretty. (Wharton, 1990, p. 1071)

I would add that the experience includes intimacy with a male, not only her little cousin but her father, whom she had to herself on that wintry day. Her nascent sexuality is suggested; the kiss aroused an "extremely pleasant sensation."

This significant memory—her "first conscious recollection"—points to central themes in Wharton's life, and no less in her fiction: her desire to love and be loved, her yearning for intimacy with a man, an intimacy augmented by sexual closeness, and her wish to be admired and

appreciated. Wharton's experiences as a child set her desires in motion, yet also created numerous obstacles to their fulfillment.

Her name at birth, in 1862, was Edith Newbold Jones. She was the last child of older parents. Her father and mother, George and Lucretia Jones, were forty-one and thirty-seven years old when Edith was born. Edith had two brothers, Frederic and Henry, who were sixteen and eleven years older than she was. Her childhood was much like that of an only child.

If there has ever been anything in the United States like the aristocracy of Europe, it would be the elite group into which Edith was born. Both of her parents were part of upper-class New York, old families who had wealth, lived in brownstones, kept summer homes (usually in Newport, Rhode Island), and socialized only with members of their own set. Edith's father never worked but lived off of real estate holdings that he had received from his family.

In the unpublished autobiographical chapters, she described herself as "a morbid, self-scrutinizing & unhappy child." She did not seem to be able to connect with her parents, brothers, or other children. Her kindest words are for her nurse, Hannah Doyle, who, she said, made her feel "safe and sheltered" in her earliest years (Wharton, 1990, p. 1091).

Edith developed solitary activities from a young age, especially inventing stories and reading voraciously in her father's library. She felt alienated from others and did not have anyone with whom she could share her favorite pursuits. Her mother arranged for other little girls to come over to play, but Edith felt they were unable to

188

Figure 13.1. Edith Wharton as a child. (Yale Collection of American Literature, Beinecke Rare Book and Manuscript Library)

talk with her about what "really mattered." After a short time she would excuse herself, find her mother, and beg her, "Mamma, please go & amuse those children." She wanted to be by herself so she could make up stories. She lived, she later wrote, in "complete mental isolation" and believed "none of the children I knew had a clue to my labyrinth," that is, her elaborate inner world (pp. 1076–1077).

There was one partial exception to her isolation that points to her embryonic interest in intimacy with a man. When she was five or six years old, a friend of her father's would take her on his knee after Sunday dinner and say, "Tell me mythology"; Edith had learned about the Greek gods. She looked forward to this event all week. "[O]ur Sunday evening guest," she recalled, "was the only person who ever showed signs of knowing anything about the secret story-world in which I lived" (p. 1077).

In looking back, she thought her parents feared her and viewed her as being like "some pale predestined child who disappears at night to dance with 'the little people.'" She was physically active and enjoyed riding ponies and hiking, and she liked to play outside, especially with boys, but she described all this as being merely her "external life." "I often wonder," she wrote, "if any other child possessed of that 'other side' was ever so alone as I." She imagines that others like her usually had some opportunity for sharing their internal world, but, she noted, "I never exchanged a word with a really intelligent being until I was over twenty" (pp. 1076–1077, 1083)

She retained some fond memories of her father but had little to do with him. The worlds of middle-aged gentlemen and their children had little overlap. She recalled that he liked to read, especially about Arctic explorations. She mused, "I have wondered since what stifled cravings had once germinated in him, and what manner of man he was really meant to be. That he was a lonely one, haunted by something always unexpressed and unattained, I am sure" (p. 813). She may have had a fantasy that, if they had ever been close, she could have helped him and they could have understood each other. That never happened; he died when she was twenty years old.

With her mother she had a troubled relationship. She felt her mother controlled her life through a set of bewildering, arbitrary rules. For example, her mother did not allow her to read novels, although other books were not proscribed. Her mother expected her to do the right thing but forbade her from asking questions that might help her discover what the "right thing" was.

Edith also felt in conflict between her mother's demand that she be careful never to hurt other people's feelings and what Edith took as the religious dictate to avoid lying. One time at a dance class she believed she had to tell the truth and announced to the teacher that the teacher's mother looked like a goat. She was surprised when the teacher scolded her furiously, instead of commending her, for her honesty (p. 1073). Late in her life she looked back at her mother and said she always intuited in her "a mysterious impenetrability, a locked room full of bats and darkness" (Benstock, 1994, p. 378).

In her childhood Edith received little appreciation from her family and did not feel valued by them. Her mother believed children should not be praised for their attractiveness or intelligence but considered it "wholesome to ridicule them for their supposed defects & affectations." Edith was made fun of for having red hair and large hands and feet, for using long words, and for caring about how she dressed. She became "a painfully shy self-conscious child" (Wharton, 1990, pp. 1087–1090).

Edith gained an early knowledge of Europe and of foreign languages. Because of financial conditions after the Civil War, her family spent six years in Europe, where they could live much more cheaply. Edith's family, while she was ages six to ten, resided for extended periods in Rome, Paris, Germany, and Florence. Edith noted that by living in Europe she had been "fed on beauty" for years. After returning to New York, she later recalled, "my first thought was: 'How ugly it is!' I have never since thought otherwise, or felt otherwise than as an exile in America. . . . I used to dream at frequent intervals that we were going back to Europe, & to wake from this dream in a state of exhilaration which the reality turned to deep depression" (Dwight, 1994, p. 20).

Intense anxieties permeated her childhood. Edith wrote that, after a near-fatal bout with typhoid fever at the age of nine, she experienced the world as being "haunted by formless horrors." She explained,

> I lived in a state of chronic fear. Fear of *what*? I cannot say—& even at this time, I was never able to formulate my terror. It was like some dark undefinable menace, forever dogging my steps, lurking, & threatening; I was conscious of it wherever I went by day, & at night it made sleep impossible, unless a light & a nurse-maid were in the room. But, whatever it was, it was most formidable & pressing when I was returning from my daily walk. . . . During the last few yards, & while I waited on the door-step for the door to be opened, I could feel it behind me, upon me; & if there was any delay in the opening of the door I was seized by a

choking agony of terror. It did not matter who was with me, for no one could protect me; but, oh, the rapture of relief if my companion had a latch-key, & we could get in at once, before It caught me!

She notes that she continued having such attacks of horror until she was sixteen or seventeen years old. And until the age of twenty-seven or twenty-eight, she recalled, "I could not sleep in the room with a book containing a ghost-story. . . . I have frequently had to burn books of this kind, because it frightened me to know that they were downstairs in the library" (Wharton, 1990, pp. 1079–1080).

Such anxieties were an inextricable part of her emotional isolation. Not having relationships in which she felt comforted, soothed, and understood, she found the world to be unsafe, and she was limited in her ability to soothe herself.

As a girl, she was cut off from formal education; the men in her social circle, but not the women, attended college. She was taught by tutors and later concluded that she learned little from them that was of value, except for languages. She continued to read widely. Her reading excluded novels, because of her mother's odd ban against fiction, but she immersed herself in poetry, history, and philosophy, written in English, German, French, and Italian (p. 820).

Becoming an Author and Marrying

Edith's old habit of making up stories soon led her to write novels. She began one at the age of eleven. It included a line in which one of the characters spoke of tidying up her drawing room. Edith's mother criticized the novel, saying, "Drawing rooms are always tidy." At the age of fourteen she completed another novel, *Fast and Loose*, the manuscript of which has survived. Edith also wrote mock reviews of her work. One included the assessment, "Every character is a failure, the plot a vacuum, the style spiritless, the dialogue vague, the sentiment weak, and the whole thing a fiasco" (Benstock, 1994, p. 135).

She wrote poems as well. A friend of the family sent five of them to the famous poet Henry Wadsworth Longfellow. He was impressed and passed them on with a letter of praise to William Dean Howells, who published them in the prestigious magazine he edited, *The Atlantic*. Edith was eighteen years old.

The age of her debut in a national magazine was the usual age for coming out in society. But a year before, apparently concerned with her shyness and bookishness, her mother arranged for her to become a debutante.

A pretty girl from a well-connected family and with two older brothers who had many friends, Edith found that men lavished attention on her. She wrote, "I tasted all the sweets of popularity. Oh, how I loved it all—my pretty frocks, the flowers, the music, the sense that everybody 'liked' me, & wanted to talk to me & dance with me!" (Dwight, 1994, p. 27).

Over the next few years, the social whirl enraptured her. She had several beaux and one engagement that lasted for only two months. During the summer of her twenty-second year, she met a young lawyer named Walter Berry, one of the few men in her social class who shared her appreciation for reading. This summer flirtation might have ended with a proposal, but it did not. In later years, though, she renewed her acquaintance with Berry, and he became her most cherished friend. She wrote in her autobiography, in reference to Berry, that "there is one friend in the life of each of us who seems not a separate person, however dear and beloved, but an expansion, an interpretation, of one's self, the very meaning of one's soul" (Wharton, 1985, p. 115).

The next man in her life was Edward Wharton—called Teddy—a Harvard graduate from a respectable family and a friend of one of Edith's brothers. Teddy did not work and had no intention of doing so. He was nice looking, pleasant, and good humored. Edith and Teddy were married in 1885; Edith was twenty-three years old, and Teddy was thirty-five.

Edith tells us she was thoroughly ignorant about sex. When she was seven or eight, a cousin mentioned to her that "babies were not found in flowers but in people." Edith asked her mother about this, and, as she recalled, "I received a severe scolding . . . and this was literally all I knew of the processes of generation till I had been married for several weeks" (Wharton, 1990, p. 1087).

"A few days before my marriage," Edith noted, "I was seized with such a dread of the whole dark mystery, that I summoned up courage to appeal to my mother, & begged her, with a heart beating to suffocation, to tell me 'what being married was like.' Her handsome face at once took on the look of icy disapproval which I most dreaded. 'I never heard such a ridiculous question!' she said impatiently; & I felt at once how vulgar she thought me." Edith claimed that she began her marriage believing that an act of God, not sex, generates a baby in the mother's womb (p. 1087).

In the early years of their marriage, living in Newport and New York and traveling frequently, Edith and Teddy were fond of each

Figure 13.2. Edith Wharton. (Yale Collection of American Literature, Beinecke Rare Book and Manuscript Library)

other and kind to each other but failed to connect sexually, emotionally, and intellectually.

As a pretty, shy, young woman in her twenties, Edith Wharton was twice in the presence of the novelist Henry James, but on both occasions he failed to notice her. Once some friends, knowing Wharton would love to meet James, invited both of them to dinner. Wharton wore a fetching hat in hopes of drawing his attention. She imagined he would compliment her on her hat, and then "I might at last pluck up the courage to blurt out my admiration for *Daisy Miller* and *The Portrait of a Lady*. But he noticed neither the hat nor the wearer" (Lewis, 1975, pp. 24–25). She thought her loveliness would draw the attention of this man, nineteen years older than she was. She did not realize that James had little attraction to female beauty. My conclusion in studying his life is that he was gay; we do not know whether he ever engaged in sexual activity with another person, and he never made his sexual interests public, but there is ample evidence that he appreciated handsome young men, not good-looking young women.

Wharton was friendly with a middle-aged man, Egerton Winthrop, who shared her intellectual interests and introduced her to science, particularly the work of Darwin, and she supplemented her reading in literature, history, and architecture with systematic reading in the theory of evolution.

Wharton wrote poems and short stories that were published in the most important magazines, such as *Harper's Monthly* and *Scribner's*. One of her little-known stories offers insight into the nature of her marriage. A woman dies, and in the afterlife she describes her husband to a spirit: "His boots creaked, and he always slammed the door when he went out, and he never read anything but railway novels and the sporting advertisements in the papers—and—in short, we never understood each other in the least." At times this woman had "exquisite sensations," but she never shared them with her husband (Wharton, 1893/1968, p. 18). She meets a true soul mate but chooses not to go with him; she prefers to wait for her husband. She does not love her husband, she explains, but "I shouldn't feel at home without him. . . . Besides, no one else would know how to look after him, he is so helpless. His

inkstand would never be filled. . . . He would never remember to have his umbrella re-covered. Why he wouldn't even know what novels to read. I always had to choose the kind he liked, with a murder or a forgery and a successful detective" (pp. 19–20).

Virtually all of her fiction during these years reflects her unhappiness and despondency; she later spoke of herself as having been neurasthenic during "the best years of my youth" (Benstock, 1994, p. 96). (Neurasthenia, thought of in the pre-Freudian world as stemming from weak nerves, was a condition characterized by fatigue, anxiety, and irritability.) Materially her life was comfortable, but, like the woman in the short story, she had no one with whom she could share her vibrant inner world. The isolation she felt would have resonated with the isolation of her childhood.

Wharton's first work of nonfiction, *The Decoration of Houses*, written with an architect, was published in 1897, when she was thirty-five. Her first collection of short stories was published in 1899. And her first novel, *The Touchstone*, was published in 1900. All three books sold moderately well and received good reviews.

The Touchstone (Wharton, 1900) tells the story of a man who, in the past, had had a romance with a woman named Mrs. Aubyn, a literary genius. When the woman died she was an acclaimed author. The man, though a nice person, was incapable of comprehending her brilliance. He encountered a problem: He could not afford to marry the conventional woman with whom he was in love. Hiding his identity, he arranged to publish the love letters that Mrs. Aubyn had written him when the two of them were young. The profits from the book, which caused a sensation because of the beauty of the letters and Mrs. Aubyn's fame, enabled him to get married. The novel expresses Wharton's sense that her husband and others in her life did not value her talents. But it also suggests her recognition of her own rare ability as a novelist, because Mrs. Aubyn's literary career foreshadows hers.

The Touchstone is infused with the underlying tragedy that this literary artist, a woman of subtle perceptions and delicate feelings, never had an intimate partner with whom she could share her inner world; her lover, though companionable, was incapable of appreciating her.

When her first book of fiction was published, several critics observed the similarity between her style and Henry James's (Benstock, 1994, pp. 99–100). James was widely considered the foremost living novelist who wrote in English. In 1900 Edith sent him one of her short stories. He wrote back with a mixture of praise and advice and suggested that she visit with him sometime (Lewis, 1975, p. 125).

James by this time had moved on to his "third manner," the style of his later fiction that some consider convoluted and others view as his greatest creation. Wharton, who admired his earlier work, was one of those disturbed by the "third manner," and, after reading one of his books, she wrote a friend, "[I] could weep over the ruins of such a talent" (Lewis, 1975, p. 125). She even composed a parody of James's style. Here is part of a sentence, in which the hero worries about his hat being damaged by the weather: "[A]ny head-gear exposed after five o'clock that afternoon to the unimpeded action of the climatic influences must, within less than the hour hand's gyration of the dial, be reduced to a condition warranting, if not necessitating . . . [the] provisionally restorative manipulations of the hatter" (Lewis, 1975, p. 126).

After reading her second novel, *The Valley of Decision*, which was set in eighteenth-century Italy, James called it "brilliant & interesting from a literary point of view" but urged her to write instead about "the *American subject*." "Don't pass it by—the immediate, the real. . . . Take hold of it & keep hold & let it pull you where it will. . . . DO NEW YORK! The 1st-hand account is precious" (Powers, 1990, p. 34).

No one knows for sure whether Wharton was responding to James's advice, but she soon wrote her breakthrough novel, *The House of Mirth*, which describes a woman's gradual descent in the New York society that Wharton knew so well. Published in 1905, *The House of Mirth* created a sensation and was a run-away best-seller. Today it is generally considered the earliest of her outstanding works. Critics have emphasized how the novel reveals the heartlessness and rigidity of the upper class in New York. Society at first takes up the main character, Lily Bart, but as time goes on, especially after questions emerge about her virtue, she is cast aside. The psychological center of the novel is different. While the novel is effective as social criticism, its psychological dimension is central. The novel expresses the experience of loneliness. Lily, who always considered herself special and found it exciting when people lavished attention on her for her external qualities, her beauty and grace, is unable to connect at a deeper level with anyone, particularly the men who pursue her. By the end of the novel, defeated by her solitude, she is overcome with despair.

In 1903 Wharton and James finally met. They had lunch together in London and were much taken with each other. James described her as "really conversable" (Benstock, 1994, p. 139). They developed a close friendship that each of them cherished, and, although never living in the same country, they visited regularly until his death in 1916. But there was a limitation to their intimacy, due in part, according to my interpretation, to the lack of sexual chemistry between them. They always maintained a touch of formality. Wharton still had not found someone with whom she could share fully what mattered most to her.

With her husband, she was even farther from experiencing intimacy. Two anecdotes help capture the nature of their relationship. Edith Wharton was an attractive woman with red hair, fine features, and a lovely, slim figure of which she was proud. Once her husband, Teddy, was walking with a friend a few feet behind Edith outside The Mount, the house the couple had built in Lenox, Massachusetts. The conversation took place after Edith had successfully published works of poetry and prose. Teddy commented, "Look at that waist! No one would ever guess that she had written a line of poetry in her life." Teddy further pointed out to the guest that they had needed a new piggery, so she had written a poem to cover the expense (Lewis, 1975, p. 272). While Teddy could be admiring and witty, his comments also reveal that her literary expressiveness lay far outside his ken.

On another occasion, Edith was fascinated by a passage in a scientific treatise on heredity, and she showed it to her husband. He replied, "Does that sort of thing really amuse you?" By this time, more than twenty years into her marriage, she had become embittered. She wrote in her diary, "I found the key turn in my prison-lock. . . . Oh, Gods of derision! And you've given me over twenty years of it!" (Lewis, 1975, pp. 228–229).

For several years Teddy, if unable to communicate with Edith, at least had been a pleasant, well-mannered companion, but in the early years of the twentieth century he began to deteriorate. He seems to have suffered from bipolar disorder, formerly called manic-depressive illness. While not the cause, Edith's increasing disappointment with him and her accompanying contempt surely exacerbated his condition, although she tried to conceal her reactions.

A Passionate Affair

Thirteen years after Edith Wharton's death, a man named William Morton Fullerton heard that someone proposed writing a biography of the famous author. Wharton, perhaps because of her status, while elderly, as a literary eminence, had died with the reputation of being stern, passionless, and aloof; it was assumed she had had a stilted marriage and no love affairs. Fullerton urged the prospective biographer to "seize the event, however delicate the problem, to destroy the myth of your heroine's frigidity." He claimed that in her love life Wharton had been "fearless, reckless even." If the writer doubted him, he clinched his point by enclosing a copy of an ardent poem Wharton had sent him reflecting on the consummation of their affair (Benstock, 1994, p. 226).

Fullerton, Paris correspondent for *The Times* of London, was an adventurous, charming, inconstant American. He led a flamboyant love life that included a brief marriage to an actress, an affair with a Parisian woman who blackmailed him for years over some compromising letters that she had in her possession, and various sexual encounters with men, possibly even with Henry James. It was James who brought Fullerton and Wharton together; when Fullerton traveled to the United States in 1907, James urged him to contact Wharton so that she might invite him to stay with herself and her husband at The Mount (Lewis, 1975, p. 182).

Figure 13.3. William Morton Fullerton, Wharton's lover. (Yale Collection of American Literature, Beinecke Rare Book and Manuscript Library)

During this first visit, Wharton immediately became infatuated with Fullerton. While less involved emotionally, he seemed to enjoy flirting with this renowned woman of letters who, at the age of forty-five (three years his elder), retained her sexual appeal. By the time of their meeting, Wharton could hardly bear the frustration and loneliness that had built up during her marriage. Fullerton was an intelligent man with whom she could communicate on a deep level, much like the man in her early story about a woman who meets her soul mate in the afterlife. After he left The Mount, she began a diary addressed to him (later she gave it to him to read). In it she wrote, "[F]inding myself—after so long! —with some one to talk to, I take up this empty volume, in which long ago, I made one or two spasmodic attempts to keep a diary. For I had no one but myself to talk to, and it is absurd to write down what one says to one's self" (Benstock, 1994, p. 175).

In 1980, forty-three years after Wharton's death and twenty-eight years after Fullerton's, about 300 letters that she had written him turned up for sale. They provide a detailed account of her emotions during and after their love affair. Despite her frequent admonitions to him to burn her letters, he saved them. Her early novella, *The Touchstone*, comes to mind. Unlike the man in her novel, he did not sell them to bankroll a marriage to another woman, but there is still the coincidence of a body of letters surviving that documents a great author's love for a man who seems unworthy of her devotion.

Fullerton enjoyed Wharton's company and could be intimate for short periods of time. At times he spoke with her and wrote to her with the ardor of a committed lover, but evidently he never intended to have an exclusive relationship with her. Simultaneously with his involvement with Wharton, in fact, Fullerton had an engagement, hidden from Wharton, with his first cousin, Katharine Fullerton. Katherine, fourteen years younger than Fullerton, not only was his first cousin but was more like a sister to him because his parents had raised her from infancy after her mother's death. As she grew up, Katherine and Fullerton even regarded each other as sister and brother, although both knew that technically they were cousins.

The period of Wharton's intense emotional involvement with Fullerton began in December 1907, after the two of them were both back in Paris. By the end of 1909, the romance was finished; they were friends or, as Wharton put it, "comrades." The two years were tumultuous ones for both of them, but for different reasons. Wharton's feelings careened between ecstasy and despair. At times they had frequent visits and outings; the peak was reached in June 1909, when they consummated their relationship and again later that summer when they had a period of love making while traveling in England. At other times they were separated, or Fullerton avoided her, or he saw her but did not care about her feelings, and Wharton was, at best, stoic and, at worst, bereft. Fullerton, meanwhile, was preoccupied with his engagement to his cousin, which did not end in marriage; with other past and probably present lovers; and with job worries.

Wharton made it clear, in her letters to him and in the diary addressed to him, that the affair with him was a life-changing experience, all the more so because it fulfilled what she had always wanted and stood in contrast to her years of isolation. She wrote about her "numb dumb former self, the self that never believed in its chance of having any warm personal life, like other, luckier people" (Lewis & Lewis, 1988, p. 138). "You woke me from a long lethargy, a dull acquiescence in conventional restrictions, a needless self-effacement," she commented in another letter (p. 161). She noted that before their relationship began "I had no personal life: since then you have given me all imaginable joy" (p. 189).

At times it seemed to her that her future life would be worse now that she had experienced love. During one of their separations she wrote in the diary, "I have stood it all these years, and hardly felt it, because I had created a world of my own, in which I lived without heeding what went on outside. But since I have known what it was to have someone enter into that world and live there with me, the mortal solitude I come back to has become terrible" (Lewis, 1975, p. 229). She wrote him in a similar vein that, since he had given her "the only moments of real life I have ever known," how could she learn to live without joy? "I knew that lesson once, but I have unlearned it—you have kissed away the memory of it" (p. 229).

As Wharton's affair with Fullerton was unraveling, she wrote how painful she found it to "have all one's passionate tenderness demanded one day, & ignored the next" and added bitterly, "My life was better before I knew you" (Lewis & Lewis, p. 208). A month later she amended her statement. "I said once that my life was better before I knew you," she wrote. "That is not so, for it is good to have lived once in the round, for ever so short a time" (p. 216).

In the summer of 1910, aware that they could be, at most, casual friends, she described her state of mind to him: "Everything ahead of me is so dark, Dear, save what you are to me & what I might be to you. *That* is little enough, heaven knows" (p. 219). It is just at this time that Wharton began writing *Ethan Frome* in earnest. The end of her affair with Fullerton was not the only factor that influenced her mood; her marriage also cast a pall over her life.

Her husband, Teddy, had gone from being a dull but polite companion to someone who could no longer function in the world. With his bipolar disorder, he was not just a quiet invalid. When manic, he got into trouble and could hardly be contained. When depressed, he was in danger of killing himself. Often Teddy and Edith were separated. During the summer of 1909, while Edith was in France, Teddy, back in the United States, spiraled dangerously out of control. He installed a mistress in an apartment in Boston. More malignantly, from Edith's point of view, he stole a huge sum of money from Edith's trust fund and lost it through a combination of profligate spending and foolish investments. After Edith learned, at the beginning of 1910, of his misbehavior, Teddy spent most of his time taking trips with companions and undergoing futile cures at spas and sanitaria (Benstock, 1994, pp. 226–229).

At one point Teddy seemed to do best when with Edith, and his family urged her to fulfill her wifely duty and take care of him. "*He* has only one thought," she wrote Fullerton in May 1910, "to be with me all day, every day. If I try to escape, he will follow." She went on, "And if you knew, if you *knew*, what the days are, what the hours are, what our talks are, interminable repetitions of the same weary round of inanities & puerilities; & all with the knowledge definitely before me, put there by all the Drs, that what is killing me is doing him no good!" (Lewis & Lewis, 1988, p. 215).

Ethan Frome

In the summer of 1910 Wharton's memories were alive with the rapture she had had with Fullerton, as well as the heartbreak, and the burden of taking care of her ill husband also weighed heavily on her. She recalled the theme of a story (only eight pages long when published many years later) she had begun three years earlier as an exercise while receiving lessons to improve her French; building on this theme, she began writing *Ethan Frome* (Wolf, 1994, p. 157). After some distractions, she returned to the manuscript a few months later, while Teddy was away on one of his trips. Just after the new year of 1911,

she wrote to a friend, "I am driving harder and harder at that ridiculous nouvelle." She was nearly halfway done and was speeding along (Lewis & Lewis, 1988, p. 232). During most of the period in which she composed *Ethan Frome*, her dear friend Walter Berry was residing in her guest suite, and each evening she read him her day's work (Benstock, 1994, p. 247).

The narrator of the novel is an educated man whose employer has sent him to work on a power plant in western Massachusetts. Stranded by a strike for most of the winter in a small town, he becomes curious about a person named Ethan Frome. Ethan is "so stiffened and grizzled" that he appears to be an old man, although he is only fifty-two years old. The narrator learns from a local that Ethan has been that way ever since the "smash-up." After spending some time with Ethan, the narrator visualizes him as seeming to be "a part of the mute melancholy landscape, an incarnation of its frozen woe, with all that was warm and sentient in him bound below the surface." He concludes that Ethan lives "in a depth of moral isolation" (Wharton, 1911, pp. 16–17). The narrator pieces together what happened to Ethan and tells the following story.

Ethan, at the age of twenty-eight, was living with his wife, Zeena, who was seven years older than he was, and her younger cousin, Mattie. The young woman's father had died, leaving her destitute, and she could find no alternative but to come live with the Fromes, where she acted as Zeena's servant in exchange for room and board. Ethan had an empty relationship with his wife. They never conversed, she had lost her youth, she criticized him frequently, and she was sickly, constantly visiting doctors and trying remedies for her many obscure ailments.

Ethan had found when Mattie came to live with them a year before that it was "like the lighting of a fire on a cold hearth." "[H]e could show her things and tell her things, and taste the bliss of feeling that all he imparted left long reverberations and echoes he could wake at will." When they walked back to their farm from town at night, he especially felt "the sweetness of this communion." He was enthralled with nature; the emotion he had derived from it before meeting Mattie "remained in him as a silent ache, veiling with sadness the beauty that evoked it." He had not known whether anyone else in the world reacted as he did, but he "learned that one other spirit had trembled with the same touch of wonder" (Wharton, 1911, pp. 36–37).

Zeena decided that as an ailing woman she needed a proper, paid servant who would help her more efficiently than Mattie was able to do. While out of town for an appointment with a doctor, she hired the new servant and announced to Ethan and Mattie that her cousin must leave at once. Ethan tried to find an alternative to Zeena's edict but finally concluded that he had to go along. "There was no way out—none. He was a prisoner for life, and now his one ray of light was to be extinguished" (Wharton, 1911, p. 146). He considered borrowing some money, so that he and Mattie might flee together, but he could not see deserting his ill wife.

So he resigned himself to driving Mattie to the railroad station and picking up the new servant, who was due to arrive. Ethan and Mattie talked in the horse-drawn sleigh; Mattie was as in love with him as he was with her, and she was also as bereft. As they came to the steep hill that led into town, Ethan reminded her that they had planned to ride a sled down there some time. He saw a sled under the trees and suggested they have their ride now; they flew down the hill and found it thrilling. After they walked back up the hill, Mattie proposed a double suicide. They could ride down again on the sled, and all Ethan would have to do was to crash the sled into the elm tree near the bottom of the hill. Ethan had the "hated vision of the house he was going back to, . . . of the woman who would wait for him there." He realized his life with his wife was "intolerable" (Wharton, 1911, p. 180). He agreed with Mattie. "She was right," he thought, after they got into the sled, "this was better than parting" (Wharton, 1911, p. 183).

But their suicide attempt failed. The crash left Ethan lame. Mattie was hurt more severely; due to a spinal injury, she became partially paralyzed. The narrator talks to a woman in town who explains what it has been like in the Frome farmhouse in the twenty-four years since the crash (Wharton, 1911, pp. 194–195). The three of them, Ethan, Mattie, and Zeena, have continued to live together, with Zeena mostly taking care of the other two. Mattie has soured, and Zeena continues to be cranky. "[S]ometimes the two of them get going at each other, and then Ethan's face'd break your heart." The woman concludes with the last words of the novel, "[T]he way they are now, I don't see's there's much difference between the Fromes up at the farm and the Fromes down in the graveyard; 'cept that down there they're all quiet and the women have got to hold their tongues."

The resonance between Edith Wharton's life and *Ethan Frome* is unmistakable. The novel is not autobiographical in a literal sense (see Anderson, 2001). Wharton never lived in a Massachusetts farmhouse, never fell in love with a servant, never attempted a double suicide. But in this work of fiction she expresses, struggles with, and lives through the same emotions that gripped her as she wrote the novel. "[T]he *soul* of [a] novel," she commented once, "is (or should be) the writer's own soul" (Wharton, 1985, p. 115). An author expresses in her fiction the emotions that matter to her most; how would anyone create an imaginative story concerning anything about which one did not care deeply? And from where could these emotions—and the conflicts and concerns that give rise to them—come, except one's previous experience? As the novelist John North commented recently, "What I hope you will accept as true is that my new novel, just like its brothers and sisters, is autobiographical in only one sense: it's made out of stuff that life has deposited inside me" (Brisendine, 2003, p. 4).

Ethan Frome not only captures, but also evokes in the reader, the feelings that Wharton had in her own life. From an early age, she yearned for intimate closeness with another person. Her marriage was arid and disappointing, much like Ethan's. She felt as if she were imprisoned there, as he did. After falling in love with Fullerton and finding someone with whom she could share her inner world, she felt that for once she was alive, and the sexual attraction was an inextricable part of the communion she had with Fullerton; Ethan's experience with Mattie was much the same. Wharton was depressed in the period in which she wrote the novel; she was still trapped in her marriage, and she knew she had no future with Fullerton. Through different circumstances, Ethan becomes depressed; he is stuck in his marriage, and the young vibrant Mattie whom he loved is gone.

Yet the writing of *Ethan Frome* helped Wharton get on with her life. Being able to express one's emotions and share them with others offers some relief. With most novels, the author shares the work with readers in general. With *Ethan Frome* the process of sharing took place in a more literal way, in that, as she was working on the manuscript, Wharton read aloud each evening to Walter Berry what she had written that day. Constructing an imaginative world that carries an author's emotions gives one a sense of some control over what before may have threatened to be overwhelming. And it is not unusual that authors discover a solution, or at least methods of coping, from their creative playing with what matters most to them. In the novel Wharton envisioned what the future could be like for her. She had been as reluctant to leave her spouse as Ethan was, yet within a few months after completing *Ethan Frome* she obtained a separation from Teddy, and in 1913 they were divorced. She refused to live a life of misery as had her character Ethan.

The Age of Innocence—the novel that rivals *Ethan Frome* for status as her most acclaimed work—captures her strategy. The outline of the underlying emotions is virtually the same in the two novels. In *The Age of Innocence*, published in 1920, nine years after *Ethan Frome*, the main character, also a man, falls in love with someone with whom he has true communion, but, due to various circumstances, he cannot marry her but instead enters a marriage devoid of passion and intimate sharing. The difference is that in *The Age of Innocence*, although he never forgets what he has lost, nor what he lacks, the protagonist lives a vigorous, fulfilling life, while retaining a touch of inner melancholy. I believe that Wharton always had some underlying regret and sadness, but she avoided Ethan's fate of becoming enveloped in depression, and she went on to live a busy, involving, satisfying life.

Psychobiography and the Study of Literature

Using Wharton and *Ethan Frome* as an example, I would like to end with a few words about the relationship between psychobiography and the study of literature. It seems to me that the two disciplines are invaluable for each other. Psychobiography offers us the potential of understanding much of the terrain of an author's inner world. That understanding, then, can help us in looking at the author's work. We can be sensitized to the emotional heart of the work, to the themes that resonate most fully with the author's emotional struggles. Knowing about Wharton's psychological experience, I would argue, helps us see that *Ethan Frome* revolves around the desire for intimacy and the desolation that comes when it is lost.

Studying an author's work is also indispensable for exploring an author psychobiographically. At times, as with Wharton, we may find, in letters and diaries, direct evidence of an author's inner struggles, but seeing how she expresses these concerns in her fiction adds depth and nuance to our understanding of what these concerns meant to her.

Henry James appreciated *Ethan Frome* more than any other of Wharton's works. "I exceedingly admire . . . *Ethan Frome*," he wrote her. "A beautiful art & tone & truth—a beautiful artful *kept-downness*, and yet effective cumulations. It's a 'gem'" (Powers, 1990, p. 195). *Ethan Frome* works in many ways, but I believe that what James responded to more than anything else was the novel's emotional truth.

References

Anderson, J.W. (2001). Is fiction autobiographical? Clio's Psyche, 8, 134–136.

Benstock, S. (1994). No gifts from chance: A biography of Edith Wharton. New York: Charles Scribner's Sons.

Brisendine, S. (2003, December 8). "Shipwreck" is all about the write stuff. Chicago Tribune, Sec. 5, p. 4.

Dwight, E. (1994). Edith Wharton: An extraordinary life. New York: Harry N. Abrams.

Lewis, R.W.B. (1975). Edith Wharton: A biography. New York: Harper & Row.

Lewis, R.W.B., & Lewis, N. (Eds.). (1988). The letters of Edith Wharton. New York: Charles Scribner's Sons.

Powers, L.H. (Ed.). (1990). Henry James and Edith Wharton, letters: 1900–1915. New York: Charles Scribner's Sons.

Wharton, E. (1893). The fullness of life. In R.W.B. Lewis (Ed.), The collected short stories of Edith Wharton (Vol. 1, pp. 12–20). New York: Charles Scribner's Sons, 1968.

Wharton, E. (1900). The touchstone. New York: Charles Scribner's Sons.

Wharton, E. (1911). Ethan Frome. New York: Charles Scribner's Sons.

Wharton, E. (1985). A backward glance. New York: Charles Scribner's Sons.

Wharton, E. (1990). Life and I. In C.G. Wolff (Ed.), Novellas and other writings (pp. 1069–1096). New York: Library of America.

Wolf, C.G. (1994). A feast of words: The triumph of Edith Wharton. Reading, Mass.: Addison-Wesley.

PART III

PSYCHOBIOGRAPHIES OF PSYCHOLOGISTS

Chapter 14

James William Anderson

The Psychobiographical Study of Psychologists

Perceptive observers have long noticed that there is an intimate connection between the personal life of psychologists—their experiences, troubles, preoccupations, and conflicts—and the psychological ideas and theories they create. Often this connection is spoken of as surprising or humorous. Henry A. Murray (personal communication, 1975), himself an influential psychological theorist, was talking with me once about Erik Erikson, whom he had known for many years. He pointed out that Erikson's theory of human development did not fit everyone but applied to Erikson and people like him very well. Then he chuckled and, referring to theories of human development in general, said, "They're all autobiographies, every one of them."

I work in Chicago, the same city where Heinz Kohut, the pre-eminent theorist of narcissism, lived. I frequently heard stories about his narcissism (along with recollections of his brilliance, I should add). He loved it when he was honored on the occasion of his sixtieth birthday; he read his new writings to his inner circle but did not want to hear any criticisms; as a young man he slept with a hairnet to preserve his pompadour. Everyone said, "Well, of course he wrote about narcissism."

Two outstanding books explore the connection between the theorist and the theory. Here is how each describes this relationship.

Amy Demorest (2005), speaking about Sigmund Freud, B.F. Skinner, and Carl Rogers, states, "In developing a model for understanding all human lives, each man drew on his own particular life. In seeking to make objective claims about all people, these theorists were influenced

by the subjective experience of themselves as individual persons" (p. 4). She goes on to argue that the differences between the three theories "result from differences in the life experiences of their originators and the personal concerns that emerged from those experiences" (p. 4).

"[T]he subjective world of the theorist," write George E. Atwood and Robert D. Stolorow (1993), "is inevitably translated into his metapsychological conceptions and hypotheses regarding human nature" (p. 5). (The term "metapsychological" refers to a theorist's overarching conceptions.) Atwood and Stolorow examine four psychologists—Freud, Carl G. Jung, Wilhelm Reich, and Otto Rank—and conclude that, through these conceptions, "each theorist's solutions to his own dilemmas and nuclear crises became frozen in a static intellectual system that, to him, was an indisputable vision of objective reality" (p. 175).

Before continuing, I would like to make it clear that I am not claiming that theorists' own lives are the sole source of their psychological theories. The work of any theorist develops in close interaction with the intellectual trends of the day. For example, there was much talk and writing about the unconscious, sexuality, and determinism at the time when Freud was creating his theories (see Arnold and Atwood, chap. 17 this vol., on Friedrich Nietzsche, who, independently of Freud, had similar insights into the workings of the psyche.) In addition, theorists do not develop their theories only on the basis of their personal experience. They always have other sources that they observe and to which they apply their ideas. It is hard to imagine that Freud would have developed his theory if he had not encountered hysterical patients who suffered from symptoms that seemed to result from unconscious forces. Likewise, Skinner's experimentation with rats and pigeons was the immediate source of many of his concepts. I am claiming, however, that theorists are drawn to explore certain areas because these areas have been meaningful in their own lives, and ultimately they become convinced of their conclusions only if these conclusions are consistent with their own experience. There is, moreover, a dynamic interaction between theorists and their ideas. Their ideas help them understand themselves and often enable them to work out vexing problems. Sometimes the ideas serve a defensive function; that is, the ideas protect them from a threat to their self-esteem or their self-cohesion. Here I give two examples of theorists and how their central psychological ideas were closely related to difficulties in their own lives: Freud and Erikson.

Freud put a great emphasis on his concept of the Oedipus complex. Once he referred to it as the "shibboleth" of psychoanalysis, in the sense that acceptance of this concept distinguished those who were adherents of psychoanalysis from those who were opponents (Freud, 1905/1953, p. 226). In the Oedipus complex, the little boy not only wants to be close to his mother but also desires her sexually, and he not only experiences rivalry with his father over possession of the mother but also wants to kill his father. Freud grew up in a familial situation ripe for the development of just this kind of a complex. His father was forty-one and his mother twenty-one when he was born. He was just about as close in age to his mother as was his father. As a boy he may have thought to himself, "Why should my father—rather than I—be the one who gets to sleep with her?" He was his mother's favorite child; she always saw him as special and called him "my golden Sigi." We know from his childhood memories that he remembered his father as being much more negative toward him. At the age of seven or eight, he once urinated in his parents' bedroom. His censuring father commented, "The boy will come to nothing" (Anderson, 2001, pp. 10–11).

During his self-analysis, Freud was shocked and dismayed when he discovered his own Oe-

dipus complex. He concluded that his "libido" toward his mother had been "awakened" during his third year when he had the opportunity to see her naked. His discomfort is palpable. Despite writing to his closest friend, he cannot bring himself to use the common German words for "mother" and "naked" but instead resorts to the more distancing Latin words, *matrem* and *nudam* (Masson, 1985, p. 268). He was similarity uncomfortable in speaking about his rivalry with his father.

Freud's personal experience of learning about his desire for his mother and his conflict with his father played a central role in his being able to formulate the concept of the Oedipus complex. On the one hand, his having had this experience sensitized him to perceiving a similar pattern in the experiences of others, particularly his patients. He was attuned to the possibility of primal feelings—lust, hatred, rivalry—arising in the hothouse atmosphere of the nuclear family. On the other hand, his development of the concept had a defensive aspect. He was troubled by his guilt; it seemed awful to him that he had felt this way toward his parents. But he could relieve much of this guilt by saying that an Oedipus complex is virtually universal. Freud had no reason to feel badly about himself if just about every little boy feels toward his parents as he did.

If the Oedipus complex is central to Freud's psychological theory, the concept of identity is equally central to Erik Erikson's theory. Identity, as explained by Erikson, refers to a person's view of oneself; constructing a workable identity may be difficult, because an identity must integrate the disparate facets of oneself while also garnering respect and acknowledgement from society. A person who has trouble forming an identity goes through an "identity crisis."

"[I]f ever an identity crisis was central and long drawn out in somebody's life," Erikson wrote, "it was so in mine" (Coles, 1970, p. 180). He noted that he had many "marginalities." Lawrence J. Friedman (1999), in his biography of Erikson, expands on what Erikson discusses and brings out a great many conflicts that Erikson had within himself, between himself and his parents, and between himself and society. Integrating various aspects of himself into a workable identity was a formidable task. Erikson never knew his father, who presumably was a Danish Gentile. His mother was Danish and Jewish. He was brought up in Germany. When he was a small boy, his mother married a German-Jewish pediatrician. To make matters more confusing, Erikson was told this man was his father, although he had memories of the time before the man entered his life. Erikson was raised as Jewish, but because of his blond hair, blue eyes, and his height, the Jewish children called him a "goy" [Yiddish for a Gentile]. The Gentile children considered him a Jew. At one point he thought of himself as a German nationalist, but the other boys spurned him as a "Dane." As he started to consider a career, he wanted to be an artist, but his stepfather thought he should become a professional, preferably a physician. He became alienated from his family, which he viewed as bourgeois.

Erikson went through a period in his early adulthood when he was significantly troubled. He notes that at times his disturbances would be characterized as "borderline," that is, as being on the boundary between neurosis and psychosis. "[S]ome of my friends," he acknowledged, "will insist that I need to name this crisis and to see it in everybody else in order to really come to terms with myself" (Erikson, 1970, p. 742).

The implication is that there was something therapeutic for Erikson in developing his concept of the identity crisis. He could understand himself and could feel at peace over his period of confusion and disturbance after he had found a way of analyzing the process of identity formation.

As with Freud and his concept of the Oedipus complex, Erikson's personal experience played a key role in his being able to develop his concept of identity. Erikson's struggles in constructing a workable identity showed him in stark relief the different aspects of identity, such as how an identity must fit with one's background while also being accepted by others. What he had encountered sensitized him to difficulties in identity formation; when he observed people going through something similar, he was attuned to their experiences. On the other hand, there also may be a defensive side to his development of the concept of identity. He felt ashamed that he had struggled through a period of psychopathology, but, evoking his concept, he could say that he merely had had an identity crisis, something that a great

many people experience. He argued, moreover, that an identity crisis can be a "normative crisis"; although painful and sometimes malignant, it offers "a high growth potential" (Erikson, 1959, pp. 116–117). (For a psychobiographical discussion of Erikson in more depth, see Alexander, chap. 18 this vol.)

As noted above, observers have often seen that there was a close connection between a theorist's life and ideas. Frequently they use their perception of this connection for partisan purposes; they invoke it in order to attack the ideas, sometimes brutally. In a passage of this kind, Emil Ludwig (1947/1973), a biographer of Freud, wrote in 1947, "The characteristics of Freud's dogmas and visions, then, might well be a product of his own aberrations, as implanted in him by childish experience." "Bluntly, thousands of neurotics each year," he insisted, "are declared sex maniacs because the founder of psychoanalysis was himself a sexopath. Thousands of the healthy are declared sick because one man was sick, and believed that the gloomy symptoms rising out of his childhood were common to all" (pp. 281–282).

Ludwig's claims are outlandish because his psychobiographical analysis of Freud is so polemical and amateurish. But what especially interests me here is his underlying argument; he assumes that if a theorist's ideas stem from his so-called "childish experience," then those ideas are automatically wrong. He has made the "genetic fallacy." Actually, a theory's accuracy is independent of its origins. The first person who posited that the earth rotates on its axis may have been hit in the head with a falling apple and, feeling dizzy, declared that the earth was spinning. The personal factors involved in the derivation of a theory neither support nor contradict its standing.

Showing a connection between the theorist and the theory does not invalidate the theory. I would argue, in fact, that with personality theories there is always such a connection. As with Freud and Erikson, a theorist is drawn to a particular area of experience because it has been prominent in his own life. He cares about this area; he is motivated to investigate it, to try to make sense of it. Why would a theorist concern himself deeply with something that did not have personal meaning for him? The theorist also becomes sensitized to this aspect of being human. He is able to perceive its workings in the lives of others, while most observers would overlook it, and he is thereby enabled to study it in others.

There is a fantasy that discoveries in personality psychology come about in another way. Many people might imagine that psychologists objectively study people and through empirical research simply find what is there. But psychobiographical studies have shown that the field does not operate in that way. Theorists use themselves as their first and most convincing model of what people are like. As Demorest (2005) convincingly demonstrates, even for Skinner, who developed his system through rigorous research with rats and pigeons, a key source of his basic concept, the controlling influence of external reinforcement, was personal.

In addition to providing insight into how the creative process works in psychological theorizing, the psychobiographical approach to the study of psychologists offers six benefits.

(1) Psychobiography helps us understand psychological theories better. Because a theorist's own experience provided major input as the theorist developed a concept, we can often find in the theorist's own life a striking and illustrative example of the workings of the concept. For example, Freud's experience shows us what an Oedipus complex might be like, and in Erikson's developmental history we can see the difficulties of identify formation.

Another example pertains to the work of Kohut, who developed an influential school of thought within psychoanalysis called self psychology. Kohut (1979) wrote a paper that purports to be an account of a patient, called Mr. Z., who had two analyses with him, one before and one after Kohut developed his new ideas. But, as Strozier (2001) has shown, there was no such person as Mr. Z. Instead, Kohut was writing about himself. The so-called first analysis of Mr. Z. is Kohut's own training analysis. The second analysis is Kohut's account of how he himself would be understood, and treated, in the light of the ideas of self psychology. We can look to this paper to see how Kohut's key ideas apply to his own experience.

(2) Psychobiography helps us find a theorist's blind spots and limitations. Knowing about the personal life of theorists brings our attention to shortcomings in their theories. There is a famous story involving Gordon Allport. As a young man, Allport visited Freud. He wanted to meet the founder of psychoanalysis. Sitting in Freud's presence, he cast around for something to say. He told Freud about seeing a boy in the tram on the way to the office. The boy was preoccupied with dirt and had a mother who seemed orderly and dominating. Freud looked at Allport and asked, "And was that little boy you?" "It honestly was not," Allport claims (Elms, 1972, p. 628). Allport believes Freud was in error and missed his actual motivation, which was to talk about something that would interest Freud. Murray, who had known Allport for decades, commented to me once on this same story. He said that Freud's remark was "very clever" because "that's just what Allport is. I mean, he is a very fastidious person; he is very clean himself. . . . Freud just hit him right on the head, right on the nose" (Anderson, 1990, p. 326).

"This experience taught me," Allport (1968) claims, "that depth psychology, for all its merits, may plunge too deep, and that psychologists would do well to give full recognition to manifest motives before probing the unconscious" (p. 384). Indeed, Allport went on to develop a valuable psychological approach, but one in which short shrift was given to deeper motives. Elms (1972, p. 630; also see Elms, 1994, pp. 71–84) argues that Allport did not just react to this one incident. Rather, his background emphasized piety, morality, hard work, and orderliness. Hence, it did not take the encounter with Freud for a "high-minded and clean little boy" to grow up to be a psychological theorist who emphasizes high-mindedness and avoids the dirty or unsavory side of life.

This psychobiographical consideration of Allport's experience helps us see a limitation in his psychological theorizing. He had a blindness to the darker side of life and tended to overlook it and downplay it. He did not like to think of people as having deep motivations, sexual conflicts, and disabling neuroses.

Barenbaum (chap. 16 this vol.) provides a more detailed psychobiographical study of Allport and takes up this same story of Allport's meeting with Freud. She argues that it reflects a common pattern for Allport, in which he tries to connect with an admired person, suffers rejection and humiliation, and then gains vindication by developing what he sees as a superior approach.

There is ample evidence that Freud idealized his relationship with his mother. In talking about the little boy's development, he has much to say about the boy's troubles with his father, emphasizing the boy's hostility and rivalry toward his father and his fear of castration. But Freud (1933/1955) describes the relationship of mother and son as "altogether the most perfect, the most free from ambivalence of all human relationships" (p. 133). Tomkins has argued convincingly that Freud was traumatically disappointed with his mother and felt betrayed by her, but it was too threatening for him to become aware of these feelings consciously, and so he protected against them by preserving the mother, in his theoretical writings about boys and their mothers, as being virtually faultless. In talking about girls, however, his various recriminations against mothers come flowing out (Tomkins, 1963, pp. 515–526; also see Abraham, 1982).

Freud's personal experience seems to have limited his theory construction so that in writing about masculine psychology he emphasized difficulties with fathers and overlooked difficulties with mothers. The case of the patient called the Rat Man (Freud, 1909/1955) provides an illustration of how Freud underplayed the role of the mother. It is the only case of his for which his original notes have survived. In Freud's case history, there is only the barest mention of the patient's mother, while a great emphasis is placed on the patient's troubled (and, one should add, Oedipal) relationship with his father. But, according to the original case notes, the patient often made reference to his mother.

In other words, a psychobiographical understanding of Freud suggests that he avoided looking at the problematical side of his relationship with his own mother. This understanding draws our attention to a blind spot in his theory. He underestimates the role of mothers in their sons' psychological lives. He is quick to see rivalry and hostility between a son and a father, but he tended to overlook the role of mothers.

(3) Psychobiography readies us to beware of overgeneralizations. It is easy to see why a theorist might overgeneralize. Anyone will come to see the world based on the model of one's own experience. If a person has grown up in the midst of war, he would tend to view all the world as rife with conflict and killing. If another person went through childhood with an affectionate, attentive mother, she would be likely to visualize mothers as loving and caring. Overgeneralization is a part of the human condition. Since theorists base their theories on their own experience, they tend to see everyone's experience as being much like their own.

Moreover, as Atwood and Stolorow (1993) emphasize, there is a defensive aspect to theory building in psychology that further encourages overgeneralization. As described above with both Freud and Erikson, theorists often derive a psychological benefit from seeing their concepts as being applicable to just about everyone. Freud, by claiming that Oedipal complexes are ubiquitous, gained relief from his guilt over having lustful desire for his mother and murderous hostility toward his father. Erikson overcame his shame regarding his period of intense psychological disturbance by claiming that a great many people go through identity crises and that such a crisis can be valuable; it can result in unusual growth and creativity.

Freud (1905/1953, p. 226) regards the Oedipus complex as being the "nuclear" complex of the neuroses—of all neuroses—in the sense that it "constitutes the essential part of their content." When someone speaks of his favored concept in such terms, it is a dead giveaway that he is guilty of overgeneralization.

(4) Psychobiography helps demystify theorists; it helps us not to idolize them. As we look at the lives of the most influential theorists, we see that they had the same personal difficulties as other people. They grappled, given the inevitably narrow range of their experience, to construct the best theories that they could. We can have a properly critical attitude toward their ideas. We can say that, indeed, these are people of unusual insight who were highly motivated to try to make sense of personality. But all of them will be limited in how much they can see. We need not be intimidated by a theorist's

pronouncements, or assume that any theorist has the final word as to what people are like. Instead, a psychobiographical approach readies us to see their ideas as having potential value while being aware that all theorists are fallible.

(5) While my emphasis has been on personality theory, psychobiography also offers benefits to our understanding of psychotherapy and psychological testing. Each psychologist develops a method of psychotherapy that is coordinated with that individual's own personality and problems. Freud suffered from repressed feelings, particularly his lust for his mother and murderous hatred of his father. Through his self-analysis, which included the study of his own dreams, he was able to get at these feelings and obtain some relief. He developed a similar system for patients that was based on gaining access to the unconscious and that included dream interpretation (Anderson, 1997).

Aaron Beck, a highly logical and controlled individual, had anxiety symptoms that started in his childhood and continued into adulthood. He was able to lessen these symptoms by using cognitive therapy, the method of psychotherapy he had developed, on himself (Weishaar, 1993).

Carl Rogers' parents had been relentlessly coercive and controlling. He grew up in a restrictive atmosphere in which dancing and card playing, let alone sex, were forbidden, and, most important, he had no freedom to think his own thoughts and make his own decisions. When he had a psychological crisis, he turned to two therapists who had learned from him how to do client-centered therapy. These therapists were able to create an atmosphere within which Rogers felt comfortable looking inside himself. "I have often been grateful that by the time I was in dire need of personal help," Rogers (1972) commented, "I had trained therapists who were . . . able to offer me the kind of help I needed." He added, "The point of view I developed in therapy is the sort of help I myself would like" (p. 58). It is not unusual that innovative psychotherapists, having found that the treatment approaches available at the time did not help them sufficiently, then go on to invent just the approach that would work best for them (Anderson, 1997).

Our awareness of the psychobiographical origins of methods of psychotherapy gives us a clear message. Any method of therapy harmonizes with some people better than others; it is particularly effective with a person who is similar to the originator of the method. Within well-developed schools of psychotherapy, such as psychoanalysis, there are a variety of techniques and methods, but still the general guideline holds: It is a mistake to think that one size fits all. Working with any patient requires finding the approach best suited to that individual.

In a similar way, psychologists design psychological tests to get at a particular aspect of experience that is most meaningful to them. Henry A. Murray, working with his colleagues at the Harvard Psychological Clinic, particularly Christiana Morgan, developed the Thematic Apperception Test. In earlier years he had lived a rather pedestrian existence, going through medical school and then studying biochemistry, when suddenly he had gotten in touch with a new realm of experience, the inner life, the area of hidden motivations and powerful emotions. Having found inspiration and excitement, he turned to psychology with the express purpose of studying this realm. He developed the Thematic Apperception Test because he was motivated to find a way of getting at and exposing fantasies, motivations, intrapsychic conflicts, and emotions (Anderson, 1999). We can use this test best if we understand that it was designed for a particular purpose.

In short, knowing about the lives of psychologists helps guide us in seeing the strengths and limitations of the psychological tests they develop.

(6) The single greatest benefit of the psychobiographical study of psychologists, in my view, is that it encourages us to be discriminating in making use of psychological theories. "[N]either the whole of truth nor the whole of good," William James (1908) once wrote, "is revealed to any single observer, although each observer gains a partial superiority of insight from the particular position in which he stands" (p. 264). Similarly, the major psychological thinkers, based on their own lives and struggles, could see deeply into certain aspects of experience. Freud made a valuable contribution in constructing the concept of the Oedipus complex, and this concept can deepen our understanding of some people, especially if we use the concept flexibly and stick close

to the evidence. But where we would go wrong would be in trying, as some psychoanalysts have done, to apply the Oedipus complex to everyone; if we did that, we would often have to distort people to fit the concept, as if we were stretching someone to put him into a Procrustean bed. At the same time, we want to keep in mind that no psychological thinker can see the whole of personality; we would be sure to limit our understanding if we adhered dogmatically to any one system and saw it as providing the ultimate answer. More than sixty years ago, Murray (1940/ 1981) advocated a similar stance toward psychoanalysis. He argued for making use of certain parts of Freud's system but warned against "going in blind and swallowing the whole indigestible bolus" (p. 296).

References

Abraham, R. (1982). Freud's mother conflict and the formulation of the Oedipal father. Psychoanalytic Review, 69, 441–453.

Anderson, J.W. (1990). The life of Henry A. Murray: 1893–1988. In A.I. Rabin, R.A. Zucker, R. Emmons, & S. Frank (Eds.), Studying persons and lives (pp. 304–334). New York: Springer.

Anderson, J.W. (1997). The analyst's own analysis: From Freud to Merton Gill. Paper presented at the annual convention of the American Psychological Association, Chicago, IL, 18 August.

Anderson, J.W. (1999). Henry A. Murray and the creation of the Thematic Apperception Test. In L. Gieser & M.I. Stein (Eds.), Evocative images: The Thematic Apperception Test and the art of projection (pp. 23–38). Washington, D.C.: American Psychological Association

Anderson, J.W. (2001). Sigmund Freud's life and work: An unofficial guide to the Freud exhibit. Annual of Psychoanalysis, 29, 9–34.

Atwood, G.E., & Stolorow, R.D. (1993). Faces in a cloud: Intersubjectivity in personality theory, second edition. Northvale, N.J.: Jason Aronson.

Coles, R. (1970). Erik H. Erikson: The growth of his work. Boston: Little, Brown.

Demorest, A. (2005). Psychology's grand theorists: How personal experiences shaped psychological ideas. Mahwah, N.J.: Lawrence Erlbaum.

Elms, A.C. (1972). Allport, Freud, and the clean little boy. Psychoanalytic Review, 59, 627–632.

Elms, A.C. (1994). Uncovering lives: The uneasy alliance of biography and psychology. New York: Oxford University Press.

Erikson, E.H. (1959). The problem of ego identity. Psychological Issues, 1, 101–164.

Erikson, E.H. (1970). Autobiographic notes on the identity crisis. Daedalus, 99, 730–759.

Freud, S. (1953). Three essays on the theory of sexuality. In J. Strachey (Ed. & Trans.), The standard edition of the complete psychological works of Sigmund Freud (Vol. 7, pp. 125–248). London: Hogarth Press. (Original work published 1905)

Freud, S. (1955). Notes upon a case of obsessional neurosis. In J. Strachey (Ed. & Trans.), The standard edition of the complete psychological works of Sigmund Freud (Vol. 10, pp. 153–318). London: Hogarth Press. (Original work published 1909)

Freud, S. (1955). New introductory lectures on psycho-analysis. In J. Strachey (Ed. & Trans.), The standard edition of the complete psychological works of Sigmund Freud (Vol. 22, pp. 5–182). London: Hogarth Press. (Original work published 1933)

Friedman, L.J. (1999). Identity's architect: A biography of Erik H. Erikson. New York: Scribner.

James, W. (1908). Talks to teachers of psychology: and to students on some of life's ideals. New York: Henry Holt.

Kohut, H. (1979). The two analyses of Mr Z. International Journal of Psycho-Analysis, 60, 3–27.

Ludwig, E. (1973). Doctor Freud. New York: Manor Books. (Original work published 1947)

Masson, J.M. (Ed.). (1985). The complete letters of Sigmund Freud to Wilhelm Fliess. Cambridge, Mass.: Harvard University Press.

Murray, H.A. (1981). What should psychologists do about psychoanalysis? In E.S. Schneidman, Endeavors in psychology: Selections from the personology of Henry A. Murray (pp. 291–311). New York: Harper & Row. (Original work published 1940)

Rogers, C.R. (1972). My personal growth. In Arthur Burton (Ed.), Twelve therapists (pp. 28–77). San Francisco: Jossey-Bass.

Strozier, C.B. (2001). Heinz Kohut: The making of a psychoanalyst. New York: Farrar, Straus, & Giroux.

Tomkins, S. (1963). Affect, imagery, consciousness, Vol. 2: The negative affects. New York: Springer.

Weishaar, M.E. (1993). Aaron T. Beck. London: Sage.

Chapter 15

Alan C. Elms

Freud as Leonardo
Why the First Psychobiography Went Wrong

Sigmund Freud's book on Leonardo (1910/ 1957b) is widely regarded as the first genuine psychobiography. Other researchers, including Möbius and Sadger, had previously concerned themselves with the psychology of "great men," but their main goal was to arrive at a specific diagnosis of psychopathology. In *Leonardo da Vinci and a Memory of His Childhood* (originally published in 1910), Freud went much further: He applied a systematic theory of personality to the entire span of a creative individual's life, and he provided psychological explanations for certain of Leonardo's achievements as well as his failures.

Almost a century later, Freud's book remains in several regards a model psychobiography. He chose one of the most important and challenging biographical subjects in the history of the human race. He provided methodological guidelines for psychobiography, by prescriptive example and by proscriptive statement, that are valid today. Through a close reading of small as well as large clues about Leonardo's life and work, and through the application of a coherent theoretical system, Freud was able to explain aspects of Leonardo's character that had long puzzled art historians. Even Leonardo scholars who are not psychoanalytically inclined continue to acknowledge Freud's insights. For example, in his classic work on Leonardo, Kenneth Clark (1967) praises Freud's study for its "passages of fine intuition" (p. 20) and for its "beautiful, and I believe profound, interpretation" of Leonardo's *Virgin and St. Anne* (p. 137). And one of the major Leonardo volumes, *The Unknown Leonardo* (Reti, 1974), begins with Freud's description of Leonardo: "He was like a man who awoke too

early in the darkness, while the others were all still asleep" (p. 6).

Yet Freud's psychobiography of Leonardo has also been the object of frequent and severe criticism over the years, beginning almost as soon as it was published. It has been attacked not only for dragging the great Leonardo in the mud (an attack that Freud anticipated on the book's first page), but also for serious factual errors and lapses in logic. The book has been used as a paradigmatic example of what is irredeemably wrong with the entire field of psychobiography—most insistently by David Stannard (1980). Stannard describes Freud's book as "among the finest indicators of the potentials . . . of psychohistory," containing "some of the brightest examples of what makes the best psychohistory so stimulating" (p. 3). But Stannard's praise is merely a device to turn the Leonardo book into a straw man, upon which Stannard then pounces in a vigorous effort to discredit not only psychohistory and psychobiography, but all of Freudian theory and practice.

Freud's *Leonardo* offers much to criticize. But it is by no means the best work of which psychobiography is capable. Indeed, its errors leave it far from the best work of which Freud was capable. By presenting a number of sound guidelines for writing psychobiographies throughout the course of the Leonardo book, Freud showed that he knew better. Then why did he violate virtually every one of those guidelines, in the very book in which they appear? The answer to this question can explain a good deal about the psychology of Sigmund Freud, who in his own way is as important a psychobiographical subject as

Leonardo. It also can tell us something about the problems and potential of psychobiography as an intellectual enterprise.

Why Did Freud Write the Book?

Before looking specifically at why Freud committed certain errors and even violated his own guidelines, it may be helpful to consider why he wrote the Leonardo book at all. Freud was already quite busy in the fall of 1909, when he began to work on the manuscript. He certainly did not need anything new to occupy his time. He was treating a heavy load of psychoanalytic patients for at least eight or nine hours a day. He was writing for publication the set of basic lectures on psychoanalysis that he had delivered extemporaneously at Clark University in September. He was overseeing publication of the third edition of *The Psychopathology of Everyday Life* and he was planning a second edition of *Three Essays on the Theory of Sexuality*, two of his major works. He was giving free training analyses to at least two colleagues, presenting regular seminars, playing an active role in the Wednesday evening meetings of the Vienna Psychoanalytic Society, working on the expansion of the international psychoanalytic movement, editing volumes and journals of psychoanalytic writings by others, and carrying on a voluminous correspondence, in longhand, with Carl Jung, Sandor Ferenczi, and many others. He wrote to Jung that October, in the same long letter that first mentioned the Leonardo project, "My week's work leaves me numb. I would invent the seventh day if the Lord hadn't done so long ago. . . . Quite against my will I must live like an American: no time for the libido" (McGuire, 1974, p. 256).

So when Freud took on the Leonardo project as well, he must have had compelling reasons to do so, even though it was not at first planned as a major work (McGuire, 1974, p. 261). He mentioned several reasons to Jung: He had recently come across a "neurotic," presumably a patient, who resembled Leonardo physically and psychologically but "without his genius." Freud had then experienced an inspiration about "the riddle of Leonardo da Vinci's character," involving the great man's sexual development. Freud had also

decided it was time for psychoanalysts to "take hold of biography," and though he feared he could not find enough useful information about Leonardo, he hoped his insight into Leonardo's character would provide "a first step in the realm of biography" (McGuire, 1974, p. 255).

Freud may have had further conscious reasons for beginning the project at that time, which he did not mention to Jung. He had become increasingly annoyed at the efforts of one member (Isidor Sadger) of the Wednesday night psychoanalytic meetings to write pathographies of distinguished writers. Sadger relied on speculative hereditary mechanisms to arrive at pathological diagnoses of these figures. Freud sternly told Sadger at one meeting in late 1907, "This is not the correct way to write pathographies. . . . [T]here is altogether no need to write such pathographies. The [psychoanalytic] theories can only be harmed and not one iota is gained for the understanding of the subject" (Nunberg & Federn, 1962/1967, Vol. 1, p. 257). A year later, in early 1909, Karl Abraham began telling Freud of his plans to write "a psychoanalytic study of Giovanni Segantini [a nineteenth-century Swiss painter], whose personality and works can be understood only with the help of the theory of sexuality" (Abraham & Freud, 1965, p. 71). Freud encouraged him, perhaps seeing the trusted Abraham's work as a corrective to Sadger's pathographies. But Abraham was slow to proceed. Toward the end of that year Freud announced that he was working on a paper about Leonardo and told Abraham that he would like to see the Segantini paper published in the same volume. "Then there would be two advances into biography writing as we see it" (p. 83). Freud may well have been inspired partly by Abraham's example to write a psychobiography of an artist; he may also have come to feel that a study of a minor Swiss painter would not be the most impressive way to replace pathography with psychobiography. There may even have been an element of competition with the considerably younger Abraham, though that is not explicit in the correspondence between them.

None of these reasons accounts for the Leonardo project's soon becoming his "obsession," as Freud described it to Jung in December 1909 (McGuire, 1974, p. 271). Nor do they account for his continuing to work on the

Leonardo book over the next four months, despite unexpected difficulties and his heavy workload. In February 1910 he reported to Jung, "Nothing is changed. I work every day to the point of exhaustion and then I write a few lines on the Leonardo" (p. 296). In March, after reviewing plans for a major psychoanalytic congress, Freud reported, "Otherwise I am all Leonardo" (p. 301). The reasons cited so far not only fail to account for the intensity of Freud's involvement with the Leonardo project but also fail to account for the errors he committed in carrying out that project, despite his own best advice to himself.

Why Did Freud Go Astray?

Freud's errors have been explained by others in various ways. No one has dared to suggest that Freud was stupid, but a number of commentators on the Leonardo book have assumed that Freud was ignorant. A thorough and accurate psychobiography of Leonardo would require broad and detailed knowledge not only of psychoanalytic theory, which of course Freud had, but also of art history, Italian culture in the fifteenth and sixteenth centuries, Roman Catholic religious history and tradition, the Italian language, paint chemistry, European Renaissance politics, and several other fields. Freud certainly did not possess full command of all those areas. So why shouldn't he make errors?

Actually, Freud was remarkably accurate in presenting solid factual information about Leonardo—more accurate, indeed, than some of his later critics. (See Eissler [1961] for a thorough review of the factual issues involved.) Freud did not try to address every aspect of Leonardo's life and work. But regarding those psychologically interesting aspects that he chose to examine, he knew what contemporary scholarship had to say about Leonardo and his times, and on the whole he used that knowledge judiciously. He also knew when contemporary scholarship was untrustworthy. One critic of the Leonardo book, Jack Spector (1972, p. 58), complains about "an omission that he [Freud] knowingly made," which supposedly led to a distortion of Freud's depiction of Leonardo. Freud underlined a passage in a French book on Leonardo, which said

that shortly after Leonardo was born his father broke with Leonardo's mother and took the illegitimate boy to live with him. Freud did not cite that passage in his book. According to Spector, "the omitted quotation that he [Freud] underlined would have contradicted Freud's hypothesis of a long period . . . when the young genius was alone with his doting and love-starved mother." Spector apparently fails to realize what Freud knew from the other biographical materials on Leonardo, that no documentary evidence exists to validate the underlined passage in the French book. It is purely speculative and does not even provide a sensible rationale for such speculation, as Freud did for his own hypothesis.

Freud was flatly wrong, however, on one important factual matter. As is now well known, he used an erroneous German translation of Leonardo's childhood memory (or fantasy) about a bird repeatedly thrusting its tail into his mouth. In the faulty translation a European bird of prey, the kite, became an Egyptian bird of prey, the vulture, and this caused problems. In retrospect, we can say that Freud should have exercised extra care concerning the translation's accuracy, because he then made heavy use of Leonardo's early memory in his book. But he did not, and some of the consequences of that failure are discussed below. Freud made very few simple, ignorant errors of this kind.

If ordinary ignorance did not lead Freud into most of his errors, what did? Several critics have suggested that it was a matter of projective identification: Freud identified with Leonardo and increased the identification by endowing Leonardo erroneously with Freud's own characteristics. That does account in part for Freud's errors and weak arguments, which remarkably often touch upon a supposed characteristic of Leonardo's that is known to have been shared by Freud. Freud himself never publicly acknowledged that he identified with Leonardo, though he admitted to identifications with Hannibal and several other important figures. But his identification with Leonardo is evident in the Leonardo book and elsewhere. Ernest Jones, who knew Freud well, has stated that "much of what Freud said when he penetrated into Leonardo's personality was at the same time a self-description; there was surely an extensive identification between

Leonardo and himself" (Jones, 1955, p. 432). Lichtenberg (1978), Wallace (1978–1979), and Trosman (1985, pp. 170–171) have discussed a number of specific points of identification between Freud and Leonardo. And in her unpublished account of her analysis with Freud, Marie Bonaparte reports having confessed to an identification with Leonardo, at which point Freud said that he too felt such an identification (Frank Hartman, personal communication).

Stannard (1980) uses this idea of identification in a lightly dismissive way, noting that "a good deal of what Freud claimed to find characteristic of Leonardo was characteristic of himself," and then listing ten such characteristics (pp. 20–21). Some of the qualities listed were indeed characteristic of Freud; some are doubtful, and some are hardly or not at all applicable. Stannard seems to imply that Freud was projecting his own characteristics onto Leonardo. But given that Stannard elsewhere claims there is no empirical evidence for the phenomenon of projection as postulated by Freud (p. 27), he cannot argue very seriously that such projection was responsible for Freud's errors in the Leonardo book, and indeed, he backs away from his own argument.

Regardless, explaining Freud's book in terms of identification and projection is a rather static approach, if all one does is list points of identification. The question again arises: Why did Freud do it? Why did he feel a need to identify with Leonardo, or to endow Leonardo with his own qualities? Why did he develop this identification so strongly at that particular time? Why did he stress certain ways in which he identified with Leonardo rather than other ways? Why did this become such an important book for Freud at a personal level?

Spector (1972), more than anyone else, has attempted to answer these psychodynamic questions about Freud's identification with Leonardo. He partially develops several interesting lines of argument, each of which is worth further attention, though in each instance his conclusions are not altogether sound. Basically, Spector proposes that Freud identified with Leonardo for three major reasons.

(1) Freud was experiencing "anxieties about having reached a turning point in his own life"

(p. xi). "His turning to the more systematic working-out of rough ideas already introduced, was like [Leonardo's] turn from the path of artistic fantasy to the logic of science" (p. 54). Freud did not really see his own life that way; indeed, he felt that in doing such things as the Leonardo book at midlife he was turning from science back to his adolescent interests in art and culture. But it is true, as Spector suggests, that in his early fifties Freud was feeling doubts about his continuing creativity and looked to the example of Leonardo for reassurance.

(2) Spector argues that Freud's unresolved problems with his parents led him to distort the picture of Leonardo's early family life. Again, there is a good deal of substance to this argument in broad outline, but Spector's specifics are not always accurate. He says, for instance, that Freud "distorted parts of [Leonardo's so-called vulture fantasy] to fit his own wish to be fatherless and alone with his mother—the typical 'family romance' he often discusses" (p. 60). At another point Spector says, "This attempt on Freud's part to play down Leonardo's father fits perfectly into the development of Freud's own personality, along the lines of what he called 'the family romance,' and as a problem of Freud's, it helps us to understand other errors and omissions of his book" (p. 57). Freud certainly admitted that as a child he had had Oedipal feelings, wishing he could displace his father in his mother's affections, and it appears that he read such feelings into Leonardo's early development as well. But by themselves such Oedipal feelings do not constitute what Freud (1909/1959b) called the "family romance," the child's belief that one or both parents are much finer and nobler than the people who pretend they are his parents. Leonardo could be said to have lived out at least part of such a "family romance," given his illegitimacy as well as the large discrepancy between his mother's supposedly peasant-girl status and his father's wealth and social position. But Freud did not identify that discrepancy as one of Leonardo's major problems. Further, in middle age, Freud seems to have been wrestling much more with the question of how to feel about his own deceased father (whether to blame him or excuse him for everything bad that had happened during Freud's early development) than with wanting to get his

father out of the way. Spector is more acute concerning Freud's relationship with his mother; we will return to that set of issues shortly.

(3) Finally, one of Spector's major arguments is that Freud identified strongly with Leonardo because of "anxiety about his own homosexual impulses, and his admiration of Leonardo's ability to sublimate them into nonsexual activities" (p. 61). It is unclear from Spector's discussion, however, why these impulses had become such a problem for Freud at that time in his life. Virtually the only thing Spector says about Freud's heterosexual impulses is that Freud "never could accept heterosexuality with full enjoyment" because of his early conflicted relationship with his mother (p. 63). Spector appears to be unaware of the full implications of this latter aspect of Freud's sexuality, which is also discussed below.

Freud's Violations of His Own Guidelines

As noted above, Freud sets forth a number of guidelines for psychobiography in the Leonardo book, some by prescriptive example and others by proscriptive statement. The prescriptive examples are mainly procedural in nature: Freud demonstrates how to examine the internal as well as the external validity of biographical anecdotes, how to compare the biographical subject's behavior with that of contemporaries in order to evaluate its relative normality or deviancy, and so forth. The proscriptive statements are explicit pronouncements by Freud about what the psychobiographer should *not* do; these are the guidelines that Freud sooner or later violates, at times quite promptly. Each substantial violation of these proscriptive guidelines appears to be a motivated violation, and each time, an important aspect of Freud's identification with Leonardo is involved. Four such guidelines are considered here, along with Freud's most likely motives for violating each one in the Leonardo book.

Avoid Arguments Built Upon a Single Clue

As Freud says, "[I]t is unsatisfactory when a peculiar feature is found singly" (1910/1957b,

p. 93). Or as Fischer put it in his book *Historians' Fallacies* (1970), "If the argument is a single chain, and one link fails, then the chain itself fails with it. But most historians' arguments are not single chains. They are rather like a kind of chain mail which can fail in some part and still retain its shape and function" (p. 305). Freud's arguments in the Leonardo book are at times of the chain-mail sort, as with his evidence for Leonardo's homosexual tendencies. But one of his most spectacular lines of argument—indeed, one that he takes up again just after he has paused to warn against arguing from "a peculiar feature . . . found singly"—consists of one single link after another, with only the first link coming from Leonardo himself. That link happens to consist of the mistranslated Italian word *nibio* in Leonardo's childhood memory, which Freud assumed to mean "vulture."

Freud's full statement is, "Remembering that it is unsatisfactory when a peculiar feature is found singly, let us hasten to add another to it which is even more striking." He then resumes a sequence of arguments already begun, a sequence composed of what amount to Freud's own learned associations to the word "vulture." Among other things, he discusses Egyptian and medieval legends about vultures as mother goddesses and as virgin mothers—a discussion Freud uses as evidence that Leonardo must have spent his first several years alone with his real mother before going to live with his father and stepmother. Freud also includes comments about the Egyptian vulture mother goddess possessing both male and female sex organs, and about Leonardo presumably assuming the same of his mother, and about all this having something to do with Leonardo's version of homosexuality. Freud even manages to relate the vulture to Leonardo's paintings of women with mysterious smiles, *Mona Lisa* and others (1910/1957b, p. 107). This astonishing assortment of inferences grows from that single illusory clue of the "vulture" in Leonardo's childhood memory.

Why did Freud so quickly and spectacularly violate his own guideline in this instance? He must have had a particularly compelling reason to do so. And indeed, as Spector (1972, p. 59) and others have noted, Freud's assumption that an Egyptian vulture was present in Leonardo's childhood memory/fantasy provided a very direct and almost unique basis of identification for Freud. The earliest childhood dream that Freud himself could remember also involved Egyptian bird-headed figures, which Freud associated with gods. In *The Interpretation of Dreams*, Freud reports the dream thus: "I saw *my beloved mother, with a peculiarly peaceful, sleeping expression on her features, being carried into the room by two (or three) people with birds' beaks and laid upon the bed.* I awoke in tears and screaming, and interrupted my parents' sleep" (Freud, 1900/1958a, p. 583; emphasis in original). In Freud's incomplete interpretation of this dream, he suggests that his anxiety upon awakening did not really reflect a concern about his mother dying as he first assumed, but expressed "an obscure and evidently sexual craving" (p. 584). Ten years later he interprets Leonardo's childhood memory/fantasy also as involving sexual contact between son and mother, and then associates this imagery with Egyptian bird gods much as he had free-associated to his own dream.

Freud describes Leonardo's actual relationship with his mother, rather than the relationship in Leonardo's memory/fantasy, as involving an early idyllic period of total love, which is then disrupted by figures from outside. Elsewhere Freud paints a similar picture of his own early relationship with his mother. But in both cases, even before the idyll is disrupted by external forces, disturbing forces develop internally. In Leonardo's case, the mother proves to be too loving: "So, like all unsatisfied mothers, she took her little son in place of her husband, and by the too early maturing of his erotism robbed him of a part of his masculinity" (1910/1957b, p. 117). Thirteen years earlier Freud had told his friend Fliess how his own libido had first been aroused at age two by seeing his mother nude when they spent a night together on a train. In the same letter he described how his nursemaid had been "my teacher in sexual matters and complained because I was clumsy and unable to do anything. (Neurotic impotence always comes about in this way . . .)" (Masson, 1985, p. 269). Here as elsewhere, Freud tends to divide his images of his early maternal contacts into a good mother and a bad mother (Abraham, 1982–1983). What his two mothers (his real mother and his nursemaid) did to him sexually in early childhood can be

seen as equivalent to what, in Freud's speculative version, the child Leonardo's natural mother did to Leonardo.

But why did Freud in late 1909 or early 1910, while he was hard at work on the Leonardo manuscript, suddenly become so interested again in issues that related to a childhood dream of his mother's apparent death, or to his mother's arousal of his libido circa 1858? His mother was still relatively healthy in 1909–1910, and in fact lived for another twenty years. His father had been dead for thirteen years. We know of no major external events in Freud's life at this time that would have provoked a renewed concern with his mother's role in the development of his sex life. However, certain more subtle events were at work to stimulate this concern. They will emerge as we continue to review Freud's proscriptive guidelines for psychobiography.

Avoid Pathographizing the Psychobiographical Subject; Avoid Idealizing the Psychobiographical Subject

Freud placed these opposing guidelines at the beginning and the end of the Leonardo book. The book's first sentences are:

> When psychiatric research . . . approaches one who is among the greatest of the human race, it is not doing so for the reasons so frequently ascribed to it by laymen. "To blacken the radiant and drag the sublime into the dust" is no part of its purpose, and there is no satisfaction for it in narrowing the gulf which separates the perfection of the great from the inadequacy of the objects that are its usual concern. (1910/1957b, p. 63)

So much for Isidor Sadger and his mean-spirited pathographies. Freud warns against the other side of this coin in the first paragraph of the book's final chapter:

> [B]iographers are fixated on their heroes in a quite special way. In many cases they have chosen their hero as the subject of their studies because—for reasons of their personal emotional life—they have felt a special affection for

him from the very first. They then devote their energies to a task of idealization, aimed at enrolling the great man among the class of their infantile models—at reviving in him, perhaps, the child's idea of his father. . . . That they should do this is regrettable, for they thereby sacrifice truth to an illusion, and for the sake of their infantile phantasies abandon the opportunity of penetrating the most fascinating secrets of human nature. (p. 130)

These are sound precepts, valuable for every psychobiographer. But from what has already been described of Freud's strong identification with Leonardo, he violated the proscription against idealization as soon as he chose to write about Leonardo, for whom he certainly "felt a special affection . . . from the very first." Freud began to violate the proscription against pathography almost as soon as he started to discuss Leonardo's character, and he intensified this violation when he approached Leonardo's early relationship with his mother Caterina.

According to Freud, Caterina did two bad things to the infant Leonardo: She initiated "the too early maturing of his erotism," and she "robbed him of a part of his masculinity" (p. 117). That is, Caterina aroused Leonardo's sexual interest at a time when he couldn't really do anything about it, and she made him into a passive, indeed abstinent, homosexual. She did the latter by loving Leonardo so hard that in self-defense he identified with her and thus later could love only little boys like himself, who were sexually unattainable. Freud held a relatively tolerant view of homosexuality, but he knew that by and large the reading public of his day did not. (He even warned one correspondent that the Leonardo book "is not likely to be to your taste. It takes for granted that the reader is not shocked by homosexual topics" [E. Freud, 1960, p. 306].) So when he firmly affixed a label of homosexuality to Leonardo, he was certainly "blackening the radiant and dragging the sublime into the dust" as far as that public was concerned. In the course of the book Freud also cited a number of neurotic symptoms displayed by Leonardo, and repeatedly discussed the frustrations and failures of the man he otherwise

referred to as a "universal genius" (1910/1957b, p. 63).

However, shortly after he identified Leonardo's core psychological problems, thus blackening his name, Freud resumed the opposite process of idealization. He did so first by adopting several positions that rarely if ever appear in Freud's writings about other individuals. Did Leonardo have an excessively strong "craving for knowledge"? Yes, says Freud, but it was not neurotic in origin; it was probably inborn, organic, "already active in the subject's earliest childhood," and was only subsequently reinforced by the attentions of Leonardo's love-starved mother (p. 77). Indeed, Leonardo's "instinct for research" was "the rarest and most perfect" type, escaping "both inhibition of thought and neurotic compulsive thinking" (p. 80). Was Leonardo homosexual? Yes, but his homosexuality "was restricted to what is called ideal homosexuality . . . sublimating the greater part of his libido into an urge for research" (pp. 80–81). Was Leonardo neurotic? Well, says Freud, "we should be inclined to place him *close* to the type of neurotic that we describe as 'obsessional', and we may *compare* his researches to the 'obsessive brooding' of neurotics, and his inhibitions to what are known as their 'abulias'" (p. 131; emphasis added). So Leonardo was like a neurotic in a number of ways, but Freud was reluctant to call him a neurotic.

Why this protectiveness about Leonardo's intense instinct for research, his presumably unexpressed homosexuality, his not-quite-neurotic symptoms? In part, Freud was simply trying to avoid sounding pathographic, while identifying certain ways in which Leonardo diverged markedly from typical developmental patterns. But he also appears to have felt reluctant to give deviant or pathological labels to characteristics in Leonardo that he recognized in himself.

Once more the question arises, why were such matters pressing so hard on Freud at this time that he needed to give voice to them and simultaneously to defend himself from their negative implications, through his identification with Leonardo? That "why" question will finally be answered in the course of dealing with Freud's fourth proscriptive guideline for psychobiography.

Avoid Drawing Strong Conclusions From Inadequate Data

Freud says, near the end of the book, that when a psychobiographical "undertaking does not provide any certain results—and this is perhaps so in Leonardo's case"—psychoanalytic theory should not be blamed: "It is . . . only the author who is to be held responsible for the failure, by having forced psycho-analysis to pronounce an expert opinion on the basis of such insufficient material" (1910/1957b, p. 135). Yet here is Freud, the founder and leader of the psychoanalytic movement, two pages away from concluding a manuscript full of "expert opinions" based on clearly "insufficient material," and eager to publish it as soon as he can. What is going on? Why is he driven to finish this study and get it out a mere six months after he began to work on it seriously?

In the fall of 1909, Freud's inner life was deeply troubled in both of the major psychological domains that he is said to have identified politely as "love and work" (Erikson, 1963, p. 265), and often described less politely as sex and ambition (e.g., Davis, 1973, p. 130). When one looks at what was particularly troubling him in these areas, one may better appreciate why Freud strove so hard at that time to show how the great Leonardo da Vinci suffered similar difficulties in precisely the same areas and how Leonardo in a sense triumphed over them. In the remainder of this chapter, Freud's problems with love and/or sex are examined in some detail; his difficulties with work and/or ambition are considered very briefly.

In the area of love and sex, Freud's personal history had been largely one of inhibition, overcome by passion, followed by frustration. It is now known that his marriage, for which he had such great hopes during his abstinent four-year courtship of Martha Bernays, proved to be a profound disappointment sexually and emotionally. The sexual aspect seems to have been largely terminated at an unusually early age for both parties—Freud was around forty, and Martha was five years younger. Freud merely alluded to this early termination of his marital sexuality in comments to his friends, but an essay written two years before the Leonardo book permitted him to say a good deal more about married sex in general:

This brings us to the question whether sexual intercourse in legal marriage can offer full compensation for the restrictions imposed before marriage. . . . [O]ur cultural sexual morality restricts sexual intercourse even in marriage itself, since it imposes on married couples the necessity of contenting themselves, as a rule, with a very few procreative acts. As a consequence of this consideration, satisfying sexual intercourse in marriage takes place only for a few years; and we must subtract from this, of course, the intervals of abstention necessitated by regard for the wife's health. After these three, four or five years, the marriage becomes a failure in so far as it has promised the satisfaction of sexual needs. For all the devices hitherto invented for preventing conception impair sexual enjoyment, hurt the fine susceptibilities of both partners and even actually cause illness. Fear of the consequences of sexual intercourse first brings the married couple's physical affection to an end; and then, as a remoter result, it usually puts a stop as well to the mental sympathy between them, which should have been the successor to their original passionate love. The spiritual disillusionment and bodily deprivation to which most marriages are thus doomed puts both partners back in the state they were in before their marriage, except for being the poorer by the loss of an illusion, and they must once more have recourse to their fortitude in mastering and deflecting their sexual instinct. (1908/1959a, pp. 194–195)

It is not known how many marital relationships Freud had observed closely enough to give him data for this dismal view of love and sex in marriage. But there is sufficient information about the Freuds' marriage to know that the passage describes it almost exactly, at least from Sigmund Freud's perspective. Some writers (e.g., Choisy, 1963; Fromm, 1959) have concluded, from the early cessation of Freud's sexual relationship with his wife, that he must have had a low or heavily inhibited sex drive throughout his life. But the passage just quoted, including such phrases as "original passionate love," "bodily deprivation," and "fortitude in mastering and deflecting their sexual instinct," does not suggest that Freud easily accepted the halt in his marital sexuality. Other evidence suggests that he struggled for several years with the question of abstinence before finally acceding to the pressures of a too-rapidly-growing family and his wife Martha's health problems (see, e.g., his letter of August 20, 1893, in Masson, 1985, p. 54). Freud's subsequent dreams, over a period of at least ten years during and after Martha's final pregnancy, often appear to express strong resentment toward her (Elms, 1980). He felt resentful because she became pregnant so easily, because she often became ill during her pregnancies, and because she refused to engage in any kind of sexual activity besides what he refers to in the passage above as "a very few procreative acts." Freud sometimes experienced partial impotence (letter of December 17, 1896, in Masson, 1985, p. 217), which added to their sexual problems—impotence probably developing in part from his anxiety lest he should make Martha pregnant again, and partly from the crude contraceptive devices available to them. But he mainly blamed Martha for forcing the almost complete termination of his sexual activity—or rather, Martha plus the mother and the nursemaid who had warped his sexual development in infancy.[1]

Beginning at about the time his active sexual life came to a halt, circa 1895, Freud entered a hugely creative period of theoretical development. One of his concepts that began to develop during this period was sublimation, the transformation of sexual energy into culturally creative acts. Freud's incorporation of sublimation into psychoanalytic theory was probably inspired in part by his personal observation that when he stopped being active sexually his creativity increased substantially. Further, he may have been able to temper his bitterness concerning his sex life by this realization that his libido was now being transformed into ideas.[2]

Over the decade following his first references to sublimation (e.g., 1898/1962b, p. 281), Freud saw himself as growing old and felt his creative powers subsiding. Initially this did not influence

Figure 15.1. Sigmund Freud. (Getty Images)

his ideas about sublimation, as expressed most strongly in *Three Essays on the Theory of Sexuality* (1905/1953): "[P]owerful components are acquired for every kind of cultural achievement by this diversion of sexual instinctual forces from sexual aims and their direction to new ones—a process which deserves the name of 'sublimation'" (p. 178). But in 1907 he wrote to Jung about his "entry into the climacteric years" (McGuire, 1974, p. 82), referring at least in part to a fading of his sexual capacities. By the time Freud next discussed sublimation at any length, he no longer perceived a direct link between sexual abstinence and genuine creativity. In the same 1908 essay where he characterized marital sex so dismally, he observed that abstinence might be useful for the "young *savant*," who "can, by his self-restraint, liberate forces for his studies." But, said Freud, "An abstinent artist is hardly conceivable. . . . [He] probably finds his artistic achievements powerfully stimulated by his sexual experience. In general I have not gained the impression that sexual abstinence helps to bring about energetic and self-reliant men of action or original thinkers or bold emancipators and reformers" (1908/1959a, p. 197). Far as he was from being a young savant, Freud would surely have hoped to be included in one of the latter categories, for which he no longer saw sexual sublimation as having strong generative power.

Interestingly, this devaluation of sexual abstinence was followed by the temporary return of Freud's sexual vigor. Nearly all that is known of this is from a letter to Jung in February 1910, when Freud refers to a discussion they had had during their trip to America the previous September: "My Indian summer of eroticism that we spoke of on our trip has withered lamentably under the pressure of work. I am resigned to being old and no longer even think continually of growing old" (McGuire, 1974, p. 292). The official English translation of that passage is fairly loose; Freud's German word *Johannistrieb* is not exactly equivalent to "Indian summer," referring rather to a second blossoming or a late love. Whatever his second blossoming of eroticism involved, it seems to have lasted from sometime before the American trip until at least the end of the year or a little longer—several months in all. It was assuredly not an affair with sister-in-law Minna or another woman. Had it been, Jung would have mentioned his knowledge of it as supportive evidence when he later gossiped about what he thought Freud had been doing with Minna several years before. Instead, it was probably the temporary resumption of sexual relations between Freud and Martha (after she had indisputably passed the upper limit of child-bearing age), or perhaps simply Freud's resurgent feelings of sexual potency that remained unexpressed in any active sexual relationship.

Whatever it was, Freud's *Johannistrieb* occurred in close conjunction with another shift in his views about sublimation. He began to work on the Leonardo book shortly after he returned from the American trip. Freud mentioned sublimation in his first description of the work to Jung (October 17, 1909; McGuire, 1974, p. 255), but the concept was at that point not prominent in his consideration of Leonardo's adult achievements. Indeed, when Freud presented a preliminary version of his work to the Vienna Psychoanalytic Society in December 1909, he described Leonardo's sublimation largely as a process occurring "in earliest childhood," when

Leonardo "translated his libido into the drive to investigate, and so it remained. With this, the greatest part of his sexual activity was exhausted for all time to come" (Nunberg & Federn, 1962/1967, Vol. 2, pp. 342–343). There Freud was at least back to sublimation as a basis for some kind of important creative activity (Leonardo's scientific investigations), but it seemed to remain unimportant to Leonardo's artistic creativity.[3]

However, by the time Freud finished the Leonardo manuscript at the beginning of April 1910—after his "Indian summer of eroticism" had subsided—one of his major focal points had become sublimation as an essential foundation for both scientific and artistic creativity. Further, Freud had added a great deal about Leonardo's renewal of artistic creativity in middle age, including what is perhaps the book's most striking passage:

> At the summit of his [Leonardo's] life, when he was in his early fifties—a time when in women the sexual characters have already undergone involution and when in men the libido not infrequently makes a further energetic advance—a new transformation came over him. Still deeper layers of the contents of his mind became active once more; but this further regression was to the benefit of his art, which was in the process of becoming stunted. He met the woman who awakened his memory of his mother's happy smile of sensual rapture; and, influenced by this revived memory, he recovered the stimulus that guided him at the beginning of his artistic endeavours. . . . He painted the Mona Lisa, the "St. Anne with Two Mothers" and the series of mysterious pictures which are characterized by the enigmatic smile. With the help of the oldest of all his erotic impulses he enjoyed the triumph of once more conquering the inhibition in his art. This final development is obscured from our eyes in the shadows of approaching age. Before this his intellect had soared upwards to the highest realizations of a conception of the world that left his epoch far behind it. (1910/1957b, pp. 133–134)

That passage is remarkable for more than its spectacular rhetorical flourishes. Most interestingly, it posits a "further energetic advance" in the libidos of many middle-aged men, a proposition considerably more emphatic than any other statement Freud ever published about midlife sexual development.[4] The passage also implies that Leonardo himself experienced just such an energetic libidinal advance, which overcame long-standing inhibitions and stimulated a regression to "the oldest of all his erotic impulses," presumably his sexual yearnings for his sensually rapturous mother. Now, there is no biographical evidence at all that Leonardo underwent any kind of libidinal advance in his early fifties, or that Leonardo's early erotic impulses toward his mother were ever rearoused. But Freud had recently described his own second blossoming of eroticism in his early fifties. One can also read the results of the self-described "obsession" that Freud developed toward Leonardo at that time—a book in which the weakest arguments and the most prominent errors involve the assertion of an ambivalent infantile erotic relationship between Leonardo and his mother, an assertion that recapitulates Freud's recollections of his own infantile feelings much more accurately than it describes anything known about Leonardo.

Here, finally, one can see why Freud felt compelled to write a book at this particular time in his life that dealt with the maternal arousal of a child's libido. It need not have had anything to do with his mother's behavior in 1909 or 1910; it need not even have involved meeting a woman who reminded him of his mother's ambivalent sensuality during his childhood, as he says was the case with Leonardo and *Mona Lisa*. It required no more than what is known from Freud himself: that his feelings of eroticism were aroused again for a time, and that he entertained renewed hopes that middle-aged eroticism could be sublimated into a resurgence of creativity. The case of Leonardo, read in that way, or projected onto in that way, must have been almost as reassuring for Freud in 1910 as was his initial elaboration of the concept of sublimation after the nearly absolute cessation of his active sexual life around 1895.

And what of Freud's insistence that Leonardo was a homosexual, but an idealized homosexual? As his marital sexuality had begun to founder in the 1890s, Freud developed an increasingly intense intellectual and emotional relationship with his friend Wilhelm Fliess. There was never anything overtly physical about the relationship, but as Freud later admitted, strong homosexual emotions were involved. In October 1910, he acknowledged to a male friend that he was working through those homosexual feelings toward Fliess again, even though he had broken off the friendship with Fliess eight years earlier (Schur, 1972, pp. 256–257). There is also evidence that in 1909–1910 Freud was experiencing what he considered to be homosexual feelings toward Jung, Ferenczi, and perhaps others among the circle of younger men around him in the psychoanalytic movement. Finding himself again frustrated in expressing his erotic urges heterosexually when the "Indian summer of eroticism" ended, Freud may have experienced not only an intensification of homosexual feelings but an intensified need to justify them. He justified them first by seeing in Leonardo a model of the great creative figure who is homosexual, but only psychologically and not behaviorally so, and second by postulating that Leonardo's homosexual as well as heterosexual impulses were effectively sublimated into creative activity, as Freud's own impulses could be, too.

The causal relationships are not at all clear here. It could be, for instance, that Freud's growing closeness to Jung in 1909 had stimulated some of the erotic feelings that grew into that "Indian summer," rather than vice versa. But the evidence does suggest that whatever causal sequence may have been involved, the Leonardo book and its psychobiographical errors derived in part from Freud's urgent attempts to deal with both heterosexual and homosexual feelings, and with the frustration he experienced in being unable to express those feelings fully.

Conclusion

Matters involving "work or ambition" constituted the other important area of Freud's life that added to his sense of identification with Leonardo in 1909–1910, intensified his obsession with getting the book written, and led him into further psychobiographical fallacies. For example, a major line of argument in the book, which leads to several marked exaggerations if not downright errors, concerns Leonardo's emotional and intellectual isolation, his rejection of religious and traditional authority in favor of empirical observation, and the inability of his contemporaries to understand his genius, which was fully recognized only by posterity. This line of argument may be linked to Freud's growing anxiety about Jung's mysticism and about the inadequacy of Jung or any other psychoanalyst to be Freud's successor. Other related concerns include Freud's disappointment over the general public's failure to give psychoanalysis its due, and his increasing worries about how his age, ill health, and death would affect the psychoanalytic movement (beyond the issue of finding a successor). Some of these concerns became much more explicit in his only other psychobiographical book, *Moses and Monotheism*, written more than twenty-five years later (Freud, 1939/1964). Freud again had personal reasons for writing that book at that particular time (see, e.g., Robert, 1976), and he fell into some of the same kinds of errors because of those personal reasons.

Two final points should be made about the Leonardo book. First, Freud's *Leonardo* is not representative of psychobiography in general, because its crucial errors derive from idiosyncratic sources bound up in Freud's personal conflicts, and those specific errors need not be repeated by other psychobiographers. Second, Freud's *Leonardo* is still valuable to psychobiographers and others interested in psychobiography, not only because it presents a number of valid guidelines for doing psychobiography well, but also because it provides a kind of cautionary tale, showing what can happen if one ignores Freud's guidelines as he did. The moral of this tale can be expressed in a final proscriptive guideline for all psychobiographers: *Avoid assuming that you are less susceptible to psychobiographical error than Freud was.* Freud knew what to avoid doing, but for his own personal reasons he did it anyway. You may know what to avoid, but you can easily fall into the same kinds of traps if you don't watch out.

Acknowledgments

This chapter is reprinted from the *Journal of Personality*, 1988, 56, 19–40. Copyright © 1988 by Duke University Press. It appears here courtesy of Blackwell Publishing. I am grateful for the assistance of a number of individuals, especially Eva Schepeler, Ruth Abraham, Ronald Wilkinson and the staff of the Library of Congress Manuscript Division, and David Newlands and the staff of the Freud Museum, London.

Notes

1. Persistent speculations about a subsequent sexual affair between Freud and his wife's sister Minna Bernays are not supported by credible evidence (see Elms, 1982). Freud may well have had sexual fantasies about Minna, but those particular fantasies are unlikely ever to have been acted upon.

2. As Sulloway (1979, pp. 176–177) has indicated, Freud was by no means the first to think of sublimation in some form, and his specific conception of it was clearly influenced by the ideas of his friend Fliess. Freud's personal situation, however, is likely to have made him more receptive to ideas from others concerning sublimation, as well as more sensitive to the co-occurrence of low sexual activity and high creativity in his own life.

3. In his conclusion to the *Five Lectures on Psychoanalysis* (1910/1957a), written at about the same time, Freud referred to sublimation as the probable origin of "our highest cultural successes." However, he devoted more space to the limitations than to the contributions of sexual abstinence as a source of energies for creative sublimation.

4. For milder comments, see Freud (1895/1962a, p. 102; 1911/1958b, pp. 45–46).

References

Abraham, H.C., & Freud, E.L. (Eds.). (1965). A psycho-analytic dialogue: The letters of Sigmund Freud and Karl Abraham 1907–1926. New York: Basic Books.

Abraham, R. (1982–1983). Freud's mother conflict and the formulation of the Oedipal father. Psychoanalytic Review, 69, 441–453.

Choisy, M. (1963). Sigmund Freud: A new appraisal. New York: Philosophical Library.

Clark, K.M. (1967). Leonardo da Vinci (Rev. ed.). Harmondsworth, England: Penguin.

Davis, F.B. (1973). Three letters from Sigmund Freud to Andre Breton. Journal of the American Psychoanalytic Association, 21, 127–134.

Eissler, K.R. (1961). Leonardo do Vinci: Psychoanalytic notes on the enigma. New York: International Universities Press.

Elms, A.C. (1980). Freud, Irma, Martha: Sex and marriage in the "Dream of Irma's injection." Psychoanalytic Review, 67, 83–109.

Elms, A.C. (1982, December). Freud and Minna. Psychology Today, pp. 40–46.

Erikson, E.H. (1963). Childhood and society (Rev. ed.). New York: Norton.

Fischer, D.H. (1970). Historians' fallacies. New York: Harper & Row.

Freud, E.L. (Ed.). (1960). Letters of Sigmund Freud. New York: Basic Books.

Freud, S. (1953). Three essays on the theory of sexuality. In J. Strachey (Ed. & Trans.), The standard edition of the complete psychological works of Sigmund Freud (Vol. 7, pp. 125–243). London: Hogarth Press. (Original work published 1905)

Freud, S. (1957a). Five lectures on psychoanalysis. In J. Strachey (Ed. & Trans.), The standard edition of the complete psychological works of Sigmund Freud (Vol. 11, pp. 3–55). London: Hogarth Press. (Original work published 1910)

Freud, S. (1957b). Leonardo da Vinci and a memory of his childhood. In J. Strachey (Ed. & Trans.), The standard edition of the complete psychological works of Sigmund Freud (Vol. 11, pp. 59–137). London: Hogarth Press. (Original work published 1910)

Freud, S. (1958a). The interpretation of dreams. In J. Strachey (Ed. & Trans.), The standard edition of the complete psychological works of Sigmund Freud (Vols. 4–5, pp. 1–621). London: Hogarth Press. (Original work published 1900)

Freud, S. (1958b). Psycho-analytic notes on an autobiographical account of a case of paranoia. In J. Strachey (Ed. & Trans.), The standard edition of the complete psychological works of Sigmund Freud (Vol. 12, pp. 3–82). London: Hogarth Press. (Original work published 1911)

Freud, S. (1959a). "Civilized" sexual morality and modern nervous illness. In J. Strachey (Ed. & Trans.), The standard edition of the complete psychological works of Sigmund Freud (Vol. 9, pp. 179–204). London: Hogarth Press. (Original work published 1908)

Freud, S. (1959b). Family romances. In J. Strachey (Ed. & Trans.), The standard edition of the complete psychological works of Sigmund Freud (Vol. 9, pp. 236–241).

London: Hogarth Press. (Original work published 1909)

Freud, S. (1962a). On the grounds for detaching a particular syndrome from neurasthenia under the description "Anxiety neurosis." In J. Strachey (Ed. & Trans.), The standard edition of the complete psychological works of Sigmund Freud (Vol. 3, p. 87–115). London: Hogarth Press. (Original work published 1895)

Freud, S. (1962b). Sexuality in the aetiology of the neuroses. In J. Strachey (Ed. & Trans.), The standard edition of the complete psychological works of Sigmund Freud (Vol. 3, pp. 261–285). London: Hogarth Press. (Original work published 1898)

Freud, S. (1964). Moses and monotheism. In J. Strachey (Ed. & Trans.), The standard edition of the complete psychological works of Sigmund Freud (Vol. 23, pp. 3–137). London: Hogarth Press. (Original work published 1939)

Fromm, E. (1959). Sigmund Freud's mission. New York: Harper & Row.

Jones, E. (1955). The life and work of Sigmund Freud (Vol. 2). New York: Basic Books.

Lichtenberg, J.D. (1978). Freud's Leonardo: Psychobiography and autobiography of genius. Journal of the American Psychoanalytic Association, 26, 863–880.

Masson, J.M. (Ed.). (1985). The complete letters of Sigmund Freud to Wilhelm Fliess. Cambridge, Mass.: Harvard University Press.

McGuire, W (Ed.). (1974). The Freud/Jung letters. Princeton, N.J.: Princeton University Press.

Nunberg, H., & Federn, E. (Eds.). (1962/1967). Minutes of the Vienna Psychoanalytic Society (Vols. 1 & 2). New York: International Universities Press.

Reti, L. (Ed.). (1974). The unknown Leonardo. New York: McGraw-Hill.

Robert, M. (1976). From Oedipus to Moses: Freud's Jewish identity. New York: Doubleday.

Schur, M. (1972). Freud: Living and dying. New York: International Universities Press.

Spector, J.J. (1972). The aesthetics of Freud. New York: McGraw-Hill.

Stannard, D.E. (1980). Shrinking history. New York: Oxford University Press.

Sulloway, F.J. (1979). Freud, biologist of the mind. New York: Basic Books.

Trosman, H. (1985). Freud and the imaginative world. Hillsdale, N.J.: Analytic Press.

Wallace, E.R. (1978–1979). Freud and Leonardo. Psychiatric Forum, 8, 1–10.

Chapter 16

Nicole B. Barenbaum

Four, Two, or One?
Gordon Allport and the Unique Personality

A recurrent theme in the work of personality psychologist Gordon Allport (1897–1967) is the opposition between the general and the unique in psychology (e.g., Allport, 1962a). In a characteristic statement of this theme, Allport described in neutral terms two tendencies in human thought: "The mind may classify its experience and contemplate the general principles that emerge, or it may be concerned with the individual happening or single event confronting it" (1942, p. 53). To illustrate these tendencies, however, he quoted from William James, choosing a passage that was far from neutral:

> The first thing the intellect does with an object is to class it along with something else. But any object that is infinitely important to us and awakens our devotion feels to us also as if it must be *sui generis* and unique. Probably a crab would be filled with a sense of personal outrage if it could hear us class it without ado or apology as a crustacean, and thus dispose of it. "I am no such thing," it would say; "*I am myself, myself alone.*" (James, 1902, p. 10, as quoted in Allport, 1942, p. 53)

Allport's choice of this passage, which shifts rapidly from a description of our reluctance as classifiers to a vivid portrayal of the outrage experienced by the object (or the crab!) we have classified, suggests the emotional intensity of his own concern with the unique self. Indeed, Allport is known as a champion of the individual personality and as an advocate of the study of individual lives (Barenbaum, 1997, 1998). As his biographer Ian Nicholson (2003) has shown, Allport's interest in personality reflected pervasive concerns regarding the problem of individuality not only in psychology (see, e.g., Stern, 1900) but also in American culture during the Progressive Era. Allport was especially insistent on the uniqueness of personality, making it a central tenet of his theory (Elms, 1994; Nicholson, 1998).

"The stress in this volume is constantly on the ultimate and irreducible uniqueness of personality," Allport wrote in his famous text (1937, p. 193). He maintained not only that individuals were unique, but even that "no two persons ever have precisely the same trait" (p. 297), a position at odds with the views of many other personality psychologists. According to Raymond B. Cattell (1946), for example, the "uniqueness of the individual does not require unique traits. For we can produce any number of unique individuals by setting up various combinations of common trait measurements" (p. 61; see also Eysenck, 1952, p. 18). In Allport's view, however, "nothing is more essential in the entire field of personality than an adequate recognition of individual traits" (1937, p. 302). Similarly, he maintained that individuals developed unique motives, and he criticized psychoanalysis and other theories that reduced "*every motive, however elaborate and individual, to a limited number of basic interests, shared by all men*" (p. 193; emphasis in original). Instead, he offered the principle of the functional autonomy of motives, "*a law that tells how uniqueness comes about*" by suggesting that motives become independent of their origins in universal "infantile" or "archaic" drives (p. 194; emphasis in original).

Allport's concern with uniqueness is evident not only in his psychological theory but also in his personal statements. His objection to intellectual labels echoed the outrage of William James's crab: "I am coy about labels, for I don't plan to be classified and thus disposed of—especially by my own profession which would love to put a ticket on me and leave me forever in a parcel room" (Allport, 1950, as quoted in Nicholson, 1997a, p. 69). Despite his frequent criticism of psychoanalysis, Allport even disliked being categorized as "anti-Freudian" (Allport, 1962b). Although psychobiographers have touched on Allport's insistence on uniqueness (Atwood & Tomkins, 1976; Elms, 1994), so far it has not been a primary focus of psychobiographical study. In this chapter, I examine Allport's position in his family as one psychological source of his preoccupation with uniqueness and with a related issue, the unity of personality.

A Prototypical Scene: Allport's Meeting With Freud

In a well-known passage of his autobiography, Allport (1967) described his "one and only encounter with Sigmund Freud" (p. 7). The passage is well worth reading in the original, but in brief, Allport claimed that as a young man impelled by "a sort of rude curiosity and youthful ambition" (p. 8), he had arranged an appointment with Freud during a visit to Vienna in 1920. Unprepared for Freud's "expectant silence," he attempted to salvage an awkward moment by describing a young boy he had seen on the tram car on his way to Freud's office. The boy "had displayed a conspicuous dirt phobia," apparently caused by his "well-starched" and "dominant" mother, in Allport's view. Freud's response—"And was that little boy you?"—took Allport by surprise, and "feeling a bit guilty," he managed to change the subject. Eventually he concluded that Freud, bent on "probing the unconscious," had misunderstood his motivation for arranging the meeting. This insight, Allport suggested, ultimately led him to develop a theory that devoted more attention to manifest motives than to unconscious ones.

The connection between Allport's preoccupation with uniqueness and his story of his encoun-ter with Freud may not be immediately obvious. However, Allport offered the story as a way of explaining the development of his "maverick" approach (Allport, 1967, p. 9),[1] a theory that emphasized the uniqueness of personality. Allport's references in his personality text (1937) to Freud and psychoanalysis suggest that his primary objection to Freud's theory was its failure as a "science of individuality"—a consequence of its emphasis on "the search for universal causes" (p. 12) and on "nomothetic" elements (p. 239; see Allport & Odbert, 1936). My examination of the connection begins with Todd Schultz's (2003) suggestion that Allport's account of his meeting with Freud exhibits several cues of the "prototypical scene." According to Schultz (chap. 3 this vol.), "The model prototypical scene will possess these five features: (1) specificity and emotional intensity, (2) interpenetration, (3) developmental gravity, (4) family conflict, and (5) thrownness, or violation of the normally taken for granted." As Schultz (2003) observes, Allport's story of the episode is highly specific and emotionally intense. Allport provided vivid descriptions of Freud's office, of the little boy and his mother, of Freud's facial expressions, and of his own emotional reactions. He quoted Freud and the little boy, using almost identical words each time he told the story. Allport's story also interpenetrates; he repeated it in classes (Ogilvie, 1984) and lectures (e.g., Allport, 1962c, 1963), in a filmed interview (Bauer 1964), in a recollection prepared for the Freud Archives (Allport, 1958), and in his autobiography (Allport, 1967).

Schultz (2003) notes that Allport's story takes place in late adolescence, thus exhibiting the feature of developmental gravity. Allport himself described the encounter as having "the character of a traumatic developmental episode" (1967, p. 7), and his account suggests that it was a turning point in the development of his intellectual identity. More specifically, Allport visited Freud soon after choosing his occupational identity; having decided to become a psychologist, he was passing through Vienna on his way back to Harvard to begin his graduate studies. In his autobiography, Allport identified "youthful ambition" (p. 8) as one of his motives for meeting Freud. He had studied Freud's work in college (Allport, 1963), and as Nicholson (2003) has suggested, he may have arranged the meeting in hopes of obtaining "a modern benediction for his new psychological undertaking" (p. 68). Complicating the developmental gravity of the episode was the fact that in taking a step toward establishing his occupational identity, Allport was also yielding to pressure from his family (Nicholson, 2003) and stepping back into a "mentor/understudy relationship" (Nicholson, 2000, p. 464) with his older brother Floyd, who had been his graduate instructor at Harvard while Allport was an undergraduate. After earning his doctorate in 1919, the same year that Allport completed his undergraduate degree, Floyd had become a member of the Harvard psychology faculty (Nicholson, 2003; see also Elms, 1994).

According to Schultz (chap. 3 this vol.), prototypical scenes need not exhibit all five of the elements he has identified. Of the two remaining features, family conflict and "thrownness," Allport's story clearly describes the latter. Unprepared for Freud's silence, he "had to think fast to find a suitable conversational gambit" (1967, p. 8), and after telling Freud about the little boy on the tram car, he was completely taken aback —"flabbergasted"—by Freud's question, "And was that little boy you?" (p. 8). If repetitive story-telling functions to decrease the anxiety provoked by such incongruous events, as Schultz (chap. 3 this vol.) suggests, Allport's repetition of this story some forty-five years later confirms his own characterization of the encounter as "traumatic" (Allport, 1967, pp. 7, 22). Thus, Allport's account exhibits four of the five elements of prototypical scenes. (I shall suggest later that it features family conflict indirectly.)

If Allport's story of his meeting with Freud is a prototypical scene, in what ways is it prototypical? George Atwood and Silvan Tomkins (1976), Alan Elms (e.g., 1994), and Allport (1967) himself have suggested that the encounter spurred his thinking toward the development of his own theory of personality (others have interpreted the incident without connecting it to Allport's theory; see Faber, 1970; Morey, 1987). Elms's (1994) interpretation is particularly thorough in linking the account to several aspects of Allport's personality and to persistent themes in his work, including his emphasis on uniqueness. In considering Allport's account as a prototypical scene,

however, I shall examine the overall pattern of the relationship he described and identify other episodes that fit the same prototype. Following Irving Alexander's (1990) method of extracting a script, I suggest that Allport's account of the meeting might be described in the following way: Approaching—arguably with some ambivalence (Elms, 1994)—an older figure he saw as a model, Allport tried to demonstrate his psychological proficiency by telling Freud a "Freudian" story (compare Nicholson, 2003). Instead of impressing Freud as a clever young psychologist, however, he felt rebuffed and humiliated by Freud's question. His eventual response was to reject Freud's approach and to strike out on his own in order to create a theory better than psychoanalysis; as Elms has suggested, Allport's (1937) personality text included a "belated (but thoroughly adult) reply" (Elms, 1994, p. 84) to Freud's question. Simplifying further, the script consists of Allport's attempt to "join the club" of an older model, his feeling rebuffed and humiliated, and his eventual vindication by asserting his own unique (and superior) approach.

If this script is a prototype, it should recur in other episodes of Allport's life story. In fact, Allport's (1967) autobiography describes at least two other sequences that reflect the same script. As a graduate student, Allport accompanied his advisor Herbert Langfeld to Clark University to attend a meeting of E.B. Titchener's experimentalists, an elite society of psychologists who prided themselves on their scientific status (Furumoto, 1988).[2] His attempt to "join the club" was a complete disaster. "After two days of discussing problems in sensory psychology," Allport related, "Titchener allotted three minutes to each visiting graduate to describe his own investigations" (1967, p. 9). Allport described his dissertation project, an experimental study of personality traits (Allport, 1922), but Titchener was not impressed. Instead, he gave Allport a withering look that punctuated "the rebuke of total silence from the group" (Allport, 1967, p. 9). According to Allport's autobiographical account, "Langfeld . . . consoled me with the laconic remark, 'You don't care what Titchener thinks.' And I found that I did not" (p. 9). Thus, Allport claimed, he recovered quickly from his own inner conflict regarding his decision to study personality, and he set out to fashion his own unique approach to psychology. However, an earlier version of this story suggests that Allport's encounter with Titchener was similar to his encounter with Freud in evoking a sense of humiliation (see also Nicholson, 2003):

> Langfeld took me to Clark. They were having a meeting of the experimental group and Titchener was presiding and in my naïveté I didn't realize what a hostile group for this kind of problem this was. . . . After they were through talking about the brightness of metals . . . the graduate students . . . had about five minutes each and I told what I was doing and one of the greatest silences you can imagine fell over the group and Titchener looked right through me and said, "As I was saying, the brightness of metals," and so on. . . . He cut me dead. . . . and, of course, that hurt. (Allport, 1952, p. 10)[3]

According to Allport, the encounter with Titchener was a "turning point" (1967, p. 9). "Never since that time," he claimed, "have I been troubled by rebukes or professional slights directed at my maverick interests" (p. 9). This story repeats the script of Allport's story of his meeting with Freud. Despite some ambivalence toward Titchener's extreme scientism, Allport attempted to "join the club," presenting a study couched in proper scientific terms (see Nicholson, 2003). Rebuffed and humiliated by Titchener, he recovered and was eventually vindicated when "the field of personality became not only acceptable but highly fashionable" (p. 9; Allport maintained his uniqueness, however, adding, "But although the field itself became legitimate, my own theoretical position was not always approved"). Indeed, during his postdoctoral year in Germany, as Nicholson (2003) has shown, Allport made a belated response to Titchener. "With barely concealed glee" (p. 122), he sent to the *American Journal of Psychology*—a journal edited by Titchener—an article reporting that the German psychologists at the 1923 Leipzig Congress of Psychology seemed to have forgotten completely the Wundtian psychology that Titchener venerated (Allport, 1923). "I took the sweetest revenge upon him you can imagine," Allport wrote to

Ada Gould, his future wife. "I never forgave him for his dig of two years ago, and what a joy it was to announce, embellish, and extol the fact that the central theme of the German Congress this year was PERSONALITY!" (quoted in Nicholson, 2003, p. 122). Allport's (1923) article described several approaches that emphasized the uniqueness and the unity of personality.

Allport's autobiography also includes an earlier episode that anticipates the script of his encounter with Freud. This account is less detailed, as Allport devoted little attention to his childhood; however, it is suggestive of family conflict, the remaining feature of Schultz's prototypical scenes. Since his three brothers were considerably older, Allport (1967) remarked, he "fashioned [his] own circle of activities" and "contrived to be the 'star' for a small cluster of friends" (p. 4). In his autobiography, he did not explain how this came about, nor did he describe his relationship with his brothers, but he did refer to "a generalized inferiority feeling" (pp. 6–7). In an earlier personal account, he traced his "great inferiority feeling" as a youth to his experience as "the object of scorn" (Allport, n.d., pp. 4–5; see also Elms, 1994). One might speculate, then, as did Atwood and Tomkins (1976), that Allport felt rejected and inadequate in comparison with his older brothers. Allport's (1952) interview with Anne Roe provides some confirmation. "I never really got on with my brothers up to that time," he reported, referring to the years before he attended Harvard as an undergraduate. "I think it was a difference in age and differences in temperament and they didn't like me and they weren't kind and I couldn't possibly compete with them" (p. 8). These comments suggest that Allport tried to join his brothers' activities but was rejected and humiliated before searching for his own way to be a "star."

Allport's autobiographical reference to his brothers does not conclude with an episode of belated self-assertion, but Nicholson (2003) describes just such an event. On a visit to his family after his first year of graduate school, Allport wrote to Ada Gould that "the suppressed youngest" had given "the older two" brothers a piece of his mind. "Exactly what Allport said to his brothers is unknown," writes Nicholson, "but it was 'good for the soul' and 'vilification to an express elevator from the sub-cellar of passivity to the roof-garden of ascendancy'" (p. 85, quoting Allport, 1921). Allport's remark reveals his concern, in relating to his brothers, with comparisons based on "ascendance" and "submission," a pair of traits that he and Floyd had introduced in rather striking terms in their article on personality traits:

> When a person comes into a face to face relation with another person. . . . there is generally a real, though sometimes scarcely conscious, conflict between the two egos. . . . In conflicts, generally speaking, there emerge a victor and a vanquished; and this is true of the face to face dual reactions described. One of the two opponents becomes the master; his interest dominates, and he carries his point. The other yields and accordingly is dominated, though by no means always against his will. The former personality we describe as ascendant. In terms of social behavior he is active. The latter is said to be submissive; his attitude in the face to face relation is passive. (F.H. Allport & G.W. Allport, 1921, p. 13)[4]

Although Allport continued to submit to Floyd's influence until he had completed his dissertation, he began increasingly thereafter to resist directives from his family and to emphasize differences between himself and his brothers (see, e.g., Nicholson, 1996, 2003). Thus, for Allport, asserting his uniqueness was one way of satisfying his need for mastery and power—an important aspect of his personality, as David Winter has suggested (1996, 1997).

According to Allport's (1937) theory of functional autonomy, although adult motives may originate in childhood, they become "self-sustaining, *contemporary* systems . . . functionally independent" of their origins (p. 194; emphasis in original). Reflecting this view, Allport's prototypical scene was not an episode from his childhood, and his account emphasized his adult concerns (Elms, 1994). However, just as Allport's meeting with Freud anticipated his later encounter with Titchener, it also reflected a repetitive pattern of relationships dating from his earlier encounters with his brothers (thus exhibiting family conflict indirectly). These encounters share a

common script: Having first approached older models and felt rejected and humiliated by them, Allport responded eventually by asserting his own independence and uniqueness. I turn now to a closer examination of Allport's relationship with his brothers as an early source of his preoccupation with uniqueness.

The General, the Unique, and the Family Niche

> I feel that unless you've got something to react against, you don't grow up.
> Gordon Allport, quoted in Evans (1971, p. 86)

Allport's insistence on the uniqueness of personality reflected a number of historical and cultural influences on his thought, including the "culture of personality" of the early twentieth century, the antimodernist and religious views he espoused, and the intellectual currents he encountered while studying social ethics and psychology in the United States and in Germany in the early 1920s (Nicholson, 2003; see also Barenbaum & Winter, 2003). Thus, I do not wish to suggest that his family position was the only source of his preoccupation with the unique personality. However, his experience as the fourth of four brothers does appear to have contributed to a heightened concern with his own uniqueness, a resistance to being labeled, and an attraction to intellectual and scientific traditions that emphasized the unique personality; these traditions, in turn, influenced his thought.

As already noted, Allport's brothers were considerably older—Harold by nearly nine years, Floyd by more than seven, and Fayette by nearly five[5]—and, according to his own account, he "couldn't possibly compete with them" (Allport, 1952, p. 8). He was also less athletic than many of his peers, but being "very clever," he "avoided fights and competition" and started "a life pattern to find out what I could do and do it well" (p. 6). Any number of theories—for example, Erikson's theory of identity (1968), White's theory of competence motivation (1959), or Adler's theory of compensation for feelings of inferiority (Ansbacher & Ansbacher, 1956)—might contribute to an understanding of Allport's decision to

Figure 16.1. Gordon Allport (far left) with his brothers. (Allport Estate)

discover his own strengths instead of competing with his brothers or his peers. Allport (1952) himself indicated that Adler's theory might be an appropriate choice for a dynamic account of his life story. However, he rejected as anachronistic—and as too general—Adler's use of early inferiority feelings to explain adult strivings: "One could conceptualize almost any life in Adler's terms as compensation for inferiority feelings" (Allport, 1962b, p. 16). Remarkably, despite having mentioned his brothers' unkind treatment and his inability to compete with them, he also expressed uncertainty regarding the source of his feelings of inferiority (1952). Viewed as an indicator of salience (Alexander, 1990), Allport's omission suggests that examining his relationship with his brothers may prove fruitful.

One theory that seems particularly useful in this regard is Sulloway's (1996) theory of sibling differentiation. Drawing on evolutionary theory and on studies of sibling deidentification (e.g., Schachter, Gilutz, Shore, & Adler, 1978; Schachter, Shore, Feldman-Rotman, Marquis, & Campbell, 1976), Sulloway (1996) argued that siblings develop different strategies of competing for parental favor in order to ensure their own survival in the family. He suggested that eldest children typically align their interests with those of their parents, adopting parental roles and relatively conservative views. Later-born children typically attempt to establish valuable family niches that are not already occupied; "they seek to excel in those domains where older

siblings have not already established superiority" (p. 353). Thus, later-born children tend to be more rebellious and more open to new experiences; for example, Sulloway found more support for revolutionary theories among scientists who were later-born siblings than among those who were firstborn. Occupying lower status positions in the family, later-born children also tend to be more sociable and more accommodating than firstborn children. Sulloway suggested that siblings of the same sex are particularly likely to develop contrasting characteristics and interests and that siblings adjacent in the birth order show greater contrasts than nonadjacent siblings, or "jump pairs" (p. 305; see also Schachter, Gilutz, et al., 1978; Schachter, Shore, et al., 1976). Rather than predict simple correlations between birth order and personality characteristics, however, Sulloway (1996) cautioned that a number of other features of the family context—for example, age differences, temperament, gender, and conflict with parents—may affect (directly or in interaction with birth order) children's strategies of differentiation.

Allport and his brothers exemplified several typical sibling strategies of differentiation. Like many eldest children, Harold played a dominant, parental role. Indeed, Floyd may have had Harold in mind when he described eldest children as ascendant personalities (F.H. Allport, 1924). After graduating from high school, Harold attended law school (at that time equivalent to a vocational school), moved next door to the family home in Cleveland, Ohio (Allport, 1952), and became his father's business partner (Nicholson, 1996). Taking over the business after his father died in 1923, he and his wife tried to enlist Allport as an assistant, apparently disregarding Allport's plans for an academic career; not surprisingly, Allport resisted. Harold disapproved of Allport's lack of business sense, and Allport, initially apologetic, later considered him domineering and conventional (Nicholson, 1996, 2003). "Floyd was a different piece of goods," according to Allport. "He was an amazing person. . . . He had always been perhaps the odd one in the family but he was much the most gifted in intelligence and aesthetically." After graduating from high school Floyd went to Harvard, which to the rest of the family represented "an utterly strange world"

(1952, p. 7). Floyd later described himself as "reclusive by nature" and noted that he had "failed to show even a decent regard for traditional beliefs and conventions" (F.H. Allport, 1974, p. 5). Thus, Harold and Floyd exemplified the large contrast frequently found between first and second siblings (Sulloway, 1996).

Like many later-born siblings, Allport's third brother Fayette seems to have had an adventurous streak; Allport characterized him as "a lady killer" and as the most "troublesome" to their father (1952, p. 8). Exemplifying the greater similarity of "jump pairs" (Sulloway, 1996), Fayette shared some of his eldest brother's interests and activities. Like Harold, he played football, and he also went to law school—but only after being "kicked out of Oberlin [College]" (Allport, 1952, p. 7). After World War I, Fayette established a diplomatic career in Europe (p. 8), where he later worked for the Motion Picture Association of America (Nicholson, 2003). Regarding the second "jump pair" in the family, Allport noted, "I was more like Floyd" (1952, p. 7), perhaps referring to his own tendency toward introversion and bookishness (Nicholson, 2003). But he added immediately that "the temperaments of the four [brothers] are extremely diverse" (Allport, 1952, p. 7), and he described all of his brothers as "a little more masculine in type" than himself (p. 8). Exemplifying later-born tendencies toward accommodation and sociability (Sulloway, 1996), Allport developed tact, social poise, and diplomacy (see Nicholson, 2003)—"highly polished political skills" that allowed him to make "peace with bureaucracy" in a way that "Floyd never could" (Katz, Johnson, & Nichols, 1998, p. 123).

Sulloway's theory (1996) would suggest that Allport's emphasis on differentiating himself from his brothers reflected a typical strategy of later-born children—an adaptive search for an unoccupied family niche. Recalling that same-sex siblings tend to show greater contrasts than do siblings of different sexes, one might also consider Allport's concern with uniqueness a contrast effect magnified by a need to differentiate himself from three same-sex siblings. It seems likely that the fourth of four sons would experience more difficulty than usual in his attempts to be recognized as an individual. Indeed, in his

fiftieth year, as Nicholson has shown, Allport still recalled being confused with his brothers: "'You remember Dad's ability to mix us all up,' Allport remarked in a letter to his brothers. . . . 'We were all "stimulus equivalents" for him'" (Nicholson, 2003, p. 25, quoting Allport, 1947). Such experiences may have been repeated at school. In an interview, Allport (1952) noted several times that he had followed his brothers, attending the same schools through all the grades. Thus, he may have encountered school personnel who tended to see him as the youngest of the "Allport boys" rather than as an individual—a tendency most likely exacerbated when Floyd returned from Harvard and took a position as a teacher at the high school where Allport was in his junior year (Nicholson, 1996). In a letter of recommendation to Harvard, for example, his high school principal compared him to Floyd (Cully, 1915). In contrast, Allport remembered with particular fondness a nurse he called "B," who worked for his family and who lavished attention on him alone (Allport, 1952; Nicholson, 2003). These early experiences may have heightened Allport's sensitivity to being "classified and thus disposed of" (Allport, 1950, as quoted in Nicholson, 1997, p. 69) and his tendency to "react against" his brothers.

"More Like Floyd"?

> All his life long [the person] will be attempting to reconcile . . . two modes of becoming, the tribal and the personal: the one that makes him into a mirror, the other that lights the lamp of individuality within.
>
> Gordon Allport (1955, p. 35)

A striking aspect of Allport's early career was his "mentor/understudy relationship" with Floyd (Nicholson, 2000, p. 464). Several authors have connected Allport's theoretical concepts of functional autonomy, maturity, and uniqueness with his efforts to emerge from Floyd's "shadow" (Elms, 1994, p. 80; see also Atwood & Tomkins, 1976). Drawing upon a close examination of Allport's correspondence in the early 1920s, Nicholson (2000, 2003) linked Allport's emerging interest in German concepts of the unique personality to his declaration of intellectual independence from Floyd. In this section, I shall consider this development within the context of Allport's early position in his family. As described above, Allport (1952) noted that he did not get along with his brothers before he entered college. Thus, his early pattern of avoiding competition and making "[his] own world" (p. 7) apparently served not only as a strategy of sibling differentiation but also as a way of compensating for painful experiences of rejection, echoed in his later responses to humiliation by Freud and by Titchener. While pursuing his own interests, Allport still admired his brothers and valued their advice and attention.

An indifferent student in grade school, Allport became interested in doing well in high school after one of his brothers commented favorably on his report card. He graduated as salutatorian in 1915 and applied to Harvard, pleased to follow the suggestion of Floyd, who had graduated from Harvard in 1913 and was pursuing a doctorate in psychology (Allport, 1952, 1967). Floyd counseled Allport on his choice of courses and became "from that time on," in Allport's words, "the bigger factor in my life" (1952, p. 8)—an accomplished and much-admired instructor, experimenter, and advisor. As an undergraduate, Allport welcomed Floyd's advice and support, as well as his pronouncements regarding psychological theory and methods. After graduating from Harvard in 1919, Allport spent a year teaching at Robert College in Constantinople, but Floyd continued to play an influential role in his career decisions (Nicholson, 2000, 2003). In 1920 Floyd advised Allport to return to Harvard to begin graduate school, helped to arrange a graduate fellowship, and offered Allport a room in his apartment. Floyd also suggested personality as the topic for Allport's dissertation and provided much of the theoretical and philosophical approach Allport adopted. "Indeed," Nicholson suggests, "a considerable part of Gordon's dissertation may be viewed as an elaboration of Floyd's research program" (2000, p. 464).

Even as an undergraduate, however, Allport combined a tendency to admire and emulate Floyd with his earlier tendency to differentiate himself from his brothers. Unlike Floyd, who professed a commitment to the ideal of a purely objective science "quite apart from any humanis-tic presuppositions, or from any utilitarian value" (F.H. Allport, 1974, p. 5),[6] Allport became interested in applying science to social service (Nicholson, 2003). He studied social ethics as well as psychology, and he participated in a number of social service activities; for some time he even considered a career in social work (Allport, 1952). Also in contrast to Floyd, who, as Nicholson (2000) observes, adopted a modernist outlook and a "strident materialism" (Nicholson, 2003, p. 46), Allport tempered his scientific orientation with a religious quest based on an "antimodernist impulse" (p. 44; see also Lears, 1981). Although Allport shared this impulse with many of his contemporaries (Nicholson, 2003), his new situation as the younger of two Allport brothers at Harvard may have contributed to his choice of vocational and spiritual pursuits different from those of Floyd. At home he had considered himself "more like Floyd" (Allport, 1952, p. 7), but this new configuration brought their differences into focus (compare Nicholson, 2000) —a contrast effect perhaps enhanced by a "narcissism of minor differences," the tendency for people who "are otherwise alike" to exaggerate their differences (Freud, 1918/1957, p. 199).[7]

At Robert College, according to Nicholson, Allport oscillated between two extremes, feeling at times like an aesthete—"a passive lover of nature's creations"—and at other times like a scientist—"a rank biologist" (Allport, 1919, quoted in Nicholson, 2003, p. 66). Having returned to Harvard as a graduate student, he collaborated with Floyd to define, classify, and measure personality traits (F.H. Allport & G.W. Allport, 1921), and his dissertation (1922) reflected Floyd's behaviorist orientation (Nicholson, 2003). However, Allport's ambivalence regarding Floyd's version of psychology intensified during this period, and he experienced considerable conflict between the scientific worldview that Floyd represented and the antimodernist, spiritual impulse he had pursued with his friends from Robert College. In letters to his friends, he complained of feeling torn between an inauthentic personality immersed in "science, SCIENCE, SCIENCE!!!!" (quoted in Nicholson, 2003, p. 75) and an authentic personality that was more aesthetically and spiritually inclined. Allport's efforts to unify these conflicting personalities soon led to his embrace of religious and scientific positions very different from those of Floyd.

According to his own account, Floyd rejected "the rather heavy religious influence in our early life," and as an undergraduate he had "long and friendly arguments" with his mother "concerning science and religion" (F.H. Allport, 1974, p. 3). As an adult he continued to hold a critical view of organized religion; he argued that "both science and religion are based ineradicably upon impulses within ourselves" (F.H. Allport, 1930, p. 354) and that the supernatural world was not an external reality but a projection of our ethical impulses. Suggesting that "God is my way of explaining my own desire to do good" rather than an actual "Superior Being" (p. 362), he advocated "a religion in which transcendental elements are effaced" (p. 361) and accepted "nothing on faith" (F.H. Allport, 1974, p. 5). Allport found just such a position inadequate. Like Floyd, as an undergraduate he questioned the religious doctrines he had learned at home, but instead of rejecting organized religion he explored "humanitarian" alternatives and adopted an "essentially Unitarian position" (1967, p. 7). Within a few years, however, he rejected this position, which in his view "exalt[ed] one's own intellect and affirm[ed] only a precarious man-made set of values" (p. 7). Identifying strongly with his mother's spiritual quest (Nicholson, 2003; see Allport, 1944), he sought a position of "humility and some mysticism" (Allport, 1967, p. 7). During his postdoctoral year in Germany in 1923 he joined the Anglican Episcopal Church, where he found a more "transcendental worldview" (Nicholson, 2003, p. 123)—precisely the sort of religious view Floyd could not accept. For Allport, an authentic religious position would become a model for the "unifying philosophy of life" (1937, p. 225), a hallmark of the mature personality.

Allport's resolution of his religious identity coincided with his exploration of German psychological approaches that emphasized the uniqueness and unity of personality. He was particularly impressed with the work of William Stern, a pioneer in differential psychology (Stern, 1900) whose more recent work focused on "real individuality"—"a kind of unique, 'spiritual' unity that defied scientific capture"—instead of "relational individuality" (Nicholson, 2003, p. 112),

based on comparing individuals on measures of separate personality traits, the approach Allport had promoted in his work with Floyd. As Nicholson has shown, Allport's new commitment to this "psychology of the spirit" (p. 103)—psychology as a *Geisteswissenschaft*, or human science—constituted an assertion of "his own intellectual identity" (p. 126). Allport's declaration of independence from Floyd was strikingly similar to his "revenge" (p. 122) on Titchener a year earlier. In a paper he described as an "attack" (quoted in Nicholson, 2003, p. 127) on the conception of personality Floyd had presented in his recent book (F.H. Allport, 1924), Allport criticized the study of personality based on scientific measurements of separate traits and promoted German intuitive approaches to "The Study of the Undivided Personality" (G.W. Allport, 1924). Submitting the paper for publication to the *Journal of Abnormal and Social Psychology*, he sent it to Floyd, who was coeditor of the journal (Nicholson, 2003). According to Nicholson, Floyd recognized Allport's declaration of independence, and his response included "several expressions of a long-established fraternal superiority" (p. 127) that accelerated Allport's disengagement from his brother.

In his autobiography, Allport (1967) maximized contrasts between himself and Floyd. After a brief mention of Floyd's role as his teacher and advisor, he devoted nearly a paragraph to the divergence of their psychological views (e.g., "His *Social Psychology* . . . was too behavioristic and too psychoanalytic for my taste") and to Floyd's greater "artistic, musical, and manual" gifts (p. 12). What is not clear in the autobiography, however, is that the course of Allport's intellectual engagement with Floyd echoed the script of his earlier encounters with his brothers, with Freud, and with Titchener. Having first tried to adopt Floyd's psychological approach to personality (albeit with some ambivalence), Allport later "reacted against" this approach and proposed an alternative, simultaneously emphasizing the uniqueness of personality and asserting his own uniqueness. Rather than a response to a particular incident of rejection or humiliation, Allport's disengagement from Floyd, beginning with his article in 1924, was part of a gradual process of developing his own approach to personality

—a paradoxical combination of scientific values he shared with Floyd and an opposing set of romantic and spiritual values (Nicholson, 2003).

"One or Two Allports?"

Allport concluded his autobiographical discussion of differences between himself and Floyd by remarking, "Over the years we pursued our own ways, but because of our common and unusual surname and divergence of points of view we managed to confuse students and the public. Were there one or two Allports?" (1967, pp. 12–13). Early in his career, Allport tried to prevent such confusion by warning his correspondents. "P.S. Perhaps I should call attention to my identity," he ended a letter to Karl Menninger in 1930. "I am not to be confused with my brother F.H. Allport of the University of Syracuse!" (see also Allport, 1928a). Despite such precautions, the confusion continued, annoying both brothers (F.H. Allport, 1931) and extending to their major works. For example, Floyd's *Social Psychology* (F.H. Allport, 1924), widely acclaimed for defining the field as "a new experimental science" (F.H. Allport, 1974, p. 9), was attributed to both brothers (Shellow, 1932), and as late as 1938, a reviewer of Allport's *Personality* text noted that "Professor Allport [had] long been known" for his behaviorist approach replacing instincts with "prepotent reflexes" (Faris, 1938, p. 239)—a prominent concept in Floyd's text. Years later, Allport (1952) still wondered whether he owed some of his rapid career progress to the confusion.

Emphasizing the divergence of their views, Allport (1967) did not mention that his early collaboration with Floyd was another source of the confusion. The brothers had coauthored not only their early study of traits (F.H. Allport & G.W. Allport, 1921) but also the *A-S Reaction Study* (G.W. Allport & F.H. Allport, 1928), a well-known psychometric test of "ascendance-submission." For Allport, the collaboration raised lingering concerns regarding his originality. He remembered being ashamed of his thesis and noted that it was "started by Floyd" (Allport, 1952, pp. 10–11). Nevertheless, he counted it among contributions he considered his "firsts":

"I believe that my own thesis was perhaps the first American dissertation written explicitly on the question of component traits of personality" (1967, p. 9). He also suggested that his course on personality, first taught at Harvard in 1924, was "probably the first course on the subject offered in an American college" (p. 9). Allport's dissertation does appear to have been the first on *personality* traits; however, a dissertation on *character* traits had appeared the previous year (Filter, 1921). And although Allport's course is widely regarded as the first course on personality (Nicholson, 1997b; Parker, 1991), Kimball Young's course "Personality and Character" preceded Allport's course by four years (Barenbaum, 2000). It is important to note that Allport made no definitive priority claims; most likely, he simply did not know of the earlier work. However, like his self-portrayal as a "maverick" (Allport, 1967, p. 9; see also Allport, 1962b, 1962c; Nicholson, 2003), Allport's beliefs regarding these "firsts" reflect an enduring concern with establishing his own uniqueness.

Work on the *A-S Reaction Study* (G.W. Allport & F.H. Allport, 1928), designed with Floyd while Allport was in graduate school but not published until several years later, complicated Allport's efforts to develop his own views. After two years of postdoctoral study in Europe, Allport returned to Harvard in 1924 and spent the next two years as an instructor of social ethics (Allport, 1967). Floyd had moved to the University of North Carolina in 1922 and to Syracuse University in 1924 (F.H. Allport, 1974). In 1926, Allport accepted a position at Dartmouth, where he taught psychology for four years before joining the psychology faculty at Harvard. At Dartmouth, he began to think seriously of writing a personality text, to develop his trait theory, and to conduct research based on the German approaches he had encountered in Europe (Allport, 1952, 1967). By fall of 1927, Allport was actively exploring "the intuitive method," his term for the German method of *Verstehen*, an attempt to understand the unity of the individual personality. He decided to use the method to teach a new course that he offered the following semester (Allport, 1928a, 1929).[8] In a talk entitled "Intuition as a Method in Psychology" (1927a), Allport remarked, "It was inevitable that mental testing should appear. By these methods persons can be compared with persons, *but can never in the wide world be understood in and of themselves*" (p. 11; emphasis in original).

Another talk, "Intuition and the Aesthetic Attitude," delivered at a symposium on art in December 1927, suggests that Allport was experiencing an intense internal struggle during this period. Borrowing terms from philosopher Eduard Spranger, he spoke of the inevitable conflict between the theoretical attitude (a scientific focus on universals) and the aesthetic attitude (an intuitive focus on individualities). The aesthetic attitude, Allport claimed, "is generally at variance with practical living and with conceptual thinking. The conflict which it creates in some men of scholarly vocation has caused a mental-break-down [sic]" (Allport, 1927a, p. 11). Making the reference more personal, he asked,

> How are we to reconcile the understanding of the particular with the understanding of the universal? The answer, I think, lies in the philosophy of the *Sturm und Drang*. The two souls that dwell, alas, within my breast (or in psychological language, the conflict of my aesthetic and theoretical attitudes) must wrestle until a resolution is discovered. This resolution will be in accordance with my own personality. Indeed it will be my personality. No one can prescribe it for me. It is the fate of each enlightened individual to work out for himself the synthesis. It may lead him to disaster, to a self divided against a self, or to the strength of genius. It is his own adventure. (p. 12)

Allport's phrase, "the two souls that dwell, alas, within my breast," was adapted from a scene in which Goethe's Faust is tormented by the conflict between his earthly desires and his spiritual aspirations.[9] A letter dated five days after Allport's talk suggests one source of his distress: "I am working along ever at the Ascendance study, which bores me to tears," he wrote to his friend A.A. Roback (Allport, 1927b). "I am not . . . a 'tester', in spite of the fact I hope soon to publish my ascendance test," he remarked in another letter. "I would rather be known as an anti-tester" (1927b). Both the test (G.W. Allport & F.H. Allport, 1928) and Allport's (1928c) article de-

scribing it, with all the requisite statistical details, were published in 1928 (see also Allport, 1928b).

Unlike Floyd, who embraced an "objective," scientific world-view, Allport first embraced, and then struggled during much of his career to reconcile, a series of opposites—science and spirituality, American psychometric and German intuitive approaches to personality, the general and the unique (Nicholson, 2003). At times he found this conflict particularly wrenching; after completing graduate school, for example, he spoke of feeling torn between two personalities, or "two natures" (Allport, 1922, quoted in Nicholson, 2003, p. 97). At Dartmouth, alternating between efforts to complete his psychometric test (developed with Floyd) and to explore the intuitive method (whose proponents attacked tests), he wrestled once again with a sense of a divided self. Allport's struggle suggests a different reading of his question: "Were there one or two Allports?" (1967, p. 13).

"Myself Alone": Unity and Uniqueness

Having completed the A-S test, Allport focused on synthesizing an approach to the study of personality instead of alternating between American and German methods (e.g., Allport, 1929; Allport & Vernon, 1931, 1933). He considered his trait theory, described in a paper in 1929 and published in 1931, his first original work: "The question of what is a trait. . . got me on an entirely different theory of personality from anyone else" (Allport, 1952, p. 11). At the same time, he began to suggest the need to create a separate field of personality, rather than continue to treat personality as a topic of social psychology (Barenbaum, 2000). Perhaps significantly, this suggestion coincided with Allport's move to Harvard in 1930 to accept a position in social psychology—"in a certain sense, Floyd's old job" (Nicholson, 2003, p. 169).

This "productive" period (Allport, 1952, p. 12) culminated in Allport's famous textbook, *Personality: A Psychological Interpretation* (1937). The book combined "a scientific message of discipline and control with a spiritual message of freedom and distinctiveness" (Nicholson, 2003, pp. 216–217), reflections of the "two souls" whose integration remained for Allport a salient concern. Devoting a chapter to the unity of personality—a focus of the German "psychology of the spirit" (Nicholson, 2003, p. 103) and one of his favorite topics—Allport argued that "unity, at best, is a matter of *degree*" (1937, p. 344; emphasis in original) and that "unity lies only in the struggle for unity" (pp. 350–351). Faust "was saved," he suggested, "because he ceaselessly strove for the completeness he never attained" (p. 351). In Allport's view, the two souls of Faust allowed him "to gain an understanding of human life" (p. 515) superior to that of his attendant, who had only one, and his striving for completeness exemplified the religious position that Allport considered "the most comprehensive" (p. 226) unifying philosophy of life.

As we have seen, a central tenet of Allport's text was the uniqueness of the individual. Allport criticized Freud, Titchener, and other psychologists for focusing too narrowly on universal aspects of mind. To supplement the "relational" view of individuality he and Floyd had promoted (Nicholson, 2003)—individuality defined in terms of departures from average scores on measures of common traits—he presented the principle of functional autonomy, *"a general law . . . that explains how uniqueness comes about"* (Allport, 1937, p. 558; emphasis in original). This principle, he argued, was "a declaration of independence for the psychology of personality" (p. 207). The principle was also Allport's own declaration of independence from psychoanalysis and other prevailing psychological views, including those of his brother, who saw "higher" interests as dependent on hunger and other "prepotent" reflexes (F.H. Allport, 1924, pp. 65–66).

In another sense, Allport's text also constituted a declaration of independence for the psychology of personality and for Allport himself. In their joint article, Allport and his brother had claimed that personality was inherently social; "only with the advent of Friday," they argued, could the personality of Robinson Crusoe "be said to stand forth in its full significance" (F.H. Allport & G.W. Allport, 1921, p. 7). Continuing to define personality as "largely a social fact" (F.H. Allport, 1924, p. 99), Floyd maintained that "the hermit exhibits little personality"

(p. 101). Allport (1937) rejected this view. It was an error, he insisted, to assume "that [a trait] must represent some kind of relationship between two people. Did Robinson Crusoe lack traits before the advent of Friday? Will the last man to remain alive on earth abruptly lose his traits when his companions die?" (p. 289). Arguing for a focus on the structure of the "personality *itself*" (p. viii), Allport proclaimed that the psychology of personality was a "new department of psychology" (p. ix), thus separating the field from social psychology—the field Floyd had defined in his text (F.H. Allport, 1924; see Barenbaum, 2000). Simultaneously declaring the independence of personality from social relationships and of personality psychology from social psychology, Allport thus became—like Floyd—the author of a pioneering text that defined a "new field of study" (p. vii).

Conclusion

Unlike authors who have focused specifically on Allport's reactions to Freud and to psychoanalysis (Atwood & Tomkins, 1976; Elms, 1994; Faber, 1970; Morey, 1987), I have treated Allport's story of his meeting with Freud as a prototypical scene that reveals a recurrent script in his life and work.[10] The script concerns Allport's preoccupation with uniqueness—an aspect of his objection to Freud that is generally overlooked (for an exception, see Elms, 1994). According to this interpretation, the meeting with Freud was one of a series of encounters, beginning with his relationship with his older brothers, in which Allport first approached and then felt humiliated by models whose views or activities he later rejected, thus asserting his own uniqueness. Similarly, psychoanalysis was one of a series of psychological views that Allport first tried to accommodate but later criticized for overemphasizing universal aspects of mind and disposing of the unique personality. His efforts to define the psychology of personality as a unique field separate from social psychology reflected the same script.

I have argued that Allport's experience as the fourth of four brothers contributed to a heightened concern with establishing his own uniqueness. Rather than suggest a direct link between his early experience and his theoretical concepts, however, I have attempted to illustrate the interplay between Allport's personal concerns and certain cultural, historical, and intellectual contexts that framed his work (see Nicholson, 2003). Allport (1937) himself objected to the kind of reductionistic interpretations that psychobiographers have since criticized (e.g., Elms, 1994; Erikson, 1969; Runyan, 1982). When David Winter asked him in 1964 "how it was that he and his brother—so similar in family and academic background—turned out to be so different in approach to psychology," Allport noted that after studying abroad he could no longer take seriously the positivism and behaviorism that predominated in American psychology (D.G. Winter, personal communication, January 13 and 14, 2004). His answer highlights intellectual and cultural trends that clearly contributed to his thought; however, as we have seen, Allport's reluctance to examine early experiences also imposed limitations on his self-understanding (compare Anderson, chap. 13 this vol.; Atwood & Tomkins, 1976; Elms, 1994; see also Elms, chap. 5 this vol.). A more complete account requires not only consideration of the personal concerns that drew him to European theories emphasizing the uniqueness and unity of personality, but also a recognition that siblings may have different experiences of their "similar" background (Sulloway, 1996).

This interpretation, I suggest, expands our understanding of Allport's response to Freud by shedding light on the evolution of Allport's critique and on Floyd's more sympathetic view of psychoanalysis. Although the evidence for a direct link between Allport's clean and pious family background and his distaste for psychoanalysis is compelling (Elms, 1994), such a direct link does not account for Floyd's more positive view (Allport, 1967). Like his unorthodox religious orientation, Floyd's interest in psychoanalysis might be linked to his disregard for "traditional beliefs" (F.H. Allport, 1974, p. 5). However, I would like to suggest an interpretation that considers the brothers' family positions as well as Allport's experience in Europe. Both Allport and his brother exemplified the tendency of later-born scientists to embrace revolutionary theories (Sulloway, 1996). As a graduate student, Floyd

"seized onto behaviorism" (F.H. Allport, 1974, p. 7), a new approach at the time, and his *Social Psychology* (F.H. Allport, 1924) translated into behavioristic language concepts from another theory that was gaining in popular appeal and beginning to have an impact on social psychology in the United States (Parkovnick, 2000). That theory was psychoanalysis.

As Elms (1994) has shown, Allport did not reject Freudian theory immediately after meeting Freud in 1920, as he implied in some accounts. Instead, he expressed ambivalence for some time afterward. Writing with Floyd, he cited Freudian concepts (F.H. Allport & G.W. Allport, 1921), but in his dissertation, he expressed a preference for more recent formulations of Freudian mechanisms by "the unorthodox psychoanalysts" (Allport, 1922, p. 7). While planning his postdoctoral travels in 1922, Allport considered studying psychoanalysis in Vienna, and he expressed both admiration and criticism of Freud during his first semester in Berlin (Elms, 1994; Nicholson, 2003). However, he did not pursue plans to study psychoanalysis, and after moving to Hamburg to study with Stern in early March 1923 (Nicholson, 2003), he wrote dismissively of Freud (Elms, 1994). What changed his mind? As noted above, Allport was seeking a new intellectual identity in Europe. He soon learned that Freud had "no recognition" in Germany (Elms, 1994, p. 78, quoting Allport, 1922); not surprisingly, he found more appealing the "new" approaches he described in the articles he sent to Titchener and to his brother (Allport, 1923, 1924). The 1923 article featured prominently the work of Stern, a champion of the unique personality and also an early critic of Freud (Stern, 1901/1988). Allport's (1937) own critique of Freud echoed Stern's objections to psychoanalysis as a reductionistic theory (Nicholson, 2003; see Stern, 1935/1938), and his concept of functional autonomy reflected Stern's refusal to reduce human drives to their most elementary form. In characteristic fashion, however, Allport (1937) suggested that even Stern relied too heavily on universal motivational concepts.

Thus, Allport's critique of Freud developed over time, informed not only by his early preconceptions of psychoanalysis and his personal encounter with Freud but also by several later experiences: his preference (characteristic of later-born scientists) for unorthodox theories, his effort to differentiate himself from his older brother Floyd, and his attraction to the work of Stern and other theorists who emphasized the unique personality. Each of these later experiences, in turn, reflected Allport's concern with asserting his own uniqueness and the uniqueness of personality—a concern raised in his early encounters with his three older brothers, expressed repeatedly in other relationships and in his work, and encapsulated in his autobiographical account of the meeting between a naive young man and the famous psychoanalyst who failed to recognize his unique motives.

Acknowledgments

The photograph of the Allport brothers (Gordon, Fayette, Floyd, and Harold) was first published in Nicholson's (2003) biography of Allport. I am grateful to Ian Nicholson for his help in arranging for my use of the photo and to Dr. Robert Allport for permission to publish it in this volume.

Notes

1. Allport's choice of the term "maverick," which originally referred to an unbranded calf, is perhaps significant.
2. Allport (1967) claimed that the meeting took place in May 1922; the date was actually April 1921 (Nicholson, 2003), a year before he completed his thesis.
3. E.G. Boring (1967) recalled Titchener's remark somewhat differently, but the upshot was the same: "Allport's communication was followed by a long silence, and then Titchener said 'As we were saying, the modes of appearance of colors are . . .'" (p. 323).
4. Each brother subsequently used this description, with minor modifications, in his own publications (e.g., F.H. Allport, 1924; G.W. Allport, 1937).
5. Allport was born on November 11, 1897 (Allport, 1967). Harold was born on January 19, 1889; Floyd on August 22, 1890; and Fayette on January 25, 1893 (Nicholson, 2003).
6. On the political themes underlying this "objective" ideal, see Nicholson (2000).
7. Allport used this concept in describing his relationship with Henry Murray: "Our fields of interest lie so close together that by unspoken

agreement we allow a 'narcissism of slight differences' to keep us in a state of friendly separation" (1967, p. 13).
8. The course was based on William Ellery Leonard's (1927) autobiography, *The Locomotive-God*.
9. See Goethe (1914). Allport (1967) mentioned that he studied Faust in England during the second year of his postdoctoral fellowship, while ruminating on his German experience.
10. On the recurrence of a script in the life story and professional work of B.F. Skinner, see Demorest and Siegel (1996).

References

Alexander, I.E. (1990). Personology: Method and content in personality assessment and psychobiography. Durham, N.C.: Duke University Press.

Allport, F.H. (1924). Social psychology. Boston: Houghton Mifflin.

Allport, F.H. (1930). The religion of a scientist. Harper's Magazine, 160, 352–366.

Allport, F.H. (1931). [Letter to G.W. Allport, December 1]. Floyd H. Allport Papers, Syracuse University Archives, Syracuse, N.Y.

Allport, F.H. (1974). Floyd H. Allport. In E.G. Boring & G. Lindzey (Eds.), History of psychology in autobiography (Vol. 6, pp. 1–29). Englewood Cliffs, N.J.: Prentice-Hall.

Allport, F.H., & Allport, G.W. (1921). Personality traits: Their classification and measurement. Journal of Abnormal Psychology and Social Psychology, 16, 6–40.

Allport, G.W. (1922). An experimental study of the traits of personality, with application to the problem of social diagnosis. Unpublished doctoral dissertation, Harvard University.

Allport, G.W. (1923). The Leipzig Congress of Psychology. American Journal of Psychology, 34, 612–615.

Allport, G.W. (1924). The study of the undivided personality. Journal of Abnormal and Social Psychology, 19, 132–141.

Allport, G.W. (1927a). Intuition and the aesthetic attitude [Unpublished symposium paper, December 12]. Gordon W. Allport Papers, Harvard University Archives, Cambridge, Mass. Courtesy of the Harvard University Archives.

Allport, G.W. (1927b). [Letter to A.A. Roback, December 17]. A.A. Roback Papers, MS Stor 66, Houghton Library, Cambridge, Mass. Published by permission of the Houghton Library, Harvard University.

Allport, G.W. (1927a). Intuition as a method in psychology. Unpublished paper, undated (internal evidence suggests 1927). Gordon W.

Allport Papers, Harvard University Archives, Cambridge, Mass. Courtesy of the Harvard University Archives.

Allport, G.W. (1927b). [Letter to A.A. Roback, undated (internal evidence suggests 1927)]. A.A. Roback Papers, MS Stor 66, Houghton Library, Cambridge, Mass. Published by permission of the Houghton Library, Harvard University.

Allport, G.W. (1928a). [Letter to W.E. Leonard, April 5]. Gordon W. Allport Papers, Harvard University Archives, Cambridge, Mass.

Allport, G.W. (1928b). Mental tests and measurements. In A.B. Hart & W.M. Schuyler (Eds.), The American year book: A record of events and progress, year 1927 (pp. 703–706). Garden City, N.Y.: Doubleday, Doran, & Co.

Allport, G.W. (1928c). A test for ascendance-submission. Journal of Abnormal and Social Psychology, 23, 118–136.

Allport, G.W. (1929). The study of personality by the intuitive method: An experiment in teaching from The Locomotive God. Journal of Abnormal and Social Psychology, 24, 14–27.

Allport, G.W. (1930). [Letter to K. Menninger, May 6]. Gordon W. Allport Papers, Harvard University Archives, Cambridge, Mass. Courtesy of the Harvard University Archives.

Allport, G.W. (1931). What is a trait of personality? Journal of Abnormal and Social Psychology, 25, 368–372.

Allport, G.W. (1937). Personality: A psychological interpretation. New York: Henry Holt.

Allport, G.W. (1942). The use of personal documents in psychological science. New York: Social Science Research Council.

Allport, G.W. (1944). The quest of Nellie Wise Allport. Boston: Author. Gordon W. Allport Papers, Harvard University Archives, Cambridge, Mass.

Allport, G.W. (1952). [Interview by Anne Roe]. Anne Roe Papers, American Philosophical Society, Philadelphia, Penn. Courtesy of the American Philosophical Society.

Allport, G.W. (1955). Becoming: Basic considerations for a psychology of personality. New Haven, Conn.: Yale University Press.

Allport, G.W. (1958). G.W. Allport recalls a visit to Sigmund Freud [Unpublished manuscript]. Gordon W. Allport Papers, Harvard University Archives, Cambridge, Mass.

Allport, G.W. (1962a). The general and the unique in psychological science. Journal of Personality, 30, 405–422.

Allport, G.W. (1962b). [Interview by Anne Roe]. Anne Roe Papers, American Philosophical Society, Philadelphia, Penn. Courtesy of the American Philosophical Society.

Allport, G.W. (1962c). My encounters with personality theory [Transcript of talk presented at Boston University School of Theology, October 29]. Gordon W. Allport Papers, Harvard University Archives, Cambridge, Mass.

Allport, G.W. (1963). Critical issues in personality theory [Anna Belle Tracy Memorial Lecture, School of Applied Social Sciences, Western Reserve University, November 8]. Gordon W. Allport Papers, Harvard University Archives, Cambridge, Mass.

Allport, G.W. (1967). Gordon W. Allport. In E.G. Boring & G. Lindzey (Eds.), A history of psychology in autobiography (Vol. 5, pp. 1–25). New York: Appleton-Century-Crofts.

Allport, G.W. (n.d.). Personal experience with racial and religious attitudes [Unpublished manuscript]. Gordon W. Allport Papers, Harvard University Archives, Cambridge, Mass. Courtesy of the Harvard University Archives.

Allport, G.W., & Allport, F.H. (1928). The A-S Reaction Study; a scale for measuring ascendance-submission in personality: Manual for directions, scoring values, and norms. Boston: Houghton Mifflin.

Allport, G.W., & Odbert, H.S. (1936). Trait-names: A psycho-lexical study. Psychological Monographs, 47(1), 1–171, no. 211.

Allport, G.W., & Vernon, P.E. (1931). A study of values. Boston: Houghton Mifflin.

Allport, G.W., & Vernon, P.E. (1933). Studies in expressive movement. New York: Macmillan.

Ansbacher, H.L., & Ansbacher, R.R. (Eds.). (1956). The individual psychology of Alfred Adler: A systematic presentation in selections from his writings. New York: Basic Books.

Atwood, G.E., & Tomkins, S.S. (1976). On the subjectivity of personality theory. Journal of the History of the Behavioral Sciences, 12, 166–177.

Barenbaum, N.B. (1997, June 19). "The most revealing method of all": Gordon Allport and case studies. Paper presented at the annual meeting of Cheiron, Richmond, Va.

Barenbaum, N.B. (1998, June 20). Idiographic and nomothetic: Gordon Allport's "introduction" of personality psychology as historical and natural science. Paper presented at the annual meeting of Cheiron, San Diego, Calif.

Barenbaum, N.B. (2000). How social was personality? The Allports' "connection" of social and personality psychology. Journal of the History of the Behavioral Sciences, 36, 471–487.

Barenbaum, N.B., & Winter, D.G. (2003). Personality. In I.B. Weiner (Series Ed.) & D.K. Freedheim (Vol. Ed.), Handbook of psychology, Vol. 1: History of psychology (pp. 177–203). New York: Wiley.

Bauer, J.L. (Dir.). (1964). Dr. Gordon W. Allport [Motion picture]. Houston, TX: KUHT Film Productions, University of Houston.

Boring, E.G. (1967). Titchener's experimentalists. Journal of the History of the Behavioral Sciences, 3, 315–325.

Cattell, R.B. (1946). Description and measurement of personality. Yonkers-on-Hudson, N.Y.: World Book.

Cully, H.H. (1915). [Letter to B.S. Hurlbut, December 17]. Gordon W. Allport Papers, Harvard University Archives, Cambridge, Mass.

Demorest, A.P., & Siegel, P.F. (1996). Personal influences on professional work: An empirical case study of B.F. Skinner. Journal of Personality, 64, 243–261.

Elms, A.C. (1994). Uncovering lives: The uneasy alliance of biography and psychology. New York: Oxford University Press.

Erikson, E.H. (1968). Identity: Youth and crisis. New York: Norton.

Erikson, E.H. (1969). Gandhi's truth. New York: Norton.

Evans, R.I. (1971). Gordon Allport: The man and his ideas. New York: Dutton.

Eysenck, H.J. (1952). The scientific study of personality. New York: Macmillan.

Faber, M.D. (1970). Allport's visit with Freud. Psychoanalytic Review, 57, 60–64.

Faris, E. (1938). [Review of the book Personality: A psychological interpretation]. Annals of the American Academy of Political and Social Science, 198, 239–240.

Filter, R.O. (1921). An experimental study of character traits. Journal of Applied Psychology, 5, 297–317.

Freud, S. (1957). The taboo of virginity (Contributions to the psychology of love III). In J. Strachey (Ed. & Trans.), The standard edition of the complete psychological works of Sigmund Freud (Vol. 11, pp. 191–208). London: Hogarth Press. (Original work published 1918)

Furumoto, L. (1988). Shared knowledge: The Experimentalists, 1904–1929. In J.G. Morawski (Ed.), The rise of experimentation in American psychology (pp. 94–113). New Haven, Conn.: Yale University Press.

Goethe, J.W. von. (1914). Faust. Part I (ed. C.W. Eliot, trans. A. Swanwick). The Harvard classics (Vol. 19, Pt. 1). New York: P.F. Collier.

Katz, D., Johnson, B.T., & Nichols, D.R. (1998). Floyd Henry Allport: Founder of social psychology as a behavioral science. In G.A. Kimble & M. Wertheimer (Eds.), Portraits of pioneers in psychology (Vol. 3, pp. 120–142). Washington, D.C./Mahwah,

N.J.: American Psychological Association/ Erlbaum.

Lears, T.J.J. (1981). No place of grace: Antimodernism and the transformation of American culture, 1880–1920. New York: Pantheon Books.

Leonard, W.E. (1927). The locomotive-god. New York: Century.

Morey, L.C. (1987). Observations on the meeting between Allport and Freud. Psychoanalytic Review, 74, 135–139.

Nicholson, I.A.M. (1996). Moral projects & disciplinary practices: Gordon Allport and the development of American personality psychology. Unpublished doctoral dissertation, York University, North York, Ontario, Canada.

Nicholson, I.A.M. (1997a). Humanistic psychology and intellectual identity: The "open" system of Gordon Allport. Journal of Humanistic Psychology, 37(3), 61–79.

Nicholson, I.A.M. (1997b). To "correlate psychology and social ethics": Gordon Allport and the first course in American personality psychology. Journal of Personality, 65, 733–742.

Nicholson, I.A.M. (1998). Gordon Allport, character, and the "culture of personality," 1897–1937. History of Psychology, 1, 52–68.

Nicholson, I.A.M. (2000). "A coherent datum of perception": Gordon Allport, Floyd Allport, and the politics of "personality." Journal of the History of the Behavioral Sciences, 36, 463–470.

Nicholson, I.A.M. (2003). Inventing personality: Gordon Allport and the science of selfhood. Washington, D.C.: American Psychological Association.

Ogilvie, D.M. (1984). Personality and paradox: Gordon Allport's final contribution. Personality Forum, 2, 12–14.

Parker, J.D.A. (1991). In search of the person: The historical development of American personality psychology. Unpublished doctoral dissertation, York University, North York, Ontario, Canada.

Parkovnick, S. (2000). Contextualizing Floyd Allport's Social Psychology. Journal of the History of the Behavioral Sciences, 36, 429–441.

Runyan, W.M. (1982). Life histories and psychobiography: Explorations in theory and method. New York: Oxford University Press.

Schachter, F.F., Gilutz, G., Shore, E., & Adler, M. (1978). Sibling deidentification judged by mothers: Cross-validation and developmental studies. Child Development, 49, 543–546.

Schachter, F.F., Shore, E., Feldman-Rotman, S., Marquis, R.E., & Campbell, S. (1976). Sibling deidentification. Developmental Psychology, 12, 418–427.

Schultz, W.T. (2003). The prototypical scene: A method for generating psychobiographical hypotheses. In R. Josselson, A. Lieblich, & D.P. McAdams (Eds.), Up close and personal: The teaching and learning of narrative research (pp. 151–175). Washington, D.C.: American Psychological Association.

Shellow, S.M. (1932). How to develop your personality. New York: Harper.

Stern, W. (1900). Über Psychologie der individuellen Differenzen: Ideen zu einer differentiellen Psychologie. Leipzig: Barth.

Stern, W. (1938). General psychology from the personalistic standpoint (trans. H.D. Spoerl). New York: Macmillan. (Original work published 1935)

Stern, W. (1988). [Review of the book The interpretation of dreams] (trans. V. Rus). In N. Kiell (Ed.), Freud without hindsight: Reviews of his work, 1893–1939 (pp. 141–145). Madison, Conn.: International Universities Press. (Original work published 1901)

Sulloway, F.J. (1996). Born to rebel: Birth order, family dynamics, and revolutionary genius. New York: Pantheon.

White, R.W. (1959). Motivation reconsidered: The concept of competence. Psychological Review, 66, 297–333.

Winter, D.G. (1996). Gordon Allport and the legend of "Rinehart." Journal of Personality, 64, 263–273.

Winter, D.G. (1997). Allport's life and Allport's psychology. Journal of Personality, 65, 723–731.

Chapter 17

Kyle Arnold & George Atwood

Nietzsche's Madness

I am thy labyrinth.
(Nietzsche, in letter to Cosima Wagner)

At first glance, a psychobiographical study of Nietzsche might appear inherently naive. After all, weren't Nietzsche's writings partly responsible for what literary theorists call the "death of the author," the current tendency of many scholars to dismiss any connection between an author's subjectivity and his or her work? Doesn't this imply that Nietzsche's work also announced the "death" of psychobiography (Sarup, 1993)?

Perhaps. Yet as we so often find when examining Nietzsche's texts, these strands of thought are interwoven with their polar opposites. Nietzsche's apparent flight from the notion of all-determining authorship is coupled with a desire to reconnect text with author, to use the lived experience of authors in rescuing their texts from what he saw as the thin, unbreathable air of impersonal and bloodless intellectuality. Philosophical ideas, for instance, are envisaged as "hav[ing] always lived on the 'blood' of the philosopher, they always consumed his senses and even, if you will believe us, his 'heart.'" They are, Nietzsche says, "a kind of long concealed vampire in the background who begins with the senses and in the end is left with, and leaves, mere bones, mere clatter" (1887/1974, p. 333).

It was this sentiment, we think, that led Nietzsche to intellectually reverse the devitalizing process he saw in philosophy by famously suggesting that "[i]t has gradually become clear to me what every great philosophy has hitherto been: a confession on the part of its author and a kind of involuntary and unconscious memoir" (1886/1973, p. 37). Philosophy robs philosophers of their vital sensuality and emotion;

Nietzsche reads that sensuality and emotion back into philosophy.

There is a sense, then, in which a psychobiographical study of Nietzsche's thought rests upon Nietzschean foundations. Like Nietzsche, we want to see the philosopher in the philosophy, the life in the logic. However, the fulfillment of this desire is not our only purpose. For we also, like Nietzsche, think that a psychobiographical study of a conceptual system can have an added benefit, that of providing a psychological critique of something ordinarily seen only in logical terms. To be sure, a philosophy can never be fully appreciated from a psychobiographical perspective. It is more than just an expression of a philosopher's personal psychology. Yet whatever else one may believe a philosophy to be, it is surely the manifestation of a specific, temporally situated human subjectivity. This suggests that an interpretation of a philosopher's personality will always have something to say about his philosophy as well.

It must still be conceded, though, that an exclusively psychobiographical study of philosophy is inherently reductionistic. Insofar as it perceives and grasps Nietzscheanism from a narrow perspective, a psychobiographical reading of Nietzsche's work will locate all of its significance in a fairly restricted interpretive space. Such a reductionistic reading, we feel, is not intrinsically wrong, as long as one is careful not to claim that what is seen in its subject matter is all that can or should be seen. Its value is in drawing a caricature of what it interprets, which, by accentuating certain little-noticed features of its subject while ignoring others,

240

illuminates patterns that would otherwise be shrouded in darkness.

The patterns at issue here comprise the psychological conditions under which it was possible for Nietzsche's thought to occur. A psychobiographical study positions us to ask what sort of personality allowed—and constrained—Nietzsche to think the way he did. Although psychobiography has little to say about the putative rightness or wrongness of a philosophical system, it invites us to critically reflect on the relationship between our own subjectivities and the theories to which we adhere. More specifically, psychobiography invites those of us who feel drawn to Nietzsche's work to think through the possible affinities between Nietzsche's ideas and our own personalities, affinities that may often parallel those that existed between Nietzsche's work and Nietzsche himself. By uncovering the connections between Nietzsche's mind and his thought, we may well start to uncover the links between our own minds and Nietzsche's ideas. In doing so, we are given the chance to examine and thereby gain some mastery over the emotional prejudices that may compel us to dogmatically adhere to one theory rather than another (Atwood & Stolorow, 1993).

For us, these issues are especially salient. Because our study, like Nietzsche's work, reads the life of the philosopher into philosophy, it is essentially a Nietzschean project. As such, it too will be critiqued here. Any conclusion reached about Nietzsche's manner of thinking will implicate our own. Thus, by calling Nietzsche's philosophy into question, this study will also be indirectly questioning its own foundations.

In writing a psychobiographical study, perhaps one of the most pressing questions is *where to begin*. A psychobiographical study deals with a life, and a life exists in time. There is a temptation to "tell a good story," to turn the life into a drama, with birth as the opening scene and death as the curtain call. However, the linear narrative conducive to good history telling is not necessarily an ally of lucid psychological thinking. For the form of psychobiographical inquiry—a search for recurrent themes found through exploring analogies between different time periods—tends to break down the temporal structure of traditional, linear narrative. Through the as-

sertion of identity between different periods of time, time itself almost seems to be called into question.

However, there do appear to be some biographical periods that are more revealing than others, eras of a life when the forms of its inner logic are exposed especially clearly. When more opaque periods of a life are viewed in the light of these eras, they often become strikingly transparent. If early childhood is one such period, then one might assume that, contrary to the ideas articulated above, this project must submit to the traditional conventions of linear narrative.

In a psychobiographical study, though, the relationship between early childhood and later periods of time is not linear but circular, as patterns of childhood experience give sense to a life's later organizations, and the unveiling of these structures in turn clarifies the formative events of childhood (Atwood & Stolorow, 1993). Accordingly, a circular order of writing recommends itself, a writing that spirals from childhood to adulthood and adulthood back to childhood. This hermeneutic circle of writing itself intuitively suggests a starting point intimately connected to the strangely circular forms of Nietzsche's own subjectivity.

These circular patterns show themselves in Nietzsche's own dizzyingly circular style of writing, a style present in all his works, from his youthful writings depicting his childhood to the intricate texts he produced near the end of his philosophical career. Often these circles involve time. Derrida (1982/1985), reading Nietzsche's late autobiography *Ecce Homo* (1908/1967), notes that Nietzsche writes "on credit," that, when still virtually unknown, Nietzsche writes as the great philosopher that he hopes to be recognized as by a future audience. Yet Nietzsche realizes that this audience will only exist after his lifetime. As an empirical person, then, he will never be able to fully realize the identity he assumes. The referent of Nietzsche's signature, Derrida argues, is riven at its core, never quite one with itself.

A nearly identical structure is perceptible in another autobiography Nietzsche wrote much earlier, at the age of thirteen. Here, Nietzsche recounts the experiences of his early family life and schooling. The style of the whole of this work is perhaps best expressed in its first sentence: "If one is an adult, one usually only remembers the most distinguishing events of his childhood" (1858/1924, p. 1).[1]

Hidden within this assertion lies a complicated pattern of thought. Nietzsche, writing this autobiography while still a boy, frames the narrative within the perspective of a wise adult, a voice experienced and worldly enough—and pedantic enough—to utter sweeping generalizations about adulthood.

The intent of that adult speaker seems almost self-exculpatory. The didactic surface of the sentence covers over a deficiency of the narrative: an inability of the narrator to recall any but the "most distinguishing events." Although Nietzsche might easily have attributed this to a child's inevitably imperfect memory, he instead portrays it as a consequence of being an "adult"—apparently, the narrator. One wonders just who is speaking here.

Leaving aside such questions for the moment, we can see that the temporal structure this sentence articulates is an odd, circular one. Nietzsche the child clothes himself in the personality of an adult and from this imagined position reflects back on his own childhood. Temporally, the present is looking through the future back to the past.

The autobiography's title—*Out of My Life* (*Aus meinem Leben*)—further elaborates this pattern. Borrowed from the title of Goethe's autobiography, the phrase amplifies the presence of a wise adult subjectivity within the text. The meaning of the title also conveys one result of Nietzsche's adoption of an adult persona. By viewing his life from the distant future rather than from the present, he removes himself from it. It is as though the future is a window placed between Nietzsche and the present.

The dual consciousness of child and adult is present throughout the text, as Nietzsche continually oscillates between the two viewpoints. The next sentence is: "Although I am still not an adult and have hardly left the years of childhood and boyhood behind me, there is much that has disappeared from my memory, and the few things which I can remember are probably only due to tradition" (1858/1924, p. 1). Here Nietzsche retreats from the adult identity. He denies

that he is an adult, and buttresses this denial with a suggestion of immaturity and perhaps inadequacy: "have hardly left the years of childhood . . . behind me." Rather than being explained away as a typical result of adulthood, Nietzsche's memory loss is now portrayed as in tension with his young age. It is as though he realizes here that the explanation he has given for his memory loss—old age—is wrong, but he is confused by this wrongness.

Similar moments of tension appear throughout the autobiography, as the perspectives of the young Nietzsche and the elderly, wise adult conflict with and subvert each other. Other passages spoken with the wise adult's voice include, for example:

> "Indeed it is always useful to contemplate the gradual development (also in sense of education) of the intellect and heart, and with this also: the overall guidance of God." (1858/1924, p. 8)
> "The spirit of imitation is especially marked in children; they think of all the things being easier, but only those things that they particularly like." (p. 13)
> "Yes, having true friends is always something very noble and elevated, and God has significantly brightened our lives by giving us companions striving with us for the same aim." (p. 14)
> "It is peculiar that, if we are somewhat advanced and have climbed to a higher step, we try to perceive our character as being somewhat more matured." (p. 14)

The adult voice is mainly audible in its utterance of sweeping generalizations inferred from the young Nietzsche's experiences. Although these generalizations are derived from Nietzsche's life, they distance him from that life. Rather than experiencing his past from the standpoint of his own particular boyhood, Nietzsche finds ways to turn his concrete experiences into instances of abstract, universal law. The wise adult subjectivity mediates the relationship between Nietzsche and his life.

Many of Nietzsche's generalizations have a preachy quality to them. They seem pretentious and inflated. Some would attribute Nietzsche's grandiloquence to the religious atmosphere in which he was raised. His father, Ludwig, was a zealous Protestant clergyman in a long line of Protestant clergymen. His mother and his other female relatives were also rigidly religious (Hayman, 1980). In Alice Miller's interesting but cursory psychological study of Nietzsche (Miller, 1990), Nietzsche's language is, for the most part, explained away in precisely this fashion. Yet, such an explanation only scratches the surface. Nietzsche's religious upbringing was, no doubt, the general formative context out of which his religious language emerged, but the more specific features of this language—the tangled, circular movements of thought and feeling which play within it—call for more elucidation.

The language of Nietzsche's later writings makes this need especially pressing. When viewed in light of the writing style of Nietzsche's later work *Thus Spoke Zarathustra* (1892/1966), for instance, the wise, sermonic adult voice of Nietzsche's childhood autobiography assumes a new, ominous significance.

In *Thus Spoke Zarathustra*, Nietzsche tells the parabolic story of a wandering holy man, a prophet of sorts who preaches a new, anti-establishment doctrine. This doctrine celebrates the body and the will, exhorting man to transcend himself and thereby become the "overman," a superior being. Zarathustra is well known for its bombastic style:

> "Verily, a strong wind is Zarathustra for all those who are low; and this counsel he gives to all his enemies and all who spit and spew: 'Beware of spitting against the wind!'" (1892/1966, p. 99)
> "But let me reveal my heart to you entirely, my friends: if there were no gods, how could I endure not to be a god! Hence there are no gods." (p. 86)

Whereas in *Out of My Life* the adult voice is somewhat hidden and restrained, in *Zarathustra* it bursts forth with disturbing power and lack of control. *Out of My Life*'s frequent moments of identification with an inflated, wise personality, strange though they appear, might still be viewed as the ordinary role-playing of a thirteen-year-old boy. However, while reading *Zarathustra*,

we begin to feel that we are in the presence of madness.

And so, the imagery of Zarathustra gives our inquiry clearer direction. The protagonist's identity—that of a holy man—recalls Nietzsche's father, who was his first experience of a preacher and who therefore provided him with the prototypical example of that role. Perhaps a clearer understanding of Nietzsche's relationship with his father will allow a more penetrating interpretation of both Zarathustra and the early sermonic voice.

Out of My Life contains several striking passages about Nietzsche's father. The first of these is the following:

> My father was the preacher of this town, and also responsible for the neighboring towns of Michliz and Bothfield. He represented the perfect image of a rural clergyman. Talented in regards of mind and temper, decorated with all the virtues of a Christian, he had a calm, simple but happy life and he was respected by all the people who knew him. His good manners and his cheerful mind brightened many of the parties he was invited to and made him popular anywhere he went, at the first moment. His leisure time he filled with the fine arts and sciences and especially with music. He was particularly skilled in playing piano, especially concerning the free improvisations. . . . (1858/1924, pp. 8–9)

The way in which Nietzsche begins this description—with an account of his father's geographical responsibilities—gives the impression that Ludwig is seen as a kind of benevolent lord. The feeling of power we sense here flows into an image of Ludwig as cultured, virtuous, and popular.

It is apparent that Nietzsche is picturing his father as a kind of ideal figure, "the perfect image of a clergyman." Yet Nietzsche's memories of this figure were not only brightened by the warm and comfortable feelings this passage evokes, but also overshadowed by what Nietzsche depicts as the "dark clouds" of overwhelming pain and loss. These clouds began to gather in the autumn of 1848, when Ludwig Nietzsche fell ill with a disease diagnosed as "softening of the brain"

(Hayman, 1980). Nietzsche himself, who was four years old at the time, describes this period as follows:

> It was in September 1848 when my beloved father became very ill due to a tumble. However, we and he consoled ourselves with the hope of a quick recovery. . . . My beloved father had to bear terrible pain, but the illness did not want to lessen, indeed, it was growing day by day. Finally even his eyesight went out, and it was in eternal darkness that he had to endure the rest of his sufferings. His state of illness lasted until July 1849, then the day of deliverance approached. On the 26th of July he fell into a deep sleep, waking up only occasionally. His last words were: "Franzschen [his wife]-Franzschen-come-mother-listen-listen-oh-God." Then he died gently and blessedly on July 27th, 1849. When I woke up this morning, I heard loud crying and sobbing around me. My dear mother entered the room with tears in her eyes and cried plaintively: "Oh God, my good Ludwig is dead." Although I was still very young and inexperienced, I nevertheless had some concept of death; the thought about being separated forever from the beloved father moved me deeply and I cried bitterly. The following days passed in tears and in preparation for the burial. Oh God! I became a fatherless orphan and my dearest mother became a widow! (1858/1924, pp. 11–12)

The psychic devastation of Nietzsche and his family is self-evident. Even when this passage is taken by itself, its length, detail, and emotional tone show that the event it recounts had a shattering impact on Nietzsche's childhood world. Moreover, Nietzsche's anguish at "being separated forever from the beloved father," especially when juxtaposed with a later statement that "[i]t is a strange peculiarity of the human heart, that after the loss of a loved one, instead of making efforts to forget the person, we visualize that person as often as possible in our soul" (1858/1924, p. 22), shows a deep emotional connection to the father, a tie that apparently made it necessary for Nietzsche to constantly hold an image of his father before his mind's eye. By means of this visualization, Nietzsche was able

to retain a semblance of his former relationship and thereby avert the dreaded experience of total and final separation from his beloved father.

His depiction of his father's funeral elaborates this web of painful emotions:

> On August 2nd the mortal cover of my beloved father was entrusted to the womb of the earth. At one o'clock the ceremony began, accompanied by the ringing of bells. Oh, this dull sound will never disappear from my ears, I will never forget the dark thunderous melody of the song: "Jesu, my confidence." The sound of the organ was roaring throughout the atrium of the church. Then the coffin lowered down into the ground, and the dull words resounded, and he, our beloved father, has gone away from all of us mourners. The earth has lost a believing soul, the heaven received a watching soul. (1858/1924, pp. 11–12)

This scene is pervaded by an uncanny, almost mystical feel. The tolling of the bells, the "resounding" of the words, the reference to "our" (rather than "my") beloved father, convey the atmosphere of an arcane rite. A dream Nietzsche had at this time possesses a similar emotional texture:

> I dreamt that I would hear the same organ-sound as the one at the burial. While I was looking for the reason for this, suddenly a grave opens and my father, dressed in his shroud, climbs out of it. He rushes into the church and after a short while he returns with a little child in his arms. The grave opens, he enters, and the cover sinks down again on the opening. Immediately the thunderous sound of the organ stops, and I wake up. (1858/1924, p. 12)

When understood in the context of the last sentence of Nietzsche's account of his father's funeral—"the heavens received a watching soul"—the dream reveals a sense that the father, though dead, is still lurking somewhere about. In the funeral passage, he is portrayed as an optical presence, a presumably benevolent figure looking down upon the world—and, more important, Nietzsche—from the afterworld. However, in the dream, he is experienced as a frightening, almost demonic entity. This is not the benevolent and containing figure we encountered before, but an inhuman, grasping creature that rips a child from its rightful place. One even senses a feeling of rupture, of a tear in the fabric of reality, and the horror of witnessing a dreadful force wrenching a defenseless child out of the world.

There is also a striking temporal circularity evident in the dream. In a sense, the past, the dead father, comes to claim the future, the child. Thus, when the dead father newly put into the grave clutches the young child recently emergent from the womb and pulls the child downward into his lair, he creates a ring or loop in the structure of time that precludes linear progression. The living of the newly dead causes the death of the newly living.

This circle is not only implied by the dream but also embodied in its visual and emotional sequence. The father leaves the grave and returns, just as the tension rises and then falls.

The world of Nietzsche's dream, with its circularity and downward pull, feels less like a human world than a dark and inhuman one, a curved space surrounding a black hole in being. Many of Nietzsche's later writings seem to struggle against the pull of the grave, the pull of gravity. Often he appears to be writing against death, as in *The Antichrist* (1895/1968):

> The Christian conception of God . . . is one of the most corrupt conceptions of God arrived at on earth. . . . God degenerated to the contradiction of life, instead of being its transfiguration and eternal Yes! In God a declaration of hostility towards life, nature, the will to life! In God nothingness deified, the will to nothingness sanctified. . . . (p. 140)

And "If one shifts the centre of gravity of life out of life into the 'Beyond'—into nothingness—one has deprived life as such of its center of gravity" (p. 167).

Ludwig Nietzsche's death not only sheds light on his son's later anxious opposition to what he saw as death-deifying ideas but also seems to hint at possible interpretations of Nietzsche's antipathy toward specifically Christian ideas. From a

Nietzschean perspective, Christianity is a religion of death, which, by placing life's goal in the afterlife, causes an impoverishment of life itself. An analogy might be seen here to Ludwig's death—Nietzsche's personal life, as his autobiography makes clear, became dramatically impoverished after his father's journey into the Beyond.

However, this analogy does not, by itself, do full justice to the labyrinthine complexity of the relationship between Ludwig Nietzsche's death and Friedrich's attacks on Christianity. The psychological intricacy of the network of symbolic connections linking the two is particularly evident in *Beyond Good and Evil* (1886/1973), a work targeting, among other things, the Christian dichotomy of good and evil. Nietzsche argues that this doublet should be questioned, transcended, and replaced with a healthier and more instrumentally sound value system. He lays out the project as follows:

> [W]hither must we direct our hopes? Towards new philosophers, . . . towards spirits strong and original enough to make a start on antithetical evaluations and to revalue and reverse "eternal values," towards heralds and forerunners, towards men of the future. . . . It is the image of such leaders which hovers before our eyes—may I say that aloud, you free spirits? . . . a revaluation of values under whose novel pressure and hammer a conscience would be steeled, a heart transformed to brass, so that it might endure the weight of such a responsibility. . . . [T]hese are our proper cares and concerns, do you know that, you free spirits? (pp. 126–127)

Despite Nietzsche's invective against Christian morality, his "revaluation of all values" is portrayed here as a moral ideal that "free spirits" must struggle to achieve. These free spirits seem like members of an elite moral order, poised to seize control of the world from a decadent religious leadership. Nietzsche's vision, then, does not eliminate the morality of good and evil but reinstates it on a new level. Stylistically, the good-and-evil dichotomy itself becomes evil, in contrast to the revaluation of all values, the good. Nietzsche's attempt to transcend the good/evil opposition undermines itself, returning him to the type of morality from which he is trying to escape.

The self-undermining dynamic we see above is a direct result of the ambivalence[2] present in the quoted passage. Although Nietzsche speaks against Christianity, he speaks like a Christian.

Perhaps ambivalence is one source of his anxiety. In *The Antichrist* (1895/1968), Nietzsche's final polemic against Christianity, this ambivalence becomes particularly evident during his discussions of Christ: "[I]n reality there has only been one Christian, and he died on the Cross. The 'Evangel' died on the Cross. What was called 'Evangel' from this moment onwards was already the opposite of what he had lived: 'bad tidings,' a dysangel" (p. 163). In this passage, Nietzsche unexpectedly sympathizes with Christ. He presents Christ as a tragic figure whose lived truth was distorted and put to evil ends. Subsequent "Christians" are heretics who pervert the true life of Christ.

> In Paul was embodied the antithetical type to the "bringer of glad tidings," the genius of hatred, of the vision of hatred, of the inexorable logic of hatred. What did this dysangelist not sacrifice to his hatred! The redeemer above all: he nailed him to his Cross. That life, the example, the teaching, the death, the meaning and the right of the entire Gospel—nothing was left once this hate-obsessed false-coiner had grasped what loan he could make use of. Not the reality, not the historical truth! (p. 166)

Paul misrepresented Christ's truth to further his own morally bankrupt agenda. In an ironic reversal, though, Nietzsche perverts the meaning of *Paul's* life by changing his title from "evangelist" to "dysangelist." After Christ's death, Paul perverts his life, and Paul's life is in turn perverted by Nietzsche long after his death.

Although here Nietzsche appears to be more the master of his circularity than he is in the passages we have already examined, he cannot ever truly encompass it. By defending Christ against the false "Christians," Nietzsche undermines his own critique of Christianity. When he portrays Christ as the antithesis of the Christian's false Christ-image, Nietzsche tacitly falls into a form of Christianity, albeit a bizarre one.

For in arguing that Paul falsified the lived truth of Christ, Nietzsche presents himself as one who knows the lived truth of Christ. He thereby places himself in a special, privileged role—that of the bearer of the true knowledge of what "to be a Christian" really should mean. Is Nietzsche, then, the true Evangelist, speaker of the true Gospel? Is he the "true" Christian?

Whether or not Nietzsche's philosophical stance here is truly contradictory, his psychological position is riddled with ambivalence and circularity. Is his role to be the defender of Christianity, or its critic? Nietzsche critiques Christianity because it is not Christianity—because, like his own argument, it differs with itself.

But what does all this have to do with the death of Nietzsche's father? For starters, as biographers (Hayman, Plestch, Forster-Nietzsche) make clear, the Nietzsche family was intensely religious and had been for many generations. Nietzsche's sister Elizabeth Forster-Nietzsche (1912) and Hayman (1980) describe how the Nietzsche family envisaged the young Fritz as a future clergyman who would follow in the footsteps of his ancestors. One may conjecture that, for the Nietzsche family, the presence of a future clergyman helped mitigate the pain brought about by the absence of the deceased one.

When pictured as a part of this family system, the wise sermonic voice narrating so much of Nietzsche's childhood autobiography takes on new significance. The preachy, moralizing tone of that voice indicates that it is the voice of Nietzsche's "own" intersubjectively imagined future identity—a pastor. By looking through the future back to the past, Nietzsche was viewing his life from the distant perspective of that imagined future identity. The autobiography's frequent invocation of God lends support to this interpretation and also reveals something of what Christianity meant to the young Nietzsche: "During this . . . misfortune God in heaven was our sole consolation and protection" (1858/1924, p. 6). "The celestial father knows how much I cried in that time" (p. 22). "Up to now I have already experienced such various things, joyful and sad things, cheerful and mournful things, but through all of them God guided me securely like a father is guiding his weak little child" (p. 32). Throughout Nietzsche's account of his past, God is watching over him. Not only was God felt to be responsible for the more pleasant aspects of Nietzsche's life, such as his friends, but also for his ability to survive pain and suffering. Indeed, God held the position of an emotional "center of gravity" in Nietzsche's life, a force giving him the stability to hold fast against the power of painful events.

The imagery in these passages is suggestive. There is a recurrent metaphor of God-as-father. The sense of being watched over by a "celestial father" also recalls Nietzsche's account of his father's funeral, where, after calling Ludwig Nietzsche "our" father, rather than "my" father, Nietzsche says that "the earth has lost a believing soul, the heaven received a watching soul" (1858/1924, p. 6).

Although Nietzsche does not explicitly say "God is my dead father," such an identity is strongly implied, as Hayman (1980) also notes. Nietzsche felt that God was a celestial father for him, giving him love, protection, and comfort in the aftermath of his earthly father's death. Nietzsche's later claim that Christianity moves life's "center of gravity" into the Beyond can be seen as a mirror image of this early experience, reflecting the shift of his own emotional center of gravity from his living father to an otherworldly Father-God.

For a five-year-old boy, one with what Nietzsche himself called the "idealizing glance" of youth (Forster-Nietzsche, 1912), one who saw his father as a powerful religious figure, one whose father had passed away, it was easy, and psychically valuable, to transform a mortal, temporal father into an immortal, eternal presence able to watch over and protect the "little child" forever.

The above notion brings an important psychological contradiction into focus. Is Nietzsche the "little child" who requires constant protection by an omnipotent otherworldly presence, or is he the worldly, wise clergyman who confidently looks back on his past experiences?

No doubt one might want to resolve this conflict by arguing that it is not the future Nietzsche who is the little child, but only the past Nietzsche, who is led through life to his future identity. Yet such an argument would do violence to the elegant circularity of time patterning Nietzsche's subjective universe. Nietzsche is the little child and the future clergyman, both the past and the future. It is only the present's meaning that is deferred, strewn away from the now, backward and forward in time.

It should be noted, however, that though such psychic entanglements are suggestive, they do not by themselves seem definitively prophetic of the later insanity to which Nietzsche would fall prey. If we examine Nietzsche's related childhood conduct, however, what we find is downright odd:

"He had a very pious, tender temperament and even as a child reflected upon matters with which other boys his age do not concern themselves. . . . He never acted without reflection, and when he did something, he always had a particular, well-grounded reason." (Pinder, quoted in Gilman & Parent, 1987, pp. 4–5)

"The other boys [in school] teased him and called him 'the little minister.' . . . One day the boys coming out of school were caught in a heavy rainstorm. Looking down the Priestergasse, Franziska [N's mother] saw the others running as fast as they could, while Fritz was walking unhurriedly and bareheaded, using his cap and his handkerchief to protect his slate from the rain. She shouted at him, signaling him to hurry. His answer was inaudible, and when he arrived, soaked to the skin, he explained that according to the rules, boys going home from school must not run or jump but proceed in a quiet, orderly fashion." (Hayman, 1980, p. 20)

"A boy who was in the third or fourth forms with him later testified that his classmates had almost deified him. 'For there was something extraordinary in his voice and his tone, as there was in his choice of expressions, that made him quite different from other boys his age. . . . According to one boy, 'He looked at you in a way that made the words stick in your throat.'" (p. 25)

Despite its strangeness, the young Nietzsche's stilted conduct becomes intelligible when placed in the context of his pastorial ambitions. The ornate manner of speaking, the meticulous, abject adherence to rules, the commitment to act only after considered reflection, have the appearance of caricatures of the behavior of a clergyman. It is clear, accordingly, that Nietzsche did not merely temporarily assume the identity of a clergyman while writing his childhood autobiography. Rather, this identity permeated his life, so much so that it was instrumental not only in shaping his own experience and conduct but also in determining his classmates' perceptions of him.

Nevertheless, whatever Nietzsche liked to imagine that he was, whatever his family wanted him to be and become, he was a child, not a clergyman. We stress this fact firstly because the biographical reconstruction of Nietzsche's childhood by friends and idolizers tends to obscure it. Moreover, it can be used to deduce a critical intersubjective aspect of Nietzsche's childhood. For if a boy is to imitate a clergyman, he must have a clergyman to imitate. There was only one clergyman with whom Nietzsche had any sort of close experience so early in his childhood. That clergyman was his father.

We do not mean to imply that the father Nietzsche imitated was exclusively the product of Nietzsche's historical father. After all, in *Out of My Life*, Nietzsche claims that his recollections of his father may owe more to family "tradition" than to his own encounters with his father. This possibility underscores the intersubjective character of the artificial identity Nietzsche assumed. Previously, we conjectured that the grief of Nietzsche's family was assuaged by the presence of a future clergyman who would replace the one who was lost. We would further suggest that underlying this dynamic was a family desire to remake Nietzsche into his deceased father, thus filling the emotional void left after Ludwig Nietzsche's death. Nietzsche's inner father may have corresponded to a piece of his mother's psychology, crystallizing her idealized memories of her husband and compensating for her inability to accept his death. If so, it may be said that Nietzsche's way of handling the loss of his father occurred in the shadow of tragic maternal abandonment.[3]

Banal as these conclusions might seem to some—Nietzsche admirers might prefer an interpretation like Jung's (1934–1939/1998), that

Nietzsche's inflated voice represented an otherworldly archetype that spoke through him—they still comprise the best possible explanation for the gestalt of meaningful connections we have uncovered. And in his later (1908/1967) autobiography *Ecce Homo*, Nietzsche includes many passages indicating a powerful identification with his dead father:

> My father died at the age of thirty-six: he was delicate, kind, and morbid, as a being that is destined merely to pass by—more a gracious memory of life than life itself. In the same year in which his life went downward, mine, too, went downward: at thirty-six, I reached the lowest point of my vitality—I still lived, but without being able to see three steps ahead. Then—it was 1879—I retired from my professorship at Basel, spent the summer in St. Moritz like a shadow, and the next winter, than which not one in my life has been poorer in sunshine, in Naumburg as a shadow. (p. 222)

Thirty years after his father's death, Nietzsche still experienced this loss as a menacing force. His identification with the dead father was so profound that he believed his decline in vitality at age thirty-six to be a recapitulation of his father's death.

Other passages expressing Nietzsche's identification with the phantom father appear elsewhere in the same work: "The good fortune of my existence, its uniqueness perhaps, lies in its fatality: I am, to express it in the form of a riddle, already dead as my father, while as my mother I am still living and becoming old" (p. 222). "At another point as well, I am merely my father once more, and, as it were, his continued life after an all-too-early death" (p. 228). The last quotation provides an apt synopsis of what must have happened to Nietzsche when his father died. After Ludwig Nietzsche's death, his son, rather than living his own selfhood, adopted his father's personality. Not only did he try to prolong his father's life by keeping Ludwig's image in his mind's eye, but he also attempted to become that image. One might say that Nietzsche sacrificed himself so that his father would live on.

The critical reader might point out that although this conclusion is consistent with a substantial body of evidence, it constitutes a partial reconstruction of emotional experiences to which we have no direct access. Such a construct can only be justified by its power to reveal networks of meaningful connections between phenomena that would otherwise appear incoherent.

Keeping the whole of the interpretation in mind, then, let us return to the scene of Nietzsche's childhood dream:

I dreamt that I would hear the same organ-sound as the one at the burial. While I was looking for the reason for this, suddenly a grave opened and my father, dressed in his shroud, climbs out of it. He rushes into the church and after a short while he returns with a little child in his arms. The grave opens, he enters, and the cover sinks down again on the opening. Immediately the thunderous sound of the organ stops, and I wake up. (1858/1924, p. 12)

Before, the analysis of this dream was limited to general characteristics such as mood and temporal structure. Now we are equipped to tease out its many subjective meanings, and through doing so begin to unravel the central knot in which Nietzsche was entangled. The first of these meanings shows itself immediately: the little child is Nietzsche himself.

Taken as a whole, the dream reveals itself to be a vivid metaphor for the childhood experiences we have reconstructed. The image of the father takes possession of the young Nietzsche, pulling him backward, downward, to live in a perpetual state of psychic death, clutched in the arms of a corpse, imprisoned in a coffinlike false identity. His psyche is possessed by an alien being, a once-nourishing relationship withers and is darkened into a macabre perversion of what had been before.[4]

No doubt this metaphor does not capture all that Nietzsche experienced of his father posthumously; he still had the fond memories and warm feelings depicted in *Out of My Life*. However, for the moment, it is the dark underbelly of the father imago on which we focus. Now that we are aware of this strange "spirit of gravity" (to use a phrase of Nietzsche's) that was forever pulling Nietzsche downward and away from life, the emotional meanings encoded in his arguments against Christianity are easier to decipher. For example:

The Christian conception of God . . . is one of the most corrupt conceptions of God arrived at on earth. . . . God degenerated to the contradiction of life, instead of being its transfiguration and eternal Yes! In God a declaration of hostility towards life, nature, the will to life! . . . In God nothingness deified, the will to nothingness sanctified! (1895/1968, p. 140)

The form of the philosophical event described here is identical to the psychological process that the metaphor of the dream expresses. This process is an emotional perversion, a transvaluation whereby what was once life-sustaining and life-affirming degenerates into a deathlike, nihilating force. This transvaluation is precisely what occurred after Nietzsche's father died. As this passage demonstrates, for Nietzsche, Christian doctrines held a subjective meaning analogous to that of his father's death—the terrible loss of an admired, affirmative presence is followed by psychic death, brought on by a morbid transformation of this presence. A similar pattern shows up in another passage previously quoted:

[I]n reality there has been only one Christian, and he died on the Cross. The 'Evangel' died on the Cross. What was called 'Evangel' from this moment onwards was already the opposite of what he had lived: 'bad tidings,' a dysangel. (1895/1968, p. 163)

The ambivalence pervading Nietzsche's attitude toward Christ becomes clearer now. Just as Christ was misrepresented after his death, Nietzsche's beloved father died and became transvaluated into his antithesis. Not only that, but Nietzsche himself, like Christ, was warped into a shape not his own. These two emotional meanings collide and converge: The symbol of Christ captures both the father identity and the son who was possessed by that identity. Christ is therefore both good and evil, both truth and lie.

This paradoxical, circular structure of father and son represents the effect Nietzsche's attempt to assume his father's identity had on his self-experience. He is not quite one, yet not quite two. The father identity and the son exist in a tension or paradox that incessantly spins out the vicious circles we have seen.

Christianity as a whole also holds these emotional meanings, as it is, to Nietzsche, an extension of Paul's misrepresentations—psychologically, an extension of the dysangel, the false identity. Nietzsche's late rejection of Christian doctrines seems to be a concrete act of rebellion against that personal dysangel. The rebellion is paradoxical, however, because of the presence of the father identity. The son rebels against the father, but the son is the father. Therefore, in trying to destroy the father, he is also attempting to destroy himself. If he wins, he loses. This version of the father–son paradox is also elaborated in Nietzsche's assault on Christian morality, in which, as we noted above, an anti-Christian content is undermined by a sermonic discursive style:

[W]hither must we direct our hopes? Towards new philosophers, ... towards spirits strong and original enough to make a start on antithetical evaluations and to revalue and reverse "eternal values," towards heralds and forerunners, towards men of the future. ... It is the image of such leaders which hovers before our eyes—may I say that aloud, you free spirits? ... [A] revaluation of values under whose novel pressure and hammer a conscience would be steeled, a heart transformed to brass, so that it might endure the weight of such a responsibility. ... [T]hese are our proper cares and concerns, do you know that, you free spirits? (1886/1973, pp. 126–127)

If we continue to read "Christianity" as a symbolic bearer of the cluster of emotional themes organized around the false father-identity, these "free spirits" able to "reverse eternal values" appear as constructions of an ideal self, free from entanglement in the father–son knot. However, as we pointed out above, this construction reinstates Christian values on a new level. Even if Nietzsche were able to eliminate the morality of the Father, he would ironically carry the essence of this morality with him into the world dispossessed of it.

One can envision an endless spiral here: The good free spirits destroy the morality of good and evil. To do so they must destroy their own destruction of the morality of good and evil, based as it is on the evil morality of good and evil. But to do so would be another act of good against the good-and-evil morality; therefore, they must destroy their destruction of their destruction ...

Son (father) destroys Father (son). To do so he/they must destroy his/their own destruction of the Father (son), based as it is on the Son (father), who is the same (and also different) as the Father (son). But to do so would be another act of the Son (father) against the Father (son), who is the same (and also different), therefore he/they must destroy their destruction of their destruction ...

A superficial solution to this sort of paradox can be found in Nietzsche's interest in the psychology of knowledge (Atwood & Stolorow, 1993), the psychobiographical study of conceptual systems. When Nietzsche suggests that philosophy is "a kind of long concealed vampire in the background who begins with the senses and in the end is left with, and leaves, mere bones, mere clatter" (1887/1974, p. 333), he appears to portray it as very much like the dysangel, the false identity. Like Nietzsche's artificial father-self, which in the childhood autobiography distanced him from his lived experiences by turning those experiences into mere instances of abstract, universal laws, philosophy allegedly distances the philosopher from his own experience through a process of abstraction that leaves "mere bones, mere clatter." By reversing this process of abstraction through reconnecting the life of a philosopher to her philosophical ideas, Nietzsche repairs the breach between father-self and child-self. The psychology of knowledge allows the child-self to reappropriate the thinking stolen from him in service of the dysangelic father-self, while at the same time revitalizing that inauthentic father-self by infusing him with the life-blood of the authentic emotions locked within the child-self.

A similar set of motives is present, we think, in the famous Nietzschian "geneological" study, which, among other things, critiques entrenched modes of understanding the world by showing that they are, in part, historical consequences and political tools of societal power relations. Reconnecting an abstract truth to its social origins, like tracing it to its personal origins, unites detached thought and lived history. Neither the genealogical nor the psychological study of knowledge, though, truly unites father-self and son-self, as both types of research operate only on an abstract, intellectual plane. They offered Nietzsche an illusory sense of unity, while forcing him further into the realm of the disconnected father-self.

It was this kind of tangled, self-defeating way of being, we want to suggest, that eventually led to Nietzsche's mental breakdown.[5] This breakdown—from which Nietzsche never recovered—occurred in 1889, when Nietzsche fell to pieces after seeing a cab driver whip a horse violently. Nietzsche ran to the animal and, wrapping his arms around its neck, fell to the ground sobbing (Hayman, 1980). Elements of the flood of delusional material that appeared during the period of the breakdown—already visible in *Ecce Homo*—can be found in several

Figure 17.1. Nietzsche. (Time Life Pictures/ Getty Images)

short letters written to friends in December 1888 (Ludovici, 1985):

[To August Strindberg]
Dear Sir:
You will hear from me shortly about your short story—it goes off like a gunshot. I have appointed a meeting day of monarchs in Rome. I shall order . . . to be shot. Au revoir! For we shall surely see each other again. On one condition only: let us divorce.
Nietzsche Caesar

To August Strindberg]
Mr. Strindberg:
Alas! . . . no more! Let us divorce!
"The Crucified."

[To Meta von Salis]
The world is transfigured, for God is on the earth. Do you not see how all the heavens are rejoicing? I have just seized possession of my kingdom, am throwing the pope into prison, and having Wilhelm, Bismarck, and Stocker shot.
"The Crucified."

[To Georg Brandes]
To the Friend Georg
Having been discovered by you no trick was necessary for the others to find me. The difficulty is now to get rid of me.
THE CRUCIFIED

The Christ identification implicit in several of the passages we examined is now fully evident. Nietzsche's use of the term "The Crucified" rather than simply "Christ" highlights an image of death and pain. Emotionally, the passages embody powerful and heterogeneous feelings. The first seems an expression of playful euphoria. The fourth looks almost like a message to a fellow conspirator.

This sort of emotional turbulence was a dominant characteristic of Nietzsche's madness. To those who took care of him after the breakdown—mainly his mother and sanitarium attendants—Nietzsche was a handful. While out walking, he often would grin merrily at various strangers, eliciting a scolding from his mother. He would at random moments remove his clothes and lie down in public places (once he tried to bathe in a puddle). He would fly into rages. He would smash windows. He would try to strike dogs and people. He would read aloud, making "loud barking or rumbling noises." He would repeat various phrases incessantly, such as "I am dead because I am stupid," "I am stupid because I am dead," "I have a fine feeling for things," and "I do not like horses" (Hayman, 1980).

These antics and others gave some observers, such as Nietzsche's friend Peter Gast, the impression that they were just that—antics (Hayman, 1980). Nietzsche's propensity for play-acting and clowning—well known to his circle of friends—makes this idea hard to shake off. As Hayman points out, though, the line between inspired clowning and insanity becomes difficult to draw at this time (cf. Sass 1992). It may be that Nietzsche ceased to play the buffoon and the buffoon began to play Nietzsche.

The figure of the clown, the buffoon, appears as a sinister and dangerous in Nietzsche's *Thus Spoke Zarathustra*, emerging at carnivalesque moments that sometimes prefigure his later mental breakdown. During an early, particularly disturbing scene, for instance, Zarathustra begins to give a sermon in a public square. A crowd is gathering round, not to listen to Zarathustra but to watch a tightrope walker scheduled to perform. Zarathustra gives his speech, feeling misunderstood by the crowd. Suddenly a jester runs across the tightrope and leaps over the tightrope walker, who drops his pole and plummets to the ground. The crowd disperses, and the tightrope walker lies dying. In a bizarre interaction, Zarathustra comforts the tightrope walker by informing him that as there is no eternal soul and no afterlife, he need not fear Hell.

The scene is rich with meaning and clearly expresses the self-defeating circularity of Nietzsche's subjectivity. It begins with an account of Zarathustra's arrival:

> When Zarathustra came into the next town, which lies on the edge of the forest, he found many people gathered together in the market place; for it had been promised that there would be a tightrope-walker. (1892/1966, p. 12)

Nietzsche's use of the character "Zarathustra" as a mouthpiece for his own doctrine is revealing. As Jung (1934–1939/1998) points out, there is a clear distinction between Nietzsche and Zarathustra—Zarathustra is not Nietzsche himself, but another figure. Yet, both Zarathustra's voice and his ideas are unquestionably those of Nietzsche. Again, we have a personality who is both one, and two.

Zarathustra's manner of relating to other human beings is tragic. Isolated for years, Zarathustra finally decides to return to human society but can only do so as a prophet—a provider of wisdom and dogma, not a participant in a reciprocal human relationship. Moreover, his audience is not there to listen to his speeches—Zarathustra is merely a temporary substitute for the real entertainment, the tightrope walker. He is a sideshow.

His speech is chiefly an exposition of the doctrine of the "Overman," an ideal of man's self-transcendence:

> I teach you the overman. Man is something that shall be overcome. What have you done to overcome him? All beings so far have created something beyond themselves; and do you want to be the ebb of this great flood and even go back to the beasts rather than overcome man? What is the ape to man? A laughing-stock or painful embarrassment. . . . (1892/1966 pp. 12–14)

The doctrine of the Overman echoes Nietzsche's portrayal of the "free spirits" in *Beyond Good and Evil*. One would expect the interpretation of the "free spirits"—as paradoxical constructions of an ideal self beyond the father–son knot—to also apply here. And much of the rest of Zarathustra's speech suggests as much:

> When Zarathustra had spoken thus, one of the people cried: "Now we have heard enough of the tightrope-walker, let us see him, too!" And all the people laughed at Zarathustra. But the tightrope-walker, believing that the word concerned him, began his performance. Zarathustra, however, beheld the people and was amazed. Then he spoke thus: "Man is a rope, tied between beast and overman—a rope

over an abyss. A dangerous across, a dangerous on-the-way, a dangerous looking-back, a dangerous shuddering and stopping. What is great in man is that he is a bridge and not an end: what can be loved in man is that he is an overture and a going-under." (1892/1966, pp. 14–15)

Zarathustra's identity with the tightrope walker, created through use of that image as a metaphor, presents an ambiguous doublet. Zarathustra is both the sideshow to the tightrope walker and the main event, the tightrope walker himself. Likewise, by mistaking words directed at Zarathustra for orders aimed toward him, the tightrope walker identifies himself with Zarathustra. Each is competing with himself for the attention of the audience.

Moreover, Zarathustra's statement that "man is a rope between animal and Overman" produces another paradox. For a rope between two points is only useful if there is somebody to walk over it. As man is a "going across," he is not only the rope, but also the tightrope walker attempting to traverse it. This mission is circular and impossible—just as a knife can't cut itself, man cannot walk over himself.

Not only that—the rope itself is strung between "two towers," which Zarathustra reads as "man and Overman." Its function is to permit passage from the first tower (animal) to the second tower (Overman). This amplifies and gives a new inflection to the above paradox—just who will make this journey? Someone from the first tower—animal? But if that someone is truly animal, how can he ever become Overman? How can anything, for that matter, ever move beyond itself? Such a movement would require that a being decouple from itself and somehow transform into an entity other than itself.

When the above paradoxes are linked, the tightrope-walker scene shows itself as the enactment of an impossible self-leapfrogging operation, psychic paradoxes multiplying in successively tighter circles. The lens of the narrative gradually zooms in on the center of the structure, the tightrope-walker.

Echoes of the father–son knot reverberate throughout the architecture of this structure. Although it would be excessively reductionistic to view Ludwig Nietzsche's relation to Zarathustra as one of complete identity, the two figures are analogous. To clarify the specifics of the analogy, it is necessary to turn back to Nietzsche's childhood autobiography.

A relevant motif of the autobiography upon which we have not yet dwelt is *self-overcoming*. The double voice we scrutinized has this theme embedded in its core, as it shows an attempt to move from one self to another—from the child (son) self to the wise adult (father) self. Although, on the one hand, Nietzsche experienced the father-self as a false dysangel to be destroyed, he also desperately wanted to become the father—as idealized figure. To succeed in becoming his father, Nietzsche would have to kill his child-self, so that it could be fully replaced by the father-self. Yet, just as the tightrope walker cannot walk over himself to reach the second tower, Nietzsche cannot walk over his child-self to reach a pure father-self.

This interpretation may seem, at first, to contradict another offered above. Previously, it was suggested that the paradoxical structure expresses Nietzsche's attempt to create an ideal self beyond the knot of father–son; however, for Nietzsche, such an ideal self would be experienced as another recurrence of the idealized Father. This is how the knot appears when viewed from the standpoint of the forward-looking child-self. From the perspective of the backward-looking father-self supposedly beyond the father–son duality, Nietzsche is already beyond the child self, which is dragging behind him, holding him back from the realization of his essential being. This element of Nietzsche's personality wishes to cast off the immature child-self so that it may move forward, unfettered, to its own actualization (cf. Horney, 1950/1991).

The child-self and father-self are in this way and many others locked in an endless battle for survival. Each must eliminate the other to truly be himself. Nietzsche's famous Apollonian-Dionysiac dichotomy echoes this conflict. In Nietzsche's original depiction of the pair in *The Birth of Tragedy* (1872/1967), Dionysus is portrayed as the spontaneous, preverbal force of nature, and Apollo is characterized as the god of form and image. Through the interaction of the two—the imposition of form and image on preverbal, spontaneous chaos—the drama is born:

We shall have gained much for the science of aesthetics, once we perceive not merely by logical inference, but with the immediate certainty of vision, that the continuous development of art is bound up with the Apollonian and Dionysiac duality—just as procreation depends on the duality of the sexes, involving perpetual strife with only periodically intervening reconciliations. . . . [W]e come to recognize that in the Greek world there existed a tremendous opposition, in origin and aims, between the Apollonian art of sculpture, and the nonimagistic, Dionysian art of music. These two different tendencies run parallel to each other, for the most part openly at variance; and they continually incite each other to new and more powerful births, which perpetuate an antagonism, only superficially reconciled by the common term "art;" till eventually, by a metaphysical miracle of the Hellenic "will," they appear coupled with each other, and through this coupling ultimately generate an equally Dionysian and Apollonian form of art—Attic tragedy. (p. 33)

Now that we have gained a basic understanding of the duality lying at the heart of Nietzsche's selfhood, we can fairly easily discern the psychological meanings of such passages. This excerpt presents a symbolic history of the phenomenology of Nietzsche's dual self, as the unformed, natural child self (Dionysus), and the finely sculptured, authoritative father self (Apollo) fight for dominance.

Not only is Nietzsche's duality apparent in this quotation, but the essential, paradoxical oneness of the dyad is also evident. The grandiloquent metaphors of the passage mark it as the speech of the sermonic voice of Nietzsche's father, and the cosmic image of a battle between gods colors Nietzsche's writing with a religious tinge. Both of these stylistic features give us the feeling that the thought of the whole passage dwells within the personality of the father, even as it attempts to symbolically externalize that figure and thereby escape it.

An especially relevant element of the above quotation is the recurring motif of artistic birth, which is portrayed as a direct consequence of the Apollo/Dionysus coupling. Here, tragedy's "birth" is not so much an event happening at a specific time but rather an eternally recurring rebirthing. Although Nietzsche tells us that this process "ends" with a synthesis of Apollo and Dionysus, it is clear from the other texts we have examined that whether or not his argument holds true historically, psychologically that synthesis never occurred. Like Nietzsche's love for the psychology of knowledge, it was a dialectical fantasy.

When one reexamines the father–son dualism from the viewpoint of this analogy, a previously concealed facet of its paradoxical structure shows itself. While the metaphor of birth may initially seem to merely be a convenient vehicle of expression, a closer look reveals that it is inextricably woven into the fabric of the father–son relationship. Because Nietzsche's dual self is composed of a parent and its child, part of his personality is quite literally responsible for the birth of the other.

Nevertheless, unlike a physical birth, this psychological birth does not begin and end in time. Rather, it eternally recurs as father-self and child-self continuously subvert each other or, in other words, as Nietzsche endlessly overcomes himself. The quality of the eternal we experienced in Nietzsche's childhood dream and in his account of his father's death can now be more fully understood. For by taking on the personality of his own progenitor, Nietzsche entered a circle in which he became his own psychological parent. If one is one's own parent, the logic goes, one grows old only to give birth to oneself once more and become a child again. Within this ring, to reach maturity is to become an infant.

It is critical to maintain the distinction between physical and psychological time in this regard. Nietzsche did not grow old in physical time to become a child once more, but rather did so in psychological time, eternally. He was always both old and young, and thus always becoming both old and young. The duality of selfhood that is the locus of our interpretation forces us to think the unthinkable—that time both does and does not exist in Nietzsche's subjective world.

This, perhaps, presents the structure of Nietzsche's subjectivity in its most basic, formal aspect. And here we can already begin to see the meaning of what is perhaps the most bizarre element of Nietzsche's philosophy—The Eternal Return.

Although this doctrine existed in linear time and therefore developed and changed, it took one particular form that we want to explore. This is the doctrine of Eternal Return as put forth in *Thus Spoke Zarathustra* (1892/1966):

"Stop, dwarf!" I said. "It is I or you! But I am the stronger of us two: you do not know my abysmal thought. That you could not bear!" Then something happened that made me lighter, for the dwarf jumped from my shoulder being curious; and he crouched on a stone before me. But there was a gateway just where we had stopped. "Behold this gateway, dwarf!" I continued. "It has two faces. Two paths meet here: no one has yet followed either to its end. This long lane stretches back for an eternity. And the long lane out there, that is another eternity. They contradict each other these paths, they offend each other face to face; and it is here at this gateway that they come together. The name of the gateway is inscribed above: "Moment." But whoever would follow one of them, on and on farther and farther—do you believe, dwarf, that these paths contradict each other eternally?" "All that is straight lies," the dwarf muttered contemptuously. "All truth is crooked; time itself is a circle." "You spirit of gravity," I said angrily, "do not make things too easy for yourself! Or I shall let you crouch where you are crouching, lamefoot; and it was that carried you to this height. "Behold," I continued, "this moment! From this gateway, Moment, a long, eternal lane leads backward: behind us lies an eternity. Must not whatever can walk have walked on this lane before? Must not whatever can happen have been done, have passed by here before? And if everything has been there before—what do you think, dwarf, of this moment? Must not this gateway too have been there before? And are not all things knotted together so firmly that this moment draws after it all that is to come? Therefore—itself too? For whatever can walk

—in this long lane out there too, it must walk once more. And this slow spider, which crawls in the moonlight, and this moonlight itself, and I and you in the gateway, whispering together, whispering of eternal things—must not all of us have been there before? And return and walk in that other land, out there, before us, in this long dreadful lane—must we not eternally return?" (pp. 157–158)

The speakers of this conversation—Zarathustra and the dwarf—provide a new, more unsettling inflection of the dualism theme that runs through Nietzsche's texts. In the childhood autobiography, we heard the voices of a child and a wise Christian moralizer. *The Birth of Tragedy* (1872/1967) presented the duality as that of Dionysus and Apollo. Now, though, the two have metamorphosed into the histrionic Zarathustra and a grotesque dwarf.

Again, a subversive identity exists between the two figures. The excerpt begins with an aggressive assertion of a difference of identity—"It is I or you!" Zarathustra goes on to say: "But I am the stronger of us two: you do not know my abysmal thought. That you could not bear!", implying that he will reveal his thought in order to destroy the dwarf, thus demonstrating the two figures' difference.

Yet by the end of the passage Zarathustra is an adherent of the dwarf's doctrine that "[a]ll truth is crooked; time itself is a circle." It seems at first as though the dwarf's thinking has subtly insinuated itself into Zarathustra's psyche. But one also is given the impression that Zarathustra already had the notion of Eternal Return on his mind. What Zarathustra says before the dwarf interrupts him seems a precursor to the thought of the Eternal Return, and in itself does not appear to have the quality of the "abysmal" that Zarathustra wants to express.

Again, an attempt at escaping a doublet circles back upon itself. Zarathustra begins expounding his doctrine of time so that the dwarf may be eliminated. His exposition, however, only reveals the essential identity of the dwarf and himself and, by confirming the dwarf's doctrine, validates rather than annihilates its being. Because Zarathustra and the dwarf are one, each can never be one. This circularity mirrors the doctrine put forth by the two speakers. In speaking of an endless circle, Zarathustra is captured by that circle.

However, although the doctrine of the Eternal Return describes time as paradoxical and circular, this excerpt portrays the pattern of the doctrine's development as somewhat linear. Such is not what we'd expect to come across in Nietzsche, especially in a passage dealing with the Eternal Return. It therefore deserves careful inspection.

The linear development to which we refer can be seen in the last two paragraphs, mainly in Zarathustra's translation of "can" into "must," when he begins to ask, "Must not whatever can happen have happened, have been done, have passed by here before?" Zarathustra translates manifold possibility into manifold actuality. Hence Eternal Return: If everything possible is actual, and if it is possible that what is happening now has already happened and will happen again, then it actually has happened and actually will happen again. It is the shift from manifold possibility to manifold actuality that creates the circle.

Let's unpack this a bit more. A more transparent instance of this sequence occurs in another account of Eternal Return from *The Will to Power* (1930/1967):

If the world may be thought of as a certain definite quantity of force and as a certain definite number of centers of force—and every other representation remains indefinite and therefore useless—it follows that, in the great dice game of existence, it must pass through a calculable number of combinations. In infinite time, every possible combination would at some time or another be realized; more: it would be realized an infinite number of times. And since between every combination and its next recurrence all other possible combinations would have to take place, and each of these combinations conditions the entire sequence of combinations in the same series, a circular movement of absolutely identical series is thus demonstrated: the world as a circular movement that has already repeated itself indefinitely often and plays its game *in infinitum*. (p. 549)

Put a monkey at a typewriter, and given enough random plunking he will produce the Gettysburg Address. Put a monkey at a typewriter for an infinite amount of time, and he will produce infinite Gettysburg Addresses—that's what Nietzsche says.

For Nietzsche, it is precisely the random, chaotic "dice game" of possibility that creates order in the universe. Because the forces constituting existence continuously interact and recombine in haphazard fashion, a finite universe requires that these forces must eventually permutate through all possible configurations. Not only that, but in infinite time they must reenact this limited group of possibilities over and over again. From out of chaos arises circular order.

In their antiphilosophical work *A Thousand Plateaus* (1988, p. 6), Gilles Deleuze and Felix Guattari note the same movement in Nietzsche's aphorisms, which, as they put it, "shatter the linear unity of thought only to invoke the cyclic unity of eternal return present as the nonknown in thought."

Indeed, if we reflect on the experience of reading Nietzsche, we notice that the feeling of circularity is often preceded by an experience of disorientation, brought about, perhaps, by Nietzsche's deconstruction of our presuppositions about the world. Nietzsche's aphorisms, especially those in *Beyond Good and Evil* (1886/1973), provide many examples of this pattern:

He who despises himself nonetheless respects himself as one who despises. (p. 92)

To talk about oneself a great deal can also be a means of concealing oneself. (p. 105)

He who fights with monsters should look to it that he himself does not become a monster. And when you gaze long into an abyss the abyss gazes into you. (p. 102)

The thought of suicide is a powerful solace: by means of it one gets through many a bad night. (p. 103)

All these aphorisms work to break down the reader's habitual mode of understanding and replace it with a new, circular form of knowing. In the last aphorism quoted, the thought of suicide, commonly understood as arising out of a desire to end life, is depicted as life preserving.

One's habitual way of viewing that desire is dislocated, and a circular structure—the thought of suicide as a defense against suicide—is substituted for it. An experience of shattering is replaced by an experience of circling.

Although the disintegration of habitual patterns of thought is an ever-present motif in Nietzsche's texts, one particular instance of such a breakdown stands above the rest. That moment is Nietzsche's proclamation of the "death of God," perhaps the most widely known element of his philosophy. The death of God is put forth as a representative example of what happens when dearly held modes of thinking about the world unravel:

> The madman jumped into their midst and pierced them with his eyes. "Whither is God?" he cried; "I will tell you. WE have killed him—you and I. All of us are his murderers. But how did we do this? How could we drink up the sea? Who gave us the sponge to wipe away the entire horizon? What were we doing when we unchained the earth from its sun? Whither is it moving now? Whither are we moving? Away from all suns? Are we not plunging continually? Backward, sideward, forward, in all directions? Is there any up or down? Are we not straying as through an infinite nothing? Do we not feel the breath of empty space? Has it not become colder? Is not night continually closing in on us? (1887/1974, p. 181)

Here we can see more clearly the experience of shattering and disorientation that is the prologue to the eternal return. The passage conveys a feeling of free-floating chaos, of "plunging . . . in all directions" haphazardly, of frightening, unknown possibilities.

When this passage is situated within the psychobiographical context of Nietzsche's opposition to Christianity, the emotional meaning it expresses becomes evident. If Nietzsche identified God with his father, then the death of God would accordingly have been equated with the father's demise. And if that is true, what Nietzsche says about the effects of God's death provides a metaphoric phenomenology of his own experience of catastrophic loss.

For Nietzsche the chief danger incipient in God's death was nihilism, the loss of values. *Thus Spoke Zarathustra* (1892/1966) was Nietzsche's answer to that threat; it was his attempt to forge a new set of values to replace those lost. However, as we have seen in the case of the "free spirits," Nietzsche's plan to construct a new system of values could only bring about a paradoxical return of the very values he was trying to replace. It is this paradox that we see in *Zarathustra's* tightrope walker scene, as an attempt to create a set of new values—to walk from man to Overman—spirals inward to Eternal Return.

When it is noted that the spiral of the transvaluation of all values is a response to nihilism, one can begin to perceive the meaning of the Eternal Return. For just as the loop of Eternal Return emerges from the turbulent chaos of matter, the vicious circle of the transvaluation of all values spins out of a response to the turbulent chaos of valuelessness—nihilism. The structural similarity between the Eternal Return and the transvaluation of all values suggests that these doctrines point to the same experience—the disorganized chaos of bereavement, followed by a circularity of experience undoing both the loss and the defense against that loss.

We were already aware that Nietzsche's psychic knots were tied in with the aftermath of his father's death. Nonetheless, although certain elements of that connection were visible, much was still hidden, and, as a result, what we did see was not fully intelligible. Indeed, the idea that Ludwig Nietzsche's personality rose from the grave to possess the mind of his young son might seem a vague and almost occult theory.

The aspect of Nietzsche's loss that we left in concealment is the experience of personal chaos described above. Even though Nietzsche's assumption of the voice of his father was explained as an attempt to keep his father alive, the experience of loss motivating this attempt was not yet fully exposed. One reason for that lack is Nietzsche's refusal to tell us explicitly about his emotional experience of loss. Although he writes in *Out of My Life* (1858/1924) that "[i]t seems like we would find quite a lot of consolation for our pain by frequently speaking about it" (p. 29), he does not speak about it. He hints, dramatizes, and covers over chaos (Klossowski, 1969/1997). While reading the childhood autobiography, one cannot escape the impression that it is far too organized. That impression is magnified by the young Nietzsche's use of elegantly stylized metaphors to bring order to his subject matter.

As we've seen, such metaphors tend to emanate from the father-self. When we look closely at the contexts in which they occur, we find that in many cases Nietzsche seems to use them to retreat from moments of pain and disorganization:

Before speaking of his father's death: "Until this time, happiness and peace always brightened our lives. Our lives were flowing untroubled like a bright summer day, but now dark clouds piled up, lightning was flashing and the bolts from the heavens were falling down in a disastrous way." (1858/1924, p. 10)

After speaking of his father's funeral: "If you steal away the crown of a tree, it will become withered and bare, and the little birds will leave the branches. The head of our family was stolen away, all joy disappeared from our hearts and we were in deep sorrow. But just when the wounds had healed a bit, they were painfully reopened." (p. 12)

"After spending a long time in the country, it was terrible for us to live in the city. Therefore we avoided the dark streets and sought out more rural areas, like a bird escaping from its cage." (p. 13)

These metaphors give the illusion of affective commentary while hiding intense emotions behind a screen of graceful figurative images. Nietzsche's life becomes an aesthetic object, not the subjective experience of a human being. Furthermore, as the autobiographical shift from the view of oneself as an experiencing subject to that of the self as distantly perceived object has shown itself to be a shift from child-self to father-self, the protective function of clinging to the father-self can be clearly discerned here. An Apollonian imposition of form and image onto Dionysiac chaos mitigates the threat of inundation by that chaos.[6]

It seems, then, that the father-self not only shielded Nietzsche from overwhelming feelings of loss but also bars us from direct access to these feelings. Nietzsche tells us they exist:

"[T]he thought of being separated forever from the beloved father moved me deeply and I cried bitterly." (1858/1924, p. 11)

"The head of our family was stolen away, all joy disappeared from our hearts and we were in deep sorrow." (p. 12)

But, he does not really show them to us. The only windows through which Nietzsche's sense of loss can be clearly seen are the moments of spiritual and psychological breakdown that Nietzsche suggests will follow in the wake of God's death.

We already had a glimpse through one of these windows; another appears in *The Gay Science* (1887/1974):

[H]ow much must collapse now that this faith has been undermined because it was built on this faith, propped up by it, grown into it; for example, the whole of our European morality. The long plenitude and sequence of breakdown, destruction, ruin, and cataclysm that is now impending—who could guess enough of it today to be compelled to play the teacher and advance proclaimer of this monstrous logic of terror, the prophet of a gloom and an eclipse of the sun whose like has probably never yet occurred on earth? (p. 279)

This passage identifies several elements of the psychic disaster it portrays. There is a *collapse* because of a dependency on that which was lost. That collapse leads to a long period of *breakdown, destruction, ruin, and cataclysm*. These terms imply that the period following the collapse is not merely empty, but filled with upheaval. Here we can see an echo of the psychic cataclysms that threatened to engulf the young Nietzsche when he lost his father.

If God dies, disaster is inevitable. Therefore, the logic goes, God must not die. Nietzsche had to keep him alive by becoming his own Father. Although by doing so Nietzsche partly protected himself from the experience of devastating loss, he also trapped himself within an identity which was not his own.

The notion that Nietzsche desired to keep God alive may initially seem counterintuitive. After all, didn't Nietzsche look disgustedly upon Christian morality as a form of "slave morality," a collective illness? He did indeed. However, as our analysis of Nietzsche's anti-Christian position has revealed, his attitude toward that religion was riddled with ambivalence. Not only did Nietzsche wish to slough off the personality of his father and achieve self-sameness, but he also needed to keep the father alive to fend off the storm of unbearable emotion that would have ensued if he fully realized his father was dead.

The Eternal Return, therefore, represents both an escape from a moment of chaotic loss and a continual flight from the danger of reliving that moment. Its structure, though, incessantly returns Nietzsche to the very object that threatens him. For, the problem the Eternal Return creates—the subject's duality—could only be resolved through the removal of one pole of this duality. If that pole were the father-self, this would amount to killing the father again, although with Nietzsche playing the role of murderer. One of the central reasons for Nietzsche's feeling that "we have killed God, we are his murderers," quoted above, shows itself. If Nietzsche tries to create a unified, authentic self—as child-self—he assumes the role of his father's killer.

But was such an act of murder possible? Was there a way out of the labyrinth of Eternal Return? In a passage from Zarathustra appearing immediately after the discussion of Eternal Return, a solution seems indicated:

A young shepherd I saw, writhing, gagging, in spasms, his face distorted, and a heavy black snake hung out of his mouth. Had I ever seen so much nausea and pale dread on one face? He seemed to be asleep when the snake crawled into his throat, and there bit itself fast. My hand tore at the snake and tore in vain; it did not tear the snake out of his throat. Then it cried out to me: "Bite! Bite its head off! Bite!" Thus it cried out to me—my dread, my hatred, my nausea, my pity, all that is good and wicked in me cried out of me with a single cry. . . . The shepherd, however, bit as my cry counseled him; he bit with a good bite. Far away he spewed the head of the snake—and he jumped up. No longer shepherd, no longer human—one changed, radi-

ant, laughing! Never yet on earth has a human being laughed as he laughed! O my brothers, I heard a laughter that was no human's laughter, and now a thirst gnaws at me, a longing that grows still. My longing for this laughter gnaws at me; oh, how do I bear to go on living! And how could I bear to die now! (1892/1966, pp. 158–160)

Like the shepherd, Nietzsche was infiltrated by another entity. His overidentification with his father can be pictured as an attempt to incorporate an indigestible being. Just as the snake clung to the shepherd's innards, the father-dysangel clung to Nietzsche's soul and could not be shaken off. On the other hand, Nietzsche's inner child was also like the snake, insofar as it crawled inside the protective enclosure of the father-self to ward off feelings of loss and loneliness.

With this paradox firmly in place, we would expect that a resolution—biting off the snake—would be impossible; that any attempt at solution would spiral into Eternal Return. Still, the snake is destroyed, apparently bringing the conflict to a conclusion. What could this mean?

Another image of a foreign entity clinging to a man shows up immediately after the tightrope-walker scene. In this case, the creature clinging to Zarathustra bears a stronger resemblance to Nietzsche's inner father:

Meanwhile the evening came, and the market place hid in darkness. Then the people scattered, for even curiosity and terror grow weary. But Zarathustra sat on the ground near the dead man, and was lost in thought, forgetting the time. At last night came, and a cold wind blew over the lonely one. Then Zarathustra said to his herd: "Verily, it is a beautiful catch of fish that Zarathustra has brought in today! Not a man has he caught but a corpse. Human existence is uncanny and still without meaning: a jester can become a man's fatality. I will teach men the meaning of their existence—the overman, the lightning out of the dark cloud of man. But I am still far from them, and my sense does not speak to their senses. To men I am still the mean between a fool and a corpse. Dark is the night, dark are Zarathustra's ways.

Come, cold, stiff companion! I shall carry you where I may bury you with my own hands." When Zarathustra said this to his heart he hoisted the corpse on his back and started on his way. (1892/1966, pp. 21–22)

Zarathustra goes on to carry the corpse across the countryside, through forests and swamps. After begging food from an old man, he tires and decides to sleep. Setting the corpse inside the hollow trunk of a tree so that it will be protected from wolves, Zarathustra lies down and closes his eyes.

This sequence of images can be read as a pictographic script narrating Nietzsche's childhood. In a certain sense, Nietzsche did take a corpse onto his shoulders—that of his deceased father. Following Nietzsche's metaphors, we might say that this burden was a heavy weight for a young boy to bear. Any growth following the death of Nietzsche's father was undermined by the other self firmly implanted in his soul, like the corpse hidden inside the hollow tree. And, just as the corpse fills the gap in the tree, the dead father-self was an attempt to fill the emotional void left by the death of the real father.

When we turn to the question of the corpse's identity, we are brought quickly back to the tightrope walker scene, for the corpse is the body of the dead tightrope walker, fallen to his death. The complex web of intertwined doublets and vicious circles constituting the tightrope-walker scene was discussed previously. We saw that the tightrope walker's place is at the apex of this spiral, competing with himself to reach the end of the rope. It is this apex, this point of tension in an exquisitely difficult balancing act, which gives us a clue as to the origins and structure of Nietzsche's breakdown.

Then something happened that made every mouth dumb and every eye rigid. For meanwhile the tightrope walker had begun his performance: he had stepped out of a small door and was walking over the rope, stretched between two towers and suspended over the marketplace and the people. When he had reached the exact middle of his course the small door opened once more and a fellow in motley clothes, looking like a jester, jumped

out and followed the first one with quick steps. "Forward, lamefoot!" he shouted in an awe-inspiring voice. "Forward, lazybones, smuggler, pale face, or I shall tickle you with my heel! What are you doing here between the towers? The tower is where you belong. You ought to be locked up; you block the way for one better than yourself." And with every word he came closer and closer; but when he was but one step behind, the dreadful thing happened which made every mouth dumb and every eye rigid; he uttered a devilish cry and jumped over the man who stood in his way. This man, however, seeing his rival win, lost his head and the rope, tossed away his pole, and plunged into the depth even faster, a whirlpool of arms and legs. The market place became as the sea when a tempest pierces it: the people rushed apart and over one another, especially at the place where the body must hit the ground. (1892/1966, pp. 19–20)

A later statement by Zarathustra, "I am still the mean between a fool and a corpse," taken together with the image of Zarathustra bearing of the corpse on his back, indicates that the tightrope walker embodies the father-aspect of Nietzsche's psyche. Therefore, by extension, it might be suspected that the jester symbolizes the child-self in Nietzsche.

With the exception of the jester's Dionysian spontaneity, however, his tone and behavior are hardly suggestive of a child's. The jester's threatening remarks, his booming voice, his insane acrobatics, surround him with an aura of threatening alienness. Nevertheless, we can see how he fits into the sequential structure of the tightrope-walker scene. The tightrope walker tries to walk over himself, and the jester jumps over him.

Moreover, there is an eerie correspondence between the murder of the tightrope walker and the event that triggered Nietzsche's breakdown. Nietzsche collapsed on seeing a cab driver cruelly whipping his horse—and doesn't the jester's treatment of the tightrope walker seem strangely akin to that of a cruel horseman toward his beast? "'Forward, lamefoot!' he shouted in an awe-inspiring voice. 'Forward, lazybones, smuggler, pale face, or I shall tickle you with my heel!'" "Forward lamefoot"? Or "I shall tickle you with my heel!"? These phrases sound more fitting coming from the mouth of a horseback rider about to spur (tickle with his heel) a slow nag.

To Nietzsche, the image of the horse and rider was a familiar one. Plato and Schopenhauer, who were both closely read by Nietzsche, use metaphors of the horse and rider to express their views of human nature; the horse symbolizes the animal instincts, and the rider refers to the conscious mind responsible for taming and controlling them.

It is tempting, then, to assume that Nietzsche's horse signified the instinctual, Dionysian child-self, and the rider embodied the controlling Apollonian father-self. Nietzsche had spent his life trying to be a horseback rider, trying to be his father. The act of grasping the mistreated horse by the neck and breaking out in tears suggests a shift in identification from father-self to child-self. We might conclude, then, that at the moment of his breakdown, Nietzsche ceased to feel himself as his father and instead was engulfed by the experience of loss and invalidation contained within his child-self.

Yet if the rider is the father-self, then what of the jester who seems his symbolic equivalent? As noted above, the jester seems more like a Dionysiac than an Apollonian. How could the jester be a jester, a motley creature of spontaneity and humor, and still embody the Apollonian identity of the father-self? He could not, but did so nevertheless. For in the very act of appropriating the horse-and-rider metaphor, Nietzsche deconstructed it. Not only was Nietzsche like a horse being ridden by a false identity, but he was also riding on the back of that idealized self-image, using its energy to propel him through life rather than expending effort on realizing his true self (Horney, 1950/1991).

Alice Miller (1990) falls into the trap that we try to avoid here. She claims that Nietzsche's breakdown can be seen as a regression to the inner child, whose true feelings and needs could only be expressed through Dionysian madness. Such an explanation, by collapsing Nietzsche's always-indeterminate madness into one half of a doublet, belies the paradoxical style of his thought and emotion. Moreover, it is contra-

dicted by the many grandiose, paranoid, and violent acts Nietzsche committed during his period of insanity. These were not the acts of a child.

The image of a loss of balance we find in the tightrope-walker scene might suggest, rather, that Nietzsche fell into a more uneven self-experience. Another passage from Zarathustra gives the impression that such a fall was an ever-present danger for Nietzsche:

> Not the height but the precipice is terrible. That precipice where the glance plunges down and the hand reaches up. There the heart becomes giddy confronted with its double will. Alas, my friends, can you guess what is my heart's double will? This, this is my precipice and my danger, that my glance plunges into the height and that my hand would grasp and hold on to the depth. My will clings to man; with fetters I bind myself to man because I am swept up toward the overman; for that way my other will wants to go.... (1892/1966, p. 142)

Nietzsche says he has "two wills," one directed toward man, one toward Overman. Although he tells us that it is the precipice, and "not the height," which "is terrible," he goes on to stress the danger of being swept upward. His wording—"my glance plunges into the height"—suggests that flying upward is akin to falling into a deep void.

The image of plunging into the sky suggests a rapidly intensifying self-inflation, an inundation of power and greatness. This rise is also a fall because, for Nietzsche, to rise to the heights of self-inflation was also to fall downward, into the omnipotent father's grave.

There is little that is unfamiliar here—since the rise into the heights is aimed toward the "Overman," the simultaneous upward and downward movement of this "rising" is as paradoxical as the tightrope walker's journey over himself to reach the Overman. However, the image of the precipice and an imminent plunge into the heights does not mirror the tightrope walker's precarious equilibrium, but rather, parallels his fall into the abyss.

Juxtaposed with the horse-and-rider incident, these passages in Zarathustra imply that the change in Nietzsche's state of mind during his breakdown was not as radical as some (Jaspers, 1935/1997) have concluded.[7] If Nietzsche's mad rantings are closely examined, this notion is borne out:

"He wrote notes to the King of Italy ("My beloved Umberto"), the royal house of Baden ("my children"), and the Vatical Secretary of State. He would go to Rome on Tuesday, he said, to meet the pope and the prince of Europe, except for the Hohenzollerns" (Hayman, 1980, p. 335).

The elegant and cultured father-self is central here, the child-self marginal. In his idealized splendor, the father-self decides to consort with the royalty of Europe, his reverse side only visible in the dreamy, childlike tone of the plan:

[note to Meta von Salis] "The world is transfigured, for God is on the earth. Do you not see how all the heavens are rejoicing? I have just seized possession of my kingdom, am throwing the pope into prison, and am having Wilhelm, Bismarck, and Stocker shot" (p. 335). Again, the father-self is dominant. The note identifies Nietzsche with God, showing us that, just as his free spirits recreate the morality they have destroyed, Nietzsche becomes God's successor after announcing his death. A deeper sense is revealed when this passage is read in the light of Nietzsche's childhood, for, by taking on the identity of his dead father, he became that Godlike figure's replacement:

After the Finos had given him a bromide he was able to talk more clearly, but, between playing fragments very softly, at the piano, he spoke of himself a successor to the dead god, and, as the effects of the calmative wore off, he clowned excitedly, leaping about, dancing, shouting, gesturing obscenely. (p. 336)

The shift in emotional state depicted in this excerpt signifies a movement from father-self to son-self. First, the calm grandeur of an Apollonian dominates Nietzsche, and then the childlike antics of a Dionysiac erupt. Another eruption occurred while he was taken for a walk: "In the afternoon, taken for another walk in the garden, he sang, whimpered and shouted, again lying on the ground several times after talking off his jacket and waistcoat" (p. 337).

Nietzsche's late insanity can be understood, therefore, as a series of radical shifts between dominance of the father and submergence of the child and dominance of the child and submergence of the father. Just as, in his childhood autobiography, Nietzsche continuously vacillates between speaking with the voice of the father and uttering the discourse of the child, after his breakdown he oscillated between the poles of father-self experience and child-self experience.

Other accounts of Nietzsche's delirium tend to support this idea:

Father-self: "According to the records of the clinic, Nietzsche apologized for the bad weather. 'For you, good people, I shall prepare the loveliest weather tomorrow'" (Hayman, 1980, p. 337).

Child-self: "During the afternoon he sometimes broke down into singing and screaming" (p. 337).

Child-self: "He stayed in bed all morning, and, taken for a walk in the afternoon, he threw his hat down and sometimes lay on the ground" (p. 337).

Father-self: "When he was led into the psychiatric department, he kept bowing politely, and he strode majestically into his room, thanking the attendants for the 'magnificent reception'" (p. 339).

It should be stressed that none of these moments represented a total victory of one self and a complete annihilation of the other. Both identities were always present; what changed was their relative prominence. During the incidents in which the father-self ruled, the child-self was still present in the fantastical, fairy-tale quality of the ideas being enacted. We do not see a God here, but a childish caricature of a God. Likewise, the yelling and wild romping of the child-self often seem more like witty imitations of childlike behavior than authentic play. One gets the feeling that there is a larger intelligence guiding these acts.

Both types of moments, then, were not quite whole-hearted. In each expression of one self we can see a kernel of the marginalized other self. This is what gave some observers the impression that Nietzsche was feigning madness—for, just as an actor is feigning because behind his role is a person playing it, Nietzsche seemed like he was pretending because behind his manifest self was always a latent self. In a way, he *was* always play-acting, insofar as what was authentic expression for one self was play-acting for the other self.

The image of a mistreated horse and its cruel rider can be taken to suggest the unbalanced domination of each self by the other. During Nietzsche's outbursts and wild antics, one self was whipping the other into submission, smothering that other self with its own subjectivity. Kicking and screaming, the child tried to overwhelm the father, who would in turn attempt to annihilate the child through hyperbolic expressions of his own maturity and power.

In his madness, Nietzsche continued to reenact the conflict between father and son, yet shifting between these extremes rather than balancing them. Instead of participating in grand wars of words, he had delusions of assassinating government officials. Rather than discoursing elegantly on the virtues of the Dionysian attitude, he sang and tore off his clothes.

We are still left, however, with the question of the jester's identity unanswered. The jester, he who walks over the tightrope walker, the royal fool, lover of paradox and irony, spontaneity and wit, seems a crucial figure in Nietzsche's madness. However, the jester's meaning remains ever elusive, despite the efforts we make to locate and define him. Here, perhaps, is that element of Nietzsche's thought that, like his wily Dionysos, is ultimately ungraspable, as it shifts and changes, seeming to resolve into a definite form only to slip from our hands once again. In one of his last letters, Nietzsche writes to Cosima Wagner:

To Princess Ariadne, My Beloved. It is a mere prejudice that I am a human being. Yet I have often enough dwelled among human beings and I know the things human beings experience, from the lowest to the highest. Among the Hindus I was Buddha, in Greece Dionysos—Alexander and Caesar were incarnations of me, as well as the poet of Shakespeare, Lord Bacon. Most recently I was Voltaire and Napoleon, perhaps also Richard Wagner. . . . However, I now come as Dionysos victorious, who will prepare a great festival on Earth. . . . Not as though I had much time. . . .

Notes

An earlier version of this chapter appeared in Psychoanalytic Review (2000), 87(5), 651–698. Reprinted courtesy of Guilford Publications.

1. All quotations from this work are the present authors' translations from the original *Aus Meinem Leben* (Nietzsche, 1858/1924).

2. We do not intend the term "ambivalence" to be understood in any specific abstract theoretical sense, but in a more experience-near manner. The same is true of the other psychoanalytic terms which are used throughout this chapter. We have deliberately left our background theory somewhat indeterminate in order to more easily direct our attention to the potentialities of Nietzsche's own metaphors and models for interpreting his personality.

3. Unfortunately, such intersubjective aspects of biography tend to be difficult or impossible for scholarly research to directly uncover, thus forcing us to speculate in order to give sufficient attention to the context out of which Nietzsche's personality crystallized. What we have in mind here is, in some respects, a more context-sensitive understanding of the processes Freud (1917/1957) originally described in "Mourning and Melancholia." Our interpretation also has many affinities with the ideas of Abraham and Torok (1994) on introjection, the intrapsychic crypt, and the phantom.

4. Pletsch (1991) also suggests that the child in the dream is Nietzsche. Klossowski (1969/1997), too, correctly grasps the child's identity, in a brilliant paper that, though ignoring most of the structures that we elucidate here, sheds light on several parts of Nietzsche's thought and personality that we do not address.

5. The reader may have noticed the similarity between such paradoxical structures and the "vicious circles" and "double binds" that several theorists have attempted to articulate, such as Horney's (1950/1991) "vicious circles," Bateson et al.'s (1956) "double binds," and Laing's (1960, 1961, 1970) "knots." Although Bateson's formulation is too narrow to include most of the patterns articulated in this study, Horney's and Laing's conceptualizations seem fairly well able to encompass many of these structures. Sass (1992, 1994) also examines psychological paradoxes of a similar nature.

6. Louis Sass (personal communication) has suggested to us that in fact these dramatic metaphors may represent, rather, attempts to express that which is too painful to be spelled out verbally. To be sure, this does seem likely. However, Sass's reading does not appear to us to necessarily contradict our own. Nietzsche's metaphors are, indeed, expressions of profound pain, but they seem to us to be expressions whose style both hides the essence of that pain and places Nietzsche's discourse within the Apollonian atmosphere of his father. While

their vividness indicates the intensity of Nietzsche's pain, they seem to smooth over the disorganization and sheer terror involved in the loss.

7. It has frequently been claimed that Nietzsche suffered from syphilis, cancer, an infection of the brain, or various other organic problems causing dementia. The main piece of evidence taken to support such claims is the supposed discontinuity between Nietzsche's behavior before and after his breakdown. This alleged discontinuity, we are arguing, was significantly less profound than is commonly believed. Although Nietzsche's behavior did bear some resemblances to dementia, the popular rumor that Nietzsche had syphilis has recently been definitively refuted by examination of his medical records and other evidence (Sax, 2003), which show that his behavior and life span are strikingly incompatible with this diagnosis. The refutation of the syphilis hypothesis means that we are left with a wide variety of explanations for Nietzsche's breakdown, among which psychological explanations can play an important if not central role.

References

Abraham, N., & Torok, M. (1994). The shell and the kernel. Chicago: University of Chicago Press.

Atwood, G., & Stolorow, R. (1993). Faces in a cloud: Intersubjectivity in personality theory (2nd ed.). Northvale, N.J.: Aronson.

Bateson, G., Jackson, D., Haley, J., & Weakland, J. (1956). Toward a theory of schizophrenia. Behavioral Science, 1, 251–264.

Deleuze, G., & Guattari, F. (1988). A thousand plateaus: Capitalism and schizophrenia. London: Pantheon Press.

Derrida, J. (1985). The ear of the other. London: University of Nebraska Press. (Original work published 1982)

Forster-Nietzsche, E. (1912). The life of Nietzsche. New York: Sturgis and Walton.

Freud, S. (1957). Mourning and melancholia. In J. Strachey (Ed. & Trans.), The standard edition of the complete psychological works of Sigmund Freud (Vol. 14, pp. 243–258). London: Hogarth Press. (Original work published 1917)

Gilman, S., & Parent, D. (1987). Conversations with Nietzsche. New York: Oxford.

Hayman, W. (1980). Nietzsche: A critical life. New York: Oxford University Press.

Horney, K. (1991). Neurosis and human growth. New York: Norton. (Original work published 1950)

Jaspers, K. (1997). Nietzsche: An introduction to the understanding of his philosophical activity. Baltimore: Johns Hopkins. (Original work published 1935)

Jung, C. (1998). Seminar on Nietzsche's Zarathustra. Princeton, N.J.: Princeton University Press. (Original work published 1934–1939)

Klossowski, P. (1997). The consultation of the paternal shadow. In: Nietzsche and the vicious circle (pp. 172–197). Chicago: University of Chicago Press. (Original work published 1969)

Laing, R. (1960). The divided self. London: Penguin.

Laing, R. (1961). Self and others. London: Penguin.

Laing, R. (1970). Knots. New York: Pantheon.

Miller, A. (1990). The untouched key: Tracing childhood trauma in creativity and destructiveness. New York: Doubleday.

Ludovici, A. (1985). Friedrich Nietzsche: Selected letters. London: Soho Book Company.

Nietzsche, F. (1924). Out of my life (Aus Meinem Leben). In E. Forster-Nietzsche, Der werdende Nietzsche. Munchen: Musarion-Verlag. (Original work published 1858)

Nietzsche, F. (1966). Thus spoke Zarathustra (trans. W. Kaufmann). New York: Penguin. (Original work published 1892)

Nietzsche, F. (1967). The birth of tragedy [1872] and The case of Wagner [1888] (trans. W. Kaufmann). New York: Vintage Books.

Nietzsche, F. (1967). The genealogy of morals [1887] and Ecce homo [1908] (trans. W. Kaufmann). New York: Vintage Books.

Nietzsche, F. (1967). The will to power. (trans. W. Kaufmann). New York: Vintage. (Original work published 1930)

Nietzsche, F. (1968). Twilight of the idols [1888] and The antichrist [1895] (trans. R.J Hollingdale). New York: Penguin.

Nietzsche, F. (1973). Beyond good and evil (trans. R.J. Hollingdale). New York: Penguin. (Original work published 1886)

Nietzsche, F. (1974). The gay science (trans. W. Kaufmann). New York: Random House. (Original work published 1887)

Pletsch, C. (1991). The young Nietzsche: Becoming a genius. New York: Free Press.

Sarup, M. (1993). An introductory guide to postmodernism and poststructuralism. Athens: University of Georgia Press.

Sass, L. (1992). Madness and modernism: Insanity in the light of modern art, literature, and thought. Cambridge, Mass.: Harvard University Press.

Sass, L. (1994). The paradoxes of delusion: Wittgenstein, Schreber, and the schizophrenic mind. Ithaca, N.Y.: Cornell University Press.

Sax, L. (2003). What was the cause of Nietzsche's dementia? Journal of Medical Biography, 11, 47–54.

Chapter 18

Irving Alexander

Erikson and Psychobiography, Psychobiography and Erikson

In recent years two publications appeared that revived public interest in the life and work of Erik Erikson (1902–1994). One certainly is Lawrence J. Friedman's *Identity's Architect* (1999), an outstanding biography of Erikson's life and work. Friedman, a historian, spent ten years producing this volume. He contacted many of the most important people in Erikson's life, including his wife Joan, who helped in providing data about more than sixty years of their life together. His use of archival sources both here and abroad was extensive and his knowledge of Erikson's work and the history of psychoanalysis impressive. The major events of Erikson's life are clearly drawn and well documented, making the book a treasure trove for the psychobiographer.

A second source of new information was provided in 1999 by Sue Erikson Bloland, a psychoanalyst and the only daughter of Erikson's marriage, which produced three other children. Her work, entitled "Fame: The Power and Cost of a Fantasy," appeared in the November 1999 issue of the *Atlantic Monthly*. In this article she discusses her father's exalted status and its impact on her psychological development. In addition, she offers a theoretical analysis of the psychological antecedents leading to the search for fame in her father's life. During the exposition, we are privileged to a view of Erikson from a vantage point heretofore unavailable to the public. It is a most welcome addition to knowledge and certainly added to my interest in trying to understand this most unusual life story as conveyed by these authors. Most of what follows has roots in these two primary sources and in a retrospective book review (Alexander, 1996) that discussed the possible role of aggression in Erikson's life.

My task in this communication is threefold. One aim is to assess what impact Erikson's two major psychohistorical or psychobiographical works, *Young Man Luther* (1958) and *Gandhi's Truth* (1969), may have had on the subsequent development of these fields and also to consider what led Erikson into psychobiographical work. The second is to reflect on the two books: What may have prompted their production, and how did they relate to Erikson's continuing battles with the problems his particular and unusual life had set for him. The third involves what I have derived from the life story—especially Erikson's childhood, youth, and early adulthood in Europe—and how that led me to attempt to paint a coherent psychological picture of Erikson's development and family life.

To approach the work in this fashion, it is necessary to disrupt the order commonly employed in biographical essays. In other words, I do not "begin at the beginning" with Erikson's entry into professional life, which can be traced to 1933 when the family immigrated to the United States, and then follow this trajectory until his retirement. Instead, I start with his work in psychobiography (on both Luther and Gandhi), discuss his appointment at Austen Riggs, and then return to his existence in Europe from the time of his birth until he completed analytic training.

Erikson's Impact on the Development of Psychobiography

The question of Erikson's impact on the development of psychobiographical or psychohistorical scholarship is in my mind not independent of the existing approved training paradigms in the parent fields in question, history and psychology. We must consider what these were like in mid-twentieth-century America. Psychology was invaded by the enforced growth of clinical psychology, supported largely by government agencies to combat the psychological problems engendered by a devastating war. While the discipline welcomed the benefits that could accrue generally to a subsidized group, the controlling forces in graduate education in psychology were well aware of the previous half-century of psychology's struggle to separate itself from philosophy and enter into the realm of empirical science. These were not exactly the conditions that would foster support of psychobiographical work. The general agreement reached in the field was to require that Ph.D. dissertations be based on empirical studies that would satisfy scientific criteria. Thus, the possibility for a subspecialty in psychobiography was slim, and, no training programs were available in psychology departments to prepare people to do scholarly work in this realm. Even today, a half-century later, one could probably count on the fingers of one hand the few university psychology departments that would find psychobiographical work acceptable as final theses. In psychology, psychobiography remains today the province of a limited number of mavericks, largely known to one another, and somewhat isolated from the central issues with which the field is concerned. Most psychobiographers were trained initially in either clinical, personality, or social psychology and later branched out into psychobiography as a matter of interest.

While some prominent historians reacted favorably to the possibility of introducing human psychological factors into the study of historical events, the general attitude was somewhat skeptical. The accuracy of the data was critical to acceptable historical scholarship. Speculative psychological theorizing seemed dangerous, and indeed, there resulted a number of psychohistorical efforts that were less than convincing. Thus, I have not identified any concerted effort to promote this field in standard graduate programs in history, although I do believe that a graduate student interested in such work could probably pursue it if he or she could find a sponsor.

Under the aforementioned conditions, it is unlikely that Erikson's entry into psychobiography could have produced rapid growth in new fields of study even if he desired to foster such an approach. Although he may have been desirous of demonstrating the importance of psychological factors in the appearance and resolution of an "identity crisis" in Luther's young life, he had no leadership interests in developing such an avenue of study. In fact, it is said that he hoped that the appellation "psychohistory" would disappear as historians became more acquainted with the importance of psychological factors in historical events. In some ways, Erikson's mission has been fulfilled. Without great notice the tenor of time present is such that psychological explanation is freely given in the press, television, and other news sources, in trying to account for important geopolitical events likely to be recorded in history. Additionally, scholars in political science certainly look at the psychological characteristics of people in power to either predict or explain the decisions they make while in office (for more evidence of this trend, see part IV of this vol.). It seems that there is general sanction for this kind of activity within modern culture without much thought about how it came about.

What may also have been important was that as a result of Erikson's work, independent scholars previously handicapped by the dominance of orthodox psychoanalytic views in psychobiographical attempts now found a simpler stage theory to explore as an explanatory device (Alexander, 1990).

What Led Erikson Into Psychobiographical Work?

How did Erikson arrive at the Luther study? He was in his fifties at the time, the mainstay member of the senior staff at Austen Riggs, in a highly regarded, revamped clinical setting. During his previous five or six years since leaving Berkeley, he had been heavily involved in treatment and training, using his own ideas about the "identity crisis" and its treatment. What could have prompted him to drop everything and apply for outside support to allow him to spend a year away from Stockbridge, where he was then located, in order to complete a psychobiographical study of a seven-year period in Luther's life? The work was centered on the time when Luther was in the early stages of his preparation for the priesthood, contrary to the expressed wishes of his father. Erikson had recently finished working with four patients who were suffering "identity crises," and he intended to prepare a book on the work. What could have dissuaded him? Clearly he had an ideal situation at Austen Riggs, one designed to his own specifications with as much security and freedom to write as he desired. What made it imperative to produce the Luther volume in a constricted time frame, one year later, especially since it took hastily generated outside financial support to even attempt the feat (Friedman, 1999, p. 276)?

One possibility that comes to mind is that perhaps his publishers were waiting for another book from him, given the unexpected level of success that *Childhood and Society* (1950) had produced in the six years since its publication. That may have been the case, but a more compelling hypothesis also presents itself, that has to do with what he may have viewed as the situation that would ultimately provide him with the greatest feelings of acceptance, congeniality, and freedom to pursue his own ideas without suffering the discomfort of the "outsider." This concern, as described below, grew out of his childhood. In my estimation, he thought that the ideal set of conditions for life and work was to be found in the professoriate and not necessarily in the clinical situation. The latter is normally administered by medical people and principally serviced by those medically trained. Throughout his earlier time in America (1933–1951), he had been affiliated with three universities, Harvard, Yale, and the University of California at Berkeley. The latter two supplied his basic income by supported research-affiliated positions. In all three settings his income was also supplemented with limited

private practice and consultation work. In 1949, after sixteen years in America, without a tenure track university appointment and without the usual educational background to compete for one, he was nominated for and awarded a professorship at Berkeley, largely sponsored by the psychology department and its affiliate Institute for Personality Assessment Research. This was no small feat to accomplish without advanced academic or medical training or even an undergraduate degree, especially since final scrutiny was conducted by an all-university committee. Although he had been active and successful in teaching graduate courses in the psychology department, we must consider the possibility that the favorable decision was influenced by the recent acceptance for publication of *Childhood and Society* by a reputable commercial house.

Unfortunately, his pleasure in the appointment was short-lived due to the controversy that grew up around the imposed loyalty oath newly demanded of all state employees by the legislature. Leading the opposition to signing the oath were various members of the psychology department, including the two senior members who were instrumental in pursuing Erikson's professorial appointment.

Although Erikson, on principle, opposed the demand for a declaration of loyalty, his reticent and somewhat private manner made expressing this uncomfortable for him, and he resigned his position one year later. This was after he was found acceptable by a committee to continue his employment. There are indications that Erikson was conflicted about what to do. That he valued the professorial appointment highly may be indicated by the fact that he was willing to suffer the possibility of a rejection for lack of academic credentials after being nominated. What may have been influential in his ultimate decision to leave was the divided climate he became aware of in the California atmosphere. He was lumped with the "foreigners," the "European refugees," the "Communist fellow travelers." It was quite a different experience for him from the earlier period in America. His initial experiences of being welcomed during the early part of Roosevelt regimes and thenceforth gave way to a feeling more reminiscent of his European experiences of being an unwanted, suspected, alien (Friedman, 1999).

One must remember that this was Erikson prior to the period of writing the Luther book wherein the finding of a voice was a crucial issue.

Other factors involved in the conflict were the difficulties introduced following the appointment. Having arrived at a secure source of basic income, the Eriksons began to plan for a more permanent home and community. Their children were in transitional stages. His oldest, Kai, was soon to enter college, and his second son, Jon, was about to begin his final year in high school. His daughter, Sue, was a beginning adolescent, and the youngest child, Neil, who suffered Down syndrome, was cared for in an adequate California facility. The immediate compromise was for Erikson to resign the professorship and accept a temporary nontenured position at the Institute for Personality Assessment Research, which did not require a declaration of loyalty. This solution allowed him to maintain his integrity and gave him the time to investigate, more thoroughly, new job possibilities. His statement explaining his decision was made in 1951 to the university committee on privilege and tenure and reprinted later that year in a psychiatric journal (Friedman, 1999, pp. 245–252).

By September 1951 all had been settled. Kai was off to college, Jon remained with the family of a friend to complete the last year of high school, and Sue accompanied the Eriksons eastward to Stockbridge. Earlier that year Erikson had agreed to an appointment in Austen Riggs, where a job description was written to accommodate his major needs, such as limited clinical service (including supervision and psychotherapy), consultative work in a distant university facility, and the right to pursue his writing projects. The latter was guaranteed by providing ample time free of other obligations. For a man rapidly approaching fifty, it seemed like the ideal situation in which to round out a career. He was clearly seen as the central figure around which a distinguished program could be built at Riggs (Friedman, 1999).

The reasons for accepting this appointment may have included other considerations. Having been associated with three of the most prestigious universities and having been appointed professor at one may have limited Erikson's choice of future employment to institutions of equal repute. Austen Riggs offered him an unusually prestigious position in a different setting, a medical, psychiatric, psychoanalytic community. It was an opportunity to mend fences with the orthodox psychoanalytic community. Suspicion of his loyalty to strict Freudian views was likely engendered by the contents of *Childhood and Society*. At the same time, however, if he accepted the job, he would also have the opportunity to further test his unorthodox ideas about adolescence and identity issues in a therapeutic setting.

Geography may also have played a role in his ultimate choice for relocation to Stockbridge. Having lived previously in Massachusetts and Connecticut, the area itself provided attraction in its beauty, its proximity to important urban centers and the intellectual mix contained in its population. Its proximity to Cambridge, with the world-renowned institutions of Harvard and M.I.T. should also be noted.

One further possibility suggests itself. Erikson may have desired ultimately to free himself of the dominance of the medical profession, and particularly the orthodox Freudian psychoanalytic community, in order to pursue his cultural and developmental ideas. Although he recognized the advantages that his psychoanalytic status afforded him generally, he was also aware of the changing position of nonmedical applicants who were no longer eligible for clinical training in established psychoanalytic institutes. Additionally, some of the people first attracted to Erikson's views were known intellectuals. These were connected with either academic or research institutes. David Riesman, a highly visible sociologist and author of *The Lonely Crowd*, and Margaret Mead, a world acclaimed anthropologist, are two such figures who come to mind. They became life-long friends of Erikson and were called upon for advice when he ran into difficult life problems. I have little doubt that they were consulted during the period of stress he experienced at the time of the California "loyalty oath" controversy. It would be my feeling that a return to a professorship in a major university was the ultimate goal upon which all three could agree. There one could enjoy the freedom to express one's thoughts, no matter where they led, without having to satisfy some dominating organizational conditions. Even Riggs couldn't really guarantee that.[1]

Riggs, however, was a setting containing various people who were eager for Erikson to join them. It certainly promised to be an accepting surround, with people who had positive regard for his ideas, which they felt were within the psychoanalytic framework. Indeed, the promise was largely realized. His relationships with the director, Robert Knight, and senior psychologist, David Rapaport, blossomed. They became more than colleagues; soon they were his close friends, walking companions, and sources of humor in the exchange of jokes.[2] There were also demonstrations by senior staff members of loyalty toward Erikson and his work. This was an attribute that we know he held in high esteem. For example, Knight supported Erikson in a confrontation with leading figures in traditional psychoanalytic publication outlets. In the early 1950s, Erikson submitted a paper to the *International Journal of Psychoanalysis* that concerned a reanalysis of Freud's "Irma dream," contained in Freud's *Theory of Dreams*, published in 1900. Erikson was trying to make a point that involved considering the value of the manifest content of the dream over and above its role in uncovering unconscious factors. The paper was rejected, after a principal review by Ernest Jones, Freud's biographer, much to Erikson's distress. According to Friedman (1999, p. 289), it was Knight, an influential member of the editorial committee of the *American Journal of Psychoanalysis* who was instrumental in subsequently ensuring its publication there.

Similarly, David Rapaport, one of the chief scholars and interpreters of Freudian psychoanalytic theory in America, spent a good deal of time reconciling Erikson's view of the ego with those of more acceptable orthodox positions, particularly that of Heinz Hartmann, who had been one of the senior psychoanalysts and one of Erikson's teachers in Vienna (Gill, 1967). It would seem to me that Erikson was always clearly aware of his uncertain position in powerful psychoanalytic circles and wished ultimately for escape from that situation. Continued membership in more orthodox psychoanalytic circles afforded him general status, and even encouragement

from some particular individuals, yet the questioning of his strict adherence to Freudian ideas continued to be troublesome to him. His chief defense seemed to be that he was trained by a member of the royal family, Anna Freud, in the home of the royal family, the Vienna Psychoanalytic Institute. He felt that his loyalty was called into question because he was bold enough to adopt Freud's pioneering attitude. He consistently declared that his work stemmed from the work of Freud and in one sense that was obviously so. Before his training in Vienna, he knew almost nothing about psychoanalysis and showed no intrinsic interest in acquiring such knowledge.

I do wonder whether his first popular venture into psychobiography, Luther's battle with identity issues, was fueled by his interest in obtaining a particular professorial appointment, one that he did secure a few years later. Two bits of unconnected information appearing in the Friedman volume (1999, pp. 305–310) lead me to consider this conjecture: One concerns the appointment in 1957 of his friend and confidant, David Riesman, to a special professorship at Harvard. The other is the fact that Margaret Mead prepared a limited bibliography of English sources on Luther for Erikson when he decided to take a leave of absence from Riggs in order to complete the book (p. 270). Since I have already intimated the possible role that the completed manuscript for *Childhood and Society*, which was accepted for publication close to the time of his professorial nomination at Berkeley, may have played in that appointment, it would not surprise me that he may have assigned similar value to the proposed work on Luther. Friedman points out that Riesman and Talcott Parsons waited for word from Erikson concerning his approval for them to begin inquiries about a possible appointment for Erikson at Harvard. This he gave in 1958 after the Luther study was accepted for publication (p. 306). The book had possibilities of attracting the attention of general readers to Erikson's ideas, a psychoanalyst commenting on human problems through the vehicle of an important historic figure. I think it also had meaning for Erikson personally.

Luther as Erikson Sees Him and What This May Indicate About Erikson

Two major aspects of Erikson's focus were on Luther's "discovery of his own voice," his ability to establish his own response to disabling authoritative positions, and the need to "mean it," to believe in the ultimate correctness of his cause over and above its particular value for him. "Finding a voice" and "meaning it" made sense in terms of Erikson's continuing struggle with psychoanalysis, especially at this time in his life. It also made sense in the light of his childhood, which we shall later examine. The unusual condition, through which Erikson's earlier identity problems were largely relieved in his Vienna years, was threatened by the directions his work was taking in the 1950s as well as how the work either confirmed or called into question his loyalty to Freud's ideas. The issue of Erikson's re-awakened identity problems during that period was recognized by Coles in his thoughtful book on Erikson's work, which appeared in 1970. Finding and expressing his own voice seemed to be a continuing process during Erikson's time at Riggs and was clearly reflected in some of his writing, especially in his reinterpretation of Freud's "Irma dream."

With regard to "meaning it," it is less certain to me that he was aware of the personal relevance to his own life at this time. What is evident, however, is that Luther's solution, open aggressive action, was neither attractive nor possible at this time for Erikson as a sign of "meaning it."

One aspect of the Luther book that stirred my interest was the extensive use Erikson made of a reputed incident in Luther's life, the "fit in the choir." This is an incident whose actual occurrence has been challenged by Luther scholars. Erikson's reported response to the reality of the choir incident seems doctrinaire. His claim was that there were enough unusual experiences, fits, in Luther's young life to allow his speculation about this contested one. Luther supposedly fell to the floor uttering a denial in either German or Latin that translates roughly in English to an often heard child's response to a derogative taunt—"I am not," or in Luther's German "Ich bin es nit." (This translation was given in 1976 by Paul Roazen for the Latin version.) The phrase itself, as used by children, is the denial of an antagonist's assertion, usually about the victim's character, ability, or origin. Consider what it must be like if the assertion has some element of truth in it, or its value for you is positive although negative for your foes. These are the circumstances that Erikson faced consistently throughout his years in Karlsruhe. He may not have had a response then. His attribution to Luther at the time of the fit is worth repeating for what it suggests about what might have been either stifled or repressed in Erikson in the past:

> Why did I introduce my discussion of Luther with this particular event in the choir, whose expectation is subject to so many large and small discrepancies? As I tried to orient myself in regard to Luther's identity crisis by studying those works which promised to render the greatest number of facts and references for independent study, I heard him, ever again, roar in rage and yet also in laughter: "Ich bin es nit." (Erikson, 1958, p. 29)

This sounds like the release of long-contained rage over accusations one could not easily deny, but that did not necessarily lead to the implications intended by the accuser: "You are an X and therefore . . ." (all negative). Yes, Erikson was the child of a Danish, Jewish mother, both positive sources of identification for him although not for many of his age mates. That accusation was difficult to deny, but it was not the entire story. The remainder of the story, untold, about a believed Danish, Christian father would have relieved only part of the difficulty.

Luther's presumed denial seems not to have been available to Erikson at the appropriate time. Consequently, its appearance later led to a burst of relief for Erikson and an attribution to Luther of roaring rage and intermittent laughter, which suggests what may have been unavailable but desirable on some level for Erikson.[3] What is implied is that the writing of the Luther book marked the discovery for Erikson of an oppositional voice that allowed him the freedom to pursue his own work without having to address the problem of loyalty to orthodox psychoanalysis.

The internal struggle of Erikson's relationship to psychoanalysis essentially found more permanent relief when he was appointed to a special professorship at Harvard in 1960 and I believe that Erikson was correct if he thought that the Luther book would enhance his candidacy. It was a book of general intellectual interest, which, among the variety of things he had in mind also promoted an understanding of a particular stage in his notion of normal developmental history. At last, at Harvard, he was located in a milieu in which his psychoanalytic credentials were acceptable and his ideas on psychological development valued.

Harvard, India, Gandhi, Satyagraha—and Erikson

Erikson's years at Harvard were mostly devoted to teaching and writing. His undergraduate course, usually oversubscribed, demanded of him little administrative time. He had a large number of handpicked graduate assistants, led by a competent, somewhat more permanent director. Each week he gave two lectures that were carefully prepared and well appreciated. On the graduate level he gave a course in which psychobiographical study was emphasized. He screened the participants and gave them much latitude in selecting the lives they wished to analyze. With regard to psychoanalysis, he retained his admiration for the boldness and the originality contained in Freud's systematic thought. However, he showed no propensity to engage in controversy regarding his adherence to orthodox psychoanalytic principles. His therapeutic work was clearly reduced and may have been abandoned entirely. Strangely enough, he mocked explanation in terms of early intrafamilial dynamics. This he termed "originology," which may help to explain why some may have thought his analysis didn't go deep enough (Friedman, 1999, p. 6). Anna Freud is reputed to have said that a great deal of his analytic time was spent in problems related to his concern about the identification of his father. Given his history, Erikson seemed fixated on the problem of origin and never seemed to focus on the ensuing early conditions, which may have been instrumental in determining how he lived and what he experienced affectively. In reading Friedman's discussion of Erikson's time in Vienna, I had the feeling that he enjoyed the attention that he received for his work at the school and also the seminars by distinguished teachers, but that he had reservations about the efficacy of the therapeutic process and its outcome.

A good bit of the decade he spent at Harvard before retirement was concerned with the culture of India, the developmental ideas contained in Hinduism, and the origin of nonviolent resistance, "satyagraha," as a method of dealing with oppressive authoritarian forces. It was a method far different in approach from that of Luther, who led a revolt and established a new religion. Gandhi, on the other hand, offered a solution to conflict that minimized aggressive power and the philosophy of retaliation in kind, or "an eye for an eye." It was a position with which Erikson could sympathize, and indeed, there is evidence that his admiration for Gandhi went back to his days as a teenager and must have been reawakened by his support for Martin Luther King's solution to the civil rights struggle. Although "satyagraha" was a stance toward authoritative aggression, Erikson unfortunately could not lead the massive populations available to Gandhi in India and perhaps to King in the United States, although the vigor and persistence of the disillusioned and discontented youth of that era in American history may have given Erikson the impression that a similar following did exist.

His trip to India was initiated in the early 1960s by a group in Ahmedabad, India, who wished to learn about Erikson's stage theory and discuss comparisons with existing Hindu views on development. Erikson's response to the invitation was positive but probably without awareness of what that visit would entail. It is not unlikely that he hoped the visit would provide more cross-cultural data on the possible universal properties of his schema: The psychological problems to be resolved at various points in the life span were universal no matter what the culture pointed to as acceptable solutions.

Apparently more difficulties were encountered in the comparison than he had anticipated, and thus the history of Gandhi's role in the famous strike of the mill workers in 1918 became Erikson's central interest. Perhaps this was not surprising in that the Eriksons were guests in the compound of one of the mill owners and his sister, who were critical figures, on opposite sides, in the 1918 controversy. It was also the case that many of Gandhi's compatriots were still available in the local area to provide their personal recollections of that historical period. It was an opportunity to revisit a limited but important point in Gandhi's life.

If one thinks of the Luther experience for Erikson as the occasion for finding and accepting his voice, the next question is that of how best to use that voice, how to "mean it." Gandhi, through "satyagraha," the pursuit of truth in a persistent, nonviolent way, held out the possibility of a solution for Erikson personally. He evidently had practiced it unknowingly in his childhood and adolescent years by not responding to the taunts of his age mates.

It is a resolution, however, whose success depends on the known attitudes and behaviors of the contending other. Contrast British rule with Nazi Germany's treatment of the inhabitants of occupied territories. Certainly one would have to take certain realities into account before responding to acts of others that are likely to induce negative affect in the victim. It should also be recognized that Gandhi had and used an additional strategy, a personal "hunger strike," when "satyagraha" failed to impress his opposition. Whether one could derive that strategy from the central idea of "satyagraha" is problematic. The possibility of starving oneself to death unless the other acquiesces has an aggressive, coercive tinge. In fact, when Erikson discovered various instances of Gandhi's aggression toward his wife, it interrupted his progress in completing the book. To deal with the situation, he finally composed a chapter, designed as a communication to Gandhi who had been dead for many years, in which he pontificated on how knowledge of psychoanalytic principles could have helped Gandhi avoid aggression. The distress that Erikson suffered at this time, the inability to continue the work, was perhaps an indication of how powerful aggression and its use remained for him. Fortunately, Erikson's oppressors lived prior to the Nazi era and were not prone to using Hitler's methods in dealing with "outsiders."

There is, however, another aspect to Erikson's distress, which culminated in the "letter to Gandhi." The example that Erikson pointed to was Gandhi's apparent treatment, at various times, of his wife. This Erikson did without regard to possible cultural differences, between India, Germany, and America. It was as though Erikson was defending what he saw as a universal principle, which seemed to have as much relationship to the sanctity of women as it did to aggression. One should recall, however, that Erikson was well aware of Gandhi's effort to recruit his countrymen for service in the British military during World War I. There obviously were situations for Gandhi that superseded the principle of "satyagraha." He was a consummate politician.

The fact, however, that Gandhi's mistreatment of Kasturba resulted in a treatise on ambivalence and marriage leads me to wonder about aggression and its relation to the most important women in Erikson's life. To this topic I shall return.

The Luther and Gandhi volumes testify to the fact that despite the resolution of identity issues by dint of good fortune and hard work in his Vienna years, the emergence of his own ideas, culminating in *Childhood and Society* and his new position at Austen Riggs, Erikson's identity problems resurfaced in the 1950s. He had discovered a voice but felt that he had to mute that voice in order to avoid expressions of an aggressive solution and its possible consequences. Escape seemed like the solution of choice. The Harvard appointment provided that opportunity.

I believe that the Harvard experience was one of the best periods in Erikson's life. It contained all the conditions he experienced in his early life. By the following year, his daughter had married and the three other children lived in California, away from home. He had the undivided attention of his wife Joan, and he was in a congenial atmosphere. But he had even more, which put him in touch with other outstanding intellectuals. He had achieved world recognition, a voice, dedicated to bringing peace and better conditions for all people. He was truly an international figure.

It was during this time that he began to comment, in his classes, on the power of the Ingmar Bergman film *Wild Strawberries* (Friedman, 1999, pp. 311–312). He saw the movie as a wonderful expression of his view of the life cycle, especially the last stage, and the path to wisdom. Because he wrote and lectured on the film for a number of years, even beyond his retirement, it seems to me that it held personal meaning for Erikson. The film, a review of various aspects of Dr. Borg's life as he travels to accept an honor from his university, may have tapped into Erikson's own concerns at this point. He may have wondered, as many people do, whether he had achieved a state of wisdom or whether he was just fooling himself. If the latter was the case, it would be reminiscent of the problem of "meaning it," the issue that he faced in the Gandhi volume when he discovered and was disturbed by the fact that "satyagraha" and aggression could exist in the same person at the same time and not be realized, as in his struggle with orthodox psychoanalysis. Friedman (1999, pp. 444–447) comments extensively on Erikson's treatment of Bergmann's film.

Erikson's Early Life: The Development or Lack of Development of Certain Personality Characteristics

To reconstruct Erikson's initial experiences with anger and its expression, one would have to examine what his early existence was like. Friedman's descriptions are helpful here. We know that he was the child of a single mother, who was a member of a prominent, financially comfortable, Danish, Jewish, family. When she became aware of her pregnancy, she completed her term and gave birth to her child in Germany. All of this, as legend has it, after consultation with her supportive but proper family.

Her social contacts in Germany, as far as we know, were with some maiden aunts in Frankfurt and with members of an artistic community in nearby Buehl. These resources remained available after the child was delivered in Frankfurt and raised in Buehl. In fact, it is highly likely that these people were accepting and even adoring of

the young child of a determined single mother, especially a child who also showed clear signs of advanced intellectual ability. Erikson (1975) has reported that the males of the artistic group gave him his first male imprinting. Evidently there were no plans made for mother and child to return to Denmark. The entire event and its resolution seem hastily conceived, largely to hide the social implications of her decision. Mother and child seemed to float in an interdependent limbo.

To interact almost exclusively with adults and to be treated with love and admiration does not seem to me to be ideal conditions for the development of aggression in a child. The constant underlying state of sadness of the mother reported in Erikson's early memories might provoke it, unless he had discovered means to direct her attention and positive affect toward himself. This, I believe, he was capable of doing with displays of his precocity, which could have induced both surprise and delight in her. The lack of experience with aggression toward adults and the relative absence of other children in his life left Erikson, I believe, less able to deal with age mates when he went to live in Karlsruhe a few years later. Not only might he have had little experience with aggressive expression, but also, given his feeling of "a foot in every door" (religion, social class—and avant garde artists), he may have felt he belonged everywhere. Luther's aggression in a response to unfair treatment later fascinated Erikson, but the means used by Luther to express his voice were not available to Erikson. What mother implicitly demanded of him in Karlsruhe was that he adjust to the new situation. By this time he was probably so dependent on her positive attitude toward him that the loss of her support would have been devastating.

The general situation that I have assumed for Erikson's early years—living alone with an adoring, supportive mother, whose time was devoted mainly to him, and a welcoming adult, artistic, set of mother's friends—would lead me to consider another possible development: expectations of being taken care of and provided for when things appear difficult. Still another aspect of his early life and his relationship with his mother would invite consideration of his expectation of privilege and of things eventually turning out to his benefit, and the assumption that privilege was his and not to be questioned. I wonder if this isn't a concomitant of narcissism, used in a descriptive and not necessarily pathological sense.

Erikson's limited descriptions of his mother during their early years together seem almost entirely positive, except for her guarding the secret of his paternity, although this latter feature seems more relevant to a later time in his life. Erikson saw his mother as beautiful, intelligent, aware of his potential, and entirely supportive. There is a long paragraph in Friedman (1999, p. 39) describing the foundation of Erikson's early life with mother. Although there is sufficient reference to her pervasive sadness, given the bond that was reportedly forged between them then, I would guess that she represented the most important source of positive affect in his life at that time and that she became a model for what he sought in a relationship in the future. I believe his experience of positive affect was stimulated early in his life by the mother's smile, an experience that he later described more generally as the origin of "identity." I would further hypothesize that the mother's sadness was distressing to him and probably resulted in behavior on his part to please and distract her, and this for the most part was successful. In fact, I would seriously consider that a lot of Erikson's dependency behavior exhibited in adulthood, has its origin in the first three years of his life. I am referring here to his reported response to being asked how he felt. He might turn to his wife and ask, "Joan, how do we feel today?" Also, he apparently didn't know much about food preferences and had to ask his wife whether he liked or would like some particular food. This may have originated in a sort of game that he played with his mother when he was a small child. His overly dependent attitudes brought pleasure to the mother even though they both knew that he possessed the ability to make his own decisions.

Erikson's greatest difficulty most likely occurred when he found his mother crying. His usual behavior may not have been successful in turning her attention to him. I would guess, however, that mimicry, crying with her, would have been enough to turn her attention toward his immediate needs and reinstate the positive affective interaction between them. I was led to this formulation by the puzzlement I encountered in reading Sue Erikson Bloland's account of her father's unfathomable behavior when she, an adolescent, alone with him, cried over the loss of a romance recently terminated (Bloland, 1999). She tells of his inability to comfort her or to do the things that he normally did in his work while listening to people in distress. Instead, he cried as well. I would propose the possibility that his daughter's behavior automatically initiated an old "nuclear script" (Carlson, 1988) derived from his early relationship to mother. His daughter's tears came from a person he cared deeply about, and vice versa. His automatic response was to cry with her without having any idea of why. To his daughter it was perhaps a sign of his ineptitude and/ or a verification of her misgivings about self. There were enough similarities in the two situations—a loved female, a family member with whom conversation was almost impossible, displaying an extreme form of negative affect in his presence, to which he felt compelled to respond to initiate his automatic response of mimicry. Perhaps his tears in fact indicated something other than ineptitude, in that they turned mother's attention to his discomfort and modified the entire scene. Certainly, under other conditions, out in the world together, he and his daughter were able to play the expected roles of loving father and daughter, no matter how they felt about the artificiality of this pose (Bloland, 1999). In one sense his response contained some measure of intended success for him. His daughter did essentially what his mother did: She turned her attention to his needs, stopped crying and vowed never again to distress him. Again, what is illustrated here is a nuclear script in Silvan Tomkins's script theory language, namely, a response to a fall from expected positive affect to the experience of negative affect and the consequent search for behaviors to reinstitute the positive affect state.

My contention is that Erikson's first three years were almost idyllic. His contacts were with adults who loved him. He had an exclusive one to one relationship with an adoring mother. However, he had little contact with age mates.

He was an adult clone, without aggressive, defensive development.

His Mother's Marriage and Erikson's Response to the New Situation

From various descriptions, including his own (Erikson, 1975), his mother Karla's marriage to Theodor Homburger (a pediatrician who had earlier treated Erik successfully in an emergency), on Erik's third birthday, was difficult for the boy. We know that he had been the recipient of his mother's undivided attention until that time. Now, he would move to a new abode in Karlsruhe and assume a life thoroughly familiar to his stepfather but entirely foreign to him. Not only did he have to share his mother's attention with an adult male but also with the community interests she grew to share with her husband. It was a new and demanding situation, which he seemed to bear mostly in silence, inwardly, to maintain the good graces of his mother, his only anchor in the world. We hear of no temper tantrums but rather of a sort of reduced functioning, a constant mild depression, and a reluctance to follow his stepfather's wishes for him to be a physician or to take a willing part in his path to Judaism.

To illustrate the magnitude and length of time that his distress lasted, I refer to some incidents contained in Friedman's retelling of Erikson's history. Although the boy accompanied the Homburgers on their honeymoon, a voyage to Copenhagen, it may not have been a positive experience. He later made a woodcut of that event showing the couple in close proximity to one another and he at a respectable distance looking away, expressionless, but with his mouth turned down. The woodcut was produced circa 1925, twenty years after the honeymoon was celebrated. That this image stayed clearly in Erikson's mind for so many years leads me to think that the loss of the individual attention of the mother, having to share her with a relatively strange man, was not a happy event in his life. There are also photos reproduced in Friedman's book, one of Erik with his mother in the year following her marriage. There

again the lips are turned down and his face appears sad. A similar comment can be made about the photo taken with the first of the three daughters born to the marriage. This child, who seemed to have difficulties from the beginning and whose slow development must have demanded the mother's attention, died during her third year of life. The other two half-sisters were born after her death, the last when Erik was ten years old. By the time Ellen, the youngest, was born, Erikson was beginning his education in the gymnasium (Friedman, 1999, pp. 288–289).

Thus, much of Erikson's childhood and adolescence was shared with a stepfather and half-sisters whose dependence on mother was at least equal to his own. From what is known about Erikson during those years, information imparted by both him and others, he seems to have been devoid of childhood playmates. It wasn't until his last year in the gymnasium that we hear of two friends, Peter Blos and Oscar Stonorov. By this time he was in his eighteenth year. That he had the capacity to make friends then was clear. Whether he had opportunities, for reasons beyond his control, is less clear. A photograph taken in 1925, with his two remaining half-sisters, is also revealing. Although he has an arm around each one, his face is impassive, while they are smiling. He was twenty-three at the time, and there are indications that the family was concerned about his stability (Friedman, 1999). He was morose and seemed greatly distressed. The *Wanderschaft* was evidently not leading to a life career as an artist.

Adolescence, the *Wanderschaft*, and Its Implications

Less available to us from the various sources of information about Erikson's life are his adolescent contacts with females his age. Nowhere is there clear comment on actual interactions with age-equal women until he began to court Joan Serson in Vienna in 1930.

Adolescence was reportedly a continuation of what he experienced from his earliest days in Karlsruhe. The children, both Jews and Gentiles, seemed to consider him an outsider, and indeed, in some sense he was. The Jewish children rejected him, perhaps because his Scandinavian appearance, unlike that of his mother, made him appear strange and suspect. Although he was born in Germany, his Jewish and Danish background made him unacceptable to the German children, who also shunned and maligned him. He was isolated. Aggression as a defense was unlikely. The consequences could have been formidable. Instead, he took his pleasures from his artwork, mostly by himself, until his last year in school when he made two friends, Blos and Stonorov, with whom he continued contact from then on, no matter where they ultimately settled. Both his mother and his acceptance by his mother's friends in the artistic community continued to serve through the years as his major source of positive affect.

The circumstances surrounding Erikson's *Wanderschaft* are worth examining. The period began in 1920 after he finished secondary school when he was eighteen years old. The custom was a well-known one in Germany, although its length was usually much shorter than the seven years of Erikson's search. Part of the reason may be attributed to the fact that a portion of the time was devoted to artistic study. However, by the third year Erikson was convinced that he could not master the intricacies of color representation, which forced him to abandon the idea of being an independent, practicing artist. During that period he seriously considered teaching art in the Karlsruhe schools, largely, I believe, to maintain his contact with the art community in which he wished to live (Friedman, 1999).

Perhaps the discovery of this inability to work with colors, which to psychologists might suggest an underdevelopment of affective expression, was a strong factor in his "identity crisis." Several things happened in the ensuing period, which led to a resolution of his situation without his "figuring out what to do." It was at this time that he began spontaneously to record his thoughts, and over a year and a half after abandoning his artistic training he compiled more than 140 pages of reflections. Friedman (1999, pp. 49–56) refers to these "jottings" as the "Manuscript von Erik." While these written pieces vary greatly in length and profundity and include elements that could be seen in later work, they were by no means distinguished. But they were his thoughts, not simply an artist's comments about the surround and its artistic possibilities. The most telltale aspect of this free expression was that Erikson assigned the work to a form of perpetuity, the Homburger library (Friedman, 1999, p. 50). Writing must have been a satisfying experience; it could produce positive affect.

The period from 1920 to 1927, the years of Erikson's *Wanderschaft*, seems to me to involve verification of his expectation of privilege, the idea that he would be supported and entitled to such support. We must remember that the length of time he devoted to charting his course was seven full years in a post-World War I inflationary economy in a defeated Germany. Yet during all of that time we know of no source of income other than that supplied by his family. The patience they exhibited was a tribute largely to the mother's concern for his eventual discovery of a life path with which he could be happy. I do not recall ever seeing anything that would indicate any concern on his part for the length of time involved in charting his path. In the last two years of this stretch of time, he returned periodically to live at home in Karlsruhe, probably coming to grips with accepting a teaching position in art in the Karlsruhe school system. There are indications that he suffered unhappiness during this time. It was perhaps the low point of his late adolescent years, an identity crisis.

Up to this time, sketching was one of the activities that he went to when distressed. The recognition that he could not be a successful artist demanded another source of positive affect. The beginning of the replacement of art by writing occurred in the last years of his *Wanderschaft*. Now two other elements were lacking in order to reproduce the conditions encountered in the first three years of his life: a new congenial group with whom he could identify professionally, and a supporting female with whom he could establish a mutual trusting relationship. By an act of chance or fate, these were supplied in the next phase of his life.

The Vienna Years

The beginning of an unexpected new life, for which there could have been no preparation, came in 1927 in the form of an invitation from Peter Blos to come to Vienna to sketch the Burlingham children, who were tutored by Blos, and perhaps to help in setting up a private school for children in analysis or children of adults connected in one way or another with psychoanalysis. It was the beginning of a new life away from Karlsruhe and the unpleasant memories it contained for Erikson.

Vienna carried with it all the ingredients that Erikson needed to be happy. He was in the company of congenial accepting adults who recognized his intellectual ability despite his lack of previous training. He had contact with children who accepted his ability to understand them, to be one of them, and yet not one of them. He also lived with one of his two known friends, Peter Blos, who did not suffer the same growth pains as did Erikson. Blos, who had come originally to Vienna to do advanced work in biology, was more of a free, adventurous soul. Within a brief period of time, perhaps a year, Erickson was helping Blos to set up the small progressive school, and he was invited to enter child psychoanalytic training, including a training analysis with Anna Freud, the leading figure in child analysis at the Vienna Psychoanalytic Institute. The situation could not have been more favorable for one in Erikson's place in life. Shortly thereafter, it seems, his path was set in a contextual framework similar to that he experienced among artists. Furthermore, he was accepted by an important woman, Anna Freud, who connected him, in a sense, with the royalty that he had assigned to his birth father in fantasy. The only thing missing was an intense, interdependent relationship with a woman.

Although they may have initially met at the Hietzing School in late 1929, the romance of Joan Serson and Erik began, according to Friedman (1999, pp. 82–83), at a Mardi Gras ball in 1930. They were both clearly fascinated with each other, and shortly thereafter she joined Erik in an abode he shared with Peter Blos. Within a brief period of time, while she was attending her mother, who was recovering from surgery in America, Joan discovered that she was pregnant and returned to Vienna. Friedman (1999, p. 83) points to some difficulty surrounding the expectation of marriage that Joan clearly entertained,

and this may reveal what Erik was like then. He supposedly responded that he was not in a position to take on permanent commitments at that time and that, furthermore, his mother and stepfather would object to his marrying a Gentile. It is possible that at age twenty-eight he was just beginning to taste the freedoms accessible to most at earlier periods in their lives and was not willing, yet, to give them up. Moreover, his reaction reflects a possibility that he was not quite in tune with the feelings of another person, a female close in age. He also failed to recognize, until friends pointed it out to him, that he was in a situation similar to that of his birth father. His response may additionally reflect a continued dependency on his parents. Whatever the case, it certainly does not reflect a mature adult, madly in love and sensitive to the distress of his partner.

The marriage, to which he finally agreed, took place late in 1930. It was, at first, a mixed blessing. I have the feeling, from reading Friedman, that Joan was a strong, organized woman who had clear feelings about various things in the world —psychoanalysis, religion, and her husband's friendship with Peter Blos and the Freuds—which sometimes engendered conflict. Given his problems expressing aggression, it seems likely that he closed off some aspects of his world of freedom in Vienna in order to be in tune with her wishes. The positive side of this equation lay in the fact that he now assumed some responsibilities related to family life and the care of home and children. When Jon, the second son, was born early in 1933, there was much to be done, and Erikson seems to have assumed some of the burdens that fell on Joan. For the first time in his life he was expected to provide sustained help to others: his students, his patients, his wife, and his children. The marriage led him into adulthood.

The situation, however, reminds me of the change in his life when his mother married Homburger and he had to relinquish the complete attention of the love object for a shared relationship with others who demanded attention as well. While he was no longer a three-year-old child and had many more options in dealing with his situation, I cannot help but wonder whether the context revived some aspects of what he felt when he was torn away from the Eden he enjoyed with his mother in the first three years of his life. This time, however, he was an adult with a budding occupation to demand his attention.[4]

A Hypothetical View of Erikson's Psychological Development

I return now to the question that fascinated me from the start: Who was Erik Erikson, and how did he get to be that way? It has always been my belief, expressed in earlier publications, that a clear relationship exists between the life history and the work products, especially obvious in the lives of personality theorists. The lives of Freud, Jung, and Sullivan certainly reflect that belief adequately (Alexander, 1990). Oftentimes clues concerning life and work connections are found in the more esoteric publications or are embedded in biographical essays. In Erikson's case, such clues are evident throughout his work and are especially salient in his main psychobiographical products, *Young Man Luther* and *Gandhi's Truth*.[5]

Any sense of Erikson's psychological development depends upon the way in which his early life, his first three years alone with his mother, is read. From the various things we have been told by Friedman (1999), it is clear that there are multiple possibilities surrounding the paternity issue. The mother's pregnancy may have resulted from a deep but impossible love affair with an unidentified Danish Gentile, from a casual sexual encounter while on vacation, or from a liaison at a family party with an unknown partner while she was in a state of inebriation. The family is said to have promoted the idea that she did not discover her pregnancy until she had almost come to term, at a time she was in Germany on vacation. According to this version she was advised by family to remain in Germany, give birth, and then raise the child in Buehl, a town outside of Frankfurt, known to house an artistic community. Whether or not any of the antecedents to this tale are true (mentioned as possibilities by Friedman), she did give birth to the child in Frankfurt and raised him initially in Buehl.

I wish to point out two things about this early situation both of which seem crucial to me in trying to understand Erikson's early psychological development. The first is that it is frequently assumed that a fatherless child is handicapped. I contend that the situation is more likely to affect the mother's general state. This may in turn have impact on the child's development. However, in my estimation, the newborn is very unlikely to be aware of the lack of a father. Life will depend on the development of the mother–child relationship. In Erikson's case it probably had both positive and negative repercussions on how the child developed. It is clear he was capable of making an intense, somewhat dependent, relationship with a female. It is also clear that he was less able to deal effectively with negative affect, his own and others', due to lack of opportunity in his early years; and his subsequent life situation made aggression even more difficult to express.

I also want to consider the conditions under which mother and child lived in the three years before her marriage to Homburger. The description of the family from which Erikson's mother came, the Abrahamsens, would lead one to believe that they were well established financially and were close-knit and extremely supportive of their own. I will venture to say that if they made plans for her immediate future upon learning of her pregnancy, it probably included ample support for her well-being and that of the child. Furthermore, there is not a hint that she was either employed and/or needed money during that time. In fact, there are intimations that mother and son may have traveled around Germany together, a matter indicating sufficient leisure time and necessary means for travel costs. Aside from reference to his mother's sadness, there is little from which to assume that this period was in any sense traumatic for Erikson. On the contrary, Friedman (1999, p. 31) supplies quotations from him referring to the basic trust established early by the mother and to nascent feelings of identity that grew from his recognition of his mother's smile to him.

Friedman (1999) summarizes this period in Erikson's life by saying,

> . . . the recognition, trust, and joy from looking face-to-face, eye-to-eye, at his helpful, intelligent, and beautiful mother was something that Erik dwelled on throughout his life. If the first three years of this illegitimate child's life

with his mother in the north of Germany, distant from the Abrahamsen's was difficult—perhaps traumatic—it was hardly hopeless. A very special bond between mother and child had been forged. (p. 31)

I would suggest that perhaps this early period was far from traumatic for Erikson and perhaps somewhat idyllic, the "good nuclear scene" from Tomkins's script theory (Carlson, 1988).[6] Any "fall from grace" did not appear until sometime in the boy's third year of life, when Theodor Homburger began to court his mother. They married on Erik's third birthday. Friedman characterizes Homburger's entrance into the lives of Erik and Karla as an intrusion on the bond established earlier by mother and son. That this event produced an upheaval in the psychological state of the child can be assumed, for the mother saw signs of advanced intellectual development in the boy prior to the time she met Homburger, whereas the period from the time of the marriage and Erik's graduation from secondary school shows little evidence of the continuation of outstanding intellectual performance. We do know, however, that he was capable of high-level intellectual ability later, as indicated by his accomplishments in life.

Erik's problems began immediately after the marriage. It was much too much for him to find a path to the return of the positive scene and the resultant feelings it generated in him—a return to the feeling of a unique bond in which mother and child shared time and space together without any semblance of knowledge on the child's part of future permanent intrusion. Instead, in the several years following the marriage he was faced with a succession of people, all with a claim on mother's time and devotion. I do not believe that he doubted her positive attachment to him, but he seemed unable to overcome the difficulty of sharing her with others.

Many children solve this situation by resort to a variety of age-equal bonds or by attachment to adult authority figures in school and in other aspects of the outside world. We hear of only one such possibility for Erik during his life in Karlsruhe. This was provided by members of the artistic set who were some of his mother's friends and who represented a continuation of a situation with which he was familiar in Buehl, where

Figure 18.1. Erik Erikson. (Time Life Pictures/ Getty Images)

an artistic community of his mother's friends lived. That acceptance by this group in Buehl and later in Karlsruhe was influential in his life appears evident. As noted above, he seems to have made a choice early in life to pursue a career as an artist. Indeed, after abandoning this notion in the years following his graduation from secondary school, he continued to sketch and to consider himself as one who approaches the world from a visual, artistic viewpoint.

What I am suggesting is that Erikson did not have the means to follow the more obvious paths through which children offset the loss of mother's exclusive attention, but resorted to an intended future solution in art, which only prolonged his misery during late childhood and adolescence. The usual means of relief were not available to him, and in fact, contact with age mates and their derision may have intensified his feelings of negative affect. The critical question is, what was his internal response to the taunts. Was it anger or shame, or both? Furthermore, what did he do when he was taunted or shunned? This we do not know.

I do believe that he is likely to have felt that it would all change for the better when he was an adult, committed to his craft, in the company of like-minded, accepting people. In the next period of time he suffered despair in trying to make his dream come true in the art world but by chance embarked upon a career that offered the possibility of fulfillment in an initially accepting environment.

In my estimation the major source of affective support available to him until the time he was eighteen came from his mother in her clear, demonstrable affection for him. Although she undoubtedly frustrated him with her steadfastness in not revealing her partner in his conception, she was his anchor in the world. Without her he would have been adrift. What he lacked, and what he hoped to produce in his search for identity was a source of positive affect which he could call on reliably when needed, just as he could in his exclusive relationship with his mother in the early years of his life. The reference point, he learned later in life, was in the smile of the mother directed toward and recognized by the child. In some ways I think that Erikson stumbled upon the substitute for the mother's smile accidentally, in his *Wanderschaft*, and perhaps was not consciously aware of the relationship for the rest of his life. There I refer to the pleasure he could derive from writing about human psychological development. The importance of development in childhood he learned to appreciate in his work at the Hietzing School and later in his psychoanalytic training. Vienna also supplied a loving female, Joan, who, like his mother earlier, remained a sustaining source of support throughout his life.

Erikson and Family Life

I never thought much about Erikson's family life other than had what struck me from his later writings, some of which focused on his early years and his Vienna experiences with psychoanalysis. I had read Coles's 1970 work and also the contributions of Paul Roazen (1976). These

sources were not terribly informative about Erikson's life at home, and as a result I guess that I invoked the consistency hypothesis and assumed his behavior to be no different than how he appeared in his daily life outside the home. Certainly my limited interaction with him as a visitor in Harvard's Department of Social Relations in the school year 1966–67 did nothing to violate my image of a pleasant, good-humored person, who was clearly aware of his prominence in the intellectual world. Thus, it was somewhat surprising to read in Bloland (1999) that he sometimes withdrew from social gatherings with friends, at home or elsewhere, to read or to write. When I discovered her article, I was amazed by her description of her father at home, how different he was from the image he presented to the world. At home, he appeared rather unsure of himself, somewhat inept, and in some ways like an unhappy child. This difference fascinated me and reminded me of the years he spent in Karlsruhe when he had to share mother's attention first with Homburger and then with his halfsisters. I wondered if solitude while exploring matters of private interest, sketching or reading, provided some measure of relief. I think what may have been critical in making the situation bearable was the fact that his mother continued her positive attitude toward him and he, as a child, had no reasonable alternative but to remain in that situation. There is a suggestion of similarity here between his childhood and adult family situations. Similar behavior patterns by mother and wife may have sustained him.

This line of thought leads me to a speculation about a peculiarity attributed to Erikson by both his biographer and his daughter (for different reasons). I first quote their positions and then offer still another possibility that recalls earlier resolutions of discomfort.

Friedman (1999) writes:

By his late forties, writing for publication had become Erikson's all-consuming passion. Much that he thought, said, read, and did was now intertwined with his writing. Joan struggled to widen his focus. She tried to make him feel less awkward, less uncomfortable, and perhaps even less unhappy with most social situations. She urged him to dance, sing, attend musical and dramatic productions, and socialize. But she always had to be watchful of Erik's whereabouts. A solitary scholar who prized sociability in his writing, *he could disappear from a dinner party or a reception that he found tedious. Usually he escaped to his study and the endless chores of writing drafts of essays and books until Joan retrieved him.* (p. 23; emphasis mine)

Sue Erikson Bloland (1999) writes:

Family friends learned to treat with good humor his disappearance from picnics or parties to find a quiet place where he could read or write. His brilliance was coupled with an overwhelming need to achieve. I suspect that the full realization of great talent is always fueled by such an intense need. And what exactly is the source of this drive? An early experience of shame so overwhelming to the sense of self that to become extraordinary seems the only way to defend against it. (pt. 2, p. 4; emphasis mine)

To this pair of observations concerning Erikson's peculiar behavior I would add a third, based on Tomkins's ideas of the importance of affects as the determining elements of scripts (Tomkins in Demos, 1995, pp. 312–388). Again, I suggest returning to the exclusive relationship Erikson enjoyed with his mother from the time of birth until the mother married Dr. Homburger. This was the first instance of having to share mother with another and then with several others as time went on. Instances in which mother's attention was captured by other family members may have been painful for Erikson. The discomfort was relieved by his retiring to his room and sketching. From his continued use of sketching in group situations in later life, it seems clear that this was an activity from which he derived pleasure even after he abandoned the idea that he could become a professional artist. Writing, as experienced during his *Wanderschaft*, was simply added to sketching as a means of return to the experience of positive affect.

I conjecture that in his adult years Erikson left dinners and picnics because he no longer commanded the attention of his wife, who was un-

doubtedly occupied with guests or other people who were friends and were not seen all that frequently. Given the fact that he was not a very aggressive person, and knowing that his withdrawal, although tolerated by others, was frowned upon generally as a socially undesirable behavior, I would guess that he was guided by an old, successful script: retire from the negative affect scene and engage in activity that could induce positive affect instead.

In all, I hypothesize two major scenes in Erikson's life. The first, a positive one, was based on his experiences in his first three years of life and included two important elements critical to his positive feelings about self. One was an exclusive, interdependent, isolated relationship with a loving female. The other was the warm, supportive atmosphere of a mostly male group who shared common life interests.

The negative scene or scenes were composed of any lasting situation that interfered with the achievement or accomplishment or maintenance of the positive scene. If such situations arose, scripts would be introduced to reinstate the positive affect scene. In Erikson's life, after his mother's marriage, he lost the exclusivity of his mother's attention but not her loving response to him and his needs. The artistic community in Karlsruhe also offered him acceptance in a like-minded professional interest group.

With both elements still present in his life he was able to carry on, but at a reduced level. Had he been able to establish friendships, or to successfully defend himself, he might have found alternate forms of gratification. Instead, he banked on a long-term solution of his difficulties, which involved an artistic career as an adult and the exclusive company of like-minded others.

It does not surprise me that his discovery of his artistic limitations produced an "identity crisis" in him. Nor does it surprise me that the first four years in Vienna appear to have solved the situation. This period duplicated, almost by chance, the elements he experienced early in life. The acceptance of the psychoanalytic group and the intensity of his unique relationship with Joan Serson replicated the support of his mother and the artistic community. In some way it was a tribute to Freud's attributed view of good mental health through *"lieben und arbeiten."*[7]

The period after his marriage and the birth of his first two children heralded the loss of some aspects of the exclusivity of his relationship to his wife. I think the next fifteen years may have been similar in some ways to his days in Karlsruhe. Only now he did not have the disparaging age mates with which to deal, and he did enjoy support from the intellectual community, from psychoanalytic circles, and from government sources during World War II. It was, however, not until the decade of the fifties that he had to face his relationship to the orthodox, psychoanalytic community, the leadership.

By the mid-fifties, however, all of the children were either entirely away from home or at school. He was in a supportive environment at Riggs and had, again, the exclusive company of his wife. It was under these circumstances that he flourished and, perhaps, discovered his voice. Certainly the years at Harvard and thereafter, until his infirmities caught up with him, fulfilled the major elements of the early positive scene.

The nature of the relationship with his wife that was consequently forged was, indeed, reminiscent of his early relationship with his mother. He seemed totally dependent on her at home, and she took care of him almost as though she had still another child. I wonder if her children didn't take on some of the properties that his half-sisters did for him. He loved them but they were indeed rivals for the attention he craved exclusively. Bloland's article made that possibility more evident to me in that she, like his half-sisters, was female, but by the time of her birth Erikson was well into his career and likely contributed little to her care. This differed from his role with the boys earlier in Vienna. I wonder if some change in his behavior at home wasn't evident after Sue, the last remaining child at home, became independent and left the fold. If so, I would imagine that he would have appeared much happier at home.

Having raised the similarity in the mother's and wife's treatment of Erikson, I would like to return to the question of his ability to recognize and deal with his own aggressive impulses, especially toward the most important females in his life, his wife, his mother, and perhaps even his analyst, Anna Freud.

Although he was clearly aware of the relationship between conscious motives and their oppo-

site stemming from unconscious sources, he didn't seem capable of recognizing the latent needs residing in himself. This I would surmise from his unexpected communication to a deceased Gandhi in *Gandhi's Truth*. Erikson's mother kept from him the secret that he longed to discover all his life—the identity of his birth father, which apparently she alone knew. Yet until his dying day he had nothing but positive images to convey about his mother. I found nowhere anything that could have been interpreted as an aggressive or hostile or negative remark. This is also true of his public attitude toward his wife. They came from entirely different backgrounds, ethnically, financially, and religiously, and Friedman mentions what I felt were subtle, disparaging attitudes in Joan's treatment of Jewish customs as well as other instances of her lack of enthusiasm for certain of Erik's propensities. Yet Erikson never seemed to consider anything but perfection for his spouse. I would wonder whether this was only a public display or whether he feared so much what aggression on his part could produce in his mother or spouse that it never became part of his conscious thought.

With Anna Freud, it was mostly the same. Although she made no secret of her displeasure in the direction his work was taking, and he knew that she was influential in having his "Irma dream" paper rejected, he never took her to task. He said only positive things about her, her work, and her contributions to psychoanalytic theory.

What I am led to at this point is that Erikson had a tendency to idealize all those on whom he was greatly dependent: mother, wife, the Freuds (Anna and Sigmund), and his Vienna teachers.[8] Whether we can ever establish the true conditions of his first three years or not, his memories of his life from age three as indicated in *Life History and the Historical Moment* (1975) certainly appear idealized. My conjecture about his first three years may find some support from the fact that he never indicated any change in his mother's positive attitude toward him. This he certainly felt, whether it was factually supportable or not.

In writing this paper I became aware of an historical trend about personality development that script theory as offered by Silvan Tomkins may inadvertently balance. The dominant position has been led by psychoanalysis and its derivative theoretical developments and tended to place major emphasis on the early years of life. Eventually, emphasis shifted to life span development, especially through the work of Jung and Erikson. In my reading of Tomkins, the major aspects of personality are formed by strategies designed to reestablish a positive affect state that has turned sour, leading to negative affect. A script is likely to emerge in an attempt to restore the individual to a positive affect state. This drama can occur anywhere in the life span and leave its impact on the evolution of personality in each individual. It need not be fixed at any point in life or necessarily dictated by the changes in demands at different junctures in the life history. Tomkins's is a view that maximizes individual differences in personality development and focuses on the neglected role of affect in human affairs (Tomkins, 1984).

When I undertook the assignment to consider the pychobiographical aspects of Erikson's life and work, I took advantage of asking about him when I met people whose paths intersected with his. One day I came across a person who knew him well and for a very long time. When asked to reflect on what he was like, the first response was, "Oh Erik, he was such a baby." The comment could have served as a testament to the profound importance of that stage of his existence for how Erikson's life was lived.

Notes

1. Erikson, in his treatment of Luther, also exemplified another often overlooked aspect of his thought about his professional calling. Lacking the imprint of a medical education, he was loath to employ symptomatology as an inevitable sign of disease. Such an attitude necessarily cried for a system in which the characteristics of typical and atypical behavior could be understood within one's responses to cultural demands at different points in the life span. Some of his colleagues saw this as a defensive maneuver to account for his own difficulties at the relevant time in his own life.

2. Whether or not humor, in the exchange of jokes, was an acceptable outlet for the expression of aggression by Erikson is entirely possible, it would take an analysis of his favorite jokes to evaluate this thought. It was an atmosphere that contained elements he had found attractive in artistic communities and in Vienna.

3. Criticism was a matter that Erikson did not take lightly, but somehow he seldom aired his responses publicly.

4. Whether this idea of a replay of an early trauma, at age three, had anything to do with his behavior at home in the ensuing years is difficult, perhaps impossible, to ascertain in retrospect. The only possibility that would provide some evidence would be a contrast between his behaviors at home, when the children were part of daily family life, and the time when they were not.

5. Friedman has already suggested that the life cycle developmental scheme may have been initiated by the birth of a Down syndrome child to the Eriksons in the 1940s.

6. Carlson's introduction to Tomkins's script theory is the simplest explanation for the beginning reader.

7. See Elms (2001, pp. 89–95).

8. In this regard, Friedman (1999, pp. 97–101) reveals a brief correspondence between Erikson and Auguest Aichhorn, one of Erikson's teachers. The letters reveal a bit about what Erikson was like shortly after leaving Vienna in 1933. The issue of Erikson's "narcissism" is discussed in this exchange.

References

Alexander, I.E. (1990). Personology: Method and content in personality assessment and psychobiography. Durham, N.C.: Duke University Press.

Alexander, I.E. (1996). Erikson's Gandhi and Erikson—revisited. Contemporary Psychology, 41, 311–315.

Bloland, S.E. (1999). Fame: The power and cost of a fantasy. Atlantic Monthly, 284, 51–62.

Carlson, R. (1988). Exemplary lives: The uses of psychobiography for theory development. In McAdams, D., & Ochberg, R. (Eds.), Psychobiography and life narratives (pp. 105–137). Durham, N.C.: Duke University Press.

Coles, R. (1970), Erik H. Erikson: The growth of his work. Boston: Little, Brown.

Demos, V. (Ed.). (1995). Exploring affect: The selected writings of Silvan S. Tomkins. New York: Cambridge University Press.

Elms, A. (2001). Apocryphal Freud: Sigmund Freud's most famous "quotations" and their actual sources. Annual of Psychoanalysis, 83–103.

Erikson, E.H. (1950). Childhood and society. New York: Norton.

Erikson, E.H. (1954). The dream specimen of psychoanalysis. Journal of the American Psychoanalytic Association, 2, 5–56.

Erikson, E.H. (1958). Young Man Luther: A study in psychoanalysis and history. New York: Norton.

Erikson, E.H. (1969). Gandhi's truth. New York: Norton.

Erikson, E.H. (1975). Life history and the historical moment. New York: Norton.

Friedman, L.J. (1999). Identity's architect: A biography of Erik H. Erikson. Cambridge, Mass.: Harvard University Press.

Gill, M. (Ed.). (1967). The collected papers of David Rapaport. New York: Basic Books.

Roazen, P. (1976), Erik H. Erikson: The power and limits of a vision. New York: Free Press.

Tomkins, S. (1984). Script theory. Paper discussed at the annual meeting of the Society for Personology, Asilomar, California.

Chapter 19

Ian Nicholson

From the Book of Mormon to the Operational Definition
The Existential Project of S.S. Stevens

I take modern physics as my witness.
S.S. Stevens (1932)

In 1935, Harvard psychologist S.S. Stevens published a landmark paper in the history of American psychology. Titled "The Operational Definition of Psychological Concepts," the paper laid out a philosophical formula for transforming psychology into a truly empirical science, and it introduced psychologists to a now ubiquitous term: the "operational definition" (Stevens, 1935a). Stevens's basic idea was to eliminate ambiguity by tying linguistic statements of psychological phenomena to observables. "Operational doctrine," Stevens wrote, "makes explicit recognition of the fact that a concept, or proposition, has empirical meaning only if it stands for definite, concrete operations capable of execution by normal human beings" (p. 517). By rigorously policing the relationship between what we see, and the linguistic terms that we use to describe our observations, Stevens believed that psychologists could be "rid of the hazy ambiguities which result in ceaseless argument and dissension" (p. 517).

In the years following its publication, Stevens's vision and language were eagerly embraced by most of his contemporaries in American psychology. Psychologist Arthur Bills (1938) observed that operationism had become part of the "framework of our current credo" (p. 378). Sigmund Koch (1941) expressed a similar sentiment in his 1939 master's thesis: "'Almost every psychology sophomore knows it is bad form if reference to 'definition' is not qualified by the adjective 'operational'" (p. 15). The dramatic rise of operationism was confirmed by Gordon Allport (1940)

in an exhaustive review of psychological research that he undertook for his 1939 American Psychological Association Presidential Address. "Concerning operationism itself," Allport wrote, "the term, though new, has a special lure.... A close-up shows that the course of this magic concept is onward and upward, leading somewhere into the world of tomorrow" (pp. 10–11).

By 1940, operationism had become a central component of American psychology. Given the significance of operationism in the history of psychology, one might well expect to discover a literature on Stevens comparable in depth and sophistication to that of his Harvard contemporaries such as Gordon Allport, Henry Murray, and B.F. Skinner (see Bjork, 1993; Elms, 1993; Nicholson, 2003; Robinson, 1992; Smith, 1992). Surprisingly, however, historians of American psychology have shown relatively little interest in Stevens. Brief discussions of his work on operationism have appeared in a handful of reviews on the history of operationism (see Green, 1992; Leahey, 1980; Rogers, 1989), but to date there have been few in-depth published studies of his career and thought (Hardcastle, 1995, is a notable exception). This neglect is unfortunate, for there is much to be gleaned from a closer consideration of Stevens's life. His career is particularly instructive for the light it sheds on the place of passion in the history of science. As historian Thomas Söderqvist (1996) has noted, in recent years scientific knowledge has been socially, linguistically, and rhetorically contextualized but rarely seen as having anything to do with the passions of the

285

individual scientist. Historians of science frequently neglect anguish and anxiety, despair and dread along with the positive passions such as joy, hope, and love. More specifically, they neglect the way in which these feelings are stitched into the fabric of scientific life. Psychobiography, of course, restores such "passions," bringing them explicitly into play.

Söderqvist (1991, 1996) used the term "existential project" to refer to the idea that science is a personal venture in addition to being a political, social, and intellectual concern. Living a scientific life involves mapping out a vision of how one can live in a way that will give a measure of sense, unity, and value to life. This vision represents the scientist's ongoing solution to a tension that lies at the heart of the scientific life. On the one hand is a desire to establish oneself in the world by engaging with other people. On the other is a concern that this engagement will lead to individual subjugation and depersonalization. It is these "enabling conditions of self-assertion" that play a crucial role in shaping scientific work.

The purpose of this chapter is to examine Stevens's work on operationism as an "existential project." My aim is to show that Stevens's "operationism" was not just a philosophy of science, nor was it purely a reaction to specific intellectual and interdisciplinary concerns. Drawing on archival and autobiographical materials, I argue that Stevens's operationist vision was also embedded in a network of personal and religious issues that extended all the way back to his Mormon boyhood in rural Utah. Operationism was, at least for Stevens, a solution to existential problems as much as it was a matter of disciplinary procedure.

The Education of an Operationist

The emotional contours of Stevens's youth are difficult to discern. His autobiography (Stevens, 1974) written near the end of his life is characteristically "objective"—factual in nature with little emotional commentary. However, the "facts" are in themselves very telling, and they go a ways toward explaining Stevens's subsequent determination to purge from psychology all that was subjective, tender, and intuitive.

Stanley Smith Stevens was born in the small town of Ogden, Utah. His father Stanley was an electrician and small businessman, and his mother Adeline was a homemaker. It was an unhappy marriage marked by ill health, infidelity, and financial insecurity. The family moved frequently, and his parents divorced, only to remarry a short time later. Stevens's extended family brought a measure of stability and normalcy to his life, and in his autobiography he described his grandfather's farm where he spent his summers as a "paradise" of "barn and corral and garden and river and irrigation ditches" (Stevens, 1974, p. 397). Unfortunately, kindly interventions by family members could not completely insulate Stevens from the turmoil of his parents' marriage, and this ongoing instability led to problems in and out of school. He failed the first grade, and although his performance in school gradually improved, he was considered "listless and dopey" with poor posture and "low in energy" (Stevens, 1952, p. 2; 1974, p. 398). Disinterested in school, Stevens (1974) joined a gang and spent much of his time "playing and warring" throughout the neighborhood (p. 399). "I used to roam the street and break into the corner grocery store and steal cars and things like that" (Stevens, 1952).

Already struggling with the unending upheavals of his parents' marriage, Stevens was dealt a further tragic blow at age fifteen when his mother died of a stroke. Two years later his father was killed in a car accident, leaving him parentless at the tender age of seventeen. The enormity of these losses can only be inferred—Stevens offered little commentary in his autobiography beyond a terse reference to his father's age:

> One afternoon I returned to the school after a hard but exhilarating day at the finals of the state debating competition only to be told that they were looking for me. There had been an auto accident and Dad was dying. He was only 42, and everyone said "so young to die." I was 17 and I wondered that a parent could be anything but old. (Stevens, 1974, p. 399)

The emotional void created by the untimely death of his parents was filled not by any of the relatives who had been so kind to Stevens as a youth, but by the Mormon Church. Stevens was raised a Mormon, in keeping with the traditions of both sides of his family. His paternal grandfather Thomas Stevens had been one of the original Mormon pioneers in Utah, and he later became a church "bishop"—a kind of minister who is responsible for everything from religious ceremony to church logistics. Orson Smith, his maternal grandfather, was also a Mormon of long standing. A practicing polygamist, Smith had three wives and twenty-eight children (Stevens, 1952). Although Stevens's own parents were not especially devout, the young Stevens developed a deep religious faith. "I was always going about going to church," he recalled. "It was a very important part of our lives" (Stevens, 1952). Determined to follow Mormon Church practices, Stevens willingly undertook one of the most important duties of every young Mormon: that of missionary. At the age of eighteen, using his own money, he traveled to Belgium and France, where he spent three years "preaching, knocking on doors, [and] passing out brochures" (1974, p. 397).

In attempting to decode the complexities of a life, Schultz (see chap. 3 this vol.) has called attention to the importance of "frequency or repetition" of issues and themes in the subject's life. Recurring patterns are psychologically significant and sometimes even "comprise nuclear constituents of personality." A dominant theme in Stevens's autobiography (1974), and indeed, throughout his entire career, was an intense reverence for a hard-headed, practical physicality coupled with a deep suspicion of philosophy, sentiment, interdependency, or anything that might point back to the indeterminate complexities of emotional life. As described below, this tough-minded ideal became the centerpiece of Stevens's career as a psychologist, but its origins had less to do with science than with the psychobiographical context of his life.

Tough-minded self-reliance was, at least in part, a reflection of Stevens's western, Mormon roots. Practicality had been a staple of Mormonism from its earliest days (Hanson & Hanson, 1980). Church apostles prided themselves on "their acceptance of a practical religion" (1972/1899, p. 429): "If Mormonism is anything at all

more than other religions," apostle Joseph F. Smith wrote in 1905, "it is that it is *practical*, that the results of obedience to it are *practical*, that it makes good men better men, and that it takes even bad men and makes good ones of them" (p. 86; emphasis added). In his youth, Stevens had to look no further than his grandfather Orson Smith to see the truth of these words. Smith combined a devotion to God with a relentless drive for material success that became the stuff of family legend. In his autobiography, Stevens glowingly described his grandfather as a "patriarchal mesomorph who had been born in a covered wagon and who had subdued his land by brains and energy" (1974, p. 399).

The emotional turbulence of Stevens's youth lent further definition to this ethic of hard-bitten practicality. With his parents preoccupied by their own troubles, Stevens learned to be emotionally self-reliant at an early age and in his autobiography he noted matter-of-factly that a "treasured need for solitude frequently overrides my need for people" (1974, p. 413). The premature deaths of his parents and his work as a missionary provided further instruction in the value of emotional toughness and self-reliance. Although Stevens dabbled in the liberal arts upon returning to the United States in 1927, he soon grew weary of the "windy" subjects that were "fitting me to talk about anything, but to do nothing" (p. 402). He felt more at home with the tough, tangible, and practical. In the summers he worked as a utility man for the Idaho Power Company, and in his senior year he switched the emphasis of his education to the natural sciences, taking courses in biology, physics, and chemistry. Stevens worked tenaciously at his studies and was promptly rewarded with high grades and an offer of admission to the Harvard Medical School. A medical career was certainly practical, but he found the prospect of four years of medical school unappealing. A vocational interest test directed Stevens toward psychology, and a conversation with psychologist C.P. Stone settled the matter. He would travel east and pursue a graduate degree in psychology at Harvard. The prospect of cheaper tuition led Stevens initially to Harvard's Graduate School of Education. However, he soon met up with the famous experimental psychologist E.G. Boring and promptly enrolled as a student in Boring's course on perception.

A legendary figure in the history of psychology, Boring was committed to advancing psychology as an experimental science—a cause he championed with missionary zeal. He worked eighty hours a week as a matter of routine, and when he married he secured a promise from his wife Lucia "never to be jealous of my devotion to psychology" (Boring, 1952, p. 34). Although Stevens failed Boring's course, he identified with his professor's spirit of certitude and utter conviction to a cause. In February 1932, Stevens queried Boring about the possibility of doing a Ph.D. at Harvard. Boring was skeptical, but he agreed to admit Stevens on condition that he pass the preliminary exams later that spring. Since Stevens had little background in natural science, the preparation for these exams was a grueling ordeal, one that served to intensify the regret he felt for the time he had wasted studying humanities. "In the midst of grubbing about in technical treatises," he wrote in his notebook at the time, "I curse the courses I took in history and damn them because they weren't courses in mathematics" (Stevens, 1932, p. 13). Stevens may have regretted what he perceived to be academic indiscretions, but his late start in science does not appear to have held him back. He performed brilliantly on his preliminary exams, much to the delight of Boring. In 1932, Stevens formally enrolled as a Ph.D. candidate under Boring's supervision, and he graduated the following year having completed a dissertation on "Volume Intensity and Tones" (1933).

Suspending Belief

In Boring, Stevens found a father figure who could equal the zeal and commitment of the Mormon patriarchs he had known in his youth. Boring was himself eager to assume this role, and he later admitted that his relationship with Stevens was "genuinely paternal. . . . Of all the graduate students who have worked with me," Boring (1952) wrote, Stevens "is the one in whose ultimate success I had the most certain belief, [and] in whose future I made the largest investment of identification" (p. 50). Despite this solid support from

his supervisor, Stevens's graduate education at Harvard proved to be a trying time. There was a great deal of scientific ground to be covered for which Stevens continued to feel ill prepared. More important, perhaps, Stevens's immersion in science brought him into conflict with his Mormon faith.

Stevens had remained a member of the Mormon Church after returning from his mission in 1927, and as an undergraduate he frequently taught in the adult class of the Mormon Sunday School. Stevens retained his church membership after leaving California for Harvard in 1931. As a Harvard graduate student, he again taught the adult section of Sunday School at the Mormon Church in Cambridge, Massachusetts. This time, however, his affiliation did not last. Unable to reconcile his "tangled intellectual inputs" with the tenets of Mormonism, Stevens left the Mormon Church, but he quickly discovered that he had spent too much time constructing a religious world-view to simply walk away from it. In his autobiography, he noted that he "was beginning to aspire to the suspension of belief," but that the "problem of belief persisted" (1974, p. 402).

What was behind Stevens's inability to "suspend" his Mormon faith? Why couldn't he just let go? To answer this question it is necessary to closely examine Stevens's life as a member of the Mormon Church and as a scientist at Harvard. A line from Stevens's autobiography provides a useful place to begin. Discussing his difficulty with religion in the early 1930s, Stevens (1974) described the process of "believing" as being "easy—and lazy" (p. 401). "It fills people with a warm glow," he continued, "so that when two or more believers are gathered together in common conviction about philosophy, politics, or divinity, they sense the cozy, comforting contagion of zeal" (1974, p. 401). For all its clichéd, scientific hard-headedness, this passage reveals a great deal about Stevens and his spiritual struggles of the 1930s. His reference to belief being "easy" is particularly revealing. Most devotional and religious literature characterizes belief as something extraordinarily difficult to achieve (see Allport, 1950). But Stevens called it "easy," because for him, as for many Mormons, it was easy. Mormon theology gave every church member a stake in his religious life. There was no clergy in a conventional sense. Everyone was a minister, and more important, everyone was given plenty of opportunities to act out the role of minister. Adults were expected to take some kind of leadership or missionary role. As one religious historian has noted, "the [Mormon] movement was not designed to encourage luke-warm bystanders or occasional attenders; it re-quired willingness to participate as teachers, branch leaders, missionaries, [and] scribes" (Arrington & Bitton, 1979, p. 42). As a young man, Stevens happily undertook all these activi-ties and he proudly recalled that "I always did my share" for the church (Stevens, 1952, p. 4).

The net effect of all this participation was the creation of bonds of loyalty and belief that were extraordinarily difficult to break. Twenty years after leaving the Mormon Church, Stevens still felt a "great loyalty to the people [who are] as good a group as you can assemble anyplace that I've ever seen (Stevens, 1952, p. 11). Stevens may have felt the weight of Mormon tradition as he struggled to "suspend belief." However, his own history of religious involvement as missionary and Sunday school teacher was not the only con-straint on his quest to leave the church. His tem-perament also proved to be an important factor. Stevens was a comparatively shy, serious person throughout his life. As a missionary, his diffi-dence does not appear to have introduced any great social distance between himself and his peers. In his autobiography, he spoke fondly of working with "close friends," on religious projects that generated the "cozy, comforting contagion of zeal" (p. 401). Stevens's shyness became much more of an issue when he left the relatively homogenous world of Utah and the Mormon Church for training as a scientist at Harvard. Scientific life required Stevens to forge new relationships with a more intellectually and socially diverse group of people than what he was used to dealing with. It also required him to take careful stock of his own abilities and decen-cies and to weigh his own ambition against the skills he had at his disposal.

Stevens turned his hand to all these tasks dur-ing his early career at Harvard, with what can only be described as mixed results. As noted, he did forge a highly profitable, familial relation-ship with the powerful E.G. Boring, and he

crafted an ambitious intellectual program for himself that was not inconsonant with his con-siderable ability. Impressive as these successes undoubtedly are, they were at least partially off-set by his inability to find anything approaching the sense of community and fellowship he had experienced in the Mormon Church. Stevens was in fact extraordinarily unpopular among all but a handful of researchers in the Department of Psy-chology. Psychologist Hadley Cantril described him as an "arch-egoist" who "has hurt me more than anyone else in psychology" (Cantril to E.G. Boring, October 1, 1937; Boring, 1930–1965). The well-known personality psychologist Gordon Allport characterized Stevens as "an unwholesome influence" (Allport to Birkhoff, March 30, 1938; Allport, 1930–1967). Even E.G. Boring, Stevens's intellectual father and principal ally at Harvard, found reason to complain about his star student's insensitive manner and aggressive personality. "You have often hurt me," Boring noted sadly. "[My wife] Lucia too knows how I come home all distrait and silent, and when she probes I tell her that it is some new wound I have received from you" (Boring to Stevens, December 3, 1936; Bor-ing 1930–1965). In a letter to Allport, Boring admitted that "people generally disliked" Stevens because he was "difficult, selfish, [and] egoistic" (Boring to Allport, October 6, 1937; Allport, 1930–1967).

Stevens was well aware of the dislike many of his colleagues felt for him. E.G. Boring sent him numerous letters outlining the damage that his

Figure 19.1. S.S. Stevens. (Courtesy of Harvard University Laboratories)

often cavalier behavior had caused to other people's feelings and to his own career prospects. "It is clear to me" Boring noted sharply, "that the time has come where your success or failure depends, not on your changing the world, but on changing yourself" (Boring to Stevens, June 28, 1937; Boring, 1930–1965). Stevens felt the isolation and in his autobiography he noted that he had "often sensed the bitter sweetness of melancholy" (1974, p. 413). Despite this realization, however, Stevens's towering ambition and missionary righteousness usually combined to defeat his "efforts at affability" (p. 413). Instead of simply chatting with students and colleagues about their interests, Stevens often felt compelled to define social situations as rhetorical contests to be won, irrespective of what "victory" might cost in terms of lost good will. As former Harvard graduate student Leo Hurvich and Dorothea Jameson (1989) noted, Stevens was "forever proselytizing," a view echoed by another former student Jerome Bruner (1983), who recalled Stevens "lavish[ing] his crotchety enthusiasm (or peevishness) on any subject anybody would care to raise" (p. 34). "His passions were total and maddening" Bruner continued, and he would "bully, bait, [and] even sulk to make his point" (p. 34).

Stevens's indifference to the feelings of his colleagues may have been extreme, but it is consistent with a larger narrative of American career success that emphasized aggressive self-aggrandizement at the expense of personal attachments (Bellah et al., 1985). In his study of American businessmen, Ochberg (1988) noted that his subjects felt obliged to strike a bargain in their quest for a meaningful life. They agreed "to abandon part of what they wanted—affectionate recognition—and instead pursue the only recognition careerism offers: that of aggressive advancement" (Ochberg, 1988, p. 202). Having made this bargain, the business executive "feels and acts as though he were on his own, as though his emotional ties and obligations to his parents were severed" (p. 175). As a graduate student and faculty member, Stevens pursued "aggressive advancement" at full throttle and throughout the course of his career he felt and acted as though he were "on his own." Disliked by most of his professional colleagues, Stevens's personal life provided little in the way of compensatory emotional sup-

port. His wife Maxine found it difficult to deal with her husband's all-consuming preoccupation with psychology, and in 1936 she suffered a mental breakdown and was diagnosed with "postpartum psychosis" (p. 410). The validity of this diagnosis and the precise details of her condition are uncertain, but there was much speculation at Harvard that it was "Stevens' unyielding ambition that is responsible for Maxine's illness" (Boring to Allport, October 8, 1937; Boring, 1930–1965). Whatever the cause, there was clearly a sense of crisis and emotional devastation in the Stevens home. Over the next several months Maxine was repeatedly hospitalized and subjected to numerous "treatments" of electroconvulsive and insulin shock therapy. Unwilling or unable to come to grips with his wife's emotional state, Stevens embraced experimental psychology and Boring's glorification of the eighty hour work week all the more emphatically. "My own reaction to the anguish of those wretched days was to plunge furiously into the task at hand" (Stevens, 1974, p. 410). Hell bent on academic success, Stevens did not allow the birth of his son Peter to interfere with his career. With his wife unable to care for the infant, Stevens brought the child to the laboratory in a basket, and in the evening he would leave the baby asleep by itself and return to the lab to work. As the baby grew more active, Stevens felt "much too tied down," and he sent Peter away to live with a "warm-hearted, motherly [Mormon] woman" in a neighboring town while he threw himself into the task of ridding psychology of subjectivity (Stevens, 1952; 1974, p. 410).[1] "Work seemed to be the only relief," he recalled, but in the minds of many of his colleagues, Stevens's unblinking commitment to experimental psychology seemed more a matter of selfishness than therapy (Stevens, 1974, p. 410).

I have always felt that he [Stevens] was a rather sly person, so anxious to be advanced and become powerful that he will not let anything stand in his way. My impression was confirmed when I learned how he had left [his wife] Maxine stranded behind this summer, at a very difficult period of her life when, no doubt, his presence and comfort to her might have prevented a relapse (Cantril to Boring, September 30, 1937; Boring, 1930–1965).

It is against this backdrop of confrontation, emotional meltdown, and "melancholy" that we should view Stevens's comment that "the problem of belief persisted." For in Stevens's Mormon-trained mind, belief was more than simply a matter of subscribing to an intellectual or theological position. To believe was to be in the Mormon Church. It was to be a member of a community, with a shared theology, social ethic, and what Stevens (1974) later described as that "cozy, comforting contagion of zeal" (p. 401). As a graduate student and later research fellow at Harvard, Stevens had acquired many things, but existential comfort and community were not among them. In their absence, the "coziness" and "comfort" offered by the Mormon Church retained a certain allure.

A Spiritual Quest

Stevens's long involvement with the Mormon Church and his gnawing feelings of emotional absence and "melancholy" set the course for much of his subsequent scientific life. The Mormon Church's influence can be seen in the very manner in which Stevens set about his career as a scientific psychologist. After he had left the Mormon Church in 1931, Stevens did not simply walk into a laboratory and begin a program of scientific research. Instead, he embarked on what he later described as a "quest . . . for an explicit philosophy that I could live with" (p. 401). An industrious life of unreflective scientific activity was clearly not enough for Stevens's Mormon-trained mind. He needed another kind of overarching metaphysical framework that spoke to his anxious, unsettled inner self while providing a context for his experimental research as a psychologist.

The culmination of Stevens's "quest" for a new philosophy was a variant of the operational philosophy of physicist Percy Bridgeman. The goal of operationism was to purge science of all metaphysical conceptions by grounding the categories of science in observables. For Bridgeman, this grounding involved the equating of concepts with some sort of empirical process. Length, for example, was said to have empirical meaning only when linked to a particular kind of method

or operation such as a ruler, radar, and so forth. Thus for Bridgeman, "we mean by any concept nothing more than a set of operations; the concept is synonymous with the corresponding set of operations" (cited in Stevens, 1939, p. 294). Bridgeman wrote his book with a view to physics rather than psychology and Stevens noted that the book was "rich in example but poor in precept" (Stevens, 1939, p. 224). With some modifications, however, Stevens was convinced that operationism could pave the way to a true science of psychology. Operationist philosophy would bring psychological discourse out of the thicket of subjectivity by providing the philosophical warrant for translating "all sentences purporting to deal with psychical states . . . into sentences in the physical language" (Stevens, 1939, p. 240). Reduced to physical terms, psychological propositions could then be subject to public scrutiny and tested for accuracy. "By carefully controlling the conditions of the antecedent operations (stimulus), accurate knowledge of the system is obtained in terms of the subsequent changes (responses)" (Stevens, 1935b, p. 328).

Stevens was not the only psychologist fascinated with the language of exactitude and order. As Toulmin and Leary (1985) have noted, most early twentieth century American psychologists were enrolled in a "cult of empiricism" that lionized experimentation, objectivity, and control at the expense of theory, generalizability, and the inner self. What distinguished Stevens from many of his 1930s counterparts in psychology was the emotional intensity with which he committed himself to the operationist cause. Stevens's papers on operationism are not sober discussions of a philosophy of science as much as emotional sermons replete with manly metaphors of physical confrontation and daring. Stevens (1939) wrote proudly of the "hard heads" and "tough minds" that were "blasting a path through subjectivity" (pp. 221, 231). Cleverly linking operationism to modernist images of masculine daring, he likened experimental psychologists to aircraft pilots, suggesting that "operationally valid knowledge is merely the starting place for new flights which will bring back increased knowledge—providing, of course, that we keep the landing field clear of unoperational obstructions" (Stevens, 1936, p. 102). The emotional intensity of Stevens's theorizing even caught the eye of Boring—Stevens's most sympathetic critic. Boring urged his protégé to "cut out the flamboyant" (cited in Stevens, 1968, p. 597). "You have had [an] emotional experience of sensing salvation in a new idea, and you are not able to evaluate critically" (Boring, 1938).

Why would Stevens be attracted to such an austere philosophy, and why did he embrace operationism with such intensity? To answer this question, we need to briefly revisit Stevens's struggle with belief. As described above, Mormonism retained an allure for Stevens even after he had repudiated its articles of faith. Mormonism promised the "cozy comfort" of community and acceptance mentioned previously, things Stevens had not been able to find at Harvard. It was this element of faith's "comforting" power that attracted Stevens to operationism. The source of operationism's appeal lay in its implicit ontology. Operationism distinguished between statements given in the physical language of natural science and "subjective" statements given in the language of thought and feeling. The former were said to be "meaningful" because they were subject to empirical confirmation. Subjective statements, on the other hand, were "meaningless" because they had "no empirical denotation" (p. 101). Technically, operationists maintained that there was no ontological difference between the things that these two types of discourse referred to. They insisted that the question of whether everything was physical was a metaphysical matter and not an empirical proposition. Despite this fine philosophical distinction, however, the physicalist thrust of operationism ate away at the ontological legitimacy of subjective categories. In labeling metaphysical statements as "meaningless" and arguing that "all sentences purporting to deal with psychical states are translateable into sentences in the physical language" (Stevens, 1939, p. 240), operationists such as Stevens had a warrant to ignore or trivialize subjectivity even if they didn't explicitly deny its existence.

The empirical and philosophical merit of this position continues to be a matter of heated debate (see Green, 1992; Kendler, 1981, 1983; Leahey, 1980, 1983). What seems somewhat clearer in retrospect are the spiritual rewards Stevens ap-pears to have derived from this austere philosophy. The principal benefit is one that some commentators have argued helps sustain operationism into the present day: the comfort of order. As Rosenwald (1986) has noted, "[W]e persist in the operationalist strategy because we hope to compress and subdue within the confines of the laboratory what plagues us uncontrollably and inescapably outside" (p. 320). Operationism promised to bring intelligibility and control to the most vexing of existential problems. All the psychologist needed to do to "throttle these problems" was translate "psychical states . . . into sentences in the physical language" (Stevens, 1939, p. 241). Once there, the problem could be subject to the discipline and control of the laboratory experiment, and its "truth or falsity" could be determined (p. 228). By defining "the criteria by which we determine the applicability of a term in a given instance," Stevens (1935b) thought himself "fortified against meaningless concepts" in religion, philosophy, and his personal life (p. 330).

Operationism and the Book of Mormon

Operationism may have provided Stevens with an escape from his past, but at times facets of his Mormon heritage seemed to catch up with him. The overarching purpose of operationism contains what is perhaps the most immediately noticeable manifestation of Stevens's Mormon background. According to Stevens, the primary goal of operationism was to eliminate ambiguity and thereby end discord within the field. He maintained that the "straightforward procedure for the definition and validation of concepts . . . insures us against hazy, ambiguous and contradictory notions and provides the rigor of definition which silences useless controversy" (Stevens, 1935b, p. 323). In a now famous passage, Stevens described operationism as the "revolution that will put an end to the possibility of revolutions [in psychology]" (p. 323). Stevens thus construed psychology in terms of a single disciplinary vision based on a set of unchanging fundamentals. Operationism was the philosophical method that would initiate order. With its help, the "notable instability of psychology" could be corrected, and the truth about the material nature of consciousness might fully emerge.

On the surface, this operationist program seems a world away from the Mormonism of Stevens's youth. Yet when Stevens's various manifestoes are positioned alongside the work of Joseph Smith, Brigham Young, and numerous other influential Mormon writers, a certain similarity of purpose emerges. According to Smith, the goal of Mormonism was to end the theological bickering that divided religious denominations (Arrington & Bitton, 1979). The way in which Smith proposed to do this was to return to what was fundamental. For Smith, that entailed a careful clarification of the early Christian message. Christ's wisdom needed to be separated from pagan rituals, Greek philosophy, Egyptian mythology and various other external factors that had served to contaminate and divide Christianity. Once this was done, Smith believed that debate over fundamentals would end, and a true unified path to the divine would emerge.

As fanciful as all this may sound, it does bear a definite thematic resemblance to the program Stevens sketched for psychology. Like Smith, Stevens said that operationism's aim was to end the discord that had divided psychology for so long. And like Smith, Stevens proposed to achieve this objective by grounding his field of interest in something he considered fundamental—in his case, the discrimination of empirical observations. This appeal to fundamentals involved a procedure akin to Smith's Christian hermeneutics. Where Smith had purged religious concepts of their extra-Christian forms, Stevens urged psychologists to purge themselves of extra-empirical forms. The discipline needed to cleanse itself of a "variable mixture of initiation, a priori postulations, [and] reified entities" that had "seeped" into the field (1935b, p. 323). Thus, for both Smith and Stevens, deliverance—be it religious or psychological—assumed essentially the same form. To be delivered, one had to stay close to the one true path, all the while ensuring that impure elements did not infiltrate and contaminate one's understanding of fundamentals.

A similarity of purpose was not the only point of correspondence between Stevens's religious past and his scientific present. Mormonism was also implicated in the physicalist emphasis of operational theory. Stevens embraced physicalism shortly after entering graduate school. In his unpublished notebook he announced that he dismissed dualism and had taken "modern physics as my witness" (Stevens, 1932, p. 25). "Electrons and protons are at the basis of consciousness," he continued, "just as they are at the basis of lead" (Stevens, 1932, p. 24). His passion for physicalism continued throughout the 1930s and culminated in his famous article "Psychology and the Science of Science," in which he spoke approvingly of behaviorism "blasting a path through subjectivity" (1939, p. 231). Such talk again seems far removed from Mormonism and its rich history of divine visitations. However, a closer inspection of Mormon theology reveals a discernible point of continuity with respect to the significance of physicality. For Stevens, our faith in something was a function of its physicality. As scientists, psychologists were not to give their trust to a psychological proposition until that proposition had been converted into a set of physical operations. According to Stevens (1939), "any meaningful psychological proposition, even though it pertains to a toothache, is reducible to public, concrete operations" (p. 240). By revering the tangible in this fashion, Stevens unintentionally reflected one of the most central and controversial facets of Mormon theology: the physicality of God. Mormons are perhaps unique in the Christian world in their belief that God, Jesus, Moroni, and various other figures in the pantheon of Mormonism are not spirits but embodied people. According to Joseph Smith, "*God the father is material, Jesus Christ is material. Angels are material. . . . Nothing exists which is not material* (cited in Hansen, 1981, p. 71). Mormons even maintained that the Holy Ghost was a person, albeit an invisible one. "There is no such thing as immaterial matter," Joseph Smith maintained. "All spirit is matter, but it is more fine or pure, and can only be discerned by purer eyes; we cannot see it; but when our bodies are purified we shall see that all is matter" (cited in Hansen, 1981, p. 71).

The Mormon notion of the physicality of God is consistent with the common sense empiricism that runs throughout the faith. To appreciate the "empirical" dimension of Mormonism it is necessary to locate the movement in the context of nineteenth century American religion. The most popular form of religious expression was the revival. The emphasis in revivalism was on conversion: a highly emotional experience where one's soul was touched by God. Mormonism was developed in opposition to revivalism's emotional emphasis. Indeed, as a number of religious historians have noted, nineteenth century Mormonism was regarded as a religion of reason (Hansen, 1981). Joseph Smith was quite explicit in this regard. He taught that one need not rely on blind faith in the search for a path to God. By consulting the Book of Mormon one could learn of the physical evidence for God— golden plates, seer stones, magic spectacles, and Egyptian scrolls. Thus, the epistemological thrust of Mormonism was not all that different from that of Stevens's operationism: we know something because it has a physical form that we can observe under the right conditions.

Operationism in Theory, Operationism in Life

Unwittingly importing the Mormonism of his past into his scientific faith for the future, Stevens's subsequent work in psychology from the 1940s onward was largely devoted to the field of psychophysics, the administration of a laboratory, and editorial work on the monumental *Handbook of Experimental Psychology* (1951). However, as Hardcastle (1995) has noted, Stevens's interest in operationism did not wane, and he was still determined to blast the same path through subjectivity in order to facilitate conceptual clarity and theoretical unity in psychology (Stevens, 1939, p. 231). Ironically, Stevens's theoretical assaults on subjectivity could not quell his inner angst, and he remained as incorrigible as ever. Instead of being an agent for clarity and unity in psychology as he had intended, Stevens's brusque manner and intellectually uncompromising ways provoked intense behind-the-scenes politicking within the university and came to threaten the very integrity of psychology at Harvard. At issue were long-standing philosophical and methodological differences between physiological psychologists, whose research was oriented toward the natural sciences, and clini-

cal, social, and personality psychologists whose research was closer to that of the social sciences. Boring (1948) had labeled these rival camps "biotrope" and "sociotrope," respectively, but the distinction was deeply rooted in the history of psychology, most notably in the German philosopher Dilthey's discussion of the *naturwissenschaften* and the *geisteswissenschaften* (see Ringer, 1969).

In the 1930s, an uneasy truce had been reached between the two camps, and an extraordinarily diverse range of topics and methods flourished within the department. However, Stevens was utterly certain of the righteousness of his cause, and he had little interest in reaching an accommodation with practitioners of what he derisively referred to as "intellectually empty do-goodism" (Miller, 1975, p. 434). He had come to regret his own brief exposure to the social sciences and humanities, and in his journal he referred to the liberal arts component of his undergraduate work as an "evil" that needed to be "remedied" (Stevens, 1932, p. 11). Stevens viewed socially oriented colleagues in similar terms, and he worked to excise the unscientific from the department just as he had removed it from his own experience. As George Miller noted, "Stevens sought out the differences and tried to overpower them" (Miller, 1975, p. 457).

In the 1940s, Stevens's uncompromising ways and disrespectful manner emerged as a crucial factor in shaping the Department of Psychology at Harvard. His blunt sense of superiority made cooperation difficult, and his policy ideas were at odds with the spirit of accommodation. One particularly contentious Stevens-backed initiative was to make mathematics as well as statistics a component of the Ph.D. exams in psychology— a proposal reflecting trends in biotropic psychology but that would seriously handicap students in social, personality, and clinical psychology. Such movements coupled with Stevens's belligerence prompted some of the "sociotropes" to wonder whether they might be better off in a separate, socially oriented department. The ordinarily serene personality psychologist Gordon Allport was a critical figure in this regard. Intellectually eclectic and one of the most highly respected "sociotrope" psychologists in the country, Allport had been associated with the department since 1920 and had been a full-time member since 1930 (Nicholson, 2003). Committed to conceptual and methodological diversity in psychology, Allport was also a strong believer in the importance of civility and dignity in matters of academic deportment. Not surprisingly, Allport found Stevens off-putting in the extreme. In a letter to Boring, Allport complained that with Stevens "breadth and mutual respect become lost causes. . . . At a recent meeting of the Department while you were away he was characteristically scornful and patronizing regarding [a] thesis subject that I brought up for approval. Only *his* candle may burn!" (Allport to Boring, March 23, 1944; Allport, 1930–1967; emphasis in original). Over time, Allport's personal distaste led to a reassessment of his own circumstances and the organizational structure of psychology itself. "There is not a single millimeter of overlap between S's [Stevens] science and mine. . . . The outlook for a balanced Department is gone, not necessarily because of the imbalance of specialties among its permanent members, but because of the attitudes of two of them" (Allport to Boring, March 23, 1944; Allport, 1930–1967).

Boring viewed these events with alarm and he worried that his most beloved psychological protégé—Stevens—would be the very person to destroy the department that he had helped create. "One thing that troubles me greatly about the future of psychology at Harvard is your lack

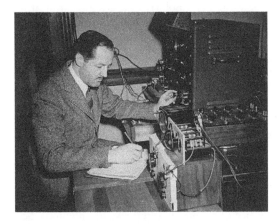

Figure 19.2. Tuning out subjectivity: Stevens in the Psycho-acoustic laboratory (Courtesy of Harvard University Laboratories)

of generous graciousness, as I see it, in scientific argument. I am haunted by the thought that this whole movement toward fission is caused by that" (Boring to Stevens, December 3, 1945; Boring, 1930–1965). In a last-ditch attempt to stave off the fragmentation of psychology, Boring appealed to Stevens to extend a measure of common courtesy to his colleagues. "It is terribly important for the future of psychology at Harvard that you should get yourself liked by your colleagues because you are considerate of their feelings, not because you have power, nor because someone else makes excuses for you, as I have been doing for a decade" (Boring to Stevens, December 3, 1945; Boring, 1930–1965).

Unfortunately for Boring, his appeal had little impact and Stevens continued on with his acerbic, domineering ways. The Department of Psychology was broken up and the social and personality psychologists joined with cultural anthropology and sociology to form a new Department of Social Relations. Although the official rationale for the reorganization was intellectual—to facilitate scholarly interchange among related fields—Harvard dean Paul Buck privately conceded that the move had more to do with psychological and political factors than scholarship (Nichols, 1998). Boring was a reluctant participant in this fissure, and he was "doubtful" about the long-term merits of the move (Boring, 1952, p. 49). However, Stevens was delighted, and a former student recalled that "Smitty felt that the fission of the department gave the scientists a chance to concentrate on the serious business of psychology" (Miller, 1975, p. 438). Physically and administratively removed from the "misguided," "unscientific" sociotropes he had come to despise, Stevens's career prospered, and he rose rapidly up the professional ranks. In 1946, he helped secure larger facilities for the psychology department at Harvard, and in 1949 Stevens succeeded Boring as director of the Harvard Psychological Laboratories (Stevens & Boring, 1947). Comfortably ensconced in his spacious new quarters, Stevens assumed the pose of a Mormon patriarch of old, dominating those around him while insisting on a high degree of conformity to his own habits of thought, work, and expression. The laboratory was his family, and members were given the duties and privileges of siblings, nephews, or cousins. Stevens was the undisputed head of this "extended family and he rewarded them or disciplined them for their own good and the good of the group" (Miller, 1975, p. 431). Never one for subtlety, Stevens ruled his "family" with a heavy hand, and he operationalized his displeasure in the crudest of ways. As former graduate student George Miller recalled, Stevens would often wait by the laboratory door to scold late arrivals:

> One rainy morning during the early days of the Psycho-Acoustic Laboratory, a staff member who had arrived late hurriedly hung his hat where water dripped onto the Webster's dictionary below. In a rage, Smitty threw the offending hat to the floor and stamped on it, loudly berating its tardy owner (Miller, 1975, p. 432).

Dominance brought Stevens a measure of repose, but no amount of operationalizing could relieve a gnawing sense of incompleteness and dissatisfaction. Stevens had sacrificed everything to the cause of "objective" psychology, but as his career wound down he came to crave for himself the very things that he had trampled on throughout his life: consideration, sensitivity, and respect. Although he was awarded the Distinguished Scientific Contribution Award of the American Psychological Association along with a number of other honors, he was infuriated by what he perceived as a lack of regard for his work, and he felt increasingly unappreciated and resentful. "There are now 30,000 psychologists who probably care nothing about sensory measurement, nor about how the sense-organ transducers operate to bring about the miracle of sensation," he noted bitterly in his autobiography (1974, p. 418). Convinced as always that he had revealed the way to truth in psychology, he was frustrated by the growing popularity of psychoanalysis, humanistic psychology, and other approaches that spoke more to meaning and fulfillment than mechanisms and invariance. He believed that psychology was abandoning the operationism that he had so painstakingly helped fashion in the 1930s.

To make matters worse, Stevens perceived these changes occurring right under his very nose. In the 1960s, a decision was taken to con-

solidate all psychologists at Harvard in a new high-rise building—William James Hall. Stevens bitterly resisted this move, and in 1962, after much rancor, he was obliged to resign his post as director of the Harvard Psychological Laboratories. "I was being fired" he recalled bitterly "for trying to obstruct what was then called progress—the transplanting of the laboratory" (p. 418). Deprived of his administrative power base, Stevens eventually concluded that psychology was beyond redemption, and in 1962 he quit the profession and in an act of petty defiance lobbied to have his title at Harvard formally changed from Professor of Psychology to Professor of Psychophysics. "Psychology has moved so far toward social relevance, and has moved so widely into media and marketplace, that those who man the old-fashioned experimental workshop must find a new label for their métier" (Stevens, 1974, p. 418). Stevens got his label, but much to his dismay he also got a new home—among the very sociotropes whom he had fought so tenaciously. In 1965, Stevens was forced out of his basement laboratory, a facility "shaped for over a quarter of a century to meet Smitty's every need," and onto a floor of William James Hall (Miller, 1975, p. 433).

Conclusion

In life, Stevens was a fascinating topic for speculation and his graduate students spent hours analyzing his scholarly abilities and infuriating ways (Miller, 1975). Stevens is no less intriguing in death, and as I hope this essay has made clear, he provides a useful vehicle for exploring the emotional context of scientific life.

His experience represents a particularly compelling illustration of what historian Lewis Feuer (1978) has referred to as "teleological principles in science" (p. 377). According to Feuer, scientific work is not strictly a matter of social context or intellectual paradigms. There is also, he insists, an emotional context to scientific work—"an underlying emotional aim"—that informs the scientist's choice of problems, solutions, and methods. Science becomes the vehicle for realizing "a particular kind of world . . . which will answer to the scientist's emotional longings" (p. 578).

In this chapter, I have argued that Stevens's career-long determination to vanquish subjectivity in psychology was born out of his intimate acquaintance with loss, alienation, and disillusionment. Orphaned from his family and his faith, Stevens turned to science and more specifically operationist psychology for an all encompassing salvation. His operationism purported to "blast" away past loyalties and existential doubts. Loneliness, despair, consideration, and respect for others—all seemed to wither under the operationist injunction to ignore "meaningless" concepts in favor of a graspable, physical world of clarity and order. Unfortunately for Stevens, subjectivity did not yield quite so easily, and no amount of bad-tempered sermonizing could change the course of psychology or quell his own sense of doubt and disillusionment.

In highlighting the emotional context of Stevens's operationist vision, it is important to keep Runyan's (1982) cautionary remarks about the danger of reductionism firmly in mind. Reductionism is at work in efforts "to explain adult character and behavior exclusively in terms of early childhood experience while neglecting later formative processes and influences" (Runyan, 1982, p. 209; see also Schultz, chap. 1 this vol.). Stevens was clearly part of a much larger empiricist tradition in psychology, and as Hardcastle (1995) has demonstrated, there is a detailed and important philosophical context to the emergence of operationism in psychology. In the present study, my ambition has not been to reduce Stevens's scientific accomplishments to a set of simplistic psychological needs, but rather to draw attention to the ways that his existential concerns informed his type of science and that of others. The emotional contours of Stevens's life energized his career and determined his choice of research topics and theoretical positions. Ever the missionary, Stevens also injected his own existential uncertainties into the lives of those around him and many psychologists at Harvard found him belligerent, uncompromising, and unfailingly selfish. Unwilling to give an inch, Stevens's emotionally driven determination to make psychology "objective" had a direct impact on the organizational structure of psychology at Harvard University.

Note

1. In a 1952 interview, Stevens reported that he saw his son "a couple of times a week for a few hours at a stretch" (Stevens, 1952).

References

Allport, G.W. (1930–1967). Correspondence. Gordon W. Allport papers, Harvard University Archives, Cambridge, Mass.

Allport, G. (1940). The psychologist's frame of reference. Psychological Bulletin, 37, 1–28.

Allport, G. (1950). The individual and his religion. New York: Macmillan.

Arrington, L., & Bitton, D. (1979). The Mormon experience: A history of the Latter Day Saints. London: George Allen & Unwin.

Bellah, R., & Madsen, et al. (1985). Habits of the heart: Individualism and commitment in American life. Berkeley: University of California Press.

Bills, A. (1938). Changing views of psychology as science. Psychological Review, 45, 377–394.

Bjork, D.W. (1993). B.F. Skinner: A life. New York: Basic Books.

Boring, E.G. (1930–1965). Correspondence. E.G. Boring papers. Harvard University Archives, Cambridge, Mass.

Boring, E.G. (1938, October 11). Letter to S.S. Stevens. S.S. Stevens papers, Harvard University Archives, Cambridge, Mass.

Boring, E.G. (1952). Edwin Garrigues Boring. History of psychology in autobiography (pp. 27–52). E. Boring, H. Langfeld, H. Weiner and R. Yerkes (Eds.). New York: Russell & Russell.

Bruner, J. (1983). In search of mind: Essays in autobiography. New York: Harper.

Cantril, H. (1937, October 1). Letter to E.G. Boring. E.G. Boring Papers, Harvard University Archives, Cambridge, Mass.

Elms, A. (1993). Allport's Personality and Allport's personality. In K. Craik, R. Hogan, & R. Wolfe (Eds.), Fifty years of personality psychology (pp. 39–56). New York: Plenum Press.

Feuer, L. (1978). Teleological Principles in Science. Inquiry, 21, 377–407.

Green, C. (1992). Of immortal mythological beasts: Operationism in psychology. Theory & Psychology, 2(3), 291–320.

Hansen, K.J. (1981). Mormonism and the American experience. Chicago: University of Chicago Press.

Hanson, A.T., & Hanson, R.P. (1980). Reasonable belief: A survey of the Christian faith. Oxford: Oxford University Press.

Hardcastle, G. (1995). S.S. Stevens and the origins of operationism. Philosophy of Science, 62, 404–424.

Hurvich, L., & Jameson, D. (1989). Leo M. Hurvich and Dorothea Jameson. In G. Lindzey (Ed.), A history of psychology in autobiography (Vol. 8, pp. 156–206). Stanford: Stanford University Press.

Kendler, H. (1981). The reality of operationism. Journal of Mind and Behavior, 2, 331–341.

Kendler, H. (1983). Operationism: A recipe for reducing confusion and ambiguity. Journal of Mind and Behavior, 4, 91–97.

Koch, S. (1941). The logical character of the motivation concept. Psychological Review, 48, 15–38.

Leahey, T. (1980). The myth of operationism. Journal of Mind and Behavior, 1, 127–143.

Leahey, T. (1983). Operationism and ideology: Reply to Kendler. Journal of Mind and Behavior 4, 81–90.

Miller, G. (1975). Stanley Smith Stevens. Biographical Memoirs—National Academy of Sciences, 47, 424–449.

Nichols, L. (1998). Social relations undone: Disciplinary divergence and departmental politics at Harvard, 1946–1970. American Sociologist, 29, 83–107.

Nicholson, I.A.M. (2003). Inventing personality: Gordon Allport and the science of selfhood. Washington, D.C.: American Psychological Association.

Ochberg, R. (1988). Life stories and the psycho-social construction of careers. Journal of Personality, 56, 173–204.

Ringer, F. (1969). The decline of the German mandarins: The German academic community, 1890–1933. Cambridge, Mass.: Harvard University Press.

Robinson, F. (1992). Love's story told: A life of Henry A. Murray. Cambridge, Mass.: Harvard University Press.

Rogers, T.B. (1989). Operationism in psychology: A discussion of contextual antecedents and an historical interpretation of its longevity. Journal of the History of the Behavioral Science 25, 139–153.

Rosenwald, G. (1986). Why operationism doesn't go away: Extrascientific incentives of social-psychological research. Philosophy of Social Science 16, 303–330.

Runyan, W. (1982). Life histories and psycho-biography. New York: Oxford University Press.

Sheets-Pyenson, S. (1990). New directions for scientific biography: The case of Sir William Dawson. History of Science, 28, 399–410.

Smith, L. (1992). On prediction and control: B.F. Skinner and the technological ideal of science. American Psychologist, 47(2), 216–223.

Söderqvist, T. (1991). Biography or ethno-biography or both? Embodied reflexivity and the deconstruction of knowledge-power. In F. Steier (Ed.), Research and reflexivity (pp. 143–162). London: Sage.

Söderqvist, T. (1996). Existential projects and existential choice in science: Science biography as an edifying genre. In M. Shortland & R. Yeo (Eds.), Telling lives in science: Essays on scientific biography (pp. 45–84). New York: Cambridge University Press.

Stevens, S.S. (1932). Journal of S.S. Stevens. Stevens Papers. Harvard University Archives, Cambridge, Mass.

Stevens, S.S. (1933). Volume intensity and tones. Unpublished Ph.D. dissertation, Harvard University.

Stevens, S.S. (1935a). The operational definition of psychological concepts. Psychological Review, 42, 517–527.

Stevens, S.S. (1935b). The operational basis of psychology. American Journal of Psychology, 47, 323–330.

Stevens, S.S. (1936). Psychology: The propaedeutic science. Philosophy of Science, 3, 90–103.

Stevens, S.S. (1939). Psychology and the science of science. Psychological Bulletin, 36(4), 221–263.

Stevens, S.S. (1952). Interview with Anne Roe. Anne Roe Papers. American Philosophical Society Library.

Stevens, S.S. (1968). Edwin Garrigues Boring. American Journal of Psychology, 81, 589–606.

Stevens, S.S. (1974). S.S. Stevens. In G. Lindzey (Ed.), A history of psychology in autobiography (Vol. 6, pp. 395–420). Englewood Cliffs, N.J.: Prentice Hall.

Stevens, S.S. and Boring, E.G. (1947). The new Harvard Psychological Laboratories. American Psychologist 2, 239–243.

Toulmin, S., & Leary, D. (1985). The cult of empiricism in psychology, and beyond. In S. Koch & D. Leary (Eds.), A century of psychology as a science (pp. 594–617). New York: McGraw Hill.

PART IV

PSYCHOBIOGRAPHIES OF POLITICAL FIGURES

Chapter 20

Alan C. Elms & Anna V. Song

Alive and Kicking
The Problematics of Political Psychobiography

The subjects studied by political psychobiographers are in many ways similar to other psychobiographical subjects. Political figures move through a lifetime of psychological development, engage in social interactions, reach and carry out decisions, make public statements, leave private records. In all those regards, the study of their lives presents the same challenges and offers the same opportunities for psychological analysis as the study of philosophers, creative artists, and scientific theorists. But a major subset of subjects within political psychobiography is distinctive in one important way: They are alive and kicking. They are not only *not dead* (in dramatic contrast to the subjects of most psychobiographies); they are also busily pursuing their political careers. They are current candidates for office, or occupants of elective or appointive office, or self-appointed leaders of nations and mass movements. However they got to where they are, their active political involvement presents their would-be psychobiographers with problems seldom encountered in other parts of the field.

Most psychobiography is *postdictive*, contemplating the connections between the past life and work of a subject who is, if not already dead, well beyond his or her productive prime. Many political psychobiographies are *predictive*, attempting to capture the subject on the wing—or rather, to trace the subject's trajectory from past history to current position to some future point of arrival. For American politicians, the primary question is often: what sort of U.S. president (or senator, or governor) is this candidate likely to become? The main goal of such research is to

assist voters in their choice of the candidate most suitable for elective office. For political figures elsewhere in the world (and for U.S. presidents when studied by non-American psychobiographers), the question is often, instead: What sort of damage is this person likely to inflict on other nations, and how can his or her power to do so be limited or blocked? Persuasive answers to such questions may advance the careers not only of academic psychobiographers but also of political journalists, publicity-seeking psychotherapists, and government intelligence analysts. But sound answers to such questions—solidly data-based, well-reasoned, and clearly defined predictions—are difficult to achieve.

Successful politicians are, almost by definition, skilled at impression management. Whether they attain leadership positions by election, by appointment, by charisma, or by violence, they are unlikely to place their personalities and their personal histories fully on view. They may simply limit access to personal information as much as possible, or they may practice some kind of public mystification, actively misrepresenting their origins and their motives. Other sorts of psychobiographical subjects are likely to do the same to some degree; none of us eagerly makes full personal disclosure, even to our therapists. But for politicians, the development and maintenance of an appealing if misleading public persona are matters of career survival. For political psychobiographers, career survival depends on the successful penetration of that persona.

Political psychobiographers have developed strategies, guidelines, and rules of thumb that facilitate such penetration. At the same time, politicians have polished their skills at impression management—including management of psychobiographers' impressions. In this chapter we briefly review a variety of ways to study the active political subject, and offer some warnings about the problems most likely to be encountered. Other chapters in part IV of this volume present more detailed examples both of research methods and of how political subjects may frustrate such research.

Psychological studies of active political figures are commonly said to take place "at a distance." For purposes of discussing both the problems endemic in such research and the strategies best suited to deal with them, we differentiate among studies conducted from a *far distance*, from a *middle distance*, and *up close*. Most psychobiographical research is done from a middle distance, physically or psychologically or both. The researcher has access to a good deal of information about the subject, including personal documents, an assortment of biographical data across the life history, and perhaps interviews conducted by the researcher or others. But researchers may find themselves studying a subject about whom information is sparse and obtainable only at a far distance, geographically and/or culturally and/or in terms of access to psychologically meaningful data. Much more rarely, a researcher may stumble into a situation where a great deal of ordinarily private information about a subject becomes available—where "up close" means direct personal access to a subject who is willing to provide detailed life-history data and answers to probing questions.

Research From a Far Distance

It is obviously preferable to do psychobiographical research from a middle distance or closer. But for politically active individuals, perhaps more than for any other kind of subject, research from a far distance may be necessary. Presidential candidates may suddenly come "out of nowhere," as they are often described when they have previously received only regional attention. If a predictive psychobiographical analysis of such a candidate is to be at all useful to voters, there may

be little time to gather more than minimal details of personal history. Leaders of foreign countries may be barely known at a time when they are first perceived as a threat to our national interests or to international stability (see, e.g., Song, chap. 23 this vol.). Charismatic leaders of social or religious movements, who may also have political ambitions or potential political impact, are perhaps even more likely to be "unknown quantities" or to possess unknown qualities. In all these cases, the potential subject may be highly protective of personal information, while the potential psychobiographer may perceive an urgent need to develop an accurate analysis of the subject's motives, intentions, and likely behavior in the near future. What to do?

First Independent Political Success.   Psychobiographers typically look at a subject's childhood for the beginnings of patterns that may persist through adulthood. But for active politicians, such information is often unavailable or may take the form of idealized representations in "campaign biographies." In looking at a wide range of past U.S. presidents and current candidates for office, James David Barber (1992, pp. 7–8) suggested that researchers can instead find valuable pointers by examining the subject's first independent political success. "Independent" here means the politician is not merely tagging along on the coattails of another politician or winning office as a cog in a political machine. The pattern of behavior culminating in that first independent success is likely to be a more direct expression of individual personality than that of later political campaigns, when the politician has learned better to cover his or her tracks. Further, that first success may strongly reinforce significant aspects of the politician's behavior which are then likely to persist through later campaigns and significant decisions. A striking example of a first independent political success outside the U.S. political system is described in Anthony Dennis's chapter on Osama Bin Laden (chap. 21 this vol.).

Quadripartite Categorization.   James David Barber is much better known for another aid to studying politicians from a far distance: his four-part schema for categorizing them into active versus passive and positive versus negative political actors (Barber, 1992). Barber first developed these categories through questionnaire responses and quantitative data on the political activities of state legislators (Barber, 1965). Legislators who spoke frequently on the assembly floor and introduced many bills were categorized as *active*; legislators who enjoyed their jobs enough to want to be returned to office more than once were rated as *positive*; and the most effective legislators turned out to be the *active-positives*. When Barber later applied essentially the same categories to U.S. presidents and presidential candidates, he shifted from quantitative to qualitative analysis, using fairly extensive biographical data to identify a given subject as active-positive, active-negative, passive-positive, or passive-negative. His qualitative depictions of presidents and candidates are for the most part middle-distance psychobiographical case histories. But it is part of his argument that with relatively little biographical data, a politician can be assigned to one of the four categories, and that once so assigned, the politician can be reasonably assumed to share a broad range of personality qualities exhibited by previously categorized presidents and candidates. Active-positives such as Franklin D. Roosevelt and John F. Kennedy learn from experience in office; active-negatives such as Richard Nixon and Woodrow Wilson tend to get stuck in controversies that threaten their public personas; and so forth. Though Barber's quadripartite categorization has been criticized for a variety of reasons (e.g., Renshon, 1996, pp. 453–454, and by Elms, 1994, pp. 197–198 and 202–203), it remains useful as a quick-and-dirty way to reach tentative conclusions about a politician for whom detailed biographical information is not yet available.

Content Analysis of Public Statements.   David Winter (1987) and others have developed reliable quantitative procedures for identifying a politician's dominant motivational structure through content analysis of campaign speeches, declarations of candidacy, State of the Union addresses, and other key public statements. In this age of professional political speechwriters, such state-

ments rarely come entirely from a candidate's own lips or pen or computer. But they are presumably endorsed by the candidate who delivers them, and they are likely to include at least some elements expressive of his or her personality. Like Barber's quadripartite schema, Winter's identification of politicians' power, achievement, and affiliation motives (derived from Henry A. Murray's (1938) categorization of principal human needs) can be useful in guiding further psychobiographical inquiry when initial details of a politician's private life are sparse.

Consistency Across Forms of Behavior.   When information about a politician's life history is both sparse and contradictory, it may be useful to identify the occasional pieces of data that show some consistency. Such analysis may usefully focus on consistency across types of behavioral data, across significant public decisions, and across domains of politics. One difference in *data types*, relevant to Winter's style of content analysis, involves the spontaneity of the material. Dillie (2000) has argued that although politicians are able to utilize well-developed impression management strategies when preparing speeches in advance, interviews and press conferences that force them to respond quickly will leave less room for public-image maintenance. Therefore, political psychobiographers should take into consideration whether these different types of data tap into differences in politicians' public and private self-construals. Consistency of behavior across these self-image domains can provide evidence of the stability of personality and its links to political behavior.

When psychobiographers focus on a major political decision, it is important to see whether this type of behavior or *style of decision making* appears in other aspects of the subject's life. In Woodrow Wilson's case, for instance, George and George (1964) found a consistent pattern of decision-making across different aspects of Wilson's life. They drew parallels between Wilson's battles with the U.S. Senate over the League of Nations Treaty and his earlier conflicts with faculty as president of Princeton University. In both cases, Wilson displayed extreme dogmatism in insisting that his decisions must prevail.

In refusing to compromise on even the most trivial of points, he failed to attain his most sought-after goals in both political arenas.

In assessing consistency across decisions, political psychobiographers may detect a tangible pattern of behaviors that can be explained through psychological theory. When assessing consistency across *domains of politics*, psychobiographers can use the complexity of bureaucratic politics to their methodological advantage. Because different types of decisions are influenced by different branches of government and by various public/private interest groups, any consistency in behavior, acts, or decisions can be attributed to the one consistent factor across domains—the psychobiographical subject. For instance, during Harry S Truman's presidency, he faced several tense public relations battles over the firing or resignation of Secretary of State James Byrnes, Secretary of Commerce Henry Wallace, and General Douglas MacArthur. In understanding these personnel conflicts, a psychobiographer must take into account that Truman felt an enormous challenge in overcoming the public perception that he was unqualified to be president. Truman's reaction to dominant figures who undermined his authority as president also appeared in the arena of foreign politics. Take, for instance, his relationship with Soviet leader Joseph Stalin. At best, Truman's interactions with the Soviet Premier were tenuous, fluctuating between admiration for Stalin and repressed hostility that emerged in private letters and later in foreign diplomacy. At the beginning of his relationship with Stalin, Truman believed that the two mutually respected each other. As their interactions continued, it became apparent that Stalin did not consider him an equal, no matter how personable or smart Truman tried to present himself. As a result, Truman began to resent Stalin and became constantly on guard toward the Soviet Union, later claiming, "They never fooled me after Potsdam" (Truman, 1953, p. 271).

Research From a Middle Distance

In middle-distance research on politicians, a wide variety of data may be available but close and substantial personal contact with the subject is not achievable. Middle-distance political psychobiographers are typically drawn from three kinds of researchers: journalists, clinicians, and academics. These categories sometimes overlap: An individual psychobiographer may belong to two categories (rarely if ever all three), or two individuals from different categories may collaborate (e.g., Mazlish & Diamond, 1979). Each kind of researcher is bedeviled by a distinctive set of psychobiographical problems, though such problems are not necessarily unique to a particular professional background.

Journalists have become the most frequent practitioners of predictive political psychobiography. They are not necessarily skilled at it, having seldom been trained in either psychology or biography. But when they deal at any length with presidential candidates or sitting presidents (or, sometimes, those aspiring to other public office), they seem to feel obligated to offer speculations about their chosen subject's psyche or "character."

The most prominent political journalist/psychobiographer in recent years has been Gail Sheehy, best known as the author of *Passages* (Sheehy, 1976) and other pop-psychology books. Sheehy has written a long string of magazine articles and books about a variety of politicians, ranging from Gary Hart to Mikhail Gorbachev to Hillary Clinton. Her most extensive effort in this regard was a series of articles for *Vanity Fair* in the presidential election year of 1988, analyzing the three main candidates for the Democratic nomination (Al Gore, Jesse Jackson, and Michael Dukakis), the two main Republican candidates (George Bush and Robert Dole), and the sitting president (Ronald Reagan). Sheehy then assembled these articles into a book titled *Character: America's Search for Leadership* (1988).

Sheehy knows a fair amount of psychological theory—mostly Erikson and Daniel Levinson, with dollops of object relations and other approaches. Further, she did more on-site observations and interviews of the major candidates and their close associates in 1987–1988 than most academic psychologists would even dream about. But several problems recur in her psychobiographical studies, and they are characteristic of other journalistic studies of politicians as well: (1) She tries to locate a *single key* to each candidate's psyche (e.g., Bob Dole's insistence on personal control, resulting from his war-induced disabilities), rather than applying a theory more broadly or looking for a complex interrelationship of psychological issues. (2) For the 1988 presidential campaign, she examined another candidate every month or two while the crucial primaries got closer and closer—thereby maintaining *too fast a pace* for careful analysis of any one candidate. (In her recent work she has devoted more time to Hillary Clinton, for instance, but she still cannot be accused of careful academic deliberation.) (3) Rather than stressing fair, even-handed, comprehensive analysis of each politician, she appears to feel she must *entertain her audience*, whom she regards—probably correctly—as much more interested in gossip than in thoughtful explications of psychological complexity. Sheehy does pretty much what one would expect in these circumstances: She reaches for easy diagnoses, she lets personal bias run away with her judgment, and she vastly overinterprets what she considers to be her unique observations of a candidate. As she interviewed not only the 1988 candidates but their close friends, relatives, wives, and sometimes ex-wives, she also tended to *overvalue* what she regarded as her *"special" knowledge* of a candidate—that is, she overemphasized the importance of bits of information that she got before anyone else did. Other kinds of psychobiographers do similar overvaluing at times, but it's a more frequent fault in the psychobiographical efforts of journalists. They are, after all, primarily interested in what they consider to be *news*.

Clinicians, perhaps surprisingly, make up another well-populated category of predictive political psychobiographer. Here we include clinical psychologists, psychiatrists, and psychoanalysts as well as any combination of those professions. A fair number of clinicians have become excellent psychobiographers—notably Erik Erikson, who never did a predictive psychobiography (unless his early paper on Hitler qualifies) but who wrote important studies of several political leaders, including Gandhi, Jefferson, and (in some sense) Martin Luther. But clinicians as a category have a poor history of making snap judgments about politicians, beginning in a big way with the presidential election of 1964, when Barry Goldwater ran against Lyndon Johnson. Goldwater was

rather far to the right, and his habit of making extreme political statements led many psychiatrists to conclude that he was genuinely crazy. A substantial number of them were willing to express their opinions in print, in a muckraking magazine called *Fact*. Some of their statements were extreme enough to enable Goldwater to sue the magazine successfully for libel (Elms, 1976, pp. 88–90). For a time, this contretemps led clinicians to avoid making psychological pronouncements about current candidates or office holders. But Richard Nixon was too great a temptation for some (e.g., Chesen, 1973), and other clinicians have followed in their wake.

Clinicians usually look for pathology, not for signs of psychological health. In studying politicians, especially those they dislike, they tend to overinterpret the available biographical data and to make overconfident diagnoses of candidates or office-holders on the basis of what they regard as their own special clinical knowledge. A recent example is a book titled *The Dysfunctional President: Inside the Mind of Bill Clinton* (1996), by a Southern California clinical psychologist named Paul Fick. (The book was first published in 1995 and then was reprinted in a slightly revised version aimed at voters in the 1996 election.) Fick considers several possible clinical diagnoses for Clinton, citing evidence that Clinton lies a lot, procrastinates, acts in ways that create chaos around himself, and so forth. Fick properly rejects most of those diagnoses, finally deciding that Clinton's main problems come from his having been the adult child of an alcoholic—or, more accurately, "an adult child of an alcoholic stepfather."

Fick continues his diagnosis by identifying denial as Clinton's primary defense mechanism, and by asserting that Clinton's "present behavior and problems indicate that the client has very little insight into the impact of his childhood problems." Further, Clinton "denies responsibility and blames others. He exhibits periodic outbursts of anger because of the long-standing nature of his pain" (p. 221). Fick does not mention that denial, lack of self-insight, blaming others, and indulging in periodic outbursts of anger can be found in plenty of other politicians, including quite a few whose parents were not alcoholic. Nor does he find it worth discussing that Clinton has shown some more praiseworthy qualities, such as empathy, "because of the long-standing nature of his pain," and that Clinton has at times exhibited considerable restraint and diplomacy, rather than the expected "outbursts of anger," in domestic politics and international affairs. Fick insists on looking at Clinton as a patient— note his use of the term "the client" to describe his psychobiographical subject. Perhaps if Clinton had really come to him as a patient, a pathographic orientation would be appropriate. (Fick actually concludes his book with "Recommendations and Treatment Plan" for Clinton (pp. 222–223), in which he proposes that the president "should be under the care of a licensed clinician familiar with the concepts of ACOA (adult child of alcoholic) treatment"—a licensed clinician such as Dr. Paul Fick, perhaps?) But as a largely successful two-term U.S. president, Bill Clinton displayed an interesting mixture of psychological flaws *and* strengths, and a clinician's concentration on his flaws is an act of professional hubris rather than a serious attempt at psychobiography.

Academics are the people who do the largest number of psychobiographies across the full range of biographical subjects. Most of the chapters in this volume were written by academics— professional scholars in a variety of disciplines. Academics have made significant contributions to the study of active politicians, beginning with James David Barber's work on legislators and presidents, and continuing through Bruce Mazlish's (Mazlish & Diamond, 1979) and Betty Glad's (1980) work on Jimmy Carter, Stanley Renshon's magisterial book *The Psychological Assessment of Presidential Candidates* (1996), and shorter studies of miscellaneous candidates and office holders by other scholars (see, e.g., Renshon, chap. 22 this vol.). Psychologists, political scientists, historians, occasional entrants from American Studies and other branches of the humanities and social sciences—whatever their specific disciplinary background, they have typically undergone sufficient training in scholarly research procedures to avoid the worst sins of journalists and clinicians. But of course they encounter problems of their own, as well as other problems characteristic of psychobiography in general. For one thing, their work tends to be cautiously slow, and that's a *real* problem when you're trying to draw useful conclusions about an active political candidate. It would have been nearly impossible for Betty Glad or Bruce Mazlish to anticipate in 1972 that Jimmy Carter would be a major presidential candidate in 1976. But if they had done so, their detailed research on Carter would have been much more useful to voters in 1976 than in 1979 or 1980, when their books on him finally came out. Somebody could have anticipated in 1984 that Vice President George H.W. Bush would be a likely presidential candidate in 1988 and therefore could have prepared a thorough psychobiography in time for the 1988 campaign season—but nobody did. We hope some judicious academic (not us!) will soon start working on a carefully considered psychobiography of Arnold Schwarzenegger, just in case the U.S. Constitution gets amended in time for him to run for president in 2008 or 2012. As voters, we'll need that information.

Research Up Close

Rarely, an insightful psychobiography emerges from a close and long-standing association between biographer and subject. For instance, Peter Ostwald's 1997 study of his good friend and virtuoso pianist Glenn Gould is just such a book. No currently active politician is likely to permit a well-qualified psychobiographer to get that close and stay that close. But it has happened once, with a politician who was still highly active—indeed, was still the U.S. president—when his psychobiographer first came to know and study him, and who continued to cooperate even as the psychobiographer's intentions to publish an analysis of him became clear. The resulting psychobiography was not published until several years after the subject's death, but the research on which it was based falls well within the time frame denoted by this category of *up-close research on an active politician*. The subject was Lyndon B. Johnson, and the psychobiographer was Doris Kearns (1976), who has continued her distinguished psychobiographical career under her married name of Doris Kearns Goodwin.

At the very beginning of her professional career, Kearns was presented with the dream of a psychobiographer's lifetime. As a Harvard political science graduate student in 1967, she was chosen to be a White House Fellow, allowed to spend a year working for a member of President Johnson's staff, and often given the opportunity to meet with Johnson himself. Despite Kearns's public opposition to the Vietnam War, which was then at its height under LBJ's direction, the president took a fancy to her. When he left the presidency in early 1969, he demanded that she join him at his Texas ranch to help prepare his official memoirs. The writing of the memoirs did not go well; Johnson insisted on presenting a proper presidential image that came across in print as stiff and boring. But as he showed Kearns around his ranch in the last years of his life, or came to her bedroom in the early mornings, he opened up psychologically. She says, "He spoke of the beginnings and ends of things, of dreams and fantasies. His words seemed to flow from some deep well of sadness, nostalgia and longing" (Kearns, 1976, p. 17). Kearns took notes about the intimate details of Johnson's life history as he called up his memories and free associations. She sometimes felt awkward about writing down what he was telling her so privately. But when she stopped her note-taking, Johnson would ask, "Hey, why aren't you writing all this down? Someday, someone may want to read it" (p. 18).

Kearns had been trained as a political scientist rather than as a psychobiographer. But at Harvard she had been exposed to the brilliance of Erik Erikson, and she made excellent use of her opportunities to interview a willing LBJ. She was able to observe closely the *context* of Johnson's reminiscences and to note the effect of changes in that context over time. Her later paper on the writing of her LBJ book includes a very Eriksonian remark: "I learned how unauthentic memoirs can be, unless one understands the stage of life in which they are written, why they are being written at that time, and what audience they aim to please" (Kearns, 1979, p. 99). As a political scientist, she was also able to recognize that the context of Johnson's behavior at different stages in his political career, combined with his strongly

rooted personality characteristics, made him a great success in certain roles (e.g., as U.S. Senate leader) and a disaster in others (e.g., as a president attempting to master foreign affairs). Her book on Johnson remains one of the best political psychobiographies—outdone, perhaps, only by her later book on Franklin and Eleanor Roosevelt (Goodwin, 1994).

But every silver lining comes with a cloud attached, and being embedded (figuratively and literally) with a powerful politician has its drawbacks. Though Kearns was aware of the dangers of transference and countertransference in such an intimate relationship, she did not altogether evade them. At one point Johnson told her "that all along he'd been hiding from me the fact that I reminded him of his dead mother. In talking with me, he had come to imagine he was also talking with her, unraveling the story of his life" (Kearns, 1976, p. 18). Kearns almost laughingly discounted this revelation as one of Johnson's characteristically manipulative maneuvers, not as a true transference reaction. But elsewhere in describing her interactions with him, she reveals (without directly acknowledging) her mirroring countertransference: "As I sat and listened to Johnson describe the details of his day, what he had done and how he had felt, the scene struck me as bewilderingly familiar. I could only think of my own childhood memory of my mother patiently listening to me, perched on a high stool in our kitchen, tell her in excruciating detail everything I had done that day in school" (pp. 5–6). She describes enough other instances of transference and countertransference—for instance, of Johnson "courting" her at White House dances and of her feeling like a lovesick teenager as she awaited his telephone calls (though neither ever let the situation become truly romantic or sexual)—to suggest that this is likely to be a primary difficulty in nearly any opportunity to do "psychobiography up close." It may not be sufficient reason to avoid such opportunities entirely. It does indicate, however, that the lucky psychobiographer who gets that opportunity should spend a lot of time analyzing not only his or her subject, but also the transferences and countertransferences between them, well before publication.

Problems Shared by All

No psychobiography is ever going to be perfect. No journalist, clinician, or scholar is ever a perfect match for a given subject. Given at least some minimal skill and talent, each psychobiographer will possess particular strengths and weaknesses as a researcher and as a writer. Each psychobiographer will be more familiar or comfortable with some types of psychological theory, less so with others. Each psychobiographer's personal background and individual biases will heighten sensitivities about certain aspects of the subject's life and personality but will lead toward distorted or incomplete views of other aspects. Especially problematic in predictive political psychobiography, every psychobiographer will have political sympathies and antipathies, political biases, and political commitments that cannot be totally expunged from his or her final picture of the thoroughly political subject. It is a worthy and patriotic endeavor to help the American voter understand the strengths and weaknesses of a candidate for high office. But in helping the voter, the psychobiographer will inevitably be tempted to tilt the analysis toward one candidate and against others, for political rather than psychobiographical reasons.

How can we deal with these personal biases and idiosyncrasies, which are always present when one individual psychobiographer studies one individual subject? We can address them partly by becoming more conscientious researchers and writers, by forcing ourselves to greater awareness of our biases, and by using the large variety of methodological guidelines and rules of thumb presented in this volume. But in the long run the best way to limit the effects of such biases in predictive political psychobiography, and indeed to improve the field of psychobiography as a whole, is to encourage *multiple psychobiographies of an individual subject*—that is, to urge a variety of psychobiographers, with different personal biases and different theoretical orientations and different methodological skills, to conduct and publish their own individual studies of the same subject.

That may seem a rather inefficient way to do psychobiography, involving much duplication of

effort. For lesser figures in a given field, it may *not* be worth all that effort by multiple psychobiographers; one psychobiography per middling novelist or assistant majority leader will be quite enough. For certain iconic figures, no encouragement is needed: Many psychobiographers, simultaneously or in succession, become fascinated by the same subject, whether it's Marilyn Monroe or Sylvia Plath or Abraham Lincoln. For yet other subjects, including potential U.S. presidents and current leaders of potentially hostile nations, multiple psychobiographies may be imperative. (That's why the CIA maintains its own staff of psychobiographers (see Omestad, 1994).) Even for no longer active political leaders, multiple retrospective psychobiographies may be worth doing, to help us understand our current and potential leaders better. Lyndon Johnson's behavior as U.S. president helped a lot of people, for instance through his strong advocacy of civil rights. But his behavior also harmed a lot of people, for instance through his insistence on fighting and expanding the Vietnam War. A clearer understanding of Johnson's behavior patterns as president, and how they developed out of his earlier life history, can be of real value as we assess prospective presidential candidates. If several psychobiographers and psychologically inclined biographers, including Doris Kearns Goodwin, James David Barber, and Robert Caro, look closely at LBJ and come up with similar conclusions, the *convergence* of those conclusions should give us greater confidence that they're all accurately perceiving something essential about Johnson. If they all look at LBJ and each one comes up with very different conclusions about him, their *divergence* should lead us to doubt the conclusions, to look more closely at how they reached those divergent conclusions, and perhaps to encourage more careful research on LBJ by still more psychobiographers.

Several chapters in this volume discuss the *iterative process* as the way an individual psychobiographer conducts the study of a single case. In a sense the whole field of psychobiography, like scientific research in general, operates as an iterative process. One psychobiographer studies a subject and reaches certain conclusions;

another psychobiographer, regarding those as tentative conclusions only, goes on to apply different hypotheses to the same subject and to uncover additional data; and so on. Gradually, if the process works as it should, our psychobiographical understanding of a multiply studied subject should improve over time, as the individual biases of each psychobiographer drop out of the emerging consensus.

Psychobiographical studies of active political candidates, as we have noted above, are often severely time constrained. Candidates may emerge on the national scene shortly before the presidential primary season begins (as happened with Howard Dean, Wesley Clark, and John Edwards in 2003). In those cases, voters may be lucky to have the benefit of even one reasonably careful—if inevitably somewhat biased—psychobiographical study of a given candidate. But certain candidates are highly visible for years before they declare for the presidency or other high office—time enough for several psychobiographers to launch and complete and publish their own individual studies of a given candidate, and time for yet another psychobiographer or an astute political commentator to integrate their findings and disseminate their shared conclusions to the general public. We are talking about ideal circumstances here, of course. We ourselves are not ready to organize and assign pools of psychobiographers to cover emerging candidates long in advance of the next presidential election. But in this age of quick and easy scholarly communication via e-mail and web-based professional journals, such pools may spontaneously emerge. Given their value in controlling individual political bias in psychobiography, and the value of predictive political psychobiography in informing voters of candidates' most important character components, perhaps a large charitable foundation can be persuaded to encourage their growth. In a better world, with a healthy national economy and a balanced federal budget, we might even advocate a government-funded Predictive Psychobiography Pool—a PPP rather than a CCC (Civilian Conservation Corps). Its benefits would be double: just as the CCC helped many out-of-work young people during the Great Depression while improving the national forests and urban infrastructure, so this PPP would provide jobs and training and experience for a generation of aspiring political psychobiographers while expanding and deepening our knowledge of our leaders' psyches. Wouldn't some aspiring political candidate like to adopt this idea as a plank in a presidential platform?

References

Barber, J.D. (1965). The lawmakers. New Haven, Conn.: Yale University Press.

Barber, J.D. (1992). The presidential character: Predicting performance in the White House (4th ed.). Englewood Cliffs, N.J.: Prentice-Hall.

Chesen, E.S. (1973). President Nixon's psychiatric profile. New York: Peter Weyden.

Dillie, B. (2000). The prepared and spontaneous remarks of Presidents Reagan and Bush: A validity comparison for at-a-distance measurements. Political Psychology, 21, 572–585.

Elms, A.C. (1976). Personality in politics. New York: Harcourt Brace Jovanovich.

Elms, A.C. (1994). Uncovering lives: The uneasy alliance of biography and psychology. New York: Oxford University Press.

Fick, P. (1996). The dysfunctional president: Inside the mind of Bill Clinton. New York: Citadel Press.

George, A.L., & George, J.L. (1964). Woodrow Wilson and Colonel House. New York: Dover.

Glad, B. (1980). Jimmy Carter: In search of the great White House. New York: Norton.

Goodwin, D.K. (1994). No ordinary time: Franklin and Eleanor Roosevelt: The home front in World War II. New York: Simon & Schuster.

Kearns, D. (1976). Lyndon Johnson and the American dream. New York: Harper & Row.

Kearns, D. (1979). Angles of vision. In Mark Pachter (Ed.), Telling lives: The biographer's art. Washington, D.C.: New Republic Books.

Mazlish, B., & Diamond, E. (1979). Jimmy Carter: An interpretive biography. New York: Simon & Schuster.

Murray, H.A. (1938). Explorations in personality. New York: Oxford University Press.

Omestad, T. (1994). Psychology and the CIA: Leaders on the couch. Foreign Affairs, No. 95, 105–123.

Ostwald, P. (1997). Glenn Gould: The ecstasy and tragedy of genius. New York: Norton.

Renshon, S.A. (1996). The psychological assessment of presidential candidates. New York: New York University Press.

Sheehy, G. (1976). Passages. New York: Dutton.

Sheehy, G. (1988). Character: America's search for leadership. New York: William Morrow.

Truman, H.S. (1953). Mr. Citizen. New York: Bernard Geis Associates.

Winter, D.G. (1987). Leader appeal, leader performance, and the motive profiles of leaders and followers: A study of American presidents and elections. Journal of Personality and Social Psychology, 52, 196–202.

Chapter 21

Anthony J. Dennis

Osama Bin Laden
The Sum of All Fears

Few would seriously dispute the impact Osama Bin Laden has had on world events since September 11, 2001. Whether one considers him a terrorist, a megalomaniac and mass murderer, or a populist hero and one of the most holy and devout followers of Islam alive today, Osama Bin Laden has left (and continues to leave) an indelible mark on human history that undoubtedly will be debated, analyzed, and discussed for decades and even centuries to come.

Biographers of Bin Laden face several significant challenges. First, because of the heinous nature of his terrorist acts, and his call for the use of weapons of mass destruction against Western civilians, Osama Bin Laden has become for many who are his intended targets a two-dimensional portrait of evil personified rather than a flesh-and-blood human being. The American media, in particular, has a tendency to portray Bin Laden as a cardboard caricature of a terrorist rather than as a psychologically complex individual acting out of motives he genuinely believes to be laudable. This sort of "pathographizing" precludes genuine understanding.

If we are to have any hope of ever understanding him, we must move beyond our own fears of terrorism and our historical experiences of 9/11. We must also avoid the temptation to read Bin Laden's biography "backward," in effect reconstructing a past based on what we judge to be an almost unsurpassingly "evil" present. He was not born a terrorist and a mass murderer. He became a terrorist by degrees as a result of his family circumstances, his searing wartime experiences in Afghanistan during the 1980s, and his unfortunate choice of mentors who just

happened to be radical Islamists who served to indoctrinate the young Bin Laden in the tenets of jihad against the West. As a young man on his way to attaining a business degree at a local university (and a promising career with the family construction firm to look forward to), Bin Laden faced many of the same questions young people in all times and places do when standing on the brink of adulthood: What shall I do with my life once I get out of school? What job should I take? Should I join the family business or strike out on my own? Should I marry? These prosaic questions and concerns are a far cry from the deadly religious decrees (*fatwas*) that Bin Laden has since issued calling for the worldwide killing of all Americans, civilian or military.

There are additional hurdles for those who want to know more about Bin Laden and his upbringing. The society (Islamic) and the country (Saudi Arabia) in which he grew up are among the most secretive and closed societies and countries in the entire world. Much of Muslim family life is hidden from the view of outsiders, especially foreigners. Saudi society by its nature has always been secretive, but it has grown even more so since 9/11, an event that led many in the West to question the role Saudi citizens and charities and Saudi Arabia's extreme brand of Islam (Wahhabism) may have played in the events of that terrible day.

Bin Laden himself constitutes a third barrier to obtaining information about his life. Bin Laden is a media-savvy individual who has spent years meticulously fashioning his public persona and nurturing his image as a humble and pious individual who relinquished a life of great wealth

311

and luxury in order to fight for his Muslim faith. The elusive nature of Bin Laden the man, both before and after he became an international fugitive from justice, has made Bin Laden the legend all the more real.

Even before 9/11, Bin Laden rarely gave interviews, a fact that made such events even bigger news when they occurred. He also tightly controls depictions of even his physical image through the careful release of several al-Qaeda–produced videotapes, the most famous of which shows him as almost a living statue standing immobile in front of his men, a latter-day Saladin the Great at war with the infidels. Biographical facts therefore are carefully guarded and must be pried loose from a variety of diverse sources other than the man himself. This I have done in the present study and in a prior book titled *Osama Bin Laden: A Psychological and Political Portrait* (2002). Such an endeavor requires a judicious evaluation of the available sources on Bin Laden, which can vary wildly in quality and content, with government-produced information (e.g., FBI, CIA, U.S. Department of State) generally ranking at the top in terms of quality and reliability, and journalistic reports and web-based sources of information falling further down the quality and reliability continuum.

As Westerners, we are also handicapped by our own intellectual inheritance and cultural assumptions in attempting to understand an essentially medieval figure like Osama Bin Laden. We live in a postmodern, secular society that tends to dismiss the role of religion as a motivator or, at least, to interpret overtly religious actions or conduct as a mask for psychological motives or base economic or political interests. Bin Laden and others like him believe in the literal words of the Koran and perceive themselves as warriors fighting in a celestial battle against the evil forces represented by the modern non-Muslim world. Such a point of view is far removed from our own. Consequently, unless one believes that an act of God, a *deus ex machine*, if you will, abruptly transformed Osama Bin Laden from a wealthy Saudi of undistinguished religious faith into an Islamic radical determined to ignite World War III, other explanations for his behavior and conduct must be sought. Western psychology can help us understand Bin Laden

by analyzing major events in his life and his family circumstances, including such factors as the presence or absence of one or both parents, birth order, formative experiences, and significant mentors. In this instance at least, the tools of modern psychology would seem to be an advantage, not a handicap.

The enormous challenge of writing a psychological portrait of a man who has benefited so completely from the attributes of the modern internet age is readily apparent. Bin Laden is both nowhere and everywhere. Legends and unfounded stories about him constantly spring up and take root on the Internet, threatening to crowd out more slender reeds of verifiable fact. From news sources both in the West and in the Muslim East, and from both private and governmental sources, I have attempted to piece together a coherent portrait of the man behind the terrorist label. A psychobiographer's job does not consist simply in assembling biographical facts in chronological order. In every life there is a "truth" beyond the known facts that can shed an animating light on the subject's mental landscape and serve as a key to understanding and anticipating the subject's actions—in the past, present, and future.

The Bon Vivant

One possible misconception about Bin Laden is that he was politically and religiously radicalized early on in life while growing up in the strictly religious society of Saudi Arabia. This represents another instance of inappropriately perceiving the past through the limiting lens of current events. Much has been written lately about the strict brand of Islam, Wahhabism, that is practiced in Saudi Arabia and the role of Wahhabism in spreading anti-Western and anti-American sentiment in Muslim educational institutions around the globe, many of these funded with Saudi money. Wahhabism is definitely a puritanical and uncompromising strain of Islam that preaches the rejection of non-Muslim ways and a return to the early roots of the faith that sprang from the Arabian desert in the seventh century A.D. However, Bin Laden did not become a terrorist and initiate a worldwide jihad against the

United States because he is a Wahhabi and was born a Saudi citizen. He became a terrorist due to other factors entirely.

Osama Bin Laden was born on March 10, 1957, to a wealthy and successful building contractor named Mohammed. The family was originally of Yemeni extraction. One of approximately fifty children Mohammed had with several wives, Osama Bin Laden was an anonymous younger son who grew up in a large household filled with several older brothers, any one of whom would be expected to take over the family construction business once Mohammed, the family patriarch, passed from the scene. There is no easily verifiable information about Bin Laden's relationship with his father. Sources state variously that Osama was either ten or thirteen when Mohammed died.[1] Given the patriarchical nature of Saudi and Islamic society and therefore the prominent role that a male head of household plays within the family unit, we can assume that Osama felt his father's death acutely, coming as it did while Osama was just beginning his teenage years. The sources are no less muddled when it comes to Osama Bin Laden's mother. She has been vari-

Figure 21.1. Osama Bin Laden. (AP)

ously described as a Saudi and a Syrian.[2] In the latter account, she supposedly divorced Osama's father, is still alive, and is no longer considered to be part of the Bin Laden family. Osama seems to have kept in touch with her as recently as the late 1990s, according to intelligence sources. Once Bin Laden discovered that his satellite phone calls were being intercepted by the CIA, his calls from Afghanistan to his mother ceased.

Osama's father had made a name for himself by winning and successfully executing several important construction contracts for the Saudi royal family, the most famous of which was the rehabilitation and repair of the Holy Sites at Mecca and Medina. The Bin Ladens were the royal family's builder of choice for just about any important construction project in the kingdom. These political contacts and the lucrative contracts that followed brought the Bin Laden family significant wealth. If not actual princes, Osama and his siblings certainly lived like princes behind the closed doors of their family compound. In a way, being wealthy but not of royal blood in Saudi Arabia was preferable to the opposite circumstance, since the teenage Osama had more freedom to engage in youthful indiscretions than a member of the House of Saud would have been permitted.

The facts that have come down to us show Osama as a worldly and possibly even dissolute youth who unabashedly enjoyed the earthly delights that his privileged upbringing afforded him.[3] The young Bin Laden was by no means a self-denying ascetic or holy warrior in training who looked forward to the institution of Allah's kingdom on earth. In the 1970s when Bin Laden was in his mid to late teens, before the start of the civil war in Lebanon in 1975, the city of Beirut was an attractive and beguiling destination for Osama and many other wealthy Saudis. A secular and Westernized city sitting incongruously in the middle of the ancient lands of Islam, Beirut was a place where wealthy Saudis could enjoy an anonymous personal freedom that was not permitted in the highly regulated society of Saudi Arabia where the religious police roamed the shopping districts and even had the right to break into private residences to check for instances of immorality, drinking, and other banned forms of behavior such as the mingling of the sexes who were not of the same family.

Beirut was the city where Osama purportedly sowed his wild oats, engaging in drinking and even womanizing (Bodansky, 1999, p. 3). Standing six foot four inches tall with a swarthy complexion, the teenage Osama must have cut quite a figure in the bars and discos of Beirut. The girls he probably would have interacted with and attracted during such jaunts were unlike those he knew back home. Sexually liberated, they would have been as likely to speak French as much as Arabic and to have been Christian rather than Muslim.

Bin Laden's radicalization also did not occur during his time as a college student at King Abdul Aziz University in Jedda, Saudi Arabia, where he studied economics and business management from 1974 through 1978. It is true that during the 1970s a number of academicians were expelled from Anwar Sadat's Egypt for their fundamentalist fervor and found their way to teaching posts at Bin Laden's university and other schools in Saudi Arabia. Sadat's Egypt was a secular society that was advancing toward an eventual peace agreement with Israel, the so-called "Zionist entity" in the political vocabulary of the fundamentalist Muslims. Muslim scholars found a more sympathetic reception for their anti-Western teachings in conservative Saudi Arabia where no *modus vivendi* with Israel or accommodation with secularism was either sought or contemplated.

Sheik Abdallah Yussuf Azzam, an individual who would later play an important role in Bin Laden's life, was one of these political refugees who came to teach at Osama's university during the time he was a student there. But there is no evidence that Bin Laden met Sheik Azzam in Saudi Arabia or ever took a course from him. At most, Bin Laden may have been generally aware of Sheik Azzam's presence at his university and the reasons for it. Sheik Azzam's curriculum involved Islam and Islamic jurisprudence, which gave him a platform to preach against secularism and modernism, the twin evils of Western society, and to advocate the expulsion of all Western influences from Islamic society and a return to a more pure form of Islam. This is the essence of the fundamentalist message and is the cause that Bin Laden publicly adopted as his own almost two decades later. But at the time, Osama

was progressing through a much more practical and secular course of study, taking business and economics courses. In summary, there is not a shred of credible evidence that the young Bin Laden was ever active in radical religious circles or even politically engaged during his time as a college student.[4]

The Muslim world in general, and Saudi Arabia in particular, was grappling with several fractious political developments during Bin Laden's student years—anger over a possible peace agreement between Egypt and Israel; the beginning of the long Lebanese civil war in 1975, which pitted religious factions in the Middle East against one another; and the increasing tension over the presence of Westerners and Western cultural influences in the Kingdom of Saudi Arabia due to the oil industry, which brought large numbers of American and European engineers to that country. But when he graduated in 1978, Bin Laden apparently was distracted by none of these events. Far from being a young revolutionary who would eventually preach unremitting war against the West and the expulsion of Westerners from Saudi Arabia, Bin Laden embarked upon a very conventional and bourgeois life working for the family construction business and entering into an arranged marriage.

By this time, Osama Bin Laden's father was long dead. But a place had been prepared for the young Osama in the family business, first by his father, and then by his older brothers who had continued successfully to manage the Bin Laden Corporation in the years since the death of the family patriarch.

From Donor to Jihadi

So what did transform Osama Bin Laden from a politically compliant young professional to a fugitive revolutionary responsible for launching the most recent world conflict in human history? One answer is Afghanistan.

When the Soviet Union invaded Afghanistan in the final days of 1979, alarm bells went off not only in Washington, D.C., but across the Muslim world. The brutal invasion and subjugation of a Muslim country by the officially atheist communist empire was an affront to all Muslims.

Predictably, the traditional Muslim religious establishment (*ulema*) perceived the conflict as a war between Allah and the forces of Satan. The Soviet Union was hated in particular for its decades-long suppression of the Muslim religion in the Soviet Central Asian republics, where most Muslims located inside the Soviet Union resided (Wright, 1992, pp. 131, 139; Kaplan, 1992, pp. 24–25; Taheri, 1989, p. 121). As the custodian of the two holiest sites in Islam (Mecca and Medina), the Kingdom of Saudi Arabia had a special role to play in resisting—or at least being perceived as resisting—Soviet aggression in Afghanistan. Saudi Arabia has always been conscious of its function as protector of Islam's holiest sites and terribly self-conscious over its close commercial and diplomatic ties to the non-Muslim West as a result of its oil wealth. Those ties left the Saudis vulnerable to criticism from Muslim fundamentalist intellectuals worldwide who accused the royal family of being puppets of the West. Accordingly, the Kingdom was eager to demonstrate its Islamic credentials and play an active role in various pan-Islamic causes as a means of stifling such criticism. Resistance to Soviet aggression in Afghanistan became the cause *du jour* for Saudi Arabia during this time period.

During the Cold War (1945–1991), no Muslim nation would dare to openly declare war against a superpower like the Soviet Union. Such a step would be suicidal. Rather, Muslim countries resisted in other ways—through political activism in international circles, humanitarian aid to displaced Afghans, fundraising and recruiting for the Afghanistan resistance (*muhajideen*), and supplying arms to them. As one of the wealthiest of all Muslim countries, Saudi Arabia's chief talent lay in rendering financial assistance. Wealthy and pampered Saudis may not have had a taste for the rigors of combat, but they could certainly write a sizable check for the cause.

Like other prosperous families inside Saudi Arabia, the Bin Laden clan gave money to the Afghan resistance and humanitarian aid groups. Unlike many other wealthy Arabs however, Osama actually traveled to the locations where those funds were destined. When Osama left Saudi Arabia for Pakistan, the staging ground of the resistance during the early days of the Soviet-Afghanistan war, it was not as a fanatical holy warrior (*jihadi*) prepared to die. Rather, Osama acted like any other wealthy professional who gives money to a good cause and wishes to verify exactly how those funds are being used by conducting an on-site inspection. Perhaps the young Osama was bored with office work, or perhaps curiosity led him to fly to Pakistan. Regardless, Bin Laden would later admit that his extended sojourn in Afghanistan was responsible for a religious awakening and was a life-changing experience for him.

Bin Laden's arrival in Pakistan brought him for the first time into sustained contact with Sheik Azzam, the same radical cleric and college professor who had held a teaching post at Bin Laden's university a few years before. A dedicated Muslim militant, Sheik Azzam received his doctoral degree in Islamic jurisprudence from the world-famous al-Azhar University in Cairo, Egypt. Forced by political conditions to move from Egypt to Saudi Arabia, Sheik Azzam later left the kingdom when the Soviet-Afghanistan war erupted and migrated to Pakistan, where he preached jihad against the Soviets and worked to recruit Muslims to join the Afghan resistance.

Born in 1941, Sheik Azzam was rather old to take part in combat, but he was at the top of his game when it came to preaching a jihad against the godless Soviet menace to the north. Sheik Azzam was a skilled demagogue and political organizer. His fiery sermons to the young, idealistic Muslim men who showed up in Pakistan and Afghanistan to fight proved instrumental in fueling the religious fervor and selfless courage that the Afghan *muhajideen* later became so well known for.

Bin Laden's initial contributions to the Afghan resistance were, again, more practical and concrete. As a young construction magnate with a management degree, Osama was able to provide organizational assistance behind the scenes. For example, he helped organize and document the flow of men and material to the front that enabled family members, among others, to keep track of loved ones fighting in the war. This clearinghouse became known as "the Base," or *al-Qaeda* in Arabic. Al-Qaeda was later to develop its own group identity and set of loyalties and become the foundation of Bin Laden's terrorist organization a decade later. What started out as a short trip to Pakistan and Afghanistan to check on conditions soon became for the young Bin Laden an extended stay. Bin Laden found that his ample bank accounts and his organizational skills were deeply appreciated by Sheik Azzam and the Afghan resistance. Still in his early twenties, Bin Laden also discovered that he was able to render a specialized and unique form of assistance that made him a legend among the *muhajideen*. During the course of his stay Bin Laden became aware that the resistance suffered not from a lack of bravery or ammunition but fortified shelter in the high mountain passes. Many men would die not during an attack on or battle with Soviet troops but in the retreat afterward when the *muhajideen* would flee back through the countryside as Soviet helicopters chased and exterminated them in the treeless and barren terrain. Accordingly, Bin Laden had heavy construction equipment flown in and went to work building underground bunkers and other shelters where the *muhajideen* could reside or to which they might retreat for safety.

Osama's political and religious radicalization took place gradually during the course of his stay among the *muhajideen* and resulted from several factors. Every day, Osama associated with men who were eager to fight and die for Allah. And every night, Osama went to sleep knowing that some of these fighters had been granted their fondest wish. The fanatical milieu of the camps and of the men around him must have had an effect on the youthful Osama over time. Second, there is strong evidence that Osama found a mentor and surrogate father figure in Sheik Azzam. Osama spent significant time with Sheik Azzam and adopted the older man's ideological beliefs as his own. Fatherless since his early teens, Osama appears to have lacked such a figure in his life ever since. For his part, Sheik Azzam found in Bin Laden a young and still impressionable pupil to whom he could impart his radical political and religious views. The relationship between the two met each of their needs.

Through his sermons in the camps and his many conversations with Osama over the years as the two men worked closely together, Sheik Azzam imparted to Osama Bin Laden his harsh, uncompromising brand of Islam and his apocalyptic world-view. Osama's religious indoctrina-

tion and political radicalization took place not at the university where Sheik Azzam once taught and Osama was a student. Instead, Osama received his religious and political education at Sheik Azzam's side in the crude and often dangerous living conditions of Afghanistan and Pakistan. Azzam taught his audience that the war against the Soviets was a war between Allah and the powers of darkness. The Soviet Union was evil because it did not follow the teachings of Islam. The United States and its allies were evil for the same reasons. But U.S. help was tolerated by the *muhajideen*, at least for the moment, since U.S. military support served their purposes.

There was a third factor responsible for Bin Laden's conversion from political quietism to fundamentalist activism. My strong sense is that

> Osama must have been secretly gratified to hear the heartfelt expressions of appreciation from the resistance forces for the bunkers he had built. At home, Osama was a wealthy but unknown Saudi businessman. In Afghanistan, he was hailed as a hero and a savior for rendering a specialized form of aid (constructing the bunkers and building roads for the resistance) that no one else could have possibly delivered for the *muhajideen* at that time. Osama's former life was marked by unsung routine. Osama's life in Afghanistan was much different and could truly be labelled a "calling." Still in his early twenties and searching to make his mark as an adult in the world, Osama must have felt a deep sense of reward and belonging in Afghanistan. He ended up staying for the duration of the war. (Dennis, 2002, p. 30)

Osama was an anonymous and overlooked younger son no more. He had found a cause worthy of his energies. Arriving as a young but wealthy donor, Bin Laden left Afghanistan at the conclusion of the war on February 15, 1989, as a hardened combat veteran. He had thrown in his lot with the greatly outgunned and outnumbered *muhajideen* and, miraculously, survived. One wonders whether Bin Laden gave his survival a providential reading. Did he remain alive while so many of his comrades died because Allah had a greater cause in store for him? Such thinking is typical of the Muslim fundamentalists. Events—whether natural or man-made—are interpreted as signs from Allah. Earthquakes, for example, have been seen as signs of heaven's disfavor. And dreams are viewed not as psychological or neurological events but as coded communications from God. Bin Laden returned home a changed man. He had made the transition from wealthy donor to holy warrior or jihadi.

The Veteran at Home

Osama Bin Laden returned home from the Afghan war to some amount of fanfare. The Saudi ruling family celebrated his role in Afghanistan as a way of emphasizing its own moral and material support for the *muhajideen*.

Any transition back to Saudi civilian life was no doubt eased by the attention and lavish praise he received from fellow Saudis. Invitations for Bin Laden to speak at mosques and at various events provided him with an important opportunity for catharsis and a chance to integrate his wartime experiences.

Settling back into the life that originally had been carved out for him by his late father, Osama Bin Laden might have been content to bask in the afterglow of his wartime adventures for the rest of his life. But major events set him on a different, less peaceful course (Dennis, 2002, p. 34).

The August 2, 1990, invasion of neighboring Kuwait by Saddam Hussein's Iraq set Bin Laden on a new and seemingly unalterable course of conflict with the Saudi ruling family. Even in that violent quarter of the world, Saddam Hussein had a reputation as a gambler and vicious bully. Many believed Hussein planned to conquer the entire Persian Gulf. His quick victory over Kuwait only increased both Hussein's bravado and Saudi fears of an imminent invasion of their own lands. Despite the taboo against inviting non-Muslims onto sacred soil, the land of Mecca and Medina itself, the Saudis decided to permit a coalition of Western countries, led by the United States, to station a massive military force inside Saudi Arabia (Friedman, 1991, p. 66; Smith, 1992, pp. 87, 91–92). Secret negotiations and compromises between the Saudi government and the conservative religious establishment (*ulema*)

in Saudi Arabia were worked out in order to ensure that the clerics would not publicly protest this decision (Dennis, 2002, p. 36). Nonetheless, many clerics argued in favor of self-defense first. Stationing atheist troops on the Arabian peninsula was tantamount to defilement. Given the transformation he had undergone in Afghanistan, Bin Laden agreed with the more radical clerics.

Osama met with members of the Saudi government and military in an attempt to sell them on a self-defense idea he had devised (Dennis, 2002, p. 35). Like the builder and construction worker he was at heart, Osama set forth an elaborate plan to reconstitute the work crews he had used in Afghanistan in order to build a series of bunkers, trenches, and defensive works along Saudi Arabia's northern and eastern borders. This would enable Osama to repeat the heroic script he had played out in Afghanistan, though this time he would be saving Saudi lives. The Saudi military and other government officials listened politely but ultimately were not interested. They preferred the safer alternative of assembling a massive military force provided by the Western allies. Osama's extreme religious zeal and his vociferous opposition to the stationing of non-Muslim troops on Saudi soil were quietly noted. Eventually, Bin Laden was welcome in Saudi government circles no more (Dennis, 2002, pp. 36–37).

By the eve of the 1991 Persian Gulf War, the Saudi government no longer viewed Bin Laden as a valuable propaganda tool to display its devotion and commitment to pan-Islamic causes. He was becoming as dangerous and uncontrollable politically as the radical clerics who railed against the arrival of Western forces. Bin Laden's outspoken stance alienated him from the governing elite and threatened the family business, as well. He had become a political liability to his extended family, which held lucrative government contracts that could be jeopardized by Osama's uncompromising political views. Denied the chance to play the hero once again in Saudi Arabia in 1990–1991 as he had previously in Afghanistan, and fearing for his own safety and the welfare of his family's business, Osama Bin Laden made the difficult decision to leave Saudi Arabia. By this time, the international spotlight had shifted from Afghanistan. Bin Laden had no desire to return to what was now, once again, a political backwater run by a combination of ex-communists and local warlords. He needed to settle in a country that shared his fundamentalist views. Sudan was tailor-made for Bin Laden. Soon after he left, the Saudi government stripped him of his Saudi citizenship.

By the early 1990s, Osama Bin Laden was living in Khartoum, Sudan, as a stateless revolutionary, much like his former mentor Sheik Azzam and so many other fundamentalists who lived hand to mouth as they were chased from one country to another depending on the political winds inside the Muslim world. But unfortunately for Bin Laden, Sheik Azzam was dead. Azzam, two of his sons, and another individual had been killed in November 1989 in Peshawar, Pakistan, by a powerful car bomb. The assassination has never been explained. With Sheik Azzam's death, Bin Laden lost yet another mentor and father figure. In Sudan, he immediately found a replacement in the person of Hassan al-Turabi, one of the grand strategists and visionaries of the transnational Muslim fundamentalist movement.

Through the Green Door
of Radical Islamic Politics

In choosing to oppose the Saudi leadership and settle in radical Sudan, Osama Bin Laden essentially had walked "through the green door" of radical Islamic politics. If the political leadership remained the same in Saudi Arabia, Bin Laden could never go home again. Sudan was an enemy of the West and of Saudi Arabia's ties to it. Like Afghanistan's Taliban government ten years later, Sudan's government ruled the country with medieval Islamic rectitude. The Islamic legal code, the *sharia*, was the basis of all laws. People hobbled along the streets of the capital city of Khartoum begging for food because they were unable to work without the hands and/or feet that had been chopped off by the government's jailers for various petty offenses. This was now Bin Laden's world and his vision of heaven on earth.

Osama was no longer a naive young man fresh out of college. He was a war veteran who had toughened up considerably, both physically

and psychologically, since the days of his pampered upbringing in Saudi Arabia. Bin Laden and his fellows in Afghanistan had taken on one superpower, the Soviet Union, and won. They believed it was not even a close contest. In opposing the will of Allah, no nation could win. Accordingly, Osama did not hesitate to oppose the Saudi ruling family over a decision he felt was un-Islamic, regardless of the personal consequences. Furthermore, given his wartime experiences Bin Laden appeared to have no trouble relocating to a primitive and economically backward country like Sudan, having lived for almost ten years in another such country, Afghanistan.

Bin Laden's stay in Sudan in the early and mid-1990s brought him his second significant mentor and filled the void left by the loss of Sheik Azzam. Now Sudan's Hassan al-Turabi assumed the function of surrogate father. Multilingual and a graduate of both Western and Islamic educational institutions, Turabi was born in 1932 and holds advanced degrees from the University of London and the Sorbonne in Paris. Turabi "imparted to Bin Laden a more sophisticated and systematic understanding of the anti-Western jihad to which both men were so committed" (Dennis, 2002, p. 47). The seventy-something Turabi was literally the "power behind the throne" in Sudan during these years. General Bashir ran the government, but Turabi provided its political philosophy and ideological content. For years, Turabi had been seeking to spread his vision of a transnational Muslim fundamentalist movement that would violently sweep existing governments in the Arab and Muslim worlds aside, abolish territorial divisions among Muslim nations, and eventually result in a modern, reconstituted Islamic empire stretching from North Africa to the Far East.[5] Turabi was the elder statesman and philosopher of the transnational Muslim movement during these years, and he used Sudan as a staging area to spread his radical ideas. Turabi organized an annual series of conferences in Khartoum that went by various names and that brought together fundamentalist groups, revolutionaries, and terrorists from around the world for the purpose of better confronting the West and coordinating their political activities.

These Turabi-inspired annual political conferences introduced Osama Bin Laden to a "who's who" of personalities from the world of radical Islamic politics and planted in him the seeds of a larger political vision. The struggle against non-Islamic forces was a worldwide struggle, Bin Laden was told. And Muslims should not be content merely to expel invaders like the Soviets from Muslim lands such as Afghanistan but should work to realize an even grander and more positive vision of an Islamic world that was politically unified and united under the banner of Islam. Turabi characterized existing boundaries between Muslim nations as artificial territorial constructs representing one of the legacies of Western nineteenth-century colonialism. These must be abolished so that the Islamic *ummah* (community of believers) could be united once again as a single political entity and unitary force on the world scene. Turabi aimed for nothing less than a modern Islamic empire. This also became Bin Laden's grand vision.

Bin Laden adopted another of Turabi's ideas, as well. The religious landscape had long been divided between Sunnis and Shiites, the religion's two major sects. Historically, this division was bitter and sometimes violent. According to Turabi, religious squabbles only divided the Muslim world to the West's advantage. Turabi called for the two sides to reconcile their differences, politically if not theologically, and work toward common political goals. Indeed, this has taken place as Sunni Sudan has worked covertly with Shiite Iran, and elements inside Sunni Afghanistan were allied with the Shiite government of Iran during twenty years of warfare.

In Turabi, then, Bin Laden had once again found a father, and he dutifully made major elements of Turabi's political agenda his own. For his part, Turabi probably was flattered to have an eager and wealthy protégé at his side who promised to fulfill Turabi's political vision long after the older generation of fundamentalists had passed from the scene. Undoubtedly, he was also an important source of emotional support for Bin Laden during his first few years of exile from his homeland.

By 1996, Sudan was coming under relentless diplomatic pressure from Saudi Arabia and the United States to expel Bin Laden from the country. Osama left Sudan and returned to the country where he had first found his calling and made

his mark on world history—Afghanistan. In Afghanistan during the late 1990s, Bin Laden discovered in the ruling Taliban a regime whose views were as medieval in outlook and as ideologically rigid as his own. The Taliban would give Bin Laden sanctuary to live and work in Afghanistan until the very end of that regime.

Osama would find a third mentor and father figure of sorts in Afghanistan when he merged the Egyptian Islamic Jihad group with his own al-Qaeda organization. (Bin Laden's outreach to another fundamentalist terrorist group was likely inspired by Turabi's own advocacy of such efforts.) This move brought Dr. Ayman Zawahiri, the leader of Egyptian Islamic Jihad, into the fold as number two in al-Qaeda. It is evident from the al-Qaeda produced videotapes and from Dr. Zawahiri's own standing in the organization that Bin Laden thinks highly of Zawahiri. Dr. Zawahiri is a medical doctor turned terrorist who was implicated in and imprisoned for the October 1981 assassination of Egyptian president Anwar Sadat. His influence on Osama Bin Laden is ongoing.

Psychological Factors

We pass now to a synopsis of the psychological forces at work in Osama Bin Laden's life.

Mentors and Replacement Fathers

Having lost his father while still in his early teens, Osama Bin Laden has consistently sought out and placed himself under the tutelage of a succession of older males who, to varying degrees, have served as replacement fathers to Bin Laden.

Islamic society in general, and Saudi society in particular, is culturally conservative and patriarchical in nature with an inbred respect for one's elders. Therefore, it should come as no surprise that the young Bin Laden would listen to the counsel of older and presumptively wiser men. But it is striking that a man as widely respected and independently wealthy as Bin Laden would consistently place himself under the tutelage of other, ostensibly less powerful individuals. And it is notable that Bin Laden seemed to develop a powerful, almost filial, relationship with one older male at a time (Dennis, 2002,

p. 46). Indeed, the world is still suffering from Bin Laden's adoption of radical Muslim leaders as his role models.

Wartime Trauma and Fundamentalist Zeal

The Afghanistan war changed Osama Bin Laden as it did so many veterans, making him indifferent to the taking of human life and callous toward the commission of atrocities against civilians like those who died on September 11, 2001, in the United States. Nonetheless, it must be acknowledged that combat experience does not turn every veteran into a terrorist or a mass murderer. Something more was obviously at work in Bin Laden's life. That something was the Muslim fundamentalist world-view he adopted from Sheik Azzam and his fellow *muhajideen* that interprets every event as a manifestation of the divine will and world political events as a struggle between Allah and the forces of darkness. Once one becomes convinced that all non-Muslims are, in essence, servants of Satan because they do not follow Islam, it is quite easy to justify killing them. This justification has enabled Bin Laden and his followers to preach and carry out mass casualty attacks against Western civilians while still believing in the morality and godliness of their cause. So, fundamentalism gave Osama Bin Laden an identity, a sense of commitment to an ideology, and an invitation to guiltlessly express his rage.

It is virtually certain that Bin Laden would credit his survival in the Soviet-Afghanistan war to the will of Allah and that he would interpret his steady rise in radical Islamic political circles to the fact that Allah had a great, world-changing mission for him to perform. Bin Laden's convictions about the righteousness of his political mission, and his belief that he is serving Allah's will, therefore make him indifferent to political negotiations or humanitarian pleas. Only death will stop him.

The Celebrity Ego

There is another psychological force at work in Bin Laden's life that became evident during and after the Soviet-Afghanistan war that no one else apparently has ever publicly analyzed or com-mented upon. Bin Laden's ego swelled along with his self-confidence as a result of his wartime exploits. During the war, he had carved a reputational niche for himself by rendering a specialized form of aid (construction assistance) to the Afghan resistance. Returning home to Saudi Arabia at war's end in 1989, he was touted by the Saudis as a brave Muslim warrior and national hero for the role he played and the deprivations he had suffered in war-torn Afghanistan. During this postwar period, he gave speeches in mosques and at other public venues around Saudi Arabia discussing his wartime exploits (Dennis, 2002, p. 53). Bin Laden found that he loved the publicity, and his ego expanded in accordance with the praise heaped upon him. He was an anonymous younger son no more.

While Bin Laden basked in the glory of his burgeoning reputation as a brave and self-sacrificing *jihadi*, the Saudi government's aim in furthering his reputation was driven less by religious zeal and more by considerations of *realpolitik*. The Saudis celebrated Bin Laden's exploits because he exemplified the Saudi government's commitment to pan-Islamic causes and its worthiness to rule over the holiest sites in Islam (Mecca and Medina).

As every movie star and politician knows, publicity can become addictive. And those abruptly removed from the media spotlight can turn in pain and anger upon their former patrons. At the outbreak of hostilities between Iraq and neighboring Kuwait, Osama Bin Laden attempted to play the savior's role once again in Saudi Arabia as he had done in Afghanistan during the war. A breach with the Saudi government was made more likely, one might even say inevitable, once the Saudis made it clear that Bin Laden would not be allowed to assume a high-profile role in the defense of the country against a possible Iraqi invasion. Bin Laden's break with the Saudis and his assumption of terrorist operations enabled Osama, in essence, to recapture the media spotlight that had been so abruptly taken from him by the Saudi government in 1990–1991.

Bin Laden's oversized ego is particularly evident in the grandiose religious decrees (*fatwas*) that he has periodically issued since the mid-1990s calling upon all Muslims worldwide to kill Americans or to engage in other violent acts as a religious duty. Bin Laden holds no religious position and is not a graduate of any religious institution. He is completely unqualified to issue any form of *fatwa*. It takes a titanic ego to presume to know the will of Allah and to issue such decrees despite a total lack of religious training or qualifications.

In other respects, Bin Laden's love of publicity and his grandiose view of himself are more camouflaged and thus require greater powers of detection and investigation. To Western eyes, Bin Laden's lifestyle can appear anything but grandiose. For example, a famous video of the terrorist master shows him speaking while reclining on his side on a humble pallet spread across the dirt floor of a cave, his head propped up by one bent arm. To a Western audience, Bin Laden's primitive surroundings seem to undermine his attempts to portray himself as the powerful leader of an international network of holy warriors committed to defeating the West. But Bin Laden is an expert showman and master propagandist. In consciously having himself filmed in such circumstances, Bin Laden seeks to remind his Muslim viewers of a famous story in the Koran called "The Cave" in which the righteous followers of Allah retreat from their enemies to live in a cave.[6] The story emphasizes the protection and victory that Allah ultimately confers upon the faithful and the damnation that Allah brings upon all unbelievers. The story describes the torments of Hell that are visited upon those who do not believe in Allah and who persecute the faithful.

In releasing the cave video, Bin Laden makes an unspoken but nonetheless direct claim to be reenacting a modern-day equivalent of this famous story. In the modern version of the story, Bin Laden casts himself as Allah's righteous leader of the faithful on earth. And like the individuals sheltered in the cave by Allah as described in the Koran chapter 18 (Surah, 1993 18) Bin Laden promises his Muslim viewers that Allah also will protect Bin Laden and his followers until they are ultimately victorious against the infidel West.

Other Bin Laden video productions are less subtle. During the autumn of 2001 after the commencement of hostilities by the Americans in Afghanistan, al-Qaeda released a video showing Osama Bin Laden and his lieutenants standing perfectly still and erect in majestic poses under bright sunshine. With his shoulders thrust back and his followers arrayed around him, Bin Laden struck a fearless pose for the camera. Never moving as the camera rotated around him, Bin Laden looked like a living statue, a modern-day equivalent of the great Muslim warrior Saladin the Great, as alluded to earlier (Dennis, 2002, pp. 55–56). Regardless of culture or nationality, everyone seemed to understand the point of this video. Again, Bin Laden demonstrated his boldness in claiming leadership of the transnational Muslim resistance to the West and provided further evidence of his masterful use of publicity to further his carefully crafted public image.

Stepping back from the particulars of Osama Bin Laden's life in an attempt to cross-reference him with other historical figures, it is clear that Bin Laden is a destructive charismatic who is very successful at nurturing his audience's imagined or perceived historical grievances and touching every wound present in the Muslim psyche. He purports to act not for himself but for the welfare of other "oppressed Muslims" around the world. He speaks incessantly of Muslims in such far-flung regions as Palestine, Chechnya, India, the Philippines, and elsewhere around the globe in a concerted attempt to make their cause his own. In the same manner, Adolf Hitler nursed perceived grievances of the German people arising from the Treaty of Versailles at the end of World War I and was extremely talented at claiming to come to the aid of "oppressed Germans" living in neighboring lands such as Austria and Czechoslovakia. There are important differences between the two men, in terms of both the substance of their respective ideologies and their biographical circumstances. Nonetheless, both display many of the same demagogical talents, and both have promised to lead their followers to a modern day utopia that, in the end, can only result in death and destruction.

Notes

1. Peter Bergen places Mohammed's death in 1967 when Osama was ten. See Bergen (2001, p. 45). By contrast, Yonah Alexander and Michael S. Swetnam (2001, p. 4) state that this death occurred when Osama Bin Laden was thirteen.

Yossef Bodansky (1999) does not affirmatively state when Mohammed Bin Laden died. However, he has him alive and well as of 1973 when Osama was approximately sixteen years of age (p. 3). Weighing the available sources, I believe this tragic event in Osama Bin Laden's life likely took place when Osama was between the ages of ten and thirteen.

2. Alexander and Swetnam (2001) state that Bin Laden's mother is a Saudi. Bergen (2001) wrote that she is a Syrian.

3. See, e.g., Bodansky (1999, p. 3).

4. In this assessment I differ from other writers and biographers, chief among them Alexander and Swetnam (2001), who suggest the opposite as does Bodansky who asserts that Osama began associating with local Islamic radicals while still a student. I do not find these accounts sustainable and believe, as Bin Laden himself stated in an interview, that his religious awakening and political radicalization began several years later during the Soviet-Afghanistan war.

5. For Turabi's biography and ideas, see generally Black (2001, pp. 336–337, 341, 343), Dennis (1996, pp. 62–63), and Miller (1993).

6. For the story in the Koran, see Surah 18 (1993). For a complete discussion of this video and Bin Laden's ingenious attempts to link himself with the individuals in the Koran, see Dennis (2002, pp. 54–55).

References

Alexander, Y., & Swetnam, M.S. (2001). Usama Bin Laden's Al-Qaida: Profile of a terrorist network. Ardsley, N.Y.: Transactional Publishers.

Bergen, P.L. (2001). Holy war Inc.: Inside the secret world of Osama Bin Laden. New York: Free Press.

Black, A. (2001). The history of Islamic political thought: From the prophet to the present. New York: Routledge.

Bodansky, Y. (1999). Bin Laden: The man who declared war on America: Rocklin, Calif.: Prima Publishing.

Dennis, A.J. (1996). The rise of the Islamic empire and the threat to the West. Bristol, Ind.: Wyndham Hall Press.

Dennis, A.J. (2002). Osama Bin Laden: A psychological and political portrait. Lima, Ohio: Wyndham Hall Press.

Friedman, N. (1991). Desert victory: The war for Kuwait. Annapolis, Md.: Naval Institute Press.

Kaplan, R.D. (1992, April). Shatter zone. Atlantic Monthly, pp. 24–25, 20–49.

The noble Koran. Riyad, Surah. (1993). 18 "The Cave," pp. 445–465 Saudi Arabia: Maktaba Dar-us-Salam.

Miller, J. (1993). The challenge of radical Islam. Foreign Affairs, 72(2), 43–56.

Smith, J.E. (1992). George Bush's war. New York: Henry Holt & Co.

Taheri, A. (1989). Crescent in a red sky: The future of Islam in the Soviet Union. London: Hutchinson & Co.

Wright, R. (1992). Islam, democracy and the West. Foreign Affairs, 71(3), 131, 139, 130–159.

Chapter 22

Stanley A. Renshon

In his Father's Shadow

George W. Bush and the Politics of Personal Transformation

In order to understand who George W. Bush *is*, one must first understand who he *was*. His story, like the man himself, is not particularly complicated, at least in broad outline. He was born into an accomplished and wealthy family, and then took some time to find his way. The most important ingredients of adult development were consolidated only very gradually by Mr. Bush.

How did Mr. Bush's life begin? With great promise, many assets, and colossal advantages. But with these benefits came demands. The complexities he faced, and the talents he brought to bear—and developed—as he faced these demands are the focus of this chapter. Understanding Mr. Bush requires special emphasis be placed on Mr. Bush's relationships with his father and mother, the challenges of being born into such a spectacularly successful family, his battles with alcohol, and his ownership role in the Texas Rangers baseball team. All these experiences propelled Mr. Bush into what can only be described as a profound psychological impasse. His life history, combined with his private ambition, pushed toward success. Yet every time he sought to gain a foothold, he found little solid ground.

The result was an erratic commitment to the outward manifestations of conventional achievement, first in adolescence, then early adulthood, and finally on to middle adulthood. Bush became the family rebel and in school the campus cutup. Later, he combined hard work with equally hard-driving living, including too much drinking. Self-medication with alcohol and acting out in middle and late adulthood became a partial substitute for the success he so desired but that remained out of reach—for a time. The story of how

Mr. Bush managed to forge a stable and successful adulthood is one of perseverance, resilience, determination, and profound but gradual personal transformation. It is seen, by some, as a tale of faith restored; Mr. Bush first rejected, then rediscovered, a personal God. Yet his is more than a story of personal faith. It is, in addition, a story of inner resolve.

Why is this story so important? It tells us a great deal about how Mr. Bush came to be the person he is. And that person is now president of the United States.

George W. Bush's Development: A Psychologically Framed Narrative

George W. Bush was born into a wealthy and extremely accomplished family. His grandfather had been a successful businessman, U.S. senator and pillar of the Eastern Republican establishment. His father, whose name he carried, had been an outstanding scholar, athlete, war hero, successful businessman, congressman, ambassador to China, head of the Central Intelligence Agency, vice president, and finally president of the United States.

Measured against these august accomplishments, George W. Bush paled and suffered the silent rebuke of lowered expectations. That is one reason why his educational program, "No Child Left Behind," has a special relevance for this president. He was not an outstanding student or an accomplished athlete. Nor did he seem to have a special talent that would help set him apart in any other way, unless it was his capacity to be the center of the group for no obvious reason except that people liked and were drawn to him. The earliest known manifestation of this occurred when he ran for class president in junior high school and won (Colloff, 1999).

More often he was taking pleasure in pranks and getting into trouble because of them. This role—as the self-described "black sheep" of the family—can be seen in retrospect as a way of embracing his difficulty in finding a way to measure up. Whatever Freudian dreams he might have harbored of surpassing his father were buried deep in his own failures to find much measure of conventional success.

The result was a profound mismatch between a father that his son admired but had little hope of emulating, and a son whose father was the North Star of his idealization and the curse of his unrealized ambitions. Because of this unresolved dilemma, George W.'s adolescence and early adulthood were unfocused, wholly ordinary, and, by family measures, undistinguished. When he graduated from college, he recalled, "I didn't have much of a life plan" (Bush, 2001b, p. 785). Many years later, that was still true. As George W. said of himself at one point in his autobiography, "I had dabbled in many things" (1999, p. 60).

After graduating from Harvard Business School, George W. set out for Texas, as his father had before him, to make his fortune. Yet, again, where his father succeeded, George W. didn't. He tried his hand at politics, running for Congress, as had his father. Yet again, where his father had succeeded, he didn't. His unfocused adolescence and undistinguished early adulthood were threatening to turn into a failed adulthood.

By the age of forty, his oil business and political prospects had reached a dead end. As he said of himself in a 1986 interview, "I'm all name and no money" (quoted in Reinhold, 1986, p. 14). Though Mr. Bush tried hard, he never located what he called "the liberator," "a major oil find that would cement his future and justify his promise" (Minuatagio, 2000, p. 201).

That term, "liberator," is suffused with psychological significance. It refers most simply to liberation from financial worries, but it carried deeper meaning as well. It meant to be liberated

from the inability to measure up to family expectations. It meant to stand on equal footing with his father's successful history. And it meant to have engineered his first major adult success.

It might also have helped to undercut the basis of what was clearly a substantial personal problem. Mr. Bush had a real issue with drinking. At various times George W. has both alluded to its seriousness and downplayed it. David Frum (2003, p. 283) quotes George W. telling a group of religious leaders, "There is only one reason why I am in the Oval Office and not in a bar. I found faith, I found God. I am here because of the power of prayer."

It is true that, duly respecting the power of prayer, George W. quit drinking suddenly and totally. This was in itself an act of determination and courage—to face his life as it was—as well as optimism that he could find a way out of his developmental impasse.

Exactly how and why his sobriety was achieved is one of the pivotal mysteries of George W.'s personal and psychological transformation. George W. credits Billy Graham; he also credits his wife, Laura. I myself credit George W. Bush, for reasons to be made clear shortly.

If George W.'s father is the North Star of his ideals and ambitions, then his mother's psychology was the instrument of his self-realization. Her famously direct, no-nonsense, and at times tart style can be easily seen in George W. He got to experience all these attributes firsthand, well into his adulthood.

One year after he stopped drinking, George W. was offered an opportunity to become a partner in a local baseball team—the Texas Rangers. Yet this time, unlike so many others, George W. grabbed his chance and leveraged this opportunity into something more important than a job—a foothold in the adult world and an opportunity to earn, due to his own skills and developing capacities, a larger place in it.

There is much more to George W.'s developmental history. But here that history begins to intersect with his turn to politics and his rise to the presidency. There is, for example, his role in his father's two presidential campaigns and what he learned from them. There is the story of his own successful run for governor of Texas and how he governed. Yet, before those things unfolded, there is the important story of Mr. Bush's psychological impasse and self-redemption.

Money and Politics: The Family Business

Family businesses are notoriously hard on the psychology of the family children. They raise issues of measuring up to success. They also raise issues of forging a separate identity in an area already successfully staked out by others. And they stoke fiery emotional currents of competition among all concerned.

Else Walker, a Bush family cousin close to George W., had this to say about growing up in that household: "This is not an easy family to grow up in. All of us had to come to grips with the fact that that there are enormously successful people in it and a lot of pressure to be a big deal. All of us have had various successes in coming to grips with those pressures" (quoted in Minuatagio, 2000, p. 158).

The Bush family business can be characterized in two words: money and service. George W.'s grandfather, Prescott Bush, had provided the family model by first making millions on Wall Street and then establishing a long career of public service. He served first as a moderator of town meetings and next as a U.S. senator from Connecticut. Tall and imposing, Prescott served as a senator for over a decade and was of course a senior member of the Bush extended family.

His son, George W.'s father, followed in his father's footsteps, first making money and then going on to public service. George H.W. Bush's political resume is a long one: chairman of the Republican Party, Harris County, Texas, 1962; U.S. Senate candidate in 1964 [lost]; congressional candidate, 1966 [won]; reelected to Congress, 1968; candidate for the U.S. Senate, 1970 [lost]; ambassador to the United Nations, 1970; Republican National Committee chairman, 1972; ambassador to China, 1974; director of the Central Intelligence Agency, 1976; presidential candidate, 1980 [lost]; U.S. vice president, 1980–1988; and finally president of the United States, 1988–1992.

That list, of course, represents only the titles, not the effort. Behind each of these resume lines lay the hours, days, months, and years devoted to a high-level, ongoing political life. This includes countless meetings, strategy sessions, consultations, and fund-raising events. Then there come the actual requirements of serving in office.

The point here is simple. A political life, especially played out at the highest levels of government, requires intense personal involvement, and in the Bush clan that meant the whole family. So for George W., the many visits of the clan patriarch Senator Prescott Bush flowed naturally into his father's political career. George W. was sixteen when his father became Republican county chairman and eighteen when his father announced his first run for the U.S. Senate. George W.'s hands-on political experience began that August by traveling with his father through Texas on the campaign trail.

Frank Bruni (2003) writes of George W. that "[f]ew had entered the White House with such a brief career in public service, such a late blooming interest in the position, such a spotty body of knowledge, and such hurried preparation, in as much as there could ever be any" (p. 3). If by public service one means elected or appointed positions, that point is correct. Yet, it is also misleading.

Consider that before gaining the presidency, George W. had the most intimate platform from which to observe, participate in, and learn about American politics—his father's extensive political career. More specifically, George W.'s experience includes the following:

Working on his father's unsuccessful campaign for the U.S. Senate, 1964 (age eighteen)

Working on his father's successful campaign for Congress, 1966 (age twenty)

Working on his father's successful reelection campaign for Congress, 1968 (age twenty-two)

Working on his father's unsuccessful campaign for the U.S. Senate, 1970 (age twenty-four)

Considering running for Texas state legislature, 1971 (age twenty-five)

Touring Texas in 1976 for Gerald Ford's presidential campaign, 1976 (age thirty)

Attending GOP candidate school, 1976 (age thirty)

Working for GOP candidate Edward J. Gurney in Florida, 1977 (age thirty-one)

Running for congressional seat, 1978 (age thirty-two)

Working on his father's 1980 presidential race (age thirty-four)

Working on the U.S. Senate race of Winston Blout in Alabama, 1981 (age thirty-five)

Working on his father's 1984 reelection campaign (age thirty-nine)

Campaigning for his Yale friend Victor Ashe running for U.S. senator in Tennessee, 1984 (age thirty-nine)

Serving as senior advisor to his father's successful presidential campaign, 1987–1988 (age forty-one)

Considering, but deciding against, running for Texas governorship in 1989 (age forty-two)

Serving as campaign advisor (not in Washington) to father's unsuccessful presidential reelection campaign, 1992 (age forty-five)

Running for Texas governor, and winning, 1994 (age forty-seven)

Running for and winning reelection as Texas governor, 1998 (age fifty-one)

Running for, and winning, the U.S. presidency, 1999–2000 (age fifty-three)

The list both confirms and contradicts Bruni's characterization. George W. does not have an extensive resume of public office, but he has a very extensive resume in politics. Indeed, one could argue that he spent an adult lifetime immersed in politics.

The questions surrounding George W.'s resume are related to how prepared he was (and is) for the presidency. Could he actually lead? Bruni's point presupposes that the best way to learn about politics is by holding office. Yet, a plausible case could be made that a lifetime of political campaigning at every level of government, for Congress, the Senate, for governor, president and vice president, would provide its own political learning experience. This would especially be the case if these experiences were, as they were for George W., repeated, and if the vantage point was as close as you could be to the candidate and the center of campaign operations.

In these positions, George W. was not only getting a high level, insider view of politics. He was also getting the same insider's view of lead-

ership. George W. is a student of leadership (Greenstein, 2003) and has clear views as to its nature and operation. These were developed and refined over many years of watching successes and failures: his father's and his own.

George W.'s political resume also makes one other important point clear: He has had a lifetime *interest* in politics. Despite being unsure of his life path at numerous points in his development, he never overtly rejected politics as a possibility. On the contrary, he took every opportunity to do campaign work, most often for his father, but for others as well, and himself considered his first possible run for office at age twenty-five. Far from being a late arrival to politics, one could say that his political interests and ambitions are discernable fairly early in his young adulthood.

This is not to say that the presidency was central to George W.'s ambitions. He was no Al Gore, trained to believe that the presidency was his goal from an early age, rebelling briefly against the assumption, only to take the quest back up in earnest and for the rest of his life at age twenty-nine. He was no Bill Clinton, seized by an ambition crystallized by meeting with President John F. Kennedy when he was in high school. Nor was he a Lyndon Johnson or Richard Nixon, seething with the desires of an outsider determined to break in and master the charmed circle of status and respectability this high office represented. Indeed, George W. says for himself that he came to his interest in the presidency "recently."

As a Bush, George W. had all the status he needed. What he lacked was the personal stature that came from being the author of his own success. The questions surrounding George W.'s resume were not only, or even primarily, seen through the lens of how well prepared he was for the presidency. More at issue was how well he had shown he was prepared for, and had prospered in, life.

George W.'s political resume reflects a historically unique, profoundly close, long-term personal and political relationship with his father. That relationship is also an intense and complex one. Its changing nature over George W.'s childhood, and his early and mid-adult development, provides an important insight into this president's character psychology.

His Father's Son

George W.'s relationship with his father is the center point of his development. Both George W. and his brother Jeb referred to their father as a "beacon" (quoted in Minuatagio, 2000, p. 101). An analysis of this relationship might therefore begin with the psychology of love and admiration. Interviewed by the *Washington Post* at his first 100 days in office, George W. was asked about his father, "Has he been helpful for you?" He replied, "He's been helpful to me by telling me he loves me, and that he's proud of me. There's nothing like a dad giving a son the kind of words that only a dad can give" (Allen, 2001).

One way to view the history of George W.'s adult development is through the lens of his desire to earn his father's pride. Love was never an issue between the two. These vital ties were forged despite, or perhaps because of, his father's long absences from home. George H.W. Bush was on the road a great deal while his son was growing up. And that didn't change as George W. got older, and his father turned his considerable energies toward politics. George W. grew up with at least one "surrogate father,"[1] but no surrogate can compete psychologically with the real person, especially when that person is incredibly accomplished, emotionally nurturing, absent, and therefore longed for and idealized. Idealization, the fusion of strong positive feelings with an emphasis on the person's admirable characteristics, is a psychological recipe for strong, close, and unconflicted personal attachments.

There is abundant evidence of the close emotional connection between the two men. In his autobiography (Bush, 1999),[2] George W. singles out for special mention the cufflinks his father gave him after he won the governorship and introduces an accompanying letter from his father signed "devotedly yours" that George W. says "still brings a lump to my throat" (p. 42). Covering then presidential candidate George W. Bush, Bruni (2003) noted how "he cried on about half the occasions when he talked about how supportive his father had been" (p. 181). Asked by eighth graders at a middle school campaign stop in 2000 about his father, he said, "I didn't like it when people criticized my dad. That's because I love

him, I love him more than anything" (quoted in Walsh, 2000).

George W. viewed his father, correctly, as a person who didn't like conflict and avoided provoking confrontations. From childhood, his father had been mild mannered, friendly, and thoughtful about others (Parmet, 2001). Nixon saw him accurately as not cut out for hardball politics. He was "too nice" and had "no killer instinct" (Parmet, 2001, pp. 293–294). Years later, in his presidential campaign, he would have to do battle with the contention that he was a "wimp."[3] As American politics turned from the ethic of service that had animated families like the Bushes to smash-mouth politics, George W.'s father had been caught in mid political stride (Helco, 2003, p. 37).

Another illustration of George W.'s strong feelings about his father was a fierce determination to stick up for him. George W. writes that he has been called the "Roman Candle of the Bush family, quick to spark and that's true when it comes to defending my dad" (Bush, 1999, p. 181). He accosted one reporter by saying that "I resent all you said about my dad" (p. 181). He would, he says, "run through a brick wall for my dad" (p. 182). "I'm a fierce warrior when it comes to my father. I'm in it for love, not for power" (quoted in Mitchell, 1999, p. 256).

Yet perhaps the most obvious and deepest reflection of George W.'s connection to his father

Figure 22.1. George W. Bush sitting at his desk in the Oval Office for the very first time on Inauguration Day, in the shadow of his father. (Time Life Pictures/Getty Images)

is the arc of his own life. In matters large and small, George W. followed in his father's footsteps. His father went to Andover and Yale; so did his son. His father joined the Navy, becoming a fighter pilot; his son joined the Air National Guard and also became a fighter pilot. His father went to Texas to seek his fortune in oil; so did his son. Both father and son turned to politics in adulthood; both also, as it happens, faced off with Iraq and Saddam Hussein, in this instance the son completing what the father had left unfinished. In family life, imitation is the most sincere and deepest form of identification.

There were smaller, more intimate parallels as well (Mitchell, 2000, p. 97). Long before he married Laura Welch, George W. was engaged to Cathy Wolfson. She was a Smith College student, as George W.'s mother had been. George W. was twenty years old at the time of the engagement, the same age his father had been when he married Barbara. George W. and his fiancé made the decision to get engaged at Christmas time, the same time of year that his parents had wed. Their plan was to spend senior year at Yale in New Haven, where George W. was, just as his parents had done. Coincidence? Not likely. Viewed in light of the other parallels in their lives, it is easy to conclude that George W. began his young and middle adult life by wanting to emulate his father.[4]

Father and son also shared a number of similar developmental experiences. Both had awe-inspiring father figures and powerful, tart-tongued mothers. Both had fathers who were often absent due to business and political aspirations. And both grew up in families valuing competition and expecting high performance.

Other similarities serving to strengthen the father–son bond include these: Neither could be called "intellectual" (though Bush Senior did well at school, in contrast with George W.); both had a leader's personality revolving around an ability to draw others toward them; both famously had difficulty with word-finding and with delivering speeches (see Parmet, 2001; Bruni, 2003).

George W. was not unaware of these father–son parallels. Of his decision to become a pilot he observes in his autobiography, "I'm sure the fact that my father had been a fighter pilot influenced my thinking" (Bush, 1999, pp. 50–51).

On his loss in his first run for political office he writes: "I was following in some *very big footsteps* when I lost my first political campaign for Congress in 1978. My dad lost his first political race for Senate in 1984" (p. 167; emphasis added).

In the first moments of the 9/11 attack George W. reached back to his father's famous vow in response to Saddam Hussein's invasion of Kuwait, "This will not stand," to give his own version, "Terrorism against our nation will not stand" (Bush, 2001c). Reflecting on those words, he said to Bob Woodward, "Why I came up with those specific words, maybe it was an echo of the past. I don't know why. I'll tell you this, we didn't sit around massaging the words. I got up there and just spoke" (Bush, 2002, p. 16).

From early in his life George W. was viewed by others primarily though the frame of his father.[5] Growing up in Midland, he was known as "little George" (Minuatagio, 2000, p. 13). On the day before his official announcement as a candidate for governor, a newspaper ran a picture of his father instead of him (Minuatagio, 2000, p. 7). When officials of Air National Guard coordinated efforts to clean up the F-102 that George W. Bush had piloted and put it on display, they painted on the wrong name, Lieutenant George Bush, Jr. (Minuatagio, 2000, p. 153). Running for Congress, he was repeatedly forced to remind people that he would be "campaigning as me," not his father (Minuatagio, 2000, p. 180). Such questions were so persistent and so troubling to George W. that he "began pulling out his birth certificate at speeches to prove that his middle name was different from his father's" (Minuatagio, 2000, p. 188). Even when he ran for governor of Texas, the *Houston Chronicle* used a picture of his father to illustrate a story about George W. speaking at a Republican woman's group (Minuatagio, 2000, p. 276).

Visiting in the White House, Frank Bruni once noticed above the fireplace a painting of George W. and his father fishing. George W. had commissioned it. The placement of the figures in particular drew Bruni's attention: "His father was in the foreground . . . reeling in a big catch. The son was behind him in profile, less easily noticed, with no fish on the line" (Bruni, 2003, p. 216).

George W. fought against being identified primarily in relation to his father, but it was an uphill fight, even for him. He said of his father, "There's no question he influenced me, but not as much as my mother" (quoted in Walsh, 2000). This is an odd view, given how he has followed in the footsteps of his father in so many basic ways. Yet his mother did have an important influence on him.

Mother and Son

George W.'s father was the North Star of his ambition and idealization, as mentioned already. But his mother was the earth-bound vehicle of their realization. Much has been made of the fact that George W. shares many of his mother's traits. He recalls a supporter telling him how he had "your daddy's eyes and your momma's mouth," which George W. considers "a pretty accurate assessment. My mother and I are the quippers of the family, sharp-tongued and irreverent. I love her dearly and she and I delight in provoking each other, a clash of quick wits and ready comebacks. Occasionally, our comebacks are too quick, too ready" (Bush, 1999, p. 183).

The psychoanalytically trained psychobiographer, of course, is less interested in who inherited what traits from whom than in the relationships those traits lead to. Throughout George W.'s childhood, Barbara Bush was the most immediate and powerful presence in the Bush household. This had a great deal to do with the fact that her husband was frequently away over the years on business, or later, political matters. As the day-to-day authority in the house, Barbara Bush received few of the advantages of idealization accruing to love coupled with absence.

This fact had a great deal to do with the strength of her personality. What was that personality? Its key elements were a direct, no-nonsense approach and a not infrequently critical (some said sarcastic) approach to people and life. Her mother, Pauline Pierce, had encouraged her to say what she thought (Radcliffe, 1989, p. 67), and she spent a lifetime as a mother and central figure in various Bush political careers doing just that. She was known for speaking her mind in an era when most political wives said

and did little to rock their husband's political boat. Among many tart public comments, she is famously recalled as having identified Democratic vice presidential candidate Geraldine Ferraro with a word rhyming with "rich" (Kilian, 2002, p. 99). Not surprisingly, her public persona reflected her more private one.

In one of those intergenerational psychological twists, Barbara Bush grew up in a household that paralleled her son's. She idealized her father and had a testy relationship with her mother (Kilian, 2002, pp. 14–15). It must have seemed paradoxical and somewhat surprising to relive her own early family experiences in the family of her making.

What happens when a no-nonsense mother deals with a son bent on testing the limits? In a word: conflict. Her children called her "the enforcer," though not in front of her. Paradoxically, it was a term she used to describe herself as well (Kilian, 2002, p. 50). This was in fact the same role George W. took on for his father when he joined his presidential campaign (Smith, 1999).

Jeb Bush called his mother "our drill sergeant" (quoted in Kilian, 2002, p. 43). Barbara Bush herself said," I would scream and carry on" (p. 50). George W. put it more bluntly: "I've been reprimanded by Barbara Bush as a child and I've been reprimanded as an adult. And in both circumstances, it's not very much fun" (p. 50).

Part of the issue had to do with the intersection of two similar psychologies. Both she and her son had rebellious streaks often leading to a

Figure 22.2. George W. Bush with the First Lady, who wears a Texas Rangers baseball jacket. (Time Life Pictures/Getty Images)

test of wills. Moreover, she was charged with almost the sole responsibility that being a mother and wife entailed because her husband was always traveling, and that was a lot.[6] To add to this set of issues, her husband, George W.'s father, had a very different approach to discipline and boundary setting. When Barbara Bush called him one day to complain that their son had just hit a baseball through one of their neighbor's windows, he replied, "My gosh, what a great hit" (quoted in Kilian, 2002, p. 52).

Throughout George W.'s life his mother spoke her mind, and her son did not always appreciate the result. In 1994, George W. recalled: "My mother told me that I couldn't beat Ann Richards" (Bush, 1999, p. 26; see also Mitchell, 2000, p. 296). He made this into a standing joke, but the lack of confidence must have been telling.

She had been on firmer ground four years before. In 1990, just after George W. had started with the Texas Rangers, he began considering a run for governor. His mother first told him privately not to and then publicly issued the following statement to a reporter: "When you make a major commitment like that [to baseball], I think maybe you won't be running for governor."

George W. responded in a fury:

"Mother's worried about my Daddy's campaign affecting my race. Thank you very much. You've been giving me advice for forty-two years, most of which I haven't taken" (Beshear, 1989; see also Minuatagio, 2000, p. 243; Mitchell, 2000, p. 252).

Of course, it's also possible there was some fear George W. would adversely affect *his* father's race. George W. had once remarked in a interview that he realized how his mother "put her relationship with her husband above her relationship with us" (quoted in Kilian, 2002, p. 52). Though he later softened his stance, the damage had been done. How could he mount a campaign after his mother, the first lady, had explicitly told him not to? That August, he publicly decided against making the race.

In fact, George W. was anxious to begin his political career but, not having accomplished enough to position himself to do so, had put out feelers to assess his chances well before his mother publicly dashed his enthusiasm. Bush

sent a veteran Texas political operator out to see what people thought of his running. Here's what he learned from her: "Everyone likes you, but you haven't done anything. You need to go out in the world and do something, the way your father did when he left Connecticut and the protection of his family. You just haven't done shit. You're a Bush and that's all" (quoted in Minuatagio, 2000, pp. 235–236).

The tension in the Bush household, particularly between mother and son, must be seen in perspective. As reporters who have covered the family attest, "[T]heir loyalty to, and support of, one another was unquestionable. . . . [You] could not fail to hear a love and admiration that transcended the competitive instincts they all had" (Bruni, 2003, p. 142). In the case of George W. this translated to a close, but not tranquil, relationship.

A Death in the Family

When George W. was six years old, his younger sister Robin became ill with leukemia. His parents took her to New York's Sloan-Kettering Hospital for treatment. Over seven anguished months, George Senior commuted to New York, his wife remaining there with her ill daughter. George W. and his baby brother Jeb were left with friends in Midland, Texas (Colloff, 1999). The treatment failed; Robin died.

The death of a child is the most devastating loss parents can suffer, and its effects ripple through families for years. It is also very hard on young children. Here is how George W. described it: "I was sad and stunned. Minutes before I had had a little sister, and now I didn't. Forty-six years later, those moments remain the starkest memory of my childhood, a sharp pain in the midst of an otherwise happy blur" (Bush, 1999, p. 14).

It's clear the tragic news that Robin was not coming back hit George W. hard. His parents had told him Robin was sick but not how sick.[7] His specific words of remembrance are worth noting. One minute he had a sister, and the next he didn't. John Kidde, a high school classmate, recalls George W. telling his friends, "You think your life is so good and everything is perfect; then something like this happens and nothing is the same" (quoted in Lardner & Romano, 1999).

It is always risky to reduce anyone's psychology to one event, however major (for more on the perils of reductionism in psychobiography, see Schultz, chap. 1 this vol.). Nonetheless, it is difficult to ignore the enormity of this tragedy or the critical period in which it occurred.

Some suggest that his sister's death was the origin of George W.'s impish, devil-may-care attitude toward life. Such an idea is tempting but inconsistent with the facts. George W. had a much earlier start on this particular element of his psychological style. In elementary school he was sent to the principal's office for disrupting a music class by painting a moustache on his face. Rather than being contrite or scared, he swaggered in "as if he had been the most wonderful thing in the world." Fearing that George W. was on his way to becoming the "class clown," the principal took a board to his behind. Mrs. Bush went to complain but, on hearing the story, wound up agreeing with the principal's action (Kilian, 2002, p. 41).

Some contend Robin's death created a strong mother–son bond.[8] As evidence they point to the fact that George W. tried to console his grieving mother, something Barbara Bush remembers him doing as well (Bush, 1994, p. 47). Yet, however close that bond became, it must have been tempered to some degree by his anger at his parents for not having been told or prepared regarding his sister's situation. And it certainly didn't keep him and his mother from having pointed and difficult disagreements over the years.

One reason George W. became free to fight with Mrs. Bush was that she realized that his attempt to cheer her up "was too much of a burden for any child to bear" (Bush, 1999, p. 47). I use the words "free to" because, as is often the case in such circumstances, young George was attempting to compensate for his parents' loss by being two children at once, himself and the "good" replacement child. Mrs. Bush's wise decision, even through the veil of her grief, no doubt redirected her son toward the psychology he had already developed rather than the replacement child he stood in danger at that point of becoming. (For an instance of a son who did

become a replacement child in order to pacify a grieving mother, see Ogilvie, this vol., chap. 12.)

Finally, his brother Marvin has suggested that the experience made George W. live fully in the present, "seizing opportunities as they came without fretting about what tomorrow would bring" (Lardner & Romano, 1999). This sounds like a plausible rationale for an unrealized life. Yet, it is clear that beneath his devil-may-care attitude, George W. had a lot of concerns about measuring up.

George W. had his own take on the lessons learned from his sister's death: "I learned in a harsh way, at a very early age, never to take life for granted" (Bush, 1999, p. 15). In another interview, he said her loss made him "fatalistic" about his run for the presidency (*Washington Post Interview*, 1999).[9] This was a lesson that would come in handy repeatedly in his own career disappointments and those of his beloved father.

What is striking about the death from George W.'s standpoint is its unexpectedness. The same could be said for many of his and his father's disappointments. One antidote for unexpectedness is routine. In George W.'s case this would include his limited, and repeatedly resorted to, favorite foods (peanut butter and jelly on the campaign trail), his exercise regime, his famous demand for punctuality, and even taking his own pillow with him as he traveled. One reporter following George W. on the campaign trail noted the importance of routine and realized its deeper implications: "[H]is almost obsessive adherence to the daily campaign schedule that had been laid out and his famous punctuality were not only about politeness, they reflected a desire to make his world as predictable and as manageable as possible" (Bruni, 2003, pp. 65–66).

One obvious question arising out of this analysis concerns George W.'s capacity for political leadership. More specifically, how, with this background, did George W. become a president willing to take so many large policy risks? What is also clear, given this analysis, is that the events of 9/11 posed a particular psychological challenge to this president. Here, in the most dramatic, bloody, and unexpected form, was the disruption of the usual. The answer to that psychological puzzle is, as we shall see, that by that time he had become transformed. Yet, before that could happen there was the problem of his drinking.

Drinking and Self-Redemption: The First Adult Transformation

As George W. tells it (Bush, 1999, pp. 133–137), in 1986, on his fortieth birthday, he, his wife Laura, and a group of friends went to Broadmoor Hotel in Colorado to celebrate. After a night of revelry he awoke the next morning, as he so often had back then, with an estimable hangover. He got out of bed and went for his customary run, as he also had almost every day for the last fourteen years. However, "This run was different. I felt worse than usual and about halfway through I decided that I would drink no more. I came back to the hotel room and told Laura I was through. I've quit drinking."

One Too Many?

Bush himself has had different things to say about the extent of his drinking problem. Talking to recovering addicts in the 2000 presidential campaign he said, "I'm just like you" (quoted in Neal, 2000). In his autobiography he writes, "I enjoyed having a *few* drinks," and "My daily run seems harder after a *few too many drinks* the night before" (Bush, 1999, p. 135; emphasis added).

In fact, the issue had to do with a lot more than his running pace. One of his speechwriters recalls that, in September 2002, Mr. Bush invited five religious leaders to the White House, and in the course of their meeting said: "You know I had a drinking problem. Right now I should be in a bar in Texas, not the oval office" (quoted in Frum, 2003, p. 283).

Frank Bruni (2003, p. 108) remembers a time on one of the campaign flights when Mr. Bush reflected back on his drinking: "You should have seen me twenty years ago, I would have been betting and drinking all at the same time." He recalled "drinking too much at Yale." He said alcohol "competes with your affections, with your family," an indication that his drinking did both. Two years before this self-revelation, George W. said about himself in an interview:

"And when you drank, at least when I did —occasionally—all I'd be interested in doing was sitting around and having a drink or two or three" (quoted in Bruni, 2003, p. 108).

When George W. had a "few too many," to use his phrase, he became somewhat loud and occasionally belligerent. The *New York Times* reported that Mr. Bush once approached an older well-dressed friend of his parents after "one too many" and asked, "So, what's sex like after fifty, anyway?" (Kristof, 2000; Mitchell, 2000, p. 105). Then there is the famous story of his chance encounter with Al Hunt of the *Wall Street Journal*, who had just written about how George W.'s father would most likely not get the GOP presidential nomination. He approached Hunt and yelled at him, "[Y]ou fucking son of a bitch. . . . I won't forget what you said and you're going to pay a fucking price for it." Mr. Hunt was seated at the time with his wife and four-year-old child (Mitchell, 2000, p. 205).

Mr. Bush apologized to Mr. Hunt a decade later (Romano & Lardner, 1999a) and in his autobiography doesn't mention the incident. He does, however, aver that "[d]rinking also magnified elements of my personality that probably don't need to be any larger than they already are—made me more funny, more charming (I thought)" (Bush, 1999, p. 135). This is, of course, a classic formulation of those with an alcohol problem. It combines a loss of inhibition with ego inflation leading to poor judgment. Not surprisingly, what Mr. Bush took to be an outsized extension of his charm was "according to my wife somewhat boring and repetitive."

Irrepressible

Mr. Bush also thought drinking made him "more irrepressible." The psychological question is, of course, exactly what was being repressed when he wasn't drinking. Aside from showing that Mr. Bush at this stage of his life could be rude and inappropriate, the stories about his drinking point to another by-product of excessive drinking, an aggressive hostility.

What caused this anger? In my view, the answer that best fits the data is that Mr. Bush felt thwarted. He was a man who had begun life with many advantages that he had failed to capitalize on, often through no particular fault of his own. He had followed in his father's footsteps, though hardly filled them.

He had gone to Andover and done all right. His father had preceded him there and had done very well. He went to Yale where his father had been a standout, academically, socially, and on the baseball diamond. George W. made his way there, but not his mark. Like his father, George W. was drawn to aviation, but his father had proved himself in combat and became a war hero. George W. mastered the complex difficulties of flying jets, but only in Texas as a member of the Air National Guard.

George's father set out from the east to Texas to make his fortune in oil, and then did exactly that. He had gone with other people's money, but parleyed it into millions of his own. George W. too had gone west to seek his fortune in oil with other people's money, but lost millions. He had, like his father, tried politics as well. As his father did, he lost his first political run, but his father had gone on from there to win two terms in Congress before being defeated for a Senate seat (for the second time). Thereafter, George H.W. Bush had held a number of senior and important positions as United Nations ambassador, ambassador to China, and director of the Central Intelligence Agency before becoming U.S. vice president and then president. His son had turned from politics after his first loss, with the realization that he needed to bide his time until he made a mark for himself as something other than a junior member of an accomplished family.

George W. Stops Drinking. Why?

A number of reasons have been put forward for Mr. Bush's decision to stop drinking. Mitchell (2000, p. 204) attributes his decision to his father's presidential campaign and George W.'s concern that his boozing might cause his father problems. George W.'s biographer concurs (Minuatagio, 2000, p. 210). Others credit his wife, Laura. Bush himself focuses on Billy Graham, who helped turn him toward religion.

While each of these explanations contains elements of truth, a closer look suggests why they aren't fully convincing. George W. did idealize his father, and so explanations that focus on his

trying to avoid the hurt he might cause to his campaign have plausibility. However, Mr. Bush had drunk "too much" at Yale and continued to do so right up until the time he quit in 1986 at the age of forty. By that time his father had been vice president for six years and had served as head of the Central Intelligence Agency and as ambassador to China and the United Nations. If George W. was worried about embarrassing his father, he spent many years running precisely that risk. Moreover, family friends report that George W.'s father had earlier asked him directly to stop drinking and spend more time taking care of his future (Minuatagio, 2000, p. 171).

Laura Bush did indeed try to help her husband stop drinking (Bruni, 2003, p. 179).[10] Yet by her own admission, she was unsuccessful (Mitchell, 2000, p. 203; Romano & Lardner, 1999a; Anderson, 2002, p. 146).[11] About the only intimates of the president who are not on public record having urged him to stop drinking are his mother and brothers. And it seems unlikely that his mother, reliably known for her straight talk on things large and small, was reticent on this critical matter, although she is quoted as being surprised that her son quit drinking because she never thought of him as having an alcohol problem. "That is not to say," she notes, "that we never maybe saw him when he'd had a little bit too much to drink" (quoted in Romano & Lardner, 1999).

Mr. Bush gives major credit for his turn away from drinking to the personal religious salvation abetted by conversations with the Rev. Billy Graham the year before he decided to quit (Bush, 1999, p. 136). Mansfield's (2003) examination of George W.'s religious beliefs leads him to agree that this religious conversion was central (p. 72).

It is hard for an outsider to judge George W.'s turn toward a more personal faith. What does seem clear is that he was searching for something fulfilling, and I mean that in the psychologically literal sense of that word. His plans to strike out on his own and succeed like his father clearly had come to a dead end.

Spectrum 7, George W.'s scrappy but hard-pressed entry in the oil sweepstakes, was a short distance from being foreclosed on by the banks before getting rescued by a merger with Harken Oil (Mitchell, 2000, p. 202). That deal was facilitated in part by Bush family friend, Paul Rea, and went through on September 30, 1986. That was the same year Barbara Bush had written in her diary that her husband, now vice president, had begun his campaign for the presidency (Parmet, 2001, p. 301). Although George W. later bragged, with little reason, about what the Harken deal showed of his business prowess (Mitchell, 2000, p. 206), the reality of the contrasting Bush trajectories could not have escaped the notice of either father or son.

George W. always wanted to succeed on his own, and on his own terms. In trying to do so, he was both blessed and cursed by the Bush family name, especially his fathers'. This name opened doors and several times helped rescue him, but it did so at a price. At forty, Mr. Bush had an immediate family with a loving, patient, and level-headed wife at its center. He had an extended family that adored him but that also no doubt wondered when he would "find himself." As for his life's work, he had very little real success that he could point to that was truly his, of his own making.

A Young Adult at Midlife

Of all the explanations put forward to account for George W.'s turn from drinking, one is conspicuously absent. That is George W. Bush himself. If there ever was a recipe for a so-called midlife crisis, this was surely it. The term "midlife crisis" is not effectively captured by the metaphor of a middle-aged man wearing earrings or chasing young women. When it occurs in real life it reflects something psychologically profound and potentially transforming. Levinson's (1979) original formulation is both elegant and complex.

He says that the task of adulthood is to build a life structure that reflects one's aspirations and emotional needs. Freud famously declared the two pillars of a well-realized life to be love and work. Analysts have come to realize how the first, love, reflects emotional relationships that allow intimacy and partnership. The second, work, can be understood as a place in which one's ambitions and skills can be realized and validated by others who matter. To these modern updates, we can perhaps add a third, this being a life structure in which a person can realize his ideals and values.

By age thirty, ten years before Bush's now legendary cold turkey turn to sobriety, Bush had come up short. As his biographer notes:

> [W]eighed against the family standards, against what his grandfather and father had already accomplished at the same stage of their careers —military heroes in world wars, Yale standouts, parents, millionaires immersed in successful careers—George W. Bush was turning thirty in 1976, and he viewed portions of his life as something of a wastrel's guidebook. He would say, simply, that he was "drinking and carousing and fumbling around" (Minuatagio, 2000, p. 173)

Laura Bush: An Anchoring Partner

George W.'s marriage to Laura Welch was a key emotional and structural development for him. Marriage reflects a commitment to the cultural, social, and legal norms by which people live together and, if they choose, raise children. But it also reflects at a more basic psychological level the attempt to blend together two separate but, ideally, complementary psychologies.

One could not think of two more complementary psychologies than George W. Bush and Laura Welch. She was quiet; he was not. He loved to talk; she didn't. He had restless unfocused energy that was yet to find its place; she had channeled hers into a life's pursuit. She preferred quiet things; he had trouble being quiet. On the other hand, this young man full of energy and quirks must have also been very attractive to someone with a conventional and somewhat staid life, and a profession, teacher and librarian, that reflected those traits. In one interview she said understatedly: "He's brought a lot of excitement to my life" (quoted in Anderson, 2002, p. 27). In another interview, she called him "incorrigible," referring to his irrepressibly impish nature, a characterization she made in an affectionate tone (Roberts, 1999).

They married three months after they met. George W. was thirty-one years old. Their twin girls, Jenna and Barbara, were born on November 25, 1981, when George W. was thirty-five.

In marrying Laura Welch and becoming the father to two daughters, George W. successfully realized the first of adulthood's tasks. The major other one, work, remained.

Her husband's view of each of their psychologies is worth examining for what it reveals about them both:

> Laura is calm. I am energetic. She is restful; I am restless. She is patient; I am impatient. ... Laura is naturally reserved, I am outgoing. ... [S]he is totally at ease, comfortable and natural, just calm. ... I, on the other hand, am in perpetual motion. I provoke people, confront them in a teasing way. I pick at a problem, drawing it to the surface. She is kinder, much more measured, arriving at a conclusion carefully, yet certainly. (Bush, 1999, pp. 80–81)

Think of Mr. Bush's comments in the context of his family experiences. It seems clear that, in a psychological sense, he married his father. Unlike his mother, Laura Bush had made clear that, "In general, I don't give George advice" (quoted in Mitchell, 2000, p. 163).

Mr. Bush's comments, written in the period before the 2000 presidential campaign, reflect an interesting and fairly accurate assessment of himself. They suggest an ability, however recently derived, to see himself clearly and, for that matter, at least one other person, as well. This ability to see clearly is an important element of the president's judgment and decision making. It is also a key to understanding his approach to presidential leadership.

Below the differences between the two, however, lay an important foundation of support. George W. needed someone to help him focus and channel his kinetic energy. His wife's calm and calming presence provided that. She still provides this balance. When her husband after 9/11 kept referring to wanting Osama Bin Laden "dead or alive," it was she who told him to "tone it down a notch" (Woodward, 2003, p. 101; see also Bruni, 2003, p. 179). She would have to do so several times, in fact.

In an interview with Barbara Walters (2001) about 9/11, Laura Bush's emotional importance for her husband became even more clear:

> Walters: Were you worried about your husband?
> Mrs. Bush: I was worried about him. I talked to him a lot of times during the day. When he first got on Air Force One to come home, I talked to him. ... He called me a lot during the day from Air Force One.
> Walters: That's how you take care of each other.
> Mrs. Bush: (Laughs) Right.
> President Bush: Well, she's been incredibly ... "steady hand," as we say in Texas. ... She's been very calm and reassuring. ...

A sense of her composure under extreme pressure came through in an interview with her husband and Bob Woodward (2003, p. 171). In talking about the aftermath of the attack, Mr. Bush said of his wife that she was never worried. She then revealed to him, apparently for the first time, that she had been "very apprehensive." The conversation continued:

> Mr. Bush: Well, I never knew it. ...
> Mrs. Bush: I didn't even talk about it that much. I woke up in the middle of the night. I know you did.
> Mr. Bush: I don't remember that. Was I up some?
> Mrs. Bush: (nods her head affirmatively)
> Mr. Bush: If you were nervous. ...
> Mrs. Bush: Well, I didn't say that to you.
> Mr. Bush: That's true, you didn't.
> Mrs. Bush: I mean I wouldn't have said that.

George W. frequently repeats in his many speeches that marrying Laura was the best decision of his life. Inevitably, he follows that up by saying that he isn't sure the same could be said of her.

In a way, Mr. Bush is onto something. He has prided himself on his ability to select the right people for his administrations and believes he has a special talent in this area. Certainly, in choosing his wife, he made a wise decision. As Bruni (2003) put it, his choice "illustrated a key ingredient of George W. Bush's luck, good instincts or talent: he chose people to accompany him through life and career who invariably made him better and set him straight" (p. 179). One need only add to this insight the fact that he must also have been the kind of person who attracted them.

The Missing Link

The stage of adult development that Levinson calls "becoming your own man" is, ordinarily, a task of young adulthood. The question at the onset of middle age, then, is whether the structure that a person has developed in his early twenties and consolidated in his mid-thirties is sufficient, with some alterations, to carry the person through midlife. If not, the resulting "crisis" consists of trying to answer these critical questions, among others: What structure will take the place of the existing one, and with what tools will it be developed?

We can see in retrospect that by the eve of his entry into midlife at age forty, George W. had not successfully consolidated one of the key tasks of early adulthood: He had not yet established himself as his own man.

I believe his drinking and boisterousness were a method of self-medication. So, too, the antics that persisted as part of George W.'s interpersonal style were a continuation of a very successful basis for finding his place in the world. The problem for George W. was that they were not wholly suitable for the adult world.

Yet, they survived almost intact long after they might have moved to the periphery, if only Mr. Bush had succeeded as an adult on his own and on his own terms. Mr. Bush's persona as the class clown, the "Bombastic Bushkin," the young man whose loafers were always barely taped together, was that of a man indifferent to conventional success. His persona masked the seriousness of his efforts, first in a hard-working but unsuccessful run for Congress, and later in an equally hard-working but unsuccessful run at making a fortune in oil.

In looking back over George W.'s developmental trajectory, it is clear that politics was always part of his vision of himself. The long and detailed history of his involvement with politics has already been documented. It began around the family dinner table and compound. It didn't stop, of course, throughout his childhood and young adulthood. Politics was like oxygen in the Bush family, part of the environment, and there can be little doubt George W. saw it in his future.

George W.'s formal introduction to politics came early, the summer between high school graduation and Yale when he accompanied his father on campaign trips in Texas (Minuatagio, 2000, p. 75). At twenty-five, George W. considered, but decided against, a run for the Texas state legislature (Minuatagio, 2000, pp. 140–141). At the age of thirty-two, he ran for Congress. In between there were plenty of political experiences.

This is the pattern of a man continually approaching and reapproaching a life's ambition. It is the pattern of a man searching to find a means by which to build the life structure that will house his aspirations. And, as we have seen, it is the pattern of a man forced to bide his time, but increasingly feeling at loose ends while doing so.

There is discernable, as well, in Bush's preliminary stage of development a capacity to watch closely and draw lessons, from his own defeats and those of his father. The traditional Bush political ethos was service. One served not because one could, but because one should. Yet, as Helco's (2003) astute analysis makes clear, American politics was in the midst of profound change, and George W. had to straddle two worlds, "the new professional smash mouth version of what he had learned the hard way in the last half of the twentieth century and the patrician responsibility version that he had inherited more naturally from the older legacy of his family" (p. 37).

George W. clearly was aware that he had a drinking problem, whatever its extent. He knew it. So did others. Whatever personal issues that problem raised for his father and his wife, in the emerging combat politics of the country it presented a large problem for his political aspirations, as well.

It has been said of Mr. Bush that "he is as smart as he wants to be." That tart comment by a congressional Democrat reflected Bush's idiosyncratic and uneven interests. When something grabbed his attention, Bush worked hard to master it—whether it was baseball statistics, the names of his prep school and college peers, the controls and working of a fighter jet, or the complex issues raised by stem cell research.

Clearly, his own political ambitions could not have failed to be a matter of crucial interest to George W., and as a consequence, it is hardly likely that he overlooked the lesson taught to him about his drinking during his 1977 run for Congress. After winning the GOP primary, George W. faced Kent Hance. During the campaign, a Bush staffer placed an ad in a Texas Tech University newspaper offering free beer at a "Bush Bash." As Bush's biographer writes, "Hance's people picked up on the possibilities right away; it was no secret in Midland that Bush enjoyed drinking, that he had once gotten up on stage with Willie Nelson" (Minuatagio, 2000, p. 190). Five days before the election, a Nance law partner sent out a letter to 4,000 members of the Church of Christ denouncing Bush for this "free beer" event for college students (Mitchell, 2000, pp. 179–81; Romano & Lardner, 1999b). Bush lost that campaign handily, for many reasons. Yet, it is hard to believe that the use of his drinking against him could not have made an impression as Bush considered his future, personal and political, in the decade between thirty and forty. As his first cousin John Ellis once told the *New York Times*, George W. was "on the road to nowhere at age forty" (quoted in Hollandsworth, 1999).

Discipline and Will

Mr. Bush faced forty with few personal successes to point to in the world of adulthood. Yet, he had the psychological foundations for ultimate success. The twin pillars of that foundation were discipline and will. Religion gave him an idiom; his psychology gave him a method.

It is difficult to imagine that beneath the surface of the George W. persona as a scamp and imp lay the capacity for strong will and substantial discipline and focus. George W.'s restless energy was poorly focused as a young adult. Yet evidence for it emerges in bits and pieces in looking back at his development.

We can start with baseball. Mr. Bush had a childhood love of baseball. Indeed, he told a group of elementary school children that he wanted to be a baseball player (Bush, 2001a, p. 374). One consequence of this attachment was

that Mr. Bush developed a lifelong interest in baseball statistics. As one profile put it, "Bush, like his father, adored baseball and played it in school, and had a formidable capacity for trivia" (Romano & Lardner, 1999c). Helco (2003) refers to the "masses of statistics he had mastered for many years" (p. 36). Mitchell (1999) notes, "What George W. lacked in real academic passion, he made up for in his skill at memorizing stats" (p. 36). When George put his mind to it, his mind could do it.

One other skill that reflected George W.'s ability to focus and learn was revealed in his relationships with the many people he met. At Phillips Academy,

> he was always remembering people's names, birthdays, habits, parents, brothers, and sisters. . . . At Yale he memorized everyone's name the instant he met them and it pleased them that he did. It was something he did even better than his father and grandfather. *Ten, twenty, hundreds of names*, he could recite them all, total recall, minutes after meeting them. (Minuatagio, 2000, pp. 13–14; emphasis added)

Two weeks before his Yale graduation, George W. joined the Texas Air National Guard. In due course he qualified to fly the F-102 fighter solo. In George W.'s otherwise dutiful campaign autobiography (1999, pp. 51–54), the only part that literally leaps off the pages is his excitement at being a pilot. Learning to fly a jet was complex and demanding, both physically and mentally. Book learning was absolutely critical, but not enough. You had to integrate what you learned in a complex series of rapid-fire decisions as you flew, and there was little margin of error: "[C]ockpits of jets are tiny and close, and they force you to learn economy of motion. They also force you to master yourself, mentally, physically and emotionally. You have to stay calm and think logically. One mistake and you could end up in a very expensive metal coffin" (p. 54). In his autobiography, George W. recalls executing a turn that the flight manual said should be a twenty degree bank, followed by a level ninety degree turn. However, "I banked at 18 . . . not level and the degree of my turn was closer to 100 rather than 90. I'll never forget the instructor's harsh admonishment: 'In the Air Force when we say twenty, we don't mean eighteen. And level is level, and anything else is sloppy'" (p. 52).

As a young adult, there were many reflections of the fact that George W. hadn't yet arrived where he wanted to be. Yet, other evidence underscores his determination at least to try. In 1977 at the age thirty-two, Bush announced that he was a candidate for Congress. He worked hard to win. He "campaigned harder than anyone expected, impressing even Reese [his opponent] with his tirelessness" (Mitchell, 2000, p. 170). He

> knocked on more than 60 doors a day in the windswept district, flat and treeless as far as the eye could see. He would often start his week in Midland, drive the 20 miles to Odessa, and then hit the 115-mile stretch north to the farms of Lubbock, rolling into every strip mall along the way. "The way he focused on what he had to do was extraordinary," Reese recalled. "He didn't relax. He worked all the time." (quoted in Romano & Lardner, 1999b)

Finally, in connection with George W.'s increasing discipline, we must note another side of his physical and mental discipline: running. Note the distinction between running and jogging. The first sets a fast pace, keeps track of time, and aims to extend endurance and capacity. The other takes satisfaction in getting exercise. George W. is a runner and has been for decades. He ran when he was cold sober. He ran with hangovers. He ran when things were going well, and he was especially likely to run when things weren't.

In an interview for *Runner's World* (Wischnia & Carrozza, 2003), Bush made the following observations on the meaning of his running to him:

> Q: What role does running play in your mental and physical fitness?
> Bush: It's very important. That's why I try to run at least five times a week, sometimes six. Running does a lot of important things for me. It keeps me disciplined. For example, I'm a person who believes in punctuality.

That's a discipline. . . . Running also enables me to set goals and push myself toward those goals. . . .

After his father lost his reelection campaign to Bill Clinton, George W. began to train hard for the Houston-Tenneco marathon. Every day, rain or shine, he ran. His own comments on his running patterns after 9/11 suggest why:

> Q: You must have the most stressful job in the world. Does running help you cope with that level of stress?
> Bush: It does. Running has helped me in times of enormous stress. *It's interesting that my times have become faster right after the war began.* They were pretty fast all along, but since the war began, *I have been running with a little more intensity.* And I guess that's part of the stress relief I get from it. For me, the psychological benefit is enormous. You tend to forget everything that's going on in your mind and just concentrate on the time, distance or the sweat. It helps me to clear my mind. (Wischnia & Carrozza, 2003; emphasis added)

Barbara Bush adds one more illustration of her son's increasing capacity for discipline: his time at Harvard Business School: "Harvard was a great turning point for him. I don't think he'd say that as much as I would, I think he learned what is that word? Structure" (quoted in Romano & Lardner, 1999d).

This is, of course, a mother speaking with justifiable pride and, most likely, a desire to help her son. Yet, Harvard was a rigorous discipline for its students.[12] So it does say something that George W. made the grade there. He probably did learn more discipline in the process.

There is another more important element to George W.'s Harvard story. He had applied to the University of Texas Law School and had not been accepted. He then applied to Harvard on his own "without telling anyone in his family" (Hollandsworth, 1999). He also didn't tell his parents he had been accepted, at first. When his brother Jeb revealed this fact and added that George W. didn't know if he would go, "the family was stunned." When George W.'s father said he should really think seriously about the opportunity, his son replied: "Oh, I'm going . . . I just wanted to let you know I could get into it" (quoted in Minuatagio, 2000, p. 148).

The decision to apply to Harvard on his own is as interesting as his comment to his parents. It seems likely that having been rejected from the University of Texas Law School, about which his parents did know, he did not want to risk another public setback. Yet, he did apply to Harvard (although secretly). His ambition, channeled in more conventional paths, seemed to be asserting itself.

Yet, his comment to his parents should not be overlooked. It reflects some sense on his part that he still had to prove himself to his parents, as well as to himself. It was, after all, his younger brother Jeb who was supposed to be the political star. George W. said so himself: "He was the brother who was supposed to have won in 1994, the Bush brother given the better shot at defeating Florida governor Lawton Childs than I had to upset popular incumbent Ann Richards. But it had not worked out that way" (Bush, 1999, p. 3).

A Gathering Discipline Reflects a Personal Transformation

All these elements, as disparate and time separate as they were, represent the small building blocks of an eventual transformation. We often think of that term as reflecting a dramatic difference, a before–after sequence whose observable consequences are clear even if the causes of the change are not. Such transformations do, of course, occur, but they are not an accurate reflection of the Bush transformation.

His transformation developed over a long period with many detours. Mr. Bush made his way at Andover by being at the center of things without having been at the center of any particular or recognized activity. The irreverent wise cracking adolescent in turn became the president of the DEKE fraternity and had a social life at Yale that, according to friends, rivaled the Wild John Belushi character in the movie *Animal House* (Minuatagio, 2000, pp. 80, 84–97). He arrived and went through Harvard Business School wearing his flight jacket and rumpled shirts, an icono-

clast and clear dissenter from the conventional attire of his classmates. George W. was a part of the institutions he attended, yet in many ways he stood apart, a combination that is an elementary part of his psychology to this day.

That persona reflected well Bush's basic stance toward people and things, engaging but selectively engaged. Yet, it provided another benefit as well. It provided George W. with a role while trying to figure out just where he fit in the world. He was not an athlete. He was not an intellectual. He liked taking risks and flying planes, but that did not seem to immediately translate to anything specific. He was smart and hard working when he was interested in something, but the very large question remained: What was he good at?

Up until his early forties, Mr. Bush had not found the answer to that question, and time was passing. It was one thing to be an ambitious and vaguely promising member of a distinguished family in early adulthood. It was quite another at age forty.

Bush's inner transformation accumulated slowly. He was good with people. He mastered what he set his mind to master, and most of all he learned how to master himself—as epitomized by his self-found sobriety. Bush discovered within himself a capacity for discipline that often stood at odds with his lack of discipline elsewhere. His running regimes, whatever his physical circumstances, his pavement-pounding work for a congressional seat, his mastery of flying jet planes, his Harvard experience, and finally beating his own drinking problem were all steps along the way to the realizing of his own inner strength and his realization that it was his to use.

Dorothy Bush Koch, George W.'s younger sister, said, "It was a transformation . . . [but] not an overnight transformation, but it was when he found happiness in his life and himself—we knew it right away. You could see a confidence. He's always had that bravado, but [this was] real confidence" (quoted in Romano & Lardner, 1999a).

Keller put it this way:

I've long suspected the essential fact about Mr. Bush is that God was his 12-step program. At the age of 40, Mr. Bush beat a drinking problem by surrendering to a powerful religious experience, reinforced by Bible study with friends. This kind of born-again epiphany is common in much of America—the red-state version of psychotherapy—and it creates the kind of faith that is not beset by doubt because the believer knows his life got better in the bargain. (p. 17)

I think Keller is wrong. I have no doubt that George W. found faith. However, I believe in addition to his faith in a personal God, he also discovered a faith in himself and in his own inner strength. Or, to put it another way, God provided the external explanation, and George W. provided the motivation.

Consolidating a Transformation

Mr. Bush's transformation was an uphill psychological battle, and there was no providential lightning bolt when he quit drinking, or later when he also stopped smoking. Interestingly, he stopped smoking the same way he stopped drinking. First, he told his wife he was going to do so. Then he quit cold.

Clearly, these were steps in a continuing process. His ability to stop drinking marked the gathering success of a developmental path, but not its end. Laura Bush had an interesting insight about her husband in this regard. She said that she believed her husband has always had discipline—he just didn't know it until he quit drinking (cited in Romano & Lardner, 1999a).

Mr. Bush had learned that he could rely on himself to overcome his most self-destructive tendencies. Did Mr. Bush become a new man? Not really. However, he did become a different one.

The irrepressible parts of his psychology became defused, less angry and less prone to inappropriate eruption. Did his capacity for anger vanish because he had found Christ or self-control? As his response to the 9/11 attack made clear, the answer to that question is: No.

Yet, he did become more self-reliant, in large part because he found qualities he could rely on. His strengths became more evident even if they had not yet found a focus and a match. That remained the one large missing piece of a real and fulfilling adult life structure.

The chance to make that match came in the form of an opportunity to buy a percentage of ownership in a second-tier baseball team with possibilities, the Texas Rangers. The economics of that deal and George W.'s part in it have been explored elsewhere (Minuatagio, 2000, pp. 239–240; Mitchell, 2000, pp. 239–244). Eventually, selling his shares made George W. a millionaire, a goal that had eluded him in decades of hard work in the Midland, Texas, oil fields.

But the Texas Rangers did something far more important for George W. Bush than allow him to make money. It provided an opportunity to match his talents and interests to a set of occupational ambitions and responsibilities. He had found a place.

This venture was also very personal for George W. Baseball was something he had loved since childhood, a place where his skills could be acutely engaged. He adored baseball, and it showed. He attended every home game, sitting in the box seats, not the owner's box, trading repartee with the players from behind the plate and with the fans, handing out autographed baseball cards with his picture on them—in short thoroughly enjoying himself. He quickly became the public face of the Texas Rangers.

Behind the scenes, George W. got involved in league politics, formulating plans for the public financing of a new stadium and helping to manage the Texas Rangers organization (Patoski, 1999). He broadened the team's appeal by initiating Spanish language broadcasts, an early harbinger of his political outreach to this important group. This was an opportunity opened up to him on account of family connections, but here, unlike his difficult experience in the oil industry, he seized the opportunity and made a success of it.

When George W. is asked to cite the career accomplishment of which he is most proud, it begins at age forty-two, when he led the investment group that purchased the Texas Rangers (Romano & Lardner, 1999c). Much has been made of the public platform that George W.'s role as a Texas Rangers owner and front man gave him. Those observations have merit. As George W. Bush often said of his role: "It solved my biggest political problem in Texas. There's no question about it and I knew it all along. My problem was 'What's the boy ever done?'"

(quoted in Minuatagio, 2000, p. 241; see also Mitchell, 2000, p. 253).

Ronald Betts, a long time friend and the son of a man who had befriended young George W. as child, said: "Before the Rangers, I told him he needed to do something to step out of his father's shadow. . . . Baseball was it" (quoted in Patoski, 1999). George W. finally starting to achieve at forty-two what had escaped him for so long. He was becoming his own man and could now turn again to another long delayed goal—politics.

George W. faced the same problems in politics as he did in life. He was his father's son. Yet, he was inescapably drawn by interest, psychology, and family history to follow yet again in his father's successful path.

No sooner had he begun to make his mark at the Texas Rangers than he let it be known he was seriously considering a run for the Texas governorship in 1990. He obviously was chaffing to get into politics despite the fact that his father was then president. His mother publicly torpedoed the 1990 run, as we saw, but that had only delayed his entry. And, as it turned out, in the interim a large psychological obstacle to his political career was removed. His father lost his reelection campaign.

George W.'s father's defeat lifted a number of constraints. Laura Bush has said that after the defeat, "George and Jeb were freed, for the first time in their lives, to say what they thought about issues" (quoted in Pooley, 1999). More important, George W. could now make his play for the political big leagues, in an important sense, on his own—as his own man. Sure, he had the Bush name. But Ann Richards was a popular and savvy incumbent. She was, in the words of one observer, "the most famous governor in America, an organic force with high steely Republican-style hair, a Texas-to-the highest-power sense of what was truly droll, and a huge approval rating" (Minuatagio, 2000, p. 270). The Bush name may have helped get George W. on the playing field, but he was otherwise starkly on his own, against a very formidable opponent.

Ann Richards relied on her popularity, her incumbency, and George W.'s famous temper. All three failed her. She called him an elitist and a "shrub." She seemed to believe that she was better than her opponent and seemed to consider it an insult to campaign against such a person. At a rally in Texarkana, she told a group of teachers, "You just work like a dog, you do well . . . *and all a sudden you've got some jerk who's running for public office* telling everybody it's all a sham" (quoted in Romano & Lardner, 1999c; emphasis added).

What George W.'s run for governor showed, although it wasn't evident at the time, was that he could temper his ambitions in the service of a more immediate goal: first, get elected. His ambition then, as now, proved to be grounded in pragmatism.

Toward a Transforming Future

Now, finally in late mid-adulthood, Mr. Bush has established himself as his own man and, it might be added, a man to be reckoned with. In both business and politics, he had leveraged lessons for his self-transformation. And in doing so, he finally found his elusive holy grail—success. His involvement with the Rangers had provided an opportunity to successfully match his talents and interests to a set of occupational ambitions and responsibilities, a circumstance that had eluded him his whole adult life.

His solid win over the popular incumbent Anne Richards had fueled his reputation in some watchful circles as a giant killer. He proved to be a successful and popular governor, and his landslide reelection confirmed that he really did have substantial political skills and talents. His political success was no fluke.

He had found a place. No, actually, he had found two places: as a successful businessman and a successful political executive. His success in both domains derived from the qualities that had been the basis of his salvation and personal transformation: focus, will power, perseverance, and resilience.

What he did for himself would become his model for dealing with his country and the world.

Notes

1. In describing George W.'s friendship with millionaire backer New Yorker Ronald W. Betts, one reporter wrote:

The bond reaches back to Mr. Betts's father, Allan W. Betts, whom Mr. Betts has described as a substitute father to Mr. Bush when his own father was preoccupied with his political career. As Mr. Betts has told it, after Allan Betts died in 1986, Mr. Betts and his wife and two daughters went out to a restaurant with Mr. Bush. It was there, Mr. Betts told New York magazine in 1999, that "George told a story about how after he graduated from Yale, he wrote my father a letter, thanking him for being his father-in-absentia. Nobody's closer to their father than George, but his father was down in Texas. Busy." (Bumiller, 2003, A18)

2. That book is credited as being written by Karen Hughes, his senior advisor.

3. Interestingly, this is a view shared by Donald Rumsfeld with Bob Woodward (2003), who quotes him as follows: "In their years in the House, Rumsfeld had found Bush [senior] to be a lightweight who was more interested in friendships and public relations and public opinion polls than substantive policy" (p. 22).

4. His mother dismisses that view out of hand (Roberts, 1999):

"Ms. Roberts: The idea that Governor Bush is trying to live up to his father's expectations you called 'nuts.'"

Barbara Bush: "It is nuts."

5. The quotes in this paragraph are all drawn from Minuatagio (2000).

6. Mrs. Bush recalls the multiple responsibilities as a period

of long days and short years; of diapers, runny noses, earaches, more Little League games than you could believe possible, tonsils, and those unscheduled races to the hospital emergency room, Sunday school and church, of hours of urging homework, short chubby arms around your neck and sticky kisses; and experiencing bumpy moments—not many, but a few—of feeling that I'd never, ever be able to have fun again; and coping with the feeling that George Bush, in his excitement of starting a small company and traveling around the world, was having a lot of fun. (quoted in Lardner & Romano, 1999a)

7. Through the years, the decision not to tell George W. just how sick his little sister was has weighed on Mrs. Bush:

"I don't know if that was right or wrong. I mean, I really don't, but I know he [George W.] said to me several times, 'You know, why didn't you tell me?' I said, 'Well, it wouldn't have made a difference'" (quoted in Lardner & Romano, 1999a; see also B. Bush, 1994, p. 45).

8. The reporters Lardner & Romano (1999a) title the part of their series on George W. that deals

with this tragedy "Tragedy Created Mother-Son Bond."

9. More specifically,

"I am somewhat fatalistic is this sense. Take this potential run for the presidency. I feel like saying, God's will be done. That if I win, I say that, I told people, I mean, if I win, I know what to do. If I don't win, so be it. So be it. And I feel that way. I do. I feel liberated in that sense" (Washington Post, 1999 A20).

10. In one interview Laura Bush did admit that she had confronted her husband with a stark choice regarding his drinking, but then quickly downplayed it (Roberts, 1999):

Ms. Roberts: It sounds like you've both been there. He's been quoted as saying that you said, "It's either me or Jim Beam."

Laura Bush: Well, that was a joke. Of course I didn't really say that.

Barbara Bush: You didn't? [Laughter.]

Christopher Anderson (2002) reports the following [unconfirmed] exchange between George W. and his wife: "'This,' Laura told George one final time, 'has got to stop.' George studied her face for a moment, his mouth twisted in that all too familiar smirk. Then he rose slowly, ambled over to the kitchen counter and poured himself another bourbon" (p. 146).

11. Laura Bush is quoted as saying,

He had been working toward it for a long time. I think for a year at least he'd been thinking, "I really need to slow down or quit." Most people who try to quit drinking first think, "Well, I'm just going to only have one drink." And I think in his mind he thought, "Well, that's what I'll do." And then, of course, it didn't really work. Like for everybody, just about, who tries, it doesn't really work. (Romano & Lardner, 1999a)

12. A somewhat more detailed examination of Mr. Bush's time at Harvard can be found elsewhere (Solomon, 2000; Minuatagio 2000, pp. 31, 145–163).

References

Allen, M. (2001, March 10). Post interview with President Bush. Washington Post, p. A6.

Anderson, C. (2002). George and Laura: Portrait of an American marriage. New York: William Morrow.

Beshear, T. (1989, April 29). Motherly advice. Courier-Journal (Louisville, Ky.), p. 2A.

Bruni, F. (2003). Ambling into history: The unlikely odyssey of George W. Bush. New York: HarperCollins.

Bumiller, E. (2003). Out of the White House, but still in the loop, New York Times, 27 October, A18.

Bush, B. (1994). A memoir. New York: Scribner's.

Bush, B. (2003). Reflections: Life after the White House. New York: Scribner's.

Bush, G.W. (1999). A charge to keep. New York: William Morrow.

Bush, G.W. (2001a, March 1). Question and answer session at Lakewood Elementary School in North Little Rock, Arkansas. Weekly Compilation of Presidential Documents, 37(9), 373–374.

Bush, G.W. (2001b, May 21). Commencement address at Yale University in New Haven, Connecticut. Weekly Compilation of Presidential Documents, 37(21), 784–785.

Bush, G.W. (2001c, September 11). Remarks on the terrorist attack on New York City's World Trade Center in Sarasota, Florida. Weekly Compilation of Presidential Documents, 37(37), 1300.

Bush, G.W. (2002, January 15). Remarks at a town meeting in Ontario, California. Weekly Compilation of Presidential Documents, 38(2), 11–19.

Colloff, P. (1999, June 1). The son rises. Texas Monthly.

Frum, D. (2003). The right man. New York: Random House.

Greenstein, F.I. (Ed.). (2003). The George W. Bush presidency. Baltimore, Md.: Johns Hopkins University Press.

Helco, H. (2003). The political ethos of George W. Bush. In F.I. Greenstein (Ed.), The George W. Bush presidency: An early assessment (pp. 17–50). Baltimore, Md.: John Hopkins University Press.

Hollandsworth, S. (1999, June 1). Younger. Wilder? Texas Monthly.

Keller, B. God and George W. Bush, New York Times, 17 May.

Kilian, P. (2002). Barbara Bush: Matriarch of a dynasty. New York: St. Martins.

Kristof, N.D. (2000a, March 3). Political memo: rival makes Bush better campaigner. New York Times, p. A15.

Kristof, N.D. (2000b, July 29). How Bush came to tame his inner scamp. New York Times, p. A1.

Lardner, G. Jr., & Romano, L. (1999a, July 26). Tragedy created a Bush-son bond. Washington Post, p. A1.

Lardner, G. Jr., & Romano, L. (1999b, July 28). At height of Vietnam, Bush picks guard. Washington Post, p. A1.

Levinson, D.J. (1978). The seasons of a man's life. New York: Knopf.

Mansfield, S. (2003). The faith of George W. Bush. New York: Tarcher/Penguin.

Minuatagio, B. (2000). First son: George W. Bush and the Bush family dynasty. New York: Times Books.

Mitchell, A. (1999, December 20). McCain is latest victim of pop quiz. New York Times, p. 33.

Mitchell, E. (2000). Revenge of the Bush dynasty. New York: Hyperion.

Neal, T.M. (2000, January 20). Bush to recovering addicts: "I understand." Washington Post, p. A07.

Parmet, H.S. (2001). George Bush: The life of a Lone Star Yankee. New Brunswick, N.J.: Transaction Press.

Patoski, J.N. (1999, June 1). Team player. Texas Monthly.

Pooley, E., & Gwynne, S.C. (1999). George W. Bush profile. Time, 153, 24.

Radcliffe, D. (1989). Simply Barbara Bush. New York: Warner Books.

Reinhold, R. (1986, April 30). In troubled oil business, it matters little if your name is Bush. New York Times, p. A14.

Roberts, C. (1999, December 19). Bush mother & wife interview. ABC This Week. Retrieved December 20, 1999, from http://www.abcnews.go.com/onair/thisweek/transcripts/tw991219_bush.html.

Romano, L., & Lardner, G., Jr. (1999a, July 25). Bush's life-changing year. Washington Post, p. A1.

Romano, L., & Lardner, G. Jr. (1999b, July 29). Young Bush, a political natural, revs up. Washington Post, p. A1.

Romano, L., & Lardner, G., Jr. (1999c, July 31). Bush's move up to the majors. Washington Post, p. A1.

Smith, E. (1999). George, Washington, Texas Monthly, 1 June.

Solomon, J. (2000). Bush, Harvard Business School, and the making of a president, New York Times, 18 June.

Walsh, E. (2000, October 25). Bush addresses silent influences. Washington Post, p. A18.

Walters, B. (2001, December 7). Interview with President George W. Bush and First Lady Barbara Bush. ABC News Special.

Washington Post. (1999). "I made mistakes:" Interview with George W. Bush. 25 July 1999: A20.

Wischnia, B.,& Carrozza, P. (2003) 20 questions for President George W. Bush: A running conversation. Runner's World on line, retrieved August 23, 2003, from http://www.runnersworld.com/footnotes/gwbush/home.html.

Woodward, B. (2003). Bush at war. New York: Simon & Schuster.

Chapter 23

Anna V. Song

Hunting the Snark
Methodological Considerations in Studying Elusive Politicians

North Korean dictator Kim Jong-Il or, as he has titled himself, "Dear Leader," presents an interesting puzzle to outside observers. As his people starve to death, he entertains Russian dignitaries with opulent train rides full of helicopter-delivered lobsters, cognac, and women. While many parents are forced to leave their children at orphanages lest they die of exposure, Kim showers his children with toys and electronics—even his illegitimate son was given a 1,000 square foot room filled with toys and slot machines. As the technological and economic gap between North Korea and the world widens, Kim is funneling all incoming resources to his military and his newly regenerated nuclear program. It is not as if Kim is oblivious to the state of his country. On the contrary, he has used his nation's desperate situation as a leveraging tool for more humanitarian aid from the international community. Yet how could a rational human being ignore such despair and indulge in luxury in front of the world stage?

Kim's indifference to the suffering of his people is just one factor inspiring study of his personality. Kim is also the leader of a nation on the verge of nuclear capabilities. Although nuclear capabilities are in and of themselves a cause for concern, it is the fact that North Korea is noncompliant with international security norms that raises this concern level even higher, both for North Korea's neighbors and for the United States. Kim presents an interesting methodological challenge for researchers conducting a psychobiographical examination. Since we have very little information on Kim, it is quite difficult to make any inferences about his personality or decision-making style.

Using the example of Kim Jong-Il, this chapter reviews several obstacles researchers face when conducting political psychobiographies. In particular, I focus on the psychobiographical study of a leader about whom we have very little information. In addition, I present four methodological guidelines that can (a) help organize the data collection process and (b) help bring behavior patterns to the forefront.

Obstacles in Political Psychobiographies

If Kim were a run-of-the-mill world leader, we could, as political psychobiographers, collect a considerable amount of data from a variety of sources. Ideally, we would analyze speeches, written text, and correspondence from various stages of the politician's life. There would probably be an assortment of friends, family members, and colleagues whose anecdotes could provide some insight into our subject's personal life. This type of data would be in addition to memoirs, subject interviews, and biographies recounting his life from childhood to adulthood. Although such an ideal scenario is rarely true for even the most scrutinized leader, a variety of material on most political figures is usually readily available for examination. Unfortunately, such is nowhere close to the case regarding Kim Jong-Il.

Propaganda

North Korea is particularly known for its propaganda machine. The few non-Koreans who have

344

visited Pyongyang have commented on the sterile, cosmetic atmosphere of the city, which suggests that Kim's administration has placed strict controls on how citizens' lives are displayed in public. Schell (1996) went so far as to question whether passing North Koreans were actual citizens or actors hired by the government to play citizens. Buruma (1994) writes of massive libraries and hotels, externally grandiose in style and stature so as to impress the world with Korean ingenuity. But, these buildings are left unfinished because of North Korea's withering economy. According to Buruma, "Pyongyang is like a huge stage set. It is the closest thing to Germania, Hitler's grandiose and happily unrealized vision of the future Berlin. Everything is gigantic in scale, and although two million people live and work in the capital, much of it is clearly intended for display" (p. 3).

Not only does the North Korean government control the presentation of its citizens' everyday lives; it also rigidly dictates the media. The official North Korean news agency never publishes items that could be construed as critical of Kim's regime. In fact, most of the news is either an attack on the United States government or an announcement of a new monument or holiday in honor of Kim Jong-Il or his father, Eternal Leader Kim Il-Sung.

To complicate matters even more, North Korea's counterpart, South Korea, engages in its own propaganda, perpetuating rumors about its northern brethren in order to garner support for certain foreign policy stances. Seoul encourages dubious rumors that will exacerbate Kim's already tarnished reputation. For example, until the mid-1990s, South Korean publications speculated that an accident that took the life of Kim's younger brother was not an accident but some malicious act by Kim to eliminate competition (e.g., Institute for South-North Korea Studies, 1985). Although Kim's younger brother did die in a drowning accident, there is no evidence that Kim Jong-Il was responsible for the death, and more current biographies omit past speculations.[1]

Isolated Nation: North Korea as a Cold War Relic

North Korea is a relic of the Cold War era. After the close of the Korean War, North Korea retreated behind the Iron Curtain, secluding itself from modernization, advancement, and globalization. As one of the last communist nations still in existence (Cuba is the other), it remains behind its own Iron Curtain, not acknowledging that the Curtain has lifted elsewhere in the world. While Pyongyang isolated itself from the rest of the world, its antiquated state left it vulnerable to natural disasters, making it near impossible to recover economically. It looked to its benefactors, namely, Russia and China, but they were distracted by their own political transformations. The dissolution of the Soviet Union left few Russian resources to help Pyongyang. Beijing worked to help keep the North Korean regime afloat for a time. Nonetheless, the country withered and deflated, causing mass starvation and desolation among its population, which in turn increased Kim's need to keep his regime under control. At such a point, most international leaders would seriously consider complying with international demands as a means to relieve their nation's poverty and avert imminent implosion. Instead, Pyongyang continues the tradition left over from the Cold War days, namely, political games shrouded in secrecy and extreme distrust verging on paranoia.

Culture and Language

Differences across cultures affect psychobiographical studies in significant ways. To Westerners, the behavior of a subject from another culture may seem odd, maybe even psychologically deviant. Yet certain practices are products of ingrained customs and beliefs, not indications of the subject's character or personality.

For example, some might perceive Kim's deference to his father as extreme and psychologically telling. It seems discordant with our knowledge of Kim Il-Sung, who was often dogmatic and harsh and sometimes abusive (Frontline, 2003). Several defectors and observers have commented on the elder Kim's extraordinarily high expectations of his son and the great displeasure he would openly display when Kim Jong-Il would fail (Hwang, 1999; Lee, 1998). However, most Asian cultures strongly promote extreme respect for elders, sometimes manifesting itself as complete subservience. In this particular case, it is the psychobiographer's job to place Kim Jong-Il's behavior in the context of Korean culture as a whole, then to judge whether this particular father–son relationship was normal (or abnormal) within Korean society.

In addition to culture, language barriers frequently present an obstacle for psychobiographers, especially during the data collection/analysis stages. The bulk of information on Kim Jong-Il is written in Korean. Non-Korean speakers will immediately find it difficult to locate biographical resources that are written in their language. Moreover, Koreans engage in a particular type of rhetoric conveying emotions that cannot be communicated in other languages. Common words in the Korean language, such as *Soksanghae*, which is a type of negative emotion, have no direct translation in English. The closest way to describe this particular feeling is extreme frustration, grief, and helplessness.

As a first generation Korean American, I am familiar with many Korean customs and traditions. If I encounter an example of behavior that is not within my range of familiarity, I am fortunately able to rely on members of local Korean communities to provide information as to whether the specific behavior may be normal according to Korean culture. Although this background offers some advantages in studying Kim, I lost my ability to speak Korean at a very early age and am considered a native English speaker. Therefore, in writing this chapter, I have been limited to sources that were translated or were written by other English speakers.

Kim Jong-Il's Idiosyncrasies: Feigning Irrationality Is Rational

The question of whether a leader is rational or irrational has been an integral aspect of research in traditional political psychology (e.g., Jervis, 1976; Schelling, 1966; Simon, 1995). The assumption behind this line of questioning is that if a leader is considered a rational decision maker, he will follow a set of decision-making rules, thereby making it easier to predict his behavior.

Following news that North Korea had resumed its nuclear weapons program, questions about Kim's rationality intensified. Several news organizations published articles analyzing his decision-making style, casting doubts as to whether he was a sane leader (e.g., "North Korea's Dr. Evil," 2003). Much of the momentum behind this line of questioning comes from the severe absence of reliable information on Kim. Given the limited data available to those outside Korea, the basic question of rationality is hard enough to address, let alone discerning personality dynamics and behavioral patterns. Making matters worse, the question of rationality persists because Kim has chosen to stay behind closed doors, cultivating a sense of mystery among analysts, adversaries, and admirers alike. According to North Korean defector and Kim's adopted daughter Lee Nam Ok, Kim wanted to maintain his hermetic reputation. When confronted with the possibility that the position of supreme leader was not compatible with a reclusive lifestyle, Kim responded by saying, "Leave it that way" (Lee, 1998, p. 2).

Moreover, Kim and the North Korean government have created an elaborate "personality cult" around Kim and his father Kim Il-Sung. Exaggerations or outright lies have been disseminated regarding Kim Il-Sung's rise to power, Kim's origin of birth, and many other aspects of the two leaders' lives. These stories serve to build a mystique that not only promotes blind faith among their followers but also thwarts analysts' attempts to understand the real Kims. In a way, Kim's commitment to maintaining this air of mystery by feigning irrationality is itself rational. If his adversaries know little about him, they cannot predict his next move, giving him a clear advantage in strategy and negotiation. (For more on the role of feigned irrationality as a means of enhancing deterrence, see Glad, chap. 24 this vol.)

Methodological Guidelines

Although these issues pose serious complications to political psychobiographies, certain methodological solutions can help psychobiographers construct a scientifically sound study from minimal data. These guidelines include consistency checks across data sources, decisions, and domains.

The concept of consistency checks in political psychobiography stems from the criticism that, unlike artists or writers whose products can be directly attributed to the subject, products of political figures (e.g., political acts and decisions) can theoretically be attributed to sources other than the politician. For example, a presidential address could be considered a product of a president, especially considering that the speech is delivered by him and encompasses the goals and motives of his administration (Winter, 1987). Conversely, one can argue that an address is a product not of the president but of his speech-writers and advisors. More specifically, the speech is a group creation, in which case the motives and goals of others may obscure our subject's personality (Hermann, 1980).

Political decisions fall prey to similar criticism. Decisions are products of the subject, but they are also shaped by different forces and factions within the political sphere, such as legislatures, party politics, international pressures, and electoral considerations. From this perspective, decisions are not an indication of the subject's personality, but a product of a giant bureaucratic system. Lastly, politicians, to at least some degree, are dependent upon public favor. Therefore, they are motivated to present an idealistic version of themselves. This type of impression management invariably affects the content of speeches and decisions (Elms, 1976; Renshon, 1998; Tetlock, 1981). For this reason, some political psychologists have argued that speeches cannot be considered products of the subject (Hermann, 1980; Dillie, 2000).

The use of consistency checks is a rebuttal to these criticisms. Politicians, like other psychobiographical subjects, exhibit behavioral patterns and stable characteristics. Consistency checks across data, decisions, and domains help the psychobiographer identify traits belonging to the subject and aberrations that may be due to other influences. More specifically, patterns and characteristics that are found consistently across data, decisions, and domains are best attributed, not to varying external influences, but to the one constant variable—the subject himself.

This technique is especially useful when there is a minimal amount of data on the subject. In this particular case, patterns are not easily discernible and are frequently obscured by contradictory information. Consistency checks help the psychobiographer focus on subtle characteristics and patterns that are indicative of the subject's personality. For example, since there is very little information about Kim Jong-Il that is not tainted by North Korean propaganda or anti-North Korean enthusiasts, themes that do reoccur across data sources (communist and noncommunist), decisions, and domains can be considered indicative of Kim's personality. In this psychobiography of Kim, the process of consistency checks itself revealed a key factor in Kim's personality—the inconsistency of his self-image and the ramifications it has on his behavior.

Consistency Across Types of Data

As the father of psychobiography, Freud (1910/1961) in his book on Leonardo passed along several methodological guidelines. In terms of the data collection process, Freud suggested that researchers collect as much data as possible, from as many sources as possible. Elms (1994) agrees, explaining that wealth of data increases accuracy and decreases the odds that findings are based on misperceptions, biases, or other errors. But in addition to collecting a multitude of data, it is also important to test whether themes run across data. This additional step can be thought of as a *consistency check*. In the case of political psychobiography, especially in cases where data are scarce, consistency across data helps the psychobiographer identify testimony that is tainted by biases or propaganda.

Given the snapshot of Kim as a despot who indulges in luxury as his people starve to death, it is not surprising that certain sources portray him as a conceited madman gone wild. Kim's former sushi chef Kenji Fujimoto (2004) provided several disturbing accounts of life behind closed doors. He writes about wild parties with beautiful women dancing for Kim and his guests. Not satisfied by the performance, Kim commands the women to remove their clothing and perform a striptease. Despite the obvious discomfort shown by the women and bystanders, he escalates the situation even further by coercing his guests to dance with the naked women.

In addition, Fujimoto presents a Kim who is incredibly selfish, endangering the lives of his family for his own comfort. According to the

chef, Kim was prescribed painkillers after a serious horseback riding accident in 1992. Fearful
that he would become addicted to the medication,
he forced family and close staff members to take
injections of the painkillers because he did not
want to be the only one to become an addict.

In contrast to Fujimoto's account, several
sources have portrayed a vastly different picture.
According to Lee Ok Nam (1998), the niece of
Kim's second wife who defected from North
Korea in 1996, Kim was not the irresponsible
playboy many thought him to be. She reports
that Kim spent an incredible amount of time
absorbing himself in research and news from
abroad in order to keep abreast of international
affairs. According to her, when Kim did have free
time, he chose to spend it with his family, making it a point to have dinner with them every
night.

Just from these two portrayals of Kim, we face
the psychobiographical quandary of deciding
which story to believe and which to dismiss. On
the one hand, both Fujimoto and Lee may have
certain biases that taint their depictions of Kim.
Even though both are defectors, they had very
different relationships with Kim and therefore
different reasons for escaping from him. Lee fled
North Korea because she could no longer live in
a house where Kim controlled every move. Just
as he controlled his regime, Kim also dictated
every aspect of his family's life and sequestered
them from public eyes. Lee also had reason to
be extremely fearful of Kim's retribution—her
brother, who defected with her, was assassinated
in Seoul. As a condition for her testimony, she
was assured that her location would not be released to the public. Fujimoto was not a part of
the Kim family, but of the staff. In this respect,
he was prone to see another side of Kim, one that
his family would not be privy to. Also, since
Fujimoto's relationship with Kim was not familial, it is likely that he has few or no lingering
twinges of loyalty, as Lee might.

In a situation such as this, the psychobiographer needs to find other sources more removed
and objective, in order to discern which aspects
of stories are reliable or faulty. In the case of Kim
Jong-Il, we have the account of former U.S. Secretary of State Madeline Albright, who visited
North Korea in 2000. Albright (2003) observed

Figure 23.1. North Korean leader Kim Jong-Il
(bottom left) poses with his family in 1981.
(Getty Images)

Kim as being intelligent and much more engaging than one would predict, considering his reputation for boorishness. She surmised that Kim
had complete control of his political environment
and was not the loose cannon most researchers
figured him to be. In fact, she was impressed at
how knowledgeable Kim was of current affairs
outside of North Korea and how quick-witted
he was during their meetings. Yet Albright also
described an event that Kim orchestrated for her,
a stadium event called the mass games, in honor
of Kim and his deceased father, Kim Il-Sung.
These games included pyrotechnics, giant television screens, and thousands of dancers, gym-
nasts, and school children dancing in shows.
Albright was taken aback by the sheer enormity
of the event, especially considering that it was taking place as North Koreans outside of Pyongyang
starve to death.

Of course, Albright's account is also tainted
by impression management—Kim would have
been on his best behavior to impress the former
secretary of state. Moreover, Kim had a specific
political agenda in meeting with Albright; he was

hoping to circumvent South Korea's and Japan's involvement in future treaties with the United States (Fujimoto, 2004). But what her account does provide is an explanation for the major discrepancies between Lee's and Fujimoto's testimony. From Albright's description, we see that Kim can be calm, collected, and knowledgeable but also has a penchant for luxury and self-worship. Thus, it appears that some aspects of both Lee's and Fujimoto's stories are reliable.

In addition to personal accounts of Kim's life, we can examine other sources of data, such as political statements emanating from North Korea, to see if they validate themes found in personal testimonies. An examination of North Korean news stories shows divergent pictures of an aggressive, prosperous North Korean regime and a persecuted, vulnerable one hoping to fend off a U.S. attack. Compare the following quotations from the Korean Central News Agency of DPRK (Democratic People's Republic of Korea):

The U.S. anachronistic hostile policy towards the DPRK is the main factor of spawning the nuclear issue between them. It is, therefore, the master key to finding a peaceful solution to the nuclear issue for the U.S. to make a switchover in its policy. On the contrary, it is set to further its hostile policy towards the DPRK aimed at stifling the DPRK militarily in the future too. The U.S. moves compel the DPRK to steadily increase its self-defensive nuclear deterrent force. ("U.S. to Entirely Blame for Serious Nuclear Stand-Off," October 15, 2003)

[T]he Songun policy enforced by the DPRK provides a sure guarantee for defending peace on the Korean peninsula where the worst situation prevails due to the U.S. highhanded [sic] and its moves for a war. Leader Kim Jong Il unrolled an effective Songun policy unprecedented in history, decisively frustrating the U.S. moves and honorably protecting the sovereignty of the country and the nation. Kim Jong Il's Songun policy is a powerful political mode that helps each country and nation firmly defend their sovereignty and right to existence from the U.S. supremacy. ("Kim Jong Il's Songun Policy Praised," January 13, 2004)

The Korean people are registering big successes in the efforts to carry out tasks set forth in the joint New Year editorial. The workers of Chollima Steel Complex are turning out large quantities of steel by raising the operation rate of converters from the outset of the year. The Sinchang Youth and other coalmines have introduced advanced cutting method into production. As a result, they are overfulfilling their daily assignments by more than 50 percent. ("Economic Achievements of Korean People in New Year," January 7, 2004)

Even within North Korea's own propaganda, we see evidence of a dualistic national image. One image presents a prosperous, industrious nation overproducing products. This kind of a nation presumably would not require humanitarian aid from other countries to feed its people because they are self-reliant and strong. The other image presents a weaker nation struggling against the imperialistic motives of a larger nation, the United States. Implied in this message is that the United States is stronger and more hostile than North Korea, the latter prevailing through sheer will.

The thematic parallels between Kim's personality and North Korea's national image are not coincidental. Kim is in complete control of his nation, and that includes the messages that are released through its news agency. Therefore, it would not be unreasonable to assume that images conveyed through the national newspaper are, in some part, an indication of Kim's own personality. In this sense, we see the theme of dualism emerge again at a personal level, suggesting that inconsistency is a consistent pattern in Kim's life.

Consistency Across Decisions

Early in his leadership career, Kim Jong-Il appeared fairly consistent in his decisions, showing a penchant for violence and state-sponsored terrorism. He is suspected to have ordered a bombing in Myanmar in 1983. The targets of that bombing were South Korean officials on diplomatic assignment. Kim is also suspected to have ordered the bombing of a Korean Airline flight in 1987, killing 115 Koreans. It is thought that Kim issued the command for this bombing to sully South Korea's international reputation prior to its hosting of the 1988 Olympic games. Kim's motivation behind both violent acts appears to have been to intimidate and coerce South Korea, giving North Korea dominance over the peninsula.

More recently, with the Bush Administration's intense focus on national security and international stability, the Korean Peninsula has garnered increased attention. Indeed, some of the actions taken by the small rogue country and its dictator, Kim Jong-Il, have given the world reason to raise a collective eyebrow. Since he assumed official power in 1993, Kim's regime has engaged in a policy of brinkmanship, teetering between positive steps toward international security and acts of military/diplomatic aggression via acquisition of weapons of mass destruction, including nuclear warheads. North Korea withdrew itself from the Nuclear Nonproliferation Treaty as a result of stalled progress in implementation of the 1991 denuclearization accord. After a series of talks, North Korea and the United States agreed to sign the 1994 Agreed Framework that called for Pyongyang to freeze its existing nuclear program and be monitored by the International Atomic Energy Agency. After several years of psuedostable relations with Washington, Pyongyang destabilized relations by launching a "Taepodong-1" ballistic missile into the airspace over Tokyo in August 1998. In response, President Clinton named former Secretary of Defense William J. Perry to conduct a review of U.S. policy toward North Korea. The resulting report, "Review of United States Policy Toward North Korea: Findings and Recommendations," suggested a quid pro quo policy: North Korea would be rewarded for movement toward peace and stability but severely punished for acts of noncompliance and aggression. This strategy mirrored then South Korean President Kim Dae-Jung's Sunshine Policy. Dialogue between Kim Jong-Il and Kim Dae-Jung flourished, resulting in a reunion meeting between 100 members of North and South Korean families long separated by the Korean War.

Although the reunion led some analysts to hope for stabilization of relations between North Korea and the international community, Pyongyang remained engaged in its strategy of brinkmanship. In October 2002, Pyongyang admitted to restarting a nuclear weapons program, a direct violation of the 1994 Agreed Framework. Subsequently, North Korea declared that treaty null and void, expelled United Nations inspectors, and threatened pre-emptive "self-defense" against neighboring nations. Moreover, when approached to resolve this potentially volatile issue diplomatically through multilateral talks, North Korea rebuffed the United States, claiming that the current dilemma was solely a reaction to U.S. threats and therefore resolution could only come through bilateral discussions. In fact, North Korea went so far as to accuse the United States of plans to invade, pointing to America's war against Iraq as evidence of Washington's predilection for invasion.

Currently, it seems as if there is no consistency in Kim's decision-making style. At times, he acts as if he wants to be embraced by the international community and partake in the economic/technological developments that other countries have been enjoying. Conversely, he also acts irrationally, threatening much stronger nations, including the United States, in order to maintain North Korea's way of life. In many ways, Kim is consistently inconsistent, as the following examples demonstrate.

Kim undoubtedly knows that his military strength could not match U.S. capabilities. The North Korean army consists of approximately 1 million troops, most of them positioned near the demilitarized zone (DMZ) just twenty-five miles north of Seoul. The United States has only 4% of the number of North Korea's troops in the area; about 37,000 soldiers serve as a major deterrent to military aggression. However, while North Korea's strength lies in manpower, it is no match in terms of technological military advancement. Of their 3,800 tanks, 2,750 were designed in the 1950s, and 250 tanks go as far back as 1934 (Center for Strategic and International Studies, 2002). In contrast, South Korea is one generation behind the United States in terms of military technology and holds a considerable arsenal of equipment. Also, nearby the United States has stationed the 6th Cavalry Brigade, which consists of the new OH-58D, the most advanced attack aircraft in the world. Indeed, even Kim acknowledges that he is militarily out-matched by the United States. Kim informally discussed the issue with South Korean newspaper publisher Choe Hak Rae. When asked why North Korea spent so much of its resources on missiles, Kim made it clear that he knew he was aware of his military's disadvantage. "The missiles cannot reach the United States," he said, "and if I launch them, the U.S. would fire back thousands of missiles and we would not survive. I know that very well" (Choe, as quoted by Maass, 2003, p. 41). Although it is an undeniable fact that North Korea would not be able to incur the military cost of noncompliance, Kim acts counter to this fact. Instead of behaving like a smaller country barely able to keep its people from starvation, Kim presents his nation as a military force to be reckoned with.

Kim Jong-Il knows that any act of aggression against South Korea would be followed by severe military retribution from both Seoul and Washington. The United States has a history of supporting international allies such as Israel and South Korea. U.S. military presence serves not only as a deterrent but also as a symbol of Washington's political commitment to Seoul. In addition, after the September 11th attack on the United States, President Bush has made international security the major focus of his administration. In his State of the Union speech in 2002, Bush promised to deter states sponsoring terrorism, including North Korea. Subsequently, in September 2002, the Bush Administration released "The National Security Strategy of the United States of America," which outlined a strategy of pre-emption against states engaged in the development of weapons of mass destruction. According to the National Security Strategy, the United States "will not hesitate to act alone, if necessary, to exercise our right of self-defense by acting pre-emptively against such terrorists, to prevent them from doing harm against our people and our country" (U.S. National Security Council, 2002, p. 6). The threat of pre-emptive strikes is not equivocal or baseless—it has been reinforced by U.S. military actions against other terrorist nations such as Iraq and Afghanistan.

But despite the knowledge that retribution would be imminent and his nation could not viably defend itself from military action by the United States or South Korea, Kim acts as if the opposite were true. Again, as in the consistency check across data sources, we see a pattern of duality in Kim's decision making. On the one hand, he seems as if he is willing to make concessions in order to join the international community. On the other, he goes out of his way to bite the hand that feeds him, even when that hand can strike a considerable blow. If we take this pattern of decision making as an indication of Kim's personality, it seems as though there are two antithetical images being portrayed. The first is that of fierce fighter who will forcibly defend himself against stronger, dominating entities. The second is that of an appeaser who is aware of his weakness and will recoil when threatened.

Since analysis both of data sources and of decisions reveals polarized elements of Kim's persona, the third check across domains becomes even more important. Lacking such a check, it remains possible that Kim's contrasting images are mere artifacts of the methodological obstacles discussed above. However, if duality is apparent across different facets of Kim's life, it more likely indicates a true personality characteristic, rather than a methodological faux pas.

Consistency Across Domains

Just as in the examination of Kim's decisions, we find yet again a dichotomy of self-images Kim projects across the different domains of his life. Granted, complete consistency in self-portrayals is extremely rare in human behavior. In fact, the inconsistency of human behavior across domains and situations has spurred heated debates among personality psychologists (leading to the so-called person/situation controversy of many years back). Mischel (1968) argued that correlations in human behavior from situation to situation are so low that stable personality characteristics cannot be said to exist. Numerous psychologists responded to Mischel by showing consistency in personality when focusing on aggregation across the life span (Epstein, 1979), on motives (Winter, 1973), and on traits (Costa & McCrae, 1992; Robins et al., 2001). In all three cases, researchers have accounted for deviation in trends of behavior; they also argue that stable personality characteristics do exist and can help distinguish individuals. In addition, most of the researchers have added that even if there are inconsistencies in behavior, individuals usually fluctuate within a narrow range of action. Barring psychopathology, humans rarely shift from one extreme of behavior to another.

In light of these findings, Kim's behavior across domains seems puzzling. Unlike most people who act only within a narrow range of behaviors from one situation to another, Kim consistently moves between two major extremes—self-aggrandizement and hubris versus insecurity and shame.

An analysis of Kim's public and private persona illustrates this dichotomy. The few public appearances made by Kim lead one to believe that he is a narcissistic dictator who is so obsessed with his physical appearance that he teases his hair into a ballooning bouffant and wears platform-heeled shoes. Many such national events include monstrous ceremonies that he himself orchestrates in his honor. Moreover, Kim has erected statues and monuments in honor of himself and his predecessor and father, Kim Il-Sung. One would think that someone who displays such overt hubris in public would expect his will to be done. Yet, despite all these ego-building demonstrations, it seems that in private Kim does not believe his requests will actually be honored and instead uses aggression to get what he wants. For example, why would a man who is seemingly larger than life kidnap South Korean and Japanese women, forcing them into his harem called the "pleasure and happiness team," as did Kim? Also, when leaders want the help of filmmakers or entertainers to project a government message, they usually ask. Instead, Kim abducted a renowned South Korean filmmaker and his actress wife, forcing them to produce propaganda movies, including the universally panned *Pulgasori*. Not even Adolf Hitler felt the need to kidnap Leni Riefenstahl to produce his propagandistic film *Triumph of the Will*.

In addition, one would expect a man who publicly displays as much confidence as Kim to carry out his wishes in the open, regardless of what others might think of him. Instead, Kim has engaged in several secret lives that are carefully hidden from the public and, when he was still living, his father, Supreme Leader Kim Il-Sung. The elder Kim hand-picked Kim Jong-Il's wife, a woman in the Worker's Party who had dem-

onstrated loyalty to the regime. Unhappy with the union, but afraid to speak out against his father, Kim secretly wed two other women and kept those unions as covert as possible. Special familial events with these women, such as weddings and births of children, became secret operations. During the birth of Kim's eldest son, the family had to slip out of the hospital to avoid detection by Kim Il-Sung's informants.

Perhaps the most poignant example of the dualistic theme that emerges across public and private domains of Kim's life is the story of his birth. According to the official story issued by the North Korean government, Kim Jong-Il was born during a fierce thunderstorm on February 16, 1942. His mother, Kim Jong-Suk, and father, Eternal Leader Kim Sung-Il, were training in a guerilla resistance camp on top of Mount Paeku, the mythical birthplace of ancient Korea. To add to the mythological connotations of the story of Kim's origins, North Korean schoolchildren are taught that a new star and a double rainbow appeared in the sky to mark the birth of such an extraordinary leader. In reality, there was no star or double rainbow. In fact, Kim Jong-Il was born one year earlier than reported—North Korean officials changed Kim's birth date to create a 30 year difference between father and son. In addition, Kim was not born on Mount Paeku but in a Siberian town where his father, then just a revolutionary fighter, was hiding from the Japanese controlling Korea.

Despite the powerful propaganda images projected by the North Korean regime, there are straight facts that we know of Kim's life. He grew up under the ever-watchful eye of his despotic father, Eternal Leader Kim Il-Sung. In 1948, Kim saw his younger brother drown under unusual circumstances. One year later, his mother died during childbirth. Leaving him with only his sister, these deaths made Kim's childhood especially lonely and isolated, especially considering his father's frequent absences as a revolutionary.

As a radical fighting to take control of Korea, Kim Il-Sung not only made his mark in politics but also left an indelible scar on his son in several significant ways. First, the elder Kim abandoned his son in a guerilla camp to be raised by a community of women. According to Kim Il-Sung himself, Jong-Il's upbringing was in semi-isolation, with very few other children around with whom to play. Kim Jong-Il grew up among soldiers and revolutionaries. Second, when Il-Sung was present, he was not a nurturing father who showered affection upon his lonely son. Instead, according to former U.S. Ambassador James Lilley, the elder Kim frequently degraded his son (Frontline, 2003). Third, in addition to this harsh treatment, Il-Sung enforced an incredible standard on his son in an effort to groom him as his deified successor.

Theory as a Guide to Data Analysis

At this point in our analysis of Kim Jong-Il, we see that he is a man of contradictions. One version of Kim is as a competent, knowledgeable family man brimming with hubris and self-confidence. This is the Kim we see in public, during diplomatic meetings, national celebrations, and political events. The other version is of a man full of self-doubt, who is easily threatened by more powerful figures and lashes out in seemingly irrational ways.

Although this double image is clearer than the perspective Kim's propagandists or opponents provide, it remains somewhat unsatisfying. Not included in this portrayal are suggestions of how these themes work in Kim's life, how they might influence his future behavior, or where these themes came from in the first place—the reasons why we do political psychobiography at all. Instead of a complete picture of Kim Jong-Il, we have scattered pixels of a photograph insufficient to allow us to connect the dots.

Here is where theory becomes an effective tool for organizing the information garnered through consistency checks across data, decisions, and domains. Theory provides the psychobiographer with a vehicle to generate specific hypotheses about the subject's behavior, allowing one to test whether the minimal amounts of data are part of a coherent picture, and perhaps suggesting what the picture might look like at the end.

In this psychobiographical analysis of Kim, one theoretical construct that might help give rise to a more coherent picture is the narcissistic per-

sonality syndrome. Narcissism has been used by psychobiographers to analyze political leaders in several ways. The traditional explanation of narcissism, initially propounded by Freud, has been further developed by psychoanalytic theorists such as Kernberg (1984) and Kohut (1971, 1977), both approaching narcissism from an object-relations perspective. More recently, several psychobiographers, including Elms (1994), Post (2003), and Glad (chap. 24, this vol.), have employed the concept of the narcissistic personality—and "malignant" narcissism especially—to explain tyrannical leader Saddam Hussein's behavior (see for more on this subject, Glad, chap. 24 this vol.). In his analysis of Hussein, Post uses Volkan's (1980) definition of a narcissist as a person whose self-esteem is so fragile that he protects it by surrounding himself with adoration and engages in complicated actions in order to avoid criticism. Unlike sociopaths, who seem almost conscienceless, narcissists have conveniently flexible senses of right and wrong. In the political arena, they do not perceive problems as threats to national security or work to resolve potential threats, but instead focus on how such problems might preserve their status or power.

Although Kim Jong-Il and Saddam Hussein are similar in leadership style (e.g., they are both dictators who rule their people through intimidation and do not comply with standards of conduct set by the international community), their lives and behaviors are different enough to necessitate different theories. More specifically, Hussein's and Kim's backgrounds reveal striking dissimilarities. Unlike Kim, who from birth had a personality cult built around his ultimate inheritance of power, Hussein came from a poor, powerless family and rose through the socialist Baath party and the political hierarchy of Iraq to become dictator. There are also key differences between the two men in relation to decision making. Unlike Hussein, who may have used external threat as a manipulative tool for maintaining power, there is evidence that Kim genuinely perceives such threats as a danger to North Korea's national security and his own regime.

These key differences suggest that any theory used to explain Hussein's behavior will not fit Kim as well. A variation of narcissistic personality theory, concerning narcissism from the perspective of self-conscious emotion researchers, may be more applicable.

Self-conscious emotions are different from basic emotions in that the former involve self-representations while the latter are responses to survival goals or to external attributions. An example of basic emotions would be anger or joy, while pride, shame, guilt, and hubris are self-conscious emotions. Tracy and Robins (2004) present a theoretical model of how dueling self-images could result in conflicting self-conscious emotions and narcissistic behaviors. They argue that people assess positive and negative events in terms of the impact these may have on their self-representations. Positive events would result in pride or hubris, while negative events would lead to shame or guilt. They also argue that differences in locus of attributions would lead to different types of emotions. More specifically, if attributions of events are internal, stable, and global, people are more likely to feel shame (negative event) or hubris (positive event). This is in contrast to feelings of guilt or pride, which require attributions that are situation specific and local.

With respect to narcissism, then, self-conscious emotion researchers argue that the path to shame and hubris is integral to the narcissist's regulation of self-esteem. Narcissists simultaneously hold both high and low levels of self-esteem. High self-esteem is more explicit and is demonstrated through the narcissist's tendency to self-enhance and self-aggrandize. In contrast to this self-image, researchers have found that self-promotion is used as a technique to suppress low self-esteem. Therefore, narcissists engage in a regulatory emotional cycle—they frequently interpret events as pertinent to their self-representation and attribute positive events as stable and global aspects of the self. Negative events are generally interpreted as external in origin, but when an event is undeniably internal (i.e., the narcissist cannot avoid responsibility), it is then attributed to unstable and specific parts of the self.

As a result of this regulatory cycle, narcissists seem to be full of contradictions. On the one hand, they may appear charming and full of self-confidence and attract many admirers who laud their accomplishments or character. On the other hand, there may be lapses in behavior that reveal negative self-representations, such as low self-confidence or berating subordinates as a means of increasing the narcissist's sense of power.

In the case of Kim Jong-Il, the dualistic themes that emerged from consistency checks across data, decisions, and domains appear to fit the model presented by Tracy and Robins (2004) very well. We have images of a man brimming with self-confidence and self-adulation: the god of his nation, self-perceived as worthy of the fervor generated by the personality cult around him and of the mythical stories of his birth. We also have images of a man who cannot live up to his apparent godlikeness: sometimes feeling insecure, acting subservient to the mere memory of his father, and resorting to coercion or violence to obtain what he wants, since he lacks the confidence to use persuasion or negotiation.

Tracy and Robins's theoretical model not only gives us an indication of what Kim's whole personality might look like, but also can be used as a guide in future data collection on Kim's life. The model provides specific hypotheses about Kim's behavior that may lead to a more complete picture of Kim as a person and leader. For example, based on this conception of narcissism, we might predict that Kim would overly attribute new positive events as relevant to himself, while new negative events would be externally attributed, or relegated to unstable and specific parts of himself. Moreover, attributions of positive events would be stable and global.

As additional information becomes available, we can then develop a more comprehensive picture of Kim Jong-Il based upon the hypotheses derived by this preliminary psychobiographical analysis. At the time of publication, recent political commentaries have discussed the impact of the U.S. invasion of Iraq on Kim's decisions and behaviors. Most analysts are in agreement that Kim perceives the invasion as a threat to North Korea's national security. Consequently, his continual noncompliance with international demands for nuclear nonproliferation is seen as an attempt to use the prospect of nuclear capabilities as a leveraging tool to secure his position in power. These independent analyses follow the lines that our hypotheses would predict: Distant events (e.g., U.S. war on Iraq) are construed by Kim as directly relevant to his sense of self (the securely positioned leader of North Korea). In order to minimize possible unpleasant self-conscious emotions, negative events are attributed to external causes (U.S. imperialism) rather than to internal, stable, and global aspects of the self (the insecure leader who is in power due to his father).

Conclusion

Although the methodological guidelines discussed in this chapter can be employed in any political psychobiography, they are essential when dealing with leaders for whom we have very little reliable data. It may appear unreasonable and methodologically impossible to even try to study such leaders, especially when many other potential psychobiographical subjects offer the prospect of vast amounts of usable evidence. However, certain situations compel a psychobiographer to accept the challenge. Very often it is precisely the most secretive and puzzling leaders who pose the gravest threat to international security. In such cases, psychobiography is a necessity—an indispensable aid to policy formation and diplomacy. Improved methods of research and data analysis, as well as applications of the most appropriate theories, are important components of such efforts.

Note

I thank Kate Isaacson, Jessica L. Tracy, Todd Schultz, and William McKinley Runyan for invaluable comments on the theoretical structure of this chapter. Thanks are also extended to members of the Bay Area Psychobiographers Group, including Ramsay Breslin, Candace Falk, and Liz Cara for editorial feedback. Lastly, I am especially grateful to Alan Elms, not only for his methodological, editorial, and conceptual guidance, but also for his training and mentorship.

  1. For a discussion of the reliability of data from North and South Korea, see Tanter (1998).

References

Albright, M. (2003). Madam secretary: A memoir. New York: Miramax.

Buruma, I. (1994, September 19). Letter from North Korea: Following the great leader. The New Yorker pp. 66–74.

Center for Strategic and International Studies. (2002). Conventional arms control on the Korean Peninsula: A working group report. Washington, D.C.: Center for Strategic and International Studies.

Costa, P.T., & McCrae, R.R. (1992). Four ways five factors are basic. Personality and Individual Differences, 13, 653–665.

Dillie, B. (2000). The prepared and spontaneous remarks of Presidents Reagan and Bush: A validity comparison for at-a-distance measurements. Political Psychology, 21, 572–585.

Elms, A.C. (1976). Personality in politics. New York: Harcourt Brace Jovanovich.

Elms, A.C. (1994). Uncovering lives: The uneasy alliance of biography and psychology. New York: Oxford University Press.

Epstein, S. (1979). The stability of behavior: On predicting most of the people much of the time. Journal of Personality and Social Psychology, 37, 1097–1126.

Freud, S. (1961). Leonardo da Vinci and a memory of his childhood (ed. J. Strachey, trans. A. Tyson). New York: Norton (The standard edition). (Original work published 1910)

Frontline. (2003). Interview with James Lilley. Public Broadcasting Station (PBS). Retrieved January 31, 2004, from http://www.pbs.org/wgbh/pages/frontline/shows/spy/interviews/lilley.html.

Fujimoto, K. (2004, January-February). I was Kim Jong Il's cook: True stories from the Dear Leader's onetime chef. The Atlantic Monthly, p. 107.

Hermann, M.G. (1980). Assessing the personalities of Soviet Politburo members. Personality and Social Psychology Bulletin, 6, 332–352.

Hwang, J.H. (1999). True picture of North Korea according to a to a former Workers Party Secretary. National Intelligence Service: Testimonies of North Korean defectors—Hwang Jang-Yop speaks. Retrieved January 15, 2004, from http://www.nis.go.kr/eng/north/defector_index.html.

Institute for South-North Korea Studies (1985). The true story of Kim Jong-Il. Seoul: Institute for South-North Korea Studies.

Jervis, R. (1976). Perception and misperception in international politics. Princeton, N.J.: Princeton University Press.

Kernberg, O. (1984). Severe personality disorders: Psychotherapeutic strategies. New Haven, Conn.: Yale University Press.

Kohut, H. (1971). The analysis of self: A systematic approach to the treatment of narcissistic personality disorders. New York: International Universities Press.

Kohut, H. (1977). The restoration of the self. New York: International Universities Press.

Lee, O.N. (1998, February). Kim Jong-Il's defected daughter. Tokyo Bungei Shunju. Retrieved January 31, 2004, from http://www.kimsoft.com/1997/namok.htm.

Maass, P. (2003, October 19). The last emperor, Kim Jong-Il. *New York Times Magazine*, p. 38.

Mischel, W. (1968). Personality and Assessment. New York: Wiley.

National Security Council (2002). The national security strategy of the United States of America. Washington, D.C.: U.S. Government Printing Office.

"North Korea's Dr. Evil" (2003). Newsweek, January 13.

Post, J.M. (2003). The psychological assessment of political leaders. Ann Arbor, Mich.: University of Michigan Press.

Renshon, S. (1998). The psychological assessment of presidential candidates. New York: Routledge.

Robins, R.W., Fraley, R.C., Roberts, B.W., & Trzesniewski, K. (2001). A longitudinal study of personality change in young adulthood. Journal of Personality, 69, 617–640.

Schell, O. (1996, July). In the land of the Dear Leader. Harper's Magazine, p. 58–67.

Schelling, T.C. (1966). Arms and influence. New Haven, Conn.: Yale University Press.

Simon, H.A. (1995). Rationality in political behavior. Political Psychology, 16, 45–63.

Tanter, R. (1998). Rogue regimes: Terrorism and proliferation. New York: St. Martin's Press.

Tetlock, P.E. (1981). Pre- to post-election shifts in presidential rhetoric: Impression management or cognitive adjustment? Journal of Personality and Social Psychology, 41, 207–212.

Tracy, J. L., & Robins, R. W. (2004). Putting the self into self-conscious emotions: A theoretical model. Psychological Inquiry, 15, 103–125 [target article].

Volkan, M. (1980). Narcissistic personality organization and reparative leadership. International Journal of Group Psychotherapy, 30, 131–152.

Winter, D.G. (1973). The power motive. New York: Free Press.

Winter, D.G. (1987). Leader appeal, leader performance, and the motive profile of leaders and followers: A study of American presidents and elections. Journal of Personality and Social Psychology, 53, 196–202.

Psychobiography in Context
Predicting the Behavior of Tyrants

Psychobiography can help solve political puzzles, as long as political behavior is not seen reductively as a simple reenactment of childhood adaptations. As Schultz (chap. 1 this vol.) points out, excessive reductionism signifies bad psychobiography. Behavior, after all, is modulated by context, and the political leader with great power is in a very special position—able, perhaps, to change the environment in which he and others operate. It is this interaction—particularly relevant in the case of a tyrant—that is the focus of this study. I look at how certain leaders affect their environment and how their behavior is in turn influenced by what they create.

Absolute power, as Lord Acton noted some time ago, corrupts those who have it. But why? An analysis of the career of prototypical tyrants enables us to understand the kinds of individuals most subject to that potential for corruption. Most tyrants harbor grandiose fantasies. Unanchored in traditional values or personal loyalties, they possess certain advantages in maneuvering their way up the political ladder. In power, they can orchestrate information and control people to attain the mirroring responses they need. Indeed, their extreme defensiveness and vindictive responses to questioning, when combined with their earlier life histories, suggest that they are deeply insecure and capable of great rage. These characteristics qualify most such individuals as malignant narcissists. But unlike malignant narcissists in the economic or artistic world, the person who achieves near absolute political power is in a position to act out many of the fantasies of which other people only dream. But therein lies the danger. Lacking clear external boundaries, the malignant narcissist in power often becomes erratic in his behavior. Acting outside the societal constraints that bound most people, surrounded by sycophants who tell him only what he wants to hear, he is apt to act on his fantasies in ways that could bring him and his nation to eventual ruin (Glad, 2002).

Aside from the injustices such a person will impose on the people, the tyrant poses a major question for international relations theorists today. These first surfaced when Schelling (1980, pp. 180–203) argued that a national leader enhances the costs of deterrent threats if he takes a flight into irrationality—for example, making commitments that burn his bridges behind him, getting on the slippery slope. At one point during the Vietnam War, Richard Nixon purportedly interpreted this to mean that a president who acts recklessly can also enhance deterrence by appearing to be impulsive, irrational. He can risk nuclear war, for instance, even if the actual result of such a war would be as disastrous to him as to those he threatens.

Today the U.S. government assumes that tyrannical leaders of smaller powers may take similar flights into irrationality, in part because they actually *are* irrational. The Saddam Husseins of this world, it is charged, are so out of touch with cost–benefit analysis that they may threaten to use nuclear weapons, and might *actually* use them, even if the costs reciprocated on them are disastrous (U.S. White House, 2002; Bush, 2001a, pp. 1291–1317; Bush, 2001b, pp. 1427–1473). Thus, they may engage in first nuclear strikes, undeterred by concerns of retaliation.

But are tyrants generally so reckless that they will attempt to secure weapons of mass destruction (WMD) and use them against militarily stronger nations? If so, this may dramatically change conventional considerations of balance of power politics in the international system. It also underscores the need for an analysis of the psychological makeup of most tyrants, including the idiopathic and contextual factors that incline some toward more threatening behavior than others.

Some Definitions

Classical political theorists identified the tyrant as one who rules in his own self-interest and does so without self-constraint. For Plato the tyrant was not a protector, but "the overthrower of many, standing up in the chariot of the State with the reins in his hand" (Plato, 1941, p. 325). Lacking concerns for elementary considerations of justice, and promoting only his own interests, he needlessly creates enemies and sets himself on a path often leading to increasingly chaotic behavior. He is compared to the monarch in that he rules outside the law and promotes a political order based on extreme cruelties and mistrust. (cf. Aristotle, 1948, pp. 121, 132, 158, 267).

Other definitional questions concern distinctions between the tyrant and the more benign autocratic, "authoritarian" dictator. As Jeanne Kirkpatrick has argued (Kirkpatrick, 1982, pp. 133–134), the leader with a totalitarian program, in attempting to transform society, culture, economy, and the human personality, vastly increases the government's reach and, through it, coercive power. Autocrats, or authoritarians, on the other hand, have more specific goals in mind. While expanding their powers, they do not extend their authority into every aspect of community life. Thus, Franco "did not attempt to undermine the social power of the Catholic Church in Spain, nor that of the large landowners. Like many military dictators in Latin America and elsewhere, he did not attempt to alter significantly the cultural, social, or economic status quo" (pp. 133–134). As he made no adjustments to Spain's traditional class inequalities, she continues, Franco did not

require the extreme repression of the people, as seen in other regimes.

This equation of tyranny with transformational leadership, however, creates problems. Certain leaders may exercise despotic power less through endeavors to completely transform the institutions they inherit than to capture them. In Nazi Germany, for example, Hitler turned both private economic corporations and the churches to his ideas of leadership by the fuehrer, while using his secret police to penetrate these and other social groups as well as the family. Moreover, at the other end of the benevolence spectrum, leaders with concern for justice and the well-being of their people may challenge the corporate institutions in their polities in efforts to promote the higher values of the people they lead. Indeed, James M. Burns (1978) would limit the term "transformational leader" to such individuals. Individuals of this sort, he suggests, relate to followers "in such a way that the leaders and followers raise one another to higher levels of motivation and morality" (p. 20).

The tyrant, in short, may seek either to transform institutions or capture them. In either instance, he turns these institutions to his own purposes. If he does take on fundamental reconstruction, he has some short-term advantages relative to the more benevolent transformational leader. Change unleashes not only hopes of a better future for many but also realistic appraisals of loss, fears, and possible hatred of large groups of individuals whose interests and values are being challenged. Tyrannical leaders can deal with that backlash through the use of terror, intimidation, and a relatively unconstrained state power to buy support from strategically placed individuals and communities. The leader committed to a democratic and peaceful change must constrain these emotions without the use of such devices. Gorbachev's problems in bringing about a democratic revolution without the use of force have been delineated in an earlier work (Glad & Shiraev, 1999a,b; compare Bauman, 1994).

We arrive, then, at the following definition. Tyrants are those rulers who seek power for their own purposes. Their goals may be a basic restructuring of an entire polity, or the simple maintenance of themselves in power. Lacking substantive grounding in shared morals, values, or loyalties of the people they lead, they possess certain advantages in their climb to power. They can kill off enemies, lie, change programs, and do whatever they see as politically advantageous.

The thesis I am developing here is as follows. Though most tyrants can be labeled malignant narcissists, they differ from each other in three ways: (1) The contents of their basic schemas (see below for definition) suggest they may pursue assorted kinds of political goals and devise various means of attaining those goals. (2) The size of their military and other politically relevant resources, as well as their strategic positions, will determine their ability to act on those goals in ways threatening to other states. (3) Their ability to see and adapt to boundaries that other states may place on their behavior will also vary with the clarity and firmness of those who impose those boundaries, as well as their own psychological inclinations and powers. An analysis of the three major tyrants of the twentieth century (Hitler, Stalin, and Mao) in terms of these factors suggests that even they differed somewhat in terms of their proclivities to respond to external constraints on power. Analysis of the three powers in George Bush's so-called "axis of evil" —Iraq, Iran, and North Korea—reveals even greater differences (Bush, 2001a, pp. 1291–1317). The central concern for the political analyst therefore has chiefly to do with the aims and modus operandi of a particular tyrant, petty or grand, and his or her potential impact on the security of the major nations of the world.

Schema

As Robert Jervis has pointed out, human beings generally deal with the world via simplifying schemas—ideations, scenarios, metaphors, or programs that enable them to simplify and deal with an almost infinitely complex world (Jervis, 1970). Tyrants, as I have argued at great length elsewhere, are particularly adept at building schemas that provide highly grandiose images of their roles and missions. Moreover, if they are politically successful, these schemas are likely to resonate with the specific peoples they lead, strik-

ing themes with broad appeal. What this means is that tyrants, despite certain psychological similarities, will spin stories that vary in significant ways one from the other. Moreover, the specific plots and subplots will shape their behavior to different degrees, providing guidance for how they act.

Hitler, for example, clearly articulated in *Mein Kampf* his view that the Aryan people were a superior race, tough, lean, blond, and disciplined. Moreover, in following him, *der Fuehrer*, they would come to establish a great Eurasian empire, a *Reich* lasting 1,000 years. Hitler at times saw himself as protected by providence, as a second messiah who would clear the world of the insidious influence of the Jewish people, the Russians, and communists. As a strong leader, he could openly admit plans to employ a variety of crude tools—including propaganda and war— to achieve these ends. Tying this Reich to "der Fuehrer," his own person, he made it clear he was working on a timetable keyed to his own health and age (Hitler, 1939, pp. 412–414, 425–455; Toland, 1976, pp. 591–593).

Stalin, by way of contrast, came to embrace the idea that the Soviet Union under his leadership was the harbinger of a worldwide revolution—a movement that would bring economic equality and an end to colonial rule over the suffering peoples of the world. Forgoing the idea, promoted by Trotsky and others, that revolution must occur overnight, he argued that communism could be achieved within Russia first. In viewing the triumph of communism in the world as a longer term effect of local revolutionary movements, aided and abetted by the USSR, he could tolerate "temporary" reversals and bide his time (Taubman, 1982, p. 149; Zubok & Pleshakov, 1996, p. 45).

Mao's view was that a nation did not need a large and radicalized proletariat to succeed in a communist revolution. Even peasants could revolt and, with an energetic and ambitious political leadership, develop a technological revolution overnight (the "great leap forward"). Communist revolutions, in short, might find fertile ground in the basically agrarian nation of Asia. To guard against backsliding bourgeois elements, the leadership would have to be on guard.

Differences between various communist regimes, Mao and his successors came to see, could even lead to de facto alliances and understandings with capitalist nations (Pye, 1976; Glad, 2005).

These three men, though they had well-developed and grandiose schemas, were politically shrewd enough to succeed in complex climates where they had to bide their time, adapting to changing circumstances with shifting alliances. As a result, they were able to sustain themselves in power for a reasonable period of time.

At the other extreme of the tyrant spectrum are men with such erratic fantasies that they could claim little credibility beyond their small domains. Jean-Bedal Bokassa of the Central African Republic, later called the Central African Empire (1976–1979), was one of these. He crowned himself emperor in a costly ceremony that practically none of the renowned invitees attended. The equally clownish and brutal Idi Amin of Uganda (1971–1979) declared himself Conqueror of the British Empire, sent farcical telegrams to world leaders, humiliated British business in demeaning ceremonies, covered his chest with bogus decorations, and complained that Kissinger and other foreign officials never came to Kampala to get his advice (Decalo, 1989, chaps. 3, 4; Orizio, 2003; Bokassa, 2003). From a psychological perspective, the impulsiveness of these two tyrants suggests a more fragile psychology structure—that is, a borderline personality —than that of either Hitler, Stalin, or Mao (Kernberg, 1975, pp. 40–44).

Unlike Hitler, Stalin, and Mao, none of the leaders of what George W. Bush has called the "axis of evil"—Iraq, Iran and North Korea— entertains the idea of a worldwide crusade. Two of the three show considerable adaptability in rising to power and in maintaining it. Also, none seem as erratic as Bokassa or Idi Amin.

The schemas of these leaders of the axis of evil provide grounds for only a regional imperialism. Saddam Hussein regarded himself as the successor to Nebuchadnezzar and other great leaders of antiquity. His original goal was to unite the Arab people in one large political entity. A student of Stalin's techniques for exerting control over a people, he centralized the power of the Baath party over which he was the absolute ruler, created a secret police, built a military organi-

zation that he would lead, and apparently stockpiled reservoirs of WMD, which were his instruments of choice in expanding in the Middle East. At home, his reach, however, would be limited by the secularist cast of his thought. Responding to the changing cultural climate in the regime, he became increasingly religious over time in his public presentations. But he had staked his future on Pan Arabism, rather than the rising tide of Islamic fundamentalism. Indeed, his history in dealing with the *Shias* in Iraq, even his support of equal rights for women, made him less than a credible leader of the fundamentalist religious revival sweeping the Muslim world (Karsh & Rautsi, 1991, p. 206; Glad, 1993, pp. 65–83).

Kim Il-Sung (1945–1994) and his son, Kim Jong-Il (1994 to present), based in North Korea, embraced *chu'che* or self-sufficiency. North Koreans would depend on their own resources for whatever North Koreans needed. Leaders would attend universities in North Korea. Farmers, technicians, and others would use tools produced in North Korea (thereby working with a "relatively unsophisticated" technology). Improvements, when excessively "Western" in nature, would be rejected (Hunter, 1999, p. 215). Externally, the major goal has been the unification of the Korean peninsula, a project Kim Il-Sung initiated with the invasion of South Korea in 1950. Korea's nuclear energy program is justified today as a defensive measure, based on the fear of U.S. intervention. To gain the money and raw materials it needs for its weapons programs, North Korea has shipped materials to Syria, Iran, possibly Libya, and other regimes that the United States sees as potentially adversarial (Albright, 2003, p. 463).

Khomeini's goal for Iran was the creation of a hierarchically organized Islamic regime in which the *Shia*, or religious law, administered by clerics, would govern every aspect of Iranian life. Crucial in securing his ultimate victory over the more secular and democratic middle classes was his tarring of their leaders as collaborators with the United States and other Western powers that had dominated politics in the Middle East since World War I. His views, embodied in the constitution of the Islamic republic of Iran, created an order based on the idea that one God was the source of all legislation and an *Imamate*—a spiritual leader who provides truth and enlightenment—would provide continuous leadership in the perpetuation of the Islamic revolution. In accord with these views, he undertook in the summer of 1980 the desecularization of all aspects of Iranian society (Arjoumand, 1988, chaps. 4–8). Perhaps his most notable action at the international level was the *fatwa*—religious law—issued in 1989, ordering any capable Muslim to kill British author Salman Rushdie for his "blasphemous" novel *The Satanic Verses* (Timeline: Iran, 2003*)*. Though Khomeini's appeals still have resonance with some Islamist intellectuals fourteen years after his death (Bangash, 2000; Ramahi, 2000), the placing of near absolute power in the hands of one Iranian cleric may not appeal to leaders outside Iran who see themselves as leading similar Islamic republics.

Capabilities

The threat that tyrants pose to their neighbors is relative to the capabilities of the entity they lead, and their strategic position. From this perspective, it is quite clear that the three major tyrants of the twentieth century constituted major world or regional threats. Hitler at the apex of his career was leading the strongest and most effective military organization in Europe and from the center of the continent could turn toward the East or the West or in both directions at once (to his own ultimate detriment). Stalin's Soviet Union had the largest population and landmass in all of Europe, and those assets were put to good defensive use in World War II. Embracing an ideology that traveled well in a world in the throes of a great depression and, later, several anticolonial movements, the Soviet Union was also in a position to expand via nonconventional means in the postwar world. Eventually, with development of its nuclear and missile capabilities, the Soviet Union was in a position where it could challenge its erstwhile ally, the United States, in its own terrain and elsewhere around the world (Taubman, 1982, pp. 49, 153).

Though Mao's China lacked nuclear weapons and ICBMs throughout most of the post-World War II period, its huge manpower, landmass, and strategic location meant that it could threaten

U.S. allies in Southeast Asia. The Chinese entry into the Korean War in the winter of 1950 and its support for Vietnam in the 1970s created limits on how the United States could fight those two wars. General Douglas MacArthur's idea of taking the Korean War into China was a pipe dream given the size of China's population, military, and landmass. Later, during the Vietnam War, Presidents Kennedy and Johnson also had to face similar limits.

No member of George W. Bush's contemporary "axis of evil" poses a threat comparable to those posed by the three major tyrants of the twentieth century. Iraq and Iran counterbalance each other in the Middle East. The two countries fought to a substantial stalemate in a war that lasted eight years (1980–1988). Even more significant, Iran, Iraq, and North Korea have not developed significant nuclear weapons (at the time of this writing) and have limited missile delivery capabilities, while nearby countries, India and Pakistan (not a democracy), openly house short- and middle-range ballistic missiles and nuclear weapons and extensive delivery capabilities. Indeed, India has sixty nuclear weapons. Israel, in contrast to the other nations in the region, has more than 200 (Center for Defense Information, 2003; International Atomic Energy Agency, 2002). Size of military organization also ranges in the millions for India and Pakistan, while Iran has a military of only about 880,000 and Iraq of about 293,000. Only North Korea boasts a larger military organization than its potential adversary, South Korea (CIA: World Factbook, 2003a, 2003b).

These members of the "axis of evil" threaten primarily their neighbors. This threat broadens only under the following circumstances: rogue leaders in the "axis" unilaterally obtain WMD, and they possess the requisite recklessness to use them fearlessly. Alternatively, such leaders might ship by-products to non-regime-based terrorist groups such as Al Qaeda.

But are tyrants from the so-called axis particularly irrational? Even impulsive leaders do not usually wreak horror if it clearly signals their own demise. Nor are they likely to hand over weapons systems to those who might turn on them at some future date. Fundamentalist groups such as the Islamic brotherhood have threatened the Egyptians, the Saudis, the Algerians, and other Middle East governments in the past. And Bin Laden has made it clear that Al Qaeda is prepared even to attack Muslim governments of which it disapproves. In November 2003, his group of apparently freelance followers took action against Saudi Arabia, Turkey, and purported Muslim cooperators with the West in Iraq (McGreary, 2003, pp. 53–56). Are members of the "axis of evil" ever likely to pair up with Bin Laden and other such groups when they engage in such activities? Probably not

Reality Testing

This brings us to a final proposition. Tyrants, as a brief historical detour should make clear, do vary in their ability to exercise an instrumental rationality when it is in their interest to do so.

Certainly tyrants are often inclined to take chances, to ignore negative feedback, and to cut themselves off from information that would curtail risky and expansive behavior. Indeed, early success and commitment may make them practically impervious to developing constraints. Thus, Hitler by the time of the Munich Conference in 1938 was feeling invulnerable as the result of his earlier successes—entering the Ruhr, the Anschluss with Austria, and the conquest of the Sudetenland in Czechoslovakia without opposition. He was disappointed when the British, with their compromise, took away from him the pleasure of entering Prague at the head of his conquering troops. "That fellow (Chamberlain)," he said, "has spoiled my entry into Prague . . . next time, no *Schweinnehund* was going to deprive me of my war" (Toland, 1976, p. 524; see also Glad, 1990, p. 68).

The two petty tyrants mentioned above—Jean Bedel Bokassa of the Central African Republic and Idi Amin of Uganda—plunged ahead with measures that destroyed their countries, challenged regional neighbors, and eventually led to countering responses that brought them down. Bokassa bankrupted his country and permitted the massacre of 100 schoolchildren by his Imperial Guard. French paratroopers finally removed him in a military coup and reinstated the president he had overthrown (Bokassa, 2003). Idi

Amin of Uganda (1971–1979) expelled foreigners who had kept the economy going, promoted intratribal conflicts, and declared war on Tanzania. Enemies foreign and domestic joined in an invasion led by Tanzanian forces, causing him to flee to Libya, where even his friend Muammar el-Qaddafi was not particularly welcoming. Amin's telephone lines were cut, and he moved to Saudi Arabia a year later. There he lived in a world of isolated grandiosity until his death (Greenfield, 2003).

Still, most tyrants recognize external constraints that limit their capacities for expansion and do adapt, albeit reluctantly, often belatedly. In 1945 and 1946 Stalin, when confronted by the United States, backed off from his attempts to secure territory in Turkey and Iran (Taubman, 1982, pp. 130, 149–151). His attempts to wrest Berlin from allied control in 1948 ended with a retreat, after the United States showed, in its year-long airlift, that it would not back down without a possible military confrontation. And though Stalin reluctantly backed North Korea in its invasion of South Korea and later, as the United States approached the Yalu River, urged China to enter the war, he nevertheless consented to the Korean armistice of 1953. It had become clear to him that neither side could win all of the peninsula without risking a big power conflict (Zubok & Pleshakov, 1996, pp. 52, 65). In 1962, Khrushchev even responded to the U.S. quarantine of Cuba by pulling out Soviet offensive ground-to-ground nuclear missiles in that country, a retreat made possible by President John F. Kennedy's agreement to provide the Soviets with a face-saving out (Chang & Kornbluh, 1998; Khrushchev, 1970, pp. 495–500).

China, too, settled for the 38th parallel when it became obvious that the Korean War had come to a stalemate. Even more dramatic, a recognition process started by Nixon and Kissinger eventuated in a semisecurity relationship during the Carter administration in which the U.S. sent nonlethal equipment to China and secured listening posts on their borders as a counter to the USSR (Glad, in press).

Most important for this analysis, Saddam Hussein, too, has shown some ability to adapt to reality. In his war with Iran, he compromised in ways favorable to Iran on the terms regarding the *Shatt El Arab* waterways. His entry into Kuwait, unlawful as it was, can be understood in terms of his political and economic interests. During the eight-year Iran-Iraq War, Iraq sustained tremendous economic losses and depleted its oil reserves. Moreover, Kuwait and the United Arab Emirate began pumping more oil shortly after the peace treaty with Iran was signed. These increases led to a decline in the price of oil, furthering Iraq's economic difficulties (Aburish, 2000, pp. 259, 277; Karsh & Rautsi, 1991, pp. 201–207). Testing the waters, Saddam Hussein sent out several signals that he might attack Kuwait. In the spring of 1990 he proclaimed, "[W]e have reached a point where we can no longer withstand pressure." At an Arab League meeting in May 1990, he accused Kuwait of declaring war on Iraq (Karsh & Rautsi, 1991, p. 206). And just before undertaking the invasion of Kuwait, Saddam Hussein told U.S. Ambassador to Iraq, April Glaspie, that he might take action of some kind. She replied that the United States had no defense treaty with Kuwait and that "we hold no opinion about . . . the inter-Arab disputes, such as your border disagreement with Kuwait" (Glaspie, 1991, p. 19). The United States never made it clear that the invasion would lead to the massive U.S. led international response that followed (Bush, 1989).

Even Saddam Hussein's evident shell game with U.N. inspectors after the Persian Gulf War can be understood from a *realpolitik* perspective. Blocking access to his military sites would limit the intelligence the United States could gain via the U.N. inspections about his military capabilities for the war that might come. The suggestion today, that he simply shipped any WMD out of the country, makes little sense. A leader bent on maximizing his control over his domain would not hand over such power to a potential competitor. As for his suicidal bent, Hussein's attempts to evade capture after the U.S. entry into Baghdad and his recent inglorious surrender suggest that this man, unlike Hitler, is determined to live for as long as he can.

In Iran, the clerics' hands are tied by widespread evidence that many resent their continued hold over political life. Mohammad Khatami, a moderate reform cleric, was elected president in 1977 after beating back the conservative religious ruling elite, winning seventy percent of the popular vote. In his reelection campaign four years later, he won by an even larger majority. In July 1999 and again in June 2003, security police were unable to prevent pro-democracy demonstrations at Tehran University. To adapt to the concerns of women, senior clerics in August 2000 issued a *fatwa* allowing women to lead congregations of female worshippers (Timeline: Iran, 2003).

At the international level, the ruling elite has adapted to other pressures. The United States in 1995 imposed oil and trade sanctions against Iran for its alleged sponsorship of terror and for attempts to acquire nuclear arms. In a nod to these concerns, Iran signed an agreement with Saudi Arabia in April 2001 to fight terrorism, drug trafficking, and organized crime. In December 2003, the Iranians agreed to permit tougher U.N. inspections of its nuclear sites and to suspend its program for uranium enrichment, a result of U.N. pressures and months of European-led negotiations. Direct U.S. pressure on Iran, however, can backfire. In January 2002, George W. Bush's "axis of evil" speech angered reformers and conservatives alike. American support of the dissident student movement, too, could strengthen the hand of the conservatives, enabling them once again to link those desiring freedom in Iran with an imperial United States. Even today, reform members of the Iranian establishment have joined conservatives in condemning U.S. support of the student demonstrations. The fear of the reformers, as BBC analyst Sadeq Saba has noted, is that U.S. support may abet hardliners in the regime (Iran Protests, 2003).

As for North Korea, its leaders and the United States, at the time of this writing, are engaged in tit-for-tat exchanges that make any resolution of differences very difficult. In 1994 Kim Il-Sung promised to put a temporary hold on nuclear building enterprises after discussions with Jimmy Carter (Brinkley, 1998, pp. 399–403). But both sides would subsequently charge that the other had reneged on the deal. And in the summer of 2003 North Korea stated it had nuclear capabilities it would abandon only in the event that the United States negotiate a bilateral nonaggression pact (Kahn & Sanger, 2003; Yoo, 2003; Curl, 2003). Not willing to give in to what it considered "nuclear blackmail," the United States declared that it would not engage in bilateral negotiations on such matters. In July, North Korea, in a somewhat more conciliatory move agreed to a six-nation meeting in Beijing. In early August, however, a U.S. undersecretary of State John R. Bolton (noted as a hardliner with ties to Secretary of Defense Donald Rumsfeld) attacked the North Korean leader by name forty-one times. "While he lives like royalty in Pyongyang, he keeps hundreds of thousands of his people locked in prison camps with a million more mired in abject poverty," was one of his charges. In response, a North Korean spokesman decried Bolton's "political vulgarity and psychopathology condition" and indicated that North Korea would no longer deal with him as an official of the U.S. administration (Brooke, 2003). The Bush administration responded shortly thereafter in another voice, stating that it might give the North Koreans some form of written agreement at the six-party talks organized by China. But North Korea refused to be mollified at this point, and the talks were subsequently suspended (Weisman, 2003).

Perhaps the United States might be more successful with North Korea if it could show the same kind of "patient but firm diplomacy" that has worked with Libya (Libyan Deal, 2003). As former Secretary of State Madeleine Albright has noted, Kim Jong-Il was well informed and "was not delusional," which suggests that talks dealing with his security concerns might be productive, shown through a number of medias, including a *New York Times* article (Albright as quoted in BBC News, 2003; see also As Bush Holds Back, 2003; see also Albright, 2003, pp. 463–472; Gregg, 2003).

Earlier, Muammar Qaddafi had been viewed by the United States in the 1980s as the most threatening leader of a rogue regime—a major supporter of terrorist attacks on targets in the West. But Qaddafi had gradually moderated his behavior—the result of several policy failures, as well as endeavors to check his excesses by several Western powers. Within his own country, the Islamic brotherhood tried to overthrow him. His coup attempts in Egypt and Sudan failed. Most of his alliances purporting to unify Libya with other Arab states were mainly paper engagements. The French checked some of his actions

in Chad, and the United States showed its muscle, shooting down two Libyan aircraft in the Gulf of Sydra (1981) and undertaking paramilitary operations in 1990–1992 to undermine him. By 1992 the United States, Great Britain, Japan, Belgium, Denmark, and Sweden had ended diplomatic relations with Libya and, in accord with U.N. sanctions, blocked arms sales and air travel to Libya (Sicker, 1987, pp. 113–126; U.S. Department of State, 1986).

In an apparent adaptation to these facts, Qaddafi denounced the Muslim Brotherhood in 1977, calling them the worst of god's enemies and a destructive force in the Arab nation. In October 1989 he admitted that he had backed a terrorist group but that he had found the group to be working for itself rather than for all Arabs. In recent years he has given additional evidence of his desire to join the world community of nations. In the fall of 2003, and after five years of talks, Libya offered compensation of $2.7 billion to the victims of the bombing of Pan American flight 103 over Lockerbie, Scotland. Finally, in December 2003, after nine months of secret negotiations with the United States and Great Britain, Qaddafi announced that Libya would adhere to nuclear, biological, and chemical weapons treaties. He would also sign an additional protocol to the nuclear nonproliferation treaty allowing U.N. experts to inspect weapons programs at short notice (Tyler, 2003). Though the White House suggested it was U.S. intervention in Iraq that played the key role in this development, the history of Qaddafi's evolution supports the view of Joseph Cirincione, director of the Carnegie Endowment for the International Peace nonproliferation project, that the success was the result of diplomacy. "The administration is changing the policy in fact, without changing the word," he said. "They relied more on carrots than sticks. . . . And it worked" (Cirincione, 2003).

In addition to tyrants who moderate their behaviors, there are other leaders who might have become full-blown tyrants but somehow did not. Kemal Ataturk of Turkey might be considered such a leader. Though he governed autocratically from 1923 up to his death in 1938 and expelled Western troops from Turkey, he also modernized the country's legal and educational systems and emancipated women. Nor was he a threat to his neighbors, deciding that Turkey would not pursue any irredentist claims. At his death, he was widely and deeply mourned as the father of the republic (Volkan & Itzkowitz, 1984, p. 343). Gamal Abdel Nasser of Egypt started out with grandiose ambitions and was ruthless in dealing with internal enemies. But he promoted industrial growth, land reform, and women's rights. When an Islamic fanatic claiming to act on behalf of the Muslim Brotherhood tried to assassinate him, he responded by cracking down on that most extremist sect. And though he denied use of the Suez Canal to Israel and engaged in two wars against that country, he had tentatively accepted in 1970, shortly before his death, a U.S. plan that would have led to peace negotiations with Israel. The Suez Canal, which he nationalized in 1956, was finally opened to Israel and all other traffic by his successor, Anwar Sadat, with the signing of the peace treaty between Egypt and Israel in 1979 (Pelizza, 2003; Nasser Encyclopedia Britannica, 2003).

To delineate possible differences between these two types of tyrants, Vamik Volkan has distinguished "reparative" from malignant narcissism. Though leaders such as Ataturk have inflated self-images, as do all narcissists, they also embrace the needs and fantasies of their followers, thus tying themselves to them in meaningful and positive ways (Volkan, 1980, pp. 131–152).

One final note: Tyrants aren't alone in their difficulties with reality testing. Wishful thinking, and/or the buttressing of preferred alternatives, as Richard Ned Lebow has pointed out, is often characteristic of democratic leaders acting in stressful and ambiguous situations. Thus, the United States ignored warnings from high-level Chinese sources in September and October 1950 that any U.S. intervention in North Korea would lead to Chinese resistance. Domestic pressure and General Douglas MacArthur's success at Inchon created a situation in which President Truman wanted to believe these were mere idle threats (Lebow, 1981, pp. 155–64, 207, 227). In another instance, the 1976 Committee B Report by the CIA widely overestimated Soviet aggressive intentions and capabilities. Persons committed to a program of building a U.S. militarily superior to the USSR were particularly prone to embrace that point of view (Glad, forthcoming).

As the latter example above suggests, enemy images are particularly prone to psychological exaggerations (Volkan, 1988, pp. 196–216). At the present moment, many in the West have replaced the Cold War threat from the worldwide communist conspiracy with the Cold War threats from tyrants with WMD potential. The proclivity to exaggerate the power and irrationality of such men and women is manifest in statements by George W. Bush to the effect that the United States finds itself in a very dangerous battle, a confrontation at the world level between good and evil. A more surprising formulation along these lines, however, appeared before 9/11 in the writing of former Unscom United Nations Special Commission chief Richard Butler (Butler, 2000, pp. xviii–xx). Piling speculation on speculation, Butler argued that Saddam Hussein's past gave us but a taste of what he might do in the future. Saddam Hussein not only invaded Iran and Kuwait, Butler said, but Bahrain, Saudi Arabia, and Turkey as well. Not only has he sought WMD, "he has already used them against Iran, and, to some extent, Israel." Saddam sees WMD as a key to his leadership of the Arab world, said Butler. "Missile, bomber, artillery shell, even crop dusters—are all means of delivering the chemical weapons he has built and on occasion used." One scenario Butler spun out involves a hit squad from the Middle East spraying, via an ordinary spray can, the contents of a one-liter bottle filled with chemical weapons agents over Times Square or Grand Central Station in New York City. Hundreds, maybe thousands of Americans would die, Butler wrote. But Saddam probably would not take responsibility for such an act, and most Americans and their allies would be loathe to punish any single nation as a result. If the crime could be traced to Saddam, however, pressures to engage in a revenge attack might be irresistible, Butler predicts. But would it be "fair to slaughter innocent civilians, the most likely victims of US bombing raids?" (Butler, 2000, pp. xviii–xix).

A closer look at Saddam Hussein, as suggested above, indicates that though he was a cruel and self-serving overlord of the Iraqi people, he was not quite as mad as Butler suggests. Though he did invade Iran and Kuwait, his attacks on other countries in the Middle East were in response to the U.N. war against him in 1991. And though he used chemical weapons against Iran in his war with that country, and against some revolting Kurdish villages in Iraq in 1988, he did not do so against the U.S./U.N.-led coalition wars against him in 1991. Nor did he in 2002, for that matter. And at this moment, we have no evidence that Saddam Hussein backed the egregious, more conventionally armed terrorist attack of September 11, 2001.

Conclusions

Tyrants, in short, are not all alike. Most have grandiose plans and can engage in many cruelties, distortions, and other lawless behavior. But tyrants also differ substantially in their schemas, the relevant capabilities of the states they head, and their ability to assess, with some degree of realism, the limits others place on their actions. Their schemas may be more or less grandiose. Their abilities to act on the schema, in the international setting, constrained by the capabilities and strategic position of the state they head. And most are sufficiently in contact with the world around them that they can see and adapt to external constraints on their ambitions, albeit with difficulty. Leaders of smaller rogue regimes, then, are unlikely to take flights into irrationality that necessitate big powers squashing them. Some do harm primarily to their own people and pose threats to their immediate neighbors. Those players, men who are particularly erratic and driven by fantasies, may be brought to account by others in their region. Tyrants who are dangerous—those with worldwide ambitions, capabilities, and poor reality testing—pose the greatest threat to the broader world order. But even these rarities may be contained by other major states, which can check and balance what they might do with countervailing power. For those few Hitlers of the world who are allowed to roam freely for too long, war may be the final response. But it need not be the first reaction, as this chapter suggests.

In making these assessments, we should also check our own proclivities for seeing threats everywhere and for thinking we can secure perfect security. Butler urged that "the world act now to prevent any attack with a chemical, biological or indeed a portable nuclear weapon, not only by Saddam Hussein, but by other states, terrorist movements, armies of liberation, lone lunatics–anyone with the motivations to launch such an attack" (Butler, 2000, p. xxi). But to guard against every tyrant, every far-out lunatic, regardless of his capabilities or possible interests, can put us on a paranoiac path in which we police and limit ourselves in ways beyond what any crazed leader really can do to us. We need to retain the ability to discriminate between various potential adversaries, to assess at a realistic level the damages they might do to our polity, all the while realizing that harm of whatever kind can only be limited, not eliminated. That is how the international system functioned for the past fifty years, and hopefully will function in the future.

References

Aburish, S. K. (2000). Saddam Hussein: The politics of revenge. New York: Bloomsbury Publishing.

Albright, M. (2003). Madam secretary: A memoir. New York: Miramax Books.

Albright, M., (2003, July 23). As quoted in BBC News Profile: Kim Jung-Il. Retrieved October 23, 2003 from http://news.bbc.co.un/go/or/fr/-l/hil/wirkd/asa-pacific/1907197.stm.

Amin, Idi. (2003). Retrieved September 4, 2003 from http://www.Britannica.com/eb/article?eu=7264

Aristotle. (1948). Politics of Aristotle (E. Barker, Trans.). Oxford: Clarendon.

Arjoumand, S. (1988). The turban for the crown: The Islamic revolution in Iran. New York: Oxford University Press.

As Bush holds back, Americans seek North Korea dialogue. (2003, November 23). New York Times. www.nytimes.com

Bangash, Z. (2000). The imam of the ummah who restored Muslims hope and pride. Retrieved October 23, 2003 from http:/www.muslimedia.com/archives/features00/imam-hope.htm.

Bauman, Z. (1994). A revolution in the theory of revolutions. International political science review, vol. 15, no. 1, pp. 15–24.

Bokassa, Jean-Bedel. (2003). Retrieved September 4, 2003 from http://www.Britannica.com/eb/article?eu=2610.

Brinkley, D. (1998). The unfinished presidency: Jimmy Carter's Journey beyond the White House. New York: Viking.

Brooke, J. (2003, August 5). North Korea moves to win some friends before nuclear talks. New York Times. www.nytimes.com

Burns, J.M. (1978). Leadership. New York: Harper & Row.

Bush, G. H. (1989, October 2). National Security Directive 26. Retrieved October 23, 2003, from http://bushlibrary.tamu.edu/research/nsd/.

Bush, G. W. (2001a). Address to the nation on the terrorist attacks. Weekly Compilation of Presidential Documents. 1291–1317. Retrieved September 2, 2004 from http://www.gpoaccess.gov/wcomp.

Bush, G. W. (2001b). Remarks announcing the most wanted terrorists list. Weekly Compilation of Presidential Documents. Washington, 1427–1473. Retrieved September 2, 2004 from http://www.gpoaccess.gov/wcomp.

Butler, R. (2000). The greatest threat: Iraq, weapons of mass destruction, and the crisis of global security. New York: Public Affairs.

Center for Defense Information. (2003). Nuclear issues. Retrieved March 19, 2004 from http://www.cdi.org/issues/nukef&f/database/.

Central Intelligence Agency (CIA). (2003) The world factbook. Country list. Retrieved October 23, 2003 from http://www.cia.gov/cia/publications/factbook/.

Chang, L. & Kornbluh, P. (Eds.). (1998). The Cuban missile crisis, 1962. New York: New Press.

Curl, J. (2003, October 20). Bush offers guarantees to North Korea. Washington Times, p. A01.

Decalo, S. (1989). Psychoses of power: African personal dictatorships. Boulder, Colo.: Westview Press.

Glad, B. (Ed.). (1990). Psychological dimensions of war. Newbury Park, Calif.: Sage Publications.

Glad, B. (1993). Figuring out Saddam Hussein. In M.L. Whicker, J.P. Pfiffner & R.A. Moore (Eds.), The presidency and the Persian Gulf war. Pp. 63–89. Westport, Conn.: Praeger.

Glad, B. (2002). Why tyrants go too far: Malignant narcissism and absolute power. Political Psychology, 23, 1–39.

Glad, B. (ms in prep). Jimmy Carter: The inner circle and the making of US foreign policy.

Glad, B. & Shiraev, E. (1999a). A profile of Mikhail Gorbachev: Psychological and sociological underpinnings. In B. Glad & E. Shiraev (Eds.). The Russian Transformation. Pp. 23–52. New York: St. Martin's Press.

Glad, B. & Shiraev, E. (1999b). The reformer in office. In B. Glad & E. Shiraev (Eds.). The Russian Transformation. Pp. 3–22. New York: St. Martin's Press.

Glaspie, A. (1991. March 21). Hearing before the subcommittee on Europe and the Middle East of the Committee on Foreign Affairs. United States/Iraqi relations, House of Representatives [Transcript]. Washington, DC: U.S. Government Printing Office.

Greenfield, R. (2003, August 18). Obituary: Idi Amin: Jovial but brutal tyrant known as the butcher of Uganda. The Independent. London, England, from Http://www. highbeam.com/library/doc3asp?

Gregg, D. (2003, February 20). Interview on Public Broadcasting Service: Frontline. Retrieved October 23, 2003, from www.pbs.org/wgbh/pages/frontline/shows/kim/interviews/gregg.html.

Hitler, A. (1939). Mein kampf. New York: Stackpole.

Hunter, H.L. (1999). Kim il-sung's North Korea. Westport, Conn.: Praeger.

International Atomic Energy Agency: Nuclear Energy Department. (2002). Country nuclear power profiles. Retrieved March 19, 2004 from http://www pub.iaea.org/MTCD/publications/PDF/cnpp2002/index.htm.

Iran protests at U.S. interference. (2003, June 16). Retrieved November 3, 2003 from http://newsvote.bbc.co.uk/mpapps/pagetool/print/news.bbc.co.uk/2hi/middle_east/292628.stm.

Jervis, R. (1970). Perception and misperception in international relations. Princeton: Princeton University Press.

Kahn, J. & Sanger, D.E. (2003, August 29). North Korea says it may test an a-bomb. New York Times. Retrieved October 23, 2003 from http://query.nytimes.com/search/restricted/article?res=F50D11FD345DOC7A8EDDA10894DB04482

Karsh, F., & Rautsi, I. (1991). Saddam Hussein: A political biography. New York: The Free Press.

Kernberg. (1975). Borderline conditions and pathological narcissism. New York: J. Aronson.

Khrushchev, N. (1970). Khrushchev remembers. Boston: Little Brown & Company. Kim Il-sung. (2003). Retrieved September 4, 2003 from http://wwv.britannica.com/eb/article?eu=46519

Kim Jung Il. (2003). Retrieved September 4, 2003 from http://www.britannica.com/eb/article?eu=46515

Kirkpatrick, J. (1982). Dictatorships and double standards: Rationalism and reason in politics. New York: Simon & Schuster.

Lebow, R. N. (1981). Between peace and war: The nature of international crises. Baltimore, Md.: John Hopkins University Press.

Libyan deal shows need for U.S. shift in U.S. diplomatic tactics analysts say. (2003, December 21). USA Today. Retrieved September 13, 2004 from http://usatoday.printthis.clickability.com/pt/cpt?action=cpt&title=USATODAY.c com++Li

McGeary, J. (2003, December 1). When no one is truly safe. Time, pp. 53–56.

Nasser, Gamal Abdel. (2003). Retrieved October 23, 2003 from http://www.britannica.com/eb/article?eu=56299.

Orizio, R. (2003). Talk of the devil: Encounters with seven dictators (trans. Avril Bardoni). New York: Walker & Company. (Original work published 2002).

Pelizza, S. (2003, December 1). The star of Nasser. Retrieved October 23, 2003 from www.geocities.com/iturks/html/modern_history_3.html.

Plato. (1941). The republic (trans. B. Jowett). New York: Random House.

Pye, L. W. (1976). Mao Tse-Tung: The man in the leader. New York: Basic Books.

Ramahi, G. M. (2000). Imam Khomeini's tradition of islah (reform): A legacy or a responsibility? Retrieved March 19, 2004 from http://www.muslimedia.com/archives/features00/khom-islah.htm.

Schelbing, T. (1980). The strategy of conflict. Cambridge, Mass.: Harvard University Press.

Sicker, M. (1987). The making of a pariah state. New York: Praeger

Taubman, W. (1982). Stalin's American policy from entente to détente to cold war, New York: Norton.

Timeline: Iran. (2003). Retrieved October 23, 2003 from http://newsvote.bbc.co.uk/mpapps/pagetools/print/news.bbc.co.uk/l/hi/world/middle_east/country_profiles/806268.stm.

Toland, J. (1976). Adolf Hitler. New York: Random House.

Tyler, P.E. (2003, December 21). Secret diplomacy won Libyan pledge on arms. New York Times. Retrieved December 22, 2003 from http://www.nytimes.com/2003/12/21/international/middleeast/21LIBY.html

U.S. Department of State. (1986, January). Libya under Qaddafi: A pattern of aggression [Special report]. Washington, D.C.

U.S. White House. (2002). National security strategy of the United States of America. (2002). Retrieved October 23, 2003 from http://www.whitehouse.gov/nsc/nss.html.

Volkan, V. (1988). The need to have enemies and allies: From clinical practice to international relationships. Northvale: N.J.: J. Aronson.

Volkan, V. (1980). Narcissistic personality organization and reparative leadership. International Journal of Group Psychotherapy, 30, 131–152.

Volkan, V.D., & Itzkowitz, N. (1984). The immortal Ataturk: A psychobiography. Chicago: University of Chicago Press.

Weisman, S. R. (2003, August 13). U.S. weighs reward if North Korea scraps nuclear arms. New York Times. www.nytimes.com

Yoo. Jae-Suk. (2003 October 26). North Korea says it will consider Bush plan. The State, Columbia, SC. p. A4.

Zubok, V., & Pleshakov, C. (1996). Inside the Kremlin's cold war: From Stalin to Khrushchev. Cambridge, Mass.: Harvard University Press.

Index

abandonment, 152, 248
  in life of Truman Capote, 51–52, 53
  themes in songs of Elvis Presley, 144
Abnormal Personality, The, 28
Abraham, Karl, 211
academicians, as psychobiographers, 306
accommodation, 229
admiration, psychology of, 327
adolescence, as critical period of formation, 75,
  275–276
adult development, 335
advantage
  expectation of, 276
  feelings of, 77, 78, 122
aesthetic attitude, versus theoretical attitude, 233
affect
  centrality of, 62
  positive, 69, 75, 281, 283
Afghan War, 314–315, 320
Agee, James, 4
agency
  tension between communion and, 77
  themes, 61, 75
Age of Innocence, 198
aggression, 32, 96, 272, 282
  accompanying drinking, 332–333
  by Kim Jong-Il, 352
  lack of, 273
agreeableness, 72
Albright, Madeline
  meeting with Kim Il-Sung, 364
  meeting with Kim Jong-Il, 348
alcohol abuse, in life of George W. Bush, 324,
  332–333, 336
Alexander, Franz, 25
Alexander, Irving, 15, 43
alienation, 116
allocation rules, 109
Allport, Floyd, 228–232

Allport, Gordon, 10, 15, 21, 91, 206–207, 223,
  285, 289
  approach to studying personality, 233–234
  family position, 227–229
  meeting with Freud, 43, 88, 224–227
  negation by, 47
  relationship with Floyd Allport, 229–232
  role in split of Harvard psychology
    department, 294–295
  work of, 25–26, 65
Al-Qaeda, 315, 319
Al-Turabi, Hassan, 318–319
ambition, 290, 334, 335
ambivalence, 129
American Psychological Association, 16
Amin, Idi, 360, 362
analysis, pace of, 305, 306
anger, 88–89, 172. *See also* hostility
Ansell, Mary, 186
Answered Prayers, 52–53
Antichrist, The, 245, 246
Apollonian-Dionysiac dichotomy, 253–254
Arbus, Allan, 118
Arbus, Diane, 47, 48–50, 112–113
  eccentricity, 123–125
  photography of, 115
  sensation seeking, 119–122
  symbiosis, 125–130
  themes of life and work, 116–119, 130–131
"Are You Lonesome Tonight?"
  changes in lyrics by Elvis Presley, 146–151
arousal, need for, 120
art
  artists' knowledge of source of, 136
  function for artist, 138
  importance of medium, 138–139
  interference with perception of, 135
  as a projection of selves, 137
  psychology and, 139–140

CPSIA information can be obtained
at www.ICGtesting.com
Printed in the USA
BVHW06*0031150818
524513BV00009B/216/P